Prison Wor

Prison Worlds

An Ethnography of the Carceral Condition

Didier Fassin

Translated by Rachel Gomme

polity

The right of Didier Fassin to be identified as Author of this Work has been asserted in accordance with the UK Copyright, Designs and Patents Act 1988.

First published in French as *L'Ombre du monde. Une anthropologie de la condition carcérale* © Éditions du Seuil, 2015

This English edition published in 2017 by Polity Press

Polity Press
65 Bridge Street
Cambridge CB2 1UR, UK

Polity Press
350 Main Street
Malden, MA 02148, USA

ISBN-13: 978-1-5095-0754-2
ISBN-13: 978-1-5095-0755-9 (pb)

A catalogue record for this book is available from the British Library.

Library of Congress Cataloging in Publication Control Number: 2016031519

Typeset in 10 on 11.5 pt Sabon by
Servis Filmsetting Ltd, Stockport, Cheshire
Printed and bound in the UK by Clays Ltd, St Ives, PLC

The publisher has used its best endeavors to ensure that the URLs for external websites referred to in this book are correct and active at the time of going to press. However, the publisher has no responsibility for the websites and can make no guarantee that a site will remain live or that the content is or will remain appropriate.

Every effort has been made to trace all copyright holders, but if any have been inadvertently overlooked the publisher will be pleased to include any necessary credits in any subsequent reprint or edition.

For further information on Polity, visit our website: politybooks.com

To L. H. and all those for whom prison makes this life, which they are in the process of pointlessly losing, so insistently precious

To F. F. and all those working in prisons who strive to make incarceration more dignified, or simply more livable

For A.C. D. and all those who work to defend the rights of prisoners and to improve prison conditions

And by "*justice*" I mean nothing other than the restraint necessary to hold particular interests together, without which men would collapse into the old state of unsociability. Any punishment that goes beyond the need to preserve this bond is unjust by its very nature.

Cesare Beccaria, *On Crimes and Punishments*, 1764

But the prison memoirs – "Scenes from the House of the Dead," as he himself called them somewhere in the manuscript – appeared to me to be not without interest. The completely strange world, unknown until that time, the strangeness of some of the facts, some particular notes on those lost souls, attracted me, and I read with curiosity.

Fyodor Dostoevsky, *Memoirs from the House of the Dead*, 1862

There people live their hard and heavy lot
cooped in deep rooms, – their gestures show they're scared,
more terrified than any yearling herd;
and outside wakes your earth, its breath is stirred,
but these, though living still, now know it not.

Rainer Maria Rilke, *The Book of Poverty and Loss*, 1903

Contents

Preface to the English Edition

A World of Prisons

Presented by its promoters two and a half centuries ago as moral progress in the administration of punishment, prison has become over the past decades one of the most vexing and unsettling issues in Western societies for both the spectacular increase of its population and the grim reality of its facilities. But while imprisonment is today in most countries the ineluctable reference and the ultimate horizon of the penal system, until recently neither its efficacy in reducing crime nor its respect for democratic principles has been seriously discussed outside a few academic circles. The correctional institution has been taken for granted and is barely visible. An elephant in the room, it has largely been ignored by the public. To take the most extreme example, in the United States, the number of people incarcerated increased more than sevenfold over four decades, reaching the impressive figure of 2.3 million inmates in the early 2010s, which made the country's incarceration rate the highest in the world, yet without provoking a major debate. New laws were constantly being passed, imposing new mandatory minimum sentencing and criminalizing new offenses. New facilities were regularly being built, involving new private actors and new security measures. An ever tougher legislation and an expanding correctional system were business as usual in government, and these widely popular policies were little questioned. Only in recent years has the problem begun to be addressed, in large part because of the colossal share it represents in the states' budgets. The political, moral, and social implications of mass incarceration have remained for the most part in the background.

In fact, what prisons entail involves two distinct, albeit related, aspects: penal and correctional – how offenders are punished and how incarceration is conducted. Studying the penal system involves analyzing how problems are socially constructed, how the public emotionally reacts to particular events, how some crimes are deemed serious and others are not, how the executive and the legislator produce norms and laws, how the police use their discretionary power to focus on specific offenses or offenders, how prosecutors and judges decide to indict and sentence certain acts while ignoring others. In the end, it is this entire complex process that leads to the filling or emptying of prisons and determines the composition of their population. Studying the correctional system implies examining the infrastructure and functioning of its facilities, the recruitment, training, activity, and supervision of its personnel, the rights and obligations that inmates are supposed to have, the daily interactions among those who are confined and with those who guard them, the formal and informal modes of regulating, settling, and sanctioning the various issues that may arise. Indeed, it is this dense network of material and immaterial elements that defines what life in prison looks like for those who serve a sentence as well as for those who work there.

Both the investigation of the penal chain and the inquiry into the correctional apparatus are indispensable to a full understanding of the prison system. However, they represent distinct challenges for social scientists, since the former, being open, is much more accessible to direct observation and other scientific approaches than the latter, which is, by definition, closed. This explains why most research is carried out on the penal chain, while little knowledge is available about the correctional apparatus. This is particularly true in the United States, where an impressive sum of sociological, historical, and legal studies exists on the logics and mechanisms that have led to the phenomenon known as mass incarceration, but where what it means to be incarcerated for the millions of individuals who enter prisons and jails each year is hardly studied. Indeed, the Federal Bureau of Prisons, most of the 50 State Departments of Corrections, and the 3,000 local jails have maintained a high degree of opacity regarding what goes on in their facilities, restricting both scientific activities and external assessment, and therefore avoiding public or legal accountability about how prisoners are treated. It is much less the case, however, in other countries, such as Britain, where observational methods and interview techniques have recently resulted in substantial works on prison.

In France, the penal chain and correctional apparatus are relatively open to outsiders' gaze. The ministry of justice, which is in charge of both, has its own small research unit, as does the National School of Prison Administration, and it finances the main public research center in criminology. Social scientists and legal scholars are regularly solicited to conduct surveys on various aspects of the justice and prison systems, notably to evaluate new policies or respond to specific questions, but independently conceived projects can also be granted permission, which has given birth to a growing field of research on justice and prison. The present book has greatly benefited from this relative opening. Over four years, I have been able to spend time, day and night for a total of seven months, in the short-stay facility of an important urban area. Such an institution is generally reserved for pre-trial detainees, the proportion of whom has recently decreased to one-fourth of the facility's population, and for convicted persons with a sentence of less than two years, although some inmates may remain five years or more. During my research I have gradually been authorized – and have progressively authorized myself – to be present in all parts of the facility and attend all sorts of its activities, from cultural programs to parole board meetings, from disciplinary hearings to the solitary confinement unit. It has been more difficult to gain the trust of the prisoners than that of the personnel, and probably also to have sufficient confidence in myself to sit with the former in their cells than to stay with the latter in the walkways. But however fascinating life in such a facility may be, and however demanding its observation may become, I have repeatedly tried to step outside, on the one hand to study the everyday work of the justice system in the district criminal court, and, on the other, to examine the considerable body of legal, administrative, and statistical documents on the evolution of punishment practices, in order to apprehend the processes that have led to the prison system being what it is. This book is thus an attempt to analyze both the penal chain and the correctional apparatus. It aims at characterizing the punitive moment through which French society – like many others – is going, and at comprehending the carceral condition as it is experienced by those who endure it.

*   *   *

France today has the highest number of prisoners of its peacetime history. Its incarceration rate is 100 per 100,000 inhabitants, which is still seven times less than in the United States. In the past six decades, there has been a more than threefold increase in the prison population, which has swelled from 20,000 in 1955 to 67,000 in 2015. One could logically imagine the reason for this evolution to be a rise in crime. Such is not the case, however. Although the curve of crime statistics is always difficult to interpret, since it is influenced by the way offenses are represented in the public sphere and constituted under the law as well as by the activity of the police and the decisions of the judges, for the most robust data available, which also corresponds to the most serious crime, namely homicides, the trend over the past century and a half is clearly of decline, except for a short period in the 1970s when a moderate increase was observed. In fact, the dramatic expansion of the prison population is the consequence of a more severe penal system. This repressive turn results from two main phenomena. First, new offenses have been criminalized. Driving without a license, for instance, was until the 1990s a rare violation of traffic laws usually sanctioned by a fine. In the following decade, with the creation of a penalty point system and the multiplication of radars on the roads, the number of suspended licenses skyrocketed, while a 2004 law made it an offense punishable by a one-year prison sentence. Today, driving with a suspended license is the cause of one incarceration out of ten. Second, for a given breach of the law, prison sentences have been passed more frequently and for longer periods. Most notably, a 2007 law establishing mandatory minimum sentencing for recidivists has contributed to an increase of 9 percent in prison sentences and 17 percent in time to be served that was observed during the following five years. But when one examines these statistics closely, it appears that, paradoxically, the smaller the offense the greater the escalation in harshness. Other factors have also played a role, in particular the growing use of immediate appearance trials, which has a prison sentencing rate twice that of the normal procedure, and the activation of prison sentences for minor offenses perpetrated several years earlier, for which probation was already in progress. In sum, an increase in harshness rather than a rise in crime caused the expansion of the prison population. French society was undergoing a *punitive moment*.

This repressive trend being what it is, two further questions need to be asked. Is punishment justly allocated? Is it fairly distributed? In other words, are the crimes that cause more damage to society the most severely sanctioned (justice), and is the same offense punished in the same manner across society (fairness)? Ample discussion of these two points is provided in the book, and I will therefore limit the answers to one illustration: drug law violations. In terms of justice, suffice it to say that in the 2000s the number of convictions for use of marijuana has more than tripled, as a result of the establishment of quota of arrests by the police, while for financial crime it has decreased by one-third, after the introduction of legal measures rendering the indictments for such law infringements more difficult. It would be difficult to argue that smoking a substance that is legal in certain countries might be more prejudicial to society than embezzling funds. Currently, in France, imprisonment sentences for drug law violations represent one incarceration out of seven, essentially for possession and resale of cannabis, with one-fourth of these violations corresponding to mere use. In terms of fairness, while epidemiological surveys show that marijuana consumption is widely distributed among the youth, being even slightly more frequent in the middle class, those sentenced to imprisonment belong only to disadvantaged groups and ethnoracial minorities. The main reason for this discrepancy is that law enforcement officers concentrate their activity in housing projects rather than around universities, and use socioracial profiling to decide whom to stop and search. Presently, in French prisons, half of the prisoners are unemployed, half of them declare to have no profession, four out of five have not finished high school, and in the short-stay facility where I conducted my research, three-fourths of the inmates belonged to ethnoracial minorities, being mostly black and Arab men. The unjust and unfair allocation of punishment explains in good part the formidable disparities observed in French correctional institutions. In this respect, it should be noted that the expansion of the prison population with its socioracial component occurred at the very moment when socioeconomic inequalities started to deepen after a long period of contraction and when ethnoracial minorities became the target of stigmatization campaigns from right-wing parties. The penal state has definitely been a way of governing the poor.

With this analysis in mind, it is possible to enter the prison system itself and better apprehend the way it operates. Indeed, it is not enough to wonder how contemporary societies have come to incarcerate so many people with such a disproportionate representation of the most disadvantaged and discriminated categories. One has to ask: what is it to be confined in a French prison today? Guards often say that the only thing of which prisoners are deprived is their freedom, and this belief has been at the heart of the very idea of the prison since its inception. Judges even maintain that the so-called incarceration shock may be salutary for the person convicted in the sense that it allows him to realize the consequence of his act. Yet, were freedom the only deprivation endured and the incarceration shock actually salutary, French correctional facilities might not have the highest suicide rate in the European Union, twice that of comparable countries such as Germany or Britain and five times what it was half a century ago. While the reasons for this suicide epidemic are unclear, it suggests that what inmates lack in prison is not just liberty. It is also privacy in their shared cell, an affective and sexual life with the constraints imposed on their rare visitors, the possibility to make decisions on ordinary needs like taking a medicine when in pain, the right to express emotions like anger when facing frustrations. What they are deprived of is their dignity, as they are subjected to body searches, and fair treatment, when they are sanctioned for misdeeds that the administration knows they have not committed. What the incarceration shock implies can be the loss of their job with the anticipated difficulty involved in finding another one, the disruption of their marital, family, and social life, and the exposure to violent encounters and criminal networks. At the end of the four years I devoted to studying prison life, the most obvious conclusion I could draw was that, contrary to the common idea that the prison system is expanding like an archipelago beyond its walls, something remains irreducible in the *carceral condition*.

For the social scientist, and probably for the public as well, the question that then comes to mind is: what is prison life like under this carceral condition in France? Much of my work has been an attempt to provide an answer to this question. Beyond the deprivations and the shock, beyond the drastic security measures and the harsh conditions of confinement, what is the prison experience for both personnel and prisoners? As one gets progressively immersed in the correctional system, whether as a new inmate, a novice officer, or a social scientist, one becomes aware of much more complex relationships and arrangements between the multiple agents and within the various contexts than what one expected. The imagined total institution appears as a field of forces, where the rules are permanently tested, negotiated, and diverted by guards as well as inmates. Of course, these rules are defined by the prison staff; certain officers do misuse them; all ultimately enforce them strictly and even brutally in the event of conflicts. In other words, power is unevenly distributed and some abuse it. Yet, in the daily life of the facility, compromises constantly occur: a shower is authorized although it is not supposed to be, an inmate back from a visit is left for a while in the walkway instead of being locked up, an officer agrees to serve as intermediary to pass tobacco or coffee from one cell to another. These adjustments are deemed to contribute to keeping the peace within the prison for the evident benefit of all. But they also reveal the existence, within limits steadily iterated, of mutual respect acquired through months or years of cohabitation.

The institution plays an important role in the production of this internal order. The threat of sanctions, which affects not only the stay in prison but also the time served and the possibility of parole, definitely counts. Yet, after having been publicly criticized at the turn of the century, and so as to conform with the European Prison Rules, the correctional system has undergone important transformations, both material and organizational, such as an improvement of the environment in the admissions unit or the presence of a lawyer during disciplinary hearings. A person familiar with the correctional apparatus in the United States would certainly be surprised to discover that French inmates are incited to vote rather than being disenfranchised, and cannot be submitted to solitary confinement for more than 30 days instead of having no maximum. Conversely, an observer of the French prison system would undoubtedly be astounded to learn that in the United States inmates may be shackled or controlled by pepper spray, and guards can beat up a prisoner and even kill him without being sanctioned by the institution or indicted by a prosecutor. National contexts differ. They matter. They influence legal guarantees, institutional regulations, and professional ethos.

Yet, beyond these differences, which are certainly crucial for those who spend months or years behind bars, one question is of universal relevance: that of the sense and function of the prison. It can be formulated in philosophical terms, but it has to be examined on an empirical basis. A common justification of the prison is utilitarian: it reduces crime via incapacitation, deterrence, and rehabilitation. For short-term sentences, which represent in France the great majority, with four out of five being less than one year, this justification is difficult to argue, since studies show that recidivism is higher after incarceration than when an alternative penalty is given. Indeed, the destructuring of family and professional life is not compensated by efforts toward reinsertion during prison time, the stay being too short to provide useful activities and plan re-entry under supervision. The months spent in prison are experienced as vainly lost: no work, no class, no sports, and no social work undertaken. Imprisonment reveals the naked truth of its sole meaning: the retribution of a wrong as a form of socialized vengeance. However, even if one accepts this justification, according to which the suffering of the person convicted must be commensurate with the injury to the victim or the damage to society, could one argue that smoking marijuana, driving with a suspended license, even stealing a cellphone or an auto radio is worth several months in prison?

*   *   *

After having spent a decade or so exploring the compassionate elements of contemporary societies via the analysis of the deployment of humanitarian reason, I have since dedicated my research to their repressive component through the study of policing and punishing – the dark side after the bright one, so to speak. In that respect, my earlier book, *Enforcing Order*, and this one, *Prison Worlds*, constitute a diptych illuminating how repression operates from the street to the cell. Both texts rely on the same ethnographic method, a similar presence in the field for a long period of time, an analogous endeavor to connect local observations to the legal framework, the political context, the demographics of the concerned populations, and, in the end, an equivalent attempt to draw conclusions of general value regarding the logics and mechanisms involved in the way punishment is distributed. From that perspective, I tend to think that the deeper the ethnographic inquiry the broader the anthropological comprehension. In the same way as the study of the daily work of an anticrime squad in the disadvantaged outskirts of Paris can illuminate the activity of law enforcement in Ferguson, Rio, Johannesburg, or Bangkok, so the investigation in a French short-stay prison can shed light on the functioning of correctional facilities in the United States, Brazil, South Africa, or Thailand. It is not a matter of suggesting that things would be similar everywhere, but that certain phenomena may be found anywhere. To deny ethnography this sort of generalizability is to try to deprive it of its unique critical edge. Indeed, some facts, details, interactions, and meanings can only be observed and interpreted via this method: they remain invisible or impossible to measure via others. And recognizing them entails not only scientific discoveries but also political issues.

In this respect, it may be that contemporary societies – some of them at least – have reached a turning point or are on the verge of doing so. The punitive moment that I have analyzed in this book is finally being questioned, at least in certain places. The cost and efficacy of the correctional apparatus are sometimes disputed. The social disruption provoked by incarceration and its role in the production and reproduction of crime begin to be acknowledged. In recent years, several European countries with already low incarceration rates, such as Germany, Netherlands, Denmark, Sweden, and Finland, have reduced even more their prison population. This trend has also been noted most recently in the United States, although at a slower pace and starting from a much higher level. Conversely, in France, like in most countries worldwide, the incarceration rate continues to grow, as the retributive ideology is kept alive via law and order policies often underlain by a politics of fear. But even if the decline in the prison population were to be confirmed and extended, it should not distract attention from the carceral condition to which I have devoted most of this book. Ultimately, society can be judged on the state of its prisons and the way it treats its prisoners.

D. F., March 2016

Acknowledgments

Prisoner: You're back, then? Are you writing another book?
Me: No, it's still the same one.
Prisoner: It's going to be never-ending, then.
Prison officer: It's like *The Lord of the Rings*: it'll run into volumes!
(returning from the yard, July 2013)

It is a remarkable paradox that in France, prison, the prime site of confinement, is a space open to research. One need only point to the number of studies carried out there and the books and articles published on the subject. The contrast with the closed world of the police is notable in this respect. I, like others before me, have benefited from this openness, both at the central level of the Directorate of Prison Administration and the local level of the prison where I conducted my research. Not only was I warmly received by those in positions of responsibility in these institutions, but I was also welcomed by the staff – correctional officers, probation and re-entry counselors, and contractors employed by the private service provider – and the civilian personnel – doctors and nurses in the walk-in clinic, the clergy of diverse faiths and members of various advocacy organizations – as well as by sentencing judges, prosecutors, and defense attorneys, and even, in the district court (*tribunal de grande instance*), magistrates sitting in immediate appearance trials.

As I indicated to all these informants when I outlined my project to them, my aim is both to respect the anonymity of places and persons, and to ensure the confidentiality of the observations and testimonies gathered. For this reason I am unable to acknowledge individually all of the many people who allowed me to conduct my research with an exceptional degree of freedom, for which I am grateful to two successive directors and their deputies, and in the atmosphere of trust and cordiality that I encountered among the staff and others involved in the prison. This desire to protect my sources, as journalists put it, has also led me to modify some personal attributes and elements of biography that would have rendered the people whose actions or words I report too easily identifiable. In particular, where duties are exercised by a small number of agents, I have usually used gender-neutral terms, except in cases where indicating the gender of the person concerned was essential to understanding and not potentially prejudicial to them. I wish to express my sincere gratitude to all those I cannot cite.

We may wonder about the reasons for the French prison system's relatively benign disposition toward researchers – an attitude that is not necessarily echoed in other countries. After all, given the information on the situation in French prisons that filters through in newspaper and magazine articles, TV programs, press statements from organizations such as the International Prison Observatory (Observatoire international des prisons), parliamentary reports, and also reports from the National Ombudsman (Médiateur de la République) and especially the General Inspector of Prisons and Detention Centers (Contrôleur général des lieux de privation de liberté) – all of them generally authoritative documents that are unsparing in their criticism of prison policy and practices – the institution might well fear the proliferation of outside scrutiny, and could easily cordon itself off from the curiosity of social scientists. That it does not is entirely to its credit.

There are two explanations for it. The first, more clearly manifest at the level of national administration, is due to a form of democratic culture, certainly reinforced by pressure from the forces listed above, combined with a will to knowledge that is evident from the fact that the Directorate of Prison Administration has its own office for surveys and planning, that the main research center in this field operates under the aegis of the French Ministry of Justice, and that calls for scientific projects on the prison system are regularly published. The second, more perceptible at the local level, relates to a degree of dismay felt in the prison service over the negative public image of prisons and prison staff, which these latter consider unjustified. Working for an institution that the French president described in parliament as a "national disgrace for France" just as I was beginning my study is not easy, especially when the staff have the feeling that the realities of the prison environment are ultimately as much the result of political choices, legislative measures, budget constraints, and court decisions as they are of penitentiary practice itself. In these circumstances, the scrutiny and reflections of researchers could hardly make the representation worse, especially as researchers are credited both with spending more time there, allowing them to immerse themselves in the environment and thus to understand it better, and being more independent of ideological and institutional interests. "We have nothing to hide," I was often told by members of the management team in the prison, and indeed they were as good as their word, letting me organize my work as I wished, including in places and at moments that did not show the establishment in the best light, and even after the publication of my book on policing, when I was applying for a renewal of my research authorization, which might have been refused in the context of the public debate generated by that book. Prison guards too encouraged me: "We hope you're going to show prison how it really is." They felt that they were still too often tarred with the traditional image of the "screw," and regularly inquired about the progress of my research.

But the world of prison is not made up solely of the prison management, its staff, and independent contractors. It is also, above all, made up of the life of the prisoners who spend months or years there. They too were generous in their welcome. Admittedly, one of their most frequent complaints was that they were not listened to by the wardens, the guards, or the probation and re-entry counselors. If a stranger comes in and invites them to talk, it is likely that he will be well received. Nevertheless, it seemed to me that the relationship went beyond a simple expectation of being heard. What was being manifested was the feeling that they were recognized as something other than just inmates. What was also expressed was the idea that the vehicle of the written word could give weight to what they were telling me. I am grateful to them for the interest they showed and the confidences they shared with me.

I hope that in this book I have preserved something of the truth of their experience, while at the same time protecting the anonymity and confidentiality of their individual histories, a procedure that has in some cases led me to omit elements of their stories or statements. The family names that appear in some of the reported conversations have of course been changed. However, I have never resorted to the practice, widespread in the social sciences, of using an invented surname or forename, or even an initial, as it seems to me that this process gives an anecdotal turn to their story. Contrary to this common usage, I have preferred to call them simply what they are: men. I use the term "prisoner" or "inmate" only in the context of administrative or demographic data relating to the prison population and in descriptions of interactions with prison staff, where the roles of each are predetermined. I have adopted the same practice in relation to the terms "defendant" and "suspect" in situations involving the courts or the police. When I recount the story of an individual or describe his relationship with me or with others, I say "the man" in order to restore to him a kind of dignity of which prison, the courts, and the police tend to deprive them – a fact they themselves complain of, maintaining that once they cross the threshold of the prison they are no longer anything but their inmate number.

This study was financed by an advanced grant that I was awarded in 2009, under the IDEAS program of the European Research Council: my proposal was to explore a domain I called political and moral anthropology. The support afforded by this grant goes far beyond the actual funding: it opens the doors of institutions, makes it possible to employ young researchers, 10 of whom were involved in this collective project, focusing on different areas and different subjects, and, finally, facilitates the dissemination and discussion of research outcomes – in other words, contributes to the production of a public space in which the social sciences have their place. The study was conducted in France, but has become a book in the United States. The freedom I enjoy at the Institute for Advanced Study, the interdisciplinary interactions that constitute the daily life of this institution, and the intellectual ethos characteristic of it were all essential to the work of reflection and writing. It is also the Institute, along with Iris, Institut de recherche interdisciplinaire sur les enjeux sociaux, and the program Tepsis, that funded the translation. As was the case with Bruno Auerbach at Le Seuil, so John Thompson, at Polity Press, accepted this project enthusiastically when I proposed it to him. And, as for several of my previous books, I have benefited from Rachel Gomme's remarkable work of translation as well as from Patrick Brown's, Laura McCune's, and Sarah Dancy's attentive copyediting. Finally, the book owes much to the conversations I had throughout the writing process with Anne-Claire Defossez, particularly during our precious mountain hikes, and beyond these discussions, to a particular idea that we share of what the world is and what it could be.

D. F., Princeton, August 2015

Prologue

Where It All Begins

"I don't know this law," said K.
"So much the worse for you then," said the policeman.
Franz Kafka, *The Trial*

"So, this case . . . is quite extraordinary! All in all, it's just another unfortunate road traffic incident, of the kind we see all too many. But, you're giving us a real adventure story." Thus the presiding judge, adopting a cheery tone, introduces the final case of the immediate appearance trials in a session she described to me later as "light, but quite representative of our work." To be specific, the session has covered armed robbery, domestic violence, resisting arrest, and driving without a license. The last glimmers of winter daylight are filtering through the high windows of the plain concrete and glass district court building. At one end of the vast, almost empty courtroom, the judge sits on a raised dais, accompanied by her two associate magistrates, whose voices remain unheard throughout the four hours it takes to try the five cases. Alongside her, the court clerk does not lift her eyes from her computer screen, while the court usher busies himself looking for a lost document.

In the defendant's box, partially enclosed by walls of wood and plexiglass, stands a man of 35 who looks 10 years younger: thin, haggard, shaven-headed, dressed in jeans and a tee-shirt. With his drawn features, doubtless the result of being held in custody, he seems lost, frowning with a sort of anxious perplexity at the judge's torrent of words, which are interrupted only by occasional questions to which he replies in brief sentences uttered in a low, uncertain voice. Behind him, the two policemen who brought him in after removing his handcuffs. In front of him, the court-appointed attorney he met a short time before, and whose assistance he has accepted. Opposite him, a young prosecuting attorney. I am the only one seated on the public benches. Not a single relative, friend, or witness is in attendance for any of the five cases heard. In contrast with the presiding judge's breezy remarks, a motto inscribed in giant letters on the wall above her offers a sententious reminder of the solemnity of the place: "The court is the ultimate arbiter, declaring and recalling the value of things."

It takes all of the presiding judge's talents as a storyteller to liven up the account of the – all in all rather banal – events that have led to the defendant's appearance before her. One Sunday in late summer, in a small town nearby, a car veered off the road and crashed into a signpost. The collision caused it to roll onto its side, but the occupants lifted it back up again and drove off. When the police, who had been called by a witness, arrived, the vehicle had disappeared, but they found the license plate that had been torn off in the collision and easily identified the car in question, which was found in a parking lot not far away. When they questioned the owner, a woman in her 30s, she explained that her partner had been driving the vehicle. She claimed to have no idea where he was, but stated that he "had friends among Roma people." The police officers then asked her to tell him that he was required to present himself at the police station. The man did not comply with the oral summons given to his partner, and four months later, the police arrived at his home at 6:30 in the morning to question him. Discovering that he no longer had a driver's license and that his car was not insured, they arrested him and notified the public prosecutor; the following day, they brought him to court for an immediate appearance trial.

Having recounted the facts, the judge asks the accused how he pleads, and when he admits to the charges, she explodes: "What a completely stupid thing to do! Did you think you could live on the run like that?" The defendant explains softly that he was not on the run; he lives close to the police station, and on his return from work in the evening he has several times met police officers who know him well and could easily have asked him to accompany them down to the precinct. "Come on, tell the truth in court!" the judge insists. "You took advantage of not being arrested to enjoy the holidays with your family." The defendant lowers his head. He has three young children, one of them adopted, and his partner is expecting a fourth. The judge feigns surprise: "Looking at you, you give the impression of someone showing remorse, but you're not at all sorry! When the police officers questioned you, you said you would only talk to the judge with your lawyer." Realizing that this remark is highly inappropriate, she corrects herself, acknowledging that this is indeed his right.

Examination of the case file reveals 19 citations over the previous 15 years, generally for similar offenses. These often resulted in a fine, once in the confiscation of his vehicle, and four times in prison sentences: of two months, four months, six months, and one longer stay of 36 months on account of violence and the activation of suspended sentences. "It's a mystery how to make you understand that you cannot drive without a license and without insurance. You're a danger to the public, and we're only going to be safe if we put you in prison. What do you think?" The man remains silent. The judge moves on to rapidly scanning the social review, which is required in immediate appearance trials and is conducted by a psychologist from a rehabilitation organization. The report states that the man's late father was a mechanic and that his mother brought up her seven children on her own. Having dropped out of a vocational school, their son began working at a very young age in temporary jobs, before finding more stable employment as a delivery driver, during the course of which he received 12 points on his license. The resulting prison sentences caused him to lose his job, and it was also one of these sentences that interrupted the lessons he had begun taking precisely for the purpose of regaining his license. He was released eight months earlier from his most recent prison sentence and looked for work for a long time before being hired as a temporary warehouseman in a company that was about to offer him a fixed-term contract the following week. He is also a former heroin user and is still enrolled in a methadone maintenance treatment. "You've been on methadone for four years?" asks the judge reprovingly. "That's pretty much a treatment for life, isn't it! One drug replacing another." Suspecting that he ran off after the accident in order to avoid being breathalysed, she adds: "And if you drink on top of that, it's hardly going to help." Overwhelmed, the man remains silent.

It is now time for the prosecution to present its case. Of the three offenses, explains the public prosecutor, only two have been proven. In this tale that she describes, in an echo of the judge's dramatization of the narrative, as "surrealistic," the offense of fleeing the scene cannot be legally established because the circumstances of the accident meant that the accused was forced to stop, and did not drive off immediately. However, the lack of a license and insurance is confirmed, and moreover these are repeat offenses since he has recently been convicted of the same crimes. Because of this aggravating factor, she asks the judge to apply the mandatory sentence principle; in doing so, she effectively extends the scope of this automatic sanction beyond that prescribed by the legislation, which limits it to crimes punishable by sentences of three years or more. Moreover, far from encouraging clemency, "the recent employment and his good integration into his family" only make things worse from her perspective and justify a heavier penalty since, she argues, these favorable circumstances have not prevented him from committing further offenses. Regretting only that she cannot request the confiscation of the car, which is registered to his partner, the prosecutor concludes by calling for a custodial sentence of six months imprisonment with immediate incarceration. The judge suggests that she add reckless driving to the list of charges, in order to allow for compensation of the municipality, the mayor having submitted a claim, backed up by invoices, for 240 euros to replace the damaged signpost.

When it comes to the public defender's turn to address the court, he begins, to the evident surprise of his client, by denigrating his partner. In an attempt to refute the offense of fleeing the scene, which has however already been dropped by the prosecutor, he accuses the young woman of lying to the police by stating that her partner was not at their home, when in fact he was; and so it was she, not he, who obstructed the course of justice. The lawyer does, however, acknowledge that the offenses relating to the lack of driver's license and insurance are incontestable, "offenses which represent a danger to society, since he's hardly the world's greatest driver," he adds with irony, to the increased astonishment of the defendant. But he bases his arguments against returning the accused to prison on the social context. He makes mention of the defendant's family and work circumstances, noting that he "supports his partner and their three children," "doesn't sit around doing nothing and living off welfare," "is following a treatment plan," and "is attempting to reintegrate into society." He therefore asks that the accused be "given this one last chance, or maybe the first chance after his troubled criminal past," in view of both the recent change for the better with the job he has just been offered and the family's precarious financial situation, with their only income being his wages. In a weary tone, he concludes his case by recalling, without conviction, the "possibility of alternative penalties that will help him become aware of the seriousness of his actions and support him on the path to proper integration" – penalties that he does not, however, specify. The judge intervenes once more to correct him on the stability of the employment, reminding him that it is nothing more than the promise of a fixed-term contract. A discussion ensues with the public prosecutor and the public defender on the meaning of temporary jobs and the need to reform labor law. The accused appears once more amazed by this unexpected digression. Finally, the judge turns toward him to ask if he wishes to add anything. In a scarcely audible voice, the man says that he regrets his action and is now "on the right track." Hardly has he finished speaking when the judge declares a recess in order to deliberate. The hearing has lasted just 35 minutes.

Half an hour later, the court is reconvened. For driving without a license and insurance, the judge issues a sentence of six months' imprisonment, and also awards damages to the civil claimants. The man appears despondent but resigned. The police officers replace his handcuffs and escort him to the prison, where he will be incarcerated.

* * *

It is there that I see him again three days later. He is in the new arrivals section of the prison, a sort of acclimatization zone between the outside world and the reality of incarceration, where inmates spend a few days before being transferred to the main buildings. The cell, where he is alone for the time being, measures about 100 square feet. The walls are painted pastel blue. It is minimally furnished: a basin with a mirror above it, a toilet hidden behind a screen, an iron bunk bed, a table and two plastic chairs, a closet. The barred window is covered by a thick rubberized grille, through which an exercise yard can be glimpsed, its high walls topped by coils of concertina razor wire. The few essential items given to each new arrival are placed in one corner. A transit zone, the cell does not have any of the decorative items found in cells where prisoners spend longer periods of time. After offering me one of the two chairs, the man sits down on the bottom bunk.

As I explain my research to him, he smiles fleetingly and says that he recognizes me, having noticed my presence in the courtroom, and wondered who I was. I ask him how he feels. "When I came in I was really down. I'm feeling a bit better now." Upgraded to meet the standards of good practice of the European Prison Rules for "caring for and accompanying the detained person during the intake phase," the arrivals section is a source of pride for the prison warden, who has had it refurbished, and for the correctional officer in charge. It allows for a less abrupt transition into detention, particularly for those who are imprisoned for the first time. Inmates held there receive special attention and meet with key personnel, from the senior management to the probation and re-entry service, as well as the private contractor that provides employment opportunities and the outpatient health clinic. "I was worried I wouldn't get my medication, because I was brought in on a Friday night," the man tells me, referring to his daily 60mg dose of methadone. "But the doctor came on Saturday. She trusted me. Lucky I had the medication on me, so she knew I was telling the truth and was on it, and she wrote me a prescription." The prospect of going without medication during their first few days in prison is indeed one of the worst fears of both prisoners on methadone treatment and guards, who dread the consequences of withdrawal.

The man soon returns to the subject of his sentence. "Sure, driving with a suspended license is illegal, but you can't call it a serious crime. It's not right that you end up together with burglars and rapists just for that. Sometimes you go into jail calm and you come out more crazy. I've been inside four times, and I've been offered loads of stuff. I've even been asked straight up to join in robberies. There are Islamists here too, they try to recruit us . . . They put you in jail with all those guys, but the judges don't realize what it's like in here!" He breaks off and then resumes: "You might as well go to jail for actually doing something. Driving with a suspended license is no big deal. This place messes with your head." Visibly marked by his three previous stays in this same prison, he describes the everyday violence: "There's a fight in the exercise yards at least every two or three days. And then there's the shakedowns. Last time on my first day, when I joined the main prison population they took the sneakers I was wearing." His frail physique obviously did not make life in prison easy for him: "In here, if you're weak, you're the maid. You have to do everything the guys tell you to. When they put you out there, it's like sending a lamb out into a pack of wolves . . . And then there aren't that many French guys in the prison. Most of them are blacks and Arabs. You can count the number of French guys on one hand. We're the victims. They put pressure on us. Either that or you just don't leave your cell." Without spelling them out, he hints at the forbidden activities imposed on the most vulnerable – picking up packages thrown over the walls or hiding prohibited objects among their belongings, at the risk of severe punishment. But he also makes broader reference to the rule of the strongest and its consequences: "Sometimes guys kill themselves and you don't know why. He's been in here for months and then he kills himself. That doesn't just happen. People kill themselves as soon as they arrive here, not after months. Unless there's a problem." He speaks of the prisoner he felt closest to last time he was in prison, who was "found dead in his cell" four days before he was due to be released. "And they claimed it was 'death by natural causes,'" he adds bitterly.

However, what seems to distress him even more than the prospect of time in prison, of which he has some experience and which he is already getting used to again, is the loss of his outside life: "When I get out I'll be out of work, I'll have to start all over again. It took me nearly a year to find a job, now it's fucked up. When I'm released I won't have anything left. Two months I was at that company as a warehouseman. The judges don't understand. They don't think a temporary contract is a real job. But fixed-term contracts don't grow on trees. Especially in my situation. That's what really pisses me off: I was just about to get a contract." His main concern is that he will not be able to see his three children grow up and take care of them: "Last year I was jailed just before my son was born. And now I won't be there for his first birthday. I won't see my new baby born either. That's really hard, you know … My kids are what keeps me going." He falls silent for a few moments, then resumes, anxiously: "I'm worried. One of the older two is starting down the wrong path. That's what I'm scared of. When I'm not there, their mother has trouble controlling them, especially my 13-year-old boy. And we can't keep telling them 'Dad's away on vacation.' They're too old for that now." But suddenly remembering what was said about his partner in court, he is furious at the way she was stigmatized: "And then they call my wife a liar. They're full of shit! Anyway I didn't have any confidence in the public defender. When he came to see me in custody he started by scolding me. I said to him: 'Hold on, are you here to judge me or defend me?' Those lawyers, they just turn up to collect their money," he concludes, returning to the familiar refrain of defendants without money.

Recalling the accusation of lying against his partner then leads him to confide something about his identity: "I'll be honest with you, we're kind of Roma. But I didn't say that in court because they're real prejudiced and it would only get me a worse sentence." This point, which was actually mentioned in passing when the facts of the case were read out during the hearing, was indeed not taken up by anyone. Yet it was explicitly identified in the police's report as a detail communicated to the court, which could therefore not ignore it. Whether or not the court took it into account, the secret of his origins was equally difficult to hide in the prison. A little later that day, in the exercise yard, I heard another prisoner call out to him, in friendly greeting: "Hey, gypsy!" Two of his cousins and their father were also incarcerated in the facility and, as I was often told, news travels fast in prison.

As we part, the man tells me of his hope that, this time, he will get the sentence adjustment he was refused four times during his previous long prison term. "I have to do everything I can to get out of here as soon as I can," he says, adding, lucidly: "But I know it's not likely, because they're all backed up." And indeed, contrary to his hopes, he was eventually released right at the end of the specified sentence term, reduced only by the sentence reduction credits – seven days per month – that are automatically allocated on condition of "absence of disruptive behavior" in prison. However, he did not benefit from any additional sentence reduction – four days per month, for a repeat offender – that are awarded in recognition of "efforts toward social rehabilitation" through work or training in prison, since the shortness of his sentence effectively made these two activities inaccessible to him. In the end, his stay in prison lasted four months and 23 days, without any provision made for helping him reintegrate into society. Constraints due to the heavy workload of the probation and re-entry counselors mean that sentence adjustments enabling a smoother transition to life on the outside, possibly in the context of a job, are only exceptionally granted in sentences of less than six months, as priority is given to inmates with longer sentences. Release is thus almost always "cold," without the period of reintegration and work that allows prisoners to be placed under electronic surveillance, in other words the "ankle bracelet." In this case, the court itself could even have stipulated the sentence adjustment, since the defendant was on the verge of signing a contract with the company where he had temporary employment. It did not.

Those serving short prison sentences are therefore doubly disadvantaged: on the one hand, they cannot work, receive training, or attend classes, and so are also deprived of additional sentence reductions; on the other, they do not benefit from the efforts of the probation and re-entry service, meaning that their sentences cannot be adjusted. Prisoners are not generally aware of this when they arrive. They ask to be able to work or study. They write to their counselor to arrange a meeting to discuss sentence reductions and adjustments. When they get no response, they ask the senior officer whether their repeated requests were indeed transmitted. Finally, as they see the weeks go by without anything being offered to them, and often without even receiving any reply, they understand that they will spend the rest of their sentence without any activity other than the twice-daily walk. Until one day, they are told they are being released, finding out when the guard, himself just informed by the prison administration, calls them on the internal telephone in their cell to tell them to pack their belongings because they are getting out.

Six months after our conversation, I was accompanying a prison officer and an auxiliary as they distributed the lunch to the inmates, when a door opened and I suddenly came face to face with this same man. As surprised as I was by this unexpected meeting, he greeted me without formality: "Dude, what you still doing here?" After the guard laughed at his question, he realized how inappropriate it was, having taken me for another prisoner. This gaffe, for which he laughingly apologized, suggested to me that he had unconsciously filed me in a different mental category from the authority represented by the prison administration. We had time for no more than a brief exchange. The cell door was already closing and the meal distribution continued. Intrigued by his presence beyond the specified term of his sentence, I learned a little later that three weeks after his release he had once again been convicted of assault at an immediate appearance trial. This time he had been sentenced to ten months' imprisonment, with five months suspended for two years. Over his chaotic career, with the prison terms he had listed to me – "2010, 2011, 2012, 2013" – he had never relapsed so quickly.

*   *   *

"I'm real pissed, because I was putting my life back together again. I had a job. I had my kids," he had said to me when we had met the first time. Obviously there is no knowing whether, despite the promise of employment and the birth of his new child, he would have had all the social resources he needed to see through this rebuilding process, if he had been let off with a noncustodial sentence such as community service, or with a sentence adjustment stipulated by the magistrate during the trial to be implemented by the sentencing judge later on. However, it is certain that imprisonment with immediate incarceration and no prospect of adjustment left no opportunity for social reintegration and made it highly likely that he would reoffend. Sentencing him to prison maximized the risk that he would return there. The presiding judge was well aware of this.

When, at the end of the hearing, I asked her why she chose prison time for driving without a license and insurance – two offenses that are linked, since the first almost automatically implies the second – despite the man's family and work circumstances, she replied, dispiritedly: "Yes, I know, we talked about that while we were deliberating. We don't know what to do in these cases. We're helpless. We feel as if it doesn't make the least difference. We know he'll do it again, but we still have to apply the punishment. With his previous convictions, what else could we do?" Without any further justification of her decision and with little illusion as to its efficacy, she felt that her only option was imprisonment, both to punish the crime (because it was a repeat offense rather than a serious one, a fact she emphasized dramatically in court), and to protect society (at least during the sentence, for she could not have been unaware that short prison sentences with no possibility for adjustment have been shown to encourage recidivism).

In fact, on that day, all the defendants except one were returned in handcuffs to the prison, either because they had agreed to be tried immediately on arrest and had been sentenced to prison, or because they had invoked their right to request a postponement in order to prepare their defense but had been remanded in custody awaiting trial. When the public prosecutor's office puts forward a case for immediate appearance trial, it indicates that they have reasonable grounds for believing the defendant is highly likely to be sent to prison, either after sentencing or in pretrial detention. Moreover, at the immediate appearance trials I attended, except in cases where there was a blatant lack of evidence that resulted in the defendant's acquittal, the judge almost always granted the prosecution's request for sentencing. The role of the defense attorneys, usually appointed by the court, seemed a mere legal formality to which evidently no one attached any great importance, starting with the public defenders themselves who readily acquiesced to this assessment when I spoke with them after trials.

During the first days of my research at the prison, in order to familiarize myself with the facility and its occupants I sat in on the interviews that members of the management team and the probation and re-entry counselors conducted with new inmates on arrival. For them the aim of these was to establish a first contact, to evaluate circumstances and needs, to identify problems, particularly risk of suicide, and more broadly, in the case of the wardens, to know "their" prison population. I was struck then by the frequency of short sentences, and still more by the trivial nature of the offenses that had resulted in them. The number of sentences for driving with a suspended license, among other offenses, was soaring, having quadrupled in France over the past 20 years, largely as a result of the increased number of speed cameras on roads. These offenses were often punished by a suspended sentence that "came down" when the individual was convicted for a second offense, in which case the two penalties were added together, creating a sentence lasting several months. People working for trucking and delivery companies – those unskilled, poorly paid jobs that are inevitably taken by young working-class men – were singularly vulnerable precisely because of the conditions of work in these professions, where they are under pressure to maintain productivity.

"Two weeks in jail for a repeat offense of driving with a suspended license: what's the point in that?" raged one of the directors after an interview with one inmate. "What's he going to learn in prison? And what can we do in two weeks? All it does is desocialize him. What's the guy going to say to his boss? And to his wife and children?" But these driving offenses, which were often punished by sentences much longer than two weeks, were for him just the most visible aspect of a pattern whereby imprisonment was becoming the routine punishment for actions whose perpetrators would never have been incarcerated when he began his career 25 years earlier. Moreover, he was aware that not all those who committed such offenses bore the same risk of being arrested and ending up in prison: "The other day, I saw among the new arrivals a man who'd been convicted of driving with a suspended license. He was black. I asked him about the circumstances of his arrest. He told me that it was a routine police road check, but he pointed out that he had been checked 15 times since the start of the year." The warden added: "I've only ever been checked once in my life," implying that if he had driven with a suspended license no one would ever have known. Thus, the selection of the prison population begins in the street, where ordinary policing leads to the profiling of individuals on the basis of their physical appearance, and continues in the public prosecutor's office through the real-time processing that is reserved for certain kinds of cases and above all certain kinds of defendants. Immediate appearance trials, which usually result in custodial prison sentences, are the ultimate end-point of this selection.

The judge's embarrassed justification of her decision precisely reflects this reality and the concern it causes: the growing centrality of prison both in the thinking of magistrates and in their arsenal of available punishments leads to imprisonment being readily seen as unavoidable for repeat offenders, all the more when, as in the case described above, they are people whose lives have been marked both by social precarity and by previous incarcerations. But the judges are not the only ones who have begun to think in this way more and more often. It is society as a whole that has become more repressive, to the extent that the courts, which have been imposing increasingly harsher penalties, are constantly accused of being too lenient. In a context where security has become a major electoral issue, new offenses have been added to the penal code, stiffer penalties have been voted in, mandatory sentences have been introduced, guidelines have been issued to public prosecutors, and judges have been subjected to political pressure. As a result, the number of people imprisoned has doubled over the last 30 years. This situation is not, in fact, specific to France: it is evident in almost all Western countries, notably the United States, where the prison population has risen almost fivefold in three decades.

However, those sent to prison are not evenly distributed throughout society. The fact that the man sentenced for driving without a license and insurance was from a poor background and belonged to a minority group is not random accident, either in terms of cases sent for immediate appearance trial or in terms of custodial sentences. These are in fact the two most characteristic features of those whose offenses are processed summarily and whose prison sentences lead to immediate incarceration: they come from disadvantaged urban communities, often living in public housing projects, and belong to ethnic minorities, generally North Africans or sub-Saharan Africans, sometimes Roma. Because they are disproportionately involved in the offenses that are most subject to repression, and because, even when this is not the case, police activity tends to focus on them (for insulting a police officer and resisting arrest, or for use and possession of drugs, for example), they are consistently overrepresented in fast-track prosecution procedures and among those sentenced to imprisonment. Here again, beyond individual variations related to national history, we see a similar sociodemographic distribution in all Western countries. In the United States it is even more pronounced, with imprisonment seven and three times higher, respectively, for blacks and Hispanics than for whites, and eight times higher among black dropouts than among those with college degrees.

The opening scene in the district court therefore has exemplary value. It both illustrates and reveals a triple reality of the contemporary world that has long been identified by social scientists researching prison policy and the world of prisons in the United States, Britain, France, and elsewhere. First, prison occupies a central place in the social imaginary and court practice, as the ultimate sanction and routine mode of punishment not only for serious crimes, but also a growing number of petty crimes, particularly when they are repeat offenses. Second, the solution of imprisonment is disproportionately and arbitrarily applied to socially disadvantaged and ethnically discriminated populations, particularly during times of economic difficulty and growing inequality. Third, these two facts have a relatively recent history that can be read on two temporal levels: that of our modernity, with the invention of prison in the eighteenth century, and that of our present, with the expansion of prison over the last 30 years.

The judge who sentenced a father of three in precarious financial circumstances to six months in prison solely for having committed a repeat offense of driving a vehicle when he had a suspended license thus acts within a larger context. She is participating, without being entirely conscious of it, since her reflection takes place in the immediate moment of the decision, in a fundamental transformation of the relationship between punishment and inequality. The fact that the justice she administers is not applied in the same way to all, as sociological studies have long shown, and as parliamentary reports have more recently noted, emerges from social patterns and political choices that are beyond her awareness. She could of course issue different penalties – and variations in the severity displayed by different judges and different jurisdictions are sufficient to illustrate the part played by each magistrate in the decisions made, even when done so collectively – but it would be wrong to see this simply as a question of individual choice. In this case as in others, the presiding judge is effectively pronouncing the judgment she thinks society expects of her.

*　　*　　*

It might seem surprising that a book on prisons should open with a court scene. After all, if there is one world that is closed, that deploys extraordinary ingenuity and a wealth of technical resources to cut itself off from the outside, it is that of the prison. It might then seem consistent with the prison project that the picture drawn of it should be equally self-contained. And indeed, a number of reports and analyses of prison present it in this way: as a world apart. This insular perspective, which views prison as a community closed in on itself and describes it as a subculture, has long been subject to debate in North American research, and has been taken up more recently in French writings. It is becoming ever less tenable as prison occupies an increasingly central place in public debate, as external scrutiny penetrates prisons, contemporary technology spreads inside them, and finally as one appreciates the extent to which the prison population, just like the social differentiation observed in delinquency and criminality, reveals the disparities that operate in the repression of crime.

Prison is the product of the work of the police and the judges, governments and parliamentary representatives, journalists and film directors, and even society as a whole, through the fiction known as "public opinion" and the impact of the statements made on its behalf. A change in the legislation relating to the penal system or the implementation of European regulations, a spectacularly violent crime committed by a convicted criminal out on parole or a book denouncing scandalous prison conditions, a judgment against the state in an international court or a case brought by a nongovernmental organization, a demonstration by correctional officers following an attack on one of their number or the reactions to the suicide of a prisoner: all of these influence not only what prison is and the way it operates, but also what those who work there and those who are serving their sentences there think and do.

The man imprisoned for driving without a license and insurance therefore owes his sentence to the recent recategorization of his offense, now classified as vehicular crime, and the subsequent revision of penalties, which changed the punishment from a fine to imprisonment. More broadly, his incarceration is due to increased media focus on road traffic accidents, to a heightened sense of insecurity, to the suspicion that the courts tend to be overly lenient, to the increasingly routine use of immediate appearance trial to deal with minor crimes committed by people with little social standing, and to the belief of judges in the salutary effects of "the carceral shock" on repeat offenders. Thus the overpopulation of prisons and the social composition of those held there represent the culmination of a whole set of decisions taken by the government or parliament, by the police and the courts, but they are also the product of the multiple representations society has of crimes and misdemeanors, and the best ways of punishing and preventing them. Hence the sense of injustice felt by prison staff, particularly guards, when the shame of the conditions in which offenders are held falls purely on them, when they are just "the end of the line," as they themselves often put it.

Moreover, the reverse is also true: both the reality and the image of prisons have an impact on public debate and the social world, on expectations of compensation for victims and on the precarious financial situation of inmates' families, on the sense of whether the punishment fits the crime, and on the reproduction of inequalities. Once someone discovers, or pretends to discover, that some prison sentences are not served or that some prison establishments suffer from a serious shortage of resources, the media is soon overtaken by polemics orchestrated by political parties, advocacy groups, or journalists denouncing the inefficiency of the court system, or the indignity of prison conditions. But prison does not just provide fodder for imagination and controversy; it also disrupts the social order. The incarceration of the man for driving without a license and insurance just when he was due to sign a contract of employment that will no longer be open to him when he gets out, while his partner struggles alone with a desperate financial situation, and his children, left to themselves, seem to be following a worrying path, contributes to the increasing fragility of what are already the most vulnerable groups in society, and to the perpetuation both of social inequality and of criminal ways of life. More generally, the way in which people think of prison, the role attributed to it by the courts, and the place it is given within the law have a major influence on society, particularly on the prospects for rehabilitation of inmates and the risks of breakdown in family relations, on the alienation of particular groups and the marginalization of particular districts, on the balance between punishment and prevention of crime and wrongdoing, and on the choice between exclusion and rehabilitation of those who commit them. Those working in prisons are aware of these issues, especially those in the probation and re-entry services, who continually raise the question of the "meaning of the sentence."

Prison worlds are thus simultaneously a reflection of society and the mirror in which it sees itself. They should therefore be thought of in ways that go beyond simply referring them to their buildings, their staff, and their regulations. We need to open the scope of our analysis to the extent that prison is open to the social space. The day-to-day life of a correctional facility can only be understood in relation to the facts, events, discourses, and actions that take place outside it. Viewed in this perspective, our scene in the courtroom is not just a way of offering a glimpse of what happens prior to incarceration and how people come increasingly to be sentenced to this ultimate punishment. It also reminds us that, for both inmates and personnel, the prison is closely linked to its environment and sensitive to the spirit of the times. For prison worlds may be closed, but they are still porous. Life on the inside intersects with life on the outside. Prison is not separate from the social world: it is its disturbing shadow.

Introduction

The Expanding Prison

> The concept "punishment" is in fact not one meaning, but a whole synthesis
> "of meanings": the previous history of punishment in general, the history
> of its employment for the most various purposes, finally crystallizes into a
> kind of unity that is hard to disentangle, hard to analyze, and, as must be
> emphasized especially, totally indefinable.
> Friedrich Nietzsche, *The Genealogy of Morals*, 1887

Prison is a recent invention. This may seem a surprising assertion, given the
extent to which deprivation of freedom appears, in contemporary society,
to be the most evident and the most universal form of punishment. Yet,
incarceration as the central modality of retributive justice has existed for
little more than two centuries. Historians certainly agree that confinement
could be used in antiquity, in the Middle Ages, and in the Renaissance, but
it was a rare and marginal practice, generally imposed either while awaiting
judgment or the execution of a capital sentence, for the early Christians in
the Roman Empire in particular, or while conducting an interrogation of
the accused through torture, in the context of the Inquisition for instance.[1]
Seldom did it serve as the actual punishment, except in the case of the dun-
geons of Châtelet and, later, the Bastille. For a long time the most severe
sanctions were corporal and public, ranging from flogging, branding, and
mutilation up to death by hanging, decapitation, drawing and quartering,
or burning at the stake. Executions were sometimes preceded by torture,
the most frequent form of which was the wheel on which the executioner
broke the condemned person's bones. Depending on the crime, banishment,
varying both in duration and in distance of removal, was a frequent alternative punishment, often rescinded upon payment of a fine.

By the early modern period in Europe, however, incarceration was beginning to emerge as a mainstay of punishment, partly through the internment
of undesirable individuals in general hospitals like Bicêtre and la Salpêtrière,
in which were gathered paupers, vagrants, thieves and prostitutes, and
partly through forced labor by convicts in the form of the galleys and, later,
arsenals in France, of the workhouses and the North American colonies for

England.[2] Imprisonment as such nevertheless did exist, used either as an additional constraint within the general hospital, with a confinement block for delinquents and criminals, or as an alternative sanction for women or old men who were to be spared the rigors of forced labor.

But it was not until the eighteenth century that imprisonment emerged as the supreme form of punishment, one both reserved for convicted criminals and dedicated to carrying out the punishment – this at least is the idea, since today short-stay prisons in France, for example, also serve to confine, sometimes for several years, individuals who have been charged but have not yet stood trial and are therefore still presumed innocent.[3] The fact that prison became the central modality of punishment obviously does not mean that it is the most used or the most serious: on the one hand, minor sanctions, particularly fines, are much more frequently issued; on the other, the death penalty was for a long time, and in some countries still remains, the ultimate sanction. Prison, however, emerged as the paradigmatic punishment, one that most clearly epitomizes the historical shift of the penal thinking from an action on the body to a suspension of freedom, and one that most acutely concentrates the ambiguities of the meaning of the sentence, perpetually oscillating between vengeance, reparation, prevention, and rehabilitation.

The invention of prison was for a long time represented as the result of a humanist and even humanitarian project promoted by philosophers such as Cesare Beccaria, whose 1764 treatise *On Crimes and Punishments* was highly influential throughout Europe, and Jeremy Bentham, whose 1787 *Panopticon* immediately met with a favorable reception, and philanthropists such as John Howard and William Blackstone, who worked to transform the penal system and prison establishment in England.[4] The ideas of these reformers, it is suggested, were borrowed by the leaders of the French Revolution in their drafting of the Declaration of the Rights of Man and the Citizen as well as by the post-revolutionaries in the United States in their construction of the famous New York and Pennsylvania prisons. According to this reading, the moral progress championed by intellectuals, politicians, and religious leaders was hence the driving force behind this great project. Appalled by the arbitrary and brutal nature of the punishments inflicted by the *ancien régime*, the reformers sought to make punishment more just and less harsh. Prison therefore represented a rational response, equitably applied and resolutely respectful of human dignity, introduced to replace cruel and degrading punishments.

This optimistic and generous account, which casts the institution of prison as a product of the Enlightenment, was contested by Michel Foucault in *Discipline and Punish*.[5] In his view, the ending of the use of torture, the establishment of a penal code that replaced the discretionary authority of the sovereign, and the universalization of confinement as an attenuated form of sanction do indeed mark a turning point in the way that punishment is implemented, but one whose significance is more complex: "The prison, an essential element in the punitive panoply, certainly marks an important moment in the history of penal justice: its access to 'humanity.'

But it is also an important moment in the history of those disciplinary mechanisms that the new class power was developing: that in which they colonized the legal institution." In fact, according to Foucault, if we wish to understand the stakes at play in the birth of the prison, we must bid a definitive farewell to the idea of moral progress, which is always tainted by the assumption that there is a direction to history, so as to grasp the political project underlying this development: "The conjuncture that saw the birth of reform is not, therefore, that of a new sensibility, but that of another policy with regard to illegalities." The point was, on the one hand, to put in place a system of punishment that broke with the arbitrary and spectacular aspects of the sovereign power to punish, as manifested in public ordeals and executions, and, on the other, to respond more effectively to offenses committed by the lower classes, which had until then been largely ignored, by enabling the introduction of differential sanctions for crimes. Prison certainly punished in a more humane way than the old penalties, but, more importantly, it made it possible to punish more often, while at the same time respecting the new judicial as well as social order, and creating a universal hierarchy of sanctions.

Following the publication of Foucault's influential work, historians, while being quick to criticize it, nevertheless set about revising the earlier overly optimistic account whereby the invention of prison was represented as the moralization of punishment. Three main reservations were expressed in relation to this narrative. First, the historical rupture is much less clear than was long believed: corporal punishment, humiliating penalties, and extreme coercion persisted well beyond the advent of the prison. In France, for example, it was only very gradually that physical punishments within correctional facilities, such as leg shackles, metal collars, or the wooden cangue, disappeared from legal texts and from practical use. And it was not until the mid-nineteenth century that exposure in a public place in the stocks was abolished, and only in the mid-twentieth century that the last colonial penal colonies were closed.[6]

Second, the dominant rationales for confinement bear little resemblance to the reforming utopias initially put forward: rather than a softening of punishment, it was a more muted, less visible form of violence that was being instituted. While deprivation of freedom was the common feature of all correctional establishments, it was accompanied by a variety of punitive constraints, which, particularly in Great Britain, imposed severe conditions of imprisonment and harsh working conditions. These constraints increased in severity throughout the nineteenth century, with the development, based on criminological theories, of policies consisting in underfeeding prisoners while forcing them to perform grueling tasks under threat of brutal punishment, the aim being to make prison sentences more of a deterrent.[7]

And third, the dominant reasoning behind the generalization of confinement did not derive primarily from the adoption of the ideas of philosophers and philanthropists, but rather formed part of deeper changes in societies that extended beyond just the institution of prison. In the United States in particular, where European thinkers had little influence, it was the combined effect of the conceptualization of criminality as a problem threatening the celebrated liberal model, and the belief in the possibility of transforming the individual through discipline. This dual ideology translated into a policy influenced by religious principles and experimental techniques, and led to the design of an extreme form of coercion based on isolation, silence, and labor.[8] Thus, over and above the significant differences between countries and considerable variations through time, the shift from bodily punishment to deprivation of freedom and from execution to imprisonment is a complex phenomenon, which, as Foucault argues, marks a new way of governing "illegalisms" rather than a simple scheme to humanize punishment.

*   *   *

What is this way of governing based on? If we are to understand it, we need to begin by examining what lies at the root of the intention to punish. In *The Genealogy of Morals*, Nietzsche asserts that it is "impossible to say for certain why people are really punished," and that the meaning of punishment itself cannot be simply defined, for "only that which has no history is definable" – and punishment certainly has a history, long and tortuous. In support of his argument, Nietzsche draws up a lengthy list of the widely varying and even contradictory reasons that may be invoked to justify punishment, from precluding further harm and reparation of damage to preventing disorder, even inspiring a sort of terror.[9] And indeed, in perusing the successive penal codes, the discourses of reformers, and the debates among legislators, one cannot fail to be struck by the diversity and often the confusion of the arguments put forward. The recourse to punishment thus finds many different justifications. Moreover, certain theorists question whether it is necessary and legitimate to punish. Hence, they seek to propose alternatives, taking the view either that moral condemnation should not automatically imply the imposition of coercion and suffering on the condemned person (the naming of his crime and the concomitant social reproach is sufficient to induce him to reform), or that the offender should receive treatment rather than punishment (physicians and criminologists have proposed theories and remedies, including surgical interventions, to conquer deviant impulses). Nevertheless, if we accept the consensus among most commentators, that punishment is a necessary response to crime, how can it be rationally justified?

It is generally recognized, as John Rawls notes, that there are two main moral justifications for punishment.[10] The first, retributivism, looks to the past, focusing on the wrong committed: the aim of punishment is to inflict a sanction proportionate to the crime. It can be considered a civilized form of revenge, its original and radical formulation being the principle of "an eye for an eye," and its contemporary avatars being manifested in the equation established between the seriousness of the act and the length of the prison sentence. The second, utilitarianism, looks to the future, reflecting on the effects of the sanction: punishment is only justified to the extent that it generates positive consequences for society. It is addressed both to the culprit, who it is hoped will be dissuaded from offending again, and to potential criminals, whom it seeks to discourage from their plans. In theory, these two justifications are mutually exclusive. The empirical reality is more complex. They sometimes contradict one another: it is possible to renounce punishment for the benefit of the individual and of society. Compulsory treatment, for drug users, and court warning, for minor offenses, are based on the idea that punishment would risk drawing the offender into a vicious circle of criminality. In other instances they come together, as in the case of compensation for civil parties, which impinges on the offender in proportion to the material or symbolic hurt he or she has caused, while at the same time serving to acknowledge the status of the victim and to restore a sense of justice in the social world. In fact, the establishment of norms of punishment often brings together the two types of justification: the aim is both to inflict punishment and to protect society.

This distinction between the two rationales holds true for punishment in general. But we need to consider how the invention of prison affected its meaning.

From the retributivist point of view, confinement deprives the individual of what society, or at least its philosophers from the Enlightenment on, regard as the greatest common good: liberty. It is noteworthy in this respect that the nation that represents itself as the champion of political liberalism, making freedom the cornerstone of democracy, is also the country with the highest levels of imprisonment in the world – as if the more that liberty is valued, the more its revocation becomes the supreme punishment.[11] Be that as it may, when compared with the penalties that preceded it, prison represents a new form of expiation of the act committed. Unlike torture and exposure, mutilation and execution, it is in fact supposed to preserve the human dignity and corporeal integrity of prisoners; the campaigns of the British reformers and the French revolutionaries of the late eighteenth century, like the European Prison Rules today, specifically state this dual aim. It is, however, far from certain that this intent is translated into reality, either in the jails of the past or in today's prisons. And so the persistence of strip searches, which prisoners find particularly humiliating, and, conversely, the controversies and resistance aroused by legislation banning the systematic use of the practice, which guards see as a threat to their security, remind us both that the work on bodies has not gone away and that dignity continues to be challenged in prisons.

From the utilitarian point of view, imprisonment should aid in the prevention of crime in three distinct ways: incapacitation, deterrence, and rehabilitation.[12] First, it renders the offender incapable of committing harm for the duration of his incarceration: with an increase in the length of prison sentences and automatic imprisonment in cases of recidivism, this period has become considerably longer, particularly in the United States where a third offense can lead to life imprisonment without parole. It is at this extreme cost that neutralization emerges as an efficient method of removing criminals from society. Second, imprisonment is supposed to discourage the offender from reoffending, and more broadly to have the same effect on others who might be tempted to commit crimes. This was the ground on which the promoters of the Victorian prison system defended the harshness of the conditions imposed on inmates in terms of both food and labor; still today, prison improvements are challenged by those who believe that ameliorating conditions too much risks making incarceration less of a deterrent. Finally, imprisonment is supposed to give the prisoner the opportunity to come to terms with his action and seek to improve through his conduct. Moral reform was the great project of the designers of penitentiaries in the United States of the Jacksonian era, who believed that isolation and silence provided a monastic atmosphere conducive to the examination of one's conscience. In its contemporary French form, work on the self, through acknowledgment of one's guilt, desire to improve, demonstration of good conduct, and involvement in prison activities, is an essential element in the program for rehabilitation of offenders and in the evaluation of any adjustment of their sentence. Exclusion from the social world, discouragement from committing crime, reform of inmates to aid their re-entry into society – three different ways of conceiving of prison from the point of view of prevention rather than simple punishment.

*　*　*

Whether the penalty is justified from a retributivist or a utilitarian point of view, as we have outlined them above, prison therefore emerges as both an innovation in relation to earlier punishments and an institution that remains relatively stable over time; the great rationales set out in the late eighteenth century continue to coexist 200 years later, despite the oft-noted humanization of punishment. But while the various justifications for the prison system recur in the theoretical arguments throughout this period, simple observation of prison demographics suggests that the respective weight given to each of them in the thinking of both the legislator and the judiciary has varied widely over time.[13] Given that, when penalties become harsher or conversely more lenient, the prison population increases or decreases accordingly, it is reasonable to assume that the economy of moral justification for the respective severity or leniency has changed.

In France, with the exception of the years immediately following the three wars of 1870, 1914–18, and 1939–45, the number of inmates saw a steady decline from the mid-nineteenth to the mid-twentieth century.[14] At the start of the Second Empire, after the repression that followed the 1848 revolution, there were 52,000 men and women in local and regional prisons. On the eve of World War II, there were no more than 12,000. This is a dramatic shift – a reduction of three-quarters over a little less than 100 years. There are many explanations, by no means all tending in the same direction.[15] The banishment of repeat offenders to penal colonies, with some sentenced to hard labor, and the introduction of suspended sentences and parole for first-time offenders, are indicative of a desire to differentiate penalties with a view toward more effective crime prevention. The criminals considered most dangerous were removed from French territory, while penalties were suspended for those convicts considered redeemable – two almost opposite rationales that nevertheless both contributed to the emptying of prisons. In the years following World War I, the reduction in the male population, decimated on the battlefield, accelerated the fall in inmate numbers. As a result of this reduction, prisons were closed in the 1920s and 1930s. However complex and sometimes contradictory the reasons for this phenomenon, one may conclude that, for almost 100 years, prison was increasingly viewed as a less than ideal response to criminality.

The second half of the twentieth century offers a stark contrast to this trend, with prison returning to the heart of penal thinking. This period is marked by a rapid rise in the number of inmates in France. There were 20,000 prisoners in 1955; 50 years later there were 58,000. In relation to the total population of the country, this amounted to a doubling of the rate of imprisonment.[16] In 2014 the total number of prisoners in France exceeded 68,000: more than one in every thousand persons was incarcerated. Moreover, these figures do not include those interned in immigration detention centers, who in the past were held in prison, but are now treated separately. The number of immigrant detainees has risen considerably since the late twentieth century, reaching a flow of several tens of thousands per year since the ministry of the interior began setting targets for deportation in the early 2000s – targets which have since become a tacitly accepted norm.[17] But even if we limit the figures to correctional facilities as such, the prison population has risen three-and-a-half-fold in little over half a century. While the increase was initially related to the political situation at the time, as a result of the incarceration of North African detainees during the Algerian war of independence, the growth in numbers over the period as a whole reveals profound structural shifts in French society and its attitude to punishment, particularly from the 1980s onwards, when questions of security became an electoral issue and political responses increasingly tended toward repression.

One could of course assume that the rise in the prison population is the automatic result of an increase in crime, particularly the most serious offenses. This is far from the case. Since the 1980s, the homicide rate has decreased markedly. Over the same period, the number of people incarcerated has more than doubled.[18] In fact, the development reflects a change in penal policy, itself linked to a change in the way that punishment is conceived in relation to the act it is intended to punish, to the perpetrator of the act (whose attenuating social circumstances are increasingly less acknowledged), and to its victim (where the concern is, on the contrary, to take them fully into account). This is what Denis Salas calls "penal populism."[19] The idea that punishment needs to become harsher, with prison sentences being handed down for offenses not previously subject to imprisonment, and longer sentences for those that already were, has, since the 1980s, translated into a criminalization of acts that were not previously deemed criminal, an increase in the severity of punishment for certain offenses, automatic prison sentences for reoffending, increasingly repressive policing under pressure from a results-oriented culture, and, finally, the development of special judicial procedures such as prosecution in real time and immediate appearance trials, where the risk of being sent directly to prison from the court is much higher than in regular trials. Thus the retributive function of prison is coming to take precedence over utilitarian concerns: the imperative is to punish and to be seen to punish, even when national and international statistical studies increasingly cast doubt on the efficacy of this policy in terms of crime prevention.

France is far from unique in this recent development. In fact, it is in the United States and the United Kingdom that the phenomenon has been both most marked and studied in greatest detail. According to David Garland, the punitive turn in these countries occurred a little earlier, arising in the 1970s with the radical contestation of the model of "penal welfarism" that had prevailed since the late nineteenth century, in which, as the term suggests, the logic of repression was subordinated to the social project.[20] This model, inherited from philanthropists and philosophers of the Enlightenment, champions a softer utilitarian version of punishment: rehabilitation rather than neutralization. Or, to put it more precisely, an appropriate and proportional punishment should serve to reform the individual with the intention of reintegrating him into society, rather than making him expiate his crime. This so-called "modernist" orientation in penal policy was reflected in both the United States and the United Kingdom by a stabilization and even, at some points, a reduction in the rate of imprisonment, up until the 1960s.

During this period, individualization of punishment lay at the heart of the system, both in terms of the initial decision made by the judge and in the later adjustments carried out by the penal institution. The aim was to avoid imprisonment as much as possible. If it were, however, deemed necessary, it was to be accompanied by psychologists, social workers, probation officers, and, more broadly, experts in health, education, and of course criminology. Crime was effectively seen as being determined by social conditions rather than only individual factors, whether genetic or psychological. Moreover, these experts continued to monitor criminals after their time in prison, with the aim of preventing repeat offenses. Thus there was a degree of complementarity and continuity between the penal state and the social state. Asserting the role of the state in the matter of social protection, the New Deal in the 1930s in the United States and the Beveridge plan in the United Kingdom in the 1940s form the historical background to this period. These initiatives expressed the optimistic vision of a society that would protect its weaker members, through a project of solidarity aimed at pushing back and even, ultimately, eliminating both poverty and crime.

The reversal of this attitude seems as sudden in its onset as it is complex in its origins. It occurred first in the United States, and then gradually gained ground in Western Europe. During the 1970s, attacks on the social model of prison converged from all sides.[21] On the one hand, a progressive critique voiced by academics, social workers, and even former inmates challenged the oppressive discipline exercised for the purpose of moral reform of prisoners, and the discriminatory way it was applied, insofar as it essentially targeted ethnic minorities and poor communities. On the other hand, a conservative campaign developed, basing its arguments on the ineffectiveness of this model to prevent reoffending, because, as is often asserted by those who dismiss rehabilitation while omitting to acknowledge that programs often fail because their funding is withdrawn, crime is increasing.[22] However, the two-pronged attack on the paradigm of rehabilitation was only decisive because it was set within the more general context of the restoration of a law-and-order thinking following two decades of social mobilizations. After the 1950s and 1960s, which saw the triumph of the civil rights movement and a proliferation of unrests, particularly among students, a period of reaction took hold in the social, economic, and political domains, as well as in the moral sphere. This wave culminated in the election of Ronald Reagan in the United States in 1981, preceded two years earlier by Margaret Thatcher's rise to power in the United Kingdom, both instituting a new doctrine of fighting crime that became so dominant that it was never seriously questioned by their opponents or their successors.

The "conservative revolution" manifested itself with particular intensity in the penal arena. The language of punishment became generalized in political discourse, and recourse to imprisonment was established as the best response to crime. Security concerns, sensationalized by the media, came to occupy a central place in the collective imagination and the public sphere. While social etiology was replaced by individual responsibility in the interpretation of crime, the figure of the victim enjoyed growing legitimacy. In the United States, the principle of "zero tolerance" formed the basis for increasingly harsh legislation that introduced heavy, automatic, and unreducible penalties. This was famously expressed in the formula "three strikes and you're out," the title of a bill voted in in California in 1994, which obliged judges to issue a sentence of life imprisonment for a third offense, whatever the seriousness of the actual crime. As a result, between 1970 and 2010, the number of those held in federal and state prisons rose from fewer than 200,000 to more than 1.5 million, an increase of 750 percent; the number rises to 2.3 million if those held in county jails are included. In addition to these figures regarding those actually incarcerated, those sentenced to prison but released on parole and on probation, whose judicial situation is especially precarious, should also be taken into consideration. Indeed, they account for the largest proportion of new arrivals in prison, following violations of the very strict conditions of their conditional release from detention. The penal population in the United States thus amounts to seven million people.[23] The dual logic of expiation and neutralization has reached its culmination.

Contrary to what might be expected, changes in government had little effect on this development. The radicalization of punishment initiated by Ronald Reagan and Margaret Thatcher was not moderated during the eight years of Bill Clinton's presidency or the ten years of Tony Blair's government. Moreover, it was set in the context of deeper transformations of the relationship to public good and national solidarity. Breaking with the previous period of penal welfarism, which limited the reach of prison while expanding social protection, the reinforcement of the penal state was thus accompanied by a reduction in the social state.[24] Poor black communities in low-income areas most directly affected by the reduction in welfare programs were also the most dramatically subjected to the hardening of penal policies. Prison was increasingly becoming an instrument for managing inequality.

* * *

The punitive turn of the 1970s and 1980s points to a structural shift, which took its most extreme form in the United States, but concerned virtually all Western nations. With the doubling of its prison population over the course of three decades, France is one of the European countries where this tendency was most pronounced and remains most lasting.[25] However, France also stands out from other countries by the sharper demographic variations in prison population following political changes after general elections. This might seem self-evident, given that what determines the shift toward harsher penalties relates principally not to objective trends in criminality, but to subjective shifts in the attitude toward punishment. Without underestimating the two circumstantial elements that influenced the prison population in opposite ways – presidential pardons pronounced immediately after elections, and tragic events generating repressive responses – it is therefore no surprise that the right should overall be more severe than the left.[26] However, the polarization of penal policy is remarkable compared to what was observed in other countries: in the United States, the alternation between Republicans and Democrats did not affect prison inflation any more than the switch between Conservative and Labour governments in the United Kingdom; while in Germany the replacement of the Social Democrats by the Christian Democrats did not unsettle the relative stability of rates of imprisonment. In France, by contrast, changes in the parliamentary majority have, until recently, exerted a marked influence on prison demographics. The election of the socialist president François Mitterrand in 1981 was followed by a fall of 22 percent in the prison population, the largest decrease in the previous 50 years, while the re-election of right-wing president Jacques Chirac in 2002 was accompanied by a rise of 14 percent, the sharpest increase in that decade. In the first case, the stamp of the then minister of justice, Robert Badinter, is all too evident.[27] In the second, the determining factor is the influence of the then minister of the interior, Nicolas Sarkozy.

This shift is noted after each national election that brought a change in government: hence a fall of 22 percent after 1981; an 11 percent rise after 1986; a 9 percent decrease after 1988; a 4 percent increase after 1993; a 1 percent decrease after 1997; and an increase of 14 percent after 2002.[28]

Within these repeated swings, it is noticeable that the impact of the return of the left to power gradually diminished over time, while the effect of the election of the right tended on the contrary to be reinforced. The polarization remains, but the punitive groundswell gradually overtakes all parties and institutions. Recent developments confirm it. Under the presidency of Nicolas Sarkozy, from 2007 to 2012, the number of inmates rose rapidly from 58,402 to 64,787. But following the election of socialist François Hollande, for the first time under the Fifth Republic, that is, since 1958, the return of a left-wing majority was not accompanied by a decline in the prison population, which continued to increase, reaching 66,572 on January 1, 2013. Since that time, the record for number of people in prison has even been surpassed several times: two years after the change in government majority, the figure stood at 68,859.[29] Moreover, these statistics only include individuals held in prison; in order to obtain the total penal population, those on conditional release and under electronic surveillance need to be taken into account. By 2013 these measures, which barely existed in the early 2000s, applied to more than 12,000 individuals – who, although they are not incarcerated, are nonetheless under permanent threat of landing themselves in prison should they fail to respect the conditions of their adjusted sentence. As of April 1, 2014, the number of people under prison sentence, whether incarcerated or not, had reached 80,740, a rise of 250 percent over the previous 30 years.

The evidence is clear: numbers speak for themselves. Just as much as the wording of new legislation, administrative reports, official speeches, newspaper articles, documents by reformers, and statements of protest from campaigners, which have rightly been the subject of a number of academic studies, the statistics offer evidence of the facts, and sometimes of the contradictions they reveal. In contrast to the solemn declarations of respect for the rule of law, the saber-rattling rhetoric of wars against crime, and the tirades against the leniency of the courts, they offer an unemotional picture of the dominance of the security agenda since the 1980s, and its reflection in penal policy. The concern is to punish more and more implacably, and at the same time to remove criminals from society for longer and longer periods. During the first decade of the twenty-first century, the increase in prison numbers was thus due to a combination of two independent tendencies in terms of flow and stock: the number of people in prison rose by 9 percent, and the average sentence increased by 17 percent – in other words, more people were being incarcerated, and for longer. However, it should be noted that the doubling in the number of short prison sentences during this period also highlights the increasingly routine use of prison as a punishment for petty crime, a factor that has a contradictory effect on these two tendencies. It increases the pressure on flows, because there are more new arrivals, and it diminishes the stocks, since short stays tend to reduce the average time spent in prison. There is therefore no contradiction in the fact that the number of short sentences is rising markedly, while the average length of sentences is increasing, with the former phenomenon tending to partially mask the latter.

The mechanisms of this twofold development will be examined in more detail later, but its most remarkable feature is without doubt its persistence in the face of both the objective reality of crime and the empirical proof that this harsher regime does not work. On the one hand, the proportion of murders and sexual assaults, which are subject to long sentences, is decreasing sharply in the total number of offenses resulting in imprisonment; hence, while prison sentences are more frequently applied and longer, they are being imposed for less serious crimes.[30] On the other hand, studies show that a stay in prison has a detrimental effect in terms of reoffending: those who are incarcerated are more likely to commit further offenses than those given a prison sentence but left on probation, and stays of less than six months show a higher than average rate of recidivism.[31] In other words, not only does retribution now prevail over prevention, but the harshness of sentences is increasing regardless of their efficacy. In short, the power to punish has broken free from its rational justifications.

*   *   *

Yet to focus analysis on changes in the nature and techniques of punishment, and the justifications for it, risks overlooking an important phenomenon that spans history and is especially evident today: the inequality of punishment, and particularly of prison sentencing. It is not enough to measure the effects of harsher laws, police practices, and court decisions on the increase in prison population. We need also to understand how the punitive turn operates differentially through society, in order to identify the categories or groups it affects most intensively or, by contrast, those to whom it shows particular magnanimity. In France, however, there are limited data available to analyze this differentiation.

It was only in 1999 that the French national census included for the first time a sample of prisoners; it is therefore not possible to evaluate developments over any length of time. Moreover, the census analysis does not distinguish between short-stay and long-term prisons, thereby masking the specific disparities that are much more marked in the former than the latter.[32] The census reveals the young age of the inmates, more than half of whom are under 30, with one in every 200 men between the ages of 20 and 30 in France being incarcerated. More than three-quarters of the men in prison have left school before the age of 18, compared to only half of those in the general population, and the risk of imprisonment is 16 times higher for those who end their studies before the age of 16 than for those who continue studying beyond the age of 20. Blue-collar workers, who make up half of the prison population, and the unemployed, of whom the percentage in prison is twice that in the general population, are substantially overrepresented in prison, in contrast to senior management and white-collar professionals. Inmates born outside France are twice as numerous as in French society as a whole, and if these proportions are taken into account, the risk of imprisonment is 2.7 times higher for those originating in sub-Saharan Africa, 3 times higher for those from

North Africa, and 3.3 times higher for those from Eastern Europe. Thus, those sent to jail are primarily young men with a low level of education, from poor backgrounds, and of immigrant origin. A lack of economic and cultural capital combines with the effects of age, gender, and origin to produce a prison population markedly different from the general population.

There are two ways of interpreting this observation: either the statistical picture does reflect the criminal population, or it reveals a bias in the way questions of crime are addressed. According to the first interpretation, the working class and immigrant minorities share a higher propensity toward crime. According to the second one, conversely, discrimination against these groups is suspected. To determine which of these two alternatives is correct, one must take up Claude Faugeron and Guy Houchon's invitation to move from "the study of punishment to the sociology of penal policy."[33] Understanding prison demographics thus implies shifting our gaze from prison itself to what comes before it; in other words, tracing, along the penal chain, back to the courts that confer sentences, the police who make the arrests, the members of parliament who enact laws, the governments that devise national policies, the commentators who feed public perceptions of security and punishment – in short the whole of society, which, through this plethora of agents and institutions, decides who should go to prison, and why.

In his 1893 work *The Division of Labor in Society*, Émile Durkheim argued explicitly for this shift of focus.[34] Searching for the foundations of any human society, he finds them in the solidarity that exists among its members and is symbolized by the law. There are two main types of law. Penal law consists "essentially in some injury, or at least some disadvantage imposed upon the perpetrator of a crime. Their purpose is to do harm to him through his fortune, his honor, his life, his liberty." Civil law consists "merely in restoring the previous state of affairs, reestablishing relationships that have been disturbed from their normal form." The former is repressive, and the latter restitutive. To restrict the analysis to penal law, "the bond of social solidarity to which repressive law corresponds is one the breaking of which constitutes the crime, that is, any act which, regardless of degree, provokes against the perpetrator the characteristic reaction known as punishment." However, given the diversity of acts considered criminal, and the variation in the definition of crime over time and between cultures, what is the generic feature by which it can be recognized? Durkheim's response inverts common-sense thinking: "We should not say that an act offends the common consciousness because it is criminal, but that it is criminal because it offends that consciousness. We do not condemn it because it is a crime, but it is a crime because we condemn it." There is therefore no substantive definition of crime: it must always be understood relationally. In a radical statement of the kind to which contemporary readers are no longer accustomed, Durkheim adds the following evidence of his previous assertion: "In the penal law of most civilized peoples murder is universally regarded as the greatest of crimes. Yet an economic crisis, a crash on the stock market, even a bankruptcy, can disorganize the body social much more seriously than the isolated case of homicide." Crime is thus not that which negatively affects society or a proportion of its members; it is that which society, or a proportion of its members, chooses to treat as such. And punishment is an essential key to understanding not only what is considered criminal, but also what forms the basis of social relations.

The social composition of penitentiary establishments can thus serve as an indicator of what a society considers should be punished by a prison sentence. Analyzing who is jailed and why means asking which of the acts that are subject to condemnation are punished and which are tolerated, which are deemed serious or minor, which incite outrage and which are looked on with indulgence. Adopting Durkheim's reasoning, it is possible to suggest non-habitual comparisons in order to interrogate the evidence of the criminalization of human acts. In the United States, those who sell cannabis can be sentenced to life imprisonment without any possibility of parole, but those whose risky or even suspect financial operations have led to tens of thousands of people losing their jobs or homes are not held accountable for their actions;[35] and while murderers can spend years on death row awaiting execution, the politicians who, on the basis of deliberately deceptive information, declare a war resulting in hundreds of thousands of civilian and military victims, enjoy impunity.[36] In France, successive governments in recent decades have prioritized the penalization of petty crime over the penalization of financial crime, passing increasingly harsher laws in relation to minor misdemeanors, but remaining tolerant of corporate corruption, at the risk of repeated condemnation by international regulatory organizations and despite the sometimes serious consequences of these practices not only in economic terms, but also in terms of human cost.[37] Since a wrongdoing that constitutes a greater harm to society may give rise to a much lesser punishment, or even go unpunished, prison demographics do not reflect the seriousness of the actions sanctioned, or at least do not only reflect this; they also reveal the choices of what and who is to be punished, and why. Crime exists not in the absolute, but in relation to the censure to which it is subject.

Technically, of course, sentencing is a matter for the judiciary, but it presupposes, prior to the work of the judges, a form of judgment by society, as expressed in public discourse, opinion polls, and the wording of laws. There are two ways of interpreting this judgment, depending on whether the focus is on the act or the agent who commits it. In the first interpretation, the judgment is moral: it assumes that the sale of marijuana or minor offenses are more reprehensible than, respectively, suspect financial transactions and large-scale corruption. In the second interpretation, the judgment is social: it implies that in society, working-class people and those from ethnic minorities are systematically more severely punished than the white middle class and political or economic elites. Several factors support the second interpretation. Contrary to popular opinion, it is social differentiation that underlies the moral distinction rather than the opposite. Repressive law focuses on acts committed primarily by people from low-income backgrounds, while restitutive justice is applied to acts principally perpetrated by middle- and upper-class offenders. To put it another way, the offenses deemed the most serious, and hence the most heavily punished, correspond to particular socioeconomic and often ethnic profiles.

For over half a century, social science research, not least that undertaken by members of the international Law and Society movement, has demonstrated the existence of this inequality before the law, the police, and the courts, and hence in relation to prison. In France in the 1980s, a pioneering study by Bruno Aubusson de Cavarlay revealed stark disparities in penalty depending on social category. While half of all "jobless" offenders are punished with prison sentences, in eight out of ten cases "industrial and commercial employers" are merely fined. These discrepancies are not due to differences in the nature of offenses, because they are consistent over all types of act, with the former group being jailed three times more, and the latter five times less, than average. In an eloquent phrase, couched in ironically old-fashioned terms, Aubusson de Cavarlay sums up these results: "Fines are for the bourgeois and petty bourgeois, imprisonment is for the lumpen, and suspended sentences are for the working class."[38] This class dimension is compounded by an ethnoracial factor, which René Lévy, also in the 1980s, analyzed in a study of the police's patterns of referring offenders caught in the act directly to the public prosecutor's office – a device known to result much more frequently in prison sentences. French people of North African origin were twice as likely as other French nationals to be brought before the courts under this procedure, which penalizes the defendant. Here again, the discrepancy is not due to a difference in the type of offense: "The effects of the origin of the person and those of the definition of the crime cannot be confused with one another."[39] These observations on the effects of class and origin were formulated just before the hardening of penal policies that focused precisely on offenses committed primarily by young low-income men of ethnoracial minority. However reluctant current research is to focus on it, the dual discrimination identified then has only been reinforced since. In France, as elsewhere, the entirety of the process that leads to imprisonment is unequal – from the creation of the law to its application, from the work of the legislator to the actions of the police and the judge.

*   *   *

Thus, prison has seen its place in society fundamentally altered since what can be called its invention more than 200 years ago. Following a long period of stability – and even decline, particularly marked in France – during which alternatives to incarceration were from time to time devised, the pendulum has swung back over in recent decades, placing prison once again at the heart of the penal system. The demographics attest to it: imprisonment has become, or perhaps has returned to being, the prime mode of punishment.

Offenders are jailed more and more often, for longer and longer periods, even for offenses previously deemed minor.

In this reversal, and despite political discourse that aims to justify it in other terms, the retributive perspective has won out over the utilitarian approach: the will to punish has prevailed over concern for prevention. Insistently reiterated during recent years, the decision to implement suspended prison sentences that are years old, and relate to acts committed even further in the past, even when the individuals concerned may have started a family and found work in the meantime, shows that the expiation of the act committed takes precedence over the risk of a return to crime that might be feared as a result of the destabilization of the individual's personal situation and his socialization in a prison environment. Of course, the utilitarian perspective has not entirely disappeared, but it is expressed primarily in terms of incapacitation, the temporary removal of individuals from society. The long-discredited principle of rehabilitation is still maintained through the commendable work of probation and re-entry counselors, sentencing judges, and rehabilitation organizations, but it struggles against a lack of resources to meet the growing needs that stem from the rise in the prison population. As for the principle of deterrence, of which criminal judges, especially in immediate appearance trials, must convince themselves when they make their decision to hand down a prison sentence, it does not stand up against the empirical evidence of recidivism rates following prison sentences.

Overcrowded correctional facilities, whose population reflects both social inequality and disparities within the penal system, and which find themselves chronically underresourced in material and human terms: such are contemporary prison worlds. To characterize it in this way is not to reiterate the customary discourse of condemnation of the conditions in which prisoners are being held, but rather to point out that prison is only what society makes it. If French correctional facilities can be represented, in an oft-quoted parliamentary report, as a national disgrace, this is first and foremost a consequence of what has played out prior to and outside of them.[40] For those who work there, the stigmatization of their institution and, by implication, of their profession, is particularly unjust because it burdens them with the weight of choices and decisions over which they have virtually no influence; and whose consequences, as distressing for themselves as for prisoners, they experience on a daily basis. They cannot be held accountable for the fact that the penal state is expanding as the social state recedes.[41] In beginning this ethnography of the carceral condition with a sketch of the moral history of prison, my aim is to situate my study in a broader reflection on the metamorphoses of the meaning of punishment.

In this respect these developments in penal policy, and their manifestation in prison worlds, are revealed much more clearly in short-stay than in long-term correctional facilities.[42] Unlike the latter, dedicated to those serving medium- and long-term sentences, the former hold both those awaiting trial, who account for a little more than a third of their population, and those sentenced to terms of less than two years.[43] They are thus much more sensitive to changes in the categorization and punishment of minor crimes, such as driving and drug-related offenses, the number of arrests for which has increased most sharply in recent decades. They also reflect the growing practice of real-time prosecution for minor crimes, which leads to much harsher sentences than normal procedures and concerns mainly young men from low-income and immigrant backgrounds.

Although the 98 short-stay correctional facilities house all types of prisoners, petty crime, often tried at immediate appearance trials, accounts for a much larger proportion of inmates than major crime does, which generally concerns those awaiting trial, while the social and racial differentiation that results in large part from the dual inequality before the courts is particularly marked in these prisons. Moreover, since only long-term correctional facilities adhere to the legal principle of one inmate per cell, it is the short-stay ones that shoulder all the burden caused by overpopulation. For prisoners, the prospects for employment, professional training, and continuing education are also much lower in short-term facilities, as are the chances of being taken on by the probation and re-entry service, whose agents are overloaded with cases. In short, short-stay facilities epitomize the key issues of the prison system as manifested in recent times through disparity of sentences and excess of prisoners, increased harshness of the courts, and insufficient resources of the administration.[44] They are the mirror image of how the power to punish operates in contemporary society.

It was in one of these correctional facilities that I conducted my research, between the spring of 2009 and the summer of 2013.[45] Situated in a large conurbation, most of its intake naturally consists of prisoners from within this jurisdiction. In terms of overall rates of unemployment and other social indicators, the population of the conurbation is disadvantaged compared with the region as a whole, and several of the towns within the area incorporate Sensitive Urban Zones, that is, disadvantaged neighborhoods composed of public housing for which the state provides special support.[46] Given this demography – and probably also owing to the picture painted by correctional officers, very few of whom are from the region – the facility has a poor reputation among prison staff, who are unenthusiastic about being assigned there, often in their first posting. As a senior member of the probation and re-entry service explained, "the tensions arise because young, inexperienced professionals come face to face with a difficult public in this highly urbanized region."

The center's theoretical capacity is a little under 600, but the number of prisoners held there is well beyond that number, reaching 800 or up to 900 at certain times of year, particularly in the summer. The prisoners comprise exclusively adult men. There is no women's block, and no longer a block for minors. One-third of the inmates are under the age of 25, while fewer than one in five are over 40. About 20 percent of them are non-French nationals, half of these of African origin. In a quarter of cases they are serving sentences of less than six months; another quarter are serving between six months and one year, but almost one-fifth are serving sentences of more than three years, in other words well above the official maximum for short-stay facilities. These statistics differ little from those for other similar establishments in the region.

This book follows a logical progression. In order to understand the evolution and composition of the local demographics during the recent period, we need first to analyze the way in which penal policies, police practices, and court decisions lead to an increasingly large and increasingly differentiated proportion of the population being sent to prison; I will focus on the processes behind the rapid growth and social selection that weigh so heavily on contemporary prison life. It is only after this preliminary account that I will truly penetrate the world of prison, to grasp its ordinary – and sometimes not so ordinary – reality, through the interactions and tensions between the prison population and prison staff. I will follow the journey of the new arrival, discussing what is known as prison shock; I will attempt to comprehend the spatial, temporal, and sensory experiences that define prisoners' lives; I will pay attention to the changes and variations that influence the lives of the guards; and I will examine the role of objects in transactions between the two, particularly from the point of view of the relations of power and resistance they make manifest. Having outlined the prison context, I will then move on to address the central issues: the reign of constraint and violence, on both the individual and institutional levels; the frictions between the law and rights in terms of work, education, social welfare, and treatment of non-nationals; the issues surrounding order and security, with the different meanings protection has for guards and those they guard; the normalization of punitive practices and the ambiguities of internal justice; and finally, the aleatory application of sentence adjustment and support on release. I will conclude by asking what the contemporary propensity for imprisonment signifies, and offer a final reflection on the meaning of ethnographic practice as a way of understanding prison.

*   *   *

There are few human experiences as rich and intense as that of prison worlds, especially for researchers who, although they only pass through without ever walking in the shoes of either those who are guarded or those who guard them, are nevertheless affected not only by the loneliness, distress, rigor, violence, and injustice, but also by the joy, pride, solidarity, friendships, and words and gestures of concern and respect. The four years over which the period of my research extended convinced me of the need to change our collective view on prison – our view of what happens there, which I attempt to describe and interpret, and of what is at stake, not only for those who are serving their sentence and those who monitor or support them through this process, but also for society as a whole. Indeed, prison offers a reading of the contemporary world, both through the process by which it is filled and through the way its residents are treated. For more than 30 years, in France, the former has steadily worsened, while the latter has seen some improvement. It is therefore a question not of whether we have the prison that we want, but rather of whether we have the punitive society that we desire.

1

For Whom the Cell Fills

> To an observer belonging to a different society, certain of our practices
> would appear to be similar in nature to anthropophagy, which we deem
> so alien to our own notion of civilization. I am thinking of our customs
> regarding justice and prison.
> Claude Lévi-Strauss, *Tristes Tropiques*, 1955

"Put me in solitary! I'd rather be in solitary than stay with this guy. I can't handle it, I can't take it anymore!" Visibly beside himself, the young man rushes out of his cell, pushing past the five guards standing in the opening of the heavy door. It is evening, all the inmates have been locked up until the next morning and in theory the night shift should not have any contact with them, apart from confirming their presence through the peephole when they make their rounds. Guards only open a cell in the event of an actual or suspected incident, and in such cases, as a precaution, they come in a group under the lead of the prison lieutenant on duty. On this occasion, an argument between two prisoners sharing a cell, and the anticipation of a fight, have led them to intervene.

When they open the door, they find themselves face to face with two very agitated men. One of them, in his 30s, arrogant and defiant, declares volubly that he does not want to stay with his cellmate any longer. By turns threatening and charming, hinting at the risk that "it'll end in tears," and trying to get the officers on his side with his repeated "you know me, I don't want any trouble," he is doing his best to push his cellmate over the edge by making him look ridiculous. In particular, he repeats several times that he is "fed up with this guy lying there playing with his balls," eliciting sniggers from the guards. The other man, who is little more than 20, seems stressed and upset. White-faced, he holds himself together for a few moments until, unable to bear this humiliating situation that the guards show no sign of wanting to put a stop to, he explodes with frustration and rushes out into the gangway to escape his bully's sarcastic remarks. Having previously verified that a place has come free after another inmate left that same day, the lieutenant is conciliatory. He asks him calmly to take his things and

leads him to the other cell.[1] In the course of this brief move, the man begs
for some tobacco. One of the guards, who explains to me in an aside that
he always has some in his pocket to give to prisoners who crave it but have
none, gives him a little tobacco. "Can't you give me a bit more?" wheedles
the prisoner. Irritated by this demand, the officer becomes angry. He takes
back his gift, and makes the man enter his new cell. As the team begins to
move away, the man realizes he has forgotten to bring his mattress cover
with him and asks, through the door, to be let out to go and fetch it. "It's
too late now," is the reply. And despite his protestations, the guards resume
their round.

"Doubling up" in cells is a major source of problems in the day-to-day
life of prisons.[2] Friction between cellmates not only results in violence
between them, but also leads to conflicts with the staff. Many "refusals
to return to cell," which can degenerate into a confrontation with a guard
and end in solitary confinement, are an expression of protest against the
imposition of a cellmate. Ensuring good cell matches is an exacting additional task for senior officers, who are required to satisfy multiple criteria
in the process. Decisions are made mainly on the basis of age, penal status,
and whether or not the individuals smoke, but also in addition, as far as is
possible, their mental health, personality, origin, religion, and even their
personal preferences are taken into consideration. All these are elements
that are of primary importance in keeping the peace and maintaining order
in the facility, but also stem from the application of the European Prison
Rules, and their incorporation into correctional law. Notwithstanding these
efforts, which I witnessed during meetings of the joint services committee,
where assigning prisoners is one of the essential tasks, there were constant
problems. Doubling up generated permanent tensions in the prison. It was
poorly tolerated, and gave rise to incessant requests and recurring negotiations with the senior officers as prisoners returned from exercise and sought
to secure, if not a cell to themselves, at least a cellmate they got along with
better. This situation, directly linked to prison overcrowding, was already
worrying when I began my research, but it worsened rapidly over the
months.

One of the wardens did not mince his words: "More than 900 people in
a space designed for fewer than 600, that's the first institutional violence the
state imposes on prisons. The principle of one prisoner per cell goes back
to the Third Republic. Over a century later, we still can't guarantee it."
During the four years between the beginning and the end of my research,
the number of people given a prison sentence rose by 35 percent, while the
number actually in custody increased by 18 percent. Over the same period,
human resources remained unchanged and even fell slightly in terms of
guards, generating a 23 percent increase in workload. In fact, despite the
growth in adjusted sentences resulting in parole, which more than doubled,
not least through use of electronic monitoring, which even tripled, the
occupancy rate rose from 125 to 147 percent, which means that the excess
prison population almost doubled. Considering, moreover, that some cells

are left vacant for maintenance reasons, that others are used for isolation purposes, and that finally some individuals held under special conditions because they are deemed dangerous are housed alone, almost all "ordinary" prisoners are in fact "doubled up." Faced with this troubling development, the prison management had installed bunk beds in almost all the cells, creating a total of 1,020 possible bed places. "I am proud to say that we have never had to put mattresses on the floor and make prisoners sleep there, as other prisons have," one of the directors said to me. As he was well aware, this pragmatic solution, which allowed him to mitigate the serious shortage of spaces, at the same time endorsed a form of exemption from the legal obligation to provide each inmate with an individual cell.

Such is the de facto norm in short-stay correctional facilities in France, since the increase in prison places has never kept pace with the growth in the prison population in recent decades. The number of people sentenced to prison in France, including those under electronic monitoring, rose from 31,551 in 1982 to 50,115 in 1992, 48,594 in 2002, and 73,780 in 2012. This represents an increase of 133 percent in three decades, with a 52 percent rise just since the early 2000s.[3] Statistics for people actually incarcerated have seen a similar progression, with record totals beaten month after month: the figure of 68,569 prisoners, corresponding to an occupancy rate of 12 percent, was reached on July 1, 2013, the time at which I was completing my research.[4] This growth in the prison population and the resultant over-occupation of cells are unevenly distributed. As one warden remarked in frustration: "It's an extraordinary paradox that, in long-term prisons, which house those people who have been sentenced, the principle of 'one prisoner, one cell, one job' is applied, whereas in short-stay prisons, where many inmates are awaiting trial, they are housed two or even three to a cell. Once they've been found guilty, they are properly treated. While they're still presumed innocent, they're all piled together." Ironically, this unequal treatment was reproduced, despite his best efforts, in the very facility he was in charge of, since the application of the European Prison Rules in the block that housed those sentenced to medium terms of imprisonment meant they had to be held one to a cell, placing even greater pressure on the remainder of the prisoners, many of whom were awaiting trial. The carceral condition of the prisoner on remand, who can retain this status for years pending trial or appeal, is in many respects unfavorable compared with that of those who have been convicted.

This troubling observation was confirmed in a report presented to the French National Assembly, which spoke of "endemic overpopulation" and reported an occupancy rate of 92 percent in long-term prisons compared with 135 percent in short-stay prisons. In another report, this time to the French Senate, a simple explanation was given: in long-term prisons, "the conditions of imprisonment and length of stay mean that the prisoner population is much more difficult and changes less; it is therefore essential to maintain correct conditions of incarceration." Conversely, in short-stay prisons, "faster turnover means that much more difficult conditions of imprisonment can be tolerated." As a result, the authors argue, these differences in occupancy rate can be explained in terms of "power relations" working to the disadvantage of those awaiting trial, who become the "adjustment variable in the prison system."[5] Thus it is a form of political cynicism, in which confirmed criminals are treated better than alleged offenders because the former are feared more than the latter, that accounts for this inequality between long-term and short-stay prisons. It is a significant inequality: as of July 1, 2012 the rate of occupation was over 200 percent in six short-stay prisons in metropolitan France, and in almost all prisons in the overseas territories. In these facilities it is not even correct to talk of "doubling up," since prisoners are often housed three or four to a cell designed for one person, with mattresses on the floor making it virtually impossible to move around these confined, densely inhabited spaces. In such conditions, it is easy to imagine the tensions that arise among inmates and with staff.

*   *   *

In theory there are two explanations for prison overcrowding: either too many people are being locked up, or not enough prisons are being built. In other words, either some of the people held in correctional facilities should not be there, or there are not enough places for all of those who should be incarcerated. For a long time it was the second of these explanations that prevailed, while the first was rarely taken into consideration. The response was therefore to build new prisons. In 1987, the Gaullist minister of justice Albin Chalandon launched the massive initiative known as the "13,000 program" in response to the situation he reported having discovered on taking up his post – to wit, the presence of 51,000 inmates in prisons designed for only 32,500 places.[6] Over the following two decades, several building programs aimed at both expanding and renovating prison real estate were announced by successive governments, without necessarily ensuing in corresponding construction. The last but one, at the height of the law-and-order policies implemented by successive right-wing governments, a plan to build 25 new prisons announced by minister of justice Michel Mercier in May 2011, overturned that of his predecessor, Michèle Alliot-Marie. It envisaged the creation of 20,000 new places by 2018, a figure raised to 30,000 by President Nicolas Sarkozy a few weeks later; a report issued the following year planned to reach the total of 80,000 in 2017, an increase of almost 50 percent over current capacity.[7] However, when Christiane Taubira was appointed minister of justice in the left coalition government in 2012, she began to question the idea that more prisons were needed, and suggested instead that there were perhaps too many people in prison for whom other penalties might have been both more just and more efficacious. The goal was subsequently reduced to 63,000 places in five years, with priority being given to devising alternatives to imprisonment and to sentence adjustment.[8] Once again, it was a question of whether individuals who should not be in prison were being incarcerated, or whether prison capacity is not being adequately adjusted to the real need for incarceration.

When I put this question to one of the wardens, his response was cautious. "Actually, it's both," he said, but he went on to expand much more fully on the first interpretation, admitting that "when you lock people up, you often feel you're committing an injustice," than on the second, in support of which he remarked simply that "in any case, there are French people who are calling for security, and we owe it to them." A few days later, meeting a prisoner in his cell, I did not even need to ask him the question: "They go on about how there's not enough space in prisons and then they jail people just for that!" he exclaimed, referring to his own case. He had been imprisoned two months earlier and was sharing his cell with a young Caribbean man. He was 51 years old, of Haitian nationality, but had been legally resident in France for many years. He worked in construction, but described himself as a "hairdresser, photographer, manager." He had a number of previous convictions for minor offenses, three of which had already led him to the same prison. This time he had been caught by the railroad police just as he jumped the turnstile without validating his ticket. Not wanting to miss his train, he had lost his temper: "They insulted me. I answered back. They jumped on me and beat me up. I was off sick for two weeks!" Yet it was the police officers who lodged a complaint against him, an almost systematic practice when the person has been injured in the course of his arrest, so as to forestall any legal claim. His time in police custody had been a trying experience, because "if you're in there for insulting the cops, they give you a hard time." Following an immediate appearance trial, he was sentenced to six months in prison. "I was hoping for just a suspended sentence. I didn't raise a hand to them, I didn't resist arrest, the cops didn't even claim compensation. I said to the judge: 'I don't get it: I'm not a drug-dealer, I'm not violent, I'm not an Islamic fundamentalist. Why are you jailing me for six months?' He said: 'Consider yourself lucky: the public prosecutor asked for a full year.'" Philosophically, he concluded: "I'm not saying it wasn't wrong to try and travel without a ticket, but six months for a train fare . . . ." As proof of the sincerity of his remorse, this self-proclaimed Catholic had decided not to go out to the yard, in order, he said "to kind of punish myself for my sin." Should this man have been in prison, as the magistrate felt, or could he have been spared this ordeal, as he himself thought? And more generally, do the courts lock up too many people, or is there a shortage of prisons?

Choosing between these two interpretations clearly implies adopting different views on the meaning and appropriateness of punishment. But it may be easier to begin with a simpler question, less likely to arouse passion and resort to ideology: what has caused the recent rapid growth in the prison population in France? The technical analyses contained in a number of official reports concur on this point. The main explanations offered for the rise in the recent period point to four principal mechanisms: the harsher penalties specified under the law, particularly for repeat offenses; the increasing severity of the courts under pressure from government; the growth in immediate appearance trials, which put defendants at a disadvantage when compared to normal procedure; and the sudden decision by the government to enforce old non-executed sentences.

Before returning to each of these elements to analyze their consequences, it is necessary to understand that underlying these various explanations is the central place occupied by prison in the social imaginary – a fact that, as we have seen, is not only linked to modernity (given that the institution was invented little more than 200 years ago), but also has taken off in the recent period (considering the remarkable reversal that has taken place over the last few decades). "What does it mean to punish in a democratic society?" asked the members of the panel at the Consensus Conference that met in early 2013 to discuss public policy on the prevention of recidivism. They noted that "prison today seems to constitute, in the eyes of both the public and the legal profession, the most obvious and the most accepted of penalties"; they, however, recommended that "imprisonment should be conceived of no longer as the penalty of reference, but rather as one penalty among others."[9] But in light of the political discourse and recent legislation, and given the practices of both prosecutors and judges, such a proposal seems, for both the government and the courts, an intellectual revolution that is hard to envisage.

Reflecting on her practice, a sentencing judge who had previously served in the criminal court mused on the dominance of this culture of incarceration. She explained how her position had differed depending on whether, in the course of her career, she had worn the judge's robes in court or had been responsible for determining a sentence adjustment: "When I'm in court, I punish using prison sentences. When I'm a sentencing judge, I tend rather to think that prison could have been avoided, especially for all these repeat offenses of driving with a suspended license." Some went further still, seeing the persistence of this attitude, despite the change in policy under the left-wing government, as a paradoxical affirmation of judicial independence. On September 19, 2012, a circular on penal policy from the minister of justice called on the courts to exercise more moderation and discernment in their decisions to impose prison sentences, with the specific aim of better tailoring sentences to individuals.[10] Noting that the number of persons incarcerated in his prison, as throughout France, was continuing to rise almost a year after the publication of this memo, one warden commented: "When we saw that circular we said: 'Finally! The flow is going to slow down a bit and we'll be able to concentrate on our job.' But since the memo it's been as if the prosecutors and judges had taken offense at the minister's intervention. They haven't just carried on as before, they've even increased their use of prison sentences." In his correctional facility, there were 3 percent more inmates than in the previous year, as against an increase of only 1 percent the year before. On the ground, this meant that 25 further cells had had to be "doubled up." In the 12 months following the publication of the circular, the total number of people incarcerated rose by a further 1.5 percent, although there had been a slight fall the year before.[11]

Although it would be difficult to confirm his hypothesis that judges had responded by taking umbrage, the figures suggest at least a degree of inertia in the judicial system.

The increased severity of the courts, and above that, the government's tougher stance on crime, is generally justified in terms of the shift in public opinion, itself partly influenced by the media.[12] Giving an account of their preparatory hearings, the authors of one parliamentary report write: "The rarity with which alternative sentences are issued is both a cause and a consequence of the society's perception of them. Many of those we interviewed said that the broader public did not see alternative penalties as true punishment. That prison would be the only response to be understood by public opinion is at least how the penal policy followed in France over the last decade has been justified."[13] The reservation introduced in that last sentence suggests that this argument should not be regarded as the real basis but simply as a legitimation of the severity demonstrated by politicians and magistrates.

But what is this public opinion? In one of his lectures, Pierre Bourdieu famously argued that "public opinion does not exist." His criticism is rooted in a challenge to three assumptions underlying the opinion polls that seek to measure it: that every individual has an opinion, that all opinions are of equal value, and that there is in society a consensus about what the problems are and therefore what questions should be asked.[14] We might add a fourth assumption: that the burden of opinions expressed is quite robust, in other words that it does not vary depending on the way the questions are formulated, or in relation to external events. Yet, the extensive coverage of criminal cases and the way they are treated in the courts render the polls and the opinions they are supposed to measure highly sensitive to news stories, particularly when they are exploited by the media and politicians.

"Never, in the almost 20 years that I have worked in prison administration, have I seen a case give rise to so many reports by the inspectorate, and shake up the prison world so profoundly," said one warden to me, in reference to what became known in January 2011 as the "Laetitia case," named for the young woman murdered by a convicted criminal who had just been released from a short-stay prison. He had been sentenced to one year's imprisonment for insulting a magistrate, half of it suspended on condition of good behavior, and had therefore logically been released at the end of his sentence, issued for a minor offense unrelated to the later crime. In the days following the murder, the media had leaped on this tragic story, with phrases like "barbaric death," and the president had condemned "serious dysfunction" in the courts, calling for "sanctions" on the judges concerned.[15] However, when reports from the public inquiry established that there had been no error on the part of the courts, the focus shifted to questioning what the warden called the "weak link" in the chain of punishment – the probation and re-entry service, whose interregional director was fired.

It was in this charged atmosphere that a right-wing daily newspaper published an article under the headline "Recidivism: courts are not strict enough, say French people." The report was based on an opinion poll conducted just a week after Nicolas Sarkozy's declaration, which showed that the people surveyed "felt that the verdicts and sentences issued by the courts are not tough enough" – an opinion expressed by 85 percent in relation to repeat offenders, and 71 percent in relation to juvenile offenders. The report also stated that 72 percent of respondents "felt that overall the courts are not working properly" – a figure that stood at only 41 percent three years earlier.[16] In the months that followed, the number of incarcerations soared, reflecting a change in judicial practice, as jail time was more frequently issued to defendants awaiting trial (in order to protect the courts against the risk of a crime being committed before the trial) as well as to individuals sentenced, even for a short time (in order to avoid having them outside under probation).[17] The speech had the remarkable performative effect whereby the pressure from the media on one side and from politicians on the other created a dissatisfied public, and made judges more wary.

However, another survey, conducted earlier in a less emotive climate, introduced very different elements into the debate on the question of punishment. While, according to this poll, three-quarters of French people believed that prison played an important role in protecting society and sanctioning offenders, only 20 percent believed that it helped to combat reoffending, while 64 percent thought that sentence adjustments were effective in achieving this aim. Moreover, two-thirds of respondents considered the material conditions of imprisonment to be poor, and 71 percent wanted to see prison changed and improved. But this survey, which was carried out in 2009 and analyzed early in 2011 by the Directorate of Prison Administration, was not published; the "opinion" expressed in the report contradicted the official discourse and was therefore not to be made public. When the new minister of justice found out about the study, she demanded that her services publish it. It didn't appear until June 2013, exactly four years after it was conducted.[18] At a Senate conference, Christiane Taubira explained that she wanted to "win over public opinion" on the subject of penal policy. The revelation of the suppressed report was represented as the first step in this process.

Penal policy, police practices, and judicial decisions are not explained by the results of opinion polls on justice and prison, any more than they are by crime statistics. On the contrary, as we shall see, it is penal policy, police practices, and judicial decisions that find, amid the plethora of objective and subjective indicators produced by opinion polls, tools that allow them to legitimate changes for which, whether through cynicism, conviction, inertia, or apprehension, decision-makers, legislators, police, and judges in various ways bear the initiative and the responsibility. So what precisely are these developments that account for the rise in prison population? Let us return to the four factors to which it is generally ascribed: the stiffening of the laws, the severity of judges, real-time prosecution, and the activation of non-executed sentences. The first two are linked, although distinct, and

I shall analyze them in conjunction in order to show how they generally interact with and reinforce one another.

* * *

"It's crazy that I'm in jail for that!" The man, of Portuguese origin, is in his 50s. He runs a small construction company. He has five children, aged between 2 and 18. His wife does not work. He has just been sent to prison for driving with a suspended license. Dismayed and indignant, he describes how he was stopped at a routine traffic check and told by the police that he had lost his license. He was arrested and held in custody, and then sentenced to prison at an immediate appearance trial. In the intake interview with one of the wardens, he explains that, because he had moved home, he never received the letters relating to his offenses, probably for speeding, and as a result was unaware that his license was invalid and that there was an outstanding warrant for his arrest. He has never been in jail before. Apart from the humiliation he feels in front of his wife, his children, his family, and his friends, his main concern is the practical consequences of his imprisonment: "I've got commitments to clients, contracts signed for projects. Some are sure to turn against me if I don't deliver on time." After the interview, the director tells me he cannot understand why the court made such a decision. In fact, this obsession with incarceration was sometimes manifested in extreme ways: a 57-year-old man suffering from pancreatic cancer at an advanced stage, who lived on a meager pension, was imprisoned for several months for a repeat offense of driving with a suspended license.

Convictions for driving offenses have increased by 58 percent in 20 years. In 2011, out of 560,000 individuals convicted of a crime in France, 232,000, or almost half of them, were found guilty of traffic violations; of these, 70,000 received prison sentences, with 18,000 actually being sent to prison, accounting for a quarter of all new incarcerations that year.[19] At the start of my study, I often sat in on the interviews with new arrivals. With an average of four new inmates each day, it was not uncommon for one or two of them to be in prison for driving offenses, almost always for driving under the influence of alcohol or driving without a license. In my conversations with them, both wardens and judges spoke of their unease at seeing people incarcerated for a simple road safety offense, particularly when they were fully integrated in society in terms of work and family, and imprisonment threatened their stability on both counts. The directors and magistrates were well aware that this shift had nothing to do with a deterioration in driving behavior, and was instead the result of tougher laws and policing.

It was only in the 1970s that road safety became a public problem, in the sense that consciousness of the seriousness of the situation, and the need to remedy it, crystallized in response to the steady rise in the number of people killed on the roads each year.[20] The appointment of a minister for road safety and the creation of an interministerial road safety committee in 1972 paved the way for a public awareness campaign and the introduction of a series of measures, foremost among them laws on speed limits and the compulsory wearing of seat belts. The graphs of mortality began to trend in the other direction. From the 1980s onwards, as a result of several spectacular accidents, but also the creation of victims' associations, national policy was given a more repressive orientation. It was at this point that people began to talk of "road violence." The white paper submitted to Prime Minister Michel Rocard in 1988 recommended more frequent traffic checks and automatic sanctions, which gradually came into force over the following decade. But the real punitive turn came in the early 2000s, when President Jacques Chirac made road safety one of his three national priorities for his second term in office.

The two central planks of the program put in place at that time were the points-based license and the criminalization of driving under the influence of alcohol. The first, instituted 10 years earlier, only really became effective as a sanction in 2003, with the proliferation of speed cameras on the roads and the introduction of automatic processing of offenses, leading to the addition of between one and six points depending on the amount by which the speed limit was exceeded. The second, with a legal threshold initially set at 1.2 g/l blood alcohol, later lowered to 0.8 g/l, and later 0.5 g/l, involved the automatic addition of six license points on top of the fine. These developments should also be interpreted in the context of securitarian thinking more generally. The consequences of the new policy were quickly felt: a growing number of drivers lost their license, often without their knowledge. In 2011 alone, 12 million points were added to licenses, 87 percent of them for speeding, resulting in the invalidation of 85,000 licenses.[21] At the same time, the 2004 law known as Perben II, after the eponymous minister of justice, made driving with a suspended license a crime punishable by one year's imprisonment and a fine of 15,000 euro. Between 2000 and 2009, convictions for driving with an invalid license rose fivefold.[22] The criminalization of road safety offenses then reached its cruising speed, with a quarter of a million new cases added to the National Criminal Records Statistics each year.

The reclassification of these offenses as road violence in common parlance, the shift from a rubric of contravention to one of criminal offense resulting in a prison sentence, and the introduction of procedures likely to lead to the loss of the driver's license thus combined their effects on repression of these offenses.[23] However, the penalization of these acts was filtered through another factor. It resulted not directly from the commission of the offense, but from the intervention of the national and local police. Driving with a blood alcohol level above 0.5 g/l, or with a suspended license, is not enough for offenders to be brought to court; they must also have been subject to a road check. How the police choose which vehicles they pull over is thus of decisive importance. And although no study has been conducted in France, it is generally recognized, on the basis of many surveys carried out in other countries, that this selection is not statistically neutral, but is disproportionately targeted at drivers from minority backgrounds. Ultimately, the imprisonment of the Portuguese man for having lost his points-based license was the product of this conjunction of multiple factors: the rise in awareness of road accident deaths, the dramatic representation of the issue, the campaigning by victims' groups, the intervention of partisan experts, the instrumentalization of the problem by politicians, the hardening of the legislation, the selection bias among the police, and the growing severity in the judicial treatment. A remark by one correctional officer prompted me to assign a concrete significance to this development of the feeling that driving offenses should be more heavily punished: "You often hear people say, 'It's just driving with a suspended license, or drunk-driving: why do they put the guy in jail for that.' But tell that to my brother! His 7-year-old son was killed by a reckless driver whose license had been revoked. Sure, it's prison, but it's also prevention."

There are, however, many other breaches of the law punishable by short jail sentences. One African man, who had lived in France with his family for a long time but whose residence permit had not been renewed, was sentenced to six weeks in jail for resisting deportation. A 32-year-old man who worked as a garbage collector was locked up for two weeks for traveling a few miles beyond the limit imposed by his electronic tag. A 45-year-old divorced salesman found himself jailed for one month for failure to pay alimony to his ex-wife. In their intake interviews, meeting with these often distraught inmates, many of whom had never contemplated the prospect of one day finding themselves in prison, the staff tried to offer words of encouragement: "You'll be getting out soon. You just need to get through the next few weeks. Think about when you get out." Nevertheless, one probation and re-entry counselor, in an aside to me, could not help expressing her frustration: "When I see all these people who are here for one month! It makes me think, 'What are the judges doing?' These are people who have a job, or they're in training, or in school, and they're putting all that at risk. Prison can ruin these people's lives." And indeed, the frequent consequences of these short prison sentences in terms of loss of professional, social, and family stability, which are themselves factors in recidivism, are well known. But these sentences are sharply on the rise, with nearly 40 percent more sentences of under six months handed down between 2006 and 2008, while sentences of less than three months can make up more than a quarter of those actually served.[24] They are too short to ever allow for the establishment of a work or training plan that might facilitate re-entry into society. "It's the short sentences that give us the most problems," admitted one guard.

Prison sentences are not only more frequent, they are also becoming longer, particularly since the passing of the law of August 10, 2007, which established mandatory minimum sentences for offenses subject to three years' imprisonment or more if the individual is legally considered a repeat offender – although judges have the option of making an exception provided they can offer a strong argument for it. A study comparing the minimum sentences issued by judges in the three years preceding this new legislation noted the following facts: between the two periods, the rate of issue of these penalties rose from 8.4 percent to 40.7 percent; it was highest for the least serious offenses, reaching 45.8 percent for offenses subject to a minimum term of three years; the toughening of sentences was particularly marked for drug-related offenses, where the rate multiplied fivefold, and still more marked for theft and possession of stolen goods, where the proportion of minimum sentences rose sixfold; it was lower for driving offenses, but still double that of the preceding period; the effect of the new law was felt most strongly in the first year after it was introduced, with half of all sentences being minimum terms, and a slight decrease being observed subsequently. The average length of prison sentences rose from 9 months before the law was passed to 15.6 months after; in other words, the length of prison time increased by 73 percent. For offenses subject to sentences of a three-year maximum, it increased from 6.2 to 9.5 months, a 50 percent rise; the length of sentence thus reached three-quarters of the maximum possible sentence, compared to an average of half the maximum for offenses subject to a maximum of 10 years.[25] In sum, the legislation has proved spectacularly effective, since magistrates impose strict sentences five times more often than before, and the prison sentences issued have increased by an average of almost seven months. Equally remarkable is the fact that, contrary to the declared aim, which was to combat repeat perpetration of serious offenses, this severity is applied proportionately more to minor crimes.

When the law of August 10, 2007 was passed, magistrates initially protested against it, complaining that it contravened the higher principle of individualization of sentences to which they were committed. However, it seems to have gradually become accepted, to the point that, as we have seen, the circular of September 19, 2012, which called on prosecutors and judges to revert to "individualization of the penal response," did not result in the expected fall in prison sentences. As one magistrate told me: "At first there was a lot of opposition, but in the end it's become pretty much accepted." It will be interesting to observe whether, during the years following the abolition of mandatory minimum sentences under the law of August 15, 2014, sentencing returns to its pre-2007 situation – in other words, whether the rate of minimum sentences will be reduced to one-fifth of its current level, and the average length of jail term will fall by six months, or whether, on the contrary, the inertia noted above will be reflected simply in a slight change in direction, the habit of punishing more harshly having already become established.

There is nothing to suggest, however, that the pendulum will swing back the other way. Although some magistrates said they felt restricted by mandatory minimum sentences, it seems that others felt liberated by this legitimation of intransigence. In the district court from which the prison where I conducted my study receives its inmates, many criminal judges had a reputation for inflexibility, which they had earned well before the introduction of this measure. One of them in particular was feared for his implacability and his aggressive attitude. The prison staff were well aware of this. At a meeting of the committee responsible for allocating prisoners to different blocks, everyone agreed on the marked disproportion between the acts ascribed to one 25-year-old man and the punishment he had received. "He really is a sad case," said, with sympathy, the guard who saw him when he arrived. Jobless and penniless, the man no longer had a place to live and was sleeping in his car. He had been arrested for riding a stolen scooter, along with his friends, on a parking lot. He had been sentenced to one year in prison for a repeat offense of possession of stolen goods. He had five previous convictions for theft of what he described as groceries, which in terms of repeat offenses were considered equivalent to possession of stolen goods. "I'm here for nothing," he said to me. "I get a year just for possession of stolen goods. It's my past that's caught up with me." Thinking back to his trial, he went on: "The judge, he says to me: 'Why don't you go back to Algeria? You don't belong here!' I was shocked that he said that to me. I came to France when I was six months old. I've always lived in France; I speak French a lot better than Arabic. This is my home." The liberties of tone and language that judges allow themselves in addressing some defendants in such circumstances testifies to how condescension and hostility had become routine. It was rare, however, for these attitudes toward certain defendants in the courts to take the form of such open xenophobia.

But in addition to the positions and attitudes more or less explicitly expressed by judges, a structural factor in the functioning of the court system suggests that a reversal in the tendency toward severity is unlikely, despite the abolition of mandatory minimum sentences: namely, the processing of huge numbers of these minor cases at immediate appearance trials.

*   *   *

"When they take you into the court, you feel like an animal being displayed to the crowd. You get out of the police cells, you've been pushed around by cops, you've had almost nothing to eat or drink for 48 hours, you feel dirty. In the end all I could think of was getting to prison so I could wash, eat, and smoke." In the experience of this prisoner, in his 30s, who had been arrested for punching a neighbor when he was drunk and had spent two days in police custody before being brought to court for immediate appearance trial, the entire procedure, from arrest to verdict, was a terrible ordeal that ended, as is often the case, in prison.

Real-time prosecution of penal cases, to use the official term for the entirety of the process from the point when the investigating police officer calls the duty assistant public prosecutor until sentence is pronounced, is a recent procedure, instituted gradually since the early 1990s and only coming into force throughout France in the 2000s. A distant relative of the old "in flagrante delicto" procedure, it is a fast-track procedure that makes it possible for a person arrested to be tried within a 24 to 48-hour period. There was a dual rationale in the creation and generalization of this procedure: the will to speed up court processes at a time when the system was unanimously criticized for being too slow, and the desire to integrate the courts into the security policies that were being introduced at the same time. Real-time prosecution makes it possible to try cases quickly, but above all to try a certain type of case: petty crime easily identified by the police and potentially subject to quick decisions, like traffic offenses, use and possession of marijuana, or insulting an officer and resisting arrest.

The criteria defined by the Code of Penal Procedure are that the offense must be punishable by at least two years' imprisonment, reduced to six months in the case of someone caught in the act, that the charges must be sufficient and the case ready to be brought to trial.[26] Thus real-time prosecution acts as both a cause of and a solution to the considerable increase in convictions, which rose by 50 percent between 2002 and 2011. On the one hand, it encourages the police, who are themselves under pressure to meet numerical targets, to take a more interventionist approach; on the other, it absorbs the resulting excess of cases by reducing the length of time before they come to trial. The priority accorded by the courts to "minor cases" is therefore detrimental to "more substantial cases," as some public prosecutors complain.[27] In the 2000s, when convictions for drug offenses and driving with a suspended license increased respectively by 255 percent and 400 percent, it is interesting to note that prosecutions for corporate crime (the most difficult cases), including fraud, bribery, embezzlement, and tax evasion, fell by 29 percent in France.[28] These data throw into relief the choices made in penal policy during that period: to punish petty offenses that the police have made a decision on whether or not to investigate, allowing them to target certain low-income communities, while ignoring cases involving wealthier individuals.

While real-time prosecution is a short sequence of events for the justice system – a call from the police, a decision by the duty assistant public prosecutor, a transfer of the case to the courts, the immediate appearance trial – the defendant's perception of it is quite different. For him, this trying ordeal seems much longer, both objectively, as it begins with the arrest and usually ends in jail, and subjectively, because the 24 to 48 hours of the process are a particularly violent experience for him. The arrest itself represents an overturning of his everyday reality: a moment earlier, he might have been sitting on a bench chatting, or at the wheel of his car beside his partner, or simply present in a public space; suddenly, he is overtaken by fear and sometimes anger, restrained and sometimes handcuffed, treated roughly and sometimes physically assaulted. The time in police custody is an especially difficult moment: over and above gathering information in order to draw up a statement, it is aimed at putting the defendant through an ordeal with its combination of the material environment, the lack of hygiene, the impossibility of resting, the humiliation of the strip search, the destabilization aroused by police interrogation, the anxiety about the outcome of the trial.

A defendant brought to court at the end of this ordeal is not in full possession of himself: he is dirty, exhausted, physically debilitated, psychologically perturbed, low in morale. He has usually not been able to prepare his defense. It is rare that he is defended by his own lawyer – supposing that he has one, that he has been able to contact him or her, and that the lawyer has been free to take the case. He is therefore provided with the services of the court-appointed lawyer who is responsible for the various cases brought to trial on that day and hence has less than half an hour to familiarize him- or herself with the case, meet the defendant at the court holding cell and prepare his defense. If there are crucial documents, which would forestall a prison sentence and which need to be produced in the court, the counsel does not have the time to procure them. The magistrates in immediate appearance trials thus see before them defendants who are often broken by what they have undergone, distraught at the prospect of what lies ahead, incapable of presenting a coherent version of the facts they are accused of, and aware of being poorly defended by the lawyer who has just been assigned to them.

Three-quarters of defendants in immediate appearance trials leave the court holding cell accompanied by police or correctional officers who remove their handcuffs when they enter the courtroom and who stand behind them until they leave.[29] The hearing is brief, averaging about 30 minutes, a little over half of which is devoted to reading the charges, the various statements, the legal case file, and the social report, with most of the remainder being given over to the arguments of the public prosecutor and the defense lawyer, and, where applicable, the lawyer for any civil parties to the case. In other words, the time available to the accused to state his case is extremely limited. It is usually restricted to a few questions from the presiding judge, generally more factual than contextual; if the accused attempts to offer any response, he is quickly interrupted in order to pass on to the next point, for the trial has to proceed quickly.[30] Moreover, the defendant's voice is barely audible. He often speaks indistinctly, without a microphone, unlike those who are free to go up to the witness stand, and has difficulty expressing himself coherently owing to fatigue, poor French-language skills, the intimidating nature of the situation, or the fear of saying something that will prejudice his case. All these factors mean that immediate appearance trial works strongly to the disadvantage of the accused.

A 45-year-old man who looks 10 years older, tried under this procedure for drunkenly assaulting his wife and his son, offered this account of the 24 hours preceding the hearing: "The hardest bit isn't when you get to prison. The hardest bit is the police custody. The police are bullies. A dog would get treated better. Even one of the young ones, I was old enough to be his father, you should see how he talked to me. They call you by your first name, they never say 'Mister.' You ask to go to the toilet, they're right next to you, they laugh and make you wait. In the night I didn't have a blanket, I was shivering, they didn't give me anything. The food is tiny portions and it's disgusting. We're not at war, we're not the enemy. OK, I did something I shouldn't have. But I'm a human being! In police custody you suffer, you really suffer." When he arrived at the court holding cell, he was visited by the court-appointed lawyer: "She asked me for money, 1,000 euro. For spending 15 minutes talking to me and speaking for five minutes at the trial! If she'd at least defended me properly." In fact, although they are supposed to work for free, court-appointed lawyers are permitted to solicit fees if the defendant has sufficient financial resources. The man continued angrily: "She told me not to ask for my case to be adjourned. But that's not right, because before you get to court, you can't get your evidence together, you can't even make a phone call." When the presiding magistrate asked him what he wanted, he did in fact choose to be tried immediately. Haggard, with two-day stubble, dressed in a crumpled sport coat, he appeared lost, almost absent, in front of a judge who admonished and lectured him: "At court, I was in a bubble. I didn't know what I was saying. Everything gets mixed up, you're in another world. I wanted to say to the judge: 'Give me a chance.' But she didn't let me speak. She was the one doing all the talking." In the end he was sentenced to eight months' imprisonment, six of which were suspended on condition that he undergo treatment for alcoholism and not contact his wife. Had he asked for an adjournment, contrary to what he imagined and as the presiding judge herself told me after the hearing, he would most likely have been remanded in custody to await trial and would again have ended up in jail, but perhaps for a slightly shorter time if he had managed to find a lawyer in the meantime.

But he probably could have avoided prison. For this to happen, he would have had not to be judged at an immediate appearance trial but according to the traditional procedure, which would have given him time to find alternative accommodation so as not to return to his home, and also to get in touch with an organization offering support for alcohol dependency. This would have taken a few more hours to put in place, which was impossible under the real-time prosecution. As the judge explained at the hearing: "The problem is, he doesn't have an address. If he'd at least had an address that could be verified, to ensure that he could be recalled to court, he could have got a conditional suspended sentence. But here we had nothing. It's a real shame." The verdict reflected this impasse in which the court found itself: the two months in custody are the product of this emergency justice in which the court-appointed lawyer cannot prepare the case and which forces the judge to lock up the accused. For the man himself, imprisonment holds serious financial consequences, as he owns a small scrap metal business that employs six people, and has a large contract he will not be able to honor. His wife is not working, his daughter is preparing for her medical school entrance exam, and his son is enrolled in a vocational training program. "I'm really worried I'll find nothing left when I get out. In my line of business, jobs don't grow on trees." His whole family will suffer from the situation in which the man accepts full responsibility, but for which he, like the presiding judge, would have hoped for a different punishment. The irony of the court's decision is, however, that, as with all short sentences, he will receive absolutely no preparation prior to release, since the probation and re-entry counselors choose to work only with those sentenced to longer terms so that they can develop a plan with them. "I don't know what I'm doing here: I'm wasting my time. Prison is a waste of time," the man said to me. It was hard to disagree. Two months after he was jailed, he left the prison in the same personal circumstances as when he entered – with the added trying experience and multiple consequences of a stint in jail.

Immediate appearance trials are being used more and more frequently. In the early 2000s, the number of cases tried under this procedure was equal to those heard under the traditional procedure. Ten years later, immediate appearance trials are used two and a half times more often.[31] Real-time prosecution is thus becoming the norm for criminal justice. It generates imprisonment primarily in two ways: through custodial sentences, and through remanding defendants in custody to await trial.

In the first place, penalties issued at immediate appearance trials are generally much harsher than they would be under traditional trial procedure. Custodial sentences in particular are very frequent: 57 percent in Toulouse, 64 percent in Nantes, 66 percent in Lyons, 75 percent in Nimes, for example.[32] As the author of one information report to the Senate wrote in 2006: "The charge that this procedure is a 'conveyor belt to prison' could not be verified in the absence of national statistics. However, the local data would seem to bear it out."[33] Since then, a report to the National Assembly has produced figures for France as a whole, based on the only information available on immediate appearance trials – the orders for immediate execution of sentence, from which the authors draw the following conclusion: "Immediate appearance trial leads to a custodial sentence in more than 35 percent of cases, whereas they represent on average only 21 percent of sentences in criminal courts."[34] In fact, given that, in the latter case, some of the sentences are adjusted prior to execution, immediate appearance trials are at least twice as harsh as the traditional procedure in terms of actual incarceration. But the detention order decided at the court is in itself an interesting piece of information, because it indicates that the convicted offender is handcuffed at the end of the hearing and goes directly to the prison. In 2010, of nearly 16,000 such detention orders decided in court, 96 percent came from immediate appearance trials.

Second, immediate appearance trials often also result in detention while awaiting trial. This happens when the case is adjourned at the defendant's request. The trial should in principle be held within four weeks, which are then spent in prison if the court deems that the defendant cannot offer sufficient guarantee of appearance or continues to represent a danger to society. But detention can also be decided before the case gets to court when police custody begins on a Thursday or Friday, since in this case defendants spend the weekend in prison while awaiting their hearing. One evening I witnessed the arrival of four young Romanians who were being brought in for three days while awaiting an immediate appearance trial the following Monday: they were charged with stealing chickens. In 2011, of the 88,000 people jailed in France, nearly a quarter were held while awaiting an immediate appearance trial. "These short stays, even if it's just to bridge the gap between police custody and trial, they mean more inmates and an added suicide risk," one warden told me in frustration.

The popularity of real-time prosecution, as evinced by the exponential rise in its use, is due to the speed with which cases can be resolved. From this point of view, while immediate appearance unblocks the courts, it must be said that it clogs up the prisons. In this context, it is all the more remarkable that the authorities now insist on tracking down people who had been sentenced to short jail terms that had not been executed, long after their conviction and longer still after the crime itself.

* * *

"When you lock them up, you have the feeling that you're perpetrating an injustice. Of course we have to punish criminals, but years later, there isn't any point any more. They track down a guy for a little sentence that goes back to the Ark! In the meantime he's put his life back together, he's moved on. When he realizes, he's furious. He sees it as an unfair system that's out to get him. In 2012 I had people being jailed for sentences of two weeks, a month, six months that dated back to 2005, 2006, 2007 ... ." One warden, by no means known for his indulgence toward inmates, protested thus against the policy of systematic execution of old sentences introduced in 2009: "We're formally implementing the law, but at what cost? It's a disaster. We're just going to regenerate crime." The number of prisoners held annually in his prison had risen yet again.

On June 22, 2009, Nicolas Sarkozy, addressing both houses of parliament in Versailles, exclaimed: "How can we speak of justice when there are 82,000 sentences that haven't been executed because there are not enough prison places?" The figures came from a report completed by the ministry of justice three months earlier, but not disseminated at that point. A few weeks later, the minister of justice announced "a circular on this subject summarizing good practices that can be implemented immediately."[35] In fact, this discovery was only news to the government. A study of the implementation of custodial sentences issued in 2001 had already shown that, 18 months after being handed down, 45 percent of these penalties had not been executed. Over half these cases were provisional sentences, and nearly one-third had been granted pardon or amnesty.[36] No one had been alarmed by these figures. But times had changed, and the new president had placed security issues at the heart of his message. In this context, to assert that there were more people sentenced to custodial terms outside the prison system than inside was to deliver a shock to public opinion, with the twofold effect of putting judges once again in a difficult position, and demonstrating the government's determination to punish criminals effectively.

Clearly, those who are unfamiliar with the system may be astonished, and even outraged, to find out that so many sentences are not executed. However, the analysis presented in the 2009 report on which the French president based his remarks offers some helpful clarification.[37] First, the authors establish that more than two-thirds of the sentences that are not executed correspond to penalties of less than six months; they point out that German law, unlike French legislation, specifies that such sentences should only be used in exceptional cases. Second, they assert that if France were to tackle the task of ensuring execution of sentence, the total number of sentences to be served would represent a 250 percent increase in the prison population at the time of the report, showing how unrealistic the project is. Finally, they note that more than one-third of these sanctions were already under review by sentencing judges, and half of these were in the process of being adjusted. In other words, the analysis of the non-executed sentences puts their significance in perspective; ultimately, the courts, tacitly and sometimes unwittingly, find alternatives to the execution of short sentences, thereby avoiding further prison overcrowding. This is not, however, the interpretation that was adopted by the government, and at a time when public prosecutors were subject to intense pressure from the ministry of justice, they were required to do everything in their power to ensure that custodial sentences be executed, regardless of how long ago they were issued and the current situation of the individuals in question.

"I'd forgotten about it, or actually I thought they'd forgotten about it." The 30-year-old man has the tired face and the bad teeth of a former drug user. It is the first time in his life that he has been in prison. He is French, born in France to Algerian parents. He lives in a housing project. As a teenager, he says, he "really went off the rail," but when he was 18 he decided to stop. "I didn't want to make my mother cry like she did for my brother, who's already got 21 convictions and been jailed 18 times." He got his driver's license, worked as a security guard, then as a bartender, and then as an air conditioning installer, before becoming a delivery driver: "It was all clean money." In 2007, at a traffic stop, he was arrested for driving with a suspended license, a very common occurrence in his profession. At the immediate appearance trial, he was given a three-month suspended jail sentence. In 2008 he was arrested once again, this time in his neighborhood, for carrying a weapon that was discovered during an identity check. Once again at an immediate appearance trial, he was sentenced to one month in prison, added to his reactivated suspended sentence, amounting to a total of four months, but the court did not issue a detention order. The sentence was therefore "adjustable." For five years he heard nothing more from the courts. He lived with his parents, continued to work, decided to get his teeth fixed. He met a young healthcare assistant he wanted to move in with. One day, he received a summons from the court. "After all that time, I thought the system had forgotten about me. I won't lie to you, I put the letter to one side and thought, let's just see if they send me another one." A few weeks later, on his way to the supermarket with his niece, he was stopped by the anticrime squad, who checked his identity and realized that he had an outstanding warrant. He was arrested, taken to the police station and then the court, where the public prosecutor told him he would be jailed. "I tried to argue, to see if they couldn't find another solution, like electronic monitoring, but they wouldn't listen." He had therefore ended up at the prison to "do" his four months.

When I interviewed him the day after he entered, he spoke calmly, softly, coming across not as angry, but rather as uncomprehending, with a deep sense of injustice. "When I arrived here, it was difficult. Prison is hard. I shouldn't be here. I'm a hard worker, have been since I was 18. I work from four in the morning to eleven, then from two in the afternoon to seven in the evening. I'm not a slacker. I get up every morning at three. I'm not scared of work. I don't belong in prison. And you know, all the guys from my housing project who are in here say: 'It's unbelievable, not you! You've always been so straight.' It's not even like I'm charged with anything serious, and I've done nothing wrong since 2008." He talks of his family, his sisters, his older brother who has settled down now, another, younger brother who has been disabled since the age of 2. He is worried about his job. "It's not prison itself that scares me. But I know that this means the end of my fixed-term contract. They won't take me back at my company. We transport precious items. We work with banks. They'll never give me my job back." But he also knows that he will have to go and live somewhere else with his girlfriend. He talks of the tense relations between the anticrime squad and the young men in his neighborhood: "I can't stay in my project. The anticrime cops are always after you, they hang around you and insult you until you respond. And then they arrest you for insulting an officer and resisting arrest. When they have it out for a family, they never let go. They push us to the limit. My brother, they used to walk past him and say: 'How's it going, shit-eater?' He answered back and straight away it was insulting an officer and resisting arrest. I've always tried not to respond to their provocations, but now that I've been in jail they'll try to bring me down again: 'There, you see, you've been inside too!' The best thing is not to say anything. When you don't answer they get discouraged." In his intake interview, he asked to be placed in the convicted prisoners block. "My whole town is here," he smiles. In this block, conditions are a little better than in those that house defendants awaiting trial; evenings are calmer, most of the inmates work. It is unlikely, however, that he will be allowed to go to the workshops or classes because his stay is too short for any of this to be put in place. "I might get my teeth fixed here," he fantasizes. At this point I know – as he probably does too – that he will leave in three months, given the likely sentence reduction credits, without having had any useful activity, without having seen health professionals or probation and re-entry counselors, only able to hope that his stay will pass smoothly. Caught up by an already distant past he thought he had escaped, he will now have, both in himself and in the view of others, the indelible mark of time in prison.

At least he should have no other sentences to be added unexpectedly to the one that has put him in jail. Not all prisoners are this lucky. Often the prison clerk's office receives notification of old penalties during the incarceration. These then lead to extensions of the jail term that are all the more distressing because they had been forgotten or suppressed, and are often announced shortly before the prisoner's release date. A man in his 40s was jailed for a repeat offense of driving with a suspended license: he received an eight-month custodial sentence, to which was added a month suspended carried over from his previous conviction. Three weeks before he was due to be released, he received notification of a five-month sentence for threatening behavior that dated back six years. Twenty days before his new projected release date, he received another notification of a four-month sentence for theft that was two years old. Finally, a week before he was again due to be released, a sentence of ten months, issued eleven years previously, again for driving with a suspended license, was dropped on him. "I can't take this any longer. It's not right, what they're putting me through," he says, devastated, when told of this latest postponement of his release. He had spent a total of 28 months in prison, two-thirds of it for driving with a suspended license, portioned out at the whim of a malfunctioning judicial system, in a sort of bureaucratically organized torture.

Shortly after I began my study, a prisoner committed suicide in his cell. No one had anticipated this. He had not been tagged as a suicide risk in his initial interviews or during his stay. His action was all the more difficult to comprehend because he was just about to be freed. However, a little later it was revealed that a few days before his projected release date, he had been notified of two old sentences: one of three months, for a conviction two years earlier, and the other of eight months, handed down in a trial that had taken place three years before. It was more than he could bear. Remarking on this tragic case, one of the wardens said to me: "The next Outreau will be for a sentencing judge." He was referring to the infamous case of an alleged pedophile network, which revealed the dysfunctions of the justice system: one of those charged had committed suicide while awaiting trial. In the case of the prisoner who killed himself at the prison, the problem was not a technical error on the part of the sentencing judge – at most it was a demonstration of zeal at a time when the judiciary was under pressure from the government.

*   *   *

Three years before the publication of his book on the birth of the prison, which had such a profound and lasting influence in the social sciences, Michel Foucault gave his third lecture at the Collège de France, entitled "The Punitive Society." It did not represent a major shift in his work, since the first two series of lectures he had given following his election to this venerable institution were devoted, respectively, to the "will to knowledge," in which two of the empirical examples considered were the judicial practices of ancient Greece, and, in the related seminar, nineteenth-century penal psychiatry and to "penal theories and institutions", focusing on the emergence of the modern judiciary, while the related seminar examined the forensic medical aspects of a nineteenth-century murder.[38] Thus the question of justice was already quite present in Foucault's reflection on power and truth. The new feature of the 1972 course, however, was that he broadened and shifted his focus by taking punishment as his subject and demonstrating how "a society in which the apparatus of the judicial state performs corrective and penitentiary functions," as he put it in his lecture of February 17, 1973, emerged in France at the end of the eighteenth century. What appears today self-evident – the administration of justice by the state, the articulation of the judicial and coercive functions, and the implementation of penal practices through the correctional institution – thus has a history, and this history is a recent one. But the essential point, one that his later work on prison has perhaps led many commentators to overlook, is that, for Foucault, the question of prison is embedded within a broader context – the punitive society. It is in this context that I have sought to locate my analysis.

In order to understand prison, we have to know who is locked up, for what reason, for how long – and certainly also, who is not. Hence the development of attitudes, discourses, policies, legislation, police practices, and court decisions is inseparable from any study of prison worlds, for it is they that determine the demographics – and sociology – of those worlds. Prison crystallizes all these changes; it is the end point of the processes they put in place, and the receptacle of the parts of the population they concern themselves with. In his lecture, Foucault analyzes specifically how the line of demarcation between working-class "illegalities" such as fraud and smuggling, which until then had been tolerated and even encouraged, because in sidestepping the law they contributed to a dynamic economy, and crime, epitomized by theft and therefore construed as a danger to the social order and the object of punitive morality, shifted with the rapid rise of the middle class and the development of capitalism in the early nineteenth century. At the same time, the ruling classes arrogated exclusive power to exempt their own "illegalities" from the law and its sanction.[39] If we continue this analysis into the contemporary period, we clearly find not a continuum, but rather, as we have seen, moments in history during which various penal theories and a range of correctional ideologies have been tested, imposed, deployed, and then contested, withdrawn and discarded. And so, after the years of social experimentation in rehabilitation and re-entry of the mid-twentieth century comes the phase of repression that characterizes recent decades. What remains structurally constant, however, throughout all periods, is, on the one hand, the establishment of lines of demarcation between what is to be punished and what is tolerated and, on the other, the existence of differentiated patterns of distribution and application of punishments.

All the symbolic work of power aims to efface these operations and to represent these lines of demarcation and patterns as part of the natural order. In recent years, it has consisted in particular of arousing fear and displacing anxiety, focusing public attention on insecurity rather than inequality, while at the same time dissociating them from one another, constituting certain groups and certain spaces as dangerous, singling out recidivism as necessitating exceptional punitive measures regardless of their effect on prevention, making it seem obvious that driving with an invalid license or use of marijuana should merit greater mobilization of judicial resources than corporate crimes, justifying the introduction of the disadvantageous procedures of immediate appearance trial for a growing number of defendants charged with often minor offenses, and establishing as common sense that even a short custodial sentence should be served in prison, however long after the perpetration of the act committed and whether or not it is to the detriment of the social integration of the individuals concerned. The point is therefore to expose this form of naturalization of problems – in the sense in which social facts are presented as "natural." Hence my efforts in this book to engage in a combined – and sometimes tedious – analysis of laws and reports, statistics and stories, official declarations and secrets confided, observations in court and moments witnessed in prison, for it is in the detail of these elements and their juxtaposition that underlying logics are revealed. The change of perspective involves just such a fine-grained work of deconstructing these false commonsense understandings.

This work is not the monopoly of the researcher. On this point, it is worth noting that prison staff themselves sometimes reveal an acute critical comprehension of the development of the punitive society. With good reason, one might think: it is they who are burdened with its repercussions, who have to face overcrowding and to manage doubling-up in cells and tensions between prisoners, who are swamped with monitoring vulnerable inmates, sentence adjustment files, and requests for mental health appointments. But this is not the only reason: they come to know the prisoners, their journey, their behavior, day by day; they cannot avoid judging who they are and what has led them to prison. In public, they abstain from commenting on court decisions. In conversation, they sometimes offer their impressions, express their reservations, reveal their doubts. They are epitomized by the correctional officer who is shocked by the one-year sentence for riding a stolen scooter, the probation and re-entry counselor who points out the human fallout from short sentences, the warden outraged that people who have rebuilt their lives are chased down to serve old sentences. One of the directors describes the change over a single decade: "Ten years ago, the average French person would never have imagined they might one day be in prison. Now, they should know they're no longer certain of avoiding a prison sentence. Ten years ago, it was inconceivable that you could go to prison for driving with a suspended license. Now, we get two or three a week – guys who just don't get it." Yet these voices are rarely heard. Prison staff more often find themselves in the position of defendant than in the role of accuser. And when they do express an opinion, it naturally relates to professional demands rather than criticizing the penal system.

The fact that the judicial institutions are ultimately those that decide the fate of people charged with offenses – the assistant public prosecutor who puts forward the case for immediate appearance trial, the criminal judge who decides the sentence, the sentencing judge who adjusts it – should not conceal the fact that much is played out before the case reaches them. There is the media with its representation of current affairs and news stories, and those in authority who respond to it; there is the government that defines policy and the legislators who vote through laws; there are the police who focus their activity on particular crimes or groups; there are also the commentators and analysts, whether researchers, experts, or campaigners, who describe and interpret these phenomena; and finally there is what is established, through surveys and discourses, as public opinion, which "thinks," "criticizes," and "demands." Thus the penal apparatus reflects this multiplicity of interventions and agents which we may term the punitive society.

But it is not enough just to name it. We need to try to understand what drives it. Why is it that in recent decades French society, in particular, and, to varying degrees, most Western societies have set themselves to filling their prisons and building new ones in order to fill them just as much? The phenomena I have described in detail, from the introduction of mandatory minimum sentences to the implementation of old suspended sentences, including the expansion of immediate appearance trials, relate to the recent period – the first decade of the twenty-first century, which in France was marked by a rise in securitarian thinking. As I have pointed out, this development was set within the context of a longer-term and wider-ranging social change, but it has greatly amplified the intensity of that shift. In order to understand it, we need to enlarge the frame of interpretation and include in it a broader range of the features characterizing society and the functions performed by the state. Society is not just punitive, it is also unequal. The state is not just a penal state, it is also a social state.

In the years following World War II, France experienced a rapid rise in average income, coupled with a strengthening of the social protection system. Between 1950 and 1975, the annual increase in gross domestic product was over 5 percent, average wages tripled, growing faster than the minimum wage, and the proportion of household disposable income contributed by social benefits doubled. However, in the last quarter of the twentieth century, growth slowed, there was little increase in wages, and social benefits as a proportion of disposable income remained steady, while unemployment tripled and income inequalities deepened. The disparities intensified during the first decade of the twenty-first century, as unemployment rose from 7.8 percent to 9.8 percent, and the ratio of the average standard of living of the richest 10 percent to that of the poorest 10 percent moved from 6.2 to 7.2.[40] This is the context in which the toughening of penal policy and the increase in the prison population occurred, the trend becoming sharply intensified from 2002 onwards; as mentioned earlier, the number of people sentenced to prison rose by more than half. In other words, while the economic situation was worsening and social inequality was deepening, a stagnation in social benefits was observed, which represented an actual contraction given the growing rate of unemployment; at the same time, there was a rise in the number of prisoners, which was not linked to any increase in crime and serious offenses.

This combination of increasing inequality, the decline of the social state, and the expansion of the penal state is also observed, with variants, in many other Western countries, and, even if we cannot draw a causal relationship, the rise in prison population at a time of deepening inequality calls for interpretation.[41] There are a few notable exceptions: in Europe, the Netherlands and Germany, and, more recently Sweden, have reversed the trend in their prison population and reduced the number of prisoners. As far as France and the majority of Western countries that have seen the opposite development are concerned, theories aiming to account for the combined social and penal developments fall, very roughly, into two groups.[42] In the view of the first, repressive policies serve the interests of the ruling classes to the detriment of the working class. When the situation in the labor market deteriorates and poverty rises, the parts of the population deemed useless and potentially dangerous are subjected to increasing coercion and, where appropriate, incarceration.[43] In what I have described above, the choice of offenses to which repressive measures are applied, and the recourse to disadvantageous procedures for minor offenses, support this thesis. The second theory is that repressive policies correspond to a change in norms and sensitivities throughout the whole of society, particularly a growing intolerance toward certain types of disorder and toward those judged to be responsible for them, with imprisonment becoming the means to dissuade or exclude them.[44] As described earlier, the rise in security concerns stimulated by media reporting of spectacular crimes, and the positive recognition granted to victims, can support this reading. In the first case we can speak of political economy, because it centers on relations of production and class conflict, and in the second of moral economy, inasmuch as we are dealing with values and affects.

These two interpretations are not as incompatible as they might appear.[45] The well-understood interests of the privileged classes may be based on the emotional foundations of social anxiety, just as the feeling or experience of insecurity can contribute to disadvantaged groups being excluded from the economic dividends of society.[46] As Bernard Harcourt showed in relation to the United States, the punitive society is all the more certain of being able to bring its project to fruition, since it rests on a convergence between the more or less conscious strategies of the elite and the more or less stirred up expectations of the majority[47] – a convergence that thus needs "minorities" in order to subject them to this "institutional violence" that was described by the warden at the prison.

2

A Well-Kept Public Secret

The truth is not a process of exposure which destroys the secret,
but a revelation which does justice to it.
Walter Benjamin, *The Origin of German Tragic Drama*, 1963

"Let's face it. Look out there in the yard. It's all blacks and Arabs." The man is standing at the barred window of his cell. It is Ramadan. He has chosen not to go out this afternoon because of the heat and thirst. He points to the inmates walking about below us, most of them in small groups, between the high walls topped with barbed wire. He turns to me, smiling, and, as others before him have often done, calls me to witness the obvious fact of the distinctive racial composition of the prison population. He is a French-born citizen of Moroccan origin. He is 28 years old. A first-time offender, he has been sentenced to three years in prison for possession and sale of marijuana. After a pause, he resumes: "Us in here, we feel the injustice of justice. I was dealing pot. I'm not saying it's not wrong, but it's only marijuana. I never hurt anybody, I never stole from anybody. I never even shoplifted. I pay my taxes and my fines. So when I see Sarkozy profiting from the riches of a senile old woman or Cahuzac and the millions he owes in taxes . . . and they're free. There, you feel the injustice."

This theme of double standards came up frequently in my conversations with prisoners. In the present case, the man was evoking two judicial affairs, one in which then conservative presidential candidate Nicolas Sarkozy was accused of receiving a clandestine donation from the funds of billionaire Liliane Bettencourt after tapes recorded by her butler were rendered public, and the other in which the socialist minister of the budget Jérôme Cahuzac had to resign after news website Mediapart revealed he had secret bank accounts in Switzerland and Singapore. Inmates were indeed well informed about ongoing events, especially when they were related to justice and prison. They watched the news and read the newspapers. They followed stories about court cases very attentively, commenting on them later. They drew comparisons: the severity exhibited toward the offenses they committed, which they did not always conceive as serious, against the indulgence shown toward the powerful for crimes that appeared to have much graver consequences – the difference between the amounts of money involved being for them an indicator of the disparity between the acts concerned. One conclusion seemed obvious to them: the reason there were so many blacks and Arabs in prison was because society treated them unfairly.

The overrepresentation of ethnic and racial minorities in French prisons is an example of what Michael Taussig calls a "public secret," that is, "what is generally known, but cannot be spoken": a "reconfiguration of repression in which depth becomes surface so as to remain depth."[1] Everyone knows, everyone knows that everyone knows, but the secret must be publicly kept – in other words, must not be made public even though it is a fact the public is manifestly aware of. If this is the case, how are we to understand this public secret, and its significance? Secrecy is rightly considered an instrument of power; it could, however, also be a sign of powerlessness. A fact is concealed because people do not know how to talk about it and what to do with it, because they fear the consequences of its revelation both for those who know it and for those it concerns. It would seem that this applies to the issue of race in prison. Moreover, the prison establishment does not just pass over it in silence; it has no knowledge of it. It is not spoken of (I almost never heard staff discuss it explicitly), but nor is it even grasped (there are no statistics that would make it possible to measure it, still less mechanisms for interpreting it). We are faced, then, with the paradox of this situation in which people do know, without having actual knowledge.

The reasons for this voluntary ignorance are of two kinds. Some are not specific to the world of prison. It is considered wrong to identify individuals in terms of their origin or appearance, particularly in databases and surveys: it is assumed that this would give credence to the existence of ethnic or racial differences and contribute to the ethnicization and racialization of society. Other explanations, by contrast, are linked to the very information concerned: it is feared that the existence, and even more the publication, of statistics linking the prison population with ethnic and racial minorities would inevitably feed a discourse of stigmatization and practices of exclusion, and it is true that crime and immigration or origin have often been conflated in the recent past.[2] These two types of argument must be taken seriously. The first emphasizes the risk of essentialization and normalization of ethnic and racial categories. The second underlines the dangers of incorrect interpretation and cynical instrumentalization of these sensitive data. Thus the public secret around the overrepresentation of minorities in prison testifies both to a quandary in the face of an uncomfortable fact and an ethical concern with regard to divulging it. The prison management does not want to know about it, and the staff prefer not to speak of it. Only the inmates have no hesitation in pointing it out.

While the keeping of this public secret is understandable, it is nevertheless still part of a twofold phenomenon: the concealment of a troubling reality and the censorship of debate on the subject, both at the risk of feeding rumor and prejudice among the majority population and shoring up the sense of injustice among minority groups. Should we then seek to better understand this reality? And how would this be useful? Four arguments can be made. First, the prison administration cannot ignore the composition of its population. Ethnic or racial category is certainly not the only factor meriting attention; data on occupation, employment status, level of education, and place of residence are also useful. Nevertheless, ethnic or racial identification is both an indicator of social situation (black people in prison in France, in Britain, and in the United States belong mainly to disadvantaged social classes) and a specific marker of a particular condition (which allows us to incorporate the specifically ethnic or racial component of discrimination). Second, public authorities need to interpret these data: the figures never speak for themselves, and must be put in perspective. The overrepresentation of certain minorities in prison may reflect greater involvement in crime (and if this is the case, it too needs to be analyzed), or a bias in the drafting of legislation, the work of the police, and the decisions of the courts (resulting in a specific penalization of these groups), or a combination of the two elements. Third, these statistics and the explanations offered for them should be debated in the public arena. Whether viewed from the perspective of crime prevention or from that of equity in penal policies and their implementation, these are issues that concern all citizens. Fourth, and finally, once such data have been produced, analyzed, and discussed, they should inform public action as much as social campaigns. Although it is doubtful whether they can always be used in this way, the fact remains that, both for the state and for civil society, they are an essential instrument for action, not least against discrimination, since to combat it, one must be able to measure it. In sum, knowledge of prison demographics is therefore not just a matter of scientific curiosity: it is a democratic necessity. This public secret needs to be investigated further.

*   *   *

"Race matters in British prisons," write Leonidas Cheliotis and Alison Liebling in a long article that presents a survey of inmates in 49 prisons in England and Wales regarding their experience of racialization, racism and, more broadly, race relations.[3] With respect to incarceration in the United States, "the most important social fact is the inequality in penal confinement. This inequality produces extraordinary rates of incarceration among young African American men with no more than a high school education," assert Bruce Western and Becky Pettit in a meta-analysis of studies on the racial composition and educational level of the prison population, and on the socioeconomic and intergenerational effects of disparities in imprisonment.[4] But who can say whether "race" matters (or not) in French prisons? And who can evaluate the "inequality" (or absence of it) of incarceration in France?

Inequality in relation to imprisonment, and particularly its racial dimension, is indeed not well studied and even often unknown: we can more easily describe the prison population in terms of the crimes committed than in terms of who the prisoners are.[5] When the public authorities do take an interest in inmates and the problems they face, they do so generically, without focusing specifically on disparities, on the principle that undifferentiated treatment should prevail in the drafting of regulations and the production of statistical data. This principle relates particularly to the distinctions that might be made within the French population on the basis of origin or appearance. The French republican ideal is, indeed, based on the indivisibility of the nation and the equal status of all citizens: it is permissible to count foreigners, but not Arab or black men.[6] This refusal to racialize the population is, of course, laudable when it comes to instituting laws and norms applicable to all. It becomes problematic when it is set in opposition to awareness of inequality. For a long time French society has been able to ignore ethnic and racial discrimination, and even simply to avoid naming it: what was not measured did not exist.[7] Prison is therefore no exception to this logic, which holds for all French institutions. Even the remarkable reports by parliamentary committees and regulatory bodies, however critical they are of penal policy and of the prison system, avoid approaching the delicate subject of the color of incarceration.[8] The entire state apparatus is blind to inequality in imprisonment and its ethnic and racial component. The silence around the public secret is thus compounded by a blindness to what it is composed of.

This situation contrasts with that prevailing in other countries that also face a growth in their prison population, but are historically more inclined to debate the issue of race. In Britain, for example, it is known that in 2010 there were 4.7 times as many black, or Afro-Caribbean, people in prison as in the general population, 3.9 times as many mixed-race people, and 1.4 times as many South Asians, while whites and East Asians were underrepresented.[9] This is not a recent development, since, as early as 1990, there were already 7.1 times more black people than white people imprisoned in England and Wales.[10] In the United States, even the ratio of incarceration according to ethnic and racial variable is known: in 2009, when compared to whites, there were 6.7 times more blacks, or African Americans, and 2.6 more Hispanics.[11] More precisely, it has been observed that for a man born in the 1960s, the probability of spending some time in prison at some point is over 20 percent if he is black and under 3 percent if he is white, that at any given moment 11.5 percent of black people aged between 20 and 40 are in prison, compared to 1.6 percent of whites of the same age, and that if a social dimension, measured in terms of dropping out of high school, is introduced, the proportion in this age class is 32.4 percent for blacks and 6.7 percent for whites.[12] In Britain and the United States, recognition of this overrepresentation of minorities has led to research studies that aim to explain it, public debates that call it into question, social activism seeking to correct it, and even to some changes in penal and prison policy.

By contrast, in France, prison administration, like all public institutions, does not gather data on minorities. Some fragmentary information is nevertheless available. The easiest data to obtain relate to foreigners. The

number and proportion of non-French nationals in prison rose consistently between 1974, when the borders were officially closed, and 1993,
which marked a shift toward a more administrative treatment of breaches
of immigration law. From this date, undocumented non-nationals are less
and less frequently incarcerated in prisons, and increasingly locked up in
immigration detention centers prior to deportation. When the practice of
imprisoning people without legal residence was at its height, they made up
nearly one-third of all prisoners, whereas foreigners now make up around
one-fifth and are generally convicted for other offenses; their proportion has
remained high partly because on average they receive tougher sentences for
the same crimes and half as many adjustments at the end of their sentence as
French nationals. More than half of them are nationals of African countries,
two-thirds of these are from North Africa.[13] However, foreigners represent
only a small proportion of the prisoners from minority backgrounds, most
of the latter being French citizens.

One way of getting round this obstacle is to use so-called proxy variables that serve to approximate populations of immigrant origin. In 2002,
for example, over half of all prisoners had a father who was born outside
France, including six out of ten on the African continent; in one-third of
cases, their parents did not speak French at home when they were growing
up. If we compare these figures to the census data available for the general
population, the probability of being sent to prison was 3.1 and 2.6 times
higher if either the father or the mother was born outside France, and these
odds reached 5.2 and 4.5 for the subgroup in which the father or mother
was born in Africa.[14] Here, too, the data do not take into consideration
all minorities, because they do not include black people of French origin,
notably those from the overseas territories, or of Roma people, both of
whom studies have shown to be subject to discrimination in a range of
spheres. Although interesting, these surveys do not encompass the entirety
of the reality pointed out by the man standing at the window of his cell.
It was a reality that I could not myself ignore, for the exercise in the yard,
the visiting hours, the returns from workshops, and of course the Friday
prayers in the multifaith chapel – each one of these offered me a visual
reminder of the substantial presence of minorities in the prison.

In order to get a more accurate picture of the overall composition of
the penal population in the facility, in July 2013 I took a census of the
men there, recording their age, nationality, and whether they belonged to
a minority. To determine the latter, I went by family name, photograph,
and any additional information, for example in the case of "travelers."[15]
However, I was not able to correlate this information with occupation,
employment status, level of education, or family situation; I will return
to these factors later, drawing on aggregated data. I therefore restricted
myself to the three variables cited above. A little over half the inmates
were under 30, and only one-fifth were over 40. French nationals represented 78 percent of the total, and, among the 22 percent of foreigners,
Europeans were the most numerous, comprising 8 percent, half of whom

were Romanian, while North Africans and sub-Saharan Africans made up two subgroups at 5 percent each. Ethnic and racial minorities made up 77 percent of the prisoners: 35 percent of them were black, 32 percent of Arab origin, and 5 percent Roma. The other national groups comprised 2 percent Turks, 2 percent South Asians, and 1 percent Latin Americans. Among the black men, 84 percent were French nationals and 14 percent were from sub-Saharan African countries, while the remaining 2 percent came from other regions of the world. Similarly, of the Arab men, 84 percent were French and 14 percent were nationals of a North African country; the remaining 2 percent were of other geographical origin. This distribution was markedly influenced by age. In the under-30 age group, 77 percent were black or Arab, and 16 percent were white. Among the over-40s, however, 40 percent were white, and 51 percent were black or Arab.

To sum up: in the correctional facility where I conducted my study, at the time when I performed this count, black and Arab men represented two-thirds of all prisoners, and as much as three-quarters of those under 30, who counted for half the total prison population. As a point of reference, in the United States the prison population is made up of a little under one-third black and Hispanic men, while in Britain around a quarter of inmates are black, Asian, or mixed-race – classified in terms of the categories used in the two countries. The point is, of course, not to compare these figures, given that, first, I am considering only one facility on one side with a national prison system on the other; and, second, a short-stay facility in an urbanized region cannot be considered representative of the entire French prison system. However, it is interesting to note that if we use the proportion of non-French nationals in the prison population as a proxy of the proportion of minorities, the prison I studied departs only slightly from the average in France (24 percent compared to 19 percent over the whole prison population), while the distribution by nationality is almost identical (with African nationals representing 55 percent and 54 percent respectively).[16] It is therefore not unreasonable to suppose that my statistics do not describe an exceptional situation, and do not differ greatly from the national demographics.

Thus we may assert that, at least in some French prisons, the proportion of minorities is slightly higher than in US prisons, and markedly higher than that in British prisons – a fact that will certainly come as a surprise to those who imagined France to be an exception.[17] Of course, we need to relate these figures to the proportion of minorities in the general population to determine precisely the level of overrepresentation; as we have seen, this ratio is almost seven in the United States and five in the United Kingdom. Because of the ban on producing such statistics in France, it is not possible to do this.[18] However, even in a disadvantaged urban environment like the department where the prison I studied is located, the two-thirds of the prison population made up by Arab and black men certainly do not reflect the local demographics. There is little doubt that they are massively overrepresented.

Of course, racial identification represents only one dimension of the minority issue. According to figures from the National Prisoner Records, more than half the people held in the facility where I was working were unemployed, and one in eight was working on a short-term contract; only one-third had a steady job; half of them said they had no occupation and one-quarter were blue-collar workers, with white-collar workers making up only 1 percent. Four out of ten had no educational qualifications, four out of ten had a degree from a vocational school and only two out of ten had a high-school or higher qualification. Finally, two-thirds of them were single. Thus, these minorities are defined as much by their limited economic and cultural capital as by their color and origin. They constitute a sort of underclass of African origin. In the prison I studied, the black and Arab prisoners, who were for the most part French nationals, were generally the children of immigrant workers who, in their time, had formed the proletariat of French society – initially North African, then from sub-Saharan Africa. The crucial difference between their generation and that of their parents is that they had no work.

Should the public secret of this delicate question be exposed? I hesitated long before undertaking the statistical analysis I have presented here, and I spent as long asking myself whether it was justified to publish the results, weighing the risk of ill-informed or ill-intentioned interpretation. However, this risk seemed to me less significant than the cost of ignoring, or feigning ignorance, of one of the most disturbing aspects of the reality of prison, and of the penal policy that contributes to producing it. I believe that it is a scholar's duty to address society's issues, even the most difficult ones, to pose them in rigorous terms, and to enable public discussion of them. While in this case the prison administration's reasons and the prison staff's scruples are eminently respectable, the sociologist or anthropologist must state the truth of the facts, even when they may be difficult to hear.

At the start of his lecture at the University of Leuven in 1981, Michel Foucault explained what is at stake in such an undertaking:[19] "How can one tell truth and speak justice at the same time? How can truthful speech be a foundation for just speech? This, I believe, is one of the great problems that has spanned our entire history." It is not enough to disclose what was hidden; we must also reveal what is at stake in hiding it. This is the sense of Walter Benjamin's statement, at the head of this chapter: while the disclosure destroys the secret, the revelation of the truth does it justice. Having presented the facts, it is therefore incumbent upon me to interpret them.

*   *   *

When I was teaching social sciences at the University of Paris, I used to present, in my first-year course, a study that served to demonstrate to students both the importance of a critical reading of statistics, and its interest for the public debate. This study was conducted by Pierre Tournier and Philippe Robert in the late 1980s, at a time when the far right's rhetoric on issues of immigration and insecurity, which was progressively taken up by some mainstream right-wing politicians, aimed to conflate the two phenomena: the rise in crime, it was claimed, was due to the increased presence of non-citizens.[20] The publication of statistics on the prison population, which were widely reported in the media, appeared to confirm the link between these two facts. There were proportionally 5.4 times more foreigners than nationals in French prisons. The revelation of this surplus did not fail to fan the flames of the xenophobic discourse. For Tournier and Robert, the point was to critically examine this figure.

The rate of incarceration is the relationship between the number of people in prison and the total number of the corresponding group living in France. In the case of foreigners, Tournier and Robert argued that it was artificially augmented by three factors: first, a proportion of the foreigners living in France was not counted by the census, thus reducing the denominator and increasing the ratio; second, the population of foreigners living in France was not structurally comparable to the French population, since it has a higher proportion of young people and men, two elements that were closely tied in with criminal behavior; third, there was one crime that artificially enlarged the representation of foreigners because it exclusively concerned them, namely the lack of legal residence documents, an offense that is currently increasingly subject to repression. When they took these three factors into account, by correcting and standardizing the non-national population so that it became comparable to the French population and by removing specific offenses against immigration law, the coefficient of overrepresentation of foreigners in prison halved, falling to 2.77 – and this without even being able to take into account social class and employment status, which would have reduced the coefficient still further.

But their analysis did not end there. In order to be imprisoned, one must have been arrested and charged, if not tried. They therefore turned to the activity of the police and of the courts, identifying three levels of differentiation that put non-nationals at a disadvantage. First, out of all the incidents reported, those that are cleared up tend to be the types of offense more commonly committed by foreigners. Second, among the incidents investigated, the proportion where charges are brought is higher than for French nationals. Third, when charges are brought, the courts tend to imprison foreigners more often than French nationals, despite the fact that they are less often involved in serious crime; pre-trial detention in particular is more common, because they are deemed more likely to fail to appear in court. If these various elements were taken into account, the coefficient decreased to 1.71. In other words, when the factors of heterogeneity and discrimination accessible to measurement are statistically controlled, the apparent overrepresentation of foreigners falls by two-thirds.

Quite apart from the facts it revealed, this demonstration was pedagogical. Behind the apparent neutrality of numbers, the deconstruction of the statistics resulted in the unveiling of the unequal processes involved in the repression of crime. The reason there were so many foreigners in prison was not because they committed more crimes but – at least in large part

– because the entire police and criminal justice system worked to their disadvantage. The end result of this discrimination in the practices of the police and the judiciary, even if it was not necessarily fed by xenophobic prejudices, was to make non-nationals appear a threat to public order. The same kind of investigation must be undertaken to understand the current overrepresentation of minorities in prison: to decode, behind the unmentionable color of incarceration, the mechanisms that explain it.

This is, however, much harder to do than in the case of non-nationals. Here there are no data to correlate all the stages that, from the work of the legislator through the activities of the police to the judgment in court, lead to imprisonment (as dependent variables), with individuals' origin, social situation, and place of residence (as independent variables), because the study of these variables is not permitted in France.[21] The silence and blindness of the institutions are therefore compounded by their opacity. Everything is set up to naturalize the overrepresentation of minorities, by making it appear a simple translation of their greater propensity to crime. First, it remains unspoken in order to avoid stigmatizing them (which assumes that this is indeed the main explanation). Second, the authorities therefore make efforts not to see it (because if they did they would not know what to say about it). Third, any critical analysis is thwarted (by dint of not producing data that might validate it). How, then, is it possible to denaturalize the overrepresentation of minorities in prison? The difficulty of this exercise, in the absence of statistics including socioeconomic and ethnoracial variables into the different levels of the police and criminal justice system, should not be an excuse for giving up on it.

By way of illustration, consider drug offenses –the very crime committed by the man who talked to me about ethnoracial disparities in the yard. This is not a trivial example, because in the United States, the "war on drugs" was the principal factor in the production of mass incarceration that has mainly affected African Americans, and to a lesser degree Hispanics. The situation is of course different in France, but for 50 years legislation on drugs, in particular its differential application at different levels of society, has contributed significantly to the increase of and the disparity in the prison population. Not enough, though, in the view of one of the prison wardens, who told me: "The other day, I saw a documentary about the penal system in the United States. Over there, 50 grams of crack gets you 20 years. I'm not saying we should go over to that system, because it doesn't do anything to cut crime anyway, but maybe there's a happy medium between them and us." Indeed, as if the punishment was not heavy enough, he exaggerated it, because under the Anti-Drug Abuse Acts of 1986 and 1988, mandatory sentences were five years for five grams of crack and ten years for fifty grams.

It was interesting that he chose this example, for it is precisely the one that is presented as the paradigmatic illustration of disparities of treatment between poor blacks and rich whites in the United States. In effect, possession is punished much more harshly by the federal authorities for crack cocaine than for powder cocaine: until 2010, the quantity for which the mandatory five-year custodial sentence was applied in the case of crack cocaine was one-hundredth of that for powder cocaine, leading to thousands of incarcerations for simple possession, almost exclusively of poor blacks. Following the passing of the so-called Fair Sentencing Act, the ratio of severity was reduced, but still stands at 18 to 1.[22] Yet, the harmful effects of cocaine are medically identical for the two forms. What differentiates the two products is not their composition or their toxicity, but their consumers: the vast majority of crack smokers are black people living in disadvantaged neighborhoods, while snorting powder, which is three times more common, is a practice more widespread in well-off white circles. Thus, at a time when security was becoming a national issue, crack was associated with crime. In France, however, it is not crack but marijuana that is the central issue. And it is not dealing that explains the increase in incarcerations, since dealers make up a minute proportion of 0.25 percent of the prison population, but use, possession, and resale, often of small quantities, in nine out of ten cases, of marijuana: these offenses are responsible for one in every seven new arrivals in prison.[23] In the prison where I carried out my study, they represented a still higher proportion, being the cause of incarceration of 21 percent of those in pre-trial detention, and 14 percent of convicted inmates.

Drug offenses, moreover, represent the crime that has seen the sharpest rise in penalization in France, on all three levels of repression: arrests, convictions, and prison sentences. First, since the law of 1970 forbidding the use and distribution of drugs was passed, with tougher sanctions being regularly introduced in the years since then, arrests have gone up sixtyfold, reaching 150,000; arrests for simple use have increased twice as fast as those for resale or dealing. Second, convictions have doubled over the last two decades, but tripled for simple use, totaling almost half of all convictions. Third, although prison sentences are used less than alternative sanctions, they have still doubled in 30 years, and here too the most rapid rise in recent years has been in sentences for simple use.[24] These figures reveal how the actions of government, parliament, the police, and the courts have combined in recent decades to organize increasing repression of violations of drug laws.

This repression was initially targeted mainly at heroin. It is now applied principally to marijuana. In other words, while penalization has shifted from a "hard drug" to a "soft drug," which several politicians in France, including ministers, have suggested in recent years might be legalized, there has not been, as might have been expected, any easing of repression, but rather a tougher attitude, the paradox being that offenses which present a much lesser danger are being punished more systematically and more harshly. Through more frequent arrests and convictions, these crimes are responsible for 12,500 new incarcerations each year, or 14 percent of the total. Custodial sentences for simple use account for 3,100 prisoners, or 3.5 percent of new arrivals.

At first sight, such a development appears neutral in terms of those who commit drug offenses. The law is harsh, but it is the law, it might be supposed, and it applies to everyone. After all, even if the majority of international experts hold that repression of use and possession have never been proven to be effective, it is understandable that a government might seek to remedy the problem of drugs, and that a parliament might take action to legislate on the matter. And people expect, of course, that priority be given to the most harmful practices, and that the law be applied universally. However, what is observed is the opposite. Already, in 1995, the authors of the *Report of the Working Group on Drugs and Drug Use* expressed surprise that consumers of cocaine were paradoxically less harshly treated than users of marijuana "because of their more favorable social situation," and noted that repression of drug use was practiced predominantly in "often difficult neighborhoods," at the risk of giving "drug users the impression of arbitrary application of the law."[25] Not only were the most dangerous substances not prioritized, but there was discrimination between drug users, to the benefit of well-off groups and to the detriment of lower-income groups, as repression targeted disadvantaged urban zones where immigrants and their children were concentrated.[26] This is also what I observed during the course of my research with the police between 2005 and 2007, in a large conurbation in the Paris region.

*   *   *

With regard to use and possession of marijuana, it is almost always the police who take the initiative to intervene, in contrast to many offenses for which it is the public who call on them to act. The first stage in the process that eventually leads to arrest is generally a stop and search of the individual, and his vehicle where applicable: it is at this point that the drug may be found. And such stops and searches are not randomly distributed.[27] Over the 15 months of my study of the police, almost all those I witnessed concerned young people of minority origin from low-income neighborhoods. These checks were not prompted by particular behaviors, even drug use, but were carried out on young people, most of them of North African or sub-Saharan African descent, who happened to be in public spaces, usually in housing projects. The discovery of small quantities of marijuana did not always result in an arrest; this depended on a number of contingent factors, including previous interactions with the police and the person's attitude during the stop and frisk, as well as the characteristics of individual police officers. However, I never saw young middle- or upper-class white people being taken to the precinct and charged with use or possession of marijuana, even when they were consuming it openly in public. At most, these offenders were issued a verbal caution.[28] I noted that the police were irresistibly drawn toward certain neighborhoods, and adopted an inflexibly harsh attitude toward certain groups, but seemed systematically to avoid other neighborhoods and to show leniency in relation to other groups. Some of them were operating in anticrime squads that had been set up a few years prior specifically with this objective. "During my training, I spent some time with an anticrime squad in the Paris region, I expressed surprise to team members that all the people I saw them check were blacks or Arabs," remembered one of the prison wardens. "'But it's because they're the criminals,' they told me." The director admitted that he had not been convinced by this explanation.

Were there in fact objective reasons for these differences in treatment?[29] In other words, did the neighborhoods and groups targeted by the police consume more drugs? If we look at marijuana, which accounts for the majority of arrests under the drug laws, the number of users in France is estimated at 3.8 million, 1.2 million of whom are believed to be regular users, the proportion of the latter rising to 9 percent among men aged between 18 and 25.[30] Use is thus widespread, and much more commonplace in French society than elsewhere in Europe. It extends to the whole of the population, especially the male population. In terms of the social differentiation in use, research reveals that it is more frequent among the children of white-collar workers and independent entrepreneurs, and less common among the children of blue-collar workers, junior employees, and the unemployed. In terms of cultural capital, studies show similar levels of use among those who have completed higher education and those who have dropped out of high school.[31] These two statistically documented observations clearly do not indicate higher use among young people living in public housing, who are known to be generally from low-income families, with lower levels of education.

Nevertheless, when the French public is asked about situations when they have witnessed drug use or dealing, or about whether they feel uncomfortable in their neighborhood as a result of these practices, residents of better-off neighborhoods state that they have less often witnessed or been disturbed than residents of housing projects, particularly in Sensitive Urban Zones.[32] It is likely, therefore, that what differentiates neighborhoods is not the frequency of marijuana use, but its visibility; use is naturally more evident in the public areas of housing projects than in the enclosed premises of private houses. It is worth remembering that the question here is the one of use, not of dealing, which has a different spatial distribution and is subject to other modes of repression. Dealers are not arrested during routine police patrols, but following organized surveillance by specialist teams, the "narcs." It is also worth noting that the differences between the perceptions of residents of different neighborhoods are small, and do not always trend in the same direction. Witnessing drug-related practices is mentioned by one person in five in the better-off housing neighborhoods, and one in four in the projects, while there is in fact less trouble with drug use in the suburbs than in the capital. Paris residents still complain about pollution three times more than about drugs, a factor that those who argue for repression forget to take into consideration, and which puts the discomfort occasioned by drug use starkly into perspective. With regard to the objective data available, and without minimizing the subjective aspect of the nuisance caused, it is thus difficult to justify public housing being the object of the almost exclusive attention of the police where repression of marijuana use is concerned.

How are we to understand this phenomenon? Drug offenses are "easy cases," as police officers put it, since in general all it takes is to search people – or their car – when conducting an identity check.[33] It becomes a crime that allows the police to raise their clearance rate. However, the problem is that stops and frisks are subject to precise conditions set down in law, which are rarely met in reality: if they cannot be justified by the suspicion or anticipation of a crime being committed, they are illegal, as the officers and their superiors are well aware. Conducting such actions among these groups that criminologists term "police property"[34] – that is, minorities viewed as dangerous, the monitoring of whom society offloads onto the police – is an easy way to score arrests, without fear of those concerned filing a complaint, as a member of the middle or upper classes exposed to the same ordeal might do. Thus stops and frisks take place in the projects rather than outside schools and universities, where they would nevertheless be at least as effective in terms of discovery of marijuana.[35]

These discriminatory police practices are nothing new.[35] But they intensified after 2002, with the implementation by the ministry of the interior of what is known as the "results-driven policy." This policy consisted in setting the police quantitative targets for arrests. In order to make up the shortfall of cases, law enforcement officers resorted to what they called "adjustment variables": the use and possession of marijuana.[36] Between 2000 and 2009, the number of people arrested for simple use of marijuana rose by 150 percent; the reverse was observed for resale and dealing, since the proportion of charges for these types of offenses has consistently fallen.[37] This change was the subject of a critical report in 2011 by the National Court of Audit, which stated: "In order to improve their numerical results, particularly for clearance rate, the services have increasingly prioritized identifying the least serious offense, the simple use of drugs without reselling them, to the detriment of seeking out and arresting those who both use and resell, and indirectly of the dismantling of dealers' networks."[38] The report does not, however, point out the socially and geographically selective nature of this repression, which is certainly ineffective in terms of the fight against drugs, but effective as social control.

Over the last few decades, and especially in recent years, the courts have been faced with a considerable increase in charges, the vast majority of which concern simple use. This mass of cases has led to a proliferation of alternatives to criminal charges, such as a police caution, and recourse to simplified procedures, such as court orders allowing the judge to decide a discharge or a fine. Nevertheless, the guidelines on tougher practice issued to public prosecutors, the introduction of mandatory minimum sentences for reoffenders, and the frequent use of immediate appearance trial have resulted in a spectacular rise in the number of convictions and incarcerations. Between 2002 and 2008, convictions for simple drug use increased almost fourfold, and prison sentences more than sevenfold.[39] Given the selection operated prior to trial by the police in their practice of arrests, this increase in the harshness of sanctions has impacted mainly upon young people of immigrant origin living in low-income neighborhoods, since generally, as we have seen, real-time prosecution of this type of case tends to penalize them. For them, at the culmination of this expedited trial, a custodial sentence with immediate transfer to the prison is the rule.

My reason for offering this meticulous analysis of the policies, practices, and statistics is that these drugs cases represent a key domain that links the production of social inequality in incarceration rates with its concealment via apparently universally applicable laws, procedures, and sanctions that are not challenged by any mechanism of evaluation.[40] This inequality results from the construction of the problem in the public arena, in the elaboration of the legislative arsenal, in the practices of the police, and in the work of the courts. At each of these levels, which are to some extent interdependent, it is the same groups that are primarily affected and which, at the end of the chain of punishment, find themselves jailed. The point here is not to describe a perfectly oiled, rigorously uniform, and totally overdetermined mechanism, but rather to grasp the interlocking, convergent, and opaque mechanisms that contribute to producing the disparities observed.

There is first the public discourse that stigmatizes neighborhoods described as sensitive and communities of immigrant origin, which is in some way legitimated by the link made between crime and drugs in these neighborhoods and among these groups: their youth embody the new dangerous classes. There is then the action of the government and representatives, who, in a climate of increasing anxiety around drugs, focus the apparatus of repression on one product, marijuana, which is less harmful than others such as cocaine, or even alcohol and tobacco, but is more easily associated with low-income groups and urban disorder. The fact that the epidemiological reality of drug use is entirely different from this representation is neither here nor there. There is also the intervention of the police who, mandated to control these areas and their inhabitants, multiply arrests of simple users under pressure from unachievable targets; users in residential areas and from the middle classes are not exposed to anything similar. There are finally the decisions of prosecutors and judges who, also pressured into severity, the former by ministerial instructions, the latter by the constraint of the law, amplify this tendency; moreover, immediate appeal trials give the defendant little chance. Thus, rather than in individual responsibility, it is in the complex, multiple, and convergent mechanisms of the chain of punishment that the explanation should be sought for the overrepresentation in prison of black and Arab minorities, in whose unequal status color, origin, social class, and residential segregation are closely interwoven. Drug offenses, especially the use and possession of marijuana, which constitute the majority of convictions under this legislation despite being objectively relatively harmless, are the most telling and the most troubling illustration of these mechanisms.

* * *

It was perhaps in some way to escape this condition that, in the criminal court where I sat observing immediate appearance trials, the man who had just heard his sentence took the action he did – an action as desperate as it was unexpected, and by which it appeared that I was not the only one surprised.

At the tail end of the year there are few cases. The last concerns a man in his early 30s, of French nationality, born of Malian parents in a large conurbation in the Paris region. Clad in a dark cotton windbreaker, he stands in the dock, anxious but calm. He responds to the questions of the presiding judge (a different magistrate from the one described in the prologue) in a low voice, searching for words but speaking in coherent sentences. He is accused of use, possession, and transport of "drugs, specifically marijuana," and of "refusal to comply with an order to stop," and "violent resistance to persons holding public authority." The facts, as reported in the police statement, are as follows.

Two days earlier, around midnight, as he was driving through the center of an urban area, a police car that had passed him in the opposite direction started up its sirens and lights. Panicking, he fled, pursued by the police. A few hundred yards further on he abandoned his car in a parking lot and continued on foot, throwing away a plastic bag as he did so. Rounding a bend in the street, he found himself face to face with two police officers and tried to escape them, but they managed to stop him by grabbing hold of him. While they, assisted by reinforcements, attempted to handcuff him, he held onto the roof rack on the police car and then, having been forced to the ground, placed his hands beneath his body. He was finally subdued, taken to the precinct, and placed in police custody where, having called vainly for some water to drink for several hours, "he lost his temper." Nevertheless, the police statements do not indicate that he offered any verbal or physical aggression at any point. Marijuana was discovered in the plastic bag he threw away as he ran off. A search of his clothes revealed 335 euros.

After reading out his name and date of birth, the judge asks insistently: "Haven't you got an address? Are you homeless? Do you live on the streets? Are you resident in an accommodation center?" The man tries to explain: "I've been on the street since August. Before that I was living with my girlfriend but we broke up." Ignoring his attempt to explain, the judge cuts in: "In any case, I don't have an address down here!" After briefly citing the charges, she asks if he wants to be tried in this session, or whether he would like an adjournment to prepare his defense, pointing out that in the latter case, the court will have to choose one of three options while he awaits trial: detention, release, or placement under court monitoring. The man does not know what to answer, so his court-appointed lawyer explains to him that, given his current situation, he can offer no guarantee that he will appear in court, making pre-trial detention the most likely outcome. The accused therefore agrees to an immediate trial. The judge then returns to the police officers' statements, punctuating her reading with observations and questions.

She asks the defendant about the circumstances in which he collided with the two police officers who were trying to stop him. He says that he was of course trying to escape them, but that they stood in his path and grabbed hold of his clothes. "So all in all, it's the police officers' fault," she comments dryly. A little later she asks the accused what the money found on him was for. He explains that as he lives on the street, he always has a little money on him, to pay for fuel. "So what does he do to pay for his gas? He deals a bit, is that it?" says the judge, suddenly addressing him in the third person. His police record comprises four convictions for driving with a suspended license and use of marijuana, but also, in the most recent case, "resisting arrest." Apart from the first incident, when he was given a suspended sentence with probation, the other three offenses resulted in custodial sentences. The social report shows only that the man is single, separated from his girlfriend with whom he was living, father of a young son whom a judge has allowed him to see only once a week because of his precarious situation, and that he has a certificate of vocational training in electronics, but is not working. The judge expresses surprise: "Really, you've been out of work for some while! How long is it?" Two years, he admits, acknowledging that because of his "legal problems" he has been unable to find a steady job, particularly as he has no fixed address. "So you're living in your car, is that right?" asks the judge, who finally seems to have understood the answer the man gave her a while before.

Pleading for the police officers who, although they were not injured during the arrest, are claiming 500 euros each in compensation from the defendant, "to hit his pocket, because that's what'll hurt him most," the plaintiffs' lawyer asks the court to order "an obligation to compensate the victims." He insists that, since the accused "has no income at all," this will mean that "the state, in other words you and me," will avoid having to pay the bill. Speaking in her turn, the public prosecutor emphasizes the four previous convictions, describing driving with a suspended license as "vehicular crime." She argues that by contesting the police officers' statements, the accused is showing himself to be "as disrespectful of the court as he is of the police," and asks for a mandatory minimum sentence of 12 months in prison. Finally, the court-appointed defense lawyer pleads with conviction, explaining that, while the refusal to comply with an order to stop is proven, the crime of resisting arrest is not, since her client simply sought to avoid being handcuffed, without offering any violence. Borrowing a phrase used by the prosecutor, she suggests that since "everything has been tried" in terms of custodial sentences, he be punished by an adjustable sentence "without actual imprisonment but with an obligation to appear before the sentencing judge," and that he be returned the money taken from him "and above all the car, because it is his only home and we're in the middle of winter after all, and it'll also help him find work." Before retiring, the judge asks the man if he has anything to add. He replies softly and hesitantly: "What I would like to say, Your Honor, is that I admit I have done wrong. It's been years I've been having problems with the law, but it's not really what I want. If I go back to prison I'll backslide. Lately, I've been trying to get back on my feet. For the sake of my child, and for my commitment to getting myself out of where I am, I ask you to do something to help me. The last time I got out of prison I went back to see my girlfriend, but she refused to let me see my son. She blocked all my attempts . . ." The judge interrupts him brusquely: "The court has heard you. It will now make its decision." The session is adjourned.

A few moments later it resumes, for the announcement of verdicts. As the defendants hear their sentence they leave the courtroom, some convicted but released under a suspended sentence, others returned to the court holding cell to await their departure to the prison. Soon only the man of Malian origin is left in the dock, flanked by two police officers. The judge tells him that he has been found "guilty on all charges." He is sentenced to 10 months in prison with immediate incarceration, and ordered to pay 400 euros to each of the plaintiffs. Neither his money nor his car is returned to him. The man stands speechless, as if dumbfounded. After a moment's silence, he begs, in a dull voice, that at least he be given back his car, which is the only thing he owns and which he will need when he gets out. The judge becomes impatient: if he wants, he can always write to the court to ask for it. The man glances around, in desperation. All at once, he gears himself up, clambers over the wall of the box, jumps over his lawyer's bench and rushes into the spectators' area, where the few observers are just leaving. As the police officers scramble to chase after him, shouting to alert their colleagues, the man runs across the foyer of the courthouse and disappears in the neighboring side streets. A dozen police officers race after him. Soon sirens are heard through the town. The pursuit of the man is organized on foot and by car. Half an hour later it ends with the capture of the convicted man, who is taken to the prison. A week later, he is tried again at an immediate appearance trial, this time for escaping: 12 months in prison are added to the ten already handed down.

This man's gesture, a tragic and pathetic protest, reveals the impossible situation he feels himself trapped in. Cut off from his family, separated from his girlfriend, kept from seeing his son, with no job, no home, and no resources, he sees the only two things he has left being taken away from him – his freedom and his car. For the court, however, the facts are simple, and prompt few qualms: he is a traffic offender and a drug dealer, guilty also of resisting public authority, with the aggravating circumstance of repeat offending (for good measure, the journalist reporting the facts in a regional daily paper later darkened the picture further by inventing a fifth conviction and a previous escape attempt). Each of the crimes of which he is convicted justifies a custodial sentence, and the repeat offense could even call for a mandatory minimum sentence.

These three crimes alone account for almost one-third of the population in the prison. They are, indeed, the offenses for which convictions have risen most rapidly in France over recent decades. Road traffic offenses, breaches of drug laws, and failure to respect public authority are responsible for one-third of incarcerations. Over 20 years, the number of convictions for these three types of offense has risen by 58 percent, 128 percent, and 74 percent respectively. By contrast, convictions for homicide and armed robbery, each of which constituted a little over 1 percent of imprisonments, have fallen by 16 percent and 48 percent respectively.[41] In a remarkable development, while the most serious crimes fell (except for rape, where the increase in convictions reflects efforts to bring more of these offenses to justice), the crimes that increased most markedly were in fact misdemeanors, where penalization has resulted from the two-pronged action of harsher legislation and targeted application of it. There is nothing to say that these offenses are actually rising, since the corresponding convictions and incarcerations primarily reflect the priority given to them – paradoxically considering the limited objective harm they cause – by legislators, the police, and the courts. In the end, this priority results in the overrepresentation of certain population categories: to wit, low-income ethnic and racial minorities.

It is important here to distinguish two phenomena that, for the sake of simplicity, I shall call "social" and "penal." The first derives from the general conditions of production and reproduction of inequalities, while the second relates to the particular conditions of formulation and application of the law. Up to this point, we have mainly been considering the chain of punishment. But this itself is embedded in a social framework that delimits it and powerfully constrains it. When the police and magistrates intervene to make an arrest or issue a punishment, much has already played out beforehand. Their potential client group is in large part defined by a set of disparities and discriminations that build up through the structural shifts of French society. In order to illustrate this dual social and penal effect, let us return to the case of the defendant who fled the courthouse.

The man comes from a city where unemployment is almost twice as high as in the region as a whole, where blue-collar workers are proportionally twice as numerous and white-collar workers three times less numerous than in the region as a whole, where only one-third of adults possess a high-school diploma or higher, and where one-quarter of the population is of immigrant origin. The city incorporates two Sensitive Urban Zones, cited by Insee as more in difficulty than the regional average for this region, which is itself seriously disadvantaged.[42] This is where the man grew up, in a Malian family. His education went no further than the Vocational Training Certificate, a level at which unemployment is only half that of those without qualification, but remains twice as high as for those with higher education, and even three times higher within the electronics sector.[43] Moreover, finding a job is much harder for people of immigrant origin, especially non-Europeans. Among those aged 15–24, unemployment is 13 percent among the children of French nationals, compared to 22 percent for the children of immigrants, and up to 30 percent for those whose parents are of African origin. Five years after leaving school, only 61 percent of the latter have found a job, compared to 82 percent of the children of French nationals, and when they have it is three times as likely to be temporary; during those five years, 29 percent of young people of African origin have been without work for more than 24 months, compared to 11 percent of the young people of European French origin. In the adult male population of working age as a whole, the probability of being unemployed is nearly four times higher among those who had two parents of African immigrant origin than among those who are not of immigrant origin, and for those who have a job, it is twice as likely to be a temporary contract.[44] The judge should perhaps not have been so surprised that the man before her found it difficult to get work.

His life path – what little of it that is made known to the court through the brief social report – illustrates a statistical reality that affects all those of his age group, origin, and class, all the more because, like many others from his background, he has had a criminal record for 10 years. One of the prison directors observed, in relation to young inmates: "I'm struck by how much they aspire to be normal, to fit in. They aren't struggling against society or capitalism. They'd love to be in our position. Their form of criminality isn't chosen: it is suffered." One of these men, a 26-year-old Algerian who came to France with his parents at the age of six months, and was sentenced to one year's imprisonment for a simple theft, offered this explanation of his action: "I stole, but I didn't want to. It wasn't to get rich, it was so I could eat. I was on the streets. Before that I did every kind of job. I've been a construction painter, a delivery driver, a truck operator, a trash collector. I was on temporary contracts. But when you're looking for work and you don't find it … So I had no choice but to go out and steal. You can get 30 or 40 euros for a car radio." In the case of the man who fled the court, the accumulation of months in prison for driving with a suspended license and marijuana use, two crimes for which he is more likely to be caught because of his skin color and origin, complete his social exclusion. When the police car came across him, on that night in December, he was already deeply embedded in a precarious and marginalized existence: for four months he had been living in his car and surviving by selling small quantities of marijuana.

However, the fact that the police officers patrolling in the city center decided to switch on their lights and siren when they saw this man they did not know is not insignificant – even if it is in itself nothing unusual. In fact, nothing in the driver's attitude rendered him suspicious, so nothing justified the check they decided to carry out. Nothing, that is, except what he represented to them, a black man at the wheel of an automobile. The reading of the charge was revealing, as the presiding judge began it with this unexpected formula: "You are charged with driving a Citroën vehicle of the C4 model . . . ." In the United States, this offense has a name: "driving while black."[45] Police officers often explain that they do it because they know they have more chance of "finding something," their intuition being logically confirmed by the fact that they can only find in the place where they are looking. Social science researchers speak of "statistical discrimination" to indicate that this selection does not imply prejudice toward a particular group, but rather the neutral appreciation of a high probability of offenses within it.

However, it is difficult to dissociate the two aspects. It would be more accurate to say, on the contrary, that the appreciation of this probability is in fact linked to a prejudice, while making clear that this prejudice is not necessarily racist but may simply be racialist: in this case, the officers seem to have considered that a black man presented certain characteristics that might legitimately arouse their suspicion. And their racial profiling paid off, since the man was in possession of a bag of marijuana. Had he been white, however, and holding the same quantity of cannabis, he could probably have gone on his way without any trouble. But this was not the case, and the subsequent events, with his attempt to flee and resisting arrest, add still further to the case file. The final stage, in court, is then an almost-too-obvious formality for all those involved. Well before the appearance, the case has already been largely played out. Just as the decision to send the case to court goes without saying for the investigating officer, real-time procedure seems the obvious choice to the public prosecutor. Indeed, all the conditions seem in place to justify an immediate appearance trial: flagrante delicto is demonstrated, the accumulated charges are sufficient, the penalty for the crime is well over six months' imprisonment.[46] After his 48 hours in police custody, the man is taken to the criminal court to be tried.

* * *

Thus, for a whole set of reasons relating both to their life circumstances and to police practices, low-income groups and racial minorities are overrepresented in immediate appearance trials; furthermore, this procedure is highly prejudicial to the defendants on whom it is imposed, particularly in terms of the likelihood of a custodial sentence. But this does not mean that this judicial stage adds to the discrimination.[47] The magistrates inherit a predetermined penal population, with regard to which their room for maneuver is limited by a punitive legislative apparatus and government. Yet it would be possible for the immediate appearance trial not to discriminate between defendants, and to treat them in an equitable manner. Let us examine whether this is in fact the case.

The most systematic study available establishes that, for offenses against the police, all things being equal, the risk of a custodial sentence is seven times higher when the defendant comes before an immediate appearance trial, and almost ten times higher when he has been in custody prior to trial, compared with the traditional criminal procedure.[48] It also shows that these penalties are issued almost twice as often to groups described, on the basis of their family name and forename, as "North Africans" and "blacks," than to "Europeans." In their interpretation of the results, the authors assert that this discrimination relates to a combination of "judicial factors" that they are able to quantify – the seriousness of the charge, whether it is a repeat offense, the presence at the trial, and the nature of plaintiffs – and that if these are taken into account the racial variable disappears. They conclude that "judges' decisions appear not to 'see' the skin color and origin of the defendants": magistrates therefore do not practice discrimination in their judgments in immediate appearance trials. However, their analysis excludes "extra-judicial factors" which, as the authors explain, are not included in the case files studied. Yet these factors play an essential role in the more stringent penalization of low-income and minority groups. The comparison of two cases tried one after the other offers a qualitative illustration of the difference in treatment.

The first case concerns a young black man aged 19, French, born in a medium-sized town that includes three Sensitive Urban Zones and where the median annual income is 12,000 euros, 61 percent of households are not subject to tax, 31 percent of the population are immigrants, a quarter of them of sub-Saharan African origin. He lives in a housing project. His parents are Senegalese, and his mother, a widow, is rearing her five children alone. He started studying for a Vocational Skills Diploma in carpentry, but says that he wants to work as a chef. He has already been in prison several times. He is charged with insulting an officer and resisting arrest during one of the many stops and frisks to which he is regularly subjected by anticrime squads. His mother, who is present at the trial, dressed in a traditional damask dress, explains to me, during the recess for the judges' deliberation, that "the police are always after him." She recounts the circumstances of the two previous times he was held in police custody for acts of which he was later exonerated because, in one case, he was in prison when the crime took place and, in the other, the culprit was later identified. But according to two boys from his housing project who are in court for a different trial, the defendant is nevertheless a troublemaker in the neighborhood: "He fucks up too much."

During the trial, the young man displays a degree of indifference, expressing himself in an offhand manner, and is sharply called to order by the judge. Although he has asked to be tried that day, the absence of one of the officers who is a civil party to the case leads to an adjournment. The magistrate must therefore decide whether he can go home free, or remain in detention, while awaiting the new trial date. After a stern speech from the public prosecutor and a lukewarm address by the court-appointed defense lawyer (things seem to have gone badly during her interview with the defendant in his cell), the court chooses to keep him in detention, asserting that the defendant cannot offer a guarantee to appear at a later trial. Realizing that her son is going back to prison, his mother approaches the judge, who is in the process of signing her decision, and begs her to let her son go home, assuring her that he will present himself when summoned, as he has always done, and that he will behave well until then. "Please leave, madam!" the judge expostulates three times, signaling her dismissal with a wave of her hand. With tears in her eyes, raising her arms to heaven, the woman cries out in protest, calling God as her witness.

The second case concerns a young white man of 23, French, born in a small commuter town where the median annual income is 26,000 euros, 32 percent of households do not pay tax, and the proportion of immigrants is 8 percent. He is a university student. He has no criminal record. He is accused of having physically and sexually assaulted his girlfriend following an argument. It is claimed that the forced intercourse was accompanied by obscene insults and humiliating remarks. The medical report revealed vaginal tears and a genital abrasion. The woman was unable to work for six days. A prior incidence of violence led to a broken finger, but the young woman did not report it to the police when she left hospital. The defendant's parents, who are French and middle class, are in the courtroom with his brother and sister and their partners, whispering to one another. They have hired a lawyer. The victim, overwhelmed, is sitting alone in the front row. She has no defender.

The accused answers the judge's questions in a humble, respectful tone, admitting that he got carried away, but describing the sexual act as consensual. Questioned gently in her turn, the young woman reasserts the violence she suffered. In a brief concluding speech, the public prosecutor demonstrates the implausibility of the defendant's version and calls for a custodial sentence. Following him, the defense lawyer gives a long, passionate speech, downplaying the facts her client is accused of, and emphasizing his good family circumstances. At the end of a hearing that has lasted twice as long as average, the young man says that he regrets his actions and promises to improve. When the session resumes, the judge announces the sentence: a suspended prison sentence, compensation to the victim and a restraining order. The young man's relatives make a noisy display of their satisfaction.

Contrasting offenses and contrasting decisions. Charged with having insulted and resisted law enforcement officers who were once again checking and searching him, the young man of African origin goes off to prison. Accused of rape and violence against his girlfriend, who has a medical certificate and evidence of temporary incapacity for work, the young man of French origin goes home to his family. It is worth noting that both cases relate to a repeat offense, but the reoffending is juridically established in the first one, the police having lodged a complaint against the defendant, and only medically certified in the second, since the young woman decided not to file a complaint. In one case, the legally defined reoffending is taken into account, but not in the other. Although they are different in nature, because the decision concerns awaiting trial for the first defendant and being tried for the second one, it is impossible not to compare the two verdicts, especially as they are announced one after the other. While, with respect to other trials I witnessed, the first case seems run-of-the-mill, in terms of both the profile of the accused and the court's decision, the second stands out by virtue of the seriousness of the facts alleged, which are not challenged in court. The difference in evaluation relates not to culpability, which seems unquestioned in both cases, but to the appropriate response – preventative for one, who goes to prison, and definitive for the other, who goes home with his parents. How are we to understand these different outcomes?

The disparity between the two decisions results from the differential way in which the three magistrates, and before them, no doubt, the police officer and the public prosecutor who have chosen the real-time procedure, understand who and what these two young men are, how they present themselves, and what they represent. Their physical and expressive presence – their body and their attitude – become essential elements in the attestation of their truth: the truth of their history and their actions, the truth of their past and their future, the truth of their manifestation of remorse and of their prospects for reforming. The young black man from the projects and the white university student are virtually polar opposites in terms of their biographies, their competences, and their resources. First, their biographical journeys: a history of educational failure and petty crime in the disadvantaged and criminogenic environment of the projects, where police harassment is the norm; a smooth trajectory in a well-off middle-class environment leading to higher education. In each case, however, the life path is socially and juridically determined, since the police harassment produces the repeat offense in the first, while the procedure ignores the prior domestic violence in the second. Second, their cultural competence: the capacity to express themselves on the linguistic, rhetorical, and emotional levels; their knowledge of the rules of the legal game and adaptation to the prescribed role; one does not know how to behave in court, while the other adopts the required attitude. Finally, their social resources: recourse to a hired lawyer rather than the court-appointed defender; the presence of a respectable family who offer the necessary guarantee of social integration, contrasting with a mother who displays her origin too visibly and casts doubt on the guarantee to appear before the court. Each of these elements, which mixes the objective with the subjective, the judicial and the extra-judicial, the characteristics of the defendants and the considerations they give rise to among the magistrates, incorporates both social and racial aspects, and influences the judges' work of evaluation, which, ultimately, relates less to the acts than to their perpetrators. But is this not, then, the paradox of individualization of punishment?

During the trial, various signs, from the tone adopted toward the defendants to the remarks addressed to them, also offer glimpses, if not of the ultimate verdicts, at least of the differences in assessment on which they will be based. Thus, the relation of alterity maintained by the presiding judge toward the youth of Senegalese origin (in another case, involving a defendant who had little understanding of French, after telling him to repeat and spell the name of his mother tongue, she turned proudly to the clerk of the court: "We need to ask for an interpreter, preferably Wolof, in parentheses: a Senegalese dialect"; and a little later, she asked the defendant with overfamiliar surprise, "Isn't it frustrating to have your wife and children in Senegal and be here in France without any work?") is as patent as the sense of identification she demonstrates toward the young man of French origin (all the more because her own son, who is also a student, is taking advantage of the university vacation to sit in on the trial with his friends, who are evidently enjoying this excursion and, in the previous case, poked fun at the Senegalese defendant's halting speech and laughed at the judge's joke about how many children he has). This play of distance and proximity, foreignness and affinity, antipathy and sympathy, mistrust and trust, which is, ultimately, just the everyday background of social interactions, is thus part and parcel of the court's final decision to lock up one and free the other, to give the second one a chance, and, once again, to deprive the first one of his.

The ethnography of this court session reveals that, contrary to what the authors of the above-cited study concluded purely on the basis of the penal case files they considered, judges too "see" skin color and origin, even if, in their practice, both factors pass through the filter of the law and juridical norms as much as that of values and affects. Such an observation does not necessarily imply that judges are racist: some do openly express their prejudices toward immigrants or minorities, but more often euphemistic forms of othering mingle culturalist comments, the expression of a social distance, and the reproof of inappropriate behavior.[49] Rather, it points to the almost imperceptible way in which judgment, understood in both its moral and its judicial senses, constructs and integrates differences and ends up, at the culmination of a process much of which is played out before the trial, discriminating in the issue of the two sanctions. This discrimination effectively makes insulting the police more serious than raping one's girlfriend, not because the second act is considered intrinsically less grave than the first, but because a hierarchy of trust, and therefore of worth, is set up between the young black man from the projects who does not know how to behave, and the young white university student who demonstrates good conduct.

* * *

One singular feature of contemporary prisons is that they house a disproportionate number of men belonging to minorities. By this I mean groups constituted in an unequal relationship to the majority. This social process is dialectic, both coming from the dominant group, through stigmatization, discrimination, segregation, and exclusion, and expressed in the dominated group, through consent, resistance, activism, or self-assertion. How, then, are we to understand the massive overrepresentation of minorities in French prisons – so massive that, in some cases, like the one I studied, it can exceed that observed in the United States, where the situation is already considered extreme? This is the question I have tried to answer, finding the explanation on two levels.

The first level relates to changes in social structures. From the 1970s onwards, in a climate of profound economic restructuring, increasing unemployment, and a fall in social mobility, low-income groups have been particularly affected, and especially immigrants. The social environment, especially the housing projects that were initially conceived as a contribution to improving material conditions and a space of transition toward homeownership, have become sites of concentration of a poor population, mainly originating from the African continent and with no prospect of objective betterment, despite piecemeal attempts in the form of local government initiatives. The young people in these disregarded neighborhoods, who are generally French nationals, often with little education and victims of discrimination in the job market, have found themselves excluded from the national community and readily stigmatized by politicians. This precarity and this rejection have contributed in some cases to the development of criminal practices, and more broadly to processes of desocialization that are all the more visible because they emerge in highly segregated environments. The purpose of this cursory account is not to offer sociological excuses for crime, as former socialist Prime Minister Lionel Jospin infelicitously suggested, but simply to offer a social reading of it. And the obscuring of this social dimension, by society and, more specifically, by judges, in favor of an individualized interpretation resting solely on the rationality and responsibility of the perpetrators of crimes, itself contributes to the production of disparities in modes of punishment, and to the inability to imagine appropriate responses to the problems of crime.

The second phenomenon relates to the way the chain of punishment is oriented. The temporality of this phenomenon coincides more or less with the one described above, and the securitarian turn that emerged in the 1980s. On the political level, choices were made in terms of defining what should be punished and how, including a growing and selective penalization of petty offenses, while a degree of tolerance was manifested toward financial crime. At the level of the police, partly because of the missions entrusted to them, and partly because of the discretionary power from which they draw their authority, some areas and some groups become subject to targeted repression, notably public housing projects and their residents. Finally, on the judicial level, the preference for real-time prosecution of crimes that principally involve these same groups puts defendants at a serious disadvantage compared to the usual judicial procedures. Ultimately, we come to understand that society, through its elected politicians and government officials, but also through its journalists and its experts, decides, for example, that the possession of a few ounces of a product freely consumed in neighboring countries constitutes a crime more serious than tax fraud, justifying not only harsher punishment but also more expeditious and more inequitable procedures, as the prisoner cited earlier complained to me.

The historical transformations in social structures and the chain of punishment largely explain this shift, in one generation, from an immigrant population that played an important role in the postwar period of growth and prosperity in France known as the "Thirty Glorious Years," to a subproletariat of immigrant origin that today supplies the majority of the prison population, which is composed principally of those who have committed misdemeanors rather than felonies. But it would be wrong to suggest that this demographic character of prisons, with their extreme social differentiation, is a recent phenomenon. Studying the demographics of French prisons in the late nineteenth century, Michelle Perrot notes that "a new kind of suspicion emerges: that of the foreigner."[50] In this she sees "the sign of an anxiety that only grew more powerful in subsequent years," especially in relation to Italians. She notes above all that "here are those identified by the evidence: the poor, and particularly working men," who "fill the prisons to such an extent that they start to be designed for them"; it is even thought that "factories had in some sense prepared them" for incarceration. The overrepresentation of non-French nationals and lower-income segments of society in the prison population, and the almost naturalized representation of them as the "dangerous classes," are thus not new phenomena, and are probably factors that would be found throughout history, and that we could interpret with reference to the interplay of the social and penal factors.

However, what is different today is that, on the one hand, we are no longer concerned mainly with European foreigners, but with French minorities originating from the African continent, and, on the other, those in question are not so much workers as the unemployed. Certainly, we continue to "punish the poor," but they now come above all from a sub-proletariat originating in the former colonial empire.[51] It is this colonial heritage (colonial subject grandparents, immigrant parents, minoritized children) that is the disturbing singularity of the contemporary prison population, a singularity that, from this genealogical perspective, resembles more the British situation than that in the United States.

At the window of his cell, my interlocutor, commenting with a smile on the demographics of the exercise yard ("it's all blacks and Arabs"), and offering me an entirely subjective interpretation of it ("us, we feel the injustice of justice"), thus demonstrated an unarguable lucidity – the lucidity of those who know that they are being deliberately deprived of the truth of what constructs their social condition, because it would threaten the social order. Without rancor, he countered the public secret with his own awareness of the obvious disparities in treatment. There is no equality in relation to punishment, and the allocation of prison sentences derives from a thinking that aims to remind each person of his place in society. For some, the system avoids as far as possible subjecting them to the fearsome experience of imprisonment. For others, it imposes the supposedly beneficial shock of incarceration.

3

Ye Who Enter Here

Through me you pass into the city of woe.
Dante, *The Divine Comedy*, 1308–21

"Tell them I'm holding up. When you call my family, reassure them." The man begins to cry. "Is that true?" the probation and re-entry counselor, seated opposite him in the meeting room, asks gently. "No," the man admits, and breaks down, weeping, his arms on the table. He arrived at the prison the evening before, having spent the day at immediate appearance trial. Like all new prisoners, he has been placed in the arrivals unit and has passed through a series of interviews with various staff members. He is Pakistani and went to high school in France, but dropped out at the age of 15; he describes himself as self-employed, but lives on welfare benefits. He is in his 30s, married, has no children but is bringing up his 3-year-old nephew. It is the third time he has been jailed, the first time in this prison. Each time was for drunk driving. "I've had a serious alcohol problem since my pop died," he admits. But he explains that this time he was not driving. He says he was sitting in a friend's car, stationary, with hazard warning lights on, while his friend went up to his apartment for a few minutes. The police refused to believe him. The court sentenced him to 12 months in prison.

He was overwhelmed. "Honestly, I can't handle prison. And this time it's one year. All my plans will go down the drain." The following week he and his wife were to attend a long-awaited appointment for in vitro fertilization treatment. He was also due soon to begin working for his brother, who has a shop. And then there is the little boy: "My nephew calls me daddy: he thinks I'm his father. When he doesn't see me he's going to flip out. I promised him I'd be there with him for his first day at elementary school." He asks the counselor to call his wife: "Without my wife, I'm nothing. She said to me: 'If you go back to jail, you can forget your family'. So please, ma'am, call her. Tell her I love her. And tell her to give my son a kiss." He breaks off for a few moments, then resumes, sobbing: "I want to end all this. I'm really through with it. I don't want to be a burden on my family. I can't do it. I don't want to live like this anymore." The counselor assures him she will call his wife, and offers a few words of comfort. The man leaves the room, if not calm, at least relieved and soothed by having been able to express the anguish of his arrival in prison.

"Incarceration shock" is a cliché of penal rhetoric. It implies that imprisonment is a way of giving the sentenced individual a salutary signal that will prompt him to reform, as he suddenly becomes aware of the seriousness of his action, or at least of its consequences. This pedagogic aspect of the sanction is a major factor in legitimizing it in the minds of the judges who hand it down. The point is not just to punish the guilty, nor just to protect society: prison is thought to have the potential to reform prisoners. This discourse on the benefits of incarceration is thus diametrically opposed to another, frequently heard in the public arena: that of prison as "crime school." In this latter view, far from being beneficial, incarceration fosters integration into criminal or sometimes fundamentalist networks that result in further deviant and unlawful behavior. So which is true? Does prison correct inmates, or corrupt them? Neither of these discourses is based on more than anecdotal facts, such as the repentant declarations of a former prisoner, or the reconstituted journey of a jihadist. Inmates themselves may also make use of them, some to persuade the sentencing judge when there is disagreement over a sentence adjustment ("This time I've got it, I'm going to stay on the straight and narrow, I don't want to go back to prison again"), others in a prison entry interview, to contest the sentence they have just been given by the court ("I'm going to be living among criminals and I'm going to come out worse than before; I don't get why I was jailed for something like that").

Within the penal sphere, the judicial sphere and the world of prisons hold diametrically opposing perspectives on incarceration shock. There is nothing surprising in this. Judges see prison as an abstract penalty. Correctional officers, counselors, and wardens live it as a concrete reality. Judges' knowledge of it is distant, filtered through the principles of the law, the wording of legislation, pressure from the ministry of justice, conversations with police officers, the imaginary of the profession, and a certain commonsense understanding. For correctional staff, prison is the stuff of everyday life, experienced through relationships with inmates, in contact with suffering and violence, in the rhythm of backdated suspended penalties activated at the end of a sentence, in the apprehension of suicide attempts and concerns about managing overpopulation.[1] A young public prosecutor offered this account of her work at the criminal court: "When you put on your robes, you're acting as the public minister. That's how I feel, anyway: I'm representing society. You're making the accusation, so you're naturally acting more on the side of repression. Your role is to protect society." By contrast, one of the directors at the prison made a point of his empirical knowledge, identifying himself with his correctional officers: "We really feel like we're in the thick of it. We're on the ground." The performance of the magistrate, who has a "role" to play, is of a different order than the experience of the prison officer, who emphasizes his "ground." The result is two distinct conceptions of what imprisonment means.

This difference of professional culture is reflected in the differential understanding of the effects of incarceration shock. An experienced sentencing judge, who had previously served as a court magistrate and a public prosecutor, and had been commenting critically on the government's repressive policies, nevertheless ruminated on the possible beneficial effects, making reference to what some prisoners had told her: "Despite everything, I've had the impression that minimum sentences and even more generally harsher sentencing sometimes did cause something to click with them. Of course, it's part of the rhetoric, and I know they're telling me what I want to hear, but there are still quite a few who say: 'It's the first time I've been in jail for so long, it's really made me think' [she hesitates] . . . In some cases, the 'shock sentence' seems to have a bit of an effect and push them to move onto something else [she laughs] . . . well, with all due reservations!" Her colleagues, pronouncing judgments in immediate appearance trials, did not seem to share her doubts, as one manager in the probation and re-entry service, who had previously run a juvenile facility, observed: "Judges are still living in a fantasy world, where the incarceration shock has a positive effect. Really, for a lot of these young people, prison sets them on a track of marginalization. Everything's perfectly set up for them to keep coming back: the bad contacts they mix with inside, the police harassment once they're out. We need to make the public prosecutors and judges realize they've got to get out of that way of thinking." But within the prison I studied, the shock of entering prison was feared above all for its immediate consequences. One of the prison directors offered this illustration of the importance of the electronic contact record (ECR), on which various staff note their observations about inmates, and which any of them can consult at any time: "In the arrivals block, it's essential. Because of incarceration shock. It's often these guys' first time in prison. It might be someone in for drunk driving, for example. He wasn't expecting to find himself in prison from one day to the next. So for him it's really difficult. In those cases there's often a risk of suicide. We flag it up in the ECR, and put preventative measures in place." Thus, depending on the position occupied in the penal world, and the principal mission that derives from it, the shock of incarceration has different meanings: a salutary punishment for judges, it is regarded by the probation and re-entry services as contributing to recidivism, and by correctional staff as exposing the prisoner to the risk of suicide. The only point on which these three groups of actors on the penal stage agree is that incarceration is indeed a shock.

Inmates, who are absent from this conversation between professionals, also offer their own accounts. One of them told me how, during his previous term in another facility, a man arrived one evening. He had just been given a custodial sentence at an immediate appearance trial, for domestic violence. He was found dead in the morning. He had hanged himself with his belt.

*   *   *

It is in order to mitigate this shock that the correctional administration has, in recent years, attached particular importance to improving conditions for the reception of inmates when they arrive in prison and over the following few days, in other words during the delicate period of adjustment to the reality of prison life. This development is part of the program of application of the "European Prison Rules."[2] At the entrance to the prison, a notice displaying an EPR logo, in red, white, and yellow letters against a blue background, has been attached to the outer wall, a sign that the facility meets the requirements of the EPR's "set of standards." When I began my study, the prison director told me how much it meant to him that his facility was one of the first in France to achieve this recognition. ~protocols~

"Good practice," to use the term adopted in the certification documents, begins as soon as the prisoner arrives at the prison.[3] He is first taken to the waiting room, while the police officers who have brought him in pass his information and documents over to the prison staff. He is then received in the prison registry, where the formalities of entry are completed and his incarceration order is checked. He is photographed and given his prison identity card, which he will later need to move around many areas of the facility. He is given a new arrivals handbook, an extract from the prison's internal regulations, a timetable for his first week of incarceration, and a "correspondence kit" comprising a ballpoint pen, paper, and stamped envelopes. Then comes the "changing room" stage, where a strip search is conducted in a cubicle, with both body and clothing being inspected for any traces of violence. He is offered, and almost always accepts, a shower. Jewelry and items of value are placed in storage and recorded, with the exception of "watches, wedding bands, and religious pendants," which the prisoner is allowed to keep. Similarly, a number of objects and personal effects "forbidden in prison," such as telephones, electronic gadgets, leather jackets, and navy blue-colored clothing, which is too similar to the guards' uniforms, are also taken away. A toilet bag and a set of clothing containing "garments and undergarments," together with "tennis shoes and flip-flops," are given to the new inmate, as well as a canteen token that allows him to purchase tobacco, coffee, sugar, and toilet paper to a maximum of 20 euros, allocated in case he has no money. Finally, when all these stages are completed, he enters detention proper, accompanied by a guard to the arrivals unit, sometimes passing by the kitchens for a microwave meal if, as often happens, he has arrived late in the day. He is then given a "bedding and linens kit," with sheets, blankets, pillow cases, towel, and tea cloths, and a "utensils set," containing plate, bowl, glass, and cutlery, before being installed in his cell.

This protocol of arrival at the prison is generally strictly followed, and once it is complete, verified on a list signed both by the various correctional officers and by the prisoner – who, as might be imagined, has a lot else on his mind besides ensuring that all the formalities have been correctly fulfilled. Perhaps more than the individual elements of this sequence of events, it is the way they are enacted that illustrates the facility's approach

to the European Prison Rules. Everyone seems to share the concern not
to add to the dreaded incarceration shock. The tone of the exchanges is
generally courteous, even affable. Explanations are often offered of the
reasons for the whole body search, and why certain objects are taken away.
Some new arrivals, furthermore, are not new to the procedure: "Here you
are sir, your new arrival kit. It contains . . . – Don't worry, I know!" Very
often, this reception procedure is especially important given the extremely
difficult ordeals the prisoner has been through in the police station and the
court. It offers them a striking contrast. One prisoner, whose case has been
under investigation for a year, recalls his surprise when he arrived at the
prison: "The time in police custody, that was really hard. When I arrived
here it was totally different. They said: 'Good day, sir.' The guard speaks
to you completely differently than a cop. He asks you: 'Would you like to
take a shower?' And then they bring you clothes and you get 20 euros for
the canteen. Can you believe it? They give you money!" Another, who had
arrived a few weeks earlier, was almost relieved to finally reach the end of
his nightmare journey: "I was shocked at the way they treated me in police
custody. It was really terrible. After that, they took me to court. I was
sentenced at 11 at night. I arrived here at 11:30. We had a shower. We got
changed. I had some food. I only wanted one thing: to get to my bedroom."
Surprisingly, but revealingly, this is the term he uses to refer to his cell.

In his book *Asylums,* Erving Goffman writes extensively about what he
calls "admission ceremonies" in total institutions, of which prison seems
the epitome. His description is identical, to within a few details, of that
described above: "taking a life history, photographing, weighing, finger-
printing, assigning numbers, searching, listing personal possessions for
storage, undressing, bathing, disinfecting, haircutting, issuing institutional
clothing, instructing as to rules, and assigning to quarters." These formalities effect a "'trimming' or 'programming,' because in thus being squared
away the new arrival allows himself to be shaped and coded into an object
that can be fed into the administrative machinery of the establishment, to
be worked on smoothly by routine operations." This first contact between
inmate and staff represents a sort of apprenticeship in the docility that will
mark the prisoner for the remainder of his stay, "an 'obedience test' and
even a will-breaking contest," exemplified by the slaps repeatedly adminis-
tered to an Irish teen entering a correctional facility, until he understood he
had to call the warder "sir."[4] All these elements, Goffman explains, form
part of a strategy that aims to depersonalize and intimidate the new arrival,
to strip him of his previous identity and reduce him to a disciplined subject
who submits to authority. But neither my observations of the process of
admission to prison, nor the comments on it offered to me by prisoners
(quick as they were to criticize the facility in many other areas) seem to correspond to this analysis; the same procedures, or almost, as those described
by Goffman tended, rather, to attenuate the impact of the traumatic experience of arrival.

The fact that, despite the stages of admission following an almost identical path in these two descriptions, the perceptions of what is being played out seem so contradictory certainly calls for explanation. A superficial reading might lead one to conclude that, since the social sciences are by definition interpretive disciplines, the logical route would be to identify discordances in the way two different researchers studying the same facts see and understand them. This argument seems to me inadequate, since I imagine that, if I had gathered the empirical data Goffman had available to him from his own investigation, and from the references he cites, I would probably have drawn the same conclusions. But the point is not just to note that things have changed over 50 years, or that the situation in the United States is different from the reality in France, though both these statements would be true. It is possible to draw from this apparent divergence more general conclusions on institutions.

According to Goffman, total institutions are those that bring together individuals who live the entirety of their time cut off from the outside world by barriers that prevent free movement, subjected to rules that are both precise and constricting, and placed under the constant authority of the staff.[5] Prison offers a paradigmatic illustration of this definition. But like any institution, it is made up of rules of play and therefore of players – in other words, of an objective part that structures interactions between agents, and a subjective part that depends on the initiative of the latter.[6] And so the fact that the form of the admission protocol remains the same does not necessarily imply that its meaning does not change. In this case, to move from the metaphor to reality, the European prison "Rules" adopted by the institution modify the point of the game. Here it is important to pay attention to the details: the distribution of clothing by the facility manifests two different intentions, depending on whether it is a stigmatizing uniform (such as the orange jumpsuit worn in many prisons in the United States) or modern everyday items (like the outfit of jeans, shirt, tee-shirt, and sneakers provided in the French facility). In the first case, it is a costume imposed on the prisoner for the purpose of making him easily identifiable, but also of shaming him; the depersonalization implied by wearing a uniform is compounded by the humiliation it imposes. In the second, it is everyday clothing that the prisoner is free to accept or refuse, and that he can wear or leave aside; the objective is that he should be able to change and dress in clean clothes, if he wishes, while his own clothes are washed, or until he receives new ones from his family. At the same time as the rules change, the agents adapt their practices. For example: on one side, we have a teen slapped upon entering a juvenile facility by a ruthless warder who wants to teach him to say "sir"; on the other, an inmate astounded by the correctional officers calling him "sir" when he arrives at the prison. In other words, the same stages of the ritual have entirely different meanings, both for the guards and for the prisoners. These indicators suggest that correctional staff understand what prison expects from them, whether that is to show cruelty or to demonstrate civility; at the same time, in a converse movement, prison tends to become what they make it. The objective and subjective parts of the institution thus play off each other, and the same sequence of events during admission takes on different meanings, though of course without eliminating the power relation at the heart of prison life: in the one case, abuse, in the other, a softening of the hierarchical relationship. Individuals subjected to this sequence of events on entering prison are highly sensitive to the difference.

But let there be no mistake. The fact that the admission procedure is more respectful of prisoners' rights does not mean it no longer represents an ordeal for the new arrival. The European rules do not change anything about the social function of prison, and the phase of reception into the enclosed premises of the facility always serves to demonstrate and inculcate the separation between the outside and inside worlds. This was the experience of two young men transferred from their juvenile facility one evening because they had just turned 18. After hearing the ominous slam of the security gate separating the reception area from the prison proper, as they walked down the long, deserted corridor leading from the place where they had just been admitted to the arrivals unit, one of them, visibly intimidated, turned to the other: "It's not like back there!" His companion, gazing somberly straight ahead, said nothing. A few minutes earlier, one of them had had his Koran taken away because of its hard cover, as well as a pair of black trousers deemed too similar to those worn by the guards; the other had been relieved of a poster of the film *Scarface*, which could have been used to hide objects, and a hooded sweatshirt, to prevent him from hiding his face; all of these were to be stored in the changing room. These restrictions, imposed for security reasons, served at the same time to mark the separation between outside and inside.

Furthermore, the fact that the moment of arrival was the focus of special attention from prison management does not preclude errors and anomalies. European certification has little influence over the day-to-day dysfunctional character of a bureaucracy that, in addition to the customary activities of this type of organization, has to manage personal belongings. At a meeting of the committee responsible for assigning inmates to cells, one correctional officer sighed: "He's the second inmate in a few days to have his glasses taken during the search and then we can't find them anywhere." It is a fact that, particularly when new prisoners arrive in the evening, the night-duty guards, especially if they are new to the facility, tend to be overzealous in their sorting of personal items, and to keep in the changing room those they are not sure are authorized. The loss of such objects can be devastating. A Malian man admitted a few days earlier told me of his distress: "When I was arrested, I had an album of photos of my family with me. When I got to my cell I realized I didn't have it any more. I wrote to the block senior, but he told me they didn't find it during the search. It's really bad for me. I had photos of my wife and children in there. I feel like my privacy has been violated." Distraught by everything that had happened to him since his arrest, however, he was not sure that the album went missing in the prison, reflecting that it could just as easily have been lost at the police station before he was brought to immediate appearance trial.

Arrival at the prison is therefore as much the start of one ordeal – that of incarceration – as the end of another – arrest, police custody, and immediate appearance trial – and the two are equally violent. The fact that, for some, entering the prison may be almost a relief says much about the way institutions treat suspects in police stations, and defendants in court. From the moment of the police intervention to the arrival in a cell, it is a brutal descent into hell.[7] Prison consecrates this fall. The step over its threshold, and the ritual of admission, imprint in the minds of those committed the auguries of the prison experience to come: a feeling of dispossession of self and submission to the institution.[8] The application of the European rules and the efforts of the correctional officers do mitigate their effects. But they do not efface them. By prolonging this liminal phase, the following week, which is spent in the arrivals unit, postpones a little longer the moment when the prisoner comes face-to-face with the reality of prison.

*   *   *

Although not the only element represented in the "good practice" certification file, the arrivals unit constitutes the most visible part of it. With its freshly painted cells, the walls of which bear no trace of their temporary occupants, its brightly lit rooms where inmates meet individually or in groups with representatives of the various categories of prison staff, its telephone kiosk in a corner of the room fitted with a few pieces of weight-training equipment that no one ever gets to use, its little exercise yard where new arrivals do not yet have to rub shoulders with longer-established prisoners and where the ping-pong table is mainly used as a place to sit and chat, it is also the area most suitable for showing to occasional visitors.

In the office on the second floor, the four documents pinned to the noticeboard testify to the exemplary character of this place: a photograph showing the officer in charge of the arrivals unit together with the national director of prison administration, on the occasion of his visit to the prison; a reproduction of the French Revolution's Declaration of the Rights of Man and the Citizen, the text embellished by figures representing the Monarchy holding the chains of Tyranny, and the spirit of the Nation wielding the scepter of Power; a cartoon showing a man leaving a prison emblazoned with the EPR logo, a bundle over his shoulder, declaring with satisfaction: "I'm going to recommend the place to the Let's Go guide"; and finally, a letter from a former inmate. It reads: "Hey to all the senior ofisers and ofisers who look after me wen I was jailed, I want 2 say thank u for everythin, I no Im no good, Im sory for that, u no Im hard but I have to try twise as hard, and I cant show my weekness to just any1, but u u help me for 2 yers, I o u everythin cos its not u wot sent me heer, and all the same u put up with me, I dont sho it, I dont say it, but I undrstand cwik, thank u all, thank u for understandin, sinseerly yors. PS I reely got the lesson durin my stay heer, Im not saing I wont go back but one things shor I wont go back to the same kin of stuf." The whole forms a sort of honor board, where the officer displays, on an equal footing, the signs of recognition conferred on him by a high-ranking official and a former inmate, while the irony of the cartoon seems to put the seriousness of the Declaration in perspective.

What the officer tells me, moreover, matches this heterogeneous and gratifying collection: "Me, I'm satisfied with my day when I've been able to sort out all the inmates' problems. And then when they're grateful, it feels good. We try to do our best, and if after they say: 'That was kind of you, that's cool, officer,' we're happy." He holds one of the few permanently assigned correctional officer positions in the facility. One major advantage of this role is that he works only during the day, and has fixed hours, rather than suffering the rotating shifts of his colleagues who work evenings and nights, and this makes his family life easier. As in the case of the visiting rooms, this is a position of trust, for which management places emphasis on interpersonal skills. In post since this unit was created, he is appreciated by the inmates there, and sometimes finds a way to get them an additional phone call – a big favor given the meagerness of the usual allocation. Indeed, the credit granted to new arrivals is one euro, which allows for only a few minutes' communication. If the inmate has the misfortune to misdial or reach an answering machine, he may not get to speak to anyone. Such a setback generates powerful frustrations, for this call is often the only direct interaction the inmate has with his family during the first month, before visiting hours are set up.

The officer is assisted in his daily work by an "aux" who has been in this facility longer than he has. In his 40s, this inmate was first held here while awaiting trial, and was then sentenced to a long jail term. From the Court of Appeals to the Court of Cassation, he has already spent seven years in the prison, where he is one of the longest-serving prisoners. His amenable character, his reassuring attitude, and the good relations he has maintained with both prison staff and other prisoners have made him the trusted man appointed to this crucial role of auxiliary, which implies not only serving meals and keeping the block clean, but also a privileged treatment with a larger cell kept open part of the day to facilitate his routine activities. In the arrivals unit, he has become a precious ally for the officer, attentive to the problems and requests of inmates spending their first few days in prison. Relations between the two men are informal, almost amicable: "The guy that's just gone back into his cell, did you see him? He keeps talking about killing himself. We need to flag it up. – D'you want me to write something? – Yeah, do that, cool. – But there's already two ECRs. – Don't matter, make another one. The more the better. – Not necessarily, afterwards it gets a bit much [laughs]. OK, I'll write a note anyway, is this OK? – Yeah, perfect!" The officer writes: "Staff alert: talks continually about suicide, often cries." He remarks to me: "The ECR is really useful for us." The electronic contact record has in fact become the main tool of communication in the prison. Everyone can consult it from his or her workspace, with level of access to information dependent on status.

The first days in prison under the auspices of the European rules are the occasion for a series of interviews with a member of the management team, a probation and re-entry counselor, and a representative of the healthcare service, as well as group information sessions on the possibilities for getting a job, doing a training course, or going to classes. Interviews take place in an office or the meeting room. The correctional officer goes to fetch the individual from his cell and brings him back. From one interlocutor to the next, many of the questions are repeated as they aim to map out the inmate's history and personality, as well as to anticipate his behavior and any problems he may have during his stay. But there are variations: interviews with the directors are more general, while those with the counselors are more focused on social background and penal history; the latter also offer to make contact with the individual's family.

The meetings with wardens, which are led by questionnaires and recorded electronically, mechanically follow a set of questions on marital status, education, employment status, reason for conviction, and criminal and prison record, before coming to those that concern the present incarceration more specifically: "Do you want to work? Are you interested in vocational training? Do you have any special dietary requirements? Do you use drugs? Do you drink alcohol? Do you smoke? Are you under medical treatment? Do you have a disability? Do you think you will have any visitors? Will you get any financial support from your family? Are there any inmates you might have problems with? Is there anyone you would like to share a cell with?" Thus the main features of a social, penal, and medical portrait of the new inmate are roughly sketched, its trace subsequently to be preserved in the electronic contact record. They will be of use particularly in the conversations between various staff members concerning the inmate's final assignment to block. Toward the end of the interview, a number of rapid-fire questions aim to identify specific risks: "Have you ever contemplated suicide? Do you have violent tendencies? Do you admit the crimes you are accused of? Do you accept being in prison?" Often a few words of comfort, vague but warmly intended, are offered in conclusion: "We'll do all we can to make sure things go as well as possible." The interview lasts about 15 minutes.

The inmate, who surely understands the functional nature of an interview during which his interlocutor looks at his screen as much as at him, often replies in monosyllables or short sentences to questions that touch on complex, intimate, and painful subjects, which frequently call for expansion that he sees clearly would not be appropriate in this constrained context: "Do you have any special dietary requirements? – No. – Are you addicted to alcohol? – No. – Are you addicted to drugs? – Not any more, since I've been on methadone. – Have you ever contemplated suicide? – Everyone contemplates it sometime. – But have you attempted suicide? – No, never. – Have you ever had problems with a fellow-prisoner? – No, but I've only been here two days. – Will you have visitors? – Maybe my father. – Do you deny the crimes you are accused of? – No. – Do you accept being here? – [The prisoner laughs.] What do you expect me to say?" The man has just been jailed by the sentencing judge for failing to comply with the restrictions of his electronic monitoring by leaving his home outside the prescribed hours.

But the exchange can sometimes be more empathetic, particularly if it appears that the inmate is not doing well. A man in his 40s presents himself in the interview room, his face marked by recent injuries, his eyes swollen, evidently in great distress. It is his first time in prison. He is weeping silently. He is in pre-trial detention for assault: he argued and fought with his wife – both were drunk; he hit her; his son-in-law hit him in turn. He was sent for immediate appearance trial, but the case was adjourned because one of the documents needed for the verdict was missing. The director strives to calm him: "Maybe you're terrified of prison, sir. I'm using that word purposely, because it'll get rid of the picture of prison you must have in your head. Look at me, I'm a young woman, the place is clean, we try to help you. Trust us." And as the man says that he is very worried because he had been on sick leave for four months and was just about to return to work, she adds: "There is always a solution to problems. Don't let yourself go under. Deal with one thing at a time." Although it is hard to see the efficacy of this psychotherapeutic support, improvised as it is, and without follow-up, it still makes some sense when one realizes that there is a waiting list of several months for a session with the psychologist.

For the wardens, these interviews are precious because they are the main point of interaction with inmates; over and above the superficial knowledge of individual cases they provide, they allow them to gain an understanding, at once global and concrete, of the operation of the penal system and the realities of the prison population. For the counselors, the interviews offer an opportunity to identify problems related to family situation, lack of social welfare benefits, or lack of residence rights, and hold out the possibility of a subsequent sentence adjustment; however, their impact is limited by the fact that, because case files are randomly assigned, the counselor who sees the new arrival generally does not continue to monitor him, and above all by the fact that fewer than one-fifth of inmates will benefit in any way from the probation and re-entry service, given the shortage of human resources. Finally, all prison staff make use of the information gathered in the interview to organize inmates' incarceration, to assign them to a block depending on their profile and their wishes, to register them for the various activities on offer at the facility, to anticipate their potential problems, and, where applicable, to categorize them among the "suicidal" or the "destitute," who will be subject to close monitoring.

As for the inmates themselves, the succession of meetings with understanding and sometimes sympathetic staff can give them the reassuring impression that they are being actively taken care of as soon as they arrive in prison, and raise their hopes for a resolution of their problems and an adjustment of their sentence. Many spoke of such optimistic prospects when I met them in the arrivals unit. But they were soon disillusioned: it would be a long time before those privileged moments when they were listened to were repeated, and for many they would remain the only ones they experienced during their stay. They would write to their counselor, as the guards advised them to do. They would complain to the block senior, and ask for a meeting with the director, usually in vain, especially when the shortness of their stay would not allow time for any follow-up to be put in place. Likewise, after being seduced by the prospects of work, training, or classes in the meetings at which these activities were presented, they would realize that the shortage of places in all of them would mean they had to wait several months, and that the first reported incident would send them back to the bottom of the waiting list for an indefinite length of time. Many would pass their entire stay without any diversion other than one hour twice a day spent in the exercise yard.

But the time had not yet come for them to discover this reality, of which only the seasoned prisoners were aware. The new arrivals were, for a few days, still in that protected space where everything was done to ease the transition from the world outside to the world inside. The correctional officer was not too strict, the auxiliary dispensed old-timer's advice, the various services in the facility came to them. They had a well-appointed cell, a daily shower, free television, the personal items they had been given on entry, emergency financial assistance if they needed it. They moved around their unit to go to interviews or meetings. They went out twice a day in their special exercise yard. There were never any fights or shouting. At the end of their stay in the block, they were asked to fill out an anonymous question-naire about their satisfaction, which ended with a so-called open question: "What did you think of your week in the arrivals unit?" Then they were transferred to a block – where everything changed. After the halt at the oasis of the first few days, the crossing of the desert began. It represented a second entry into prison. And the harder they fell.

*　*　*

"They renovated the arrivals unit to create a good impression," one pris-oner, who arrived at the prison two weeks earlier, comments ironically, noting the difference between his accommodation during the first few days and the everyday reality of incarceration. He calls me to witness. "Over there, it's all like it should be. The guards are cool, the cells are clean. But here, look at the state of the washbasin, the walls, the floor, even the bed. I asked for some cleaning products to clean it all. OK, I'm in jail, but it should be at least basically clean." Like almost all the other inmates, he is sharing a cell. And like almost all those who are doing so, he did not wish to share.

A man who had entered the main prison a week earlier told me of his surprise when he discovered who his cellmate was: "I ended up with a 40-year-old junkie. For five days, from Tuesday to Sunday. I asked the guard why they put me in with him. He said the guy had problems and they thought I could help him. Why should I help him? I don't give a shit about him. Anyway, you can see he's fucked up. And also, I'm paranoid and I was scared he'd put his medication in my food. I said to the guard:

'Either I go into the hole, or you put me in a different cell.' So they put me with a guy from my town. Now things are better." Another, who came in while awaiting trial a year previously, had moved several times before he found an amenable cellmate: "When I first came, I got beat up one of the first times I went out in the yard. So they moved me into a different block. To start with I was with a young junkie, that wasn't good. Then, I was with an older man who was depressive, we each kept to our own corner, that wasn't great either. And then they put me in a cell on my own because at that time I had a problem with hemorrhoids. But I couldn't take it. I asked to be with someone from my wing who I got on with. He wanted to share too." Sharing one's personal life with another in a 100-square-foot space for 20 hours a day is a difficult ordeal. Sharing with someone whom one cannot tolerate or of whom one is afraid is unbearable.

Who should be put in with whom, and where, is perhaps the thorniest day-to-day problem for the prison staff. It takes up the first part of the session of the committee that meets twice a week, attended by a warden, the senior officers for each block, the guard from the arrivals unit, and representatives of the probation and re-entry service, the walk-in clinic, the education department, and the section responsible for work place-ments. Each new arrival is briefly introduced by the various members of the committee who have met him, and after this round of the table, his block allocation is decided on the basis of his situation, the senior officer of the block being then charged with finding him a suitable cellmate. In addition to the one for the arrivals, there is a "protected prisoners" unit, one for "leavers," and one for "confirmed convicted prisoners" serving sentences of at least two years, all of whom, for different reasons, enjoy more favorable conditions. The remainder, amounting to over half the facility, houses the majority of the inmates, made up predominantly of young men, most of them awaiting trial or serving sentences of six months or less, with a higher density of habitation, stricter regime, lower levels of employment, and virtually no re-entry support – particularly as these parts of the prison do not observe the European rules. In other words, the unfavorable situation in short-stay prisons compared to long-term facilities is compounded by an internal differentiation that increases its penalizing properties for inmates awaiting trial or convicted of minor crimes. The remark of the director who deplored the fact that individuals presumed innocent are treated much worse than those judged guilty was therefore confirmed – and the same could be said of petty offenders compared with those convicted of serious crimes.

Within these constraints, the committee and the block seniors do their best to manage the permanent shortage of places. This is all the more complex because the European rules require that within cells, pre-trial prisoners be separated from those already sentenced, and young adults from older individuals; that cellmates be appropriately matched; and that prisoners be consulted about their initial cell assignment.[9] These formal constraints sometimes conflict with the intuition of the staff. One inspector of prisons, visiting the facility, criticized the "doubling-up" of a convicted prisoner with a man awaiting trial in the arrivals unit. When he left, the correctional officer explained to me that with no empty cells, the pre-trial prisoner in question, a young man considered "suicidal," could not be placed with the only other pre-trial prisoner who did not have a cellmate, a "hobo" who the guard thought was likely to make the shock of incarceration even more distressing for the new arrival. The latter had therefore been placed with an older convicted prisoner who had already served several jail terms and seemed likely to be a more reassuring cellmate. "That kind of rule is bureaucratic and counterproductive," said the guard, vexed that his discernment had not been recognized.

The general principles of the European standards are, moreover, augmented by local standards that require that those working be grouped together in order to facilitate their movement around the prison, that smokers do not share a cell with non-smokers in order to avoid additional discomfort to the latter, and that religious observance be taken into account, less out of fear of conflict between faiths than out of pragmatic considerations relating to the different dietary and ritual observances. More specifically, within the prison, efforts to maintain harmonious environment lead to grouping together certain types of crime, especially in the case of sex offenses, since they are always the object of stigmatization in prison, and certain personality types, particularly where individuals deemed vulnerable are concerned. Finally, inmates involved in the same case are sometimes put together, because they are known to be friends or family, as are individuals of the same national origin, partly for ease of communication, and residents of the same town, mainly so as to group them together in a different block from that housing the residents of a neighboring town, with whom there is known to be rivalry. "How can we take all these criteria into account at once?" a chief officer asked in exasperation, as he left one of these meetings. It is true that even a computer program into which all these variables would have been fed would generally be unable to come up with an ideal prisoner distribution on a daily basis, particularly given that juggling arrivals, departures, and transfers complicates matters still further.

A great deal of practical sense is thus required in assigning prisoners to blocks and pairing them with a cellmate, particularly given the growing number of special cases: "He says he wants to be with Turkish prisoners"; "He'd like to be in a block with other inmates from his district"; "He's been convicted, but he says he wants to be with his son, who's pre-trial." Other requests provoke amusement: "He would like to be with someone watching 'Orange Is the New Black.'" Others may be still more surprising: "He's very religious, an observant Jew. – Yes, and we were taken aback that he wanted to be with Mr Abdelkader, who is also very religious, but an observant Muslim. – You have to admit there aren't always ethnic problems between them." Toward the end of the meeting, with few places remaining, distributing them becomes particularly difficult. One block senior, who was being asked to accommodate a young man convicted of vandalism, said: "I have spaces, but only with people with psychological problems. – That's too bad, we'll have to double them up," says the director resignedly. Another sergeant, trying to find a place for a young man of African origin imprisoned for possession of drugs, and described as calm and a non-smoker, says: "I've got a non-smoker on his own, but it's a sex offense. – We've got no choice, it's either a smoker or ... ," replies his colleague, regretfully, without finishing his sentence. And in relation to a man who claims he has received death threats because he is accused of being a "snitch" and therefore asks to be put with convicted prisoners because he has "got" a one-year custodial sentence: "You have to earn your place in my block – it's the cherry on the cake," jokes the block senior, confirming the privilege granted to convicted prisoners and irritating his colleagues, who bear the costs of this selection that works to the detriment of the many pre-trial prisoners.

Tedious as they are, discussions around cell assignments are punctuated by sparks of humor on the part of the committee members. Speaking of one new arrival who will have to double up with a man who has already been in the prison for several weeks: "He wants to be on his own, the other one too. So they'll be on their own together." Referring to the application of the European rules: "It says in the rules that a convicted prisoner and a pre-trial prisoner can only be together if they give their consent. – The truth is that a lot of them are together without having given consent. –In fact they consent since they are together!" With regard to an Albanian man convicted of burglary: "We never have any problem with Romanians in pre-trial detention, they never give us any trouble. – But he's not Romanian, he's Albanian! – Well, we don't have any Albanians. – So let's put him in with a Romanian. Albania's near Romania, isn't it? – Well, there aren't any borders now anyway." Sometimes committee members also express incomprehension, and even anger, not with regard to crimes perpetrated or suspected, which are never subject to any moralistic comments, but in response to court decisions that seem to them inappropriate. A 56-year-old Tunisian man on conditional release is sent back to jail because he failed to comply with the requirements of his adjusted sentence. He is suffering from laryngeal cancer, at a stage sufficiently advanced for the liberty and detention judge, to whom an appeal has been made following the decision by the sentencing judge, to request an urgent medical opinion: "It's a death foretold," remarks the guard, soberly.[10] An Algerian man in his 30s is sentenced to a month's imprisonment for refusing to give a DNA sample.[11] He was jailed in the middle of December. "It's a joke! What's the point of that? – It's ridiculous to make him spend Christmas and New Year's in jail when we know how high the suicide risk is then. – No prizes for saying that if anything happens we'll be the ones held responsible again!" Despite his short sentence, in order to mitigate its potentially damaging consequences, the man is placed in the convicted prisoners block.

But the assignment of inmates that takes place at the end of the committee meeting is just one element in the turbulent tale of cell changes, requests for reassignment, and, among the few who enjoy the privilege, battles to remain alone in their cell. At each return from the exercise yard, the block senior, or his deputy, receives more or less insistent complaints from prisoners who want to move, cannot stand their cellmate any longer, and are frustrated by promises not kept because they are often impossible to keep. But the prisoners receive the same delaying responses, the same assurances that their request is being dealt with, the same promises that it will not be long now, or, conversely, the same remarks about the prison not being a hotel. Sometimes, a working prisoner returning from the workshop is angered to discover a new arrival installed in the cell he left empty; the new inmate is himself embarrassed to feel his presence unwanted, and intimidated by the aggressiveness of the prior occupant, unless, on the contrary, it is he who brutally imposes himself. Tensions between cellmates and with the guards then arise, sometimes going as far as "refusal to return to cell" which can, if it is not managed with due care, end in solitary confinement.

One prisoner meets me alone in his cell, taking advantage of everyone being in the yard because it is the only way of getting a few minutes of privacy, though by this very act he deprives himself of the outing. In the course of our conversation, he describes a situation that arose recently in his unit. A young Polish man who spoke almost no French had just been assigned to a cell on his own, probably because the committee suspected he was vulnerable. Nevertheless, a few days later the pressure from shortage of places resulted in him being assigned a new arrival as cellmate: "A really big black guy, who took all his things as soon as he arrived. Mateusz came to see me to explain the problem. I told him to go and talk to the block senior." The following day, the latter summoned the two men, intending simply to remind them of the general principles of life in prison. The young man, who understood little of what the block senior said and had hoped to be offered a more suitable solution, asked insistently to be moved to another cell. "The senior told him it wasn't him that decided. That was how it was and not any other way, and if he wasn't happy he'd go to solitary. Mateusz carried on and now he's in the hole. He shouldn't be there. But while he's there, the other guy is here, nice and warm, he's taken over the cell." Prison is an apprenticeship in the survival of the fittest, which the prison staff can, through an inopportune intervention, reinforce further.

* * *

The fact that entering prison acts as a shock is a commonplace of the penal sphere, which some consider beneficial, and others seriously damaging. The few epidemiological studies of this subject, and the somewhat more numerous personal testimonies, tend to support the more pessimistic view.[12] In concentrating their efforts to mitigate this shock on the reception of arrivals on the day of their incarceration and over the ensuing week, within a block specially designed for this purpose, prison management, following the European rules, deems this a particularly delicate period, which justifies special attention. This is undeniably the case. But the ordeal suffered by individuals and their experience of institutional violence go well beyond these first few days following their arrival. The temporality of the disturbance to which the prisoner is subject extends both before and after the moment of incarceration.

In the period before, it all begins with his interaction with law enforcement officers, often as unexpected as it is implacable, especially when it is at the police's initiative. "It's violent, the way they take you in," says a 45-year-old man who was arrested in the parking lot of his workshop during a road check, just as he was setting off his scooter. The police told him that there was a warrant out for his arrest. Two years earlier, he had been sentenced to eight months' imprisonment for credit card fraud. He served his sentence in a short-stay prison. Following his release he became a skilled tradesman, and set up his own business. However, he was unaware that an earlier suspended sentence had been automatically activated by the more recent one; neither the court session judge nor the prison registry had been apprised of this prior conviction before he was released. The arrest, in consequence of the new policy of implementing old sentences, came as a bolt from out of the blue on the expanding horizons of his social situation. Moreover it happened when he was with his 17-year-old son, who saw with astonishment his father being taken away by the police and had to walk the three miles back to the family home. For this man, then, the experience began with the shock and shame of the arrest. All of this preliminary phase, which extends through the twofold ordeal of police custody and trial, is of course out of the hands of prison management, but the staff are well aware of how heavily it influences arrivals in prison.

Following arrival, the brief transition through the arrivals unit does at least offer a foretaste of the prison – the impersonal communal spaces, the sound of doors slamming, the shouts of inmates calling to one another through their windows, the rap music that blasts out late into the night, and, above all, for many, of the distress, loneliness, anxiety, and depression that form part of the experience of imprisonment. But this first impression gives no sense of how the rest of the stay will be, except for old hands, of course, who compare one term to another to assess what has improved, and what has gotten worse. One 35-year-old inmate categorized as destitute, imprisoned for assault two months earlier, described his transfer into the main prison. "It was a shock. Here there's no TV, no hot plate, not even any tobacco. When I arrived the cell was completely empty, it was hard for me. I asked the guard: 'Why are you putting me in solitary?'" He breaks off, contemplating the little room, which seems barely more fitted out and furnished than when he first came, and after a moment of reflection, resumes: "Of course, when you're homeless like me, you don't have anything when you're outside, either. But at least when you live outdoors, even if you don't have anything, you have your freedom." Fortunately, he gets on well with his cellmate, a placid, taciturn man. But the beginning of his stay was difficult. During one exercise period, he was forced to climb the high fence surrounding the yard to fetch "parcels" thrown in from outside the prison. The guards saw him do it, and he was put in solitary confinement. His time in the arrivals unit was well in the past.

The sociologists Antoinette Chauvenet and Cécile Rambourg, evaluating the implementation of the European rules in two short-stay facilities, note that "while the creation of the arrivals unit allows for a softer 'landing' in prison, the 'incarceration shock,' at least insofar as it relates to the conditions and regime of imprisonment, is not eliminated: it is simply extended, or in other words, partially postponed." They conclude that "being placed in a dirty cell, with mattresses taking up most of the floor, abandoned by their cellmates, after 10 days in a newly built arrivals unit, where they are looked after by attentive guards, can seem senseless."[13] And indeed, what sense is there in improving the conditions in which inmates are received, and creating a transitional stage before they move into the everyday reality of prison? An initial response might be to take into account the new prisoners' viewpoints, as expressed in interviews with researchers or in the questionnaires distributed by the guards; these indicate relative satisfaction and a degree of gratitude for the efforts made by the institution and its staff. A second response would focus on the public relations strategy that this innovation makes possible for a prison administration that is always alert to anything that could help to improve the poor image of correctional facilities – and in fact there has been a noticeable effort to make this initiative known, through statements from heads of the Directorate of Prison Administration, and publication of a letter on the subject of the European rules.[14] While recognizing the validity of this dual perspective, a more wide-ranging reflection could be proposed.

In the first place, implementation of the European rules emerges from a contemporary form of government characterized by the introduction of principles of law and ethics simultaneously with the deployment of mechanisms of repression, to which they serve as both counterpoint and counterpart.[15] Seeing them as a counterpoint emphasizes the role of organizations that champion human rights, of mediation and monitoring bodies, and even of some within the prison system, all of them committed to respecting the values of dignity and humanity. Describing it as counterpart is an invitation to see in this process the concessions that the authorities have to make in a democratic society in order to render their punitive apparatus politically and juridically acceptable to both the tribunal of public opinion and the tribunals of the legal system. It is this double tension, between the ethics embedded in the law and the repression effected by policy, on the one hand, and between the defenders of human rights and the promoters of the punitive order, on the other, that makes possible the creation and application of the European rules. Let us not forget that this structure was instituted in France during a period of unprecedented intensification of retributive justice. In this regard it is important to note that it was Rachida Dati, the same justice secretary who introduced the penal law of August 10, 2007, which "stipulated a minimum sentence for the first repeat offense" and abolished "the reduction of sentence for minors aged between sixteen and eighteen" from their second repeat offense, who also brought in the 2009 law on prisons, which "guarantees prisoners the enjoyment of certain rights," including "the principle of one prisoner per cell" – a measure that was subject to a five-year moratorium. On one side inflexibility; on the other, magnanimity. Analyzing the dual tension at the heart of the changes in the punitive state thus means not only giving an account of the complexity and ambiguity of changes in the carceral world, but also doing justice to its protagonists, avoiding the cynical reading that notes only its instrumentalization by those in power, and restoring the critical work of both human rights advocates and prison professionals.

Second, the creation of a mechanism for receiving inmates based on a set of standards for good practice can also be read as a response to questions about incarceration shock. By creating the arrivals unit – a special space dedicated to this function, distinct from the everyday operation of the institution – the prison management confirms the existence of this shock and its damaging nature, because the aim is to reduce it. This assertion has two implications: internally, it denotes a recognition of the deficiencies of the system as it is, since another system has to be invented in order to prepare the inmate for it; externally, it represents a retort to all those, notably a majority of judges, who justify imprisonment as a salutary experience for the convicted, and whose discourse on learning through suffering is thus contradicted. The paradox of the introduction of the arrivals unit is that, by focusing on the initial moment of imprisonment, it offers a reverse image of the entire carceral experience. These units shed new light on the whole system. From incarceration shock, the focus moves to the shock of prison. In this new framework, it is difficult to defend the idea that the few months of a short sentence will be beneficial, when for one prisoner they lead to the likely collapse of his business because of failure to fulfill contracts, for another to the loss of a job hard won after years of precarity, for a third to the obligation to give up the apartment where his wife and daughter live, and for many others to more subjective ordeals such as humiliation, loss of self-esteem, the feeling of discouragement, and, above all, a sense of injustice.

"The worst thing is to be in prison and to feel justice is unjust: innocent people must suffer horribly in prison," said one director to me the first time we met. Speaking of the case of two young men who, after pressure from both politicians and the media, had been sentenced to long prison terms after a highly politicized trial that was heavily weighted in favor of the prosecution and based solely on the testimony of a police informer, he added, convinced of their innocence: "In this case, I'm just a public servant, and I have to deal with it." In fact the sense of injustice felt by inmates, which I observed when they arrived or later, was – it is tempting to say, fortunately – rarely of this nature. Aside from the short sentences for minor crimes, for which the punishment seemed excessively harsh to those sentenced, most acknowledged that they had not been incarcerated without reason: "It's simple," said one. "If you don't want to come back, stop committing the crime. There are no innocent people in prison. I did wrong, I take the consequences."

Feelings of injustice did, however, exist. One Turkish prisoner was serving a two-year sentence for sexual assault. The victim had claimed that she recognized him, and, despite a number of conflicting details (she recalled a dialogue, whereas the man spoke barely any French; the attacker was in a car while the accused could not drive, etc.), the man, who did not attend his trial, having not received the summons because he was homeless, had been found guilty and punished with a two-year custodial sentence. A year later, during the heated discussion about adjustment of his sentence, his lawyer stated solemnly: "Each day that Mr. Demir spends in prison is one more day of the imprisonment of an innocent man." When I later asked the sentencing judge about the case, she admitted her difficulty: "It's true that this case is troubling, but as far as I am concerned, the sentence has been pronounced, and I have to recognize it." The man had told me how hard it was for him to be obliged to attend regular sessions with a psychologist, and participate in a discussion group with sex offenders, absurd situations in which not only was any attempt to deny his guilt unheard, but his denial itself was taken as confirmation that he was not yet ready to change, and therefore to be released under electronic monitoring; it was better for him to pretend to obediently submit to the exercise.

Usually, however, inmates recognized what they had done wrong, and acknowledged the principle of punishment: "It's normal, I fucked up, I have to pay." In such cases, feelings of injustice almost always comprised two elements. First, the custodial sentence – when they felt that other punishments would have been more in keeping with the degree of seriousness of the crime, or less damaging to their future prospects, or both. Second, the conditions in prison – what they said about how society thought of prisoners, through the material and human conditions imposed on them, through the debasement they felt subjected to, and through the devaluation of their existence that all this time, empty of activity and meaning, signified to them. The shock of prison sits precisely at the conjunction of this dual sense of injustice: the disproportion of the punishment, and the indignity of its execution.

4

Life in Prison: A User's Manual

> When someone gets in one day to the Fortress he will find first of all nothing
> but a sequence of dim, long, empty rooms. The sound of his footsteps
> echoing under the tall concrete roof supports will fill him with fear.
> Georges Perec, *W, or the Memory of Childhood*, 1975

"There shouldn't be all this wasted time here. It should serve some purpose. Prison serves no purpose at all. Absolutely none. Unless it acts as a wake-up call, but that's personal; if that doesn't happen, it's pointless." The man sighs wearily. It is the exercise period, but he has not gone out with the other inmates. We are sitting on the two plastic chairs in a large, light, peaceful room in the convicted prisoners block. In one corner there is a telephone booth, which at this point in time was a privilege extended only to this category. On the opposite wall, a window, the only one anywhere in the prison accessible to inmates where the view is not obstructed by a rubberized grid, the close-textured grating that prevents prisoners from throwing out their trash and passing objects to one another. Here only thick vertical bars break up the view, but they are far enough apart to allow the field of vision to open when one comes close enough. After a pause, the man resumes, smiling suddenly: "Look, this is where we often come in the afternoon. We stand here, in front of the window, and we stay just like that, looking out, not doing anything – just looking outside." He remains silent for some minutes, attention focused on the outside environs.

The window looks out not onto the interior of the prison, but onto the outside. Beyond the high walls, the horizon of fields that surround it can be seen. Yet it is not on this bucolic landscape that my interlocutor's gaze rests, but on an asphalted area of ground closer in: he is looking at the parking lot. It is at this point that I realize that this wing of the building is the only one from which it is possible to catch a glimpse of a human presence outside the prison, since the others look out onto exercise yards or the edge of the nearby forest. "From here, you can see everything," the man explains. Gesturing to sketch the layout of the spaces he has mapped out, he points to the vehicles below: "That's where the visitors park. Over there, it's the lawyers, chaplains, and prison visitors. In front you've got the catering company staff. You can't see the guards and wardens, their parking lot is behind the trees. You see, from here we know everything that's going on." He stops for a moment, with an air of satisfaction, and then, regarding me with a mischievous smile, says: "You, for example, drive a gray Peugeot 406." When, after parking my car and before entering the prison, I sometimes took a moment to contemplate the imposing mass of the facility, standing out starkly against the summer daylight, or at night, haloed by uncanny reflections from the lamps, I had never imagined that I too was the subject of scrutiny – just as the prison staff were, although they were aware of it, and even saw this glimpse into their life outside the prison walls as a potential threat, which some occasionally mentioned to me. My interlocutor's remark thus aptly reminds me that inmates are not only subject to observation and surveillance: they also subject others to it.

A few months earlier I got to know the man who is regaling me with his expert knowledge of the vehicles belonging to the prison staff and outside service personnel. He was then working in the kitchens. We have had several conversations, sometimes just the two of us in his cell, sometimes in the company of other inmates in the larger cell occupied by the auxiliary. At that time he was in a block for pre-trial prisoners. He had been arrested for dealing marijuana and had been held on remand for more than two and a half years. It was the third time he had been in prison, always for the same offense. This time, he had no doubt that he would pay dearly for his recidivism. He was, moreover, aware that this long pre-trial investigation was already a punishment. He was questioned by the examining judge only twice a year, in a regional court several hundred miles away, and the long journey, handcuffed and flung about, uncomfortable and vomiting in the back of the police van, constituted an ordeal in which, he believed, those transporting him took pleasure. Such a long-drawn-out interrogation process delayed the trial still further and extended the duration of his stay in pre-trial detention.

This status had a number of prejudicial consequences: he had no access to the telephone; he remained housed in a block where conditions were much worse than where convicted inmates stayed; he could not work with the probation service toward a sentence adjustment and re-entry into society; he was subjected to individual constraints specifically requested by the examining magistrate, especially with regard to visits. Moreover, he anticipated that, once he had been judged, the remaining prison time he would have to serve would not allow him to be sent to a long-term facility, where he could have benefited from more favorable conditions in terms of accommodation, employment, and freedom of movement within the blocks; indeed, the verdicts often meant an additional prison term too short to require a transfer. This penalization of preventive detention affected not only those whose cases, like this man's, were under investigation, but also – for short periods – individuals who had been charged but whose immediate appearance trial had been postponed for some weeks, and – for longer periods – convicted prisoners who had appealed the court's decision and remained in provisional detention until the appeal had been judged.[1] Almost one-third of the inmates in the facility were in pre-trial.

For all those who remain for years in this precarious position, the time in detention often leads to despair. The length of their stay is compounded by its vacuity. The slow erosion of time, at first suspended while awaiting a trial for which no date has been set, then dissipates as they give up the prospect of a long-term prison which would offer better conditions, and weighs all the more heavily because this time is empty of both activity and meaning. Only after several months was this man allowed to work in the kitchen. His tasks were more those of a porter than of a chef, but he was at least able to earn meager sums of money, almost all of which he sent to his wife. He had asked to attend classes, but had not been accepted for the proposed sessions, probably because they clashed with his working hours. He loved sports, but had to wait two years before being authorized to play soccer once a week, and had succeeded then, he told me, only because he had written to the National Ombudsman (Médiateur de la République). This feeling of wasting his time, learning nothing, doing unskilled work, improving neither body nor mind, and spending sterile days engaged in meaningless actions fed into the sense that his life had no value. The uselessness of his activity contaminated his sense of what he had become – useless.

This self-disparagement was reinforced by the daily experience of frustrations and humiliations provoked by the comments and actions of correctional officers, which he knew he had simply to endure. While he acknowledged that some had good qualities, he added: "But I also know what they're capable of. There are some that push you to break the rules. You have to learn not to answer back." He had developed a cautious approach: "I've always kept my distance with them. As far as I'm concerned, a guard is always a guard." The violence of certain situations that he had to accept without reacting was no less intolerable for that. "The other day, one of the block seniors couldn't find her keys. Cue for all of us to be strip-searched. And not just anyhow – bent over! In the end she found them and apologized to us. But she was certain we'd stolen them." Indignity was often meted out more slyly, for example in the jokes and remarks of the chef: "With his dirty jokes and lewd comments, it's unbearable. When we're not working fast enough, it's: 'Get your fingers out of your asses, boys!' The other day, he said to one guy: 'If I was your father I would have killed you at birth.'" An employee of the delegated management contractor confirmed to me later the everyday contempt the chef showed toward inmates. Indeed, some of the contractor's employees, or even members of prison staff, knew that they could take such liberties with impunity, while the prisoners were well aware that reacting risked landing them in serious trouble. He learned to keep quiet. "Here in prison, you don't have the right to be human anymore, you don't have the right to have feelings, you don't have the right to blow your top. Anger is forbidden. But by holding it in, you end up hypersensitive." This was often how disorder erupted.

However, this man had never had an "incident report" against him, the infamous "IR" that constitutes the unit of measurement of docility in the prison system. He owed this quite rare achievement, which led one director to describe him as a "model prisoner," to the exercise of self-control and a strategy of avoiding problems. He was a dedicated runner, having discovered the sport when an external support worker had come to give them classes: "During the exercise periods, I run. Eight or ten miles, for an hour. After that I chat a bit with other inmates, and we come back in. It helps me not to get too involved with others. That way, there are no arguments. And running is what helps me get through." I had indeed noticed a dozen pairs of top-brand running shoes neatly lined up by the door of his cell, brought to him by his wife over several months: "Some study, others watch TV. Me, I run. That's my outlet." Like the athlete in Georges Perec's novel *W*, running allowed him a temporary escape from the constraints and humiliations of prison.[2] This was how he kept going, resisting as best he could the process of disintegration he witnessed in himself: "We resign ourselves to being punished for our crime. We accept the punishments that shatter our lives. But prison turns us bad. When I arrived I was kind, polite, well-mannered. Pardon my language, but they fucked me over. I've become mean, hard, aggressive." This feeling of being corrupted by the prison environment was widely shared among prisoners.

[handwritten margin note: v H Claude Gueux.]

His trial having finally taken place, the man is now in the convicted prisoners block where conditions are a little better and he can begin working toward the adjustment of his eight-year sentence. Sitting at the window, he is no longer scrutinizing the parking lot. His gaze unfocused, he says: "Here, you can dream. Me, what I want is to pick up my daughter at school in the afternoon, so she can tell me what she did during the day. I want to go off with her and my wife for a picnic on Sunday, and sit by the water. They're simple dreams." His daughter had been born shortly before he was incarcerated. "I won't see my daughter grow up. When I was jailed, she was four months old. I don't know how old she'll be when I get out." We stay for a few moments watching an exchange between two cells about 10 yards apart, conducted by means of a "yoyo." A long cord made from a strip of sheet is hanging from the window of one cell, a sock filled with a heavy object tied to its end. A swinging movement begins and gradually widens. A more rapid gesture sends the device toward another window, from which the handle of a broom is sticking out. After several attempts, the cord finally rolls around the stick, allowing the filled sock to be cautiously drawn into the cell. "Probably hash," says my interlocutor, who is commenting knowledgeably on the maneuver. This is surely evidence that the window grid is not as effective as management imagines – unless, as some prisoners suspect, its efficacy is measured in another way: by the level of opacity created in the cells, which reinforces the feeling of being enclosed.

We leave our observation post and go back down to the first floor. The man knocks on the thick plexiglass of the door to the walkway. The guard opens it for us from his monitoring desk. I thank him for allowing us to talk, while the man slowly returns to his cell. I learn later that, after spending almost five years in prison, he has been given a limited release order, a probationary measure that could lead to conditional release. The order was issued a few days before Christmas, allowing him to celebrate the holiday with his wife and little girl for the first time.

* * *

The world of prison is a space–time existence – a confined space for a specified length of time. It is this dual dimension that demarcates the inmates' world. This is what defines the concrete sense of the punishment. Being a prisoner boils down to this: being confined in a space and being constrained in time.

The space is first and foremost the 100 square feet of the cell sealed by a heavy metal door with a peephole. Unlike the bars in the prisons of the past – or, for that matter, of many countries still today – it assures both the enclosure of the prisoner and his privacy. It shuts him in entirely, but protects him from others' scrutiny. At least this would be the case if inmates were housed alone. But, as we have seen, this is rarely the case. The door therefore is more evident in its role of enclosure than in that of protection. The tiny vestibule of the cell holds a small sink with a shelf and mirror above. The toilet cubicle is semi-separated from the rest of the room by two screens that only partially hide its occupant, but often hang skew when they have been broken.[3] The main space is taken up on one side by iron bunk beds, with the upper one used for storing belongings by the few prisoners who have no cellmate, and on the other by a table and two chairs, and a hotplate. Two narrow closets stand against the back wall. A television, its flat screen fixed to the wall and almost always on, dominates the cell. The window is obstructed by the double enclosure system of bars and grid.[4] The congestion of the small room, and the blocked view from its single window, give the visitor a painful sense of oppression.

The state of the cell depends on its previous occupants, how long it has been since it was refurbished, and the way those housed there have maintained and arranged it. Some appear very dilapidated, others have been recently repainted (one inmate expresses disappointment that prisoners are not, as in the prison where he was previously incarcerated, allowed to repaint their cells when they first arrive: "You never trash a cell you've decorated yourself"). Some are entirely bare, others covered with posters (of top-league soccer players or NBA basketball players, the violent protagonist of the GTA III video game, or a nude couple from a Dolce & Gabbana ad, occasionally a political slogan: "No law ever created so many outlaws"). Some are organized with care. "I was able to arrange my cell how I wanted," says one feared and respected prisoner who, perhaps for this reason, has managed to avoid having a cellmate imposed on him. His walls are decorated with pious Muslim images, and a low table has been constructed using a plank placed on a garbage can and covered with a richly embroidered cloth. But to claim, as one deputy warden asserted to me, that "the average cell today is better than the average hotel room" is to make a statement that even regular users of the low-cost hotels springing up in the no-man's-land around cities would probably not be prepared to endorse.

Apart from the recurrent problems of malfunctioning equipment, whether hired or purchased, and leaks from the sinks or toilets, the most frequent subject of complaint in prison is cohabiting with another prisoner and the loss of privacy this entails. When they are doubled up, prisoners are not alone at any point in the day.[5] One inmate, a student of Spanish origin, who was jailed two months earlier awaiting a trial that he thinks, given the offenses he is charged with, will not take place for at least four years, has a glimpse of what these long years will be like: "One hundred square feet shared between two! Even if it was your best friend, you'd end up not being able to stand him. And he won't be able to stand you either. Sharing with someone else, there's no privacy, there's nothing." Another, a man of Moroccan origin in his 30s, who has also been in pre-trial detention for nearly four years for a drug-dealing case that is still under investigation, explains that he has already had several roommates imposed on him: "Either they give me an 18-year-old kid, or a guy old enough to be my father." Currently he is sharing with a smoker, though he himself does not smoke. "He's OK, but it's not right." His cell is clearly well looked after, but sharing impinges on even the most trivial details of everyday life: "As far as comfort goes, I can't complain. As long as you've got a bit of money, you can get some stuff. But the hardest thing is having to share a cell with somebody . . . I'll tell you something. When I want to go to the toilet, I wait until my cellmate's gone out to exercise, in the afternoon. I can't do it when he's here." The price of this brief moment of privacy is the loss of his one chance during the day to go outside, because he works in the morning. "I'm campaigning to get my own cell," he concludes, adding that he is going to write to the International Prison Observatory and the European Court of Human Rights.

But for the inmates, the space of the prison also includes the communal areas. The architectural layout adopts the contemporary form of the panopticon, as it was developed in the short-stay prisons constructed in the late 1980s under the so-called "13,000 Program." This was the most extensive real-estate development in the history of the French prison system, under which 25 prisons were built.[6] Each of the three blocks is composed of four wings, each of which has two superposed walkways with a row of cells on both sides. The two walkways, one above the other, open onto a four-sided space where the garbage cans are stationed, and where notices detailing regulations are posted. The four wings fan out in a star shape from the surveillance post, generally known by the acronym "MAP," short for "monitoring and accommodation post" (*poste de contrôle et d'hébergement*). The post, an enclosed booth, is permanently staffed by a prison officer who manages movement around the block by opening and closing the doors, and answers his colleagues' telephone calls and the prisoners' calls on the intercom. From this central space, a double-door security entrance opens onto the exercise yard, and a second leads, via long corridors, to the other blocks and the various spaces dedicated to work, healthcare, sports halls, and places of worship. Each space thus delimited – walkways, centers, corridors – is enclosed by a heavy door, its upper part made from bars covered with plexiglass. To get the door opened, one must knock loudly or call out, and the guard in the monitoring post releases the lock.

Thus, all the inmates' journeys within the facility consist of a series of doors to be passed through, whether they are going out into the yard, to the workshops, to see the doctor, or to the visiting rooms. When an incident arises somewhere, all movements are simultaneously halted, including those of the staff, and an announcement is made over the public address system, followed by one a little later indicating that normal activity can be resumed. Movements around the prison begin early in the morning, immediately after the 7:00 a.m. prisoner check, and continue until the final returns to cell shortly after 6:00 p.m., in order to allow for the last cell check of the day, with a pause during the guards' mealtime. And so, apart from the lunch break, there is a constant procession of inmates circulating alone or in groups under the watchful eye of the guards sitting in the monitoring posts. It is a dance of colors, moreover, for while most of the inmates wear the garments of their choice within the limits of the regulations, some can be recognized from the color of their clothing: yellow for "canteen assistants," white for the "laundry operatives," green for the "cleaners," red for "maintenance," blue for "workers."

But it is the exercise periods that generate the greatest flows and the most significant risks of incidents. The correctional officers in the mobile team in charge of this task enlist the support of the mobile brigade in each block to organize exits from cells, presentation of prison identity card, passage through the metal detector, and finally the descent to the yard, all of it amid a hubbub of inmates calling out to one another, jokes with the guards, appeals to the block senior, and calls to those who have set off or sidestepped the metal detector. A cell door closed by an officer who decides the inmate is taking too long to come out, a clothing deemed against regulations by one guard when it has been accepted by another, or a refusal to pass through the metal detector can quickly degenerate into conflict. The onset and, above all, the resolution of such situations depend on the character or mood of those involved, the desire of some officers to pick a fight, or the determination of certain inmates not to lose face. On the way back, the game is played out in the opposite direction, with prisoners often delaying the return to their cell and taking advantage of the last minutes before being locked in again. This may be the moment when one of them who has been waiting weeks for a response to a request refuses to go back into his cell in protest, once again setting up a power struggle that can very quickly become a confrontation. Usually, however, the exit to and return from the exercise yard proceed smoothly, a rowdy choreography where each individual has his place and knows his role, in a subtle mix of familiarity and distance, cordiality and defiance. Then comes the distribution of meals, a moment of return to calm, as the auxiliary, accompanied by a guard who opens the cells one after the other, hands each inmate his dinner. And the long period of isolation begins.

* * *

The spatial dimension of prison is inseparable from its temporal dimension. This temporality operates on two scales. The first is that of the day, rhythmically structured by the repetition of almost identical cycles: get up, shower, exercise, meal, break, exercise, meal, lock-in. The second extends over the length of the incarceration: it is the time of the sentence, or at least that part of it that is actually to be spent in prison. These two temporalities overlay one another in an interminable routine, where one day follows another, always the same, until the moment of release, whether final or under a sentence adjustment.

There are of course some variations in the temporality of the day, relating to structural factors such as whether the inmate works, goes to classes, or is on a training course, and circumstantial factors like an appointment at the clinic, a visit from a relative, or even a summons before the disciplinary board. For those granted the privilege, there is also the half day of sports, and for those who practice a religion, the periods devoted to worship; Friday afternoons for Muslims, Sunday mornings for Catholics. Even with these variations, the cycles repeat unremittingly and are marked by the length of time for which prisoners are actually locked up. What might be called "night," if it did not begin with the locking of cell doors when the 6:00 p.m. meal is distributed and end around 7:30 a.m. with showers, is already a long period of enclosure each day. But the remaining 10 hours, which might be described as "day," are also spent mostly in closed cells, particularly for those inmates who, having recently arrived, have neither work, activity, nor visit, and whose only moments outside the shared 100 square feet are the 10 minutes allowed in the shower every two days (provided they get up in time when they are called) and the two hours of exercise (assuming they are not too scared or depressed to go out into the yard). Thus the facility, as a short-stay prison, adds enclosure in the cell to enclosure in the prison itself, doubling the loss of freedom. As one inmate who had been there three years put it, "the ultimate weapon is the key."

This confinement, interrupted only by brief collective movements from place to place, is as out of step with the pattern in long-term prisons, where prisoners are generally allowed to move around the prison as they wish, for example to go and prepare their meals in the shared kitchen, as is the practice in other European countries, which some inmates who had experienced them looked back to nostalgically.[7] In the short-stay prison, being locked up almost all of the time is the rule. The effects of this practice are intensified by three main factors: the daily reiteration of the same series of events and gestures that seem pointless; the sheep-like collective accomplishment of actions which leaves little scope for individual autonomy; the imposition of cohabitation with a cellmate which removes any possibility of privacy. Much more than the simple loss of liberty that prison is supposed to entail, it is also the loss of meaning, the loss of autonomy, and the loss of privacy that determine the experience of incarceration; it can be aggravated still further by additional constrictions imposed on certain categories of individuals, such as the special notice prisoners, or SNPs (*détenus particulièrement signalés*, DPS), or in some parts of the prison such as the solitary confinement block.

There is another loss that prisoners often mention, and which they describe as directly linked to the experience of time: the loss of moral feeling. This manifests itself as both lack and excess. On the one hand, they speak of a dulling of affect, particularly of the sympathy they might feel for others. Standing at a window in his wing that looks onto the exercise yard, a man who has been awaiting trial for two years observes thoughtfully: "For some guys, prison time is real hard: they get lynched in the yard. At first you're shocked when you see a guy beat up and kicked about like that. And then there comes a time when you don't feel anything anymore. You see the scene, you see the guy being taken to the infirmary, and you're looking at it, and then you carry on shooting the breeze. That's what prison does to us." On the other hand, some spoke of their changed personality, the aggressiveness they could no longer control, the hostility they felt toward others. Put through the ordeal of four years in preventative detention for a drugs case, with transfers to three different facilities and several periods in solitary confinement, one man said with bitterness: "Sometimes I don't like the person I've become. Even my sister says, 'I hate that you've gotten to be like this.' I've changed. I'm crazy. I blow off at the least little thing. I can stand the hole, but it's made me anti-social. I'm scared that when I get out I won't be able to stand other people anymore." These disruptions of personality probably add to the other obstacles to re-entry into society.

The long temporality of imprisonment extends over weeks, months, years. For pre-trial prisoners – and for those convicted who are awaiting appeal or the Court of Cassation, who share the same "nondefinitive" status – this temporality is not just one of long duration. Without a fixed end-point, it is beyond their grasp, leaving them unknowing and powerless. Even the date of the trial is often known only shortly before, and individuals whose case is under investigation might spend several years before finding out when they will be tried. Of course, the experience of this temporality depends on the effective length of the prison sentence, and, for the purposes of simplification, we can distinguish between short stays, generally between three and six months, sometimes preceded by a few weeks in preventative detention before immediate appearance trial, and long stays, which may last from two to five years or even longer, and are the result of drawn-out investigations and appeals.

For prisoners in the first category, the relatively short interruption of their family, work, and social life leads them to focus their temporal experience on the outside world, seeking to reduce the damaging effects of imprisonment on their loved ones, work situation, and social integration.

For those in the second category, awareness of the long time of their sentence leads to a perception of time centered on prison life, aiming to make it a little less empty of activity and meaning, and probably also as a way of not thinking too much about an outside world to which they know they will not soon return. This is not to say that the prisoners in the former category have no concern about the realities of incarceration, or that those in the latter do not value their family relationships, but rather that a pragmatic polarization emerges, reinforced by the fact that short stays hardly ever allow prisoners to engage in work, training, or classes, while long stays often lead to one of these activities. In one case, prison is an unfortunate hiatus that prisoners need to be able to forget. In the other, it is an indefinite period in which they must invest.

Yet over and above these differences, a sense of meaninglessness prevails: the waste of time is probably the most frequent topic of conversation among prisoners.[8] First, the time wasted in relation to what they might do outside. "The people I was with before I came in here, they're getting on with their lives. Us, our lives are on 'pause'. They'll have gotten ahead of us when we press the 'play' button again," says one pre-trial inmate who has been in the prison for three years awaiting his trial in criminal court; his metaphor is one that is frequently used to represent the prison experience. Then, there is the time wasted in relation to what they are not doing inside. "There's nothing to do here. I've asked to work and to go to classes: I got nothing. It took me nine months to get permission to practice sports, and that's only once a week. How can you reintegrate? A guy that comes in here for driving without a license, once he is released he gets into burglary," asserts another pre-trial prisoner who has been awaiting his trial at the district court for 21 months, taking up another commonplace – that of prison as the school of crime.

* * *

If prison is an experience of space and time, it is also a sensorial experience. Here again, it is made of both lack and excess: too much noise and not enough light, disinfected areas and foul-smelling corners, bland and overcooked meals. The senses, which Jack Goody calls "our windows on the world," through which we "acquire information as well as sensations" and which, ultimately, interact with our "sentiments, feelings, mentalities," are an important element of prison life.[9] Their importance often goes unrecognized, both by experts and by those involved in the carceral world, even though it is from them that prison derives its singular atmosphere; all those who have worked and still more those who have lived in a correctional facility immediately recognize its specific ambience, through hearing, sight, and smell.

Such was the case with the sonic experience of the prison I studied.[10] The soundscape varies depending on the time of day, the population of the wing, and any specific events that occur. In the calm periods, for example when most of the inmates are in the exercise yard and all that is heard are the distant echoes of their voices, the relative silence is perpetually interrupted by a succession of muffled knocks on the doors separating the various spaces, accompanied by loud calls specifying the compass direction of the place the individual wants to enter, followed by the dry click of opening and the dull slam of closing. When I began my research, a very distinctive sound could often be heard during the exercise periods: the metallic rattling of bars being tested while prisoners were out of their cells. The guard responsible for this task would run a stick over the metal cylinders that block the windows, listening for a variation in sound that betrayed an anomaly. Some years later, this routine practice had disappeared, though the prison officers could not explain why; no doubt other security measures had taken priority. Moreover, shortly before I arrived an improvement had been made that was mentioned to me by several inmates: intercoms had been installed in the cells, helping to reduce the sound level in the blocks, as previously prisoners would bang on their door and shout to call the officers, a practice that added to the din of incarceration. Now the guards receive messages and respond to them from the monitoring post. But the sound environment of the prison is much more varied – and also more testing – than a simple alternation of metallic sounds linked to movement around the prison. Apart from the public address system that gives out information on collective events such as exercise, visiting hours, and occasional incidents, two types of sound characterize the prison world: voices and music.

Inmates are in the habit of talking loudly in echoing spaces: the return from visiting rooms, workshops, and especially exercise is often animated and thundering. It is at these times that interactions with guards usually take place, often jokingly, as well as with the ranking officers, for various requests: "Chief, the light bulb's gone in my toilet, it still hasn't been changed. It's been a week. – Yeah, I know, Traoré: it's crap! . . . I'll write again." Or else: "Have you thought about my request to change block, chief? – We'll try to work it out at the next committee meeting, Meraoui." But the most remarkable verbal exchanges happen through the windows, which offer the only possible means of communication when the inmates are locked up in their cells: they call from floor to floor or even from one block to another to pass information, request a service, or just talk or joke. Here is an example of a dialogue between three inmates through open windows, one summer day, after a soccer match that degenerated into trouble: "Wesh, dude, was it you called me? – Hey, Chinky! – Hey, Jackson! – What went down? – It was Blacky! – What happened? – Chinky got into a fight with him. – What did he say? – He said, 'I'll eat his balls.' – Yeah, but the faggot hurt me. – And you didn't get your own back? [silence] – Get a coffee, it'll calm you down. – Or better, a reefer. – It's OK, there was no blood!" Short and shouted, these exchanges animate the façades of the blocks, but can also be heard inside the cells. Not everyone appreciates the loud, syncopated communications. A 25-year-old inmate, whose participation in the cultural activities offered by the facility suggests that he departs somewhat from the predominant norm in detention, emphasizes this difference, which relates both to the perception of sound and the use of language: "It would be great if there was quiet sometimes. There's no discretion here, everything's over the top. It's even difficult to have a conversation."

Moreover, the sound systems with twin 10-watt speakers that had recently appeared in the prison canteen had been a hit among the young inmates: at least five were sold every month. In some blocks housing pre-trial prisoners and those serving short sentences, where the human density is highest and the inmates least controllable, the small hi-fi systems engage in a competition of noise, with different rap tracks mingling in a deafening cacophony. Closing the window of his cell as we sat down to talk, an older inmate sighs: "You see, there's the noise! Some people don't respect other people's privacy. In the moment when they're doing it, they don't realize. They're into their thing. They need to share their music." He concludes pedantically but indulgently: "As Malraux would say, once you've understood, you can't judge anymore!" The staff is similarly unappreciative of this noise nuisance, especially in summer, when windows have to remain open in order to render the air breathable. At a meeting of the assignment committee to which the music coming from a number of cells formed a noisy soundtrack, the block seniors joked: "Looks like the neighbors are having a party. – I don't know if we're invited. – If we are you can go without me!" After a moment one of them got up, and went to the phone, dialed a number and said to his colleague: "Shut off the power to the second floor, please!"

While the sonic environment is an experience of excess of decibels, the visual field is characterized rather by shortage of light. The communal areas of the blocks, with their great glazed bays and pastel-colored walls, are lit well enough, but the cells are generally gloomy. The installation of the grid over the bars has significantly reduced the natural light, as well as substantially limited and broken up the view that inmates have of the outside world during the 20 or so hours they spend shut in each day. This restriction of light is certainly not without its effects on their psychological and cognitive functioning.[11] Gesturing to the window through which little squares of blue sky were all that could be seen, one pre-trial Basque prisoner whose case had been under investigation for four years expostulates: "Why do they impose that on us on top of everything else? It's banned under the European rules. I've told them that, but they said they'd rather pay a fine." In fact, the rules set out by the European Council are simply recommendations and have no force in law; the answer he was given should be taken as a form of cynicism rather than anything else. The man continues: "My buddies who get out of prison, sometimes they sit for hours at a window looking at the sky." There is no doubt that contemporary prisons no longer allow prisoners to watch "the sky above the roof, so blue, so calm," as the poet Paul Verlaine was able to.[12] Over the years the man has seen his field of vision and the light levels in his cell progressively reduced; now, apart from the two hours of daily exercise, he has only a fragmented image of the outside world, and even in the middle of the day he can no longer read without artificial light.

Although they speak readily about the deafening noise and oppressive gloom, prisoners say little about their olfactory and gustatory experiences. The communal areas of the prison do not usually have any marked odor. Even at meal times, the circulation of metal trolleys hermetically sealed over their cling-wrapped meal plates does not alter this sterile neutrality. Only in solitary confinement are any distinctive features revealed in this regard: "The hole stinks of urine, it stinks of excrement. You're in the shit," says one inmate who has mental health issues and has been isolated several times following uncontrolled outbursts of violence. As for taste, it is hardly stimulated by the dishes prepared in the kitchen, in which the inmates detect few gastronomic qualities. The head of the catering service, however, boasted of its merits to me: "We use 20 percent organic ingredients. Our poultry is certified French, and the beef is certified Charolais. We even offer a choice of dishes: for people who don't like fish with saffron there are spicy sausages, or for those who don't want kidneys in mustard sauce there is fried chicken." Less appetizing than they sound, a substantial proportion of these meals disappeared into the garbage cans, with inmates accepting only the mass-produced bread they were given and preparing dishes themselves with products bought at the canteen shop, which they passed from cell to cell with the assistance of the guard. In view of the origin of most inmates, these rich flavors were usually Mediterranean.

* * *

In the day-to-day functioning of the prison, which is dominated for the majority of prisoners by inactivity and boredom, exercise and television are the two most predictable sources of entertainment, but they emphasize rather than ameliorate the idleness of the prisoners and the vacuity of incarceration.

For those who are not assigned work, training, or class, the twice-daily trips to the exercise yard represent the main opportunity to be outside their cells, and they are valued for this reason. However, some inmates avoid them for fear of being attacked because of the type of crime that has brought them to prison, in the case of sexual offenses, or because they are afraid of being put under pressure to go and pick up packages thrown over the prison wall, at the risk of being caught and punished. During the exercise period, most inmates' activity consists of talking while walking around the yard. Some jog, others do push-ups. Sometimes there is a ball that can be used for a soccer game, but I counted more than 20 lost on a neighboring roof. "Lucky there are the grilles you can hang onto, to do some exercises. We asked them to put in a bar. They wouldn't agree to it," complains one man who says that sport is a release from the everyday tensions.

Television, by contrast, is a much more consistent feature. Throughout the day and into the night, it is a permanent, reassuring presence. As one inmate, who has arrived a few weeks earlier, expresses it: "Sometimes we put on the TV. It gives you some background sound. You sleep better that way." Comparing the tensions that reigned at the time when I began my research, when free-standing television sets rented to inmates by the prison support association were a constant source of complaints, and the situation that prevailed once flat screens hired out by the private service provider had been fixed to the walls of the cells, it has to be recognized that the change did much to calm relations within the facility. "Television buys social peace" is a frequent refrain among both the guards and the prisoners. Yet it should not be reduced to this function. It does more than just entertain prisoners, or dull their senses; it is a source of information and even contributes to a level of critical awareness.[13] Inmates know all about the current news stories, especially those that concern the justice and prison system, and are quick to compare the treatment of legal cases involving politicians, of which there was a proliferation during the period of my research, with the treatment to which they had been subjected. Television was the opening to the outside world that the cell window no longer provided.

However, the most valued activity is sports. A crucial diversion for inmates who spend most of their prison time within their 100 square feet, sport is all the more precious because it is so rare. The waiting list can often be longer than six months. When a prisoner has been accepted, and provided that no reported incident has been sanctioned by withdrawal of this activity, he has the right to one single session per week. The reason for this limit is that the only place where sports can take place is a small gymnasium with an adjacent weight room. The soccer field, behind one of the blocks, is almost always desolately empty, as management considers it impossible to guarantee adequate security there, because it is not fully visible from the prison observation towers.[14] Since no provision has been made for additional security cameras, this large space is used only on the rare occasions when tournaments are organized under special supervision. The gym, on the contrary, is permanently occupied. It is not in good shape, does not conform to standards, and the strip lights in the ceiling threaten to fall down. Management has removed the radiators and pipes along the walls, which not only present a danger for those practicing sports, but have caused a flood following a leak. The flooring, damaged by the water, has become uneven, sometimes causing injuries, and nobody can say when it would be replaced. The hall is left unheated, making it virtually unusable in cold winters. One of the coaches, who complained that there was no allocated budget for sports and that "even for three soccer balls, you have to beg on your knees," added: "If that doesn't tell you how little the support staff are valued. . . ." Inmates felt the same was true as far as they were concerned.

Everyone recognizes that sports are not a priority. One coach told me that previously there had been a punching bag in a little annex off the gym, which allowed prisoners to train in boxing, a welcome release from the tensions of prison. It had been removed when the space was restructured and an office installed. The coach had been waiting six months for it to be rehung in another place but nothing had happened. "All it needs is four screws put in, a maintenance-team inmate is ready to do the job, but he isn't allowed." The prison management had asked the private contractor to do the work, but the latter had insisted that, as this task was not included in the contract, a new clause would need to be added. This would result in an additional cost that the warden, already facing cuts in government funding for prisons, could not take on. But the gym was not used only for sports. It was also where cultural events took place, usually in the afternoon. When a show, an art exhibit, or a musical program is planned, the hall becomes unavailable not only on the day of the presentation, but also the day before, which was taken up with the installation of the folding chairs that would seat the audience of inmates. "The guys wait all week for their sports session. And it's cancelled so they can put 20 chairs in the gym for a show the next day! It wouldn't cost them anything to let us set everything up on the day of the show: it takes 10 minutes," complained one inmate, who is regularly deprived of his sports session.

These cultural events are the focus of special attention from the national as well as local prison administration. They demonstrate both openness to the outside world and concern for the intellectual enrichment of the inmates. Some prestigious occasions even bring personalities from the world of culture and representatives of the ministry of justice to the prison.[15] At one brief exhibit, lasting just one afternoon, of three works by a contemporary artist who had just won a prestigious prize, those in attendance included, in addition to the artist, the chief executive officer and the head conservator of the Pompidou Center, the deputy directors of the National and Interregional Directorates of Prison Administration, and a dozen external guests. Talking with them, I realized that they were delighted by the exotic experience of spending the afternoon in a correctional facility. "I believe this is the first time in history that an artwork from a museum has been shown in a prison," boasted the CEO of the Pompidou Center in his introductory speech. This proud assertion was probably exaggerated, since we cannot be certain that all such artistic presentations had been systematically recorded, or that any precedents had been exhaustively researched, but it clearly indicated that this initiative aimed to promote both the policy of the museums, demonstrating that they were fulfilling their social mission toward "excluded audiences," as they were euphemistically called, and the policy of correctional facilities, for whom this cultural gesture expressed what was often termed the "humanization" of the prison world. The correctional staff themselves felt honored by the visit of these distinguished guests, and gratified by the presence of serious, attentive inmates that testified to the efforts it was making for them.

In order for the presentation to succeed, it needed sufficient viewers, but not too many. There had therefore been some promotion of the event, and those who had already participated in activities with an educational content were invited, while prisoners considered hard to control were excluded. Those present comprised 25 of these hand-picked prisoners, noticeably older than the average for the facility, with a very limited contingent from minority ethnic groups, but a significant proportion from the "protected prisoners" unit. Behind the seven rows of chairs they occupied, around

15 correctional officers watched over the event to ensure it ran smoothly. Facing this audience sat the officials and guests. A cameraman filmed the scene. After the welcome and congratulatory speeches, the artist talked about his work, referring both to some of his installations, images of which were projected on a screen, and the three works exhibited, whose resemblance to certain comic strips clearly disconcerted the audience. Describing his modest background and expressing himself in simple language, he sought to bond with his audience: "So art is what's enabled you to meet us here. It's not just about painting a nice picture. It's about making things possible." Following his presentation, the inmates were invited to ask questions. Some ventured to speak: "I don't know anything about art. Do you manage to make a living from it? I know Picasso, van Gogh. They're dead, but they were poor when they were alive. Do you make enough to live on?" Or: "Hi!, Sorry for bothering you. I do a bit of drawing. Your pictures look a bit crazy to me. I guess you must have a few strong drinks sometimes, do you?" While the guests exchanged smiles, the artist answered as best he could. In conclusion, he put a question to the audience: "I'd like to know if you get something out of this kind of event." Behind me, one inmate whispered: "We should say yes, to make him feel good." Then, aloud: "Us, you know, we're here to pass the time. But we're in jail. You came here. That's good." The event ended with a buffet of soft drinks and cheap canapés, which the prisoners were shy to approach.

Other cultural events were less impressive. There was a concert with a singer, accompanied by a pianist, who sang songs from well-known French films, with commentary from a presenter in between each one. The repertoire ran from Melina Mercouri to Jeanne Moreau and Cora Vaucaire. Some of the 20 or so inmates sitting in the middle of the freezing cold gym were baffled by these old-fashioned songs (there were some snickers at the beginning), but most of them, especially the older ones, were happy to hear them again (smiling with pleasure as they recognized them). "Irma La Douce" ("I'm cold alone, without you, my honey") and "A Weakness for Strong Men" ("The ones whose knife comes out, who hit to kill, all the guys from the docks . . .") were particularly well received, but the highlight of the show was "I've had it up to here" ("Moi j'en ai marre"), a hit for Mistinguett: "Keeping quiet all the time / I've had it up to here / It's gotta come out / I'm tired of taking it all / Without a word / Everything I have to stand . . . ." The guards were equally appreciative and, to the surprise of the prisoners, two of them took up the famous theme song of the 1939 film *Extenuating Circumstances*.

There was also a forum theater show, consisting of sketches performed by inmates aimed at creating exchanges with the audience. The theater director, who had spent several weeks in the prison preparing this show, had trained six of the twelve inmates who initially signed up in "prepared improvisation," the other six having dropped out. The chosen theme was "transmission." The first scene portrayed the tensions in a cell where three "old-timers" were faced with a "young inmate" who spent his time on his games console and failed to do his share of the domestic tasks; several members of the audience contributed to the discussion on how the crisis should be managed, some suggesting that the older inmates should have been harder on the new arrival, others taking the view that the prison staff should have intervened. The second scene showed an inmate leaving prison and arriving home to find himself caught between his two brothers, one a criminal and the other with ambitions to become a doctor, while the father, an illiterate immigrant in a blue-collar job, appears helpless; discussion with the spectators centered on recidivism. In both cases, the audience found the performance highly diverting, laughing and commenting on the scene.

While these events might be considered popular in terms of the intention of the organizers and the audience response, they were not so in terms of participation. As a result of a twofold process of self-selection by the prisoners themselves and cooptation by management, it was always the same couple of dozen men who formed the audience for the event, in the middle of an almost empty gym. All these entertainments, which took extensive preparation and were certainly costly, benefited 1 prisoner in 40, whereas, by comparison, sports, even though rationed, involves 10 times more inmates. Moreover, this process means that the shows bring together a small group that is not representative of the prison population in terms of age, ethnic origin, social or geographic background. Virtually none of the young men of North African or sub-Saharan origin who made up the vast majority of those in the facility ever came. The programs on offer, at which they knew they would not be welcome and which in any case were of little interest to them, did not relate to their culture – nor to that of the majority of their generation, for that matter. They reflected a traditional vision of cultural forms, showing the social and generational characteristics of those who conceived them.

By coincidence, on the same day as the forum theater session, three inmates appeared before the disciplinary board for having filmed and broadcast outside the prison a short sequence from a comedy sketch they had devised and performed in the exercise yard, dancing in grotesque costumes. More than the show itself, which parodied the Internet meme known as "Harlem Shake" that was viral at the time on social media throughout the world, it was the fact that it had been broadcast outside the facility, indicating the use of forbidden cellphones and above all giving an image of the prison that did not conform to the rigor expected of a punitive institution, that had led management to consider sanctioning those involved. Of the three inmates, two were punished by a suspended sentence of four days in solitary confinement and a withdrawal of their sentence reductions, while the third, who appeared to be the organizer of the event, was discharged with the benefit of the doubt, because he had disguised himself better in his costume. A fourth inmate, who had just been released under electronic monitoring, also had his sentence reductions withdrawn by the judge, but was not sent back to prison. The youngest of the suspects, who did not deny having been one of the protagonists but was unaware that the scene had been posted online, said: "It was just a bit of Sunday morning craziness between ourselves." In response, the deputy warden, who was chairing the disciplinary board and seemed to be trying to convince herself too, attempted to explain to him the gravity of his action: "It's a very serious matter. There is a complete mismatch between the reality of prison, with the risk of stigmatization and desocialization that it involves, and the completely immature state of mind you demonstrate by letting yourself be filmed. It risks making people think prison is a summer camp." Devastated by the prospect of the punishment that would postpone the adjustment of his sentence and his release, the young man replied simply: "It might go against me, but I prefer to let off steam that way than by hitting guards, like other guys did last week." The deputy warden had to acquiesce, but added that their actions could "be assimilated to a movement" – the euphemized term to designate a rebellion.

If it was a rebellion, it was a quite harmless and peaceable one. It would probably be better thought of as a simultaneous release and resistance. Release, because "letting off steam" meant relieving themselves of the tensions of prison; resistance because the "bit of craziness" sought to mock the institution by defying it. The warden probably realized this as she was judging the culprits for what elsewhere would have been qualified as a schoolyard prank, but took on particular significance in the context of the prison. It would not, in fact, be unreasonable to classify this amusement, however clumsy, with the tradition of clandestine spectacles performed in places of incarceration, which have this dual cathartic and ironic function.[16] The fact that in this case the prison tolerated the outlet but punished the resistance is ultimately in the order of things in the context of an institution dedicated to punishment. But there might be a lesson for management in this apparently minor incident – that there are other ways of thinking about the culture and entertainment of the prisoners entrusted to them, by choosing less elitist and discriminatory forms, which might interest and involve larger sectors of the prison population.[17] This is indeed being done by many local groups working with similar audiences, and is starting to be developed in some correctional facilities.

*   *   *

However, the most intensely charged moments of prison life are not the leisure activities, but the visiting hours. These are the only times when inmates can meet with people who do not belong to the prison world (either prison staff or external service providers). They are thus powerful affective experiences of reconnecting with a wife, a partner, a child, or a mother.[18] The 30 minutes that these interactions last are often the most precious, the most comforting, and the most emotional of prison life. As I walk down the corridor that runs alongside the cubicles, in the company of a guard entrusted with ensuring they run without incident, I glimpse a couple entwined around one another and kissing passionately, a father with an

8-year-old girl on his knee sitting opposite a woman who is simply smiling at him, a man silently and motionlessly weeping as he gazes at his mother who is also in tears, a woman chatting quietly with her husband as their two children play on the floor. The partings are sad, often tender, sometimes harrowing: a little boy who came with his mother and uncle sobs inconsolably as he watches his father, who had held him in his arms throughout the half hour, walk away; a mother begs that her son, who has been sentenced to solitary confinement, not be punished further, because he doesn't realize what he's doing, an assertion confirmed by her son's distraught appearance; a man with still reddened eyes explains that it is the first time he has seen his mother in the two months since he was jailed, as it is difficult for her to travel (given that he is accused of a rape he denies having committed, it is easy to understand how this visit, which suggests a possible reconciliation, takes on a crucial significance for him). The personal investment in visiting hours is also manifested in the attention prisoners pay to their appearance. Inmates generally wear their best clothes, often comprising immaculately clean track pants in bright colors, a tee-shirt that shows off their muscles, and spotless, expensive, fashionable tennis shoes. The obvious efforts made by many of the young women to appear beautiful is equally revealing of how these encounters center on issues of seduction and desire. The elegance exhibited by some soberly dressed parents – he in a suit, she in a tailored skirt and vest – indicates an attempt to create an air of distinction that aims to restore a family image tarnished by the shame of prison. The billowing damask robes in subtly harmonizing colors worn by African mothers and the austere straight djellabas worn by the older Muslim men indicate the same concern for dignity. In these brief half hours, the visiting rooms mingle affect and performance, abandonment to the emotion of the moment, and attention to the impression produced.

But achieving access to them is a path strewn with obstacles. While prisoners have a right to visits, this right is subject to regulations and procedures that are always constraining and sometimes insurmountable. The general conditions for visits are defined by law, while the specific arrangements are set by the facility's internal regulations. The first stage in the process, obtaining a permit for a visit, involves submitting a request in writing to the director, accompanied by a series of documents such as photocopies of the identity card and family book, which those not native to France may have difficulty in getting. In principle, this stage takes a number of weeks, during which the inmate receives no visitors. It sometimes ends in failure, for example when a magistrate investigating the case of a pre-trial prisoner forbids a visit by a close connection for reasons related to the inquiry. Once authorization is obtained, a date has to be arranged. Since the number of places available for each of the daily five half-hour visit slots is limited, and the telephone line used to arrange visits is often engaged, this second stage can be frustrating for the visitors, especially as reservations can only be made one week in advance, unless they have an electronic card that allows them to book visits via the self-service machines in the prison grounds. Saturday appointments are of course much in demand, and therefore hard to secure.

Once the permit and time are settled, there remains the final stage, the visit itself. Like most facilities built since the 1980s, the prison is located outside the city. Many of the visitors are on limited incomes, have no private car, and do not have the money to take a taxi. Getting to the correctional facility by public transportation is complicated for them because it is so far from the city center, with an infrequent bus service. Even for those who live in the region, the journey sometimes takes more than two hours each way, including waiting for connections between the different transportation systems. For some, the distance may be much harder, involving long journey times and high travel costs, as one national survey revealed.[19] Almost half the visitors live more than 30 miles from the prison, and a quarter more than 60 miles away; to visit the facility, nearly two-thirds of them spend more than 50 euros per month and a quarter more than 100 euros per month. In the case of inmates incarcerated very far from their home for particular reasons, such as Basque political prisoners, the difficulties may be greater still.[20] The distance also means there is a higher risk of hold-ups, for example a problem on the railroad line. Arriving late, even by only a few minutes, results in mere cancellation. Visitors sometimes spend half a day on public transportation, only to find out when they arrive that they cannot meet with the husband or son they have come to see.

Reception of the prisoners' families, which is entrusted to the private company that won the delegated management contract for this facility, takes place in a small building close to the prison entrance. It is a bright room with chairs, a drinks machine, a magazine rack, and a play corner for children, and two offices. The company's employee team works in one of these, answering calls and registering visitors. The family support association occupies the other: its members provide information for visitors, lend toys to the children, offer coffee and cookies. "We're here to listen without judging, inform people about their rights, point them toward other organizations they can approach," explains their president. The only time prison staff are present is when they guide the group of visitors into or out of the prison after their identity has been registered. The waiting room fills and empties in line with the visit timetable. It is a place where one can witness the anxiety of the moments leading up to a meeting, the emotional reunions between prisoners' wives, the exchanges of information on life in prison or means of transportation. When it is not too cold, the children play on a small roundabout while their mothers chat and smoke outside the entrance to the building. The men often prefer to wait in their car in the parking lot, listening to music with the doors open. On some days, young women spend long hours in the family room or close by. But they do not follow the other visitors into the prison. They have come with their little boy or girl, who is led alone to the room where a "father–child visit" takes place, discreetly monitored by a psychologist. During the time this monthly meeting lasts, they wait. Then, when the child returns, they leave again without having seen their husband or partner.

The visit itself is made up of a succession of moments, each precisely defined and timed. For the 3:00 p.m. visiting slot, for example, visitors have to report to reception half an hour earlier. Ten minutes before the visit time, they enter the facility and pass by the cloakroom to leave any packages they have brought, the content of which will be checked before they are passed on to the inmates. A quarter of an hour later, they enter the visiting area proper, and a guard opens the door of the cubicle where they wait alone for five to ten minutes, until the prisoners arrive. At the end of the half-hour visit, the prisoners leave first, and the visitors stay alone for a moment, before being gathered back together in a room where they spend nearly an hour while the prisoners are searched, in order to ensure that no illicit substances have been brought in. If they had, the police would be called to arrest the visitors concerned, and all would have to remain confined. At 4:30 p.m., they are finally allowed to leave and can return home. The 30-minute visit thus turns into two hours of alternating waiting, tensions, emotions, frustrations, anxiety, and irritation. As one family support volunteer says, "for the families, it's really a double punishment."[21] The affliction of imprisonment of a loved one is compounded by the vicissitudes of the visit experience.

On the inmates' side, the visit follows symmetrical procedures. Prisoners leave their cell to go to the section of the block where the visiting rooms are located. A guard confirms their identity biometrically, and checks that nothing contravenes regulations: prisoners are forbidden to "eat, drink, smoke, bring any item" during the visit; "watch, jewelry, cigarettes, lighter, vest, windbreaker, coat, mail, food" are also prohibited. It is at this point that the inmates leave the bag of their dirty laundry, which their family will take away. Once these various checks have been completed, they enter the cubicles where their visitors are waiting. At the end of the visit, they pick up the package brought for them, together with their clean clothes, and then one by one undergo a strip search in a cubicle, while their clothing is inspected manually. This is the most delicate stage. It is the moment at which a banned substance or forbidden object may be discovered. It is also an opportunity for some malevolent guards to be overzealous in their inspection. Even without either of these ultimately rare occurrences, the search represents a brutal re-immersion into the prison world after the emotional moments through which the prisoners have just lived. As one director put it: "For most inmates, it's moving from the best of prison, with their children on their knee and their girlfriend in their arms, to the worst of prison: 'Come on! Strip off! Give me your clothes!'" The correctional officers are aware of the violence of this situation, and, feeling uncomfortable themselves, often restrict their search to a cursory inspection of the prisoner from behind. The officers entrusted with overseeing visiting hours are chosen with particular care; these are guards known for "not having problems with inmates." They readily show goodwill toward inmates and their families, reassuring the latter ("Don't worry, he'll be here soon") and joking amiably with the former ("Go and show off your six-pack!"). At the end of a visiting hour in late December, guards and prisoners warmly wished one another a happy new year as they departed.

For both visitor and inmate, the often bittersweet time of the visit can become painful – as a result of reproaches expressed, a break-up sensed, bad news brought. One particular ordeal is the phantom visit: when he enters the visiting area, the inmate is told that the person he is expecting has not come. This is a moment of distress, for not only does he feel the deep disappointment of the meeting that will not happen, but he also has no idea of the reason for the absence: simple delay or mishap, an accident on the journey or some other serious incident, a forgotten arrangement that betrays a growing indifference or the sign of a separation to come. If he has no access to a telephone, he probably will not find out anything for several days. Nobody will try to discover the nature of the problem, which might reassure him. One employee of the private contractor said bitterly: "I think it's shocking, the way they treat phantom visits. The prisoner doesn't even know what's happened. If at least there was somebody who could call the family and check . . . But no, the general feeling is: 'They're being punished, they asked for it, they're paying for it.'" In the best case, the inmate is warned just before leaving his cell to go down to the visiting area, sparing him the humiliation of showing his distress or anger in front of the guards and other inmates.

Poignant situations can also arise. When all the visitors' cubicles are opened one by one, an old man dressed in a traditional Muslim qamis finds himself suddenly alone in the little corridor, with his young son who has come with him. As I later learn, he has recently suffered a stroke and has difficulty traveling. The chief officer goes off to ask his colleagues what has happened. When he comes back, he explains to the old man that his nephew has not been able to come down because "he's hurt his foot." The uncle's face crumples. He has understood the real reason for this absence: the last time they came, he and his son took the wrong road, arrived late, and were not authorized to visit the inmate. "My nephew harbors grudges," he says soberly. He moves away with dignity, but limping much more visibly than when he entered a few minutes earlier. Sympathetic, the sergeant accompanies him back to the prison entrance in order to spare him the additional fatigue and distress of the long wait with the other families when they leave the visiting rooms.

At the opposite extreme, the most joyful visit experience is that of the father–child meeting. All the inmates who spoke with me about it told me how happy it made them. This is a relatively recent arrangement, set up by a voluntary organization partly funded by the prison's probation and re-entry service. Sessions are monthly, and last nearly two hours. In the presence of a psychologist, who stays in the background "so they can forget about her," the father interacts with his child in a room kitted out for play and sports, called "baby-gym" for the under-5s and "karate" for those aged up to 12. The limited availability of staff means that only 22 fathers can be signed up; this means that an average of 40 or so men are able to benefit from this activity each year, far fewer than the number who could claim access to it on the grounds of being fathers. Those serving short sentences are virtually excluded, owing to the long waiting list. Priority is given to pre-trial prisoners and convicted inmates who otherwise do not see their child at all, for example if there is a problem with the mother, but most do not fall into this category, and this encounter with the child also contributes to maintaining the link with the partner. According to the coordinator of the program, "Often, it's these fathers' first child. It's also often their first time in prison as a father. Even if it's not necessarily their first time in prison altogether."

Late one afternoon, I run into a man coming back to his block with a paper bag in his hand. He is radiant: "Today is my daughter's third birthday! We celebrated with a cake in the baby-gym. There was a bit left, so I brought it back to eat with my friend. It's just two little cakes, but I'm so happy!" He explains that this time in prison is different from previous ones: "Now I'm married and a dad. It's not the same at all. I was selfish. It's like I abandoned them." With no money, his wife had to leave the apartment they were renting and take her daughter back to live with her mother. "Luckily, I've got my wife. She prepared everything this morning: drinks, cake, little plates and everything. That takes time. We don't always realize." Suddenly pensive, he adds sadly: "And she stayed in the parking lot for two hours, waiting. I know what she's going through. She's in prison too." When the children are a little older, the relationship is different. A man with a long criminal record describes the change that came about when the karate was set up: "I follow my daughter's education closely. She's in second grade. Before, she was anxious, she wasn't doing well at school, she had bad grades. Now, when she comes she shows me her school report, she's got all As and Bs, with great comments from the teacher. I'll tell you something. I'm 35, I've been in jail 10 times, it never touched me. But this time, there's my daughter. It's different. I went to see the warden and I told him: 'All I want is to get the maximum sentence reduction so I can get out as quick as possible.'"

Rare and fleeting, the moments of visits – particularly those with children – offer an occasional bright interlude in the dull experience of prison life. Not everyone has the good fortune to benefit from them. Some choose not to. One man serving a one-year sentence explains that he does not want any visits: "It's more painful than anything else to see them sad." Another, sentenced to four years, limits this restriction to his 10-year-old daughter: "I don't want her to see me in prison." But one can never be sure that these declarations of fortitude are not covering up the suffering caused by deeper reasons that would make these meetings impossible in any case: it is better to say you don't want visits when you know that nobody will request one. But most of those who do not receive visits acknowledge that this is an ordeal for them. One pre-trial prisoner who has been forbidden for three years to see his wife, by order of the examining judge, and is despairing at this privation, expresses it in a sort of melancholy defiance: "Here, you're dead. You wait. You wait, patiently. Sometimes I get the urge to write to the director to start putting money aside for a coffin."

*   *   *

Experiences of incarceration certainly vary.[22] "Les Baumettes, it's like Guantánamo. Here, it's the Holiday Inn!" exclaimed a 22-year-old man who had just entered the prison and was comparing the reception to what he experienced in a previous stay in the Marseilles prison of Les Baumettes. "Just the canteens, the tobacco, and all that, when you arrive. Even the cells are cleaner. And back there we were three to a cell." His enthusiasm would no doubt cool a few days later when he would be transferred from the arrivals unit to the block where he would serve out his sentence for aiding and abetting a burglary. But he would certainly appreciate finding that he would have only one other cellmate, rather than two as before, and would find his impression of a relatively modern, clean facility confirmed, contrasting with the dilapidation and abjection of a prison that is regularly condemned by French and European organizations. Conversely, comparing his incarceration in Paris with his current imprisonment, a 25-year-old man recalled: "I've been in La Santé. I got a shock when I arrived here!" He added: "Of course, compared to there you're in a five-star hotel here. There we had mice, roaches, holes in the walls. Here it's really clean. But the most important thing is the prisoners. Back there the inmates weren't youth from the hood. There was a much better atmosphere amongst us. And then there were a lot of different activities. Tai Chi, painting, pottery, theater, dance, classes with the education volunteers. And it was easy to get. Here, there's none of that. And for the few activities we do have, the waiting lists are endless."

In fact, these two assessments of the prison are less contradictory than they appear on first reading. The two men agree with the fact that material conditions in the short-term prison where they are currently are better than in the facilities where they were previously incarcerated. But that is not enough to automatically improve their life. The latter of the two is probably more aware of this than the former, first because his long experience in the facility has given him the measure of the paucity and poor quality of the activities, and second because his maturity makes him more sensitive than the youth of the other to the make-up of the prison population and the disadvantages that result from it. These two factors are without a doubt key to understanding the experience of the carceral world. The first points to the reality of the facility, particularly to the idleness that is one of its characteristic features. One inmate in his 30s, who through various stays in half a dozen French and European prisons has gained a comparative perspective on the subject, puts it placidly: "Here it's not bad, but the problem is, they've got no money. You can't complain. The only drawback is there's no work. And everybody wants to work." The second point relates to the demographics of prison, particularly the overwhelming presence of young men of minority background convicted of minor crimes. Another inmate, similarly well versed thanks to a long history of imprisonment, but already in his 50s, articulates this difference: "In a short-stay prison, you've got guys who are presumed innocent, you've got young men who shouldn't be here. And here they do nothing. At 11 in the morning the guys are still asleep. It's crazy! Prison's lost its meaning. There's no punishment anymore, no readjustment to the outside world." One of these criticisms is directed at the correctional policy, the other at the penal policy. The first points to the emptiness of prison existence. The second questions the aberrations of the punitive system.

A diptych thus emerges from prisoners' comments on their experiences of incarceration. There are the conditions of imprisonment on one side. These can be divided into material and regulatory aspects. The former has been manifestly improved: the short-stay prisons built in recent decades are much less uncomfortable and much more hygienic than what came before and are still in use, such as Les Baumettes and La Santé. The latter has also been marked by significant advances: the application of part of the European Prison Rules, and of successive French legislation, leads to the recognition of certain rights in terms of both legal representation of prisoners and maintenance of family relations or access to culture. Few inmates deny that these are positive developments, even if they emphasize rather than erase the spectacular differences between the new facilities, which polish up the image of prisons, and the old ones, of which there are still many, and which are regularly condemned as a disgrace by national and international organizations.

How, then, are we to understand why those incarcerated and those who advocate for them continue to repeat their indictment of prison? The point is that there is another side to the experience prisoners have of it: the meaning of the punishment. Here again two components may be distinguished, one relating to the correctional aspect, the other to the penal dimension. They are closely linked. First, prison is pointless, say prisoners, because we don't do anything here. Work is scarce, training sporadic, classes limited, and activities insufficient, whether sports or culture. We waste our time here between the television and the yard. Second, they point out, this dearth is linked both to the increased length of prison sentences and to the presence in prison of people who should not be there. The combination of these two factors results in, or aggravates, not only overpopulation in correctional facilities, as has already been noted, but also the structural shortage of activity. The sense of the pointlessness of the sentence time thus undermines the prison's designated mission, whether from the point of view of moral education or of social reintegration.

Many among the correctional staff would probably subscribe to this twofold analysis. Inmates and officers share not only a space, but also, albeit for contrasting reasons and sometimes from opposite sides, certain problems, or at least their consequences in terms of stress. The two mix with one another in the everyday, while at the same time attempting to maintain an impossible distance between them. In this respect, one essential mediation, to which too little attention is paid, is that of the objects that often serve for inmates as a way of inventing modes of resistance, and for prison officers as a way of exercising forms of control – paradoxical transitional objects.

5

In the Nature of Things

Always go back to the object itself, to its raw quality, its difference ...
Recognize the greater right of the object, its inalienable right.
Francis Ponge, *Mute Objects of Expression*, 1952

"It's their way of resisting us," explains the guard sympathetically, as I accompany him on his night round. As the half-dozen officers responsible for verifying that inmates are in their cell each evening walk quickly around all the wings of the prison, glancing through the door viewer to check that the occupants are indeed present and alive, they often find themselves faced with an opening that is blocked or obscured, forcing them to call through the door to the inmates to free it up: "Peephole, please!" Inside, the occupants often take their time to respond.

Sometimes, a voice retorts: "What about our privacy?" or, stressing the last word, "Peephole please, *sir*!" Usually, however, the prisoners move in silence but without haste to comply with the officer's request, the latter concluding: "Thank you, good night!" Sometimes an inmate may try to strike up a short conversation, for example when he detects an unknown figure in civilian clothes: "Oh it's you tonight, officer! And who's that with you?" But the exchange does not last long: "None of your business." This fleeting interaction can also be the occasion for a request: "Officer!" "What?" "I've had a headache for a while. Have you got a pill?" "No, I'm doing the night round, I don't have anything." A resigned sigh: "Thank you, good night, officer!" Occasionally, a recalcitrant inmate refuses to unblock the viewer: "You can hear me, isn't that enough?" "No, I need to see you." "You can hear my voice, that should be good enough." "No, unblock your peephole." "I don't give a shit. You can spend the night outside my door if you want." The officer gives up and moves on, justifying himself for my benefit: "We heard his voice, we know he's in there and alive." On rare occasions, a prisoner on his own in the cell will "play dead" by keeping quiet, a provocation with consequences he is aware of. In such cases the guards are obliged to call the sergeant to open the door because, for security reasons, they are not authorized to do so themselves at night.

This game of micro-resistances, which I noted in some wings took place in more than three-quarters of cases, extends the time taken to check on the more than 800 prisoners, at the end of which the count is validated by the duty senior. It is only after this validation, and provided that it reveals no discrepancy with the count made an hour earlier by the day shift before they left, that the officers can finally return to their staff room and eat their meal. At each cell where the viewer is obstructed, 10, 20, or 30 seconds are thus lost. Furthermore, the inconvenience is mutual, since the inmate has to get up and go to the door in order to show himself, when he might have been watching television or already sleeping. But being disturbed in this way apparently weighs less heavily with inmates than the inconvenience they cause. "They just do that to annoy us," a guard commented to me, philosophically. His colleagues, accustomed to these games, are generally equally unruffled, only rarely expressing exasperation. This minimal protest by the prisoners effectively forms part of the routine of the rounds, and the staff have come to accept it as such.

When I began my research, peepholes looked like a sturdier version of those typically installed in the front door of apartments, with a metal ring surrounding a plexiglass disk, closed by a hinged cover – the only difference being that the cover was of course controlled from the outside, at least in principle. In fact, apart from the newly refurbished arrivals unit, where the temporary occupants stayed too little time to alter or vandalize the premises, most of the viewers were no longer in this state: the cover had almost always been torn off and the glass itself often removed, leaving simply a gaping hole in the door. This damage might, of course, have been done by a previous occupant of the cell, and therefore whatever interpretation one could make of it applied not to current inmates, who sometimes even considered it a nuisance, but rather to the prison population as a whole.

One significant advantage of the peephole was that a cigarette or a small packet of coffee could be passed through the opening, a gift between neighbors which the guards sometimes agreed to pass on. But it had two negative consequences: first, the occupants felt they were permanently open to the gaze of the guards or even of other inmates returning from exercise, a visit, or the workshops; second, anyone trying to look through the hole, from inside or outside, exposed their eye to injury from a blunt instrument or a spray of liquid – incidents that had been known to occur in the past. In order to counteract these problems, at least in part, inmates often used the top of a soda bottle attached by a string that a light tap would knock out, or a piece of card the size of the original disk, which could be lifted up; in both cases these devices were located inside the cell and hence under the control of the occupants. Some even used fragments of mirrors to give them a view onto the walkway and those present there.

My reason for this detailed description is to suggest that we should pay attention to even the most mundane objects in the world of prison.[1] Prison is clearly constituted by an infrastructure of buildings and security devices, on the one hand, and a population of inmates and prison staff, on the other, but it also includes objects essential to the functioning of the architectural and human ensemble. There are two particularly interesting aspects to these objects: they have a social life, and they are endowed with a political significance.[2] By the social life of objects, I mean the way they are appropriated, put to alternative use, or damaged by individuals. In considering the political significance of objects, I aim to grasp the meaning conferred on them by individuals and how they transform relations of power or emancipation. In the case of the peephole, both correctional officers and inmates are involved in these two aspects of its existence.

For prison management, the purpose of the door viewer is to be able to check what is going on inside the cell at any moment, for reasons of security of the facility (particularly any threat of escape), protection of inmates (especially from risk of suicide), as well as to count and monitor the population. The peephole is thus an instrument of government, in the sense Michel Foucault gives to the word, when he emphasizes the importance of analyzing the "physics of power," that is, "a power thought of as physical action" rather than simply ideology.[3] In prison, the manipulation of this object is driven by various motivations: protecting inmates' privacy by preventing intrusive scrutiny; thwarting correctional officers by disrupting the smooth progress of the rounds; exerting psychological pressure through the possibility of attack; demonstrating an ability to contest surveillance by the prison institution. In contrast, for inmates, the door viewer is an instrument of resistance, not of the order of rebellion, but rather in the more mundane expression of what James Scott calls the forms of "prosaic but constant struggle," that is, the "ordinary weapons of relatively powerless groups," which include indiscipline, obstruction, and vandalism.[4] The peephole, an apparently innocuous and trivial object, offers an insight into the relations of power that arise within the prison, which are generally passed over if attention is focused on brutal manifestations of dominance, on the one hand, and spectacular manifestations of revolt, on the other. It reveals subtle plays where the relation of authority is negotiated, where the violence remains contained, where cooperation is still possible, where even humor has its place.

As a sign of this constantly shifting equilibrium, when I returned for my last periods of research in the prison, management had installed door viewers described as "integral, high-security, with vandalism- and aggression-resistant cover" in all cells. This was a model similar to the one used previously, but with an added stainless steel mesh to protect the plexiglass disk and to prevent attacks through the aperture, and a metal plate fixed partially over the cover so as to discourage attempts to break it. In short, the institution had regained the upper hand. Or more precisely, it had done so on the walkway side. For on the cell side, prisoners still had their bottle cap or scrap of card they could use to control the intrusion of scrutiny from outside. Requests to free up the viewer were therefore still as frequent, and the round still as long, but the doors were no longer vandalized and prison officers no longer at risk of underhand tricks. I discovered, moreover, that this new technical fix was introduced in the context of a practice of economic internalization, by which I mean a sort of internal subcontracting: under the auspices of the Prison Employment Service, the Prison Industries Authority has inmates themselves manufacture security hardware, including the various models of peepholes described above, in the workshops of nine French prisons.[5] In the ultimate irony of the social life of this object, and an indication of its multiple political meanings, prisoners are induced to contribute, through their work, to their own surveillance. But the door viewer is far from being the only object with this ambivalent quality.

*　　*　　*

"Some day, phones will be allowed. And they will have sentenced all these people to solitary confinement for something that will have become normal." The man, who is 25 and has already been in prison for three years, interrupts his litany of the privations generated by the prison ("They should put a straitjacket on the word 'frustration'") to utter this prediction. When, a little earlier, he was describing the turbulent path of his childhood and adolescence, shunted from one children's home to the next ("They used to pass me from one to another like a stinky old sock"), he had stopped short: "One day we'll have cellphones, we'll have the Internet. We'll get there. It's the way of the world." The idea is obviously close to his heart. He does not tell me whether he himself possesses such an object, but it is statistically likely that he does, given the number of cellphones in circulation in the facility. Especially if we take into account the fact that he occupies the post of auxiliary, allowing him to move more freely around his wing to ensure that it is clean, and giving him regular contact with other inmates, since he serves their meals. Many things pass through the "auxes," as the auxiliaries are called. The trust placed in them by prison management, which is rewarded by the allocation of a cell twice the size of others, in which it is also guaranteed they will remain alone, derives from their sense of responsibility and their loyalty to prison staff. But it does not go so far as imagining they will forgo an object that is as commonplace in prison as a cellphone. Not that possession of this object is accepted by management, which organizes regular cell searches to hunt out the forbidden devices, but they know perfectly well that it is the most widely shared thing in the carceral world. Despite the risk, few prisoners do without one.

One director, in my first interview with him, explained the issue: "For phone calls, we have a telephone policy that conforms to the European Prison Rules. We have installed booths in the arrivals unit and in the convicted prisoners yards. Inmates buy call credits at the canteen." He added, philosophically, "That doesn't stop them buying cellphones that they manage to get in. Obviously that's against the rules. But we recognize that they can be a calming factor. Yet, when we find them, we still take them. The phones we collected during searches over one year filled four big garbage bags." While he was reluctant to translate the volume of these containers into numbers of phones that could be related to the number of inmates in the prison, the unit of measurement chosen to represent this quantity gives an idea of the scale of the illicit trade. In fact, during the last year of my research, management did count up the phones collected: in 12 months, more than 500 cellphones were seized during searches, and nearly 250 were picked up after being thrown over the wall into the prison grounds, giving an average of roughly one cellphone found per inmate.

Significantly, the prisoners' understanding of the scale of the phenomenon, its beneficial consequences, and the danger of overregulating it chimed closely with management's analysis. As one of them put it: "Short-stay prisons are a total sieve! The wardens have to let it go, or there would be riots. All the same, if they catch you, you pay for it." He even quoted the guard's jokes at the end of visiting hours: "Hey, can you lend me your phone? I need to make a call. – Sorry, I left it in my cell!" But he admitted that he had only once been subjected to a full strip search at the end of a visit, probably because he was in pre-trial detention for a sex offense. One indirect indicator of the widespread distribution of cellphones was the consumption of telephone credits in the booths installed by the prison: in the accounts I viewed, it fell from an average of 4,000 euros per month in 2010 to 3,000 euros in 2011, and 2,000 in 2012. The usage of authorized telephone communication was falling rapidly.

Cellphones entered the prison mainly through packages thrown over the facility's walls and through direct transactions with visitors during visiting hours.[6] Paradoxically, packages thrown over the wall seemed a more certain method of delivery. They were often sent over at night, from the side of the facility that looked onto the neighboring forest, but there were also some more adventurous expeditions during the day, as was the case one day when packages were thrown from the parking lot, from a vehicle that then made off at top speed before the security cameras could catch the registration plate. Passing objects during visits was riskier, given that the items brought in by visitors were thoroughly checked before the visit, and the prisoners themselves systematically subjected to a full strip search afterwards. One solution employed for a while had been to attach the phone to the underside of the table with sticky tape during the visit, with the auxiliary responsible for cleaning the rooms commissioned to bring it later, but that stratagem had been discovered and could no longer be used. Whether packages were thrown over the walls or passed during visits, those who brought in the illicit objects risked arrest and an immediate appearance trial, which could end in a prison sentence, as I witnessed. However, there was a third option, rarely mentioned: transfer via members of the prison staff. "How do you think cellphones get in?" asked one prisoner, who had been found with a sophisticated state-of-the-art model during a search. "Where d'you think I'd get an iPhone like that? A package? Would you throw a phone that costs that much over a wall? A visit? I'm not going to ask my wife or my mother to take that kind of risk! No, management turns a blind eye to phones being passed by the guards." He did not go into further detail.[7] A few days later, I noted myself that management was reluctant to acknowledge these practices, and a director with whom I raised the subject dismissed it, firmly and indignantly.

However they got in, once inside the facility, cellphones moved in complex circuits that brought into play the networks and hierarchies operating within the prison. Some inmates were identified as "victims." These were the ones who were sent to pick up the packages from the other side of the fence surrounding the exercise yard. "The first time I went out in the yard, there were young guys coming up to me," says a man who has recently arrived. "They made me crawl under the fence to pick up packages. I didn't get what was going on. I went, but I got caught. After that they started calling me Spiderman. One guy came up to me a few days later, and said: 'You've got balls! Respect.' That's because I didn't duck out in front of them." Phones were also often hidden in the cells of prisoners deemed "vulnerable," so that the actual owner would not have problems in the event of a search. In this way, the weakest took on all the risks. When they were caught, they came before the disciplinary board, where the representatives of the prison management often guessed what had happened, and the role the accused had been made to play. But the latter were careful not to confirm these interpretations, and particularly not to give up the names of those who commissioned them. For those who controlled it, this was a lucrative market. According to one prisoner, boasting in front of another that he knew the "real prices," the going rate was "100 euros for a basic phone, 200 or 250 for a Sony-Ericsson-type smartphone, 500 to 700 for an iPhone or a Samsung Galaxy, depending on the model." These prices were not exorbitant, being in line with those charged in stores. It is therefore to be assumed that the profits were made earlier, in other words at the moment of acquisition: these were phones that "fell off a truck," to use the time-honored phrase. However, in relation to the modest resources of many prisoners, or more significantly, the wage paid to those who worked, cellphones were expensive. Top-range products cost the equivalent of half the average wage for the general population outside, but double the average wage for the prison population.

In short, the cellphone, an illicit object that has become commonplace, has its own life within prison. A means of communication with the outside, it is also a source of prestige for those with the most recent, high-performance models, of profit for those who trade in them, and of dominance exerted over those who take on the risks. It can thus be understood as capital that is at once symbolic, economic, and social. The symbolic advantage is without doubt very similar to that enjoyed in the rest of society. However, the economic and social dimensions are specific to the fact that it is a product that it is illegal to possess. Of course, it is no surprise that prohibition of a commodity generates trafficking, and hence relations of inequality and power among those involved. The same is true of other products, notably marijuana, which is the object of a very lively trade. The difference between these two products is that the cellphone is lawful in the outside world, while the drug is not; as such, there is a discontinuity in the legal status in the former case that does not exist in the latter, with the consequence that there is greater moral tolerance of the former, even within prison management.

Given these conditions, why does management resist the introduction of cellphones, while promoting the use of telephone booths? Before answering the question, it should be emphasized that the introduction of the booths represented a major advance in the improvement of prison conditions: "The installation of telephones was quite a revolution," enthused a deputy warden who had known the prison before and after this innovation. Initially restricted to convicted prisoners, the right to use the telephone had been extended to pre-trial prisoners by the 2009 law on prisons. It nevertheless remains tightly controlled. First, the prisoner must draw up a list of authorized numbers, no more than 20 in a short-stay prison. In order to do this, he must supply supporting documentation for each of the people he wishes to contact. Moreover, the examining magistrate in the case of pre-trial prisoners, or the prison management in the case of convicted prisoners, may add restrictions. Many of the inmates I met, particularly those awaiting trial, were unable to communicate with the people they were closest to, such as their partner, for months or years. The magistrates' justification for this ruling was that it was necessary for the investigation, but it often also appeared to be a way of putting pressure on the accused. One pre-trial prisoner who had been in prison for several years, and whose parents lived 500 miles away and were therefore only rarely able to visit him, complained: "The examining magistrate banned me from calling my family, except my mom. He said: 'You've got visiting hours. You don't need to call.' But the journey's expensive. My sisters can't afford to come. Fair enough my freedom is taken away, but they shouldn't take my relationships with my family and my girlfriend away too." Second, telephone conversations can be listened in to and recorded. These procedures, the possibility of which is known to the inmates, are described by management as random, but can also be focused on particular prisoners, for example if management believes there is a risk of escape or suicide. One warden declared himself particularly sensitive to harassment of victims by their attacker, several cases of which had been communicated to him: "People think about the prisoners, their rights, their well-being. But they don't pay attention to the victim's point of view. When you're getting calls from someone who's in jail and is threatening you, that's unacceptable. If we allow ourselves the means to apply the court's decisions by shifting the focus back onto the victim, it will give my job back its meaning." In such cases of telephone persecution, management can disconnect the call, if they are aware of it. Obviously, cellphones do not lend themselves as easily to this kind of limitation and surveillance.

However, the advantages inmates perceive in them have less to do with avoiding their conversations being monitored than with being able to contact their loved ones when they want. The telephone booths present various constraints in this regard. Apart from the fact that calls are costly and time-limited, access is in fact restricted. Prisoners have to make calls at times when the booths are available, mainly during exercise periods, offering little possibility of reaching a wife who works or a child who goes to school. "Let me tell you something. My daily treat is to call my little girl in the evening, ask her what she did during the day and say goodnight," confided one inmate who had arrived in prison four years earlier, shortly after the birth of his daughter. Moreover, under the restrictions decreed by the courts or the wardens, the people that some prisoners want to speak with are precisely those excluded from their list. "Sometimes I'd give anything to make a call. It's hard not to be able to talk with my wife. It's a year since I've had a conversation with her. But I don't want them to be able to say at the trial that we've been in touch, and give me a longer sentence," says, dejectedly, one pre-trial prisoner, whose partner is suspected of complicity. He asserts that he has refused to get a cellphone. Furthermore, given the supporting documents and checks involved, gaining access to the telephone booths takes several weeks or even months, especially when individuals, for example non-nationals, have difficulty in obtaining the documents. One Malian man, whose wife's residence document consists only of a mere receipt from the immigration department that the prison authorities have deemed insufficient, is not authorized to call home. "In three months since I've been here, I've never been able to call. I haven't been able to talk with my wife or my little girl. At the beginning it drove me crazy!" He is aware that, without resources, his wife and daughter are in a very precarious situation. Ultimately, for most inmates, the desire to have a cellphone with them probably relates to factors that are not necessarily specific to the world of prison: their widespread use, the freedom they offer, the privacy they allow. The telephone booths, with their restrictions and limitations, their overheard and recorded communications, are far from fulfilling these functions.

But the understanding attitude of some of the directors and guards does not indicate indulgence on the part of the prison management. A notice displayed on the wall at the entrance to the wings of all blocks reminds inmates of the punishments they risk. This "Notice to the prison population," which repeats the terms of the legislation, in simplified form, lists offenses and relevant punishments. At the top of the list, "possession of a cellphone" incurs a maximum disciplinary sanction of 14 days in solitary confinement, one month withdrawal of automatic sentence reduction, and a penal sanction involving police custody, immediate appearance trial, and frequently an additional sentence. In other words, anyone contravening the rule risks a triple punishment. Moreover, it is also likely that discretionary sentence reductions will also be reconsidered, that sentence adjustment will be deferred if it is under consideration, and, in the case of auxiliaries, that they will be removed from their post if their role is deemed to facilitate potential trafficking. So, potentially a sixfold punishment – approximately the same consequences as for "possession of narcotic substances" or "insulting and threatening a member of prison staff." The disciplinary boards tend to err on the side of clemency, suspending the sentence to solitary confinement for a first-time offender, and allowing the administrative and court authorities to decide whether or not to translate this sanction into a deduction from sentence reductions. But it is still a high price to pay for those who were caught.

In an attempt to contain the phenomenon, management sometimes organize prison-wide cell searches. This is how the four garbage bags were filled and the 500 cellphones found. Occasionally, the assistance of an elite squad from the Regional Intervention and Security Teams (ERIS, Équipes régionales d'intervention et de sécurité), who are usually called in when there are disturbances, is enlisted for such searches. On one occasion they were even requested to search 10 auxiliaries' cells, where eight phones were eventually found. "The operation was justified," one director explained to me. "The point was to show all the prisoners that we are here and that nobody is above the rules." The disciplinary boards charged with ruling on these cases nevertheless demonstrated the difficult position in which they found themselves: the auxiliaries were inmates who were appreciated by prison staff, serving as mediators, averting conflict, flagging problems, showing a sense of responsibility. Choosing these allies was a delicate business, and punishing them by removing them from their post meant getting rid of individuals who were essential to maintaining the peace of the facility. However, since the elite squad had been brought in, the procedure had to be taken to its conclusion. The auxiliaries were therefore downgraded, but the warden promised to reinstate them a month later. As far as I was able to verify, this promise was kept.

The telephone, then, is an ambiguous object. It is forbidden, but most inmates have one. It is tolerated, yet management represses possession. The ban on cellphones makes them a valued and desired commodity, the focus of a major trafficking operation whose ramifications extend beyond the prison walls. The illicit trade that has grown up around them is highly profitable. The mafia-type organization it helps to consolidate is a strongly hierarchical structure. Some prisoners enrich themselves with impunity, because they avoid keeping prohibited objects in their cell, while others pay in their stead without gaining any advantages other than possible protection. Like all prohibitions, the ban on cellphones generates not the disorder the prison administration strives to prevent, but a parallel order with sellers and buyers, strong and weak, exploiters and exploited, which the ban unwittingly consolidates. But the spread of cellphones does more than generate inequality and domination within the prison. It also creates users for whom these devices serve not only as a link to their loved ones, but increasingly as help in taking advantage of their many computing and photographic functions. Thus, for prison management, the problem is perhaps less the escape of prisoners than the escape of images that reveal to the public the day-to-day conditions of prison life. These are sometimes comic sketches, which management feels make it an object of mockery, sometimes scenes of violence, which they know contribute to the prison's discredit. Images appear on social media, or even make the headlines of daily papers or television news, and give rise to internal inquiries followed by sanctions.[8] And so a new political meaning emerges: it is no longer merely about freedom and privacy, but about provocation, protest, and public dissemination.

Many among both staff and inmates know that the ban on cellphones is a lost battle, even a futile rearguard action, and that, just as it was once unthinkable that games consoles and computers would ever be tolerated, only for them to now be on sale in the canteen alongside toiletries and cleaning products, these phones will be the next product to be sold by the prison itself, or by the contractor to whom the internal commerce is delegated. Within management, some are apprehensive or reject this development: "I dread us getting to that point, and I am very much against it," states one director. But others anticipate that, like many other reforms in the past, it will be assimilated by the institution, and even beneficial for it: "It will make for calmer, less anxious inmates. It will be the end of one underground economy," a deputy warden predicts. For there is no point in battling against a virtually universal practice that reemerges after each attempt to quash it: the solution is to adapt to it.[9] At that point, as the auxiliary mentioned earlier predicted, most people would forget the thousands of sentences to solitary confinement, and the thousands of additional months served in prison, that have punished the use of cellphones. And a new life will begin for an object that will have become commonplace – and that some will remember was, for a time, forbidden.

* * *

But the life of things that are authorized by prison management is not necessarily any less remarkable than that of those that are banned. A notice posted in the sergeants' office offers an interesting indication of the hierarchy of consumer goods within the prison. It concerns "canteen trades," in other words purchases made legally by inmates, and establishes "an order of priority in the case of insufficient resources," when the individual does not have enough funds in his account, or the sums available to be spent are too low: "1. Tobacco; 2. Correspondence; 3. Television; 4. Toiletries; 5. Drinks; 6. Food; 7. Cleaning products; 8. Fresh produce; 9. Household items; 10. Religious items; 11. Newspapers; 12. Refrigerator." This list, which is indicative of the variety of consumer goods available in the prison, also signals their relative practical, rather than symbolic, value. It is interesting to note that the practical value of symbolic goods – those relating to religion and information – seems secondary to that of practical goods, first and foremost tobacco. One can imagine the fascinating discussions that must have taken place among the prison management when they were drawing up this list, to decide whether toiletries should come before or after television, whether cleaning products should take precedence over household goods, whether soda consumption was more important than reading newspapers, or whether fresh produce will remain fresh for long in summer, in the absence of a refrigerator, which appears last on the priority list.

In this heterogeneous catalogue, tobacco is indisputably the highest-valued commodity, especially for smokers, naturally, who make up a large proportion of the prison population, some of whom even report that they took up smoking in the facility. Of the nine products offered on the canteen coupon filled out when a prisoner arrives at the prison, four relate to tobacco, either rolling tobacco or cigarettes; tobacco is also one of the three products authorized in solitary confinement. This is because it is held by correctional officers to be a pacifying factor, calming prisoners who are in withdrawal, as well as a form of reward or bargaining counter, with the poorest inmates receiving a bonus for good behavior. "Block seniors give it to destitute inmates to buy a bit of social peace," one director explains. "But it is a lethal manna that encourages a form of assistance." At the start of my research, the administration had in fact just taken up the problem, adding tobacco to the so-called monthly indigents' allowance. The list of those receiving this aid was reviewed each month, and included inmates with less than 45 euros, as stipulated by the ministry of justice regulations. The facility's annual budget allocation for purchase of tobacco was 3,000 euros. The assistance mentioned by the warden was thus shifted from an individual relationship with the staff to a bureaucratic relationship with the institution. The meager sum allocated, 10 euros per month, enabled prisoners "to buy one cigarette a day," according to the head of the committee responsible for distributing them. Even if it served in fact to buy the substantially cheaper rolling tobacco, this sum was not sufficient to meet the needs of destitute inmates, whose usual consumption was a pack of cigarettes per day, and who would beg additional tobacco from guards or other prisoners.

For poor prisoners without the funds to buy it – around 25 percent were classified in the "destitute" category, with 5 percent even having less than 10 euros on their account – tobacco sets up a double dependence: a physical dependence on the substance itself, and a social dependence on those who hold it, primarily the staff. It thus serves as a means of controlling the poorest sector of the prison population. But it is also a vector of sociability within the prison. On the return from exercise, or during meal distribution, little packages containing the precious substance are often circulated, generally offered without apparent return, as a sign of comradeship that recalls the sentiments of honor and virtue lauded by Sganarelle in his praise of tobacco, in Molière's play *Don Juan*.[10] During the first round of the night, when brief verbal exchanges often take place through the cell door, it is not uncommon for an inmate to ask a guard to pass a little tobacco to a neighbor, the officer usually agreeing with good grace. The package, slid under the door, is picked up by the officer and passed to the recipient by the same means. The transaction, which involves both inmates and guards, is part of a form of civility that seems paradoxically to be facilitated by the sealing of spaces and the invisibility of bodies – a final communication before the long prison night. But tobacco is often passed without the intermediary of the personnel. From one cell to another within a block, "mice" are thrown underneath the doors in the form of small packages attached to a string that allows the sender to keep control of his gift as he attempts to pass it; such devices sometimes follow complex routes that allow the object to reach relatively distant targets, cooperation and skills of other prisoners allowing, by successive stages.[11] From one window to another in the same block, "yoyos" are also used, consisting this time of packages, also attached to a string, that are swung like a pendulum skillfully accelerated until they can be caught; here again potential intermediaries may help the maneuver until the precious object gets to the ultimate recipient.

These multiple modalities of circulation of tobacco emphasize how central it is to the economic and social life of the prison. One inmate, who has just been called through the window of his cell, comments to me on what the inmate who called him is seeking, saying: "Here, it's currency." Because it is not only tobacco that is smoked: "There's hash. One pack of cigarettes equals one reefer." The risk taken to bring in, possess, and sell marijuana in prison raises the price compared to outside. Thus tobacco, less suspect and less visible than sums of money, can be a way of laundering the drug trade. But tobacco is not only involved in transactions relating to illicit substances. The same inmate offers other examples: "A DVD can be exchanged for a pack of cigarettes. Everything can be exchanged." Nevertheless, it is likely that even if it plays an important role in local transactions because it is legally available in large quantities, tobacco is embedded in a broader context of consumer goods, "including Tercian, Imovane, and Subutex" (three psychotropic drugs), that are exchanged within the facility for other goods, for services, for protection. But its singular feature is that it is both discreet, in that it does not draw attention, and discrete, in that it is divisible into small units. It becomes a substitute for money in a world where the usual financial instruments, from cash to credit cards, have no currency. These glimpses suggest the outlines of a possible economic anthropology of tobacco in prison.

When I began my research, one correctional officer, repeating a commonplace of the prison world, told me: "Tobacco and TV are the key weapons here." At the time, this may have been the case. Although different in nature, addiction to television was no less prevalent than dependence on tobacco. However, the welfare committee of the facility took a significantly different approach to them. In principle, poor inmates had free access to both, but if they had not expressed the desire to work or if they received a sanction for some reason, they were deprived of television but never of tobacco. For management, the latter was a need, while the former was an indulgence. Nevertheless, at this time both goods circulated physically and, as it were, monetarily. The old cathode-ray televisions belonged to the prison's sociocultural association, which rented them to inmates at the prohibitive rate of 32 euros per month, for a cost price of only 7 euros, with the profit being put toward the facility's charitable work (essentially, support of prisoners without resources). In response to failure to pay rental fees, to sanctions on poor inmates, and to frequent breakdowns of the worn-out sets, of which there were in any case not enough, they would be removed from cells, and reinstated as debts were cleared, or the impecunious prisoners served out their punishment, or the sets were patched up. These constant movements, together with the rental fees, fostered a serious black market, which the officers responsible for installing and removing television sets attempted to root out, while block seniors spent a considerable part of their time responding to complaints from frustrated inmates. The transfer of the service to a private operator when the scope of contracted work was renegotiated revolutionized this chaotic system. Flat screens were fixed to the wall in all cells, ending the circulation of sets. A new rental rate of 18 euros per month, which well-informed inmates complained was still twice the rate specified by law, came into force, making it easier for prisoners to watch their favorite programs. There were no more grumbles from inmates. Officers no longer bustled about with equipment. There were no more sets that had mysteriously disappeared and were missing from the inventory. Television had become an integral part of the world of the cell. It was no longer a weapon.

There remains tobacco. It is of economic interest because it combines use value and exchange value: as a consumer product of smokers, it plays an important role in bartering, and its divisibility even makes it equivalent to a currency.[12] But it also bears a political meaning: the staff consider it a means of keeping the peace in the prison, at least among the poorest inmates, whether officers distribute it themselves or act as intermediaries. Finally, its social importance among prisoners should not be underestimated: it creates bonds, offers a sign of welcome to new arrivals, demonstrates solidarity with those without funds. The circulation of tobacco involves a variety of actors, both prison officers and auxiliaries, and of objects, such as "mice" and "yoyos." It is easy to understand, under these circumstances, why the prison administration puts tobacco at the top of its list of priorities for consumer goods.

* * *

The carceral world is fundamentally a material world. The individual entering prison is immediately encircled by this compact, repetitive, and resonant complex of walls and surveillance towers, corridors and metal grilles, walkways and heavy doors, exercise yards and monitoring posts, rubber grids sealing the windows and concertina wire atop the fences.[13] But this materiality is reiterated in the everyday objects, from the most modest to the most sophisticated, from the most permitted to the most proscribed, from the most apparent to the most unnoticed. Ethnographies of prison tend, with reason, to focus on relations between individuals, among inmates, or between inmates and guards.[14] In doing so, they often pass over this other aspect of the experience of prison – the cold, hard mass of the architecture, the coexistence of bars and barbed wire, the long views down the galleries and the blocked horizons of the cells, and everywhere, these mundane things that end up being taken for granted as part of the prison landscape.[15]

It is these ordinary objects and banal things that I have attempted to restore to presence. The three whose remarkable trajectory I have mapped here are in no way spectacular or singular. They belong to the everyday world of prison. All cell doors have a peephole. Most inmates possess or use a cellphone. Many of them consume tobacco, or use it in transactions. And contrary to what might be assumed, these objects and things are not inert: they have a life. It is their biography that I have attempted to sketch – the story of their life in prison.

In evoking the life of objects – and the nature of things – my aim is not to reify one or another, to make them exist as such, to situate them outside the human sphere, or to make them the agents of a new ontology.[16] On the contrary, I seek to show that they only live insofar as they are enmeshed in social relations, and that it is the men and women who acquire them, manipulate them, or transform them that give them their own existence. Thus, the door viewer is an instrument of surveillance for management and a means of resistance for inmates; the two sides wage a sort of undeclared war for its control; each one adapts to the other's maneuvers; management devises new strategies, making the device stronger and punishing vandalization; inmates deploy new tactics, blocking the aperture and refusing to respond to summons. However, the peephole is also used for verbal or even material exchanges between prisoners and guards, the former requesting a service, the latter granting it. Similarly, the cellphone is a tool for interaction with the outside, but also a potential source of prestige; the prohibition on it makes it more precious, and trade in it produces new relations of wealth and power within the prison; management sees it as a simple illegal alternative to the phone booths it has installed, and discovers that its other uses, especially in relation to social media, represent a challenge to its authority and a threat to its legitimacy. In an unprecedented shift in the approach to security, possession of a cellphone, which is condemned by management because of the imagined risks of escape and harassment, is officially championed by the independent authority monitoring the prison system, in the name of maintaining family relations and preventing recidivism. Finally, tobacco ends up at the top of management's list of priorities for consumer goods, because of its assumed power to pacify, while it serves for transactions between inmates. It has its place in the former's charitable activities, and in the latter's etiquette of comradeship. With phones, inmates accumulate capital; tobacco is used as currency. Objects thus have a social life that is also a political and economic life.

But if they live, objects can also die. This is the case of the traditional equipment used to heat food. As one deputy warden told me, the administration has long ignored these techniques: meals were prepared in the kitchen and served in the cells, where they often arrived lukewarm; hot water from the tap, assuming there was any, was supposed to suffice for making coffee. Improbable alternatives were available to purchase, one of limited efficiency, the other of acknowledged toxicity. Inmates therefore resorted to designing their own heating systems. One of these was the immersion heater, also known as a "stinger," used to boil water and, potentially, to heat food in a bain-marie. There was a "canteen," official version, consisting of a resistor that was plugged into the power circuit at one end and immersed in the water at the other; the procedure was slow and relatively expensive owing to the limited life of the device. There was also a "pirated," illegal version, made from strips of tin can separated by a piece of wood and connected to an electrical wire; use of it was subject to punishment.[17] "The problem was that there were often three or four in a cell and they were being plugged in together to heat the water more quickly; that was a heavy load on the power circuits and sometimes caused the fuses to blow." The other system was a portable stove that could be used to cook food. The model available in the canteen worked with fuel tablets of the type generally used for camping, but produced dangerous fumes in the confined space of the cell, and had therefore been banned by the courts. The variation that inmates had invented, known as a "heater," consisted of a receptacle filled with oil, in which a scrap of floor-mop or sheet was inserted to serve as a wick, and over which a pot was placed on a support.[18] "But it often smoked, it made everything black, and then there were the fire risks."

In the opinion of the deputy warden, the authorization of hotplates was consequently "the most crucial reform" that had been introduced in his facility. To begin with, the block seniors were resistant, insisting that "it would never work." But within a few months the new equipment, easily obtained using a simple canteen token, had become standard in almost every cell: "For the sake of human dignity, it's important to be able to make decent coffee," the deputy warden concluded. Thus, with the advent of the hotplates, it was the "stingers" and "heaters" that disappeared from the facility (while they persist in many other prisons across the country). Their existence emphasized the administration's indifference to the well-being of prisoners, while also revealing the inmates' inventiveness and resilience. They therefore had both a moral and a political significance. The introduction of hotplates produces a form of normalization of cooking practices, which is also a normalization of social practices: management has found a technically satisfactory solution that ensures greater safety and less conflict; largely won over to this change, inmates gain in health and comfort, and have less difficulty in accepting their circumstances. This is one further step in the improvement of material conditions in the prison – which also contributes to making it easier to govern.

The life – and death – of objects thus reveal the conflicts and shifts in value systems and power relationships, in social relations and economic structures within the world of prison.[19] These conflicts and shifts do not follow a linear path of development. The hotplates make the cells more agreeable to live in, but the mesh on the windows makes them darker. The end of wide-open peepholes reduces the risk of accidents, but the more robust models limit interactions with staff. The telephone booths facilitate communication between prisoners and their loved ones, but the development of a parallel market in cellphones causes them to fall into disuse. The monthly indigents' allowance reduces disparities among inmates, but the bureaucratic norm dominates over local sociability. This shift back and forth does not mean that ultimately everything remains as it is. On the contrary, it invites us to think about flexible configurations that can never be summed up in a simple observation of improvement or deterioration. It also suggests that we should consider the politics of objects and the morality of things. Finally, it prompts us to develop a different understanding of the material mediations between the two worlds, much more connected than is often imagined, of inmates and prison officers.

6

A Profession in Search of Honor

Given a code of actions, and with regard to a specific type of actions,
there are different ways to "conduct oneself" morally, different ways
for the acting individual to operate, not just as an agent, but as
an ethical subject of this action.
Michel Foucault, *The Use of Pleasure*, 1984

"I never tell anyone what I do for a living. – So what do you say? – Sometimes I might say I'm a public official. It's too shaming, it's too embarrassing to say you're a guard. You hide it. You don't tell anyone." This correctional officer, who was around 40, was generally appreciated by inmates for his amenable nature (he occasionally allowed them an extra shower), and sometimes criticized by the administration for being overfamiliar with them (he tended to call them by their first name). He loved his job, and hoped to move up the career ladder to work one day as a senior officer. After starting out in the catering trade, where he had risen rapidly through the ranks to become manager of a chain restaurant, he chose his new profession as a way to spend more time with his two daughters. There was an element of chance in this move. He was looking for a job in public service, thought he was too old to become a police officer, and instead registered for the examination to become instead a correctional officer. When I met him, he had been working in the short-stay prison for three years. He declared himself quite satisfied with this posting. Outside, however, like half of his young colleagues, he did not tell people what his activity was because of the embarrassment this revelation would cause him.[1] Only his closest family and friends knew what he did for a living.

One warden, in our first meeting, had drawn my attention to the fact that the profession of correctional officer was marked by a kind of opprobrium inherited from the past of prison and guards, and from the history of hard labor camps and their brutal overseers, and reignited through a series of media scandals, shocking testimonies, and critical official reports.[2] He liked to illustrate his remark with an anecdote: "I always remember one old block senior who said to me: 'How do you expect prisons to be well run when in the movies the con is George Clooney and the guard is Danny de Vito?'" Another director, equally disillusioned, made a similar observation in our final conversation: "I don't think there will ever be a TV series where prison officers are the stars." The contrast with movies and television shows about the police, which have been hugely successful in recent decades, was remarkable: even when they are corrupt and violent, as in *The Shield*, the police remain popular.

During the course of my research, I noted many signs of this poor image, which extended to all prison staff. For example, one director told me how, at the end of her third year at a central Paris law school, a professor spoke with the top students in the class, in a workshop devoted to their future careers: "Most people wanted to be tax attorneys. When he came to me, he remembered: 'Oh yes! You're the screw!'" My interviewee was not amused by this "joke." Similarly, when the public television channel wanted to make a documentary about the prison, management had asked one lieutenant and one sergeant to be interviewed, but they had categorically refused: "I don't tell my friends I work in a prison," the sergeant said. While in many other institutions, employees would have been happy to appear in the media, here embarrassment prevailed. And their refusal had much less to do with reasons of security, which are sometimes invoked in relation to public appearances, than with the unease that arose when they mentioned their job. One correctional officer explained to me that, on the few occasions when she had told friends what she did, the often naive questions and the sometimes aggressive remarks she received in response eventually dissuaded her from repeating the experience. Some inmates played on this vulnerability of the staff, referring to them dismissively as "key-rings," and declaring condescendingly that they would not like to "be in their shoes." One of them stated unequivocally: "The guards do a job nobody wants to do." Working in prison is not a path to glory.

It was Everett Hughes who pointed out that in many societies "good people" delegate certain undervalued tasks to certain groups of people who are charged with carrying out what he calls the "dirty work."[3] This thesis, originally focused on tragic historical situations, has been taken up by a number of sociologists of professions as a lens through which to consider stigmatized professions. The job of correctional officer seems to fall into this category. The stigma marking those who exercise this profession relates not only to the acts they perform, such as strip searches, and the manner in which they execute them, often accompanied by a brutal imposition of discipline; it is also, and probably even more, due to the places where they carry out their work, the dilapidated state of prisons seeming to tarnish them by association, and the people they spend their time with – delinquents and criminals. Thus prison officers appear contaminated by the conditions in which they carry out their work. Yet they certainly do not choose these conditions. It is indeed reasonable to assume that they would prefer to work in prisons that are in good condition and not overcrowded, as their unions demand.

Hence it may be considered that French society, like others, produces a mechanism whereby an increasing number of individuals who have committed offenses, or are suspected of having done so, are incarcerated. It does so in an inadequate material setting, with insufficient resources that penalize not only prisoners, but also staff. Although the prison where I carried out my research did not show the worrying signs of disrepair typical of many of the outdated buildings that give French prisons their dark reputation, one director told me that from August onward, his budget no longer allowed him to honor all the contracts with his suppliers, and he had to make careful choices of which of them to pay, as some threatened him with surcharges and even legal action. When a television broadcast reveals the decrepitude of some facilities, or a parliamentary report condemns the squalor of prisons, the shame also extends to those who work in and manage these facilities.

While all staff are potentially touched by this stigma, it affects correctional officers more than others. Analyzing the "moral division of labor" in prison, Antoinette Chauvenet, Françoise Orlic, and Georges Benguigui identify both horizontal and vertical dimensions to it.[4] On the one hand, correctional officers, by virtue of their very tasks of control, discipline, and sometimes repression, perform an activity less socially valued than that of the probation and re-entry counselors, the healthcare professionals, or the private service providers, whose activity is deemed to contribute more to inmates' well-being. On the other hand, the hierarchy within the prison staffing structure naturally places the lieutenants and captains at the top, while correctional officers are at the bottom of the ladder, working in closest proximity with the prisoners. The paradox is that, ultimately, the stigma is borne by the personnel most directly responsible for the execution of the sentence – which itself results from the conjunction of assumptions about the public's expectations, choices made by governments and parliament, and finally the decisions of judges and juries – while society fails to grant them the conditions necessary to do their job satisfactorily.

This state of affairs may seem unjust on principle. It burdens a profession with a moral discredit without taking into account what it actually is, treating it as the inheritor of the grim history of prison, and holding it responsible for its problematic contemporary reality. Awareness of this stigmatization is nothing new, nor are efforts to rehabilitate the profession's reputation. These efforts have passed through changes of name, from "warder" or even "overseer" to "correctional officer," and of role, with the addition of the task of "moral improvement" to that of "guarding" (in a 1919 government memorandum). Numerous measures followed, including changes to the uniform in 1938, the opening of a specialist training school in 1945, the creation of a separate role of instructor in 1949, the introduction of a special status in 1958, the alignment of the command ranks with those of the police in 2003, and the creation of an operational staff structure for correctional officers, with four grades, in 2006. Along with these changes have come a series of regulations aimed at improving conditions for prisoners, viewed by correctional officers with some reservation and often even suspicion. These included the reform of prison discipline in 1996, the creation of the post of General Inspector of Prisons and Detention Centers in 2007, and the abolition of systematic body searches under the 2009 law on prisons.[5] What was granted to inmates in terms of rights often appeared to correctional officers as so many prerogatives being taken away from them. In their view, however, the denigration that they felt they were subject to could, to some extent, be mitigated by material measures, for example increased salaries and the provision of official housing, but also by symbolic acknowledgments. One correctional officer remarked bitterly that after more than 20 years on the job, management had not thought to award him the "prison medal of honor." He saw this as a "lack of recognition" on the part of his facility.

In this regard, one apparently technical innovation assumes major importance, by virtue of both its practical implications and its political import. The memorandum of September 2, 2011 states: "Under the interdepartmental decision of September 30, 2010, the task of prisoner transfer, hitherto the responsibility of the ministry of the interior, overseas territories, territorial communities and immigration, has been transferred to the ministry of justice and freedoms. This measure forms part of the program of rationalization of resources and staff engaged with prison administration."[6] In other words, responsibility for transporting prisoners from the prison to the jurisdiction where they would be questioned by an examining magistrate or tried in court is being progressively transferred from police to correctional officers. This work also includes guarding the prisoner at the courthouse prior to and after his appearance before the magistrate or in court, and the return to prison. It comes under the auspices of the Prisoner Transport Regulation and Organization Authority (Autorité de régulation et de programmation des extractions judiciaires, ARPEJ) and is organized through a system of Prisoner Transport Hubs (Pôles de rattachement des extractions judiciaires, PREJ). Correctional officers quickly took up these administrative acronyms, and often use the term "PREJ" to designate both the task and those who accomplish it.

One director at the prison, at the end of my interview with him, drew my attention to this new regulation: "There's one thing I must mention: prisoner transport is coming back into our remit. We're coming under PREJ management. That means that the prison officers who take on this role will be armed. They'll have a SIG-Sauer in their holster! And for them, that changes a lot. Carrying a gun gives you prestige."[7] He stressed the significance of this move: "These are developments that could help restore the reputation of the profession." His remark revealed how much the fact of not being armed, unlike the national police and gendarmerie, felt to correctional officers like an indication of a lack of public esteem. In the weeks that followed this conversation, I discovered that several guards in the prison were already signed up to receive the training that would allow them to carry out this task.

But the new role also increased prison officers' value in the eyes of others on a more moral level. The warden explained to me how judges had experienced the changeover of staff supervising prisoner transport: "The judges at the district court told us: 'It's nothing like it was when the police did it.' They said the prisoners were much calmer. Inmates feel that the PREJ understand them better, and that makes trials run more smoothly. Also, the magistrates know that prisoners will be debriefed in the transport vehicle, which is important given what sometimes goes on in hearings. And then the PREJ know that their colleagues are going to get the fallout back in the prison, so they handle them carefully." In the view of both this director and the judges, the deeper understanding that correctional officers had of the world of prison meant that their approach was better suited than that of the police to transporting inmates.

I was able to observe this difference myself at the beginning of my research. The first serious incident that occurred was precisely during a prisoner transport operation. It involved two men of African origin, who were accused of assaulting law enforcement officers, and had to be taken to the court for an interview with the examining magistrate. Although they had already been strip-searched by the correctional officers, who had informed the police about it, the latter, who arrived in riot gear, insisted on doing a second search in conditions that were both humiliating and brutal. This provoked a reaction from the two men, who were immediately brought under control and roughly handcuffed. A warden and a sergeant separately told me later that the prison officers themselves had been shocked at these police practices, especially as these were inmates whose irreproachable behavior in the prison was much appreciated. All movements around the facility had been halted for half an hour, as always when a serious incident occurs. With the new measure that placed prisoner transport under the responsibility of trained correctional officers, it was hoped that such problems would become less common.

* * *

When I began my study at the prison, I had just completed a long period of research in a police precinct in the Paris region, and more specifically with its anticrime squad; because of this, I was constantly drawing a mental comparison between prison guards and police officers. And I was not the only one to do this.[8] One deputy warden responsible for human resources told me that correctional officers were "constantly comparing themselves" with law enforcement officers, especially as they felt the police treated them as "sub-professionals." The parallel between the two professions was certainly justified, on a number of levels. First, correctional officers and police officers have similar sociological profiles: they are generally of working-class background, many of them coming from small or medium-sized provincial towns, often in northern France.[9] Second, the same individuals have often taken the exams for entry into both prison administration and law enforcement: in this case they are generally falling back on the former, having failed at the latter.[10] Third, members of the two professions deal with the same clientele, because it is ultimately a selection of those stopped by the police who end up incarcerated under the supervision of guards: these are mainly young men of minority urban working-class background.

The same profile, the same exams, the same clientele. On first reading, it is mainly accidents of fate, such as passing or failing a test, that differentiate the two career paths, placing some on the street and others in prison. Of course this picture needs to be refined, shaded, and adjusted. A higher proportion of correctional officers originates from the Overseas Territories; some have distinctive career trajectories that do not correspond to the path sketched above; some prisoners, particularly those accused of sex offenses or terrorist activities, do not reflect the kind of people the police typically deal with. At the risk of simplifying the issue, we can nevertheless say that these are two professions with similar sociological characteristics, dealing with comparable groups, in radically different environments. And their relation to the world, and especially their relationship with their clientele, are altogether distinct. This is what my two studies, as well as others, tend to show.[11] The inmates seemed to confirm this, for example when they compared the treatment they were subjected to by the police, especially in custody, with the way they were looked after in prison, even after the arrival phase.

Police officers perceive society as hostile, maintain a relationship of distance with those they deal with, often offer provocation or act aggressively toward them, and openly express racist or xenophobic opinions amongst themselves. Prison officers suffer from the lack of regard from society, often treat prisoners with familiarity, are frequently flexible in their attitude toward them, and rarely raise issues of origin or color in their conversations. These are generalizations based on my observations, with exceptions and variations in the case of both professions, to which I shall return. In particular, the fact that prison staff are generally accommodating (as I have seen and as most of the inmates I interviewed confirmed) does not mean, on the one hand, that they cannot be inflexible or even contrarian, making the daily life of inmates unbearable, or, on the other, that even agents who usually behave appropriately may not manifest violent reactions in tense situations. In prison, everyone was aware of this, both the guards and those they guarded.

All the directors to whom I pointed out this parallel between the two professions were intellectually interested and personally concerned, since, even if they did not raise the subject with me directly, the competition for image and status between prison guards and police officers was repeated at the top of the hierarchy, in the relations between wardens and commissioners, here again to the symbolic and professional advantage of the latter compared to the former. One of the prison directors offered me his theory: "There's a difference in scale between law enforcement and correctional facilities. When you're in law enforcement, you can be a detective, a patrolman, a technical expert, a top sleuth, a secret agent, a super-trained agent with the

Anti-terrorist Brigade, a social worker with the roaming Police Assistance unit. A correctional officer does all of that in just one job. In prison you have to be a beat officer keeping the peace, a psychologist and confidant, a firefighter with a paramedic's certificate for cell fires, a riot officer dressed like Robocop to maintain order. Public opinion doesn't appreciate everything a guard is asked to do. The reason I've been in prison administration for 20 years is because of the esteem I have for this profession, which sorely needs recognition." Another warden suggested a different interpretation: "The difference in the relationship police and prison officers have with the people they deal with is a question of space–time. The police officer travels to get to somewhere where something is wrong; he arrives at an event with a problem; the relationship is always going to be conflictive. In prison, on the contrary, the relationship is calm, and it can only be that way because otherwise things very quickly go downhill since they live together; they share the same space of communal life." The two directors agreed that prison staff were more worthy of esteem than law enforcement officers.

These two representations of correctional officers incorporate a measure of idealization, or advocacy, for a profession that is unjustly devalued in their eyes. On the one hand, asserting the multitasking of guards probably understates the fact that most of their work consists of accompanying prisoners to the showers, the yard, or the workshops, and responding to mundane requests relating to a medical appointment, a canteen order, or a leaking washbasin. On the other, all criminologists emphasize the diversity of tasks and skills that a police patrolman also needs to master. As for the calmness and equilibrium in the guard–prisoner relationship, they are contradicted both by the observable tensions between the two, which can quickly flare up into incidents, and the power relations, which are always present, even when the two parties exhibit a form of reciprocal respect. In these two aspects, the parallel with the police suggests similarities rather than the differences. But to explain the latter, and particularly the fact that guards in their prison display greater civility than the police on the street, even when they are dealing with very similar individuals, two elements in the two directors' analyses are worth considering: the qualitative and quantitative aspect of the work and the way it is embedded in the dimensions of space and time.

Police activity is sporadic, composed of occasional incidents punctuating long hours on patrol during which nothing happens. Furthermore these incidents, when they arise out of telephone calls from residents, often prove to be errors, hoaxes, or simply requests for assistance that are made too late, generating frustration rather than arrests. When they arise from the officers' initiatives, they consist mainly of stop and search of individuals and their vehicles, which may give rise to charges for possession of drugs, illegal residence, or insulting the police and resisting arrest if the interaction degenerates into confrontation. Law enforcement agents' relationships are thus less often with the victims of crime than with selected groups of the population, especially in working-class neighborhoods, independent of whether or not any criminal act has been established. Arrests must be generated in numbers sufficient to meet the institution's expectations. By contrast, the activity of guards is ongoing, with the rapid and continuous succession of a series of tasks set by a well-honed protocol. Incidents, including those provoked by correctional officers, are not desirable events from the point of view of the institution, for which they only create complications. In short, police officers' experience is one of boredom and unpredictable events, and prison guards' experience one of movement and routinized work. Pressure from the institution tends to favor disorder in the first case, and focuses on maintaining order in the second. In a supposed assault on a police officer, the latter is always given the credit (it is an action that is included in his activity record), whereas a violent altercation is never a positive event for a correctional officer (at most he may be acknowledged to be the victim in the case). More generally, in one profession, an offense is a good that is valued, while in the other, an incident is a problem that is deplored.

The two kinds of work are carried out in very different spatial and temporal contexts. The police circulate in open spaces: the street, the neighborhood, the town. They usually travel in a vehicle that distances and protects them from local residents. They have intermittent, brief interactions with them, rarely lasting more than a few minutes. Correctional officers work in a confined environment: the monitoring post, the walkways, the prison. They move among the inmates, who pass close by and even brush past them as cell doors are opened and closed, as prisoners go down to and return from exercise, enter and leave the visiting areas. They are constantly together, and, although they rotate daily between blocks and the population of the prison is large and shifting, the correctional officers come more or less to know the inmates, to be cognizant of the offense that has led them to prison and of their history before they arrived. These differences have two types of consequences.

First, in terms of the perception of their security, police officers rarely feel endangered by those they deal with. On the contrary, they emphasize the fact that they fear nothing; this is all the easier for them because they have little contact with the people they deal with and, when they do, it is generally in a power relationship that is strongly in their favor, by virtue of both their numbers and the weapons they carry, which they resort to in case of difficulty. Outside their work, they often live far from their precinct, are unlikely to meet individuals they have dealt with, and, if they do, are unlikely to be identified by them given the fleeting nature of the prior interactions in the neighborhoods. Conversely, correctional officers always feel potentially under threat: this is the case within the facility, because of the physical proximity, but also because of the imbalance in numbers and the lack of weapons; it is also true outside, and this is one of the reasons prison staff often give for not deliberately provoking prisoners since, they say, they might meet them one day in the shopping mall or on a street corner; stories of such encounters circulate, and two-fifths of the staff live in the area in which the prison is located. In both cases, the assessment of the danger is subjective; indeed, in

France, on average, two police officers are killed in the line of duty each year, almost always by people involved in organized crime, while it is more than 20 years since a prison guard has been killed by an inmate.

Second, with regard to their awareness of those they deal with, since the police know little if anything about the individuals with whom they interact, they can have a preconceived idea of them as criminals or even enemies, thereby justifying their distant or aggressive attitude toward them; indeed, they are usually incapable of distinguishing among their clientele because the only clues they have to interpret them are descriptors such as neighborhood, age, clothing, or skin color, which are the subject of unfavorable prejudices and lump together all those who present the same characteristics. Guards, by contrast, can go at least partially beyond these assumptions, insofar as living amongst prisoners allows them to develop a degree of discernment that incorporates the presence or absence of particular human qualities such as seriousness, honesty, humor, self-control, and above all relationship skills like discretion, politeness, avoidance of conflict, respect for discipline, authority within the group – all features that will inform the approach they adopt toward a given individual. This knowledge does not prevent, and even sometimes promotes, hostile attitudes, persecutory practices, and discriminatory conduct, but it usually allows officers to adjust their behavior by not restricting inmates to the generic categories of their social background, minority origin, or crime.

As Alison Liebling states, the sociology of guards has much to gain by taking inspiration from the sociology of the police.[12] She notes in particular that a number of elements identified in studies of the law enforcement agents also apply to correctional officers, whether that be the use of discretionary power, the preference for informal rules, or recourse to verbal authority rather than physical force. But in my view an important, and complementary, question involves thinking also about the differences between the two professions, which may of course vary depending on national contexts, but which present structural features related both to the work itself and the way it is directed by the institution, and also to the relationship with space and time, with all the issues it raises in terms of security and intersubjectivity. One marked difference in this respect concerns the question of race and ethnicity.

*   *   *

The most sensitive position in the prison workshops – and from the point of view specifically of security, in the whole of the facility – was that of "verifier," a role the guard supervising this part of the prison described to me as equivalent to "foreman." In addition to the technical skills required, it involved a special relationship of trust on the part of the prison administration, because the inmate who occupied this position was the only person authorized to go out (accompanied, of course) into the delivery yard, where the trucks loaded with products coming in to be modified in the workshops, or going out again, arrived and departed. During my research period, this inmate was a Roma of Romanian origin. Considered from an outsider's perspective, this might seem remarkable, but from the point of view of the prison, it was unsurprising.

It was indeed a noteworthy fact at a time when stigmatization of this population had reached an unprecedented level in France, to the point where the policy of "breaking up Roma camps" spearheaded by President Sarkozy had been condemned by the vice-president of the European Commission in 2010, and interior minister Manuel Valls's remarks about their "lifestyle" had been the subject of a complaint for inciting racial hatred filed by the French Movement Against Racism and For Friendship Between Peoples (MRAP, Mouvement contre le racisme et pour l'amitié entre les peuples) in 2010. The main accusation against the people targeted by Sarkozy's policy, and Valls's remarks, was that they lived "from plunder and theft, not just on fresh air," as the parliamentary deputy and mayor of Marseille put it.[13] The fact that a position incorporating two levels of trust, since it involved both transport of goods and relationships with people outside the prison – in other words, a risk of both theft and smuggling – should be entrusted to a Roma appeared all the more significant given that this group was massively overrepresented in the facility, and that the inmates belonging to this minority had often been convicted precisely of theft.

However, from the viewpoint of the staff, there was nothing remarkable in this decision. Everyone knew that the Roma rarely posed problems in prison. At the assignment committee meetings they were generally provided a place, as they wished, in blocks with their "gypsy cousins" – an expression habitually used by the Roma inmates themselves as well as the guards; and they were given priority on the waiting list for the workshops when they expressed the desire to work, not only because they were "indigent" and therefore took precedence, but also because they worked quickly and competently. Admittedly, the tasks assigned to them did not require any specific skill, but their productivity was sometimes double that of other inmates, and as they were remunerated on piecework rates, they were the best-paid workers in the prison. Under these conditions, it would have been both illogical and deplorable on management's part to deprive itself of such a productive, docile, and honest workforce.

The positive image the Roma enjoyed within the facility was in stark contrast, to say the least, with the powerful prejudice they suffered in the public arena. It suggested two things, one concerning the Roma as a group, the other relating to the staff. First, when placed in conditions similar to those of other inmates, the Roma were capable of inverting their position in the moral hierarchy, moving from being the most excoriated to the most appreciated, and this inversion concerned, moreover, both diligence and probity, two qualities they are supposed to lack. It was hence impossible not to conclude that, once equality of treatment and respect was established, albeit in the particular context of prison, they became in some sense virtuous citizens, thus refuting the essentialist discourse of politicians, according to whom their lifestyle was incompatible with the dominant culture.

Second, when faced with the necessities of the prison world, the staff disregarded popular opinion and judged the qualities of individuals on their merits. They noted that if they were given work, the Roma worked, and that if they were trusted, they earned that trust. They responded to the racist ideology swamping the public arena with a quiet pragmatism. And they did so without even making any great show of it. By a striking coincidence, three days after I had made these observations in the prison workshops, I read in the newspaper that the supposedly center right mayor of Cholet, visiting an area in his town on which traveler caravans had set up camp, had commented: "Looks like Hitler didn't kill enough of them."[14] The courts, with whom the department prefect lodged a complaint, had been extremely lenient toward this public official when he was charged with glorifying crimes against humanity. But the prison seemed impervious to this wave of hatred, and the tolerance it enjoyed from state authorities.

The staff adopt the same attitude toward inmates of African and Arab origin as toward the Roma. While three-quarters of the young men incarcerated in the prison belong to these two minorities, I never observed, either in the many meetings of the committees I sat in on, or in the informal conversations I witnessed, any of the racist remarks or jokes that are so common in the world of law enforcement.[15] Yet there were plenty of comments about prisoners, and no shortage of humor with regard to them. But remarks disparaging individuals on the basis of their skin color or geographical origin seemed to have no place. Moreover, even attenuated forms of racialization, that is, categorizing individuals on the basis of their appearance or any other essentialized trait, were virtually unknown. No one spoke of "blacks" or "Arabs." At assignment committee meetings nationality might be mentioned, or even occasionally religion, but mainly in relation to the practical implications of these attributes, with regard to residence rights and cell allocation respectively – just as reference was made, with similar intentions, to origin in discussions about "travelers" who said they wanted to be housed together. In fact the only expressions of racialization or occasionally of racism, in either discourse or practice, came from inmates themselves, or at least from some of them. White inmates sometimes claimed that they were marginalized, or even harassed, by black or Arab inmates, and took this for a sign of racism, but in these cases it was difficult to distinguish between what related to skin color and what to their alleged offense, given the types of violence and ostracization against individuals accused of sex offenses that are commonplace in the carceral world. Moreover, this interpretation was supported by the fact that black and Arab inmates complained conversely of the privileged treatment that prison staff gave inmates incarcerated for sex offenses, whom they referred to in terms of the crime they were charged with, rather than the color of their skin.

So how are we to understand that prison staff are both color-blind and impervious to racism, even as they deal with an overwhelmingly black and Arab prison population, when one might imagine that (as in public discourse and popular opinion) a confusion could arise between who these prisoners are and what they do, between their appearance and their crime? The fact that there is a significant proportion of men and women originating from "overseas" among the guards might lead their colleagues to restrain themselves so as not to give offense, but it would be as wrong to reduce racialization to an issue of color, forgetting that there are very few prison officers of North African or sub-Saharan origin (whereas the majority of prisoners are of African descent), as to assume without further analysis that the lack of it reflects the impact of diversity policies in the recruitment of correctional officers (such policies having been subject to contradictory evaluations in the countries where they have been introduced).[16] It is possible that the French Republic's ethics as inscribed in the constitution, which asserts the equality of all citizens and rejects all "distinction of origin, race, or religion" plays some role, but the same absence of racism among prison officers is observed in countries with a multiculturalist tradition, where these differences are acknowledged.[17] Moreover, there are also Caribbean officers within the police, and the same constitutional principles of indivisibility are invoked there, but this does not prevent racism and racialization. While these explanations hold some element of truth, we must therefore find others, more cogent and more specific to prison as an institution. I propose two principal reasons: the first relates to the ethos of the profession, and the second to the experience of correctional officers.

On the one hand, like many others, the profession of correctional officer does not consist only of performing rational gestures in order to ensure the operation of a facility, maintain order, and guarantee security. It also incorporates a set of norms and values that inform and influence the way each individual carries out his or her work. These norms and values are manifested less through an explicit, constructed discourse in which they might be uttered spontaneously or described in response to questions from a researcher, than through everyday gestures, such as responses to requests over the intercom or the opening of doors at shower time, or in specific situations such as a refusal to return to a cell or a request to pass a plate of food to another inmate.[18] They are passed on through initial training, professional development courses, exchanges with colleagues, and relationships with senior management, but they also derive in large part from the context provided, and even the spirit manifested by the prison administration at both national and local level. From the point of view of the institution, the individuals entrusted to its care have already been judged and punished for actions linked to their social context in the broader sense. They are therefore already all guilty. When they enter prison, it is accordingly the beginning of a new episode, and it is on this new phase of their lives that they will be tested and evaluated, and perhaps judged and punished.

The separation between outside and inside is sharp enough for differences between individuals on the basis of skin color, national origin, social backgrounds, or even the act that brought them to jail, to have little relevance. On the practical level, inmates are categorized according to the problems they pose, the behaviors they adopt, and their previous history of prison time – all features that have a concrete influence on the work of correctional officers. An inmate may be "destitute," "suicidal," "fragile," "calm," "interesting," "opportunist," "manipulative," "potentially danger-ous," "ill-behaved toward female staff." He is not "black," "Arab," "dealer," or "diddler." Thus, in prison there is no equivalent to the "institutional racism" that has been reported in relation to the police.[19] Within the prison I studied, the directors said they remained vigilant in this regard. But the norms and values instilled by the institution are not the whole story.

On the other hand, correctional officers also have a concrete and direct experience with inmates. Even though they are supposed to maintain some distance with them, for example never shaking their hand, spending time among them every day results in a degree of familiarization, at least with some prisoners.[20] This was demonstrated by the conversations I witnessed at meetings of the assignment committee, for example about bad news that one inmate had received, which prompted sympathetic reactions, or about threats another claimed to have been subject to and cited as grounds for requesting a change of block, which conversely aroused suspicion. It was also revealed by the remarks certain correctional officers made to me, encouraging me to go and see a given inmate because he had a trajectory that I would be sure to find interesting, or explaining why another was in tears with his mother in the visiting room. I ascribed more significance to these gestures than to their pronouncements, for example when a sergeant told me, emphatically: "I never forget that I am dealing with human beings," immediately adding: "Even if in a different context they might not show the same humanity." The second part of his assertion seemed to me to under-mine the credibility of the first.

The directors themselves were proud that the staff were able to develop such relationships with inmates. One of them told me about his experience of the 1998 soccer World Cup – held in France and won by the French team – in the prison he was then managing: "It's a great memory, that World Cup. It was really emotional. At the beginning, all the inmates supported their own teams. But after a few rounds, there was only France. There was such a silence, during every match! The guards were holed up in the cells watching with them. The auxiliaries agreed to help speed up the meal distribution. Every goal, the atmosphere was unreal. It wasn't guards and prisoners anymore. It was the whole national community coming together! Guards and inmates hugged each other every time the French team won. [He paused reflexively.] We share a great deal." But this kind of fraternization arose only in genuinely exceptional circumstances, and I never witnessed any sign of it.

However, if we consider only the elements common to all correctional staff – the ethos of the profession, the experience of prison – we risk losing sight of that which, within this context, makes up the singularity of life stories, career paths, and, ultimately, the various ways of being with prison-ers. These moral variations between individuals are crucial.

*   *   *

"Is Mr. Afouani going to be OK? I heard his niece just passed away. Is he holding up?" Sitting at her computer, the lieutenant is speaking to a guard standing in the open doorway. She is using the opportunity of a brief conversation regarding inmates having problems in her block to inquire about the psychological state of a pre-trial prisoner whose recent loss she has heard about. The vague, reassuring response does not convince her. "Well, I'll try to go and see him, cheer him up a bit," she decides. The office, which she shares with the chief officer, is cluttered with bags of clothing and jugs of white spirit, no doubt because of the decoration work that is under way. The paint on the walls is yellowing and crisscrossed with cracks. The window, which looks onto a small patch of weeds scattered with detritus, is closed despite the summer heat. The reason for the swarms of flies outside, the officer explains, is a septic tank that has not been cleaned in a long time, and which the new service contractor refuses to deal with, arguing that it was the former contractor's job. Working conditions are far from ideal. "This morning a guard swallowed a fly," the chief officer states without emotion.

The return from afternoon exercise is announced on the public address system. The lieutenant goes down to support the team that accompanied inmates to the yard and the correctional officers stationed in the block. She stays in the background. The prisoners come up the stairs from the yard, and greet her as they pass. She responds with a smile. Sometimes they approach her with a request: "Chief, have you had time to reply about my TV?" or: "Chief, am I going to get my cell reassignment?" Often it is she who initiates the exchange: "Mr. Sissoko, I haven't been able to resolve your problem yet," or: "We considered your request this morning, Mr. Desprez, you'll have an answer soon," or: "Did you get your appointment with the doctor, Mr. Belhaj?" In this way, snippets of information are exchanged, concern is shown, and gestures of care expressed in an informal and spontaneous way. Once the cell doors are closed, the block senior summons two men of whose insistent requests she has been notified, and receives them in an almost empty office that serves as a reception room for new arrivals.

The first, a convicted prisoner in his 30s, seems very upset because the money he released from his "savings" is not yet available, owing to an accounting error on the part of the prison, meaning that he has not been able to use the telephone. The lieutenant asks how urgent his call is. The man explains, in a toneless voice, that just as he was getting news about his 5-year-old daughter, who is in the hospital in a coma after falling from a climbing net at the recreation center the day before, the line to his wife had been abruptly cut off because he had insufficient credit. He has consequently been unable to find out about the progress of his child's condition. He seems extremely distressed. The block senior speaks gently, promising him that he will be able to call the next morning. The second petitioner, a young inmate with an arrogant attitude, wants to change his cell. The guard has reported that he threatened to attack his cellmate if he was not reassigned immediately, and that he was insolent to a warden who told him to wait 24 hours. Transfers take place in the morning, but in any case are not made in response to blackmail. The lieutenant reprimands him sharply. The man understands that the battle is lost, and acquiesces to being moved the following day as planned. Request time is over. In the walkways, the final meals are being distributed. Before leaving the wing, the block senior visits the inmate whose niece has just died, offering him her condolences and a few words of comfort. She then rejoins the staff at the main entrance of the facility, waiting for the prisoner count to be validated so that they can leave.

The lieutenant had taken up her post a few weeks earlier, shortly after leaving training school. When she embarked on studying law, her aim was to become a judge. Following her bachelor's degree, she received a master's in sentencing, which she found fascinating: "I got interested in the meaning of punishment," she says. She initially planned to take the examination for judicial protection of minors, but a short course on educational support with the National Student Association for Education in Places of Incarceration (Groupement Étudiant National d'Enseignement aux Personnes Incarcérées, GENEPI), whose volunteers carry out various kinds of pedagogic work in correctional facilities, changed her mind: "I wanted to see if I liked the atmosphere in prison, and I did." She therefore took and passed the examination for the National School of Prison Administration (École nationale de l'administration pénitentiaire, ENAP), where she followed the lieutenant training track. After internships in prisons in the south of France, she was awarded her diploma and was posted to the short-stay prison. There she was discovering a world previously unknown to her, particularly in terms of the prison population: "Here it's the hoods, the projects, petty crime." But she was adjusting well to this new environment and had quickly won the appreciation of her colleagues and subordinates. Like many correctional officers, she said she liked the collegial atmosphere of the work, including the relationship between senior staff and guards. With the prisoners, she was courteous, even considerate, but also able to be firm. In assignment committee meetings, she was one of those block seniors who tend to be conciliatory, especially when the subject under discussion was withdrawal of an inmate's right to work: she often proposed giving the offender another chance.

Clearly, in her case ethos and experience can play only a limited role in her approach to prisoners. It is her first job, she has recently arrived, she does not know the inmates. A deputy warden offers this explanation: "She has a good prison sense. It's instinctual, it can't be taught, it's a gift." But a more sociological interpretation could be proposed. The feeling of empathy she expresses and the sense of justice she exhibits do not result principally from her professional socialization or acquired knowledge. They derive rather from what led her into this profession, in other words what might be called a vocation: her academic orientation toward a degree in sentencing and her discovery of the world of prison through dedicated voluntary work are evidence of an interest in the social aspect of prison work. According to Max Weber, a relationship exists between profession and vocation; in the German word he uses, *Beruf*, this dual connotation – both neutral and ethical, or even secular and religious – is indissolubly present, and the term can be applied equally to a craftsman or a storekeeper, a scientist or a politician. And for the German sociologist, both profession and vocation necessarily have ethical implications for the way people think about their work.[21] To speak of a vocation in relation to a profession is thus not only to emphasize the existence of a calling, as opposed to random chance or constraint, but also to introduce an idea of inclination as opposed to mere rationality. It is possible to want to work in a prison. One can even love the job.

Certainly those I heard speaking of a choice and expressing an inclination were more often to be found among the senior officers and the wardens than among the guards. Not only do the professions and their corresponding ranks enable senior officers to avoid the most difficult elements of prison work, most notably proximity with prisoners and routine tasks, and accede to activity that is more rewarding in terms of both power and prestige, but the sociological and academic profiles of those who take up these posts also offer them a greater range of objective career possibilities. In studies of recent graduating classes of guards, the question about their motivation unsurprisingly produces answers emphasizing "job security" in one-third of cases, and "career advancement" in one-quarter. But it is worth noting that "interest in professions that deal in human relations" comes in third place, roughly equal to "helping to maintain public order."[22] Some older studies, interesting in that they take a longitudinal view, with interviews repeated at different points in officers' careers, even observe that "human contact" tops the list of "what you like about the job of correctional officer" for those entering and graduating from training, subsequently falling off somewhat, but still in second place 10 years after graduation, and cited more often by those with high school diplomas than by those with lesser qualifications. These results might be seen as a refutation of the frequently heard refrain "nobody becomes a prison officer by vocation," with which half of guards say they agree at the start of their studies, and four out of five after ten years on the job.[23] We should not, of course, overestimate the significance of these declarations, as we know that they depend partly on the formulation of the questions, and especially that they reflect the difficulty of gaining access to subtle realities through closed questions. Nevertheless, the responses suggest that individuals' reasons for becoming correctional officers or appreciating the work are deeper and more complex than is usually claimed, even by those working in prison administration.

It might perhaps be better to think about interest in the profession less in terms of a revelation that leads to a sudden desire to work in a correctional facility (a vocation in the literal sense of a calling) than in terms of a prosaic discovery of the realities of the job through daily practice of it (as implied in the contemporary sense of inclination). In other words, it is often through being an officer that people come to find interest in a profession many came into by chance, and in this regard it should be noted that almost all those who become guards have previously worked in other jobs. These previous careers offer useful clues for interpreting the reason why they chose to work in the carceral world.

For example, one correctional officer tells me she first worked as a care assistant, and then as a nurse, but "life circumstances" that she does not further specify led her to move away from her home region and into another job. When a friend mentioned the profession of correctional officer, she thought "it must be interesting." After a disappointing first internship in a prison where she was so bored that she contemplated leaving this career, a second posting in a short-stay facility persuaded her to continue. A few years later, in her new job, she talks enthusiastically about her work: "There's always something to do, it's so lively, and there's the social side too, that's what I like about it." In the canteen distribution post she occupies, a sensitive job because it exposes her to frequent requests and complaints as she moves through the walkways giving each inmate the products he has ordered, she neutralizes conflict by remaining even-tempered and smiling, sometimes harnessing irony with the more insistent prisoners: "I have a good relationship with them. When they get annoyed, I tell them they can lash out at me all they like, but it doesn't do any good. And the few times they've used bad language to me, they've always come to apologize within 10 minutes." While she enjoys joking with them, she does not allow herself any familiarity. "I always call them 'Mr.' I couldn't call them by their first name. Sometimes they ask me: 'Why don't you call us by our first names, officer?' I tell them I'm not their girlfriend. It's my way of showing them respect. For me, it's a question of good manners." She has won the appreciation of the inmates, who clearly enjoy exchanging a few words with an amiable woman. I several times witnessed these interactions, during which she dissipated the tensions that were always high around canteen orders. On one round, a man I know to have a tendency toward provocation comes up to her, saying in a demanding tone: "My refrigerator's leaking, can you change it for me?" She replies brightly, "Sure, Mr. Berghout, but I'm not giving you another until you've paid last month's installment on the old one. So it's up to you. You pay and I change it for you, or you keep the one you have." Understanding that he will not get the last word, the man ventures one or two joking comebacks so as not to lose face, and then goes quietly back toward his cell.

Another guard, with whom I spent long periods in the monitoring post or in the walkways at shower time, has a very different style. He has been working in the prison for five years. Previously, he was an officer in the gendarmerie. He liked the collegiate aspect of the work, and the sports. He was a martial arts enthusiast, and practiced karate. Unfortunately, he explains, his girlfriend "did not like the barracks life and the shifts." He decided to take up another career, in "prisons, because it's more stable," which, he adds with a smile, did not stop his girlfriend leaving him. While apparently more settled, the profession of guard is certainly no less demanding than that of gendarme, and he says that he is more tired after a day at the prison than after a night on patrol in his old job. He now plans to become a sports coach. He describes himself as a "bigmouth" who has even "made the mistake of getting mad with the director." He sums up his relationship with prisoners with a motto: "Me, I'm an asshole with assholes!" As a general rule, he is somewhat cold with prisoners but does not provoke them. However, one day, as an altercation begins, while his colleague attempts to reason with a prisoner who does not want to return to his cell because he believes he has been unjustly treated, I see him immediately intervene with force, pushing the recalcitrant inmate up against the wall. The incident can only end in a transfer to solitary confinement. A further indication of his relationship with prisoners emerges during one of our conversations. He is recounting the story of an incident a few months earlier: as he was with-drawing bills from an ATM machine not far from the prison, he felt a hand on his shoulder, and when he turned around, was punched in the face. He did not recognize his attacker, but heard him say: "You don't belong here, screw!" But he reassures himself, telling me that this incursion into enemy territory was an accident; indeed, he lives with his wife in a neighboring town, at a distance from his former inmates.

It appears that neither of these officers had an initial calling for working in prisons. It was a path they took for want of anything better. One wanted to be a nurse, the other a gendarme. But these initial choices inform the way they experience their new profession – with enthusiasm in one case, disillusionment in the other – and the way they behave with prisoners – one aiming for calm, the other seeking out confrontation. There is little doubt that for the former nurse, an ethics of care continues into the work of prison guard, while the former gendarme reveals a politics of power deriving from the legitimate use of force. This results in two distinct ways of engaging with the profession: "When they get annoyed, I tell them they can lash out at me all they like, but it doesn't do any good," is in this respect the opposite of "As I always say: 'Me, I'm an asshole with assholes.'" It is of course tempting to see this contrast as the effect of a gender division in the profession: the female officer, in a feminine role that combines solicitous-ness and charm, and the male officer, in a masculine posture that plays up physical power through martial arts and bodily control. But rather than a gender division, what is at stake here is a distinction of style, since the two sexes can also play against type.

One of the officers most hated by inmates was a young woman nick-named "The Rod" in reference to both her verbal aggressiveness and her masculine appearance. She compensated for her short stature by adopting an attitude of offensive superiority toward the prisoners. Readily combat-ive, she inflamed their frustrations by refusing them the meager favors her colleagues would grant. One man told me how one day during Ramadan, when, as on previous days, he had "gone down to exercise in flip-flops," the block senior had seen him and let him pass, but the female officer had called him back, telling him he was not allowed to go out in that footwear and must return to his cell. He became angry: "She got riled up. I spat at her. I got two weeks in the hole for that." She was one of the officers prisoners claimed would provoke them. On one occasion, she had been challenged close to her home by individuals formerly incarcerated at the prison, who retained a grudge against her for her brutal, insulting ways.

In contrast, there was a young Caribbean man who was gentle and affable, and was well liked by prisoners for his human qualities and his good humor. Formerly a salesman for a private company, he had imported the motto of his previous profession into his new one, and told me: "This job is all about communication, you have to talk to the inmates." He told me of one incident that had touched him. One day when he went to his district tax office, a man came up to him and said, "Officer, don't you recognize me?" Seeing the officer's look of puzzlement, he told him his name and added gratefully: "It's thanks to you that I got through!" I do not know what had earned the officer this tribute, and he himself claimed to still have no inkling of the debt the former inmate owed him, but the pride with which he recounted the episode clearly showed how much this social aspect of the profession – the possibility of helping, or even redeeming the men entrusted to his care – mattered to him.

Prisoners are well aware of this ethical aspect of the work of correctional officers and sergeants, as well as of the directors. They are able to distinguish between different members of prison staff. One inmate in his mid-30s, aiming to demonstrate to me the influence he wielded in his wing, told me how a few weeks earlier, coming back from exercise, one of his fellow inmates had insulted a guard who did not allow him to take a shower: "He yelled at him: 'You're a son of a bitch.' I said to him: 'Why are you talking to him like that? He's one of the cool guards.' The guy stopped. As long as the guard shows us respect, that's all that matters. We show him respect in return." Another about the same age, despite being highly critical of the institution as a whole, acknowledged: "I have to say, the guards deserve credit, because there are some prisoners, you should see how rude they are to them. Me, when some of them call me by my first name, if they're friendly, I don't mind. But there are other ones that talk to us like you'd talk to a dog." Thus a moral topography is sketched within the prison, with its good guards and its bad screws. Inmates sometimes even put forward a sort of spontaneous sociology that is not without accuracy: "There are some here who wanted to be cops. But they failed, so they became guards. And they behave like cops."

The prison management plays an important role in the dissemination of a particular spirit among staff and in the regulation of their practices. The weekly meeting at which they discuss problems in the facility was described by the warden as a "values meeting": he asserted that it enabled them to "put across principles" regarding "relations between officers and inmates," for example with regard to "abstaining from any racist remarks." Nevertheless, the guards more easily accepted this general discourse than the evaluation and sanction procedures applied to any inappropriate behavior, an area for which one deputy director had more specific responsibility.

This was particularly true in cases where it was clear that the officer concerned had voluntarily provoked an incident, or simply managed it badly, by being rough or insulting. These were often officers "known for repeated incidences of such conduct," or occasionally "a young officer who was out of his depth in the situation." In such cases the guard had to be called to order, or warned; personal interviews and even special training would be recommended. Nevertheless, at the disciplinary board a sanction on the inmate, possibly suspended, would be deemed necessary in order to avoid appearing to contradict the guard, and thus displeasing him. This was a delicate balance that was not always satisfactory for those responsible for maintaining it, but they knew it was key to the smooth operation of the facility.

As a general rule, we can analyze the moral work of prison officers, particularly their relationships with prisoners, as the product of two levels of moral thinking, as distinguished by Foucault.[24] At the institutional level, there is a moral code that goes beyond what the law defines as a code of good professional practice. This is a set of norms and values produced and put into practice by both the national administration and the local management, which define not only appropriate conduct, but also practices for evaluating and sanctioning behavior. In this respect, the European Prison Rules, and the law on prisons, represent significant developments. But it is clear that the introduction of these is not sufficient to account for the actual discourses and practices of officers, which are notably diverse. Thus, at the individual level, it is possible to identify ethical subjectivities, that is, ways of being and behaving, that cannot be summed up as the simple application of a code. Depending on their personal and family history, their religious or political convictions, their previous experience of other professions or organizations, the sensitivities and social relationships they have developed within the prison, the experiences or events that have marked them, prison staff – from directors to guards – may be more caring or more indifferent, more inclined to treat inmates with respect or with disregard, more aware of the social dimension or more attached to the repressive aspect of their work. Rather than a code, then, this is an ethic. It may manifest itself in what one inmate described as "trivial things, a look, a smile, a sympathetic remark." Conversely, in an officer who does not share this ethic, it may be expressed through indifference, brutality, provocation, or cruelty. And this ethic depends in large part on the view that officers have of prisoners and their condition.

*   *   *

There is a widely shared trope among prison staff in this regard. It accounts, at least in part, for a representation of the carceral world that is widespread within it, and perhaps also for the different ways of behaving with inmates. It more frequently arises among guards than among senior officers and directors, but it may be heard in more or less explicit form at all levels of the hierarchy. Significantly, however, I never heard any of the probation and re-entry counselors use it. It could be called the trope of happy captivity. It rests on a sort of simple syllogism. Major premise: inmates live in deplorable conditions in their usual place of residence. Minor premise: in prison they are given good living conditions. Conclusion: "They are better off here than at home."[25] This is the most hackneyed cliché among prison staff.

One deputy warden offered me a quite comprehensive version of it: "Here, inmates live in comfort, they are given food and linen, and get their laundry done. They even benefit from a degree of attention from directors, correctional officers, re-entry counselors. They've got all of that in the prison, when they often don't have it outside. Even security – the projects where they live are much more dangerous than prison." A common variant asserted that prisoners lacked nothing, except freedom. One guard, who had recently entered the profession late in his career, even believed that this explained recidivism and the repeat incarcerations: "Prisoners are deprived of nothing apart from freedom. They have everything. For a lot of them, coming here is like going on vacation. They spend two or three months here. They leave. And then they come back for another few months." Some felt that the well-being prisoners were alleged to experience in prison led to abuse that called for appropriate responses. Another officer, who had been on the job longer, expounded on this pedagogic mission: "You know, they feel good here. And they take advantage of that. They think they're in their own home. They haven't understood the difference between here and outside. That's what we have to get through to them." The first of these two officers was generally accommodating and benevolent, the second more inflexible and sometimes impulsive. Their common viewpoint was no indicator of how they would behave toward prisoners.

Even if it is not universally shared (or, at least, not universally expressed), this representation of the inmates should lead to reflect on two points. First, there is, in the world of prison, a significant social distance, both objective and subjective, between those who guard and those who are guarded. Objectively, whether their cultural capital is more limited (the guards), or more substantial (the directors), prison staff rarely share the sociological characteristics of a prison population that is largely of Arab or African origin and living in disadvantaged urban neighborhoods. Subjectively, they consider this population even more different from themselves than they in fact are; implicit moral disapproval of the actions that have led these individuals to prison widens the gap a little further, probably more obviously among the guards who, coming from similarly modest backgrounds, feel the need to accentuate the distinction between themselves and those they are in charge of. This twofold distancing can thus generate a preconception, born of ignorance and tinged with contempt, that in their own homes prisoners live in material and social abjection. Second, the prison staff show a sort of cognitive indifference to inmates' experiences. Even when they do witness the material conditions in which many of the prisoners find themselves, the emotional distress they face, and the multiple hardships they themselves have helped to create, it is as if they cannot see them. Or as if, though seeing them, they repress or relativize them through various forms of denial: prisoners are manipulative, they play the victim, they have everything they want, and so on. The reality in front of their eyes seems not to penetrate to the level of knowledge about the carceral world that they might draw on in both their discourse and their actions. The social distance explains the first premise of the syllogism (they live in deplorable conditions in their own homes). The cognitive indifference underlies the second (they live in good conditions here). The combination of the two explains the conclusion (they are better off here than at home).

If we consider the actual conditions of the carceral world, and the way they are experienced by most inmates, it is remarkable that the viewpoint shared by so many prison staff involves such a denial of this reality and of how it is perceived. I suggest that where it pertains, this denial has two distinct functions. For some (I believe the minority), the trope of happy captivity justifies a harsher approach, both in their interpretation of the prison rules and in their own behavior toward prisoners; they sometimes show a propensity to create conflict or exaggerate tensions and sometimes inflexibility in their grasp of situations and the application of sanctions. For others (who I think are the majority), it makes the daily spectacle of incarceration of the individuals they are in charge of, and with whom they have been taught not to get too close, seem bearable; they try as well as they can to make prison life a little more tolerable, or at least not to make it worse. This attitude is therefore a defense mechanism that, in the first case, justifies harshness (what prisoners have is always already too much), and, in the second, neutralizes sensitivity (all in all, they don't have too much to complain about). It is perhaps this capacity of the trope of happy captivity to operate in both these almost contradictory moral registers that explains its widespread dissemination.

One variant that I heard on occasion added an interesting element of international comparison. Some guards praised the prison system of the United States. One of them, who was reputed to have good relations with inmates, once said to me apropos of nothing: "I think we should be harder on them. Not like they are in the US, but harder than we are in France today." I asked him for an example: "Well, they should have to wear a uniform. Maybe not fluorescent orange or yellow like over there, but still ... So everyone's dressed the same." A few weeks later, another guard, who similarly had no problems with inmates himself, described an episode during his training: "At the school, there was an American guard who'd come to France on a two-year internship in France. He told us about the system in the US. I think it's better. There's more distance between guards and prisoners. Here, we're too close to them. They do what they like." Thus, while it was surprising given the situation of the prison system in the United States, and the recurrent revelations there of scandals involving prison staff, this American dream expressed a desire for order. If the inmates were too comfortable in the prison, they might become overfamiliar, not keep to their place, no longer be different enough, in appearance and behavior, from correctional officers. This fear of contamination, and desire for demarcation, was also fed by the nostalgia of older officers, who would reminisce: "When I started 20 years ago, they'd never have insulted a guard." The trope of happy captivity thus revealed a diffuse anxiety about a carceral world where changes felt to have been too rapid were seen as introducing new dangers. These dangers, which the correctional officers raised in their conversations and which were echoed in the demands of prison staff unions, were expressed in terms of both security problems and proximity with inmates.

The paradox was that, as correctional officers, and prison staff in general, acquired increased respectability in society through a series of practical and symbolic modifications to their professions, this sense of danger gained greater hold. The two phenomena were due to the same changes. For example, recognition of inmates' right to defend themselves, or challenges to systematic strip searches, moved them a little further away from the image of the "screw," but were perceived as exposing them to new perils. The law on prisons tended to "humanize" the tasks they were charged with, but worried them. Not all exhibited the same anxiety. Some of the correctional officers saw the improvement of their status, the recruitment of more female officers, the raising of educational standards for entry into training school, the transfer of responsibility for prisoner transport, and the publication of a code of professional practice as signs that their profession was becoming more honorable. They observed concrete evidence of this in the normalization of their relations with prisoners; a degree of familiarity, which some dreaded, also made their work easier. In the end, they had to face the fact that their fate was linked to that of the inmates, and that they too lived in prison.

One correctional officer put it to me in simple terms. Before entering this profession, he had had other jobs: clerk at the ministry of the interior, security assistant in the national police, and, finally, agent at the vehicle pound. He might have liked to enter the police force, like his three brothers before him. But the examinations he passed were those for the prison service. He had graduated five years earlier, and had learned to love his work. Inmates seemed to appreciate him: "I always call them 'Mr.' It's a question of respect!" Perhaps he felt close to them to some extent. Like one-third of the inmates, he was of Arab origin, and like around half of them, he was Muslim. He fasted during the month of Ramadan, but in order not to stand out from his colleagues, most of whom knew nothing of his religion, or at least nothing about its practices, he had not asked for his shift times to be adjusted. At the end of the morning we spent together in the workshops, where he was supervising activities, he remarked: "There are some guards who say this isn't their life, here. But of course it's part of our lives. Prison is actually a big part of our lives." To recognize this meant also recognizing that they themselves were part of the institution for better or worse – that is, in both its production of violence and its protection of rights.

7

Violent, All Too Violent

There is I know not what of Servile in Rigour and Restraint; and I am of
the opinion, that what is not to be done by Reason, Prudence and Address,
is never to be effected by Force.
Michel de Montaigne, *Essays*, 1580

"He's not a bad guy: it's just he's fed up with being in his cell," said a guard
whose slight, youthful frame offered a marked contrast with the impressive
musculature of the prisoner of whom he spoke. The man was standing in
front of the monitoring post where the young guard was on duty. Since the
rule was that, with the exception of auxiliaries, all inmates must be locked
into their cell as soon as they reached their block, the presence of this
imposing man who remained standing for some time in front of the duty
officer was somewhat unexpected. Several times, seeing him moving around
the wing as he pleased, I had wondered at the unusual tolerance he enjoyed.
The reason I had just been given hardly qualified as an explanation, for if all
that was required to be allowed out of one's cell was no longer to be able to
bear being locked in, such license should have been granted to practically all
prisoners. But ultimately, the guard's comment said more than it appeared
to. Beneath the trite formula, it revealed a level of goodwill unusual in the
facility, the specific reasons for which I discovered only later.

Apart from his weightlifter's physique, one other detail made the man
immediately remarkable: one of his eyes was covered by an enormous dressing, giving him a sinister appearance. That day, he was wearing a tee-shirt
with the French national flag on the back, overlaid with the words: "Too
much social injustice and racial discrimination leads to revolution"; on the
front was the word "France," and beneath it "It's gonna blow." As I passed
him, I heard him mutter unnervingly, "Weirdo!" Later that day, I decided
nevertheless to speak with him, and he offered me an interview, not in his cell
as most other inmates did, but in the office where the directors meet with prisoners. Given the efforts he had gone to in honing his formidable appearance,
I did not dream of objecting, even though I sensed that there was a substantial
element of performance in his self-presentation as a "tough guy" in the prison.

With a skillful mix of sincerity and theatricality, he offered me selected morsels of his story, beginning thus: "I'm not proud of it, but I'm a regular. If you want to know about prison, I'm your man." No doubt in order to impress me, he recounted how, during a previous stay in a long-term facility, he had given an interview to a journalist investigating long-stay prisons. But he also seemed genuinely motivated by the idea of contributing to the dissemination of knowledge about the conditions of life in a carceral environment, and taking my project to heart, expressed concern about its outcome: "There are stacks of people writing books about prisons. How are you going to get people interested in yours?" Perhaps this was why he confided to me that he himself also wrote. Rap, he said specifically. When I asked him if he could show me any of his writing, he explained that the texts he had were illegible, but after regaling me with a brief improvisation on a dozen or so rhymes, he promised to write me out a text that evening – and he was as good as his word.

As I learned a little later from the prison staff, the man, then 27 years old, was a long-term habitué of the facility. Having grown up in one of the housing projects in the region, he had been incarcerated for the first time when he was only 16 years old, and had served a number of terms, of increasing length owing both to the harsher penalties he received for offenses legally defined as recidivism and to suspended sentences that were then activated. His most recent conviction, he told me, was for driving under the influence of alcohol, compounded by an offense of resisting arrest followed by an altercation with police officers that had been classed as assault, for which he had been sentenced to two years' imprisonment, reduced to 18 months on appeal; an old suspended sentence had been added to this. "When I was young, I was easily led. I fell into a vicious cycle. You leave school early, you get involved in petty crime. It's a spiral, real hard to get out of once you've got sucked into it." At the time, he was relatively undersized and weak, and other juveniles in the facility had taken advantage of his vulnerability by making him their "victim." One day, a trap was set for him by calling him through his cell door. He came up to look through the peephole, and was wounded in the eye by a blunt instrument. He lost the sight in that eye. In reaction to this traumatic incident, he had gone to great lengths to effect a radical transformation of his image, starting with altering his physical appearance through bodybuilding and protein supplements, until he achieved the sculpted form revealed by the athletic gear he wore. His attitude of defiance toward the institution and its agents derived from the same effort to reverse others' perception of him as a vulnerable inmate. The staff had mostly adapted to this situation, and the exception to the normal operation of the facility that it entailed.

He himself was lucid about his position. When I asked him why he enjoyed these small privileges, he replied: "Three reasons. There are some who've known me for 10 years. There are also some who are scared of me. And then there are the ones that are cool." Sympathy from the first, fear from the second, indiscriminate tolerance from the last: he aroused various reactions which, taken all together, accounted for the special treatment he received. Even when he seemed to be defying them, the institution and its agents paradoxically considered him their protégé, provided he did not go beyond certain limits. On the day I interviewed him, he had had a long conversation with a deputy warden, who had, with some difficulty, managed to persuade him to begin a training course, as the first stage toward potential re-entry into society that had obviously been impossible during his previous terms. Nevertheless, this emerging project, and the delicate balance on which it rested, was destined to fizzle out. Not all the staff shared the same view of his case. Some found it difficult to accept the privileges he had acquired over the years.

The day after our conversation, when I arrived in his block, I learned that he had just been assigned a cellmate. "There are sure to be problems," said the young guard who was once again in the monitoring post. Among the favors the man enjoyed was that of being alone in his cell. It is, one might note, remarkable that a right that has been enshrined in legislation for more than a century should now be seen as a favor, but this was the inevitable consequence of prison overcrowding; very few were actually able to exercise this right. In the present case, apart from the fact that making the man share his cell with another inmate seemed problematic, given his physical strength and difficult temperament, there was a more technical justification: he had a medical certificate from one of the physicians working in the prison stating that he should remain alone in his cell because of a chronic infection in his injured eye. None of these factors, however, carried much weight in face of the intransigence of the personnel, who were determined that this time the recalcitrant inmate would be put in his place.

When the chief officer informed him that he was to have a cellmate, the man became angry. He reminded her of the commitments the medical and prison staff had made to him. It was no use. He had in fact immediately understood the personal stakes in the power relationship between them: "I know you don't give a shit about me. But you don't speak to me, I don't speak to you: that's OK." Confronting him, however, the chief officer did not even attempt to justify or discuss the decision. The more angry he got, the calmer she became, despite being visibly tense. Her silence provoked the expected effect, increasing the exasperation of the man, cornered by her inflexibility. When she asked him to go back to his cell, he refused, saying he preferred "to go to the hole." Without offering him any possibility of backing down honorably, she then called for reinforcements. It took no fewer than four officers to subdue and handcuff the man, who was accompanied by a dozen guards, pushing him in front of them down the walkways in an uproar of yelling and shoving, to the solitary confinement unit, where he was locked in an empty room. This was the last stage before isolation: the humiliating strip search. Given the man's strength, exceptional measures were taken. Three correctional officers went off to put on the impressive body armor, with its breastplate, shin guards, and protective padding at the wrists and shoulders. This level of force was deemed necessary in order to subdue the man if he resisted. He did not.

Obviously, I did not witness this final operation, which took place in an atmosphere of febrile tension. Disturbed by the sequence of events, the refusal to negotiate, and the brutality of the intervention, I understood that it was no coincidence that this conflictive situation had been generated only a few hours after a training course had been negotiated and promised to this difficult inmate. Evidently, some felt too much was being done for him. The deputy warden told me a little later how sorry she was, in light of her "personal investment," that things had turned out so badly: "I would like to have been informed that he was going to be doubled up, so that the arrangement made sense with mine, and I could have taken it up with him in support of the chief officer. I would also have preferred that rather than managing the situation by physical conflict, in line with his expectations, and putting him in isolation, staff had pursued a dialogue with him until he accepted being doubled up." The deputy warden took the view that "we have to take into account the fact that it is the prison system that has made Mr. Rezaoui what he is." The chief officer would not necessarily have disagreed. But she had drawn diametrically opposite conclusions on the attitude to take with him in order to break his resistance. It was from this clash of approaches that the tensions arose.

Prior to his verbal altercation with the sergeant, the man had had time to send me the text he had written. Although it has rhyme and rhythm, the manuscript is written in linear form, rather than in verses, with no punctuation and no crossings-out. Beyond the somewhat stereotyped rap sentiment and style, it expresses, with a mixture of a raw realistic view of the carceral condition and understated reticence about his own story, something of the experience of prison.

The State wants to kill us with years in prison Jail ain't that easy boy thats the vision Endless pain and depression Meds and tension With the administration Strip search screws looking up your asshole On their round they spy on you through the peephole Welcome to jail Where your dreams fail Locked up You hold up Or you cut up France so-called land of human rights Didn't tell you her cells were sorry sights Im just a man One of more than sixty-seven thousand women and men Between reality and nightmare There's no way out of there Cell exercise disciplinary Let's not talk about the hole too insanitary With these lines my truth I give you In court the prosecutor pisses on you The magistrate shoots at you The state walks over you Status of free man cancelled out by decision Of the judge who day after day sentences with the same determination Normal you get thin With all the worry youre in In your cell alone at night No more of those hot nights In that girls arms When she was giving you the benefit of her charms Now you're jerking off over Hustler Alone in your cell like a loser Only escape the rare moments of the visit Half an hour thats it You get a bit of comfort from a letter But you dont forget the pain inside you dont feel better Freedom cant be bought or sold Locked up inside you feel cold The joint pushes you to the limit Into situations where you can lose it Either youre strong Or youre gone The hidden face of France Its shut your mouth accept your sentence For remorse there is no repentance Walk or die True pain of a poor guy Who takes the rap for getting high And in my head it makes me die

Pirate

If, as the deputy warden said, prison has "made" this man who signs his texts with the pseudonym "Pirate," it is surely through the experience of violence. Violence in the relations between inmates, which not only causes him to lose an eye but also locks him into the mortifying role of victim, his only way out being the transformation of his appearance in order to invert his position: the man who was scared has become the man who scares others. Violence in the relations with staff, as correctional officers alternate provocations and concessions, and management switch between negotiation and inflexibility, with the almost inevitable outcome of a physical confrontation when the imposition of a cellmate without discussion leads to a power struggle: resistance, ending in solitary confinement, is his only way to save face. Violence of the institution, which renders such relations possible and almost necessary, making prison much more than a place of privation of liberty – a world that can be lived only in pain, precisely because of the permanent ordeal to which all in the carceral world are subject. Violence everywhere.

Once he had returned to his block, the man was offered training as a kitchen assistant. Shortly after the start of this course, suspicion was raised that cellphones were circulating among the trainees. He was one of those on whom a device was found. He was therefore temporarily removed from the sessions, with a promise that he would be reinstated a month later. In the meantime, the prison registry realized that he was eligible for release. To everyone's surprise, including his own, he therefore left the facility without completing his training. A few months later, the deputy warden who had to some extent taken him on as a protégé told me how relieved she was not only that the man had apparently not committed any further offenses, since he had not been seen at the prison, but also that he had told his instructor that he now understood how his physical appearance scared people and identified him as a former prisoner: "He's started to see the bigger picture," she concluded with satisfaction.

* * *

It is well known that, in prison, the principal victims of violence between prisoners are "diddlers" and "snitches." "Diddlers" are those guilty of sexual assaults, especially rape or sexual abuse of children, with the latter being placed at the top of the scale of disgust: "It's a code among lowlifes: you don't touch women or children." "Snitches" are individuals suspected of informing, either in the case for which they have been sentenced, or in prison, for example if an incident arises: "They see you at night in the sergeants' office talking with the block senior, and the next day you get massacred in the exercise yard."[1] The two men with whom I am speaking are in the wing for "protected prisoners," where the "vulnerable inmates" are placed, mainly those with mental health issues and those convicted of sex offenses. The antipsychotic drugs and emotional disturbances to which one of them refers during our conversation suggest that he suffers from psychosis. The episode recounted by the other tells of how a prisoner who had just learned what he was charged with beat him up on one of the first occasions when he went out to exercise, leaving little doubt as to why he is in prison.[2] Most of the inmates in this wing are mature: these two men are 30 and 42 years old respectively.

Sitting almost side by side, one on a plastic chair, the other on the bottom bunk, the two men gesture to the well-kept cell they have just invited me to enter to speak with them. "This is our little home," says the first with satisfaction, while the second adds: "Being two together makes it easier to handle prison. You give each other support. When one person isn't doing so well, the other cheers him up. We're like buddies. We talk like buddies, we respect each other like buddies. We share everything – except our sentences!" The younger is serving a seven-year sentence for extortion; he has already been incarcerated in another facility; he hopes to be able to apply for a sentence adjustment in 18 months' time. The older has been in pre-trial detention for a year, awaiting his trial on charges he does not specify; he has no previous experience of prison. They are known by names that are not those they used prior to their incarceration. The first calls himself Tito, a nickname he adopted because, he says, there is no way he will allow "people to call me by my given name." The second introduces himself as Jeremy, but adds that in fact "that's my middle name." They have been sharing a cell for three months. "We'd already known each other for a while. We realized we got on well together." It is not often that inmates ask to share a cell. The guards did not need to be asked twice to house them together.

During the course of our conversation, they recall a young man who was jailed after being charged with sexual assault. "Pascal. He was 24. An ex-soldier. They put him in with a guy who was violent. He was raped by his cellmate. And then when he came to trial, he was acquitted. Can you imagine?" Since cases of sexual assault are generally subject to an investigation, those charged with these offenses spend a long time in the facility as pre-trial prisoners, and since, from the point of view of other inmates, there is no smoke without fire, they can be punished by the same means as they are assumed to have used in their crime.[3] The cell that houses my two interviewees has its own tragic history, to which they refer a little later. "Where you're sitting, there, that's where Yazid Cherkaoui killed himself. He was part of a bank hold-up. He was accused of ratting on his brother who was involved as well. They said that during the trial his brother spat at him. The guy couldn't get over it. When he arrived he was doped up to the eyeballs, he was a zombie. He set fire to his cell and he died. He was 20 years old."[4]

In an implicit reference to the violence he himself suffered when he arrived at the prison, the older of the two gestures as if to wave away the memory: "It's the living I'm scared of, not the dead."

In order to interpret the treatment reserved for those suspected of sexual offense, we need to take into account the valorization of masculinity in a prison world in which homosociality is the norm, at least among prisoners. Men are compelled to demonstrate their masculinity to one another at all times: this is how we might summarize gender relations within the prison. Under these conditions, a man who has assaulted a woman or a child has renounced his masculine status by attacking weaker individuals whom, in terms of traditional roles, he is supposed to protect. Physically, or sometimes sexually, molesting someone who has committed such acts both diminishes that person's virility and enhances one's own. It re-establishes a normal order of masculinity. But it would be wrong to limit the expression of violent virility only to assaults on inmates deemed responsible for sexual offenses, and to reduce the norms and values on which this expression is based solely to a matter of sexuality. The punishments inflicted on those suspected of having betrayed and denounced their comrades, or of having revealed the name of a guard involved in smuggling, are based on the principle of failure to respect masculine loyalty and the code of honor between men.

Thus the whole structure of the relations of force and power games, particularly among the young inmates, derives from a masculine morality that is often imported from outside the prison, and is manifested through the performance whereby an inmate stages his masculine status in the presence of other men.[5] The inmate who signed his rap "Pirate" is an extreme illustration of this; through the radical transformation of his body, he felt he had managed to reverse the stigma of the victim he had been, and to win some kind of recognition in the prison world. Sometimes, however, this masculine image might crack, allowing an unexpected fragility to filter through. A young man who had boasted, a few minutes earlier, of his already long experience of prison, and of a series of aggressive acts against correctional officers that had led to him "bleeding the hole dry," confided to me: "During Ramadan it's real hard to be here, alone, without your family. I cry in the evening, when it's time to break the fast."

These issues around masculinity were rarely addressed within the institution. "Prison is an ultramasculine world in which nobody talks about masculinity," write the authors of a key text on the subject, noting that "people who work with men in prison – religious leaders, correctional educators, counselors, therapists, corrections officers, and parole officers – give far too little consideration to the ways that manhood and the patterns of men's relationships with one another influence how men ended up in prison in the first place, how they function 'inside,' and what happens to them if and when they are released and return to their communities."[6] Revealed not only in the valorization of attitudes seen as masculine, including the use of violence, but also in the enhancement of the male body, through a widespread practice of intensive bodybuilding, the effects of which are magnified by the ingestion of protein supplements, masculinity seems to go without saying for those working in this world of men, particularly as the prison staff do not entirely escape this way of thinking. The job of correctional officer remains a predominantly male domain (72 percent of those employed at this prison), owing not to a lack of interest in the profession among women but, rather, to regulation quotas at a national level (which restrict their presence to 30 percent of the staff in men's prisons, for security reasons). However, as one director pointed out, "increasing the number of women, especially among the chief officers, has very positive aspects, because it creates spaces where tensions and anger can be calmed."

But in general gender and sexuality were not mentioned.[7] The assignment committee meetings never addressed gender and only brought up sexuality when an inmate suspected of sexual assault had to be placed in the protected prisoners wing, more rarely when an individual thought to be homosexual was deemed more suited to being allocated a cell alone, or exceptionally when discussing possible dismissal of a worker for harassing female staff. The same was true when the probation and re-entry service took on cases: they were more alert to the issue of sex offenders, as the guidelines from the ministry of justice required, than to problems related to masculinity. For example, the Exchange and Reflection Group set up under the aegis of the Program for Prevention of Recidivism for "sex offender inmates" operated as collective therapy, in which each person could talk of his experience, as a support group, where the aim was to restore their self-esteem, and as an information session, when they were given details of the sanctions and obligations written into the law over the last 20 years. It was only deviant sexuality that was to be corrected, and the ultimate aim focused less on life in prison than on life after release.

The only context in which I witnessed questions of gender and sexuality being addressed together in public was at a Catholic gathering, and it turned out to be from a fairly peculiar angle. The prison has a fine, large ecumenical hall that is used for Catholic, Muslim, and Jewish religious services. On Sunday mornings, those Christians who wish to do so attend a Mass that the chaplain has decided to precede with a discussion around a theme relating to life in prison. One Sunday in January 2013, he set the tone straight away, referring to a conversation he had a little earlier with one of the lay assistants who join him in the prison on these occasions: "When I spoke with Alain on this topic today, he said: 'That's a real touchy subject!' [He pauses] Today, as you can see, I put on a coat and big shoes to go to the demonstration against gay marriage. So that's what we're going to talk about. An inmate left me this message: 'Shouldn't we let homosexuals live how they want to? After all, it's their life, their body.' What do you all think?" Hardly has he finished his sentence than a volley of responses bursts forth, many highly indignant: "It's bullshit! It's unnatural. That's not God's will. They should be snuffed out like germs!" "I think a man should be with a woman, so I don't support it, but I think everyone can love who they want." "In the world we live in, there's no morals anymore, it's going from bad to worse. They try to get homosexuality into the home, through the TV . . . ." As the congregants get more excited, the priest attempts to calm things by summarizing in his own way: "So if I understand right, you're against it, you think it's not a good thing, but you respect those who do. And you know, the people who came to Jesus included sinners, prostitutes, collaborators, lepers. He didn't reject them, but he asked them to live better lives." But the level of agitation continues to rise. One man starts shouting: "Everyone here watches porn movies. When it's men and women screwing, we cum, but when we see men fucking each other, we don't like it! The asshole, the anus, that's for doing your business!" Loud applause. Another man aims for a more conciliatory tone: "When I was little, kids of divorced parents were rejected. Today they're accepted. It's the same for homosexuals now. We can accept them. We know it's a sickness, it's a hormone problem. So it's fine for them to have a civil partnership. It's just marriage that's not OK." For half an hour arguments raged back and forth, often virulent, sometimes moderate, each person agreeing that relations between persons of the same sex were at best pathological, at worst wrong. Closing the debate, the chaplain concluded by resorting to an unexpected comparison: "Ultimately, it's like in prison. There's something that hurts me, something bad. But in my deepest self, even when I'm suffering, I know that I am someone who is loved by God." Alain intones: "Look down upon me, O Lord," and the congregation responds.

This discussion offers a moment of free speech, allowing the faithful to express overtly their hostility toward homosexuality and homosexuals, whom they hear being assimilated by the priest to sinners and prostitutes and compared to collaborators or lepers. Among the 50 or so men present, most of whom remained silent during the debate, I calculate mentally that there are probably several who indulge in homosexual practices, and I recognize some who are housed in the protected prisoners wing. I wonder how they feel in the face of this animosity toward what they represent. After the mass, the lay assistants tell the chaplain they were disturbed at the direction taken by the conversation, and the effect it might have produced among the faithful. The priest seems surprised. In a conversation I had with him a few days earlier, he emphasized the importance of not judging prisoners on their offenses and not lecturing them on reforming their behavior, but rather listening to their questions and hearing their suffering. This, he believes, is what he has done today, putting forward a generally applicable moral proposition based on the teaching of the Catholic church. But in the view of his colleagues, who are embarrassed by the way he led the debate, he realizes that he has probably underestimated the legitimizing power of institutions – seemingly ignoring how condemning alternative sexualities on the basis of the authority of religion can contribute to justifying animosity toward those who embody them.

The prison management, aware of this power, was much more vigilant. One director gave me the example of two members of staff sanctioned for using inappropriate language with sexual connotations: "One correctional officer was involved in two cases where he publicly called an inmate a 'diddler.' Another officer insulted an inmate by referring to his sexual attributes." In the first case, the individuals concerned had lodged a complaint; in the second, the block senior had filed a report. But the director acknowledged that it was "difficult to get people to say anything about these situations, especially in writing." Inmates feared reprisals from the staff; guards were reluctant to denounce a colleague. As a general rule, management exhibited a degree of concern for individuals charged with sexual offenses, while the other inmates felt they enjoyed positive discrimination and privileged treatment. "Sex offenders and rapists, they're far too pampered here by the directors and the guards," said one pre-trial prisoner charged with marijuana dealing, who complained that, unlike these inmates, none of his requests for work and training had been considered.

In their cell Tito and Jeremy, my two interviewees, would certainly not have denied this. However, they found justifications for these relative favors, based not only on mental distress, in Tito's case, and the sex offense, in Jeremy's, but also on their status as middle-class white men: "In the yard, there's a real problem with racism. It's blacks together with blacks, Arabs together with Arabs. Guys from one town won't mix with guys from the town next door." This account, though relatively common, is not necessarily correct. In prison, affinities between inmates, and sometimes conversely, rivalries or conflicts, pass through multiple identities and lines of demarcation.

Territorial affinities, whether relating to neighborhood or town, play out in congregation rather than divisions. New prisoners often express a desire to be with inmates they know from outside. Some cities are overrepresented. One correctional officer joked about one of them, known for its Urban Sensitive Zones: "You're quite safe going there: all the lowlifes from there are in here!" Although much is made of disputes between housing projects, they are quite rare, and I never heard any hint of them. Loyalties of origin seem to have even less sway, except in relation to certain groups such as Romanians (partly on a linguistic basis) or Basques (for essentially political reasons), but they do not result in tensions with other groups. As to the racial or ethnic alliances my interviewees referred to, they never seemed evident to me. Their impressions rather reflected the social distance they felt between themselves and these young black and Arab inmates, relating more to differences of generation and background, and hence of lifestyle, than to ethnic or racial barriers. The two men's shared interests were reading, board games, and rock music. Elsewhere in the prison, particularly among the young inmates of African origin, sports, bodybuilding, and rap predominated. My point is not to minimize either the racialization or the racism that are apparent in the discourse of some inmates. But I did not observe them giving rise to violence. The violence related much more to the application in prison of what sociologist Elijah Anderson calls the "code of the street."[8] Masculinity is fed by respect, which it nourishes in return. Neither one nor the other seems to be damaged by attacking someone weaker, sometimes in company with others.

*   *   *

While violence between inmates is set in the context of relations between equals (in statutory terms, for of course length of time spent in the prison, physical strength, financial resources, and social networks are all sources of inequality), violence between inmates and staff is radically asymmetrical. In the office of the arrivals block, the guard has stuck a note on his computer that reads: "Code of Penal Procedure Article D.243: Inmates must comply with everything operatives or agents holding authority in the prison require them to do for purposes of execution of the regulations." This reminder probably serves more to bolster the authority of the guard who pinned it up in his own eyes than in the minds of the inmates; prisoners do not enter this room and, in any case, cannot be unaware of this basic rule. As soon as they arrive in prison, the ritual of identification, search, and cloakroom signals to them and instills in them the submission expected of them, however hard some correctional officers try to attenuate their effects. Henceforth, they will be known by their prison number, they are aware that their privacy can be violated at any moment, and they can only have access to their belongings to the extent authorized by management. In the day-to-day life of the prison, their relationship with the institution is conducted mainly through the guards. Violence toward the institution is therefore expressed principally through verbal or physical attacks against guards.

One officer whom I greet in the monitoring post seems at first not to recognize me. I remind him that we had talked for a few minutes during my previous stay in the prison, five months earlier. He remembers then, and tells me: "Well, I've been off work since then. A prisoner broke four of my teeth, with a jab from his elbow that I didn't see coming." He explains that this was a man he had never had any problems with, but who had been behaving aggressively a little earlier. The length of his absence from work seems due both to the psychological consequences of the shock he suffered and to a dispute between the prison management and the medical insurance about who would cover the cost of his dental care. Such incidents are not uncommon, although they are often less serious. The possibility of one arising generates a permanent state of psychological tension in some correctional officers. One guard, who told me she had twice failed the police examinations and had finally resigned herself to taking the exam for prison administration, "for job security, not because I had a choice," talked of the stress she felt in her work: "It's constant, because what might happen is always unpredictable. Everything can be going fine, and then all of a sudden it kicks off. But once I get in my car I forget all about it – well, I try to." Another officer, whose previous job had been as a dog-handler in the army, offered me his ethological theory: "With prisoners, I found the same psychology as with the dogs I looked after before. Er . . . I don't mean they're animals. But when you go into a compound, you might have done it a hundred times before, and then the hundred-and-first time something can happen, a dog might attack, you don't know why. Here it's the same. Everything's going fine, and then bam! Everything is out of control." The unpredictability of violence from inmates is a recurrent theme among the staff. Observation of many interactions between guards and those they guard reveals, however, that incidents are rarely random occurrences. They almost always arise in particular situations and with particular staff members.

One day, a young man appears before the disciplinary board. He is charged with having said of a correctional officer who had been hit by another inmate: "It serves him right. You reap what you sow. I hope he dies!" The man presents himself alone at the hearing, as his counsel has not come and the court-appointed lawyer has not been called. He explains that he only said: "It serves him right," but never added "I hope he dies!" The deputy warden, offering little hope of a favorable outcome, retorts: "You know, it's the word of a sworn prison officer against yours." The man then says that for the last month, "people" have been trying to "bring him down." It all started after a visit at the end of which, during the strip search, the officer checking him had made a remark to which he responded and, while he was naked and putting his underwear back on, had slapped him twice. The man complained to his block senior, who told him to write to the prison registry to report the incident. He did so, but the case was not followed up. It was the same officer who was hit in the later episode, and the man is convinced that the guard wants to make him pay for his complaint. At the end of a hearing without any speech for the defense, the man is sentenced to eight days in solitary confinement, with four suspended, to which various provisions cutting his automatic and optional sentence reductions will subsequently be added. The maximum punishment for this offense being 14 days, the jury's relative leniency is explained both by the man's lack of previous disciplinary sanctions, since no incidents have ever been reported against him, and by the poor reputation of the guard, of which the members of the committee are aware. But the rule, in such situations, is still to punish the inmate, in order to avoid angering correctional officers and prevent an intervention by their union. In this case, several conversations I later have with other guards and other prisoners confirm that the former consider the injured officer "difficult," and the latter think he is a "sadist." The attack on him does not surprise either the guards, who say they are sorry about it, or the prisoners, who admit to being glad about it.

The behavior of some correctional officers creates a predictable risk of clashes with the prison population, and everyone knows it. As the inmates are going down to exercise one day, a young guard shoves one of them in the back, as if to make him hurry up, even though the man is rushing with the others toward the yard. He cannot be unaware that the one thing prisoners cannot bear is being touched by guards. The separation between the two worlds is manifested in the form of an invisible, inviolable boundary between the bodies of the one and the other. For example, an officer never shakes an inmate's hand; still less does he jostle him. The man cannot keep from showing his irritation as he shakes off the contact. Adopting an innocent air, but avoiding eye contact, the officer pretends surprise: "They're touchy just now!" Inmates present at the scene call the officer coordinating the exit from the blocks to witness: "One day that guy's going to get what he's asking for!" Management is aware that some staff indulge in such inappropriate behavior, and partly takes it into account when assessing incidents. One deputy warden cited the case of a correctional officer who was bitten by a prisoner during a strip search after visits. Going well beyond customary practice, with the intention of humiliating him, the guard had attempted to check whether the man was hiding anything in his anal cavity or his mouth. It was at that point that the incident had arisen. "We judged that it was a case of professional misconduct," concludes the deputy warden.

The inmates did not always have the necessary detachment to be able to resist provocations or frustration. One man known for his impulsive behavior, stemming from a mental health condition, told me how, one morning when he was first to take a shower, he had had to wait more than five minutes for the water to heat up. As a result, he had only just soaped himself when the water stopped before he had time to rinse off. The guard had refused to turn the tap back on. Forced to return to his cell covered in lather, the man had become angry and head-butted the officer. The disciplinary board sentenced him to five days in solitary confinement, where the maximum penalty for assaulting prison staff is 30 days. The committee had taken into consideration the fact that this officer had already had several altercations with inmates in similar circumstances of unjustified intransigence. The man said he regretted his act, but did not exonerate the officer of responsibility, adding with humor: "It blew up in his face, and it blew up in my face too!"

There is thus both a profile of the officer and a type of situation that tend to be conducive to violence. Far from being unpredictable, explanatory factors, or at least a fertile ground, can be found for many confrontations. Some officers "push us to break the rules," prisoners say, by provoking them or offending them for no reason. They may behave this way uniformly with all inmates, or have "their pet hates." Three situations are particularly susceptible to provoking prisoners' exasperation: visits, because of the emotional charge they bear, and the strip search with which they end; exercise, because not being prepared at the moment the cell door is opened may prevent the inmate from going out, and because the combined effect of the number of prisoners hurrying to the yard generates tensions with the staff; and finally showers, because they depend on the absolute discretionary power of officers. In these particularly vulnerable moments, faced with inflexible or malicious guards, the rigid application of a rule that is usually interpreted more flexibly can lead to an incident, especially if the inmate is quick-tempered, or has just been hit with bad news.

The fact that, in describing altercations as unpredictable, the staff seem unaware of these circumstantial factors – the profile of the officer and type of situation – can be explained. What they see as unexpected is in fact simply the intervention of a minor event that destabilizes a configuration in which all the elements were already in place, merely awaiting a spark that will lead to an explosion of violence. Here is one example. It is exercise time during the month of Ramadan. In their cells, all the inmates are ready, often standing up, shoes on their feet, careful to respect the prison's dress code. They know that when the key turns in the lock and the door opens, a delay in leaving, or wearing unauthorized clothing, can lead to the cancellation of this rare moment of diversion. As soon as they hear officers enter their wing calling out "Exercise, gentlemen!" they hurriedly get themselves prepared. One after the other, they pass in front of the sergeant, to whom they give their card, and then through the metal detector, before entering the corridor leading to the yard.

Suddenly, I hear shouting. An inmate, clearly exasperated, is expostulating furiously. He has come out, as on previous days, with his Quran, but an officer who sees him with the book in his hand tells him he is not allowed to take it, and orders him to go and put it back. "It's Ramadan, you can't do that to me. Why is it today you don't let me take my Quran?" The sergeant supervising the exit to the yard asks him to calm down, but the man is beside himself. "You've got to be kidding! You can't screw up my exercise! Do what you want, I don't give a shit, I'll go to the hole!" – a classic threat that inmates with no further argument issue at such moments, to the staff but also to themselves, as if to demonstrate their resoluteness. Without attempting to argue, the sergeant then decides to return him to his cell. The man refuses to go back. Immediately, the two other officers present jump on him, pin him to the ground, and handcuff him. Then, pushing him before them in the midst of the other inmates witnessing the scene, the three staff members rush him, through security doors and corridors, to the solitary confinement unit, where they enter just as half a dozen guards called as back-up run up, adding to the tumult. Dismissing these back-up officers, who barely fit into the already cramped space, the lieutenant in charge of the unit tries to take the situation in hand, attempting to calm the rebellious inmate and explaining that he will have to search him. He has only just managed to quiet him when the sergeant who brought him in winds him up again: "Hurry up, I don't have all day!" At that point a deputy director, who has just arrived himself and has witnessed the officer's intervention, loses his temper: "That's enough!" he shouts to the sergeant. "Get out, sir! Get out now! I'll see you in my office later." The pandemonium gives way to an astonished silence. Mortified and furious, the sergeant leaves, while his colleagues watch him go with consternation. The lieutenant asks the inmate to accompany him to the little room where strip searches take place before placement in a solitary confinement cell. The man follows him.

A little later, I talk about this sequence of events with the deputy director. "To begin with, it was a trivial incident," he says. "One day religious books are let through, the next they're forbidden. It's ridiculous! Some inmates hide them in their pants. He did it without hiding. You have to admit that's better!" He comes back to the way the incident was handled: "Once you're in the disciplinary unit, it's the lieutenant who's responsible for handling the situation. The sergeant should have held back. He should never have carried on being mixed up in it, especially not to make things worse." After reading the block senior's report of the incident, he decides to allow the inmate to return to his cell, to the severe displeasure of the sergeant, and the satisfaction of the lieutenant. In the evening, when they gather at the entrance to the prison awaiting permission to leave after the inmate count, discontented officers talk about the incident, calling me to witness: "You see, that's exactly what they shouldn't do. If they want to call a guard to order, they shouldn't do it in front of the prisoners. Otherwise we lose all credibility."

Clearly, this "trivial incident" took on proportions beyond the prison's capacity to maintain order. The escalation is the result of a series of factors and an accumulation of errors: the arbitrary decision to forbid the religious book, about which it is difficult to say to what extent it was a simple mistake or a provocation; the inflexible attitude of the sergeant, who did not try to hear the man's reasons but immediately deprived him of exercise; the brutal physical intervention by the two other officers, who prioritized coercion over negotiation which might have allowed the prisoner to return to his cell; the reinforcement of tension in the roughly conducted journey through the buildings, under the gaze of other inmates; the provocation of the prisoner by the officer who originated the incident, at the moment when he had calmed down; finally, the anger of the director which, paradoxically, had the effect of calming everyone but at the same time emphasized the disagreement among the staff. At first glance, it was no more than a correctional officer wielding discretionary power in relation to an apparently insignificant detail. But one cannot be unaware of the religious significance, the reading of the Quran during Ramadan. The prison management, which is generally careful to respect Muslims' practices, was in this case overwhelmed by the zeal of one of its agents.[9] The director's intervention restored a certain sense of justice, an essential condition for peace in prison, in the face of an arbitrary decision.

*   *   *

"When people think about prison, all they see is violence. But there's more to it than that, make no mistake! Usually prisoners get on well among themselves. Even with the guards, they're sometimes friendly, have a joke with us." Sitting on his bed, the man saying this has just recounted various violent episodes between inmates, and with correctional officers. But he wants to correct the false impression that the account of these striking and memorable episodes of life in the prison might create, hence supporting the common idea the public has of the carceral world. Many other commentaries, both verbal and written, carry the same message.[10] It is, however, true that the French press mainly talks about prisons when dramatic events, especially assaults, occur there. It is also true that violence against prison staff is much more systematically covered in the media than violence among inmates, which is rarely addressed unless murder is involved. The cinema also contributes to constructing this image, from *Law Abiding Citizen* to *A Prophet* ("a concentrate of prison violence," according to one director), to mention just two movies that came out just as I was beginning my research.[11] Moreover, official statistics can themselves be deceptive.

Statistics from the Directorate of Prison Administration for all French prisons for the year 2012 report 8,861 incidences of violence between prisoners (an increase over the 8,365 the previous year) and 4,403 attacks on prison staff (also increased from 4,083 a year earlier).[12] These figures, however, should be interpreted with caution, since they reflect both the perpetration of violence and the efficacy of recording. If incidents are reported more often, or certain acts are more readily identified as assault, the statistics rise; on the contrary, if the administration is less concerned about violence within prison, or the staff play down certain actions toward themselves, the numbers fall.[13] There has been a strong tendency in recent years to pay greater attention to violence committed in prison, thanks to a growing awareness of the deteriorating conditions in correctional facilities, and also because of the work of institutions responsible for monitoring them and to union campaigns concerned about the working conditions of correctional officers.

As a result, between 2007 and 2012, the national total of reported incidents of violence among inmates increased eighteenfold, and against staff twelvefold.[14] Contrary to what might be suggested by the overhasty reading often advanced by the media, but also sometimes by the national prison administration and prison staff unions, this development reflects not a worsening of the situation, but a greater interest in these questions, which is evident from the fact that these data have only recently become widely disseminated, and that such actions are now subject to comprehensive and systematic recording.[15] Several sets of evidence, based on more robust indicators, and hence on more reliable figures, demonstrate this. During the period under consideration, the number of homicides of inmates remained stable, between one and four per year, while the number of attacks on staff leading to temporary incapacity for work also remained constant.[16] Since, simultaneously, the number of prisoners has risen by 11 percent, it can even be argued that this apparent stability indicates a relative decrease. We may note in addition that, while the figure for violence between prisoners was one-third lower than that for violence against staff in 2007, it was more than double in 2012. Here too, we may assume that this reflects greater awareness of the realities of prison life, although the proportion of attacks going unrecorded is probably still higher for aggression between inmates than for assault against staff.

However justified the demands for better security for correctional officers and (albeit rarely heard) for prisoners, the fact remains that, in terms of physical manifestation and particularly in its most extreme form (homicide), prison violence has fallen over the last half-century.[17] We need only remember the uprisings, murders of prison officers, and bloody reprisals against rioters of the early 1970s in France to get a sense of this development. One director told me that, in the Directorate of Prison Administration, there is a stone engraved with the names of correctional officers who have died in service. He spoke of the time when a "law of iron" reigned in prisons: "Every year, there were one or more guards killed. Today, it's completely changed. Since 1992, I am happy to say, not one prison officer has been killed in the line of duty. The names that have been added since then are one officer fatally wounded during training, a secretary murdered by her prison officer lover, a doctor killed by a guard who was blind drunk . . . ." He had recently paid his respects at the memorial, contemplating what would happen if a guard was killed by an inmate: "It's what we dread. The reaction would be terrible." In fact, the only deaths that had occurred in the prison world were those of prisoners, from homicide by other inmates (averaging fewer than three per year) and especially from suicide (more than 120 per year). This suicide rate revealed a different reality of violence, much more significant than that discussed hitherto.

Focusing only on interpersonal assaults, whether they involve prisoners or correctional officers, in fact obscures the violence that is experienced most harshly and most consistently: that of the institution itself. This violence underlies and often explains the physical attacks, and thus weighs heavily, albeit highly asymmetrically, on both inmates and staff. "They do everything they can to destroy the little bit of humanity that is left in us. After a while, all you feel is this frustration, this hatred of the prison management. It's a quite twisted world, prison. And when we arrive, it very quickly makes us twisted, too." The profound pessimism expressed by this man, who has been awaiting his trial at the supreme court for four years, echoes similar observations made by many inmates during my conversations with them, albeit not always with the same degree of eloquence. It is a refrain heard from cell to cell, striving to put words onto a carceral condition which they understand to be much more than the prison sentence issued by the judge: "Prison is privation of freedom. It should not be privation of dignity," says another, who has also been in pre-trial detention for two and a half years. "It's constant humiliation. Everything brings us down. The searches, the showers, the doubling-up in cells. When you're a prisoner, you don't have the right to protest about anything. A guard never lies, can't ever be wrong."

Yet neither of these two is a troublemaker. Neither has any reported incidents against his name. One enjoys reading, the other plays sports. They do not know one another, and the similarity of their viewpoints is no doubt due both to their already long experience of the prison and to their capacity to analyze it (both left school early, but one has set himself up as a public writer, commissioned by inmates to create poems for their girlfriends, while the other followed philosophy classes at the prison where he was previously incarcerated). Considered exemplary prisoners and entrusted with the sensitive post of auxiliary, they swallow on a daily basis their "short-term frustrations" and their "long-time frustrations, the most devastating ones, the ones that go to your core," as the former puts it. They are lucid about an institution that is punishing them well beyond the letter of the law, arguing that it "buys peace with hash," by tolerating the circulation of marijuana, and that for its staff "the ideal would be if we were all medicated," as the latter says.

In both common parlance and legal definitions, violence is generally perceived as the brutal, excessive, and unjustified use of physical force. Applied to the world of prison, this definition covers attacks between inmates and against staff, but rarely includes assaults by staff on inmates, since the coercion exercised by prison officers is held to be justified for the purposes of maintaining public order. The famous Weberian description of the state as the holder of the monopoly of the legitimate use of physical force applies not only to the police and the army, but also to correctional staff. It is to prisons that the monopoly is delegated insofar as it concerns those who are being punished (convicted prisoners) and those who are deemed likely to be subject to punishment (pre-trial prisoners). From the point of view of this institution, which does not recognize this violence as such, the legitimacy of the use of physical force is doubly reinforced, since, on the one hand, in the normal progress of their prison term, inmates are serving out a penalty, necessitating if not the use of force, at least the threat of using it; on the other hand, when they break the rules, for example by refusing to return to their cell, the use of force becomes concrete and is deemed necessary. Thus, apart from exceptional cases, the institution and its staff are not seen as exercising violence: when they resort to coercion, they are within the law.

Now, if we consider, following a long philosophical tradition of which Walter Benjamin is both inheritor and critic, that "all violence as a means is either lawmaking or law-preserving," then the institutions of the state that use the law as a basis for justifying their exercise of physical force on citizens need to be analyzed in terms of violence.[18] More specifically, we may distinguish, on the one hand, the lawmaking violence of the contract whereby certain acts are constituted as crimes while others are not so defined, and whereby certain crimes earn their perpetrators a prison sentence while others do not result in this sanction, independently of their consequences for society; and, on the other, the law-preserving violence through which certain institutions are tasked with applying the principles of the law thus defined, by the use of constraint (always) and force (sometimes). Prison is the passive receiver of the first form of violence (it does not choose who is housed there), and the active agent of the second (it determines how inmates will be treated). The privation of freedom in its strict sense (being prevented from moving freely in the world) is part of lawmaking violence. The ways in which it is implemented (material conditions, forms of organization, principles of operation, regulatory mechanisms) derive from law-preserving violence. These are not mere semantic details, or even juridical debates, but concrete issues with practical and political consequences. Apprehending the violence of prison as an institution, to be understood as including the buildings, the regulations, management, and the staff, means analyzing what is over and above the simple privation of freedom prescribed by the law. The institution is itself conscious of this violence, because it is continually reforming itself, sometimes to increase respect for inmates' dignity, sometimes to enhance staff security, and, in the best case, linking the two. I have already offered many illustrations of this, starting with overpopulation and its deleterious consequences for prisoners, which one director himself described precisely as "institutional violence." Let us consider two aspects I have not yet touched on: healthcare, and affective life.

* * *

Outpatient Consultation and Care Units (Unités de consultations et de soins ambulatoires, UCSA) are medical and nursing care services that have come under the remit of hospital administration since the law of January 18, 1994. This legislation ended what was hitherto known, inaccurately but significantly, as "correctional medicine," which came under the authority of the national prison administration.[19] The law also integrated prisoners into the healthcare system, both by allowing them their rightful access to health insurance and by, theoretically, offering them the same care as they would receive outside prison. "I go by the principle, and I also try to pass it on to all of my team, that with any person who comes seeking treatment, we must ask ourselves: 'What would I do outside?' If I say I would make such and such a decision, then I should do the same here," says the nurse who coordinates the unit. It is also a feature she emphasizes in order to facilitate relations with inmates: "Often, they come in positioning themselves in a power relationship. We tell them: 'You're at the hospital here. Everything that happens in this consultation is confidential.' We try to gain their trust. There's a level of respect. In our relationship, there's a whole art to changing the prisoner into a patient. But it's a fragile relationship. They're super-sensitive. They're not just deprived of freedom."[20] This philosophy of a universal right, including the attention to the individual, was widely shared by the general and specialist contract physicians, the psychiatrist and the psychologists, the dental technician and the radiographer, most of whom worked part time at the prison.

Despite the staff's efforts, healthcare was nevertheless one of the most frequent subjects of complaint among inmates. Sometimes it was the quality of the service that was brought into question. One man told me how, after he twisted his ankle in the exercise yard, he had been told it was sprained, but was simply given a dressing. It was only by insisting for two months that he persuaded the medical service to X-ray his ankle: "We'll do it to make you happy," he was told. The examination showed a fracture of the malleolus, now too old to be treated surgically. He was left with a painful limp. No doubt such errors could also occur outside prison, but the prisoners often felt that their problems were treated as trivial. The doctors, for their part, believed that these somewhat special patients were using them: "You have to be able to put things in perspective, because they're great manipulators," said one practitioner. Much more frequently, however, the inmates' complaints related to the length of time it took for them to get access to the healthcare team.

Yet there was a well-established procedure: a written request had to be placed in the "medical" mailbox located on each level; the mail was collected each day by the nurse; appointments were made in accordance with the order in which the requests arrived and the apparent urgency; inmates would have to wait "a maximum of three or four days" to see someone. In reality, however, the wait could be much longer. One inmate recalls: "When there was the gastroenteritis epidemic I was sick, seriously ill. I wrote them. I got an appointment for three weeks later. In the meantime, I got better." Another tells me about one of his neighbors in the next cell, who "has been in agony" with sciatica for a week, and has been given only acetaminophen. Often, at the monitoring post, I would hear over the intercom an exchange along the following lines, between an inmate and the correctional officer: the inmate would ask when his "medical appointment" would be; the guard would answer "your request's been submitted"; the communication would end with a disillusioned "thank you."

Two types of appointment were particularly difficult to secure. A meeting with a psychologist would take at least six months, as the unit coordinator herself admitted to me. This delay automatically excluded those serving short sentences. But it also dissuaded pre-trial prisoners, despite the fact that their long wait for their trial rendered them more fragile: "I asked to see a shrink eight months ago, and I've had no answer even though I've asked several times, they always tell me to wait," said one of them, who spoke of his sadness, anxiety, and insomnia. Similarly, seeing the dental technician was no simple matter. Many of the inmates had very poor dental health, a problem that is known to be statistically correlated with socioeconomic background. "In here, if you're going to have a toothache, it's best to know in advance, because it can take a couple weeks to get treatment," an inmate commented sardonically.

One evening, when the guards are making their round to check that all prisoners are present and alive, they become aware of an acrid smell of burning as they enter one of the wings. They call the duty lieutenant, who comes quickly to open the cell from which the smoke is seeping. Through the haze they make out the standing figure of a young African man, his face disfigured by a huge tooth abscess. In the middle of the cell there is a closet that has been tipped over, a broken glass, and a number of objects that are slowly burning. In the walkway, the voices of other inmates can be heard, curious or concerned: "What's wrong with him?" "Is he OK?" "We couldn't hear him anymore, is he better now?" The story is rapidly pieced together. The man has been complaining of a toothache for several days, but has received no treatment. In the morning the guard, concerned by the swelling and the pain, asked for the paramedics to be called. Management, the lieutenant tells me, "judged that it was not an emergency." That evening, terrified at the prospect of spending another night in pain, the man, despite his reputation for being calm and "trouble-free," makes this gesture of exasperation and despair which could, given the absence of correctional officers in the blocks at night, have ended in tragedy. Full of concern, this time the staff call the town's medical emergency service. Half an hour later, an on-call private practitioner arrives. He explains that he himself has a pulled muscle, and cannot climb the stairs to the wing. The guards are not authorized to administer treatment, even if it is passed to them by a medically qualified person. As an exceptional measure, the man is therefore taken out of his cell so that the physician can give him painkillers and antibiotics. The night team takes advantage of the circumstance to "show" another sick inmate awaiting treatment, and two new arrivals. The doctor takes no more than 20 minutes to complete the four consultations. A few months later, I learned that, as the prison was no longer able to pay the substantial bill for this out-of-hours care, the external contractor's services had been withdrawn.

Such dysfunctions in the healthcare system are common in correctional facilities.[21] But they are not unique to them: communication difficulties between services or an overload of work can produce similar problems outside prison. What makes the carceral condition particular in this regard is the combination of powerlessness and abandonment that prisoners feel when they are in physical pain or psychological distress – a feeling that overwhelms them and goes unanswered – their absolute dependence on prison and medical staff, even to obtain a tablet that would relieve their pain, for which they sometimes wait several days, and the profound sense that their problems do not receive the attention they deserve and that they themselves are not deemed worthy of consideration. Even if they sometimes lash out at the individuals embodying it – prison or medical staff – it is in reality the institution (prison, medicine, or medicine in prison) that they blame for laying bare their vulnerability in this way. But there is another, more private, manifestation of this vulnerability: affective deprivation.

The family life units (unités de vie familiale, UVF) were set up to remedy this deprivation. The memorandum of March 26, 2009 specifies their mode of operation. They are furnished, two- or three-room apartments located within the prison complex, in which inmates, whether pre-trial or convicted, can see their loved ones, especially their partners and children, on the first occasion for six hours, subsequently between 24 and 72 hours. Family visiting rooms offer a more limited version, comprising simply a locked lounge, available only for a duration of up to six hours during the day.[22] The point is to encourage "maintenance of family bonds," which are held to play an essential role in subsequent re-entry into society, and hence in preventing recidivism. This new approach, limited to around 20 prisons, is a radical departure from what remains the rule in more than eight out of ten correctional facilities – the prohibition of all intimacy and the supervision of visits.

The prison where I conducted my research had recently removed the low walls in the visiting rooms that had hitherto separated the inmate from his visitors, and replaced them with a simple table that established a more convivial distance. But it had neither a family life unit nor family visiting rooms. During visits, a guard passed up and down the corridor checking through the glass door of each cubicle, often with embarrassed discretion, to make sure there was no suspicious closeness. "You're with your wife, and you don't even have the right to a bit of privacy, they're always passing up and down, watching what you're doing." This did not always inhibit sexual relations. One inmate told me how, in another facility, one of his friends who belonged to a banned Basque political organization had a so-called "visiting hours baby." The examining magistrate had punished him by forbidding him from seeing the newborn for six months, asserting that he could not have – or should never have – conceived the child.

Indeed, in the case of couples, emotional deprivation also implies sexual deprivation.[23] From the point of view of the institution, the latter is even more significant than the former, since it is generally possible to see one's partner in the visiting room, but not to have intimate relations during this time. One inmate who had spent more than 20 years in prison for various crimes clearly linked the two deprivations in an expressive metaphor: "The lack of affection, that's the worst. You leave your balls in the search room," adding: "All we've got left is jerking off." He had also developed his own theory to account for carceral violence, particularly among the youngest inmates: "Sex is a huge problem in prison. The young guys, they're full of testosterone. Why are there so many fights? Because the guys aren't getting laid. When you put a guy in prison, you take away all his qualities as a man." In fact, among the subscriptions that could be bought at the canteen, the private management contractor had included the adult titles *Union* and *Newlook* under the heading "X-rated magazines."

But the power of the penal institution was most strikingly manifested in the prohibition of visits from female partners. In the cases of some pre-trial prisoners, the examining magistrate would justify such a decision on grounds of the "needs of the investigation," a vague cover-all formula. "What I was saying about breaking someone down, that's how they do it," explained a man who had not been able to see or speak to his wife for three years. "It's so stupid because her mother and sister are allowed to visit me." In his view, if the point was genuinely to prevent interference in the investigation, it was hard to understand why two people who were so close to his wife were allowed to speak freely with him. In fact, rather than "stupid," he understood that the decision was cruel: it was an additional torment imposed on him by depriving him of all contact with his wife. "Forbidding someone to love, for me that's real serious. Loving someone means – I don't know – it means respect, it means life. It isn't right to forbid someone to make love." After a damaging childhood, when he was taken away from his mother and placed in a children's home, he was experiencing a further deprivation: "For me, not having children is real painful. I would so have liked to have them while I was young." He anticipated a sentence of at least seven years.

In choosing healthcare and affective life as a way of illustrating institutional violence, I have sought to describe structures that, for different reasons, are not apparent as such – unlike, for example, the disciplinary unit, where the project of coercion is explicit. In the first case, making the healthcare service independent of prison administration and rendering it as similar as possible to the system outside certainly represent progress as far as inmates are concerned. If they still feel they are not well cared for by the medical practice in prison, it is because carceral constraint is constant, often leaving them feeling without resources and without recourse, without any presence other than that of an illness or pain and an apparently interminable wait for relief. In the case of affective life, by contrast, the intention to extend the punitive regime beyond privation of freedom is obvious. The triple restriction on emotional life, sexuality, and procreation – a partial restriction in the first case, a total ban in the second and third – was, moreover, so taken for granted for so long by French society and by the prison administration that challenging it seems incongruous and reveals how prison extended far beyond its definition in law.

Thus, in the moral history of the carceral condition, healthcare is somewhat in advance of affective life. The principle of discrimination, prisoners being treated differently from the rest of the population in matters of fundamental rights, previously seen as legitimate, is no longer self-evident in relation to healthcare. With the various family life arrangements, a similar kind of change is under way in relation to emotional life, sexuality, and reproduction. Hence the erosion – already begun in the first case, and soon to emerge in the second – of law-preserving violence, which allowed these multiple additional privations to be imposed, ineluctably reveals the other form of institutional violence: the lawmaking violence that justifies the privation of freedom.

*   *   *

There is a large body of literature in English devoted to violence in prisons – a literature that French commentators often seem unaware of as they raise the subject when an incident occurs or national statistics are published. Yet the research conducted by criminologists in Britain and the United States, in particular, might usefully illuminate reflections and decisions related to this complex question. As the authors of one synthesis of research into the causes of prison violence write: "Prisons bring troubled human beings, often with a long history of violence as victim or offender, into confined spaces against their will. These scarred individuals are brought into close contact with staff whom they greatly outnumber but who also must, on a daily basis, maintain a peaceful and orderly routine. The wonder is there is not more violence in such an environment."[24] This way of posing the problem makes it possible – usefully from the point of view of prevention – to avoid dissociating the explanation of the violence from the reasons it can sometimes be averted.

However, there is no unified theory of the interpretation of violence. The oldest model, known as the "privation" model, emphasizes the way that the material and relational conditions of prison lead inmates to develop specific values and practices that enable them to adapt and survive, which may include violence.[25] An interpretation that arose at the same time, known as the "importation" model, underscores the fact that inmates introduce norms and habits they maintained outside, in a social milieu already marked by violence, into the carceral world.[26] These two theses are obviously not incompatible: the man who signed his texts with the tag "Pirate" acknowledged that, as a teenager in his neighborhood, he "fell into a vicious cycle," while the deputy warden argued that "it is prison that made him who he is"; more generally, the "code of the street" finds fertile soil in which to grow in "prison culture."[27] But these approaches are both limited, in that they ascribe the origin of violence essentially to inmates, even when they take the prison environment into account.

A number of recent studies have encouraged a reevaluation of this dichotomy between privation and importation, seeking to analyze what Anthony Bottoms, in an influential article, has called "the minutiae of the average prison day" and "in detail how violence can arise within this social order."[28] This is what I have attempted to do here, offering detailed reconstructions of the eruption of what were considered assaults, and recounting the interpretations put forward by the various actors, including guards and inmates, which are, it should be noted, less contradictory than might be expected. Countering the common conception that these episodes are unpredictable, this approach has revealed singular configurations of circumstances: moments during the day where tensions are heightened, members of staff who are known by both inmates and their superiors for their confrontational tendencies, sequences of decisions that leave no space for negotiation or simply the possibility of saving face.[29] But beyond these reconstructions and interpretations, which concentrate on the events themselves and those involved as actors or witnesses, it is important not to lose sight of the broader context of institutional violence within which these interactions are embedded. While this violence is inherent in imprisonment and privation of liberty, its intensity, and its effects on both inmates and staff, vary in relation to the policies implemented by the prison administration at both local and national levels. The "moral performance" of prisons, as Alison Liebling puts it, proves decisive here.[30] It is manifested, depending on the facility, in the extent to which the organizational structure encourages respect of inmates, the supervision of correctional officers promotes a particular professional ethos, the discretionary power of staff members is guided, the restrictions imposed on the prison population are limited to what is justifiable, and, ultimately, the way in which a sense of justice prevails within the prison.

Toward the end of my period of research, a series of altercations arose, all in similar circumstances, and with a similar sequence of events: violent reactions from inmates to incidents that were apparently trivial, but which aroused and revealed deeper tensions with the staff. Predictably, they occurred at the vulnerable moments around visits, exercise, or showers; they involved staff members known for having poor relations with inmates; they were characterized by a succession of actions that contributed to provoking or aggravating the incident. The most serious episode, which I did not witness, arose one day when prisoners were returning from the yard. A lieutenant told me that a prisoner had refused to go through the metal detector. A guard had attempted to compel him, the man had resisted, another officer had tried to bring him under control, three other prisoners had jumped in, and reinforcements had eventually arrived, taking the four men to the disciplinary unit where, that same night, another incident arose during the meal distribution. In total, three correctional officers were injured, four prisoners sanctioned and transferred "to the four corners of the country." The most serious consequence was the damaging atmosphere that resulted from this disorder. On the one hand, the guards became nervous. Angry at the attacks on their colleagues, they were filled with what one director described as a "desire for revenge." On the other, the inmates felt a sense of injustice, taking the view that the violence had been provoked by the guards, whom one chief officer told me were "known for looking for trouble." During the following week, further clashes occurred, and several prisoners were sent to solitary confinement. It is worth noting that this was during the summer, a period reputed to be susceptible to such events because of the heat, the peak of prison overcrowding, the decreased number of visits because of public holidays, and the delays in decisions on conditional release and sentence adjustments resulting from court vacations. That year, for Muslims, the fatigue associated with the ritual fasting and short nights of Ramadan added to the mix.

One director, meeting me in a corridor after this series of incidents, told me: "I'm glad you've been able to see what you did, so that you can get an idea of what the correctional officers suffer every day, and see that the inmates behave inside the same way they act outside." My interpretation of what I had seen was, however, markedly different. It is possible to acknowledge that the work of guards is a source of real stress for them, but to observe at the same time that the life of prisoners is not devoid of such tensions; it is even reasonable to imagine that the officers' anxiety, while not to be understated, is far less intense than the inmates' anguish, which this director seemed not to take into consideration; the suicide statistics leave little doubt in this respect. One might even agree that prisoners bring to the prison the norms, values, and habits of the environment within which they lived before entering the correctional facility, but also observe that the material and relational conditions of existence imposed on them by the latter are difficult to abstract from an understanding of events such as those described. The importation theory does not exclude the privation theory, and neither should elide a third set of explanations relating to the ethos of the staff and the operation of the facility; in holding the inmates alone responsible for the disorder, this director was ignoring conflict factors that his management was nevertheless working to minimize.

As one of his deputies, who, thanks to his long experience with the world of prison, had a more measured appreciation of the situation, said: "Both the prisoner and the guard are locked up. On their floor, they are all in a sealed chamber, in the middle of four walkways. But the inmate is the more fragile. He knows that he depends on the staff for everything – his shower, his visits, and even, if an incident arises, his parole and his sentence adjustment. He's subject to the rules of the facility." For their part, the prisoners often resorted to a lighter, more succinct formula, rendered by the eloquently ungrammatical: "Prison, they've got you by the balls." It is this dependence and subjection that, according to circumstances, personalities, and moods, nourish a violence that is not limited to the explosions in which it becomes visible, but is at work, unspoken and diffuse, in the day-to-day reality of prison relations. It is to this violence that the demands for rights are addressed, whether they come from inmates, their families, prisoner advocacy groups, or the independent bodies charged with monitoring places of incarceration.

8

Rights, Interrupted

In a state, that is in a society where there are laws, liberty can consist
only in having the power to do what one should want to do and in no way
being constrained to do what one should not want to do.
Montesquieu, *The Spirit of the Laws*, 1758

"The problem is that prisoners have more rights all the time. And they know
it . . . The law on prisons was the biggest mistake!" A chief officer, an affable
man who is generally appreciated by both his superiors and the inmates,
offers this disillusioned comment on the changes in an institution he began
working in more than 20 years ago. He recalls the short-stay prison where
he started out, the 60 men he was responsible for on his walkway, the
cells with a double bunk and two mattresses on the floor, the inmates who
obeyed the guards, and he remarks nostalgically: "That's all gone now." For
him, the carceral world in which he now works is a troubling environment,
where prisoners have rights, where correctional officers have to justify their
actions, where external stakeholders observe and challenge them. "Now
you have to note it down in the electronic contact record every time prisoners refuse to go down to activities. It's extra work, but if you don't inmates'
support organizations complain to management and say we're stopping
the guys from going to meet them. But really it's them screwing things up,
because they believe the prisoners instead of listening to us!" Like many of
his colleagues, he feels that the 2009 law on prisons shifted the balance of
power too far in favor of inmates. At this point, five years after the law came
into force, it is indeed increasingly difficult to avoid applying it, particularly
as regards the ending of the systematic strip searches that provoke vehement
reactions in the facility.

But prima facie, this discourse appears to diverge hardly at all from that
of some older inmates, who also deplore the excessively liberal regime of
modern prisons. One of them, who has spent such a large part of his life
incarcerated that he jokes that prison is his "principal residence," has for
the last six months been writing a letter to the minister of justice, though he
keeps on putting off sending it, telling himself "it won't do any good, she'll

think 'it's just another convict writing to me.'" In this missive, he laments the changes of which he has been, so to speak, a privileged witness, writing: "Today, the old restrictions are no longer in place. What have the extreme changes in prison policy over the last 30 years led to? Giving prisoners rights without the obligation of duties!" The pleonasm of the final sentence reveals how much he misses the inscription of the obligations in the current carceral contract. With more pride than regret, he recalls the prisons of old: "To give you a picture of the difference, the cells then looked like the solitary confinement unit does now. Fittings fixed to the walls and floor, no one allowed to sleep during the day, regulation uniform for everyone, all prisoners required to have an activity – work, training, classes. Life in prison was real hard, and for some young guys of my generation, those restrictions just fed their hatred of a society that only knew how to punish." Yet he is troubled by the younger generation that comprises the majority of the prison population: "Instead of an environment that could put them back on the right track, they find a place where anything goes. Sleeping until noon, watching TV all night, listening to music at full blast, being out of their brains on hash. 'Idleness is the mother of all vices.'" However, if we examine it more closely, this opinion, which can also be heard from other mature inmates, is quite different from that of the chief officer.

The same word, "rights," is used to refer to two almost opposite realities here. The rights the sergeant complains of relate to the desire to make oneself heard, to contest a manifestation of authority, to insist on the provisions of the law being respected. The rights the old inmate disapproves of refer to the license to do nothing, to disturb others, to destroy oneself. Clearly, having the right to legal representation at a disciplinary board and having the right to watch television in one's cell are not of the same order. In a famous lecture at the University of Oxford in 1958, Isaiah Berlin distinguished two forms of liberty: a "positive liberty" consisting in having the power to choose the form of one's government and a "negative liberty" based on the possibility of acting without constraint or interference from others.[1] One might speak of citizenship in the first case, and license in the second. This dualism can be – and indeed has been – articulated in the sphere of rights, where a distinction is made between positive rights, in the sense that prerogatives can be exercised, and negative rights, implying that the individual is not subjected to interference from another. Writing to the General Inspector of Prisons and Detention Centers to complain about one's conditions of imprisonment sits in the domain of a claim for positive rights. Playing on a PlayStation in prison to occupy one's long periods of boredom derives, rather, from the enjoyment of negative rights. My point here is not to reify this distinction, and there are of course zones where these two modalities potentially intersect: for example, the right not to be attacked in the exercise yard is both a negative right (an inmate has the right not to be the victim of aggression by another inmate) and a positive one (an inmate has the right to demand that management defend him against violence).

These theoretical distinctions have material political consequences in the everyday life of prisons. When the sergeant talks of inmates having all the rights, he is referring principally to positive rights, which may place additional constraints on him, but not to negative rights, which he is willing to grant them within certain limits. When the long-serving prisoner complains of inmates having only rights without obligations, he is essentially speaking of negative rights that reinforce their dependence, particularly through idleness, as opposed to positive rights that would encourage their emancipation, for example through work. It is easy to understand why guards might be more inclined to recognize negative rights (which demarcate zones of relative freedom within prison and can even make their work easier, by rendering the inmates more docile) than positive rights (which they consider as encroaching on their territory): they can shut their eyes to the fact that inmates smoke marijuana in their cell, but resist the idea of prisoners challenging systematic strip searches. In the second situation the institution and its agents are directly called into question, whereas in the first they are not, provided that the matter is not made public.

There have been important developments in the carceral domain in recent years in terms of the recognition of both positive and negative rights of inmates. The former are often formalized through the European Prison Rules, the 2009 law on prisons, the Code of Penal Procedure: the right to have meals suited to one's religious convictions is enshrined in these texts. The latter are often more informally established, through the internal regulations or routine practices of the facility: the right to purchase a games console or a hotplate from the canteen forms part of local usage. The Directorate of Prison Administration publishes a comprehensive, detailed, and informative document numbering almost 200 pages, which summarizes the rights and duties of the incarcerated individual. However, I have never seen it in the cells. In general, management did not appear to take a proactive approach in this area, even when the documents concerned were available. "At first, you could borrow *Conditions of Incarceration in France,* but they realized the book was encouraging prisoners to make demands. Now it's only available as a reference book," one inmate told me. When I went to the library, I noted, however, that the didactic *Prisoner's Guide* was still available to borrow, and that the 25 copies were all out on loan.[2] Be that as it may, the idea of the rights of the incarcerated individual now formed part of the shared culture in the prison. Both management and inmates were aware of it: management implemented them, sometimes with conviction, for example in the case of access to the telephone, and sometimes reluctantly, especially when it came to the ending of systematic strip searches. The inmates benefited from those they were granted, such as the presence of a lawyer at the disciplinary board, and demanded those they were denied, such as individual cells. External actors were also involved in this domain, both public bodies (through a representative of the National Ombudsman) and nongovernmental organizations, especially the advocacy group Cimade, which supports non-French nationals in this facility as well as 72 others.

To speak of the culture of rights is to emphasize both that rights belong to the local culture of prisons (notwithstanding the reluctance of some staff, they are now much more widely accepted than these protestations would suggest), and that, reciprocally, the national culture influences what are considered to be the rights of the incarcerated individual (in this case, the stamp of the European Union is evident in the French texts that articulate these rights). This latter dimension of the culture of rights was made manifest to me in the course of a conversation I had in the United States with a political scientist, who was astonished to learn that in France a prisoner had the right to vote. In his view, being sentenced to a jail term necessarily implied the suspension of this right. Indeed, in his country nearly six million people, representing 2.5 percent of the voting-age population, are disenfranchised following a conviction, whether or not they are still in prison. In 13 states, the restriction applies only to those actually in prison; 24 extend it to individuals on parole; 11 impose it after the end of the prison sentence, including two where it continues for the entire lifetime; only two states have no restriction at all.[3] For my colleague, and certainly in the view of many in the United States, it went without saying: privation of the right to vote was a logical consequence of the privation of liberty. By contrast, I noted the efforts of the management of the facility where I conducted my research both to disseminate information on the presidential and parliamentary elections and to facilitate proxy voting, or even day release to vote. The level of participation in elections, which was very low even taking into account the 20 percent of non-national inmates, suggested that these efforts had borne little fruit, but they testified to the importance accorded to this democratic principle – a principle which, it has to be acknowledged, was easier to implement than the right to work.

*   *   *

"What principles of the execution of sentences give grounds for maintaining a structure that has more in common with labor relations during the industrial revolution than with those in today's France?" asks the General Inspector of Prisons and Detention Centers in a press release following the decision by the Constitutional Court on June 1, 2013 to reject a challenge by two prisoners to Article 713-3 of the Code of Penal Procedure, according to which "the labor relations of incarcerated persons are not subject to a contract of work."[4] This absence of a contract, the General Inspector explains, makes it possible for auxiliaries to be required to work seven days a week, for workers to receive no sick pay, for the termination of work not to be considered dismissal, for workplace inspections to be virtually non-existent, and in general for the employer to be exempt of all obligations with regard to the employee.[5] He notes further that prison work is an essential element both in keeping the peace and in the subsequent rehabilitation of inmates, two objectives that will be more fully achieved the more the worker's rights are recognized. And he concludes by calling on the government to introduce further rules that would respect both the security requirements of correctional facilities and the principles of inmates' dignity, in order to protect prison work, "far from the relic of another age that it is today." The government's reaction, however, was not what he hoped for: in a press release, the minister of justice declared that she herself was satisfied with the Constitutional Court's decision.[6] Thus prison work still sits outside labor law, unspecified by a contractual relationship, without the protections provided for other workers. The relationship between the inmate and his employer is a simple contract of engagement that carries virtually no legal implications.

Article 27 of the 2009 law on prisons states that "any person convicted of an offense is required to engage in at least one of the activities offered to him by the head of the facility and the director of the probation and re-entry service," provided that it contributes to his reintegration into society and corresponds to his capacities, while Article 717-3 of the Code of Penal Procedure specifies that "within correctional facilities, all arrangements shall be made to provide work, vocational or general training for those incarcerated individuals who request it." In other words, inmates have a duty to work, and the administration is required to provide them with employment. This mutual commitment is, however, diluted by two factors: on the prisoners' side, the duty only applies to those convicted and excludes inmates waiting for their trial; on the administration's side, the obligation regards means and not results. In fact, the system is far from fulfilling the stipulation of the law: in 2012, the proportion of inmates engaged in remunerated activity, including professional training, was 38 percent, with substantial variations as it reached 53 percent in long-term prisons, but stood at only 28 percent in short-stay facilities.[7] Hence we may estimate that in the latter, almost three-quarters of those incarcerated, have no remunerated activity and that, if we exclude vocational training that consists of short sessions on meager hourly pay rates and serves rather to compensate for shortages of employment, as many as four out of five inmates have no real remunerated work.[8] In this respect, convicted prisoners are scarcely better off than pre-trial inmates, especially when they are serving short sentences.

The work offered is of four types: general service, which accounts for around one-third of the workforce, and involves duties in the kitchen, laundry, cleaning, maintenance, canteen, and library; the production workshops, which employ more than one-third of all those working, and provide labor for private companies; the prison employment service, which operates mainly in long-term prisons; and, finally, work outside, in the case of prisoners on parole. In short-stay prisons, there are only general service and production workshops. While in the former the level of occupation remains stable, corresponding to the tasks required for the smooth running of the prison, in the latter it varies considerably in terms of number of positions, both from one facility to another and over time. Contrary to what was expected when it took over, delegated management of these services has not improved the situation, because the contractors concerned invest little in researching businesses that might be interested, and the central administration rarely applies the penalties specified for failure to meet employment targets.[9] This might seem surprising, given that it might be imagined that the prospect of a captive, docile, and inexpensive work-force, and free premises for carrying out the work, would be economically attractive.

The National Court of Audit offers several explanations for why this is not the case: the low productivity of prison workers, which is aggravated by their low levels of pay; their lack of qualifications, especially as priority is given to poor inmates with no training; and the prejudice against prisoners compared to other vulnerable groups such as disabled people, who have a better public image and social benefits. But the mediocre performance of the contractors in this area seems predominantly to result from a lack of active attempts on their part to canvass businesses that might provide work.[10] These businesses remain reluctant to make use of the prison workforce, and, when they do so, are discreet about it. As one manager for one of the companies which had contracts with prisons explained, this is dangerous territory: "Public opinion is very harsh. Some customers are shocked that operatives are paid, while at the same time observers accuse us of exploiting them."[11] Such issues play an important role.

As the prison I studied had delegated management, a private contractor was in charge both of general service and of the production shops, except of course for the building itself and the correctional officers. The average rate of remunerated employment among inmates was 18 percent over the year 2011. Three-fifths of the work was in the facility's general service. The remaining two-fifths was in the workshops, primarily consisting of tasks involved in wrapping and packaging.[12] By the end of my study, the level of employment had fallen even lower. There were only 30 posts available in the workshops, compared to the usual 60, representing a total of 117 jobs for the 850 individuals housed in the facility – barely 14 percent. Rather than a temporary circumstantial situation, this was a structural feature of the facility. Even if there had been plenty of contracts with outside busi-nesses and the 120 posts in the workshops were open – something that had never been the case since the prison opened – this would provide a total of 200 jobs, enough for just one-fourth of the inmates. And even if the surplus of prisoners over and above the facility's official number of places was miraculously eliminated, these jobs would still cover just over one-third of the potential workforce. In other words, although management sincerely regretted the shortage of jobs, it is clear that the short-stay prison is set up so as not to be in a position to offer work to every inmate.

In these circumstances, the agents of the management contractor in charge of informing newly arrived prisoners about the prospects for employment, subsequently assessing candidates and finally participating in their "pre-selection" (*classement*) – that is, their pre-assignment to a post following a meeting equated with a job interview – expressed frustration at the substantial gap between supply and demand, between the promises made to new arrivals and what they discovered over the months, between the declared mission of their company and the actual performance it appeared to be satisfied with. With waiting lists that grew longer as the prison population increased and the number of posts in the workshops fell, they also saw how employment became an additional means of exerting pressure on inmates: "The least little incident, and management takes the guy off the list and replaces him with the next one, who doesn't have an incident report," lamented one of these agents, who said that she was interested in the "human side" of his job and the "prospects for re-entry" it made possible. Thus, rather than a right that was guaranteed to incarcerated individuals and an obligation on the prison institution, work became a favor granted on the basis of disciplinary criteria. For there had to be some rationale for rejecting or delaying more than eight out of ten requests, and discipline was the disqualifying principle that seemed most legitimate to management. It extended a basic principle to the so-called special notice prisoners, whose long pre-trial detention never allowed them to work, whereas other activities such as sports remained available to them.

In this context of scarcity, there was one factor that did confer priority: "destitution." This was not a local, but a national policy that pointed to the charitable aspect of allocation of these rare opportunities. Incarcerated persons who had very little savings and did not receive any external support had priority in employment in the general service or the workshops. Some of them were highly desocialized, making it difficult for them to be integrated into work. They would fail to get up in the morning to go to work, or would readily talk back when spoken to in a harsh way, which exposed them to the risk of dismissal. Others, however, were much appreciated by the staff, notably, as we have seen, the "Romanians," who were not necessarily nationals of Romania, since the term was applied generically to all "traveling people" originating from Eastern Europe. "We like the Romanians," said one guard who supervised this section of the prison. "They don't give us any problems. They work real hard. Since the guys are on piecework rates in the workshops, they can make double what the other prisoners do. They send money to their families and keep a bit for buying stuff in the canteen. They never cause any trouble." The restriction of work to the most needy left few places available for those who were not.

The distinction between pre-trial and convicted prisoners, which the law required should be taken into account (since only the latter were supposed to be guaranteed paid employment), barely operated, given the scarcity of jobs. Indeed, even among convicted prisoners, very few were offered work. The assignment committee took into consideration how long the inmate had been on the waiting list, especially when prisoners remained insistent in their demands and persuasive with their block senior. This was perhaps not the case with one man, who, although he had been in detention for 21 months, had still not obtained the work he had asked for. Thus, in terms of employment, there were three possible positions: an inmate could be an applicant, a "preselected," or a worker. The first status accounted for the majority of inmates. A select minority achieved the second status and were on a waiting list. At this point, in principle all that was required was to be patient and not to be involved in any incident, to hope that after a few weeks or months they might accede to the third status, entering the circle of the chosen who enjoyed paid work. But they remained at the mercy of an incident report, and hence potentially of a malicious employee of the private contractor, which could cause them to lose the dearly won privilege.

* * *

The most obvious reason why inmates valued employment so much was the income it provided. They sent part of it to their families, for whom it was sometimes the only resource. They kept the remainder to buy products in the canteen and enhance their day-to-day lives. In the general service, there were three levels of pay, depending on length of service and skill: in the kitchen, for example, a kitchen porter would be in class I, while an experienced kitchen assistant would be paid at class III. At the first level, the day rate for five hours' work was between 8.02 and 10.46 euros; at the second, it was between 10.47 and 13.70 euros; and at the third, it was up to 13.71 euros. These amounts, which were set nationally, were a little below those specified by the law on prisons, at respectively 20 percent, 25 percent, and 33 percent of the national minimum wage. Thus the sum inmates received each month, provided they had not been off sick, was between 200 and 300 euros, as I was able to confirm when I examined inmates' payslips. In the workshops, payment was by piecework, on the basis of an hourly tariff corresponding to a specified level of production. Depending on the task and the businesses that commissioned it, this tariff was between 2 and 5.5 euros per hour, when the 2009 law on prison recommended a minimum of 4.20 euros. Inmates who produced more than the standard rate were paid more; those who produced less were paid less. Monthly pay therefore varied, and in exceptional circumstances, for example for the so-called Romanians, could be as high as 600 euros, but in general it was around half this amount. Obviously, these wages were only paid for the months in which the inmate worked, and, given the scarcity of contracts, the 30 or so posts available were rotated around the 80 "pre-selected" individuals; as a result, a worker in the production shops could go months without any activity, and hence without any pay.

The low level of remuneration gives a sense of how underappreciated the work produced by inmates is. On the one hand, the tasks performed are neither skilled nor stimulating: a laundry operative places the dirty laundry of those who have no family to do it in the big machines; a cleaner empties the trashcans into the dumpsters provided and mops the floors in the communal areas; a packager wraps small bags of sugar, milk, and coffee into larger packets; an assembler folds marketing boxes for a major whisky brand. On the other, employees of the contractor often emphasize their distinction from, and in some cases their contempt for, the workers. As one of these salaried employees said of his colleagues: "Most of them reckon: 'Whatever, they're only prisoners, you can't expect anything of them except their work'; they don't think about the fact that one day these guys are going to be released." In this respect, there was a marked contrast between the formulaic discourse of the head of one of the delegated management services ("The human aspect is important to us," "We forget about prison, we're working on a business footing," "Work is a keystone of social reintegration"), and the comments I gleaned from interviews with inmates working in this service ("You should hear how they talk to us," "You can't treat a man like a dog," "I was sacked for not closing packets properly"). The combination of these factors – the low pay, the nature of the work, and the attitude of the company employees – contributed to devaluing and demotivating the workers, and concomitantly reducing the quality and productivity of their work. The contractor and even the prison management used this as a retrospective justification for the very low wages. It is therefore easy to understand why inmates needed to have other than material reasons for wanting to work, notwithstanding the obstacles and the humiliations.

These reasons were of three orders: practical, symbolic, and tactical.[13] First, having a job means that one is occupied; it kills time that refuses to pass. The five hours of those who work in the general service, from 7:30 a.m. to 12:30 p.m. or from 1:30 p.m. to 6:30 p.m., fill half their day. This means so much time not spent in their cell, and even if it deprives them of one of their exercise periods, it offers them a daily opportunity for socializing with the other workers engaged in the same activity. While they are occupied in packaging the products that pass along the conveyor belt of a small production line, an inmate jokes with his neighbor, in reference to the former socialist budget minister who had to resign over tax fraud allegations involving tax havens: "Hey, you've got a message. Your payment to the Cayman Islands arrived OK. It's signed Cahuzac!" Second, working means having a certain status, not feeling idle and useless, establishing habits conducive to re-entry into society, coming closer to normal life outside prison. Having a job and also being paid allows them to regain a form of dignity. This is no doubt what one director is referring to when he says emphatically: "I like going to the workshops. They're places where you see the working relationship really taking precedence over everything else. It's the other side of things. It's just life."

Finally, being a "worker" is a crucial contribution that can be highlighted in applications to the probation and re-entry service and the sentencing judge, with the aim of securing additional sentence reductions, day release, and parole. It is both evidence of efforts made by the prisoner to prove himself responsible and a demonstration of his desire to make reparation by paying part of his wages to any civil parties to his case. "Everyone wants to work so as to get out quicker," acknowledges one inmate. But this tactical dimension of work has two disadvantages. On the one hand, some staff and judges are doubtful about the sincerity of prisoners' desire to work, though it can rarely be demonstrated. "I don't like it when they fulfill obligations just to get a sentence reduction," says one counselor, and this type of comment, if it is made at the committee on sentencing, can detrimentally influence a judge's decision. On the other hand, those whose requests for work are not met are doubly penalized, because not only are they not working, but the fact is held against them, especially in not granting them all of the sentence reductions they could claim. When I asked a deputy warden why this was the case, he replied: "All those who really want to work, work: they hassle us and they end up having a job." That day, there were officially 194 posts for 820 inmates – a shortfall of 626 jobs.

However, above and beyond these empirical observations, a more general question needs to be posed as to the meaning and function of prison work. There are at least two parts to this question. Why prison work? And what for? The first part addresses the moral sense of the work, and the second its practical ends. Indeed, in the history of prison, forced labor long held both a punitive significance and an economic function. The prisoner's toil formed part of the punishment, but it also benefited local agriculture or industry. The two aspects could to some extent be distinguished, either to prioritize the punitive dimension, as in nineteenth-century British prisons, where inmates turned a treadwheel in an exhausting, useless, and dangerous toil, or to highlight the economic contribution, as in the United States prison system where work in the fields of the penitentiaries replaced slavery, which had been abolished, to the benefit of farmers.[14] In France, as Patricia O'Brien has shown, work "was the core, the essence, of the new punishment." Neither a purely retributive activity, nor simply capitalist expansion, it established an equivalence between the form "work" and the form "prison."[15] More specifically, in the move from the galleys to hard labor, and even in the effort to transform forced labor in the early nineteenth century, a shift can be seen from an essentially shaming penalty to a punishment that aimed to improve convicts while at the same time rendering their labor more productive – to the point that later, free workers would protest against what they saw as unfair competition. However, the transformation of prison does not follow a linear trajectory, and after a period of relative softening of the carceral condition under the influence of philanthropic ideas, the mid-nineteenth century saw a return to tougher attitudes, work once again becoming a punishment, without, however, losing its contribution to production.[16] Let us now consider conditions today.

Contemporary French prisons promote the moral significance of work, but understate its economic function. Talk is of mutual rights and obligations: the right to work and the obligation to provide work, but also the obligation to work and the right not to institute a contractual relationship. Emphasis is placed on the importance of work in helping the inmate to gain a sense of responsibility and to reform, to admit his wrongdoing and make amends for it, to commit to the path of re-entry. The possibility of this work producing wealth and serving society is played down.[17] People prefer to think that it is out of moral duty that the prison administration offers employment to inmates and out of a sense of civic responsibility that companies provide work for them. And these very arguments are harnessed to oppose any reform of contracts or wages for prison work. Yet, without denying the moral dimension, a more dialectical approach can be suggested.

"According to the General Inspector, everyone should have work, the labor code should be respected and prisoners should be paid the minimum wage," says one director. "The problem is that if we did that, there would be no work. We need to attract businesses. We don't have specially selected, motivated, productive workers like the private sector, where an underperforming employee can be sacked. Here we have no choice. And our inmates have a difficult relationship to work, they're not efficient workers. If we want businesses to come and to stay, we need a win-win-win situation: for the inmate, for the company, and for the prison management." The latter two may perhaps have felt they won out in the transaction, but this was certainly not the case for the inmates, who complained not only about the scarcity of jobs and the low wages, but also about the practical and psychological dependence in which they were placed by the workplace relationship. The unsatisfactory quality of this relationship was in fact a major contributory factor to the poor performance with which the inmates were reproached. Moreover, toward the end of my period of research, posts in the workshops represented only one-quarter of the paid jobs at the facility, with three-quarters in the general service, and hence under the sole authority of the prison. In other words, even if we accept the director's reasoning, the effectiveness of the policy of "social dumping" followed by the prison system has not been demonstrated, despite the very profitable terms offered to outside companies.

In fact, greater insight would be gained by distinguishing the two sectors. The general service is entirely under the authority of the prison management, either directly, or through the intermediary of the delegated contractor; it is management that fixes the rates of pay and the conditions of work. "How do prisons run?" asks one man whose long experience of prison gives him a realist approach. His answer: "It's inmates who do the work. And for almost nothing." One can indeed imagine what the cost would be if public servants were recruited, or if private companies were contracted to perform all the tasks that prisoners undertake. The workshops are a different category, at least as far as the labor concession is concerned, since the practical organization and regulation of the working arrangements are largely under the control of the prison administration. The facility offers the private sector a workforce for which the outlay on wages is one-quarter to one-fifth of that on the free market, with a number of further advantages such as supervision by correctional officers, absence of unions, and free workspace. The prison population functions as a reserve industrial army,[18] far too numerous to be incorporated into normal relations of production, but always available when an urgent packaging or manufacturing job arises. In contrast to the United States, where companies close factories and relocate their activity in prison facilities, and where the corporations that run private prisons employ thousands of very low-paid prisoners, in France it is unlikely that this intermittent exploitation of captive workers significantly influences employment and wage levels on the free market, but it certainly contributes to its poor public image. It is worth considering whether conditions closer to those of work on the outside might help to rehabilitate these jobs in the eyes of the public, and hence render them more attractive to businesses.

Be that as it may, it is clear that work in prison is a matter not only of a moral economy of self-reform and atonement for one's actions, but also of a political economy for which one has to take into account both the profit it generates for the management and the companies involved and the resulting financial and symbolic devaluation of inmates as workers. For the prison system, the room for maneuver is admittedly limited in a difficult economic context and hostile ideological climate, and clearly, with less overcrowded and better resourced facilities things would be very different, but the justifications put forward for refusing to bring prison work in line with standards are unconvincing. And perhaps it is precisely by articulating the moral and political economies that one could moralize, so to speak, the politics of employment in prison.

*   *   *

But the social mission of the prison is not confined to work and vocational training. There is another strand, partly related to these two: support for poor inmates. Prison has always faced the problem of poverty on a mass level. The selective orientation of penal policies, and the differential conditions in which they are applied by the police and courts, have led to the poor being highly overrepresented in prisons since their inception.[19] An institution for the poor, prison is also a poor institution, and the lack of resources allocated to facilities, with its consequences in terms of material conditions in the carceral world, has often been interpreted as indifference and contempt toward these disadvantaged and marginalized classes. Governments have begun to pay more attention to this question, a development that has been marked by a linguistic shift in the designation of the phenomenon: "destitution" becomes "poverty," and the "destitute" are termed "persons with insufficient resources." This terminological change has been accompanied by development of the statutory oversight, with the confirmation that it is the responsibility of the state, that a more rigorous codification of the category is needed, and that a more formalized definition of the procedures for addressing the issue is required. Article 31 of the 2009 law on prisons stipulates: "Incarcerated individuals with resources less than an amount specified by the regulations shall receive in-kind support from the state intended to improve their material conditions of existence. This support may also be provided as a cash payment under the conditions stipulated by government order." The Code of Penal Procedure specifies the threshold: 50 euros. The measures combine financial assistance, in-kind support, and priority access to remunerated activity.

I began my research during the last days of the old system.[20] Assistance for the "destitute" was managed and financed by a not-for-profit organization formed by prison staff, which earned its money from the profits on renting television sets: this was called "the prison's charity." A committee met once a month in the facility to assess individually each of the case files preselected by the accounts office, on the basis of an income threshold then set at 45 euros per month. It comprised a deputy warden, a probation and re-entry counselor, a prison visitor, and a representative of the charity. The block seniors, who were not present, would sometimes leave a message encouraging the committee to support an application or reject a case. The sum available in each inmate's account was calculated, with an automatic deduction of 20 percent for civil parties, and 10 percent for his release pot: the first of these enforced compensation of victims, while the second constituted savings to be used at the end of the sentence time.

Each month, around 60 of the 800 inmates were classified as "destitute." This categorization potentially gave them the right to a monthly allowance of 10 euros, if they had less than 10 euros, and a supplementary grant of 5 euros from a charitable organization, paid if the amount available was less than 5 euros, as well as free television, which the other inmates rented. "That means that in the best case they had 15 euros and TV," remarked a member of the committee with satisfaction. In addition to the strict financial criteria, granting of aid was dependent on a double moral requirement: merit was judged on the basis of willingness to work and good conduct in prison. If the inmate had not requested or had rejected an activity, he would lose the grant. If he had an incident report, he would be deprived of television. The individuals concerned only learned of these rules at the point when the sanction was applied.

Under what conditions should the poor receive assistance? This question lies at the heart of all systems of welfare assistance that adopt what might be termed a meritocratic paradigm. It has a long history: the distinction between the "deserving" and "undeserving poor" that flourished with the development of the social question in the nineteenth century goes much further back.[21] There are two methods for granting resources to individuals in need. They can be allocated assistance purely on the basis of economic criteria, by fixing a threshold below which the person has a right to assistance. But moral criteria can also be added, used to evaluate the deservingness of the individual, and generally restricting the range of the right to assistance, but in some cases extending it.[22] Social welfare policies have evolved along this line. "We don't want to create welfare dependence," argues the deputy warden responsible for the committee. "When we say: 'We'll give it to him if he looks for work or if he studies,' it's like the conditions for the minimum social income or a scholarship outside of the prison. There has to be giving on both sides." The efforts made by individuals are therefore taken into account, as well as the degree of submission they demonstrate. The committee expects them both to express a desire to work and to accept the employment offered, to behave well and to comply with authority. In this respect, this assistance for poor prisoners derives not only from a concern for charity; it also implies a desire to discipline.

But by including moral criteria, even apparently objective ones like a refusal to work or an incident report, the committee introduces a measure of discretionary power and generates deliberations aimed at taking or justifying a decision. In the case of one individual with resources of 4.86 euros, who has not requested work and has refused to return to his cell, it is decided that he will receive neither allowance nor television, but there is a discussion around the 5 euros from the charitable association. One member proposes firmness in order to assert the principle, on the grounds that the inmate is letting himself go; another, touched by the situation of this isolated immigrant, who has no visitors, pleads in favor of the grant. In the end, the 5-euro sum is awarded and a letter sent "to tell him that we are making an exception." With another inmate, whose disposable funds amount to 5.85 euros and who has refused a job, the problem of the reasons for his attitude are raised: is it unwillingness, or is this, as in another case, a prisoner who is being victimized by another? Committee members wonder if it is really his fault, but in the absence of information, decide to give him nothing, albeit with regret because "we should have sent him a message: 'You'll get it this month but it's the last time.'" A man who works in the production shops but failed to get up one morning, saying to the guard: "Yo, man, let me sleep!" is let off, and awarded television and the allowance. In relation to another, whom the committee learns is in the protected prisoners' wing, one member exclaims knowingly: "He should get everything!"

Thus a great deal of time and energy, affects and arguments are expended in deciding on the award of just 5 or 10 euros. But with 10 euros, the deputy warden has calculated, an inmate can buy one cigarette a day – unless, he adds, he prefers chocolate or a few phone calls. So the significance of the committee's efforts lies less in the amount of aid granted than in the fact that it allows them to either sanction or support individuals. Television is a luxury: the undisciplined inmate is deprived of it. The allowance meets a need: it is withdrawn from the lazy inmate. Through its treatment of the poor, the prison reveals the degree of detail engaged in the implementation of its moral project – the paradox being nevertheless that those who are punished are generally not informed of this, unless they ask to use their savings for canteen purchases and then discover that they do not have enough funds in their account; even in this situation, they are unaware of what has happened. Only those whose television is switched off understand that they are being punished, when they ask the guard for the reason.

However, it would be wrong to underestimate the impact of the steps taken to assist poor inmates. First, sanctions were relatively rare. According to my observations, depriving an inmate of television on grounds of poor behavior occurred in approximately one case in ten, while withdrawal of the allowance for failure to request or refusal of work also affected 10 percent of the potential beneficiaries; about 80 percent of so-called destitute inmates received the entirety of the assistance they were due. Second, the sums, however derisory they might appear to an outside observer, did not seem so to the inmates whose savings were scanter still. In relation to the 2.74-, 0.42-, or 0.03-euro savings cited one by one on the list of the potential recipients, the 15 euros from the committee represented a not insignificant sum for those who received it. Moreover, the modest sums of financial assistance were augmented by in-kind support provided on arrival in the form of clothing, shoes, toiletries, and correspondence kit. A man sentenced to three months' imprisonment for vehicle theft acknowledged: "Compared to life outside, I'm better off here. When you've got no home, no job, no family . . . The car I stole was my home. When it's cold you turn the engine on for a bit, to warm up. I tell you, prison is like a breath of fresh air for me. The first week, they gave me a bit of money for tobacco, they supplied me with pants and sneakers. Here, because we're classed as destitute, we have TV." This former social work assistant, 42 years of age, of African origin, had successively been fired, separated from his wife, and been evicted from his apartment. "It would be better if I had a bit of privacy, a cell to myself," he admitted, but he accepted gratefully what the facility gave him as did other inmates, for there was a sense of solidarity within the prison.

By the end of my research period, the procedure had changed significantly. The term now used was "poverty." Reference was made to the circular of May 17, 2013.[23] Cases were reviewed once a month by the assignment committee rather than a dedicated one. The poverty threshold had risen to 50 euros. The sums allocated were substantially higher, with management granting 20 euros and two charitable organizations adding 5 euros each for the impoverished – double the amount in the preceding period. Most importantly, the 20-euro allowance served to bring individuals' resources closer to the 50-euro threshold. Previously, an inmate with 12 euros would not have received any financial assistance even though he would be considered destitute; now, he would be granted the 20 euros of the management's allowance. The financial assistance allocated by the prison for the purposes of "combating poverty" amounted to almost 25,000 euros per year, including the allowance made on arrival.

The sanctions, however, remained the same: a refusal to engage in activity would lead to loss of the allowance, and an incident report to removal of television privileges. The effect of the clarification of the procedures, through a five-page document, the replacement of the paper document by a computer screen, the incorporation of the decisions into the routine procedures of the committee, and the elimination of input from actors from outside the prison management had rendered the granting of assistance a remarkably more automatic process. There were no more digressions on the significance of a refusal to work or the message to be sent, no more hesitations over decisions. More was allocated, and less was discussed. The committee coordinator, a captain, had warned me: "You'll see, things are simple, decisions are made quickly. It's not necessarily that interesting!" The tone had shifted from operating in the manner of a support organization to a bureaucratic protocol, from the affectivity of a charitable approach to the neutrality of a technical procedure. Assistance to poor individuals had become standardized. It was no longer a gift conferred out of generosity, but a right accompanied by restrictions.

* * *

In education, other rationales are at work. The pedagogic function of the prison is particularly crucial because a substantial proportion of its population comprises young men whose low level of education represents a considerable handicap in entering the labor market, and hence an aggravating factor in their social marginalization.[24] The education provided within short-stay and long-term prisons has therefore long been considered both a way of alleviating the failures of the national education system, of which crime and imprisonment are in part collateral effects, and a tool for rehabilitation of inmates, encouraging their eventual return to society. Added to this general concern is the particular issue of non-French nationals, who are known to be overrepresented in prison, and for whom a lack of French language skills constitutes an added difficulty: one prisoner in ten does not speak French, or speaks it poorly.[25] "Inmates should acquire or develop the knowledge they will need after release to ensure better social adaptation," states Article D-450 of the Code of Penal Procedure. "All resources compatible with the requirements of discipline and security must be provided for this purpose for those inmates who may benefit from education and vocational training, in particular the youngest and those with the lowest levels of schooling." Given the available means, this is a major challenge.

Over the history of prison, the place of education has fluctuated in relation to the dominant ideology. It became more prominent in the early nineteenth century, when the philanthropic principle came to the fore, since at that time schooling formed an integral part of moral and religious education in the fight against the corruption that the prison environment was supposed to represent. Subsequently, however, it receded in importance at times when the strict punitive paradigm regained the upper hand. Similarly, in the twentieth century, a renewal of interest in the prison reform movement can be observed in the somber period following World War II; this was marked by the creation of a body of correctional educators distinct from the social services in adult facilities, while the reform schools for minors were transformed.[26] But it was not until the early 1960s that the ministry of education made teachers available to prisons.

In 2013, there were 405 elementary-level teachers and 66 high-school teachers working full time in prisons; in addition, supply teachers worked an annual total of 4,407 hours. Ten years earlier, the figures were respectively 346 and 36 correctional educators, supplemented by 2,696 supply teacher hours. Thus there has been a 23 percent increase in the number of full-time teachers during this period. During the same period, the number of prisoners has increased by approximately 20 percent.[27] In terms of the number of full-time teachers, therefore, the level of educational provision for the prison population has remained relatively stable. But this assessment needs to be adjusted to take into account the fact that one-third of the increase concerns the recruitment of correctional educators in facilities for juveniles, reducing the number of those available for adults by the same proportion. These data obviously only relate to licensed teachers and so do not include the work of volunteers, notably the 1,200 students from GENEPI, the National Student Association for Education in Places of Incarceration, who play a major role in some facilities.[28] One-quarter of the prison population is classed as being in education, an increase on the figure of 10 years previously. In terms of levels of training, among those inmates in education, one in eight is studying French as a foreign language; one in two is taking classes in basic skills for students without educational qualifications; one in four is taking elementary or middle classes; only 8 percent are taking high school classes, and fewer than 2 percent are in higher education. Each year, nearly 8,000 prisoners pass national education examinations or other qualifications.

However, these figures vary depending on the facility, short-stay prisons presenting particular problems both because of a shortage of teachers and because the turnover of inmates is high. In the facility where I carried out my research and where GENEPI was not active, the efforts of the two full-time teachers and the supply teachers came up against various obstacles. There were long waiting lists, especially for training that led to qualifications. Priority had been given to the "low levels," that is, literacy, French as a foreign language, and study for basic skills, which accounted for two-thirds of the students; according to the head of the education service, they were particularly "motivated," as the low drop-out rate indicated. However, the few inmates who tried to pursue higher-level studies came up against a series of obstacles, both practical (sharing a cell with a cellmate who kept the television permanently on, making it difficult to concentrate) and regulatory (although legally permitted, purchase of a computer was forbidden by the local prison management, and access to the Internet was prohibited by the national prison administration).[29] The level of educational activity was high. In terms of flow, more than 700 students were enrolled in one or other of the courses over the year, accounting for at least half of those who entered the facility. At any given moment, around 200 inmates, fewer than one-quarter of those in prison, were taking more than one class, including in English and computing.

Despite the high numbers, training sessions ran without tensions or clashes. "We're not the prison. The students are well aware of that. We respect them, they respect us. We support them to progress, help them pass exams," explains one teacher, adding: "But even so, it is clear that we're part of prison management. We are inevitably wearing both hats. If our students get good results in their exams, it's also thanks to the administration." But this was no blind loyalty. Raising the issue of some correctional officers' behavior, another said angrily: "We see things that we find shocking, but we can't say anything." And after a short pause, he adds: "There are some really terrible things that go on." Their intermediate position, external to the institution, on the side of the staff, yet critical when they departed from standards, enabled them occasionally to have discussions with inmates, who took advantage of this rare opportunity to speak with staff members from outside a relationship of authority or supplication: "We have really deep discussions with the Basques. And we like to get into an argument with the Muzzies. They defend their values, we defend ours – with the Basques, it's the state, with the Muzzies, it's secularism." They described themselves as "committed"; one of them pointed out: "It's not by chance that we're here. We can't be ordinary teachers. We put some energy into our teaching," while another said: "They need people like us coming in. We do extraordinary work with extraordinary people. When you meet a prisoner, you often find he's an exceptional person."

Education gave rise, once a year, to a ceremonial event for the award of diplomas. In the gym, representatives of the national education system, members of the prison management staff, and of course teachers from the education team, sat opposite the 20 or so inmates to be honored. There were almost as many of the former as of the latter. "Now we're going to award a certificate to someone who has made us real proud. He took all the exams: the First Diploma in the French Language, the Certificate of General Training, the Middle School Certificate, and finally his Certificate of Vocational Skills." "This is someone who was anxious – but he made it!" "This person passed with flying colors!" For each of the students the same formula is followed: a brief personal introduction, the calling of the name, an applause from the audience, the handover of the certificate, the choice of a book as a prize. Returning to his seat, the inmate would show his delight with a modest smile or a gesture to his companions. The correctional educators seemed as moved and happy as their students by the recognition that the inmates had achieved through their work. In the last year when I attended this celebration, they were still more satisfied, for it was the first time in this prison that they had been able to offer the Vocational Skills Certificate, which had cost them a great deal of bureaucratic effort to arrange. Nine inmates, who had assiduously followed the theoretical training and the practical course, had taken the exam. All the newly qualified students were present to receive the fruit of their labors – all but one, whose certificate could not be handed over.

At the end of the ceremony, the director made a short, impassioned speech: (addressing the correctional educators and guests) "Ladies and gentlemen," (turning toward the inmates) "gentlemen – it was through the police and the courts that you entered prison. All of you know why you are here. You are here to serve out a sentence. But prison can also be an opportunity, the opportunity to do something you could not have done outside, like taking a national education degree. I'll tell you something; the reason I came to work in prison administration is not because I like to see people locked up. It's for moments like this. It's because I believe that it is possible to make prison a place that gives those who are locked up here another chance. So I offer you my sincere congratulations that you have seized that opportunity and gained the diploma you have just received. And when you leave this hall, go and tell your fellow inmates. Tell them that they too can take advantage of what the prison has to offer. Gentlemen, I offer you my compliments for the work you have done, which is rewarded today." The celebration, with its inspirational tone, was not without emotion for inmates and participants, concluding with a profession of faith in the rehabilitative mission of prison and sending the happy elect out among the people of inmates. This secular liturgy indicated the extent to which educational activity in the carceral world was still a moral work, and especially how, notwithstanding ideological developments and bureaucratic changes, a mystique of atonement was perpetuated beneath the discourse of deserved punishment and cold rationality. Prison was capable of giving a second chance to those who were capable of taking advantage of it. It offered them a form of redemption.

However, I could not detach myself for long from the empire of punishment and rationality. The day after the ceremony, I was present when a man in his 30s, sentenced to 10 years' imprisonment for a series of offenses, appeared before the disciplinary board. He had been in the prison for 18 months and it was the first time he had been summoned before them. The charge against him was as follows. Five days earlier, as he left the visiting rooms after seeing his lawyer, he had wanted to go to the gym, for the weekly activity he so valued. He had therefore taken his sports bag with him to the visiting rooms, and warned the guard of his block that he would arrive late. On his return, the officer guarding the entrance to the gym had refused to let him in. The man had become angry, thrown his belongings on the floor, and started yelling at the guard. The latter had called his colleagues who had immediately handcuffed the protester and taken him to the solitary confinement block. Nowhere in the incident report was there any mention of insults, threats, or violence, but simply of an outburst of rage. He appeared before the committee on the final day when such preventative solitary confinement could legally be imposed.

At the hearing, the man said he had not understood why he was forbidden entry to the gym, given that he had notified the guard in his block that he would be late and had been allowed to take his sports kit. Nevertheless, he apologized for losing his temper, explaining that he had received "bad news" during the visit. His lawyer, who was present at the hearing, explained. The man had just learned that the transfer to another facility he had been requesting since being sentenced several months earlier had been postponed once again. His wife, who was sick, lived in another region and in order to visit him had to travel two and a half hours each way with their 2-year-old child. There was another family complication that his lawyer had told him about. He had a son from a previous marriage, and his ex-wife had just confirmed that she refused to let him see his father. This accumulation of distressing news had profoundly upset the man. It explained why he had become angry when, a few minutes later, the guard had deprived him of his only release: sports. "I understand that, but we're not here as a sponge for your problems," exclaimed the deputy warden chairing the committee to the inmate. Examining the case file, he softened as he noted that the man had an 18-month record of blameless behavior, with no incident report, and had taken up many activities. "You've even passed your Vocational Skills Certificate. And two days before the certificates are awarded, in front of regional education inspectors, you screw up!" I understood then that this was the inmate who had been missing from the awards ceremony; he had not been able to attend the event because he was in a solitary confinement cell. The man objected meekly that he had taken his training very seriously, and was proud to be able to tell his family that he had passed the examination. "You deprived yourself of a fine ceremony," the director told him, cruelly. As happens so often in such cases, he was sentenced to eight days in solitary confinement with five suspended, allowing him to return to his cell immediately. Had his case been heard the day before, without waiting until the deadline for summoning him, he could have celebrated his diploma with his colleagues and teachers.

The succession of the celebration in the gym and the judgment at the hearing was a timely reminder that all the rights that inmates could enjoy – in this case the right to education, but it would have been the same with the right to work, the right to financial assistance, and others – always remained subordinate to the logic of the carceral order. Even though in this case the man had behaved irreproachably for 18 months, had worked hard to pursue a demanding training, and had passed the final examination, it meant nothing when it came to the urgency of sanctioning his momentary outburst, for which the multiple painful disappointments he had suffered did not constitute an extenuating circumstance. When facing the prison's law, the rights of inmates remained fragile.

*   *   *

Legal sociologists, and more generally legal scholars, generally tend to consider the institution of prison in terms of judicialization. Their focus is on examining, through the evolution of legislation and the development of legal arguments, how the law is encroaching on prisons.[30] In this respect, the changes that have arisen since the early 2000s, mainly under the combined influence of the European Prison Rules and reformers seeking to transform the world of prison, incontestably show that legal norms and judicial practices have penetrated an administration that was for a long time able to be independent of them. Take, for example, the almost systematic presence of a lawyer, either chosen by the inmate or appointed by the court, to assist prisoners appearing before disciplinary boards, and the possibility, however rarely taken up, of appealing a sanction imposed at such hearings; or the establishment of a procedure involving arguments for both parties, once again in the presence of a lawyer, in the meetings where the sentence adjustments to be decided by judges are discussed – meetings which, furthermore, generally take place within the facility, with magistrates and counsels coming to the prison.

Conversely, there would seem to be a trend for the institution itself to counterattack, as it were, in the arena of the law, since it resorts more often to the public prosecutor and the judge in order to punish acts perpetrated within the facility, such as violence, in which case the penalty issued at immediate appearance trial is added to the sanction pronounced by the disciplinary board. The new procedures, by bringing prison administration closer to the judiciary, probably also generate new tensions between the representatives of the two institutions, wardens and magistrates in particular, as I often observed. Moreover, it may be that the most profound changes regarding the penetration of the law into prison are the least visible, such as the metamorphosis of the profession of probation and re-entry counselor, which previously combined the traditions of social worker and youth worker, and is now increasingly composed of practitioners trained mainly in legal disciplines. This is a logical consequence of the growing expectation that they will help to prevent recidivism. This contemporary reshaping of the legal landscape, of which these are only a few illustrations, seems to bear out the words of the director who told me of his reservations about a remark he had heard at the ministry of justice: "A director from the National Prison Administration told us: 'Prison is simple: you have court decisions and a Code of Penal Procedure.' I wanted to say to him: 'Come and work with us on the ground, you'll see it's a bit more complicated than that!'"

But rather than the question of the law in prison, what I seek to understand here is the issue of the rights of the incarcerated.[31] The move from law to rights is crucial, because it shifts the focus of the investigation from a discipline, with its methods and its actors (law and jurists), to society in the broader sense (the law operates on the same basis as economics or politics or morality). In examining the rights of inmates, my aim is to move away from the law as a body of knowledge and practice. As Belgian criminologist Dan Kaminski puts it: "The question of prisoners' rights must be addressed more seriously and less legalistically."[32] But the point is not to contrast these two approaches, particularly given that rights are obviously partly expressed through the law and that those who defend them generally have recourse to it, but simply to differentiate them in order to better understand how prisoners' rights escape or resist the law of prison.

The right to work, as we have seen, is not the labor law. Prisons have a duty to provide a remunerated activity for inmates (even if they actually fail to do so), but there is no employment contract in prison (for political reasons that are in fact far removed from the economic justifications provided). Similarly, the right to assistance for the poor has, admittedly, been legally consolidated and even procedurally standardized, but the concrete application of it always draws in moral considerations (relating to the deservingness of the inmates concerned as evidenced by discipline and commitment). Finally, the right to education is regularly asserted by the administration and implemented by motivated teachers, but comes up against limits in the restrictions applied in the name of the carceral order (whether this be the ban on computers or sanctions for offenses committed). In other words, rights sit in an uncertain zone of the social space where the law is only one element among others and rarely the deciding factor; the administration is at liberty to skirt round the legislation by arguing on the basis of economics, morality, or security, as in the three cases I have cited. Conversely, inmates may move away from the legal approach, demanding rights in political terms, for example. While it may rightly be asserted, therefore, that the law occupies a growing place in the relationships in the world of prison, one could hardly formulate a similarly categorical statement and describe such a linear development in relation to prisoners' rights. The changes that have taken place appear complex, sometimes contradictory, and often ambiguous.

The complexity, contradictions, and ambiguity find a clear manifestation in the case of non-nationals. Two distinctive statistical features are relevant regarding the latter. On the one hand, they are overrepresented in prisons, making up 19 percent of the prison population compared to 6 percent of the population living in France. I have discussed the reasons for this excess presence above. They relate partly to the specificity of certain offenses, partly to the targeting of law enforcement activity, and partly to judges' more frequent choice of incarceration, particularly when there are questions about the guarantee of appearance in court.[33] On the other hand, the proportion of foreign inmates in the prison population has fallen sharply since the 1990s, though the actual total has remained about the same. The rate of incarceration has reduced from 31 percent to 19 percent, but the number of non-nationals under prison sentence remains remarkably stable at a little more than 15,000. However, the fall in the incarceration rate and the stability of the statistics obscure the reality of the incarceration of foreigners, since a large proportion of those who were previously imprisoned for lack of residence permit are now in detention centers awaiting deportation from France.[34] In effect, offenses against immigration law have largely been shifted to other places of incarceration; non-nationals have suffered the punitive turn in France just as the rest of the population has, but more intensely.

In the prison where I conducted my research, non-nationals made up 21 percent of the population. Some of them were in breach of immigration law, although usually incarcerated for a different reason. For obvious reasons they were particularly vulnerable, because their status meant they were at risk of re-arrest on their release from prison, and even their conviction could be accompanied by a deportation order, under what is often described as a "double penalty."[35] In many cases, their immigration situation could be resolved, either because it was a matter simply of renewing a residence permit that would expire during their prison sentence, or because appeals could be made to immigration tribunals to take into account their personal and family circumstances. However, if these administrative procedures were started from inside the prison, they became complicated or even risky, because they revealed that the individual had been sentenced to imprisonment.

There were three categories of agents who could, in principle, help undocumented inmates to do this: members of the prison staff who met with inmates on their arrival, especially the probation and re-entry counselors, since they undertook an evaluation of their social circumstances; the prisoners' lawyers, but this was only in theory, as prisoners without a residence permit hardly ever had one; and members of the human rights organization Cimade, whose volunteers offered a weekly legal consultation session devoted entirely to these cases, under the aegis of a program administratively designated "access to the law."[36] In the absence of legal counsel, there remained the prison staff and the Cimade volunteers. Regarding prison staff, I noted in the many interviews I witnessed in the arrivals block that individuals were rarely asked about their immigration status, and, when they were, the question was not always followed up with further suggestions, for example seeking a solution to the problem (perhaps because the counselors were overburdened with work), or directing the individual to a consultation with the Cimade volunteers (an idea which did not immediately spring to the mind of the interviewers). When I met with inmates and discovered that they were in a precarious legal situation, I would suggest to them that they make an appointment with Cimade. But the latter organization struggled with the difficulties of a not-for-profit body whose activity depends on the commitment and availability of its members. In this case, the three volunteers who offered weekly sessions when I began my research were unable to cope with the number and complexity of cases. Over the months, they managed to get some residence permits renewed or deportation orders lifted, but many situations were not brought to their attention, and, even if they had been, would have been beyond their capacity for intervention. Toward the end of my study, the number of volunteers had diminished, reducing the efficacy of this intervention still further. Thus, for lack of information and resources, many inmates who could have had their immigration situation resolved while they were in prison were released without residence permits, sometimes precisely because of their incarceration, as their permit had expired during their sentence.

The prison management was aware of the problem, and itself tried to find a solution to it. "A French prisoner should leave here with his papers in order: his identity card, his registration with the national employment agency, his minimum social income payments set up. I'd like us to be able to do the same for non-nationals, and enable them to leave with a valid residence permit where possible," one director told me. An agreement had been signed between the prison management, the district court, and the prefecture, with the aim of "simplifying the administrative procedure leading to the issue of a residence permit for incarcerated individuals." Each of the parties to the agreement committed to "facilitating the submission and assessment of requests for documents from incarcerated individuals not subject to a ban on remaining in France," and gave "any inmate who does not have residence papers or is subject to a deportation order the opportunity to apply to the prefect for exceptional leave to remain." According to this director, the procedure was as follows: "If an inmate thinks he meets the legal requirements for being allowed to remain, he applies to us. We direct him to Cimade or to a lawyer. This first filter acts as a preliminary assessment. If the case seems winnable, we send the file to the prefecture. The prefect either accepts or rejects the application, and in either case he informs the prison registry. On top of that, if the prefect wants to see the inmate and gives him an appointment, we organize a day release order so that he can go. As he has no legal residence documents, that means that by special derogation, our authorization takes precedence over his lack of residence rights." The procedure seemed well thought out.

In practice, however, it had very limited impact, partly for the reasons noted above, and partly because of the procedures at the prefecture. In order for an inmate to embark on this process, he had to be informed that it was possible, but it rarely occurred to those responsible to let him know, and he himself would be unlikely to venture information on his situation spontaneously, either because he did not imagine the prison management had this kind of prerogative, or because he mistrusted it, assimilating it with the repressive system alongside the police and the courts. If he did overcome this first obstacle, he still needed to meet with a volunteer or a lawyer, and have his case assessed as potentially winnable; but demand exceeded supply, with some complex cases involving multiple and lengthy processes, for example in the immigration tribunal, while others were excluded on principle, particularly if there was a deportation order, even when an appeal for lifting the order might have been possible.

In the rare cases where, once these stages had been passed, application was made to the prefecture, the chances of a favorable outcome, particularly in the case of requests for exceptional leave to remain, were extremely slim. Residence permits were already granted parsimoniously to non-nationals in general, but applications were examined with still more suspicion when they came from the prison. "I don't know if it would be better to play dead so they don't know I'm in jail, or to submit my request for renewal of my residence permit and explain that I can't attend in person because I'm in prison," mused a man from Ivory Coast with perplexity; his 10-year residence permit was due to expire two weeks later, and, being well versed in administrative procedures, he had gathered together the relevant documents in case he made an application. Finally, the entire procedure took time, and the inmate might be released before it was concluded. I never heard of any case where an inmate obtained a residence permit under the terms of this agreement. I suppose there must have been some, especially when cases concerned simple renewals of 10-year residence permits, although, if the latter expired before the request was submitted, as frequently happened in this context, the fear was that it would be rejected.

I did learn, however, that a quid pro quo had been negotiated with the prefecture. It was not mentioned in the text of the agreement, but was explained to me by a director and confirmed by correctional officers. In exchange for facilitating residence permit procedures, the prefect had asked that the police be informed of the date and time of release of prisoners who were not legal residents. Hitherto, the prefecture, and hence also the police, had been unaware of the release of such inmates, while being under constant pressure from the ministry of the interior to meet the targets for deportations. The solution they had come up with through this procedure was efficient and economical, much more so than even targeted stop and frisk operations. Henceforth, in line with this agreement, the prison called the prefecture before each undocumented inmate was released. When the individual crossed the threshold of the facility, he was awaited outside. A police vehicle would take him directly to the nearest immigration detention center, where his deportation could be organized. Under these arrangements, while the cases of undocumented migrants were rarely resolved, they were frequently arrested. In one interview in the arrivals unit, I observed the probation and re-entry counselor openly warning a man subject to a deportation order: "You should know that the facility will contact the prefecture to tell them when you are released. So you risk being arrested and put in detention." She did not, however, inform him of the existence of a nongovernmental organization specialized in cases like his, nor of the possibility (which admittedly would not have been desirable) of submitting an application to the prefecture via the prison. The man was serving a 45-day sentence for refusing to get on the plane that was to return him to Mali. He had lived in France for 10 years, on temporary receipts for applications for residence. He was the father of two boys born in France and therefore holding the right to become French citizens, and he was married to a legal resident who was pregnant with their third child.

Thus non-nationals without legal residence pay dearly for the recognition of their rights. Officially, the rule of law is respected. But in practice, the political rationale wins out over the juridical rationale. Paradoxically, with the establishment of this procedure formally respecting democratic principles, non-nationals in the most precarious position, most of whom have a family in France and some of whom have spent most of their life there, are much more exposed than previously to the risk of deportation. Carceral order proves to have much closer links with public order than might have been imagined.

9

Land of Order and Security

> The fact that, in the same social group, a plurality of contradictory systems
> of order may all be recognized as valid, is not a source of difficulty for
> the sociological approach. Indeed, it is even possible for the same
> individual to orient his action to contradictory systems of order.
>
> Max Weber, *Economy and Society*, 1921

"I've called you in because we're dealing with a serious situation." In the large hall outside the prison proper, used for hosting meetings with external guests, the director, flanked by his deputies and several sergeants, is solemnly addressing five men and women in uniform, who are listening attentively. These tardy visitors – although it is still daylight, it is already night for the 800 inmates whose cell doors have just been closed, not to reopen for the next 13 hours – are a captain and officers from the Regional Intervention and Security Teams, whose individual members are also known as "ERIS," the acronym of this organization. This body was set up in 2003, following the Clairvaux prison mutiny, to assist in maintaining and re-establishing order in the case of mass disturbances, but also to support the organization of searches during special operations and to provide backup for local staff when tensions arise.[1] The four prison administration buses parked in the facility's deliveries bay have brought a further 20 or so officers – correctional officers who have undergone special training – who are in the process of donning their intervention gear and gathering together their equipment.[2] A little way off, two of them hold the leashes of a pair of German Shepherds, who are visibly uncomfortable in the heat of this summer evening.

The director explains to his visitors that serious and mutually corroborating intelligence from both the Central Directorate of General Information (the "RG," or Renseignements généraux) and an examining magistrate gives reason to believe that two inmates currently housed in the facility are preparing an escape using explosives. Correctional services throughout France are still reeling from the shock of two similar incidents in short-stay prisons in the preceding months. In one case, the escape attempt succeeded and the fugitive was only found and arrested six weeks later; in the other, the security door held out and the attempt failed. After helicopters, which are now prevented from overflying prisons by metal wires strung above the exercise yards, explosives seem to have become the latest method of spectacular escape for the boldest inmates with the most outside support. The aim of the ERIS intervention that evening is therefore to search the disciplinary and isolation units, where the two suspects have been placed. Cell searches are of course conducted regularly by guards from the prison, but the particular profile of these two men, and the suspicions as to their intentions, lead the management to fear that this will be a more delicate operation. Hence the call to the special forces.

After a brief exchange, the 20 ERIS members enter the prison's deserted corridors in silence, accompanied by guards, ranking officers, and management. The yard where they have parked their vehicles and prepared their gear is out of sight of the blocks where prisoners are housed, and the operation needs to be kept discreet in order to avoid any reaction among inmates. Once they have donned their balaclavas, put on their helmets and pulled on their boots, the agents, heavily encumbered in their body armor, enter the disciplinary and isolation units which now hold only the two men suspected of preparing their escape. One after the other, they are taken out of their cells and led to two small yards. Neither of them offers any protest. The number and appearance of the ERIS officers, whom they have immediately identified, brook no argument. Exploration of the cells begins. The dogs enter first, on the search for suspicious odors. The guards then proceed to meticulously inspect each object and every recess of the cell. The operation is conducted in total silence. The search for dangerous substances proves fruitless. However, the discovery of a cellphone arouses some anxiety among the staff. Of course they all know how ubiquitous this forbidden object is in prison, but its presence in a part of the facility where every inmate who enters is subject to a strip search, and into which, in principle, only officers enter, cannot but be disquieting. The search lasts two hours, and the ERIS team then leaves the premises. Normal life resumes in the prison.

In the 10 years since they were set up, intervention by ERIS units has become routine in correctional facilities. Clearly, once such a resource had been created, it was unthinkable that it be reserved purely for riots, which had been the reason for constituting the teams but which were much too rare to justify their continued existence. They were thus logically drawn to extend their domain of action. They would be called essentially for preventative purposes, for a search (a much less delicate operation than the one described above had been conducted a few days earlier by the special forces to search the auxiliaries' cells), for a transfer (the day after the intervention in the disciplinary and isolation units, one of the inmates, who had refused to return to his cell after exercise, was sent to another facility, once again with the same team called in for support), or simply on grounds of perceived tensions in the prison (as was the case in this summer period, when a number of incidents had occurred).

There were various reasons why ERIS were summoned for actions that not long before would have been carried out by the correctional officers themselves, usually without difficulty. In relation to the search of the auxiliaries' cells, one director told me that the point was to create an impact and impress on inmates that management was prepared "to pull out the big guns" in the fight against smuggling. For the prisoner transfer, an officer explained that this time the message was meant for guards, who had been affected by an attack on several of them shortly before, and that management wished to demonstrate that they were being "spared" any potential risk. A few months earlier, following an assault on a staff member, ERIS had once again been called in because, according to one director, "the incident aroused a desire for revenge among the staff," and "we were concerned that it might end in a punitive expedition against inmates"; in this case, the aim was "to create a distance between the staff and the inmates." In other words, under the guise of controlling the latter, the former were being contained. Making an impression on inmates, reassuring correctional officers, protecting prisoners from the vindictiveness of guards: clearly, the scope of intervention went well beyond merely bringing an end to mass disturbances, even if this function remained. The role of the ERIS teams was not only preventative, but also, in large part, symbolic.

However, the symbol was perhaps more ambiguous than management realized. The show of force could intimidate some and reassure others, but, for the inmates, the disproportionate nature of the intervention had something humiliating and even provocative about it (was there really a need to call in special units to search the cells of auxiliaries who were supposed to be trusted by the staff?); while, for the guards, the systematic recourse to external colleagues to resolve their internal problems could be felt as devaluing and demotivating (was this the right time to request special forces for a transfer, just at the point when they had, to their great satisfaction, won responsibility for prisoner transfer between prison and court?). A director told me that on the occasion of a "sector search" of about 20 cells, he had heard his staff say to the ERIS officers: "Do things properly, guys, because tomorrow we're the ones working here!" But the routine recourse to ERIS had a broader significance. It revealed a new way of conceiving of order.

A dialectic was emerging between, on one side, a strategy of pacification through early and in some sense pre-emptive intervention by special forces who, through saturation, killed off the slightest nascent inclination toward resistance, and, on the other, the use of a militarized unit, since the use of helmets, shields, body armor, protectors, and so-called sublethal weapons, as well as the intervention tactics, mimicked theaters of war. Moreover, things sometimes went less smoothly than in the cases I have described. There have been several incidents where violence perpetrated by members of ERIS has been condemned by the European Court of Human Rights.[3] The phenomenon also extends well beyond the walls of prison. Law enforcement has seen a development in a similar direction, which began even earlier: the increasingly dramatic operations to restore order in disadvantaged neighborhoods, with recourse to special units, the display of military-style gear, and the use of special weapons, and the effect of mass presence aiming to saturate the space, all derive from the same thinking, which has reached an extreme in the United States in recent years with the SWAT teams.[4] From public security to prison security, the slippage was no accident, since the National Gendarmerie Intervention Group (Groupe d'intervention de la gendarmerie nationale, GIGN) had trained the ERIS teams. The latter had become more and more regularly involved in maintaining order in prisons.

There is a double paradox here. Whereas the rarity of riots, the lack of deaths of correctional officers in the last several decades, and the unchanging rate of assaults leading to temporary incapacity for work all indicate that prisons have become more secure despite the unfavorable context of overpopulation, security issues have at the same time been perceived as more prominent in the everyday activity of facilities. And while the administration has been developing a policy of standardization in prisons, with at least partial implementation of the European Prison Rules, improvement in conditions of incarceration in some facilities, and formal recognition of certain inmate rights, the response to crises, whether actual or anticipated, has seen the exception made routine – through the ever more frequent use of units designed for the control of mass disorder. Indeed, while the increasingly systematic recourse to force, even if it is generally more on the level of display than actual use, is broadly effective in maintaining order, it hampers other possible forms of interaction based on listening and discussion, when often a refusal to return to cell is precisely the prisoner's response of last resort to an injustice that has not been heard and to a power relationship that leaves no space for communication.

Clearly, then, order and security cannot be separated. When people raise issues of security in prison, it is also with the aim of introducing or reinstating a certain order. And when a principle of order is defended, the question is always what is gained and what is lost in terms of security.

* * *

Without doubt, the article of the 2009 law on prisons that aroused the most reservations and fears within management, and particularly among guards, was Article 57, which stipulates: "Searches must be justified by the presumption of an offense, or by risks that the behavior of inmates generates for the security of persons and the maintenance of good order in the facility. The nature and frequency of searches must be strictly appropriate to these needs and to the character of the inmates. Strip searches are only permitted if patting down or the use of electronic detection instruments are insufficient." In other words, one of the practices with the deepest symbolic significance in the carceral world and most habitually imposed by guards, one in which the relation of power between the inmate and the institution is most manifestly articulated, namely the full body searches, which had hitherto been systematically conducted in certain situations, was now forbidden. Not that strip searches were banned, as guards would complain, but the systematic use of them was. The custom (though it varied in different facilities, and at different times) had been to conduct these searches routinely – for example, when inmates entered prison, when they left the visiting rooms, when they were placed in solitary confinement, and when they returned from day release. This routine was taken for granted to such an extent that, one evening, I saw a trainee preparing to search an inmate who was about to be released, when an officer stopped him, explaining discreetly that this was not appropriate for those who were leaving the facility.

For the guards, these strip searches represented a measure of security. For inmates, they meant utter humiliation. Staff emphasized the weapons that they could reveal. Every attack with a blunt instrument, whether it took place within the facility or was reported in the press, supported their conviction that this was the only effective method of detecting them. "What about that doctor who got cut with scissors, I read about it in the paper yesterday. It's like the guard here who was attacked with a razor blade: the guy had fixed it onto a toothbrush by heating it. If we don't do routine searches, we won't find these weapons anymore," protested one sergeant. What he did not point out was that the incident in question had actually occurred before the new regulations were introduced, and that routine strip searches had failed to reveal the weapon. As for inmates, they saw the requirement to strip and the gestures that accompanied it – at minimum showing the soles of their feet, and at most bending over for an examination of the anus – as simply an added act of violence on the part of the institution, particularly as, while most of the guards were reserved and discreet, some used this as an opportunity to demean those with whom they had a score to settle.[5] "Why do they still search us after every visit, when it's forbidden by law?" asked one man who had been repeatedly subjected to this practice, having spent a long time in pre-trial detention. The law, effectively, had changed the rules of the game.

But it had taken its time to do so. As one director lamented: "For three years, the right-wing government that brought in this law asked us not to implement it. And all of a sudden, we have a left-wing government that's forcing us to put it into practice, but without concerning itself with how we're going to bring about this revolution." It was indeed only in summer 2012 that the subject, which had been swept under the carpet by the previous administration, had become the focus of ministerial initiatives. Aside from the fact that this was simply a matter of applying the law, the deferral was becoming increasingly problematic in view of the repeated condemnations of France in the European Court of Human Rights. The Council of State's decision of June 6, 2013, ordering the director of the Fleury-Mérogis correctional facility to put an end to this practice, forced the national prison administration to stop procrastinating.[6] The question was how Article 57 was to be applied. The same director went on anxiously: "The law says, 'No systematic strip searches, they have to be done for a specific reason.' Of course there are dangerous inmates that we can pick out. But there are also the vulnerable ones, who are forced to pass forbidden objects. They're asking us to be mind-readers! And if there are problems later, like, for example, if explosives get into the prison, we're the ones who'll be held responsible." His bitterness, which was shared by many of his colleagues and subordinates, had deeper roots, which, he felt, were revealed by this directive: "It's exposed the gap between the 33,000 prison staff and those who command them. We're told to respect human dignity, which guards work hard to do just like anyone else, but no one's bothered about protecting them. They'll say it to your face: the state prefers to defend inmates' rights, at the cost of sacrificing a part of the officers' security. Guards feel people always think they're violating human rights." The issue seemed to be one of morality rather than of security.

How, then, was dignity to be reconciled with security, respect of inmates with recognition of the guards? Concretely, how were prisoners who would continue to be subjected to systematic strip searches to be selected? After long discussion, it was decided that inmates to be included in this category were those who had been found in possession of drugs or cellphones, vulnerable persons who had complained of being put under pressure, individuals who had exhibited suspicious behavior in the visiting rooms, and, of course, the special notice prisoners, or SNP, whose names were included on a government list.[7] "That meant we'd still be searching 80 percent of inmates," admitted a director. A further filtering operation was therefore conducted, this one pragmatically drawn up on the basis of the most recent searches. By this method, management arrived at a list of around 60 inmates out of the more than 800 housed in the prison at the time. In principle, it was possible for an inmate to be removed from this list on grounds of good behavior, or, conversely, to be added to it if he was caught trying to bring in objects. The information was disseminated to the inmates. The new regime was being put in place when I left the prison.

The problem of strip searches is emblematic of the issues in prison security. Security has always been an absolute priority in the carceral world, and no reform is possible unless it is perceived as not representing a challenge to this function. For what is at stake is indeed the representation that staff have of security, rather than a reality, which is ultimately very difficult to pin down. The systematic practice of strip searches in a whole range of situations where inmates had contact with the outside world had been the rule in French correctional facilities for decades, although it had not prevented the constant introduction of a wide range of objects and products, including weapons: "These days you can get anything into prison: explosives, ceramic knives, mini-cellphones," said one sergeant, disillusioned. "None of them can be picked up by the metal detectors." Linking the problem of staff security, particularly the risk of assault, to systematic strip searches may therefore seem logically coherent, but it is not grounded in empirical evidence. What is known, from studies conducted in other countries, is that the mode of organization of facilities, the quality of relations among staff, the involvement of inmates in rewarding activities, the delicate balance between applying the rules and allowing a degree of autonomy for both guards and those they guard, and, more generally, what could be called the ethos of the prison, are all much more effective in preventing violence than regimes of strict control.[8] If, then, the security of staff is better protected by a particular way of conceiving of their work and their relations with inmates than by systematic strip searches, we need to grasp what this resistance to the ending of the practice means.

When guards raise their fear that their security is now threatened, they are actually speaking of something else: the fear that a particular prison order will be overturned. If the act whereby they most clearly manifest their authority over inmates is challenged, their legitimacy is also affected. The new law signifies to them, as it were retrospectively, that the systematic practice of strip searches, as they have always known it, was an abuse of power that they must give up – even, in some extreme cases, what could be qualified as "inhuman and degrading treatment" and subject to condemnation in the courts.[9] This public repudiation undermines their moral credit. It strikes at the image that correctional officers have of themselves, and the regard, or lack of regard, in which they feel society and their superiors hold them. What is at stake is therefore much more than the risk of weapons coming into the prison, and the "danger" argument conceals the feeling among guards that, once again, the balance of their relations with inmates is tipping to their disadvantage. Thus, for them, order and security go hand in hand. Yet, when correctional officers complain about the new procedure, they probably do not have a clear understanding that the consequence of the solution found by management (to select those prisoners who will continue to be strip-searched) is precisely to reinforce the institution's power. By choosing whom to include or leave off the list of inmates subjected to this ordeal, management provides itself with a new means of putting pressure on the prison population, through a double play of punishment and reward.

In arguing that the invocation of security refers to other stakes for guards, I do not mean to say that the problems are merely symbolic. The 4,000 assaults on staff recorded on average each year in France, of which just over 100 give rise to temporary incapacity for work, testify to this reality. Correctional officers know that there is an element of danger in their profession. The practice of calling one another "officer" in front of inmates, never using forenames or family names, is equally part of a collectively maintained precaution that allows them to remain anonymous. The aim is to avoid ill-intentioned inmates finding out the personal details of particular officers so that they can subsequently exert pressure or exact revenge. Stories circulate about officers who have been threatened or even attacked outside. While these are few – the same two constantly returned to the lips of those staff members who raised the topic, and in both cases the officers were known for their aggressive relationships with inmates – they nevertheless help to maintain a diffuse sense of apprehension. And correctional officers were not the only ones who felt anxious. A probation and re-entry counselor told me that, since she had worked at the prison, she no longer took public transportation but came in her car instead, saying she was "stressed at the prospect of meeting a former inmate." This tactic of avoidance had not spared her from being approached by one of them who was being released as she returned to her car in the prison parking lot: "You, probation lady, I'm going to come and find you!"

But over and above these individual concerns, security was a collective anxiety.[10] The institution itself is entirely organized around this question. Technologies aiming to ensure maximum security had been developed over the years, until they created a complex network. Rolls of concertina barbed wire installed to heighten the fences, walls, and roofs form a sort of briar crown – a term that was used by some manufacturers – above the facility; plastic bags caught in it flutter in the wind like the remains of dead crows. The wires stretched above the exercise yards weave a loose spider's web; an official report had required that the mesh be made smaller, and be overlaid with a net. The openings into the buildings themselves had been progressively enclosed in a thick and dense lattice by the addition of a rubberized grid over the window bars. The prison is thus covered in a heterogeneous, irregular fabric, enclosed in a metallic envelope made up of all the successive additions, each aiming to reinforce the facility's security.

The outer wall is topped by three observation towers, where armed agents, ready for any eventuality, keep watch day and night over the barren plain that surrounds the prison. The wallwalk running between the wall and the fence around the yards forms a no-man's-land scattered with the remains of packages thrown over the wall; the only people who enter this area are the officers going to or from their post in the observation tower, sometimes to the accompaniment of jokes or catcalls from inmates, invisible behind the obscured windows of their cells. There is also the great entrance gate with its double security door, used only by authorized vehicles, and the guard post where two officers checked those who enter and exit. Within each block, there are more heavily reinforced doors controlled by the officers in the various monitoring posts, the mirror-topped metal detector gates through which inmates have to pass on their way to and from the exercise yards, the myriads of video surveillance screens that provide a panoptical view of the different spaces of the prison, and the various alarms carried by staff in case of danger; the latter two systems are linked to a central monitoring post. In short, the entire fabric of the prison is designed to guarantee a security that seems nevertheless to be indefinitely insufficient.

In addition to these multiple material structures, security insinuates itself into the smallest details of prison life. Surveillance extends to mail, which is read, and telephone conversations, which are listened in on. The list of garments that visitors are forbidden to bring for inmates include navy blue- and khaki-colored clothing, hooded tops and jackets, lined caps, leather belts, and towels more than five feet long. The prison's only sports ground is unusable because it cannot be monitored from the observation towers, and the audience for any of the shows organized by the facility is limited to 20 or so people so as to avoid any untoward behavior. Omnipresent and meticulous, security is the pre-eminent factor in all activities. And each time a gap in the system is discovered, a mechanism for filling it is invented, adding to the security provisions and imposing new constraints on both inmates and guards. And this is an endless cycle, as revealed by the generalized circulation of cellphones, which many, both experts and decision-makers, had long believed to be both unavoidable and uncontrollable.[11] But the institution remains unfailing in its perseverance.

*   *   *

Ultimately, only two spaces escape this extreme vigilance: the exercise yards and, above all, the cells. On the one hand, the exercise yards are of course still subject to surveillance; a correctional officer supervises the hundreds of inmates circulating there, and cameras transmit images of them to video surveillance screens. But staff do not venture to intervene in this space, given the balance of forces, and it is here that all the altercations and attacks on other inmates take place. On the other hand, the cells represent the greatest potential danger for inmates, insofar as they are locked in with their cellmate for up to 20 hours every day; while serious accidents are the exception, tensions and even bullying are more common. In principle the intercom can be used to alert staff, but I never heard it employed for this purpose. In the yards as well as in the cells, it was clear that inmates' security depended above all on themselves and, if threatened, on their capacity to inform guards of the danger they were in. The assignment committee is generally accommodating when inmates in this situation request a change of cell or block, even when they doubt whether their fears are genuinely grounded.

Recently, the domain in which the greatest investment has been made into inmate security is suicide prevention. It has to be said that the problem, long ignored by the prison system, has become a grave cause for concern. Over a 50-year period, the suicide rate went up eighteenfold in French prisons: at the lowest in 1946, it was 1.4 per 10,000 persons incarcerated; at its peak, in 1996, it reached 26 per 10,000. There was an almost steady increase from the early 1970s, a period that coincided with the increase in the prison population, which had accelerated over the same period. In 25 years, while the number of individuals receiving a custodial sentence doubled, the suicide rate quadrupled.[12] This fact was all the more concerning given that, with these statistics, France had the highest prison suicide rate in Europe, substantially above that in countries with similar socioeconomic situations. It was about twice as high as in the United Kingdom, Germany, Sweden, Italy, Switzerland, Belgium, and the Netherlands, and roughly three times that in Austria, Spain, Portugal, and Greece; only Denmark and Norway had levels close to that of France.[13] In these circumstances, and at a time when, in the 1990s, suicide prevention was becoming a national public health priority, it was difficult not to include prisons in this policy. A targeted program was therefore launched in 1995.

When I broached the subject with one of the deputy wardens, he was defensive: "Actually, there are no more suicides in prison than outside, but people don't realize that." Several times, in the years that followed, he repeated the same argument. "The suicide rate in prison is marginal compared with society at large." He said he was exasperated by the media focus on these deaths of prisoners: "The media talk all the time about suicides in prison, but how many are there outside?" I found his insistence troubling. It is true that, at the time, each time a prisoner took his own life, it was reported in the local press, and sometimes also in the national newspapers. This often prompted public criticism of the prison system, which was judged responsible for these tragedies. It was also the occasion for an investigation on two levels, first by the national prison administration, and then by the judiciary. Management thus found itself subject to pressure from three sides – the media, the administration, and the courts. During this period, when the situation in prisons regularly gave rise to critical reports by independent bodies, complaints from nongovernmental organizations, and condemnations from European authorities, a suicide was an event to be dreaded. "A death in prison is always difficult," my interviewee remarked, adding: "We wonder if we are going to be held responsible." Guards also found these incidents a difficult experience. Some of them raised the matter with me spontaneously, giving an almost clinical description of the circumstances in which the body of an inmate had been found during an inspection round. They spoke of the trauma they felt, but I realized that this was derived less from the scene they had been confronted with or from grieving for an inmate they generally did not know well, than from the anxiety aroused by the series of summonses to meet with police and the public prosecutor, and the possibility of legal proceedings if the family filed a complaint.

The deputy warden's claim prompted me to check whether it was correct. I found that, for males aged 15–59, the suicide rate was in fact seven times higher among incarcerated persons than in the general population. This is all the more noteworthy because the suicide rate in France is already one of the highest in Western Europe. Actually, the fact that the country is at the top of the European rankings for prison suicides results both from a greater propensity toward suicide among French people, and from a specific effect of incarceration.[14] The word incarceration should be understood in both the active sense, of putting someone in prison, and the passive sense, of being imprisoned – an essential distinction, because the former relates to penal policy, and the latter to correctional policy. This is a point that is missed by many analyses: people commit suicide in prison not only because of the nature of prison, but also because they have been sentenced to imprisonment.

This may seem a truism, but it needs to be understood that a substantial proportion of suicides seem more directly connected to the sentence of imprisonment than to the experience of prison.[15] Indeed, suicide often occurs early after incarceration, with 7 percent happening in the arrivals unit, and 25 percent in the first two months. Moreover, the suicide rate among pre-trial prisoners is more than double that among convicted inmates. It is also higher among those who have committed offenses against persons, particularly spousal abuse, and who are more often incarcerated now than they were in the past. Finally, one-third of those who took their own lives had a history of mental illness prior to incarceration, and half of them were under the care of the psychiatric service in prison.[16] A penal policy that locks people up more often, for a wider range of offenses, makes more extensive use of pre-trial detention, and ignores individuals' previous psychiatric history is one that is bound to produce more suicides. In one of the two cases of which I had direct experience during my research (out of the eight that occurred over five years), the inmate concerned had been told shortly before he was due to be released that convictions dating back several years had just been "brought down," and that he would have to stay in jail: this was a direct consequence of the policy recently adopted by the ministry of justice, of executing sometimes very old sentences. Ultimately, the deputy warden's denial suggested that the correctional system did not want to be the scapegoat for prison suicides: the whole of society was implicated. Nevertheless, the part played by the conditions of prison life could not be understated, given that certain practices were major risk factors. The second suicide where I was aware of the circumstances came after the inmate had been placed in solitary confinement.

While reluctant to acknowledge its responsibility, the management had nevertheless signed up to the Suicide Risk Prevention (SRP) program, a nationwide initiative. The procedure consists of identifying individuals who are considered to be at risk of taking their own lives, either when they arrived or during their sentence, and putting specific measures in place, in terms of cell assignment, psychiatric follow-up, and individual monitoring. This protocol is based on the recommendations of a psychiatrist who had written an influential report for the ministry, and after whom the training received by those staff interested in the program was named.[17] At-risk individuals were often identified during arrival interviews, and discussed at the assignment committee. There were of course statistically identified criteria that the officers could list – such as alcoholism, relationship break-up, the loss of a job, being over 40, a sentence the individual did not understand, and first prison sentence – but I observed that identification of SRPs, as the inmates concerned were called, was mainly intuitive, unless, of course, there was a psychiatric evaluation, which was always followed up. According to prison staff, one inmate was "anxious because he's waiting for his trial," another had "several sentences dripped out one by one," a third was "very distressed by the death of his mother," a fourth had just "had a call from his girlfriend to tell him she was breaking up with him." One prisoner had "twice set fire to his cell," another was threatening "to cut his throat in the court, and he's already self-harmed," yet another was "still in denial about his sentence, but once it clicks into place it could be hard for him." SRPs were thus generally identified on the basis of what was known about their history, rather than impersonal criteria.

Once they have been identified, the rule is to avoid placing them in cells on their own (which, as might be imagined, is not too difficult), and to find a cellmate who could be supportive (a more delicate matter). The need for individual monitoring is noted in the inmate log. Each month, the committee reassesses the circumstances of the 50 or so inmates concerned, adding or removing names from the list. Particular attention is paid to nighttime monitoring. Once the general round has been completed, during which guards check that all inmates are present and alive in their cells, the SRPs are visited every two hours. The protocol requires that they be woken each time, because they have to be seen and heard. The guard looks through the peephole, switches on the light, and calls the inmate, who will sometimes have to get up to unblock the viewer and prove that he is alive. The man who is thus roused would often protest, explaining that he suffers from insomnia and had just gotten to sleep. But rules were rules, and two hours later, he would once again be hailed through the door and once again start awake as he finds himself suddenly dazzled. The committee was aware of the daily disturbance caused by this well-meaning harassment. In his report the chairman noted: "Inmate anxious. The repeated rounds are increasing his anxiety."

Management certainly takes the Suicide Risk Prevention program seriously.[18] While local figures of between one and two deaths per year make rigorous evaluation of the efficacy of the measures impossible, the 2014 annual report noted that "on average, three suicide attempts per month were avoided." Significant results had been obtained at national level, offering more robust evidence since the numbers were higher: in absolute terms, the number of deaths from suicide remained steady, at around 120 per year among individuals under sentence, about 10 of whom were not incarcerated; but in relative terms, the rate, which peaked in 1996 and then remained steady until 2002, fell in the 2010s to around 16 per 10,000 individuals under sentence. However, it is not difficult to see that the primary concern in this procedure is not so much the prevention of suicide risk for inmates as the prevention of administrative and judicial risk for the staff. Remarks by the director and correctional officers leave little doubt on this score. The monitoring protocol offered further evidence: waking the individuals concerned in the middle of the night is not the best way of preventing them from taking their own lives. For one thing, interrupting their sleep only aggravates their distress and renders them even more fragile. For another, if they want to end their life, all they have to do is wait until after the round. However, in the mechanical performance of this task, which is as exhausting for the guards (they called the second part of the night, with its long routines, the "death watch") as it is disturbing for the presumed suicide risks, management is "putting up its umbrella," as some put it: if a tragedy occurs, no one can hold the prison system or its agents responsible.

* * *

But carceral order is not manifested only in the dramatic scenes of intervention by special units, the formal regulations governing the practice of strip searches, or the scrupulous protocols aimed at preventing suicide attempts – the clearly spelled-out, rigorously defined modalities of life in prison. It is also at play in minute gestures, invisible interactions, and unwritten norms. It is often revealed in the smallest of events, almost imperceptible or insignificant to the outside observer, virtually inexplicable or inexpressible when one attempts to reconstruct them – but events that can nevertheless take on serious proportions. In prison more than anywhere else, the devil is in the detail.

Nothing offers a better illustration of this than the everyday, ritualized, and highly charged practice of showers. On my first visit to the prison, a correctional officer with 10 years' experience told me: "Here, the biggest cause of disorder is showers." And over four years, whether I was talking with one of his colleagues near a monitoring post or interviewing an inmate in his cell, I heard the same refrain. There seemed to be something fateful in the way everybody asserted that showers could only be a problem, that they were the source of the greatest frustrations and the largest number of conflicts. One inmate, who was standing at the entrance to his wing waiting for the end of the exercise period so that he could return to his cell with the others, a man who had been in pre-trial detention for two years and was on his way back from the visiting rooms, offered me an eloquent explanation: "In prison, it's all the little details that make a difference. Having a shower, for instance. To you that might seem normal. But here, if you ask for a shower it's like asking for the moon. There are some guards who are cool: if they see you're sweating and they're not in too much of a rush, they'll let you have one. But there's a small minority who are real sadists: they'll say no and they're happy, you can see it, they smile as they say it."

Article D.358 of the Code of Penal Procedure specifies that inmates should be able to "take a shower at least three times a week, as well as after sports sessions and on return from work." The prison applies this minimum standard to the letter. Prisoners have access to the showers every other day, and never on a Sunday. Showers take place between 7:30 a.m. and 8:30 a.m. Because the guard, who is alone on the walkways, has to pass a large number of prisoners through in this time, there is a rapid turnaround of small groups of inmates, whose cell doors he opens so that they can go and wash as soon as his colleague in the monitoring post has turned on the tap for 10 minutes. On entering the wing, the guard sings out: "Showers, gentlemen!" When their cell doors open, inmates have a few seconds to get out. Still half-asleep, some of them are slow to get up. In this case, the guards usually allow a brief extension, with the payoff for the tardy inmate being a shorter time in the shower, but some inexorably punish such delay by shutting the door, to the great dismay of the inmate, who knows he will have to go two more days without showering. Sometimes the boilers malfunction. One morning, one wing has cold water, while in the other it is scalding, and in the end nobody can take a shower; the guards make a note on a slip of paper, asking their colleagues on the afternoon shift to take this into account once the boiler is fixed; but the rapid succession of activities means that not all prisoners can be allowed a shower, generating protests. More frequently, the first inmates to leave their cell have to wait several minutes before the water reaches a reasonable temperature, and are thus short-changed on their shower time. The combination of these chance eventualities makes the morning a delicate time, even if things usually pass off smoothly.

Late requests for showers are often the occasion for exchanges over the intercom between inmates in their cell and the guard in his monitoring post. It is 11 a.m. and the intercom buzzes: "Officer! – Yes? – I didn't get my shower today. – OK, I'll have a look." He checks through a pile of little notes placed next to the console. "Yes you did! The officer came by at 8:45 and you refused. – Which officer was it? Was it you? – No, it was my colleague. – Which one? – It was my colleague. – But I haven't had my shower. – It's down here that you refused. – What time? – 8:45." Silence. The inmate hangs up, resigned to waiting two more days. Sometimes protests take a more violent turn. One evening, in the office on the second floor, a sergeant meets with a man who is very angry. "Mr. Hammouche . . . – Merrouche, I'm Merrouche! – You're an intelligent person, you know it does no good to get angry. – No, I'm short-tempered. The last time I had a problem like this with a guard, I broke one of his fingers. If your guards behave right, I'll behave right. They've got to understand I'm not their bitch. – Calm down, that's why we're talking about it, so the situation doesn't get out of hand. – I'm not asking for anything special. I haven't had a shower since Saturday. It's after seven o'clock. He says: 'I'll be back in 10 minutes.' He comes back half an hour later. I made the mistake of going back to sleep. You can't expect me to stand to attention by the door for half an hour. – But you know very well that the officers don't have much time in the mornings. – That's not my problem. Luckily he didn't touch me. But I warn you, the next one that lays a hand on me, I'll lay him out! It would be a shame for a guard to get a fork stabbed in his throat. – Don't start threatening us, Mr. Hammouche. – Merrouche, chief!" As I later realize, observing him in a variety of situations, this man habitually offers this kind of provocation, which the staff usually pretend not to notice. He seems calmer as he leaves the office. Expressing his frustration to an understanding sergeant has been sufficient to quell his rage.

However, it is not the regular morning shower that causes the most problems, but the discretionary additional showers that inmates request, often on return from exercise when they have been physically active in the yard, especially in summer. As one sergeant said to a young trainee she was supervising: "Showers are at the discretion of the guard. He can decide whether to grant them or not. And no one should go over his head." I noted that she herself was relatively liberal on this issue, but she believed that, for the sake of good order in prison, the decision of the guard who received the request should be final: she would never have overruled a refusal by one of her colleagues. And in the carceral context, this apparently trivial prerogative becomes all the more an object of power because showers are seen by inmates as both a necessity that allows them to retain a degree of dignity, and a right, which they believe management deprives them of unfairly. Thus showers serve as a measure that allows inmates to evaluate the quality of a given correctional officer. One auxiliary, in his 43rd month of prison, puts it this way: "A good guard is one who, if I come back from exercise and I'm sweating, he lets me take a shower. He's understanding. It's not one who's always negative." But a block senior I heard talking with a sergeant a few days later seemed not to be entirely in agreement with this view: "There are guards who are very strict and always say no. And in general they don't have any problems. Then there are the ones who sometimes say yes, sometimes no. So they're seen as unfair, and with them there are a lot of incidents."

The value attached to showers makes them a uniquely powerful instrument of subjection in the daily life of prison. Usually, the guards don't take advantage of this. If they think they have the time, they allow the inmate his shower; if they do not, they justify their decision on that basis, which is usually enough for the individual making the request. "I couldn't give you a shower before because there was an incident going on. I had to go and help a colleague. It's not that I didn't want to – you get that, don't you?" a young guard explains to an inmate who requested a shower earlier that morning. But some use showers as a means of retaliation, whether undifferentiated or targeted: the discretionary power becomes arbitrary, and refusal a provocation. "When I know it's him on my wing, I don't even ask. I know he'll make a point of saying no," says one man of an officer whose preferred punching bag he has become. This is the kind of situation in which an attack can come from an exasperated inmate who sees that the guard is ignoring him, or even taunting him. "In prison, a problem this big," a man with long experience of prisons tells me, bringing his index finger and thumb together to demonstrate the triviality of the matter, "can become a problem to the power of 10."

Consequently, for inmates, showers represent the marker of the indifference the institution shows toward their basic needs, and the arbitrary power some officers can exercise over them. "Not being able to take a shower," sighs one. "I heard that in some prisons they have showers in their cells. That sounds like paradise to me." And in effect, in some recently constructed facilities, this is the case, but given the construction work such an operation would involve, it is highly unlikely that a general remodeling of older prison buildings will be undertaken to provide this relative comfort. One deputy warden, despite his long experience of working in prison and his awareness of the tensions that persist around this issue, unexpectedly expressed reservations about such an improvement to the material conditions of incarceration: "The designs for new facilities incorporate showers in the cells. I'm not convinced that's a good idea. Showers are a means of communication with the guard, and a time when the inmate gets to move around outside his cell. The opening of the door, in the morning, serves a purpose in the relationship between them. It's also an additional opportunity to prevent suicide. Showers in the cells would just be yet another way of locking them in." Yet he was a fervent supporter of innovations in prisons, and had enthused to me about the benefits of telephone booths and hotplates. When he put forward this argument, there was no question in his mind of a punishment or a privation. He did, in any case, recommend that guards "be more flexible" on the matter of showers, because "that's how you become appreciated and respected by the inmates." It seemed to me, rather, that he was defending a model of community life in prison that some long-term facilities where he had worked had practiced, and perhaps still were practicing. This model was dying out, and he realized it with regret. Whether he was right or not, his view certainly did not chime with the expectations of those who found themselves incarcerated in overcrowded short-stay facilities, and wanted nothing more than a bit of privacy.

However, the case of showers is an opportunity to consider the discretionary power of the guards not only in negative terms for the refusal it allowed some to oppose without explanation but also positively through the gestures of goodwill or simply accommodation it makes possible. Prison order can only be maintained to the extent that a degree of flexibility remains possible, that staff are prepared to discuss, negotiate, and make concessions, that the rigidity of principles and norms does not become an intolerable and unjustified control, that the institution conceives of its relationship with the prison population as a form of contract binding the two parties rather than a unilateral relation of authority. At one meeting of the assignment committee, in a discussion of those selected for work, a block senior brings up the case of a young man of Malian origin who had a number of incident reports for fighting with other inmates and had been assigned to a different block with the promise that he would be offered a job if he behaved well. In the young man's letter, he points out his good behavior since his transfer, and reminds the committee of the undertaking he was given. Unconvinced by the application, the deputy warden chairing the session says he does not want to "keep promises made by others." The lieutenant, clearly frustrated by this refusal, which will put her in a difficult position with the inmate, replies: "We gave the guy some hope. If we don't keep our promises there will be problems." But the deputy warden refuses to reverse his decision: "I'm against promises. I don't like these little arrangements." Yet a few minutes earlier, in relation to a prisoner who had just come out of solitary confinement, where he had been placed for insulting a correctional officer, the same director had argued for sending him the message: "If he behaves himself over the next few weeks, he will be selected for work." So he is, in fact, well aware that "little arrangements" are indispensable to keeping the peace in prison.

* * *

One afternoon, during the exercise period, I am invited by an inmate serving as an auxiliary to meet with him in his cell. This cell, a perk of his post, is twice as large as others and is generally occupied by only one person. On entering, I am surprised to find my host in the company of two other inmates. It is Ramadan. On a small stereo system, Quranic chants play softly in the background. The three men are making two cakes. One of them tells me he trained as a pastry cook. Illustrating his words with gestures, he explains to me how to make a "base of dark chocolate," topped with a "white chocolate ganache," and finally a "spider-web pattern like on a millefeuille," using a piping bag containing chocolate. He shows me how, at the same time, he is cooking an apple tart in the "oven" he has constructed. By placing together two devices consisting of a hotplate on its lowest setting with a frying pan on it, one turned upside down on top of the other, he obtains an enclosed cooking vessel held between two heat sources.

The sophistication of the recipe and the ingenious assemblage are proudly admired by his two assistants. Their role as sous-chefs allows them both to anticipate the celebration of breaking the fast that will take place later in the evening, and to take a little time out of the alternative between the solitude of their cells and the hustle and bustle of the exercise yard. They clearly take pleasure in sharing this moment of calm in the deserted block, the only sound being the religious music. Through the open window, we can hear more than we can see of the other inmates in the yard below. The door to the cell is open. Another man, on his way back from a visit, comes in. The four men speak of their experience in prison, recall the cases that have brought them there, describe their lives before their incarceration, and imagine what they will do after they are released. The apple tart is set to cool, the chocolate fondant cooks gently. Forty minutes go by before the noise of inmates returning from exercise is heard, indicating that this peaceful interlude is nearing its end. And sure enough, faces soon appear in the doorway, jokes erupt in bursts of laughter, comments are exchanged, orders are put in for cake.

Of course, this moment of culinary conviviality among inmates preparing cakes as they talk about their experience of prison is not part of the prescribed order in short-stay facilities, where staying permanently in one's cell is the rule except during activities specified by management and authorized by guards. This is a license granted by prison staff. Auxiliaries do of course enjoy certain personal prerogatives, and, as they generally do not go out to exercise, they tend to spend this time outside their cells. But only the two men assisting their pastry cook friend occupy this post, unlike both the auxiliary and the last visitor. Moreover, of the three and then four inmates, only my host is in the wing where he is actually housed. All these small concessions are left to the discretion of the guards, and when they trust them, ranking officers and management close their eyes to such harmless irregularities. My presence among this happy company is also out of the ordinary, as I realize when the officer who comes to ask the inmates to return to their cells shows surprise at seeing me sitting there, savoring a slice of the still-warm tart they have insisted on me tasting. He was obviously not informed of my presence by his colleague at the monitoring post.

Thus correctional officers do not restrict themselves to applying a rule;

they interpret and adapt it to the circumstances and the individuals concerned. The discretionary power they hold, within certain limits, resides precisely in this scope for interpretation and adaptation. The management is generally understanding of these practices, which contribute to keeping the peace in the facility: "If you want prison to run smoothly, you need to not say no all the time, because one day you'll get a punch in the face," says a director. "But you can't always say yes either. You have to be flexible. I know that not all officers are. And inmates play on that, they'll ask the guard who's flexible, not the intransigent one." One of his colleagues goes further, offering a typology of staff: "We've got three types of guards. There are the immovable ones, who refuse every request. There are the indulgent ones, who give too much. And then there are the inconsistent ones: on Monday they give an inmate his shower, but on Tuesday they say no." Like any typology, this one describes ideal-types that are rarely encountered in reality.

In fact, I often observed hybrid practices, with staff allowing themselves substantial room for maneuver. This was particularly evident at meal distribution times. Being repeatedly asked by inmates to make various exchanges on their behalf, and on their own unless they are being observed by a colleague or a superior, they often pass a dish of food, a pouch of tobacco, a packet of sugar, a hotplate, or even a bag containing items they are told of, but do not inspect, from one cell to another. For a few minutes, there is an intense and rapid circulation of objects, with guards not entirely in control of the flow, and readily falling back on the auxiliary for assistance. Nor are they themselves excluded from these exchanges of traded goods. One guard holds out a soccer magazine to an inmate. Noticing me watching, he explains: "He lent it to me." And then, as if justifying himself, "Soccer is important here. When the local club is playing, we know every time they score: everyone bangs on their doors!" There are both pragmatic and moral reasons for these little bendings of the rules.

First, guards know that they get what they give. If they are appreciated by the inmates, they can count on their support in difficult situations. As one prisoner, who has a reputation for holding authority among the prison population, says: "Here, we have a little group and we've got an agreement. It's us the guards turn to if there are conflicts or problems." Auxiliaries are crucial allies in such cases. During the midday meal distribution, a Malian inmate in his 40s comes furiously out of his cell, pushing his young cellmate along the walkway in front of him; the latter is carrying two bundles containing his belongings. The former protests vehemently that this is not the companion he had requested and been promised, another Malian man. Without listening to the explanations the guard is attempting to give him, he shouts that he will not return to his cell, adding the ritual challenge: "I don't give a shit if you throw me in the hole!" In the end it is the auxiliary who quiets him, repeating to him, in terms he appears to grasp better, what the guard has been struggling to tell him: "The lieutenant said this morning she'll swap your friend this afternoon. The guy they've put in with you is just for the meal this lunchtime." Evidently calmed down, the inmate returns to his cell, followed by the young man, who for his part is not at all reassured. The man clearly made more sense of, but also put more faith in, the words of the auxiliary than those of the guard.

Second, guards are often understanding of what they see as reasonable requests. Various moral considerations come into play here, mingling a feeling of sympathy and a sense of justice. For example, in the isolation unit, as the evening meal is being distributed, an inmate asks the guard to pass a slice of chocolate cake to one of his neighbors. The guard does so, with a few words and a friendly smile, and then says to me: "In principle it's not allowed, but I do it because it brings a bit of humanity into relationships between the guys in isolation." These are often individuals who have themselves requested this draconian regime because they feel threatened in the prison at large. The inmate's vulnerability arouses the guard's sympathy. One of his colleagues, in charge of taking visitors into the visiting rooms, has a different reason for his choices. There are 22 cubicles, which are opened successively in numerical order once the half-hour visit is over, so that the prisoner can be taken out. The result of this procedure is that those who were last to enter the cubicles enjoy up to 10 minutes' additional visit time. For a long time, the choice of which inmate to place in which cubicle lay with the guards in charge of the visiting rooms, encouraging arbitrary decisions and provoking recurrent conflict. In a concern for equity, management introduced a system of drawing lots. But the guard retains a degree of initiative. One day a young woman, who visits her husband, comes up to him saying that she always draws the low numbers; the guard reassures her and, after checking his chart, takes her into cubicle number 19. The woman smiles gratefully at him: "It's true," he tells me. "She never has any luck in this lottery. When I can balance things out, I do it, if there are gaps." He corrects the luck of the draw by introducing his own sense of fairness.

While these various adjustments to the rules, whether they derive from pragmatism or moral scruples, or, as is often the case, from both, make day-to-day life more bearable and the prison calmer, inconsistent, unintelligible or even malicious application of them can foster disorder. One day I am spending the second half of the morning at a monitoring post, talking with the officer there who orchestrates the flows of people and trolleys, while at the same time answering intercom calls from the cells. During the meal distribution I see inmates moving around, asking to go to a different wing from their own to see a friend or take an item. From his monitoring post the guard opens the relevant door, allowing a short time for the exchange to take place. Just as the last dishes are being served, a man runs in from the central part of the prison. He explains that he has just come back from the court, where he had been at a hearing with the judge, and that he absolutely has to give an urgent message to one of his friends who is in "the east," while he is in "the south." Before the guard in the monitoring post can open the door, his colleague on the walkway steps in and refuses, on grounds of the late hour: "Officer, please, just two seconds. – What did I say? – Officer, please, just two seconds. – What did I say?" They continue stubbornly talking at each other, repeating the same phrases five times over, word for word.

The inmate starts to plead: "Officer, I never ask for anything. I'm not one of the guys that gives you trouble. If I'm asking for something for once, please believe me, it's because it's important. I was at a court session. I ran back to get here in time. I've got an urgent message to pass on. Just two seconds." From his imploring tone, it is clear that his request relates to a matter of great importance to him. The exchange has now gone on for much longer than it would have taken him to pass the information to his friend. "Listen, we've been arguing for five minutes, I'd have easily gone there and back in that time! I promise you I'll be quick." But the officer does not yield, instead becoming even more intransigent, taking the inmate by the arm and pulling him toward his wing. This physical contact, absolutely taboo in the relationship between guard and inmate, completely transforms the tone of the interaction. The man frees himself, yelling: "Don't touch me! Don't touch me! Let go my arm!" The officer threatens to call for backup: "Shove your backup up your ass!" From the monitoring post, his colleague, who is watching the scene, has already called for backup. Half a dozen guards rush in. They bring the prisoner under control. The block senior, who has just arrived, tells them to take the man back to his cell, thus preventing him from being placed in solitary confinement. She asks for an explanation of what happened, and demands a report. When I later discuss the case with her, she says she does not yet know whether the man will have to appear before the disciplinary board. In the end, he does not.

The sequence of events in this incident, which will stay on the inmate's record throughout his time in prison, including in the case of any future applications for day release or sentence adjustments, reveals how such reported incidents can spring from the most minor details – the application of a rule to which exceptions were being made a few minutes earlier, the failure to take into account the urgent nature of the request, the refusal to back down once the decision had been taken and pronounced. To be sure, the guard followed the rule, the late hour could be seen as justifying his refusal to accept something his colleague had been tolerating moments earlier, and there was nothing to suggest that his inflexibility was maliciously intentioned. There was no misconduct on his part. Yet his intransigence rendered the outcome almost inevitable. If it is too strictly applied, respect for order can generate disorder. The block senior understood this, which explains why her intervention leaned toward calming things down and opting for leniency. She knew that in similar circumstances more accommodating officers would have said: "Go on, but be quick," eliciting the inmate's gratitude.

*   *   *

The issues of order and security go hand in hand in the carceral world. Once individuals are locked up against their will and constraint is used to regulate the entirety of their existence, it becomes necessary to institute an order, and a preoccupation with security seems justified. In this regard more than others, the prison system is sensitive to media exposure of its problems, and the political attention that accompanies it, from the government and the opposition parties as well as from national and international campaigning organizations. Having been subject to intense criticism since the early 2000s – as they have in fact been at many moments in their history – correctional institutions are highly sensitive to the way in which they are challenged in the public arena. As a result, the configuration of the issues of order and security varies over time.

At the outset of my research, a deputy warden said to me: "Today we're haunted by the specter of suicide. A few years ago, we were obsessed with escape." At the time, following a series of tragedies and the revelation of France's poor statistics, which had been made much of in the press, the national prison administration had launched a nationwide program of suicide risk prevention. All the directors lived in fear of another death that would have placed their facility under the media spotlight and under pressure from the courts. When I had my final conversation with this same deputy warden, at the end of my study, he said: "When I started in this facility, our priority was preventing suicide. Now, the main issue is avoiding escapes." In the intervening period, the number of suicides among prisoners had fallen hardly at all, decreasing from 109 to 106 per year, but the publicity given to a number of admittedly spectacular escapes and escape attempts had shifted the balance of political sensitivity. Suicide prevention activities of course continued, but more mass searches had to be organized, and the ERIS teams called in more often.

Within the prison, the work of correctional officers bore the trace of the system's fluctuating focus. But rather than one key issue being replaced by another, what happened was a sedimentation of successive layers of directives. For example, at night, during the "special" rounds, the officers on the "death watch" checked up on both the SRPs and the SCPs – those under the suicide risk program and those designated as special notice prisoners. I accompanied one of them in his peregrinations through the wings, and he showed me a slip of paper with a list of 60 or so names and cell numbers. I asked him which corresponded to SRPs and which to SCPs. He did not know. Ultimately, the distinction mattered little, because his task did not differentiate between them; he had to wake up both every two hours to confirm that they were indeed present and alive. But the parallel between the two subjects was interesting. The deputy warden joked about it at a committee meeting: "Ultimately, suicide is also a form of escape." In 2012, there were 17 escapes from and 106 suicides in French prisons – six times as many suicides as escapes. Even if the problems posed are different in nature, the security of imprisonment seems to be better assured than the security of inmates.

But security can never be separated from order. Generally, the extension of security measures – in the form of higher walls, more thickly obscured windows, larger numbers of cameras, stricter check practices, more frequent mass searches, and greater readiness to call on special units – also contributes to increasing constraints on inmates – and sometimes on guards too – and hence tends to reinforce carceral order. But the relationship between the two phenomena is not unilateral or simple. Reinforcing order generates more potential for abuse of power by staff, higher risks of frustration among the prison population, increased incidence of interpersonal conflict and mass disturbances – justifying harsher repression in response – and ultimately tends to weaken the security of facilities. In other words, the two developments are not symmetrical, because greater security usually generates more order, while more order can paradoxically lead to greater insecurity, resulting in return in the implementation of harsher measures.

One potential outcome of this circular logic is the US model, with its 60 "supermax prisons," where inmates spend years in solitary confinement, locked up in their cells 23 hours a day, with a minimal or total absence of contact with other prisoners or with staff; here, the prospects for escape, violence, and disorder seem low. As for the problems of recidivism that such extreme conditions could foster, given the desocialization generated by such a regime, they are hardly at issue for many of these inmates, sentenced to life imprisonment without parole.[19] A contrasting model would be the "open prison regime" developed in a number of European countries, particularly Scandinavia, where facilities have a minimum of passive security provisions, or even none at all. The system requires selection of inmates who are prepared to respect it, is based on consensual discipline, and involves remunerated employment as a necessary condition; the likelihood of incidents and disorder is greatly diminished by the risk of incurring the sanction of transfer to a closed facility.[20] Short-stay prisons in France sit midway between these two models, but the new facilities seem to tend more toward a soft version of the US supermax prisons than the Scandinavian open facilities.

In French prisons, passive security remains a major feature and relatively strict order is maintained. Inmates spend much of their time in their cell, they are controlled on many different levels, the activities open to them are limited, and the rights that are acknowledged in practice are restricted. So whatever leeway for maneuver the system allows depends mainly on two factors: the overall spirit with which management, and the hierarchy more generally, imbue the facility, and the way in which correctional officers deploy their discretionary power in the everyday life of the prison. This leeway appears minimal in relation to the entirety of the constraints imposed by the prison system. But it is nonetheless essential, and experienced as such by inmates: the attention given by management and guards to the allocation of visiting rooms, the authorization of an additional shower by an officer, the benevolent evaluation of a conflict situation by a sergeant or lieutenant, the tolerance of minor irregularities in the prison are all elements that, while they introduce a degree of flexibility into the maintenance of carceral order, contribute to preserving its security on a daily basis. But what limits this leeway for both the national prison administration and the prison population is the permanent reminder that prison serves not only to punish for acts committed before entering; it reserves the sovereign right to punish for acts committed inside.

10

The Never-Ending Punishment

Since penal law is only codified so as to establish a sliding scale of penalties,
it is therefore because a custom by itself can give rise to doubt.
Émile Durkheim, *The Division of Labor in Society*, 1893

"Before, it was a hearing. Now, it's a proper tribunal," says a director proudly, the first time we meet. He is describing the recent innovations in the functioning of the prison system – from the tracking of inmate requests, under which the management is obliged to reply to all mail received, to the installation of telephone booths, the use of which at the time was still limited to convicted prisoners. He is particularly enthusiastic about the disciplinary board. It can now be considered a proper tribunal within the prison, according to him, first because it "adopts an argumentative procedure," with the inmate being supported by a lawyer, and second because it "rests on a procedure that has to be precisely followed in form and in substance," or risk an appeal to the administrative court. The prison has therefore equipped itself with a more just system for rendering its justice.

When it was set up in 1842, the "hearing" (*prétoire*) itself, now relegated among the historical relics of the prison system, although the term is still used by older inmates, was intended to render the distribution of punishments in prison less arbitrary and hence less unfair. The decree under which it was instituted spoke of "disciplinary justice," specified the composition of the board of assessors, described their position at the table in relation to the director, and listed the punishments authorized as well as those prohibited by law.[1] The text did nonetheless state, tellingly using the word "convict" to refer to the inmate: "After hearing his explanations, the director shall rule forthwith, aloud." Thus the director made the decision alone and straightaway, his assessors in fact serving as no more than witnesses to judicial morality. Nevertheless, almost from its inception, the prison system was concerned to present the decisions made in the deepest recesses of its facilities as a solemn form of justice, and even to imitate the appearance and procedure of a real court. In my interviewee's opinion, the introduction of the inmate's lawyer at the disciplinary board, and the possibility of appeal in case of a failure to comply with the law, though belated (being introduced only in the early twenty-first century), marked the culmination of this process of establishing due legal process.

But this was not the view of one of the court-appointed lawyers who, as we waited at the entrance to the disciplinary unit for the disciplinary board to finalize its decision in the case of an inmate she had just been defending, exclaimed: "This board is the most antidemocratic institution in France, because it's the plaintiff who gets to judge!" She added: "You can put that in your report." Married to a correctional sergeant, she told me that she felt well acquainted with the world of prisons. In her view, the fact that the board was chaired by a director, assisted by a correctional officer, to judge on offenses reported by a colleague of the latter, and alleged to have been committed in a facility managed by the former, removed all credibility, if not from the procedure, at least from its assimilation to a model of justice. This was not a new criticism: one observer had formulated it as early as 1902. "The disciplinary hearing is a theater where the actors ape justice. Whereas in the courtroom the magistrates have no direct interest in the case that has brought an individual before them, the prison staff is at once plaintiff, accuser, and judge. Nothing could be less just!"[2] More than a century later, the concurrence of these two opinions was not just striking; it also revealed the difficulty of making radical changes to the system. Despite multiple decrees, circulars, orders, and laws aimed at reforming prison law, judgment in prison remained an administrative operation, the aim of which was less to decide on guilt than to assign an appropriate punishment.

In effect, the verdict was virtually a foregone conclusion: according to the prison's own statistics, only 1 in 20 inmates was acquitted. Indeed, the inmate was almost always already guilty when he entered the room where judgment was supposed to take place. This was for two reasons: first, because it was his word against that of a correctional officer, and members of the prison management were more inclined to believe the latter than the former; second, because even if the board members had doubts about the veracity of the facts as recounted by the guard, it was very difficult for it to be seen to disavow him. A deputy warden, speaking of herself and the colleagues with whom she alternated in chairing the disciplinary board, stated baldly: "Any one of us who says he or she judges only on the facts and the inmate is not telling the truth." Asserting that they had to "take into account the realities of the facility," especially when there were tensions between inmates and guards, she continued: "Issuing a disciplinary sanction involves taking all these elements into consideration. We know that the key point at the disciplinary board is to send a message to correctional officers."[3] This message signaled to them that management was on their side. And it was unambiguously so: in the prison, 85 percent of the sanctions issued were spells in isolation or solitary confinement. But there was nothing unprecedented about this either. At the beginning of the twentieth century, Perrier noted: "In two tempi and three movements, whatever the excuses claimed by the prisoner, the director's mind is made up. He cannot put his officers in the wrong."[4] Being both judge of and party to the decisions it made, the disciplinary board could not do otherwise.

The parallel between the board of the early twenty-first century and the hearing of the latter nineteenth century should not, however, be understood to mean that nothing has changed in this domain over the last 100 or 200 years. Like the rest of the carceral world, the disciplinary authority has evolved, particularly over the last 20 years, since the reform of the disciplinary system is generally dated back to 1995, with the Council of State's "Marie" ruling.[5] The jury, which, when I began my research, comprised a director assisted by a ranking officer and a guard, is now composed of a chairperson, who is the head of the facility or someone delegated by him, an internal assessor, who is generally a guard or a sergeant, and an external assessor, who, in this case, is a civilian accredited by the prison management. Interestingly, this innovation of external participation had been proposed, in more substantial form, in a famous thesis dating back to 1850, which was echoed a century and a half later.[6] At today's disciplinary board meeting, the presence of a counsel chosen by the inmate or named by the chairperson is also required, with the accused and his defender receiving their summons and the case documents at least 48 hours in advance. In fact, this is almost always a court-appointed lawyer who has 10–15 minutes just before the hearing to familiarize him or herself with the case file, understand what the inmate has been charged with, hear the latter give his version, put the incident in the context of his penal and prison history, and prepare a defense that is, of necessity, short and general. The lawyers I met on these occasions took this work seriously, but had few illusions about the impact their intervention could have on the disciplinary board's decision. On various occasions I heard a director or guard suggest that the lawyers came to the prison "for the money," but the modest level of remuneration, given the half-day spent in getting to the facility and returning to the office, made this an unlikely interpretation. More than anything else, this comment did reveal a tension between management and the counsels around these questions of discipline, which the prison continued to consider its own business.[7] Finally, the board is regulated by a procedure laid out in the 92 pages of the circular dated June 9, 2011 "on the discipline process for adult incarcerated persons": the writing-up of the account of the incident by the correctional officer involved, the preparation of the inquiry report, generally by the chief or ranking officer, the procedure for the hearing, the modes of sanction, and the routes of appeal were all described in particular detail.[8] So while it would be hard to compare the disciplinary board to a real tribunal, as my interviewee did, it could nevertheless be observed that it had been subject to a real judicialization; the law and its actors were much more present than they had been only a few years before. But did that mean the inmates' rights were better defended? The lawyers were doubtful, and the verdicts suggested they were right.

This proliferation of texts, seeking to define the operation of the disciplinary board down to the last detail, does not just highlight the desire of the prison administration to conform to the injunctions of justice and the European Prison Rules, particularly given the regular condemnations of France by national and international authorities; it also reveals the importance, for the prison system, of perpetuating and legitimizing an internal right to punish. The more the regulations are refined, take into account decisions made with regard to the procedure, and are brought into line with European standards – in other words the more disciplinary law reinforces its formal structure – the more sanctions are issued. Over the recent period, sanctions have increased from 48,974 in 2008 to 55,511 in 2010, rising more rapidly than the prison population itself.[9] In the facility I studied, the number of disciplinary sanctions had also increased twice as fast as the number of persons incarcerated between 2008 and 2012. Prisons may be punishing better, but they definitely do so more frequently.

*   *   *

Unlike penal law, which deals in terms of infractions, misdemeanors, and felonies, prison law refers to "misdeeds" (*fautes*), which are ranked in three "grades," the first being the most serious. This language of misdeed, which introduces a moral as opposed to a legal dimension, also allows the domain of discipline to be extended, from "exercising or attempting to exercise physical violence on a member of staff" to "failure to ensure or maintain cleanliness in the cell or communal areas." As a parliamentary report noted a few years ago: "An inmate can do two weeks in 'the hole' for a grade 3 error. For example: 'throwing trash or any other object out of the windows of the facility,' 'inappropriate communication with a fellow inmate or any other person external to the facility' . . . So many doors open – so to speak – to arbitrary carceral authority."[10] Since then the maximum penalty for these misdeeds has been reduced to seven days, but solitary confinement remains one of the sanctions applicable in such cases. Given how frequent, common, and trivial they are, it is clear that such incidents rarely lead to inmates being brought before the disciplinary board, but it is precisely the broad scope for interpretation of such situations that fosters the exercise of guards' discretionary power and the sense of injustice among the prison population. While the two sides obviously ascribe a different significance to the observation, both guards and inmates have the sense that it is always possible to find a good reason to punish.

In the case of the impromptu "Harlem Shake" show that had caused agitation in the facility (it had taken place one Sunday in the exercise yard, been filmed by an inmate who was just about to be released, and posted on line a few days later by the latter when he was out of prison), the two incarcerated individuals who were convicted of participating in the improvised drama had been severely punished, with a penalty of 14 days in solitary confinement, suspended, accompanied by removal of their sentence reductions. Yet the categorization of their somewhat unprecedented action was not a foregone conclusion. Objectively, all they had done was dance for a few seconds while allowing their tomfoolery to be recorded. Since they did not own the cellphone, they could not be charged on this ground, nor for having facilitated the release of the video, for which another was responsible. Consequently, as it did not fall under any of the rubrics predefined by the Code of Penal Procedure, the musical turn, in which they were simply players, was "adjudged comparable to a group disorder," qualifying as the grade 1 misdeed of "participating or attempting to participate in any collective action preceded or accompanied by violence toward individuals or of a nature to compromise the security of the facility." Such a misdeed was punishable by 20 days in solitary confinement. The classification was manifestly exaggerated: no disturbance had occurred within the prison, since the facts were only discovered when the video went viral. What they were actually being blamed for was contributing to an event that damaged the authority of the system and put its administration in a difficult public position. Since the ministerial circular had not provided for such a case, the disciplinary board had to improvise in order to justify its sanction.

While the overall principles of the procedure are generally followed, each step was in fact subject to adaptation – starting with the first stage, the writing up of the incident report by the guard. The official specifications stipulate: "Inasmuch as the incident report can only be written up by an agent of the prison staff, the author must be clearly identifiable. On principle, the report must therefore be headed by the name and rank of the person writing it." The aim of this rule is mainly to avoid what would amount to anonymous revenge. But in the facility where I conducted my research, protection of the identity of guards in relation to the prison population seemed so rooted in customary procedure that I one day heard a guard complain to her block senior that her name had appeared in the report of an inquiry into an incident for which she had written the report; incensed, she said she feared reprisals from those close to the inmate, for she lived in the city and could easily be located. While this anonymity for accusers did not raise problems in cases where bags of marijuana were discovered during cell searches, a fact that would be backed up by photographic evidence, it did have much more damaging consequences for the inmate when the charge was based purely on the testimony of a guard who claimed to have personally been the victim of an insult or a threat.

On one occasion, the disciplinary board is adjudicating in the case of a man in his 30s charged with having said to a correctional officer, 10 days previously: "Dirty nigger, motherfucker!" Neither the incident report nor the summary of the investigation offers any contextualizing information. All that is under consideration is the claim that the slur was uttered as the inmate was returning from exercise. Without knowing who he is supposed to have insulted, or the circumstances in which it happened, the man is hard pressed to defend himself, especially as he speaks with more vehemence than eloquence. "I don' even know who we talkin' about!" he exclaims, exasperated, of his accuser. Trusting that it must be a mistake that will be easily rectified at the board, or perhaps wishing to challenge his judges, he has not felt it necessary to request a lawyer, and has represented himself. He asks for details, so that he can try to remember the incident, but the deputy warden who chairs the board has no further evidence. The latter, faced with the man's repeated denials, therefore changes tactic. In order to convince the other board members that they are dealing with an undisciplined inmate, he begins to list the 37 incident reports accumulated over his long period of imprisonment. The deputy warden's lengthy monologue is not followed by any questions from the assessors, and the man, dumbfounded at not being listened to, is taken back to his cell while the board deliberates. As we await the verdict in the corridor, a guard on placement at the prison where he is working toward promotion to chief officer, comments that in the facility where he has been working for 10 years, "we would never take a decision on the basis of so little evidence; we'd have adjourned it and asked for an additional inquiry."

When we are called back into the tiny hearing room, the man returns to stand opposite the table behind which the three board members sit. When he hears his sentence of seven days in solitary confinement, he is unable to repress a gesture of anger, instinctively bringing his fist down on the little wooden desk that serves as a "bar," shattering it into pieces. Immediately, the correctional officers present rush over, push him up against the wall, roughly handcuff him, and, while he protests loudly against the injustice, take him off to the nearby disciplinary unit. The external assessor tells me later that, with no specific details of the incident and no valid investigation, the man should never have been found guilty. The probationary chief officer similarly observes in private that if he lodges an appeal, the man is sure to succeed given the breaches of due process. However, lacking the necessary social resources – his frustration at the injustice he feels being manifested in a show of anger rather than a procedural challenge – the man will not appeal the decision. Had he done so, however, given that an appeal does not result in halting the execution of a penalty, he would at best have received a response from the interregional director of prison administration or the administrative judge, several weeks after being released from solitary confinement.

This episode, which arose in a context of high tension in the prison, points to three conclusions: one, that the board can rule purely on the basis of the word of a guard, even when it is refuted by the accused and is not supported by any circumstantial evidence; two, that it does so in consideration of how the decision will be received by correctional officers, and the negative reaction that the acquittal of an inmate accused of having insulted one of their colleagues could arouse; three, that the external assessor is inevitably in the minority, in the company of the two members of prison staff, with his voice merely contributing to the debate, but never having any decisive weight. For the inmate, conviction for an act that no one has been able to describe the circumstances of adds a 38th incident to his already long case file, with negative consequences that are felt not only in the short term, with the spell in solitary confinement, but also in the long term, with the elimination of his sentence reductions, the likely refusal of any day release, the postponement of adjustment of his sentence, and, more generally, the confirmation of his status as a problem inmate. The next time he appears before the board, his past will stand out once more as a liability on his balance sheet.

But let there be no mistake. In highlighting the limits of the extension of judicial practice into prisons, I do not mean to say that the recent changes are only the formal legalistic arrangement of a procedure that is ultimately less different than imagined from the old "hearing." I mean simply to point out that the structural agendas of prison jurisdiction are perpetuated regardless of additions such as the presence of the lawyer and the external assessor; with a director in the chair, flanked by a correctional officer, the decision taken necessarily prioritizes order over justice. And this applies both to order among the prison population (giving rise to the exemplary value of the punishment) and to order among staff (hence the message of severity sent to correctional officers). In these circumstances, the wording of the circular of June 9, 2011, according to which "each member of the board must remain impartial, refraining from showing any bias" can be understood to mean the opposite of what it says.

The fact that order in the facility must prevail over justice in the decision implies that the law, while it is certainly not simply a fig-leaf for the system, cannot present an obstacle to the smooth operation of prisons. On another occasion a man appears alone before the disciplinary board, accused by a guard of having made an offensive remark about him, though there was no direct insult. He explains that he asked for his counsel to attend, or, in his absence, the court-appointed lawyer. But the former has not come, and it appears that the latter was not informed. Nevertheless, the hearing goes ahead, the deputy warden chairing the session explaining that there is no reason to postpone it, since the lawyer's absence is not the responsibility of the prison administration, which has done its work, but of the president of the bar, who has not fulfilled his obligation. It is therefore the inmate who pays the price of the failure of communication between the prison and the courts. It cannot be said for certain that a lawyer would have altered the verdict, since the disciplinary board, clearly embarrassed by the scant evidence, issues a symbolic sentence of the shortest possible time in solitary confinement, the custodial element of which has already been served. As is always the case, the board does not want to disavow the decision to place the inmate in preventative solitary confinement by acquitting him or merely giving him a warning; the main point is therefore to validate the sanction already imposed. Whatever the reason, for the inmate, the sense of injustice in substance, with this penalty that he deems unjust, is compounded by a sense of injustice in form, since he is deprived of a defender.

Rather than justice, then, given the pre-eminence of the concern for order, the disciplinary board's work should probably be characterized in terms of appropriateness and fairness. Indeed, while the presumption of guilt weighs heavily on the accused, making an unfavorable decision almost inevitable, the board members do strive both to give each individual the appropriate sentence and to be consistent in the penalties they impose. On these two points, whatever their membership, there was little variation between different boards.

The appropriateness of the penalty was defined in accordance with the sliding scale specified in the ministerial regulations as well as the facility's customs. For example, two-thirds of cases resulted in sentences to solitary confinement, generally less than the stipulated maximum (for example, 7 days out of a possible 14), suspended when it was the first incident reported (or at least the first to come before the board). In relation to a case concerning a cellphone found in a cell, the chairman stated: "The inmate admits the facts, and the misdeed is thus established in line with article D.249-2 #9 of the Code of Penal Procedure; the sanction will be just a short 15 days in solitary confinement, suspended as he has no prior incident report" (the "just a short 15 days" relates to the maximum possible penalty of 30 days which at that time applied to grade 2 misdeeds).

As to fairness, it was expressed in the boards' efforts to give the same sentence to all those accused of the same or similar acts. This concern could in fact penalize some inmates, since, due to preparatory investigations that were too brief, questioning during the hearing that was too quick, and the inmates' reluctance to give too much detail on the events for fear of later being accused of informing, it was often difficult, in a situation involving numbers of inmates (for example, a brawl or a mass refusal to re-enter the block) to distinguish the ringleaders, those who had participated in the incident, and those who had merely witnessed it. When a fight broke out during a soccer tournament, a number of players appeared before the disciplinary board. To the first of them, with whom he seemed to show some signs of sympathy, the chairman announced the decision in this way: "The acts you are accused of are not contested, but we took into account the fact that you generally are of good conduct, that you have no prior incident report, that you apologized to the guards, and that you have just made amends. We are therefore sentencing you to 15 days' solitary confinement, but suspended, plus one month withdrawal of sporting activity." Hearing this verdict, I wondered how the board had assessed the weight of the extenuating circumstances cited. I was enlightened – but disconcerted – when I observed that the two others who were judged that day, although their prior incident records, their roles in the altercation, and their attitudes during the hearing were all different, received exactly the same sanction. All that changed was the argument justifying their punishment.

Yet, like judicial courts, the disciplinary boards did of course vary in terms of severity depending on which director was presiding.[11] Some guards who had sat on boards with different wardens were joking about it one day. Clearly delighted, they said of one of them: "She's the strictest, especially for insults or attacks on women. The other day, she gave an inmate 30 days in solitary for insulting a female guard." Conversely, they were less enthusiastic about a second, commenting sarcastically: "Him, he gives them a cookie and takes them back to their block." A third they found difficult to interpret: "With him, it depends how the inmate behaves in the hearing.

If the prisoner gets annoyed, he tells him: 'We're going to keep you in.'"
Having talked with each of these three deputy wardens, and having seen
them at work in the boards, I found that the guards' analysis chimed quite
closely with my own observations.

When we were speaking of the disciplinary board, the first of the three felt
her colleagues were "too indulgent," declaring, "if you bend, you're giving
in," whereas the second argued that "yes, there is a misdeed, but you have to
understand the reasons for it, you have to take into account the person's suffering, you have to move from sanctioning to listening." The third, who was
a former law assistant professor, maintained that he kept strictly to prison
rules. The three chairmen's decisions seemed consistent with their remarks:
the first rarely acquitted, the second was more generous in this respect, often
giving the benefit of the doubt if he thought an inmate had been victimized
by another, and the third reserved this option exclusively for cases where
there were shortcomings in the investigation, hence on grounds of insufficient evidence. The differences were also manifested in their manner of
questioning inmates, and the efforts they made to comprehend the situation
that had led to the offense. The first was as firm in her interrogation as she
was uncompromising in her decisions, using this opportunity to dispense
a sort of moral education; the second paid more attention to the accused
inmate's history and personal situation, and was able to determine whether
there were any extenuating circumstances; the third limited what the inmate
could say and ascribed little importance to the context, basing his decision
more on the evidence and the weight he gave to it. Thus three paradigms
emerged, depending on whether the board chairmen tended toward inflexibility, benevolence, or technicality in their approach to cases, and whether
they valued pedagogy, understanding, or evidence in the conduct of the
hearing. But despite their divergent philosophies and practices, all three
shared the same sense of the importance of their disciplinary work for the
sustainability of the prison system.

* * *

In prison, a penalty never comes alone. Contravening carceral order exposes
the inmate to a series of sanctions in various domains governed by different
authorities, influencing the modality, length, and place of incarceration. An
incident report, even if it is not followed up, can thus lead to restrictions
affecting work, sporting activity, day release, and even sentence adjustment.
But it is the appearance before the disciplinary board that has the most
serious consequences, except in the rare cases where the inmate is acquitted,
since a sanction, even if it is suspended, brings many others in its wake.

The ministerial circular offers an eclectic and imaginative range of possibilities in this regard. General sanctions include a warning, withdrawal
of allowances, a ban on canteen purchases, removal of an amenity device
ranging from the television or refrigerator to the electric razor, suspension
of a cultural, sporting, or leisure activity, confinement in an isolation cell,
and, finally, placement in solitary confinement. Specific sanctions involve

suspension of employment or training, a ban on physical contact during visits, or the imposition of cleaning duties. In the prison I studied, however, punishment was restricted to the basics of prison discipline, in the form of "the hole." Indeed, as in the majority of French prisons, solitary confinement was by far the preferred sanction; it was pronounced in almost two-thirds of cases, though this did not exclude the possibility of an occasional additional penalty, for example withdrawal of an activity. But sentences to isolation were also rising rapidly, doubling in proportion over the course of my research. Now issued in nearly one-quarter of cases, this punishment was seen as a substitute for solitary confinement for inmates with mental health issues, where management anticipated that the psychiatrists would oppose the sanction.[12] Removal of amenities, especially television, accounted for one-tenth of the sanctions issued. The other options were used only occasionally, with warnings, for example, being given in 1 case in 20. In short, punishment was the rule, and its most severe form was the norm.

But punishment did not end at the doors of the hearing room. A notice displayed at the entrance to each wing of every block reminded the prison population of the sanctions incurred for the most common violations of internal regulations: possession of a cellphone or accessories, possession of intoxicating substances, insulting and threatening a correctional officer, and, finally, assaults on staff members. The three columns in the summary table showed the disciplinary sanction, always including a certain number of days in solitary confinement; the potential penal sanction, which might include police custody, immediate appearance trial, and an additional custodial sentence; and the withdrawal of months of credit toward sentence reduction, extending the sentence by the same amount and delaying any possible adjustment. The penal sanction was optional, depending on the seriousness of the offense, management's desire to set an example, and the specific circumstances, since in the case of insults or an assault the victim had to file a complaint. However, the removal of sentence reduction credits was automatically applied. An inmate in whose cell marijuana was found during a search risked a maximum of 14 days in solitary confinement, a potential extension of his prison sentence, and subtraction of one month's sentence reduction credit.[13] This was the official scale of penalties.

While it was already a deterrent, the table depicted in the poster gave only a partial picture of the sanctions incurred. Various other punishments were added for the same actions; these were often invisible because they were unwritten, but they could have significant deleterious effects on the remainder of the offender's time in prison. They related particularly to activities in prison. In principle, the disciplinary board could not remove an inmate from work or training unless the infraction had been committed within the context of the post occupied, but this restriction could be circumvented. Since it was always possible that the inmate might appeal to the administrative tribunal, particular attention was paid to justifying the sanction. Thus, when the auxiliaries in whose possession cellphones had been found were judged, it was argued that their activity offered them more freedom within the prison and therefore more opportunities for trafficking than was the case for other inmates, justifying their sentence not only of a suspended term in solitary confinement, but also of dismissal from the post they valued so much. Usually, however, the disciplinary board did not rule on dismissal from work; it was the interdepartmental board that took misdeeds into account in its deliberations. If the individual had not yet been preselected for work, he was systematically removed from the waiting list for a given period of time; if he had been, his actual assignment to a job was postponed. Given the severe shortage of work and training places, incident reports became important criteria in selecting candidates, and conviction by the disciplinary board carried still more weight. Some employees of the company contracted to manage remunerated activities were unhappy about this dismissal of inmates who might have made good workers, and whose misdeed had nothing to do with their work, but it was management that had the last word on work assignment. The disciplinary board's sanctions could similarly have repercussions on sporting activity, delaying an inmate's inclusion on the waiting list or suspending the activity for up to one month.

The length of the inmate's sentence and the manner in which it might be adjusted were also affected by a sanctioned infraction, or even one that was merely reported. Sentence reductions can be gained in two ways.

The first, sentence reduction credit (SRC), is automatic, calculated by the prison registry and validated by the judge, but can be withdrawn on grounds of "poor conduct" under the terms of Article 71 of the Code of Penal Procedure. The principle of this credit was introduced after a series of mutinies that occurred in French prisons in the early 1970s, as a way of encouraging good behavior in prison. The credit is allocated on the basis of one week per month up to a maximum of three months in the first year, and two months in subsequent years; these figures are reduced for repeat offenders. In the prison I studied, there was a system of equivalence for withdrawal of sentence credits when an infraction was punished; the amount of credit withdrawn was equal to the length of the solitary confinement sanction if it was suspended, and double the length if it was applied. For example, discovery of a cellphone in a cell was punishable by a maximum sentence of 14 days in solitary confinement, engendering a possible subtraction of one month from the SRC.

The second option, additional sentence reduction (ASR), is granted by the sentencing judge on the basis of examination of the case file, and aims to reward "convicted prisoners who demonstrate serious efforts toward social reintegration," to quote Article 721.1 of the Code of Penal Procedure. According to the rule, evidence of such efforts includes passing an examination, following a course of therapy, and paying compensation to victims; in practice, work is also included. The additional reductions to be awarded are left to the discretion of the judge, based on the recommendations made by the prison management and the public prosecutor at the sentence adjustment committee. The maximum is the same as for SRC. In principle, this decision is not influenced by disciplinary sanctions, but, in addition to the fact that, as already noted, infractions affect the inmate's chances of being preselected for remunerated activity, incidents tarnish the prospects for social reintegration, even when other factors are positive in this regard. Thus, for a psychotic inmate who demonstrated behavior described as unpredictable, a potential additional sentence reduction of 63 days was reduced to 20, despite positive evidence in the form of medical care and compensation of victims. Finally, it should be noted that day release, which offers an opportunity to visit with family or meet with an employer, also suffers, even more directly, when disciplinary issues are brought up at meetings of the committee that rules on this subject.

Finally, the place of incarceration itself can be changed in the case of a serious incident. Transfer to another facility is virtually systematic in the case of assault on a staff member, and automatically applied in the case of mass disorder or an escape attempt. It is enforced immediately after a sentence of solitary confinement. A change of facility has a number of consequences, since the individual loses everything he had acquired in terms of work or training assignment, but also relational capital, and is usually housed farther away from his family, making visits less frequent and the isolation more of an ordeal.

One man tells me that before coming to this prison, he was incarcerated for 23 months in a recently constructed long-term facility. His term was going well, he had never had any incident report and had good relations with the staff. He was able to spend one weekend per month in the family life unit with his wife and young son. One day, when he arrived late for the father–child visit, the guard supervising granted him a short extension. But the sergeant, who had just taken up his post at the facility, refused to honor this concession, insisting on making him leave at the specified time, and, despite his protests, pushed him out of the room. In his urgency, the sergeant slammed the door of the visiting room, banging the little boy on the head, and prompting a sharp reaction from the man and a still more forceful response from the sergeant. "He pushed me to the ground and said in my ear: 'Just you wait, you motherfucker.' And then I was put in the hole. But I only got three days because the guards and the directors, who knew me well, knew that I wasn't guilty. The sergeant filed a complaint. The court gave me an extra four months and a 500 euro fine. The worst thing is that I got transferred. I lost everything – my family life time, my SRCs. If I listen to the old-timers, I think: 'I need to calm down, there's nothing I can do.' Listening to the young guys, I think: 'I have to smash everything up.' You see? That's what prison's like. Everything can be going fine for months or years, and then one day there's a problem, and you lose everything."

One magistrate, reflecting on this chain of sanctions issued by different authorities for the same action – in this man's case, the disciplinary board, the sentencing judge, and the immediate appearance trial judge – commented: "It has to be admitted that it's a triple or quadruple penalty." In fact, if the additional repercussions on work, day release, and sentence adjustments were taken into account, it was often a sixfold or sevenfold sanction, announced in successive waves over time. Most of these punishments were out of the hands of the disciplinary board, whose initial decision brought a cascade of others that its members did not always bear in mind when they pronounced sentence. Even when a director felt he had shown clemency, issuing a suspended spell in solitary confinement because he thought the accused had been victim of another inmate or knew that the guard accusing him had a tendency to provoke conflict, he was still initiating a chain of sanctions that retained no trace of the reservations he had expressed and the leniency he had wished to show.

Within this system of punitive inflation, two forms of sanction were banned on principle: collective punishment and selective random punishment. The absence of these was all the more remarkable given how common they are in the world of law enforcement. Collective punishment – that is, punishing a group for the wrongdoing of one person or a few individuals – was not tolerated in this facility. One day, the assignment committee had to rule on a request from the contracted management company to sanction 18 workers following the "disappearance of a bottle of perfume" in the workshop; the chairman of the meeting said he was shocked by this request, which was rejected. But management was well aware that at moments of high tension in the facility, especially around attacks on staff members, there was a risk that the guards would take revenge on the inmates; the fear of such reprisals could even serve as justification for calling in ERIS, the special unit created to control mutinies. Random punishment – that is, punishing one individual chosen at random from a group in which several have committed an infraction – was also not acceptable. When group disturbances occurred, which usually amounted to no more than a few individuals staying in the exercise yard instead of returning to their block, the cameras could help to identify the protagonists, and actually, the fact that the prison had a captive population under constant surveillance tended to minimize discretionary selection of alleged culprits. But conducting sector searches or targeted searches could be seen as an attenuated form of it; in effect, since management knew that cellphones and marijuana were ubiquitous in the prison, a decision to inspect certain cells essentially amounted to choosing who they wished to punish. In other words, collective punishment and random punishment, two manifest expressions of arbitrary order, had no place in the prison, but it was clear that they could become possible at any moment if this principle was relaxed. Constant vigilance was required to ensure that just punishment was implemented.

* * *

The extent and range of the prison's punitive arsenal should not conceal the fact that solitary confinement remains the keystone of the repressive architecture erected by the prison system a little over two centuries ago. This is not only the most frequent, but also the most normal penalty, in the sense of it being both the custom and the standard. Locking the inmate up in a solitary confinement cell is the sanction that goes without saying, both for the staff and for the inmates. In the view of the staff, nothing that is not "solitary," whether suspended or not, is truly a punishment; a warning, which is rarely issued, expresses a doubt as to guilt more than a desire to punish less harshly. For the inmates, "the hole" is the punishment they expect; it can even, as we have seen, be the threat and the challenge thrown down by those seeking to get a right recognized or a request acknowledged, and who have no other way of getting heard, as they still hope. But this process of normalization of the use of, or call for, solitary confinement still does not make it a mundane sanction. The experience of those placed there is always grueling, and sometimes traumatic.

One afternoon, when I am sitting in on a disciplinary board meeting in the small room at the entrance to the disciplinary block, we suddenly hear agonized cries. I cannot tell whether they are cries of pain or despair, but the howls are both terrifying and harrowing. For a moment, the hearing continues as if nothing is happening; whether this is from a desire to maintain a professional distance, or being accustomed to such manifestations of suffering, I cannot tell. In the recess for deliberation on the case in hand, the deputy warden chairing the session and the officer responsible for the block ask the guard what the problem is. From where we are, we can now make out, amidst a somewhat formless wailing, the repeated words "My head! My head!" According to the first information we receive, the man whose cries we hear has just been placed in preventative solitary confinement, but the cause of his moans and the source of his pain are uncertain. Do they result from the fight that has led to his confinement, or from blows he has inflicted on himself by knocking his head against the wall of his cell? The officer telephones the healthcare unit, explaining to the physician that the inmate "is suffering from a headache." The director asserts that it seems to be "an epileptic seizure." For my part, I am thinking of the case of an inmate whose story I read in the news a little before, who died as a result of an undetected cerebral hematoma. The two guards present in the room, who appear less concerned, murmur to each other about "making a scene" to deceive the staff: "If we give in to their little games, they'll think they've won!"

Once the healthcare team has been alerted, we go to see the inmate. In the austere and constricted space of the cell, I glimpse, behind the director and the two guards, a young man of African descent, half-undressed, gripped by an uncontrollable panic, and appearing at once tormented and terrified. The attitude of the staff increases his anguish. The guards are yelling at him to calm down, producing the opposite effect. The lieutenant, by contrast, displays a frigid coolness, immobilizing him with a control technique that frightens him still further. The deputy warden, who was at first observing the scene, trying to avoid contributing further to the disorder, asks the young man to tell him what has happened. Between sobs and groans, the man explains, hiccupping, that it is Ramadan, he is trying to show goodwill toward everybody, he is making efforts to behave well and control himself, and that after all he has found himself here, when he did nothing and he was the one who was hit. He does not show, and has not at any point shown, any aggressiveness toward the staff. But every so often, he can no longer control himself and bangs his head against the wall. Despite his extreme agitation, he speaks coherently, though under these conditions it is difficult to reconstitute the circumstances that led him to the disciplinary unit. Ten minutes later, when the exchange with the director has quieted him a little, the physician arrives, asks about the problem, and injects him with a tranquilizer. After a few vague reassurances by the staff that someone will come by later to see him, everyone leaves.

At end of the day, when no one has yet returned to visit the man, I spend a moment talking with him through the grille of his solitary confinement cell. He is now perfectly calm. He is dressed in a "suicide kit" of paper pants and tunic. He has also been given paper sheets, but has been refused a blanket, and he tells me he is cold. He speaks softly and apologizes for the morning's events. I explain to him that I am not from the prison management, so he does not have to justify himself to me. I piece together a few fragments of his story. He is from Mozambique, and came to France with his mother when he was one year old. Probably as a result of a report regarding child neglect, he was monitored by social workers and placed in a foster family, and later in a children's home. Two sisters born after him have French nationality, but he himself failed to renew his residence permit when he reached the age of majority. Although he has spent 19 of his 20 years in France, he is now an illegal immigrant. The risk is, of course, that when he is released, in line with the agreement between the prison and the prefecture, the police will be waiting to take him to an immigration detention center and organize his deportation to a country he does not know. But he is unaware of this possibility, since, as I realize a little later, the probation and re-entry counselor he met with when he arrived did not ask him about his immigration status, and his file bears no sign of any attempt to set things in order. For now, he is in pre-trial detention awaiting trial for sexual assault.

But his main concern is neither his legal status nor his judicial situation. He is overwhelmed by the fear that being placed in solitary confinement will "ruin" his case. Knowing that he will be in the facility for a long time, he has done all he could to behave well in prison, he says, showing respect to the guards and not arguing with the other inmates. A practicing Muslim, he adds that during the month of the fast it is particularly important to him to conduct himself irreproachably toward others. This twofold concern – with the institution and his faith – explains why he was so upset at being punished that morning: both his image in the prison and his effort to purify himself were compromised. "I screwed up my prison time when everything was going well until then, and worse, during Ramadan," he keeps repeating. He is especially despairing because, according to him, he is not in the wrong. He recounts the events that led him to solitary confinement. Owing to the constraints of the fast, with the meal that has to be taken before dawn, he was still sleeping that morning when the guard called inmates out for showers. Being late to join the other three prisoners in the cubicles, he says he was insulted and jostled by one of them. But when the officer intervened to halt this incipient fight, he interpreted matters otherwise, considering the young man responsible and sent him down to the disciplinary unit. As the incident occurs on a Friday morning, the man will have to wait three days until his hearing. Before leaving him, in view of the emotional fragility he demonstrates, I tell him how the disciplinary board operates and what to expect, so as to help him avoid a misstep that could go against him.

Six days later, an almost identical scene occurs. Once again it involves a pre-trial prisoner, also young, this time of French descent. He too is yelling out in pain. That morning, he was placed in solitary confinement for answering back to a guard. He has injured his hand by hitting it against one of the cell fittings, probably in a gesture of rage. He has been given a medical appointment, but a more urgent case arose in the meantime, and his consultation was pushed back without his having been told. He has therefore been waiting an hour and a half when he is brought out. As they try to handcuff him, the officers hurt him further and his cries redouble. He struggles. The lieutenant, assisted by the two guards, intervenes to immobilize him using the usual procedure, which involves twisting his hands to prevent him moving them. Cue for renewed yells prompted by the pain, and a rough return to the cell. At that moment, a deputy warden arrives. The young man is by then extremely agitated, weeping, yelling, banging his head against the wall, throwing himself motionless to the floor as if he has passed out. The deputy warden's soft but firm words eventually soothe his crisis. A little later, the young man is taken by a guard and a sergeant to the healthcare unit, to receive treatment at last. In the little waiting room the sergeant, furious, comments on the deputy warden's attitude, saying she is "trying to be a social worker," and adding that this is not the best approach with this type of inmate. A few minutes later the doctor sees the young man, and, having examined him, declares his condition "incompatible with being kept in solitary confinement," thus allowing him, to the great dismay of the prison staff, to return to his cell to await his appearance before the disciplinary board.

These two scenes reveal how painful the experience of being placed in solitary confinement can be, for some inmates at least. Very few situations can result in such acute distress. These young men's howls bore no relation to the noisy protests and vociferous arguments that were sometimes heard when a disagreement set an inmate against another individual. They expressed unquenchable suffering, irrepressible exasperation, and an entirely self-directed violence. There was not the slightest aggressiveness toward the staff: all the destructive force was turned against the individual himself.

When I sought to understand the source of this violence, it seemed to me that it did not lie only, or perhaps even mainly, in the material conditions in the disciplinary unit, rightly criticized as unfit by the International Prison Observatory and the General Controller of Prisons and Detention Centers, especially in some more dilapidated facilities. Certainly, the double-locked system of enclosure, where the cell door opens onto a vestibule separated by a grille from the space reserved to the inmate, the limited natural light filtering through the small window obscured by the rubberized mesh placed over the bars, the rudimentary supposedly safe furnishings, and the austerity of the room all made the cell feel oppressive, while the successive defacements, the dirt, and the odors of previous presences added further layers of degradation. But rather than these factors in themselves, it was what they signified and what they implied, especially for young and fragile inmates, that determined their experience when they entered the cell.

The reason the solitary confinement cell generated such extreme suffering was the triple ordeal it inscribed on the inmates' bodies, which was translated in these self-destructive actions.[14] First, a sense of injustice, either because the individual did not consider himself guilty of the actions he was charged with, or because he found the sanction completely disproportionate to the misdeed committed. Second, a feeling of powerlessness, the impossibility of making oneself heard, both literally and figuratively, and of being unable to change anything about the inexorable course of the punishment, which the virtual absence of relations with other human beings contributed to producing. Third, an irreducible kernel of pure despair, beyond words, caused by the radical isolation and the lack of diversions, the privation of others' presence, however annoying it might be at other times, and of television images, however boring they usually were: the inmate had a physical experience of the bareness of the carceral condition. The brutality of the methods used to immobilize the prisoners and take them to the disciplinary cells, and the symbolic violence of the humiliating strip search on entry to the block, even when they were conducted to the letter of the regulations, marked the move from the prison world to the disciplinary space, and revealed the change of regime it implied.

Given the ordeal represented by placement in solitary confinement, one would suppose that it is used to sanction serious misdeeds that gravely endanger the security of the facility, its staff, or its inmates. In fact, it generally resulted from more benign acts, such as a refusal to return to cell, which, as staff were well aware, could be the last resort for getting a response to a request that had gone unanswered; an angry remark, which would later be discovered to have been made following the receipt of bad news; an impatient gesture toward a guard who might in some cases be known for his propensity to foster conflict; or other infractions with limited consequences that arose in troubling circumstances.

Moreover, those most at risk of this ordeal were generally the most vulnerable. Their vulnerability could be social, when some became temporarily or permanently victims of other inmates, for whom they would pick up packages thrown over the walls or hide cellphones among their belongings. But it was more often psychological, in the case of individuals presenting with mental health issues such as psychosis, or less defined psychic disturbances, sometimes linked to addictions, that implied poor self-control. Some were quick-tempered, constantly at risk of reacting too sharply to an insult from a fellow inmate or a remark by a correctional officer. The disciplinary boards recognized the existence of social vulnerability, and some even acquitted prisoners in such cases, while others paid it little heed. However, psychological vulnerability was almost always completely ignored, for two reasons. First, the prison staff had neither training nor awareness in this area. Second, psychiatrists and psychologists did not communicate information on their patients, on the grounds that separation of the functions of surveillance and care are necessary to protect confidentiality.

However, psychological vulnerability was common. An epidemiological study of mental health among 800 inmates selected at random in 23 French penal facilities reveals a high rate of mental illness in the prison population.[15] In this representative sample, 36 percent of incarcerated persons have at least one psychiatric problem, 29 percent have anxiety issues, including panic attacks, and 28 percent have mood disorders, mainly of the depressive type. Moreover, 15 percent are dependent on narcotics and 12 percent on alcohol. Finally, the most serious manifestations, of psychoses such as schizophrenia, psychotic episodes, or others, are observed in 17 percent of inmates. With regard to the gravity of the symptoms, 23 percent are described as "manifestly ill," 10 percent as "seriously ill," and 2 percent as "very seriously ill." When compared with international surveys, this study suggests that the proportion of mentally ill people in French prisons is particularly high.

There are varying interpretations of this observation. It is difficult to distinguish the part played by penal policies and court practices, which lead to large numbers of mentally ill people being locked up, from that played by prison policies and disciplinary practices, which themselves generate or aggravate psychiatric disorders. Whatever the explanation, if more than one-third of prisoners in France suffer from psychiatric symptoms, including mood disorders in eight out of ten cases, one-third of which are considered serious, it is easy to imagine the singular vulnerability of these individuals, to the risk of both committing an act that will lead them to solitary confinement and developing worrying symptoms at this time as a consequence of their segregation. Research in the United States, where solitary confinement is generalized, has shown that these practices of isolation have severe pathogenic effects on mental health.[16] In the long run, they contribute to greater desocialization of inmates and, consequently, to difficulties in readjusting to the outside world, with a subsequent risk of recidivism.

But the immediate effect of solitary confinement is distinct: it leads to suicide. The day before the young Mozambican man presented with what appeared to be a panic attack, while the lieutenant and guards were busy placing another man, who had been involved in a fight, in a punishment cell, someone shouted "fire!" A confined inmate, who was considered psychologically fragile, had set fire to his mattress. As correctional officers evacuated his neighbors into an adjacent small yard, others quickly donned fire-resistant overalls and entered the smoke-filled, blackened cell with a fire hose. The inmate was extracted before he burned to death or suffocated.

But the preparations for this rescue operation had taken 10 minutes that might have cost him his life. Such incidents are not uncommon. Analysis of the national prison administration statistics shows that more than 16 percent of deaths from suicide occur in disciplinary units, nearly half of them on the day the inmate is placed there or the day after, although these units account for only 2 percent of prison cells.[17] In other words, a prisoner is at least eight times more at risk of taking his own life in a disciplinary cell than in a regular cell – the excess of risk is actually much higher, since disciplinary units are most of the time partially empty, while inmates are almost always doubled up in the regular blocks. Thus placement in solitary confinement emerges as by far the most important factor in the increased probability of an inmate killing himself in prison. Psychiatrists working in correctional facilities are generally aware of this. They readily write up certificates stating that the individual's mental state is incompatible with being held in solitary confinement, sometimes eliciting protests from guards. Despite these precautions, this sanction, which remains the reference penalty in the punishment system, contributes to making France the country with the highest prison suicide rate in Europe.

Yet the maximum sentence to solitary confinement has fallen markedly since the 1990s. "In the short-stay prison where I started out, it was 45 days for a cellphone," remembered one director, pointing out that the penalty had now been brought down to 14 days. "And I found an internal regulation from back in 1969, where an assault on staff got you 90 days in solitary, the first three days on bread and water. That changed in the early 1970s. We were almost 40 years with a maximum of 45 days, and went down to 30 days in 2009." After a moment's reflection, he added: "There's no reason why that development shouldn't continue." The prison staff often noted that penalties had gotten softer. Some were happy about it, while others had reservations or were nostalgic. Many seemed ambivalent, looking back with regret to a past when order was better respected, but acknowledging the problematic abuses of those times. However, even reduced to the current level, sentences to solitary confinement continued to generate suffering and suicides, particularly among individuals with mental health disorders, who were also those most likely to be placed there.

A few weeks after I finished my research, a young man who had been sentenced to a short penalty and had mental health issues was placed in solitary confinement following an altercation with another inmate. According to the account I received from a number of members of management staff, shortly after his transfer, in a gesture of despair that resembled so many others, he had set fire to his mattress. His neighbors called to the guard present at the time for help. The officer rushed over, but since he did not have the second key to the grille, he was unable to pull the young man out and save him from the flames. With the inmate crying out in fear and pain, the guard went back to ask for assistance. When the lieutenant arrived in the disciplinary unit with the key, he found the young man unconscious, with 80 percent second- and third-degree burns. The man survived for a little while in the resuscitation unit. In light of his circumstances, the judge ordered his release – shortly before he died.

* * *

A person entering prison generally thinks he will serve out a sentence consisting of privation of freedom, as he has been told by the judge who sentenced him. But in addition to quickly realizing that the privations he is to suffer are much more numerous and varied than he had imagined, he also discovers that the sentence pronounced by the court is only one of the many penalties he risks incurring. After the court judgment, he now faces disciplinary judgment and its various ramifications. There are at least two differences between these two procedures. First, the sanctions issued in prison relate more to questions of order than of justice. It is not that the prison administration is not concerned to render just decisions, but the lack of impartiality of the disciplinary boards, the presumption of the guilt of the accused, and the need to offer reassurance to correctional officers set disciplinary procedures that depart considerably from the principles of justice. Second, the large number of authorities involved in disciplinary action leads to a multiplication of sanctions, whether official or unofficial. After the disciplinary board, there is the work assignment committee, the sentencing judge, and the court judge, among others, whose decisions sometimes result in multiple sanctions that affect the modality, duration, and place of incarceration, thus departing from the principle that one cannot be punished more than once for the same offense. These differences are hardly surprising: prison is a place of constraint rather than a space of rights, and discipline is focused on maintaining internal order rather than instituting a just process. But it would be wrong also to deny the relationship between discipline and justice, as this would fail to take into account the prison administration's efforts to bring formal law into the disciplinary procedure, following the pattern of judicial practice.

Hence, prison discipline derives from a concern for internal order in a place of constraint. But it is important to point out that inmates are not the only ones concerned by this order, as is often imagined and as most prisoners themselves believe: it also involves guards. Whereas discipline appears to affect only the prison population, by both sanctioning and deterring misdeeds committed or allegedly committed, in reality it is also indirectly focused toward staff, seeking to control the risk of personal revenge or collective reprisals. The punishment imposed by the disciplinary board in some sense substitutes for the mistreatment meted out by correctional officers, just as the judicial system is used to prevent individuals taking the law into their own hands. Studies of guards' punitive practices in the United States reveal the brutality and cruelty they can exhibit, but also the tolerance, and even encouragement, they are accorded by the prison hierarchy.[18] The introduction of formal procedures, which, while recognizing prisoners' rights, also aim to satisfy staff by punishing violations of the rules and particularly challenges to their authority, tends to delegitimize the punishments and the bullying doled out by correctional officers themselves. It is not that these have completely disappeared, but they are not seen as acceptable. For the inmates, the price of this transaction is sanctions that have become almost systematic, at least in the form of suspended penalties, even when the case is based on inconsistent or nonexistent evidence. Indeed, the fact that prison is a place of constraint implies that there are people imposing this constraint, and others who are subjected to it. Since authority is structurally on the side of the staff, the management has no choice but to discredit the claims of inmates, even when it is supposed to render justice.

Criminological studies of prison have focused much more on infractions, attacks, riots, and their causes than on the procedures and practices of discipline. In other words, far greater interest has been shown in the problems of order posed by inmates than the issues of justice at work on the side of the administration and its agents.[19] This imbalance tends to understate the profound tensions at the heart of the punitive apparatus in French prisons. On the one hand, there is no question that the most degrading punishments, from flogging to leg irons, have been abolished; that penalties have been reduced, as the steady decrease in the maximum solitary confinement sentence shows; that new legislation has introduced an outside scrutiny of judgment, with the presence of a lawyer at the hearing and the external assessor on the disciplinary board; that appeals to the administrative court, even though they are rare and in principle do not result in the lifting of the sanction, have established case law that is generally followed by correctional facilities; that inmates, even if they appear before the board in a highly unequal position vis-à-vis their accusers, are less subject to the arbitrary authority of the system; and finally that the structure itself remains sufficiently flexible to allow directors to lean more toward clemency if they so choose. On the other hand, however, it cannot be denied that the range of infractions extends to minor misdeeds for which the sentences are disproportionately severe, on the principle that nothing must be allowed to pass; that the most socially and psychologically vulnerable inmates are more at risk of sanction than others, contributing to making them still more precarious; that disciplinary boards pay little heed to the defendant's explanations and reasons in their decisions; and that for anyone who gets sucked in, the punitive mechanism operates as a spiral that brings with it an uninterrupted series of sanctions on all levels of prison life. Since the 1990s, these tensions have contributed to calming relations in the carceral world, but also to the reinforcement of inequalities between those who manage, through a continual effort of self-control, not to commit misdeeds or not to get caught, and those who, through fragility, clumsiness, or failure to adjust, are ensnared by the disciplinary machine.

In the system as I have just described it, with all its tensions, one apparent aberration – in the sense of an exception – remains: the disciplinary cell. It is a modern dungeon, a survival from the prehistory of the prison system, a reminder of what prison was before prison.[20] Of course, in most Western countries, contemporary facilities have "civilized" punishment cells compared to those of their ancestors. It is, one might add, noteworthy that the country that has paid greatest attention to their material and technical quality at the same time as their oppressive and alienating power is also the country that makes greatest use of them – it is currently estimated that in the United States there are 80,000 people in solitary confinement, often for very long periods. The average duration in California is nearly seven years, and the record is 31 years without interruption for a prisoner in Colorado.[21] In Europe in general, and in France in particular, the trend is in the opposite direction, with solitary confinement several times condemned as "torture" or "inhuman and degrading treatment" by a number of European authorities. Still, it persists.

If one considers the relatively anodyne or debatable nature of many of the infractions that lead prisoners to be placed in solitary confinement, the mental health consequences and suicide risk associated with it, and the range of sanctions the prison has available as alternative penalties, one might wonder why the prison administration is so attached to this punishment.[22] Surely, in a few years' or decades' time when it has disappeared, observers will consider it with the same degree of moral distance as our contemporaries feel with respect to flogging and leg irons. In the meantime, it remains almost everywhere the reference punishment.

11

An Unfinished Business

I ask you to remember, not every man who bears the mark
of the castaway is a castaway at heart.
J. M. Coetzee, *Foe*, 1986

"Prison prepares you for coming back to prison. They should put a notice at the exit to the facility: 'See you soon!' For me it's easier to be in here than outside," says a man in his 50s who has already been convicted seven times for robbery with violence, and is awaiting a decision on his appeal against a new 10-year sentence. While he admits his previous "hold-ups," adding: "we robbed dealers, not little old ladies," he denies committing the one for which he has recently been sentenced, but admits, "they become doubtful about people like me." He certainly cannot be deemed an example of the efficacy of prison in preventing recidivism. But nor is he a typical case, with his history of repeated serious offenses that have earned him long sentences up to well into middle age. Many inmates of the prison do return there, but these cycles generally involve young men and petty offenses. One morning, noticing a familiar name on the list of those who arrived the previous day – a man of African descent aged about 25 – the guard in the arrivals block remarks impassively: "That's five times I've seen him leave, and five times he's come back!"

Since the 2000s, and particularly since the law of December 12, 2005 (which extended the time limit for definition of repeat offending, and toughened repression of recidivism) and that of August 10, 2007 (which introduced minimum penalties and increased the range of exceptions to the exemption from incarceration for juvenile recidivists aged 16 and above), the question of preventing recidivism has lain at the heart of penal policy. At least up until 2014, policy was becoming increasingly inflexible toward those who, after committing one offense, go on to commit another within a given time period. This severity is often translated by a custodial prison sentence, frequently coupled with the revocation of a previous suspended sentence with parole. The utilitarian justification of these harsher sanctions is based on a twofold argument of neutralization and deterrence: the longer the inmate is in prison, the more lastingly he is removed from the risk of committing an offense; the more inflexible his punishment, the less he will be tempted to begin again. Imprisonment thus becomes the main weapon in the fight against recidivism, on the basis of such apparently self-evident arguments. But evaluation of public policy goes somewhat against this simple common sense, especially when it is contradicted by the experience of those primarily concerned; both inmates and guards realize that a custodial prison sentence is often the best route back to prison, especially for young people. This is confirmed by research.

Recidivism has been studied in France for several decades,[1] and the available surveys provide important data that can be used to measure and understand the phenomenon. A retrospective analysis of individuals convicted in 2007 shows that 35 percent of them had already been convicted in the five years prior to this conviction; another, prospective, on a cohort of individuals convicted in 2004, projects a repeat offending rate of 45 percent over the subsequent seven years. Moreover, comparison of the five-year trajectories of those released from prison and those who are convicted but not incarcerated, adjusted to take into account the nature of the offense and the criminal record, reveals a further prison sentence in 61 percent of cases for those released from prison, compared to 52 percent for those who were given a suspended sentence with parole, 44 percent for those sentenced to community service, and 36 percent for those given a simple suspended sentence. Finally, taking only those leaving prison and the events supervening in the five years following their release, there is a 59 percent rate of reconviction, with a custodial sentence pronounced in 46 percent of cases. These rates are higher among the youngest groups and the unemployed; they are also higher in the case of those sentenced to less than six months and to one to two years in prison. Most significantly, when the comparisons are standardized by assuming all other things equal, release after a sentence without adjustment multiplies the risk of reconviction by a factor of 1.6, and doubles the risk of another custodial sentence.

In short, these studies indicate that, for similar background and equivalent offenses, individuals who are imprisoned are generally more likely to reoffend than those given alternative penalties, and that among those incarcerated, short sentences and sentences without adjustment produce more recidivism. They are corroborated by statistical surveys conducted elsewhere in Western Europe and North America, which show that prison in general as well as the length of sentence and the shock of incarceration in particular lead to more repeat offending, while parole or probation give better results.[2] We may add that the ethnography of prison and interviews with inmates clearly demonstrate how incarceration often causes breaches in family life and professional career that result in individuals becoming desocialized, while at the same time generating a resocialization in criminal environments. These two series of factors render re-entry into society difficult and foster the return to criminal activity. The empirical work of social scientists therefore runs counter to the common sense of policymakers.

But knowledge does not necessarily lead to action. The paradox of recent decades is that successive governments, particularly but not exclusively conservative ones, have systematically developed discourses around prevention of recidivism, while passing laws and publishing circulars that go against the available knowledge on the subject. Prison sentences have become tougher and more automatically applied; individuals are increasingly locked up for short and even very short periods; people convicted in the past who have since reintegrated in society have been sought out to be incarcerated; the probation and re-entry services tasked with orchestrating sentence adjustments have been swamped with work. Thus, at the same time as declaring their wish to avoid recidivism, those in power have introduced measures that encourage it. It is interesting to note that this focus on recidivism, which is also found in other European countries, contrasts with the recent tendency in the United States where, within the framework of the "new penology," the trend is to invert the significance of the figures on repeat offending. Indeed, the view taken there is that the efficacy of penal policy should no longer necessarily be measured by a fall in these statistics, which would suggest a reduction in crime, but by a rise, which quantifies the activity of the services; the more recidivists are locked up, the more the effort to repress is demonstrated. It might be argued that this amounts to an admission that mass incarceration has failed, but it would be more pertinent to see it as a way of governing inequality, by prioritizing repression over prevention.[3] By contrast, even if it fails to furnish itself with the means to do so, France seems to have not yet entirely given up on the idea of reducing recidivism.

But the importance ascribed to this reduction by those in power is not new, nor is the failure of penal measures for preventing it. Although the renewed interest, which no doubt is as much a matter of public relations as of concern for the common good, is relatively recent, the question has regularly resurfaced in public debate since the earliest days of prison. Thus, in the second half of the nineteenth century, legislation proliferated, culminating in 1885 in the successive enactment of the law imposing penal transportation of recidivists, and the law that instituted conditional release combined with sponsorship and rehabilitation. The first of these established the ultimate method of neutralizing recidivists, since it stipulated "permanent internment in the territory of the French colonies or possessions" for some of them, depending on their offenses. The second, on the contrary, derived from an innovative philosophy of reintegration, defining the conditions of a release once "half of the sentence has been served," or two-thirds for repeat offenders, and the procedures for payment of an "annual subvention" to sponsoring organizations that contributed to the rehabilitation of newly released prisoners. The practical failure of the first measure led to emphasis being placed on the second; it was supplemented soon afterwards by the law of March 26, 1891 that introduced suspended prison sentences.[4] Thus the arsenal of alternatives to custodial prison sentences, and adjustment of the end of the sentence, was put in place at this time, meeting with some success in terms of both a decrease in recidivism and a reduction in the prison population.

A century later, then, an almost diametrically opposite perspective prevails in the conception of penal policy: custodial sentences are pronounced more and more often, and the end of the sentence is rarely adjusted. In a belated correction that effectively amounted to an admission of failure, the 2009 law on prisons partially inverted this tendency, facilitating the adjustment of sentences of less than two years and making provision for release under electronic monitoring four months before the end of sentences of up to five years, at the same time as reasserting a number of rights – notably rights to work and to the maintenance of family relations – that are conducive to future reintegration.[5] One striking element in this new legislation, which went against previous measures enacted by the same government, was the way in which the burden of preventing recidivism shifted from penal policy to prison policy. The sentencing judge and the probation and re-entry service became the key components in this process, the former as contractor of the project and the latter as project manager.[6] At a time when the prison population was rising rapidly during the first decade of the twenty-first century, preparation for release, which had been pushed aside by tougher penal practices, became subject to heightened expectations of prison services swamped by the number of people serving sentences.

*   *   *

The sometimes extreme frustration of inmates faced with the continual postponement of their sentence adjustment clearly articulates the limits of this response. One day a 23-year-old man of North African origin appears before the disciplinary board for having refused to return to his cell after exercise. He was demanding to "see the chief," and declared he was "ready to go to the hole" if his request was not granted. In response to this "refusal to cooperate," he was placed preventatively in solitary confinement. The incident was somewhat banal, but the fact that it occurred on December 31 was not. The choice of this date for provoking an incident immediately draws the attention of the director presiding over this hearing, as it suggests a gesture of despair: it is no small thing to get oneself locked up on New Year's Eve. Expressing himself articulately, resolute but without anger, the man explains: "it's the only way I found to make myself heard." Indeed, he remarks, "it's been months since I heard anything from my counselor." Sentenced to three years in prison for armed robbery, he could have had a sentence adjustment more than a year ago, but he had not been able to obtain it given the impossibility of getting a meeting with the counselor in charge of his case. "I screwed up and I'm paying, that's only right. I was 20, I behaved like a jerk, I was with buddies in a hold-up. But since I've been here I've done everything right. I've done the training for table service, I take part in sports, I'm making regular compensation payments to the victim. In prison, I'm respectful to the guards, I always try to calm down disagreements." One of the assessors, a guard who knows him, confirms his "good behavior," while the director concedes that he is a "model inmate."

The man continues, with tears in his eyes: "I've done everything my counselor asked me to and I've had a promise of a job for a long time – but nothing's happening. I see the others getting released on adjusted sentences, and I've got nothing. I'm not jealous, I'm pleased for them, but I don't know why I'm being left behind like this. You have to understand. My dad is in the hospital dying of liver cancer. My mom is sick and can only come visit me twice a year. My little brother's been threatened by guys in the neighborhood and could get himself killed any day. I'm the eldest. I'm responsible for the family. I can't sleep at night anymore with all these problems." The board members are sympathetic, though they challenge his choice of method of communication without much conviction, given his many appeals for help: "In substance, I understand your situation, but in form, refusing to return to your cell so as to get your request heard is not a good solution." As is often the case when the board, while not deeming the accused guilty, nevertheless sentences him on principle in order not to contradict the decision to place him in preventative segregation, the sanction pronounced is eight days' solitary confinement with five suspended, allowing him to leave the disciplinary unit immediately, but not preventing him from losing weeks of sentence reduction credits. Attempting benevolence, the director concludes: "I understand your problem, but I can't solve it. I'll contact the counselor so that she can do what's required. For now, you are going to return to your regular cell."

After inquiring with the director of the prison probation and re-entry service, it turns out that the counselor in charge of this man's case has been on maternity leave for six months without being replaced. So nobody has been working on the adjustment of his sentence. The director of the service decides to take things in hand himself. But since less than three months remain until the man's designated release date, there is no longer time to do anything. Despite his efforts to meet all the requirements for adjustment of his sentence, the man will therefore be among the contingent of inmates given a "cold release," in other words without the benefits of a progressive transition and social support for their return to the world outside. The service's excessive workload and staff shortage will have led him to spend 18 months more than necessary incarcerated, at a time when his family is facing grave difficulties. Even his desperate gesture, made too late, will have no effect – except that of underlining the shortcomings of the prison system and its tragic consequences for the carceral condition. In this case, not replacing the counselor on maternity leave means that more than 100 inmates are in the same situation as he is, abandoned without any follow-up.

According to one of the senior managers of the prison probation and re-entry service, the problem is essentially one of numbers. In four years, their caseload of individuals under sentence has increased by 250, and that of inmates by 84, while the number of counselors working in the prison has remained the same. Each of them is in charge of around 100 cases.

This situation has led to drastic choices being made. "Around one-quarter of inmates are being followed up by counselors: 20 percent are sentence adjustment cases, and 5 percent well-prepared releases. In another quarter of cases, the counselors' activity is limited to access to rights and directing inmates to potential support for the future. As to the remaining half, they're pre-trial prisoners, those serving short sentences and those who are undemanding, and very little is done for them." These figures in fact seem optimistic given the reality actually measured; according to the facility's statistics, only 16 percent of prisoners due for release – fewer than one in six – are assessed for sentence adjustment in the form of electronic monitoring, work placement, or conditional release; but this figure is for cases considered, regardless of the judge's final decision: one application in five is rejected. Overall, only one-eighth of inmates released actually benefit from an adjusted sentence.

For most of the prisoners who see a counselor the day after they arrive at the prison, and often nourish the hope that their case will be quickly taken up (some of them telling me later of their plans as they look ahead to a quick release), disillusion gradually settles in, giving way to resignation, bitterness, or anger. Let us return to the three categories outlined by the senior manager. For pre-trial prisoners, who account for nearly one-third of those sent to prison, adjustment is of course not an option because sentence has not yet been pronounced. Similarly, for those serving short sentences, who make up one-quarter of convicted prisoners, there is no provision because the time is too short and the counselors too busy: "Service policy is that there is no adjustment of sentences of less than six months." Finally, those inmates described as "undemanding" constitute a vaguely defined category, hardly benefiting from any support: "Where it really falls down is if the person doesn't ask and the guard doesn't report the problem: they can fall through the net."

This last category emphasizes how the inmate must find the correct level of insistence. If, because he does not understand how the service functions, because he is unaware of the possibilities for adjustment, or because he lacks initiative (as is frequently the case in individuals suffering from depression), he does not ask for anything, he risks continuing to the end of his sentence without receiving any assistance toward his release. If, on the contrary, he is too insistent, he risks annoying his counselor, who will always be under pressure from the multiple requests she is dealing with. One man, serving his first sentence of three years for selling marijuana, has already been at the prison for 20 months, and is therefore well beyond the date when his sentence adjustment could have begun. His case has been prepared for four months; he has a promise of a permanent job with his former employer, and his wife and child have moved to a new apartment. All he is waiting for is to present his case to the sentencing judge, which requires the counselor to conduct an investigation, draw up a report, and list the case on the order of business. He has therefore written to her, and spoken to the guard and the block senior, and has finally contacted the director. "Everyone spoke on my behalf. It must have annoyed my counselor. The other day she was walking past, and she said to me: 'I don't want to hear anything more about your case, or I won't come and see you.' I was going to reply: 'Why are you talking to me like that? What's your problem?' But I didn't say anything, because I was worried she'd take it out on me."

This frustration is a common experience in prison. The probation and re-entry counselor is effectively the link between the inside and the outside worlds. She is seen by those incarcerated as the person who holds the keys giving access to earlier release. She is the one who assesses his situation with a view to the most appropriate adjustment, who organizes contact with the re-entry support organizations that collaborate with the facility, confirms that the potential future employer has a serious commitment to recruiting the inmate, ensures that, where appropriate, mental health treatment or ongoing compensation for civil parties is under way, submits requests for day release, and, although she is absent from the parole hearing, nevertheless plays an important role through the report she draws up about the inmate and his plans. Inmates therefore often have a powerful but ambivalent affective engagement with the counselor: it is she who can support or delay, defend or weaken the case; she is a social worker devoted to smoothing the path of release, but she is also a member of the prison management who forms part of the surveillance exercised over the prisoners. Inmates' moral sentiments toward her range from gratitude to resentment. These feelings are sometimes expressed through violence.

One day, at the end of the morning, a guard is counting the inmates on his floor. More diligent than many of his colleagues who content themselves with a superficial check, he moves from cell to cell, opening the door and exchanging a few words with the occupants before locking the door again. Although this quasi-convivial practice is generally appreciated by the inmates, one of them, furious, bursts out onto the walkway. This is a man of 55, who is expressing himself with vehemence. His complaint concerns his counselor, whom he has been asking in vain to meet with for several weeks. She has made an appointment for him several times and he has canceled his exercise period to meet with her, but she has not turned up. The officer in the monitoring post has just informed him that she passed by that morning unannounced and did not find him since he had gone out to the exercise yard. The man is beside himself. Despite the soothing words of the guard doing the counting, he seems unlikely to calm down any time soon. After a few minutes, he returns to his cell and goes toward the corner where he is preparing his meal on the hotplate, threatening to "throw a pan full of hot oil." The officer quickly locks the cell door. Inside, the man can be heard yelling in rage. Silence falls again. A slip of paper is passed under the door: "The oil is boiling." Sounding almost embarrassed, the guard says: "I'm going to draw up an incident report, Mr. Mansouri. I have no choice. I wanted to warn you." And he moves off, while the man continues to protest.

By virtue of their – albeit relative – accessibility, the probation and re-entry counselors are not just the "project managers for the execution of measures and sentences," as the circular defining their mission states, but are also, as far as inmates are concerned, the human face of their sentence adjustment. This is why prisoners hold them responsible for delays or difficulties that hold back their potential release under electronic monitoring, on work placement, or conditional release. But the backlog of cases and delays in dealing with them are not just due to the counselors' excessive workloads. The sentencing judge too has his limits. In this facility, there are on average three parole hearings per month, at which around 10 applications for sentence adjustment are examined each time. Thus the sentence adjustment committee scrutinizes around 30 cases per month, although of course not all are accepted. In comparison, around 140 inmates are released each month. Moreover, during the summer there is only one hearing per month. This explains why, ultimately, only one prisoner in eight is released on sentence adjustment. The criteria outlined by the director of the probation and re-entry service are used to make the necessary selection; those concerned are, in principle, individuals sentenced to more than six months' imprisonment, provided that they are sufficiently insistent in their requests.[7] But "cold release" remains the rule for the majority of inmates.

The tension between the penal policy of recent decades and prison policy over the same period therefore emerges on two levels. Intellectually, the two agendas appear to contradict one another, since one focuses on incarcerating more people, and especially for longer, while the other seeks to promote alternatives, and particularly to release prisoners earlier. Practically, they are opposed, in that penal policy represents the main obstacle to the realization of prison policy, since those charged with implementing it no longer have the means to do so. The two linchpins of sentence adjustment – the sentencing judge and the probation and re-entry service – are thus unable to take on all cases, especially given the burden of risk of a tragic incident occurring when an individual serving a sentence is outside, and the concomitant danger that, if it does, they will be held responsible. This prospect disposes them toward caution. "Pornic has played its part," remarked one sentencing judge elliptically. "I realized then that you could find yourself served up on a plate by the government and the media talking about things neither of them knows anything about. The public outcry makes judges feel insecure. The probation and re-entry services were deeply troubled by that case."[8] Consequently, two new measures have recently been introduced to short-cut the normal procedure.

The simplified sentence adjustment procedure (*procédure simplifiée d'aménagement de peines*, PSAP) allows the probation and re-entry service to propose release plans directly to the public prosecutor's office for those serving sentences of less than two years, or less than five years if fewer than two years remain to be served. The public prosecutor decides whether to submit the application to the sentencing judge, whose role is to ratify the plan. If he does not respond within three weeks, it is assumed he agrees. As the director for the service said, "the sentencing judges don't like that," because they have to make a decision without meeting the inmate. End of sentence electronic monitoring (*surveillance électronique de fin de peine*, SEFIP) allows those serving a sentence of fewer than five years who are within four months of release, or a sentence of fewer than six months of which they have served one-third, to be released with an electronic tag. However, this release is closely monitored, with the individual authorized to be away from home for only four hours each day – leading the director of the probation and re-entry service to call it "prison at home."

Nevertheless, these two measures have met with only limited success. In 2011, 12 percent of cases handled by probation and re-entry services nationwide under the PSAP system were submitted to the public prosecutor, who accepted one-third of them, amounting to 820; these represented only 1 percent of all releases. That same year, 19 percent of the cases examined by these services with a view to SEFIP were submitted to the public prosecutor, who approved half of them, a total of 3,069, corresponding to just under 4 percent of releases.[9] Overall, during this period when the measures were being put into place, PSAP and SEFIP accounted for only one release in 20. But these apparently strictly technical arrangements also have a political dimension. "Of course, the idea is to ease the burden on sentencing judges," says one such magistrate. "But at the same time, our prerogatives are being taken away. A whole series of activities that fall within our remit have been gradually whittled away." In effect, PSAP and SEFIP form an integral part of a policy that aims to reinforce the role of the public prosecutor's office – in other words, the government's intervention in the judicial system.

For now, however, the marginal efficacy of the two new measures, which reflects a degree of reticence on the part of public prosecutors in applying them, leaves the problem of sentence adjustments virtually untouched. At the same time, it reveals the difficulties encountered by probation and re-entry counselors in preparing "adjustable" cases and getting them recognized as such by the public prosecutors.

* * *

The job of probation and re-entry counselor is the youngest of the prison professions, having been introduced only in 1999. It is also the one that has been most exposed to the changes and tensions of penal policy. In 2006, nine years after the decree of April 13, 1999 that instituted probation and re-entry services, which was supplemented by four circulars within the space of a few months, reports by both the National Court of Audit and the General Inspectorate of Judicial Services evaluated it as an "incomplete reform," and called for "standardization of the activity."[10] A further circular, dated March 19, 2008, subsequently attempted to clarify the "mission" and "methods" of probation and re-entry services. From this point on, prevention of recidivism was to be their "end goal," with "two components: the criminological aspect, and the social aspect." Work on the former, focused on "acting out" and its "risk factors" in the form of "sexual delinquency, spousal abuse, street violence," is based on encounter groups and, if necessary, psychological treatment. Work on the latter, centered on "re-entry" and "preparation for release," particularly as concerns "programs of seeking employment or training, and all community resocialization activities," operates through collaboration with organizations outside the prison.

If staff in the probation and re-entry services have experienced so many changes in the profession, and seen their practices challenged to such an extent, it is because they are the product of a sedimentation, and to some extent a fusion, of different categories of agents with very different profiles and roles.[11] From the nineteenth century onward, religious organizations, lay groups, and sponsoring bodies worked both within prisons, supporting prisoners, and around them, to assist their reintegration into society. But it was only with the major reform of prison administration initiated by Paul Amor after World War II that the position of these agents gradually became formalized. The prison social service was defined in the circular of June 29, 1945 as "the fraternal link between the prisoner and society, the prisoner and his family, as well as being an active instrument for raising up the inmate and giving him a new orientation on his release." Committees for support and placement of newly released prisoners were set up under the circular of February 1, 1946, in order to create a "complete network of organizations working to facilitate readjustment to life outside," and were endowed with a "unitary body responsible for coordinating their activities." Finally, the corps of correctional educators was instituted by the decree of July 21, 1949 in order to conduct "observation and reeducation of inmates in the perspective of social reorientation."[12] At the time, as the national program for prison stated that "the central aim of a penalty of privation of freedom is the reform and social reorientation of the convicted prisoner," no emphasis was placed on recidivism (the word does not appear in any of the 14 points of the program), but rather on the moral improvement of the inmate, and his social reintegration after release. The three bodies complemented one another: the correctional educators working most closely with prisoners, the social workers helping to maintain their link with the outside, and the support and placement committees, which in 1958 became committees for probation and support of released prisoners, taking charge of them following their release. Little by little, however, they came to overlap: the boundary between correctional educators and social workers became less clear in terms of the tasks they undertook, while some of the probation officers for the new committees were recruited from among the correctional educators.

Probation and re-entry services thus descend from this triple genealogy of special education, social work, and sponsorship, with a division of labor based on a twofold distinction – of gender, with correctional educators tending to be men and social workers women; and of institution, with the public prison service coming to prevail over private bodies working within and around prisons. The short-stay prison I studied retains the mark of these historical strata. Some counselors were formerly correctional educators. "Back then, when I started, our mission focused on the relationship with family, the plan for after, and occupation," remembers one senior manager. "We were at the heart of the prison. I had four inmates working with me as secretaries, and at one time I even had a bedroom in the facility – which was actually a cell!" Other counselors still saw themselves as social workers. As one of them said, seeking to emphasize the unique approach of her profession: "The main difference in our practice is the interview. The data we gather helps us to get a complete picture of the individual in prison, to take into account his personal trajectory and his family background. Sometimes, in an interview, I even forget what it is that has led the person to prison. But most of my colleagues are more factual, relate the case more to the sentence." In effect, with the reform of the services and the reorientation of their mission toward prevention of recidivism, a new professional profile has emerged: the probation and re-entry counselors recruited over the past decade are legally trained, often with a master's degree; some of them have taken the examination to become a judge and plan to do it again. This development, which prompted a national campaign of protest for a time, has aroused some apprehension among the more long-serving counselors. As one of them put it: "We're moving from being social workers to becoming criminologists!"

The staff composition of the probation and re-entry services is now triply differentiated by gender, generation, and education, with the most recent entrants to the profession being younger, of both sexes, and trained as lawyers. In short, three professional cultures are superimposed on one another, each one representative of a different moment in the history of prisons. But as older staff retire and new graduates arrive, the "jurists" are supplanting correctional educators and social workers. Yet these differences should not be overstated. When the probation and re-entry service was set up, one of the key principles was that it should be autonomous. "The warden can't order me to do anything, and I'm not accountable to him," explains one manager in the service, who remembers the time when the team working outside prison for parole and probation was overseen by the sentencing judge, and the team inside prison with inmates was under the authority of the director of the facility. This separation of probation and re-entry from surveillance activities has clarified both the mission and the position of the new service, with two significant consequences. First, it has unified the professional body. "Everyone's doing the same job," asserts the director of the service. "Whether they think of themselves as social workers or probation and re-entry counselors, the tasks are exactly the same." Second, it has generated a renewed sense of allegiance with the correctional institution. "We're campaigning to be considered prison staff," states one counselor who continues to think of herself as a social worker. "There are people who've fought hard to get to have keys. I'm happy to open up cells myself."

In this way, despite the variations in professional profile, probation and re-entry counselors develop relatively consistent practices. Gradually, the strictly social functions are being dropped; for example, counselors do not process applications for universal health insurance, minimum income benefits, or requests to obtain or renew residence permits; at most, they direct inmates toward nongovernmental organizations that can carry out a "pre-investigation" in preparation for a subsequent meeting with the relevant authorities. Now, the major part of counselors' work consists in preparation for sentence adjustment, from the interview with the inmate to determine the best release strategy and contact with re-entry support organizations and potential employers, to the formulation of their opinion regarding day release and the reporting about the case for the hearing with the sentencing judge. But the dominant orientation toward prevention of recidivism has led to new programs: the father–child visit, for the "maintenance of family bonds"; the encounter group for "treatment of sex offenders"; sociocultural activities, in the form of one-off events such as concerts or regular activities such as writing workshops, focused on "stimulating intellectual curiosity" and "rebuilding self-esteem." Thus the legal shift given to training and to the profession itself does not prevent staff from drawing on multiple skills, from psychology to group facilitation, from conflict resolution to writing reports.

Hence of all prison staff, the probation and re-entry counselors are generally those who have the most in-depth knowledge of incarcerated individuals – at least the small minority they take on. While the guards develop an acquaintance based on daily observation of inmates, the counselors construct their knowledge from a number of interviews. The former thus develop a degree of familiarity with prisoners that nevertheless remains superficial, while the latter, who focus on their trajectory and their plans, put together a biographical picture. The relation of authority is also of course more marked with the guards, while a relationship of solicitation prevails with the counselors. The knowledge accrued by the latter in this way, together with the fact that they are personally associated with the probation and re-entry plan, often generates an affective aspect to their work. "We invest in our inmates, even though we're supposed to be emotionally detached," says one of them, who nevertheless admits to feeling more committed to those who "want to do something" than to those who act in an "unbearable or disrespectful" way. Another one states that, at first, as the mother of a young daughter, she feared she "would not manage" with individuals convicted of sex offenses, but that "if they show respect for the victim" and "they're not real perverts," she is able "even to feel empathy" for them.

This apprehension of inmates generally emerges at meetings of the sentence adjustment committee. Speaking before the correctional officer, the representative of the prison management, the assistant public prosecutor, and the sentencing judge, the probation and re-entry counselor is the person who has a comprehensive overview of the case, and hence can present the most coherent account of it, and often also the one who offers the most substantial evidence in support of the day release requested or the additional sentence reduction to be granted. While she is not an advocate for the defense, she tends to adopt a position more favorable to the inmate than the other protagonists, particularly representatives of the prison management and the public prosecutor's office. For example, for day releases, she will emphasize activities and training followed ("he's done computing classes and taken part in workshops in fencing, sculpture, and puppetry"), find words to justify the outing ("it'll allow the family to be together again"), point to an adjustment plan in preparation ("it will give us a chance to see if it's worth applying for probation"), and offer reassuring evidence in support of the request ("he's thought a lot about how he ended up here, and addressed a lot of his issues, especially with his father"). Aware of the committee's expectations, she is thus an effective mediator for the inmate. Overall, the counselors are the ones who express the most favorable opinions. When I spoke of this "generosity" to a manager of the service, he replied: "There are objective reasons for that: they see the individuals, they are in contact with them, so they don't have that colder approach taken by the warden or the prosecutor. They don't just have a file with details of assault and battery, or a repeat offense of rape in front of them. They come face to face with the human side to it." The reasons he raised had actually more to do with intersubjectivity than objectivity, but he was keen to emphasize the rationality of the positions they adopted: "To be a good professional, you have to guard against all emotion. It gives us a degree of distance." Yet it seemed to me that this was a prescription for correct conduct rather than a description of the practices I actually observed.

Indeed, it was clear that the counselors were often committed to defending not only a case but a person. The human dimension mentioned by the manager was embedded in an ethos that led one of them to say that her goal was to "help them to leave in a better state than when they came in." But the intersubjective relationship could work the other way. A man of African descent sentenced to five years' imprisonment for drug offenses is asking for day release for the purpose of "maintenance of family bonds." He has already been in prison for four years; he wants to see his wife and 6-year-old son. At first sight, his case seems unimpeachable. He has secured an auxiliary post that attests to the trust he is held in by management. He has father–child visiting privileges, and has participated in a sports outing to the beach, demonstrating that his paternal attachment is genuine. He has never had any incident report against him. Two previous day releases went well. The only hitch is an application for parole made at a hearing eight months previously, which was rejected. But there is no reason why that refusal should influence the present request.

The counselor, however, casts each element in the case file in a negative light: "the work is not done properly," "his behavior leaves something to be desired," "his sentence adjustment plan was not well prepared." With regard to a new promise of employment obtained by the inmate, she says she "always has doubts about promises magicked out of personal contacts" (indicating that the employer in question is a family member, as is very often the case), and adds that "the police investigation isn't too stunning" (a shorthand alluding to the check always made on the legality and moral standing of the putative employer). She concludes: "Notwithstanding some ... [she hesitates] notwithstanding behavior that is not in line with my expectations, I support the day release." She immediately adds that the funds authorized to accompany the release, to be taken from the inmate's savings, should be reduced from the 80 euros requested to only 50. Taken aback by this damning speech, the judge observes tongue-in-cheek: "Your reading is not very favorable." The exchange that follows sheds light on the origin of the counselor's evident animus against the applicant. She is convinced that he holds her responsible for the rejection of his sentence adjustment plan (and it is likely that she is right, just as it is possible that he is right in holding her responsible for this failure, given the way she has just undermined his application in this session). In a sign of the inmate's mistrust of the counselor, and a final unacceptable challenge to her, the man has presented his promise of employment directly to the sentencing judge. Undistracted by the personal conflict, the warden and the prosecutor nevertheless state that they are in favor of the day release, and ask for the whole of the sum requested to be granted: "He can buy a gift for his son," says the director magnanimously.

* * *

The inmate who thinks that, once he has been through the trial where he receives a prison sentence, he is done with justice, will be set straight as he approaches his release date – at least if he is hoping to have his sentence adjusted or reduced. Unless he is convicted again for an offense committed in prison and occasioning a return to immediate appearance trial, it is normally the sentencing judge whom he will face in preparation for his release. The two key structures involved in this process are the sentence adjustment committee and the parole hearing. The first rules on requests for day release and additional sentence reductions. This is an administrative procedure during which a probation and re-entry counselor and a correctional officer, as well as representatives of the prison management and the public prosecutor's office, state their opinion on each case. The second decides on sentence adjustments and revocations of these adjustments following a breach of their conditions. A proper court in miniature, it brings together the judge, the assistant public prosecutor, the representative of the prison management, and the inmate accompanied by his counsel or, more often, a court-appointed lawyer.

There is of course a precise legal framework defining the rules and modalities for allocation of day releases and sentence reductions, and for validation or revocation of adjustments, laid out in the Code of Penal Procedure. For example, a pre-trial prisoner can only be granted day release in exceptional circumstances. A man who was granted such an exception, who has been in pre-trial detention for nearly three years, describes the ordeal of attending the funeral of his brother who had taken his own life: "I wish I hadn't gone: I was surrounded by four police officers who held me on a red leash and put a security zone around us. My mom could see me from a distance: how shameful, for her and for me!" But the margin of interpretation is usually very broad. "The text gives us plenty of room for maneuver," stressed one sentencing judge.

This freedom of maneuver sometimes gives rise to apparently generous decisions, or conversely to inexplicable restrictions. A man serving three years in prison who is 18 months from the end of his sentence requests day release for the purpose of "preparing for social reintegration." He has to meet with his employer, prior to applying for release under electronic monitoring. As his appointment is for 2:00 p.m., he requests a release from 11:00 a.m. to 5:00 p.m. The request is approved, but the deputy warden only wants to authorize release from 1:00 p.m., which risks causing him to arrive late. The prosecutor therefore proposes keeping to the time requested, noting: "It'll mean he can have lunch with his girlfriend." Another inmate, sentenced to three months' imprisonment, can claim 14 days of additional sentence reduction. Given the short amount of time he has been in the facility, all that is known is that he has requested to work but has not yet been preselected, and has also requested sporting activity but has not been granted this either. The case is examined rapidly. The counselor proposes two days, management one, and the prosecutor two. In the end, the judge grants him a reduction of one day, 13 fewer than the maximum possible. "He's not working," he says, without taking into account that this is not the man's fault, since he has submitted a request on which the assignment committee has to rule. "He does more workout than reading," adds the prosecutor sarcastically.

Depending on the case, then, the decisions seem to turn a right into a favor, and a legal scale into an arbitrary sanction. Over the course of a few seconds, and on the basis of principles that are often difficult to grasp, decisions with major significance for the lives of inmates are made. A man sentenced to three months' imprisonment asks for a 48-hour release to be with his wife when she gives birth – she will be induced just after the New Year's holiday. In view of his minor offense, his short sentence, his good behavior in prison, and the strong justification for the request, this is an apparently simple case. The counselor is in favor. But without giving any specific reason, the deputy warden says: "Better to give him an emergency release once the baby is born." The public prosecutor agrees, commenting: "Whatever you think; anyway, I'm not convinced men are much use at the birth."

Given this broad leeway for decision, where it is difficult to identify indisputable objective criteria, the work of both the sentence adjustment committee and the parole hearing rests in large part on subjective assessments of the inmate's character, in order to determine whether the day release or adjusted sentence is likely to go well, whether the sentence reduction is justified or whether the measure should be revoked, but also in order to establish whether the individual really deserves what he is being granted. "A sentence adjustment has to be earned, sir! You have to make an effort.

It doesn't just fall from the sky," the public prosecutor tells an inmate he finds "nonchalant" at a parole hearing. Engaging in prison work, having completed courses, "never remaining idle," or "being respectful of staff" add value to the application, while, on the contrary, failure to demonstrate "investment," giving the impression of "just getting through the sentence," showing "little respect of the rules," or having had "several incidents" contribute to undermining it. But the moral referents differ depending on the context. On the one hand, for day release requests, merit is judged on the negative basis of an absence of discipline problems in prison, which is considered predictive of good behavior on the outside. But the significance ascribed to an incident may vary and, in the case of one applicant, about whom a member of the committee observes that he has an incident report, the deputy warden saves him by explaining that it actually happened because he interposed himself during an assault on a guard: "His intention was good, he wanted to help." On the other hand, for sentence reductions, merit is evaluated in positive terms, in relation to efforts demonstrated to obtain work, take classes, engage in activity. Inmates deploy appropriately adjusted tactics. One of them, who goes to the library, wants to take part in the chess workshop, has requested training in house painting, and attended courses in prevention of alcohol dependency, obtains the maximum possible 42 days despite the counselor's reservations: "I'm not convinced he's really committed to his treatment program," she comments disapprovingly.

But it is in the parole hearings that the moral dimension emerges at its fullest, both in the assessment of the situation and in the pedagogical instruction of the prisoner. With the inmate present, the sentencing judge and the public prosecutor are not seeking principally to determine whether the adjustment plan is viable, relying for this largely on the opinion of the probation and re-entry counselor, but are, rather, attempting first to get a sense of the improvement in character achieved, and then to give the inmate one final lesson on his criminal past, and toward his future life. Thus, the moral evaluation of the inmate incorporates recognition of responsibility for the offense of which he was convicted, compensation of civil parties at least under way, psychiatric care or addiction clinic attendance (particularly in the case of violent offenses), activities in prison (on a hierarchy that places intellectual activities above sports), and the absence of incident reports, at least over the recent period. Similarly, the moral education of the inmate focuses on the seriousness of the misdeeds committed, the harm suffered by the victims, the need to clean up his act, the last chance represented by the sentence adjustment. "Sir, you were a youth worker and you gave in to pressure to carry cocaine. If someone asks you to do that again, are you going to say yes? – No, I have a family, I have plans. I'm going to move on. I'm going to rebuild my life when I get out. – It's no small thing carrying cocaine. – I know, I truly regret it. If I could go back, I wouldn't do it. – Let's hope so!"

The inmate himself generally understands the role he is required to play and what is expected of him. He must make amends: "I recognize the wrongs I did. I'm the only one responsible. But I've worked on myself for 18 months. I'm trying to make amends to society. I'm asking you to give me a chance." It is also important that they show they have mended their ways in prison, and that this has been beneficial: "In prison, you question yourself. I've been going to school for six months. I've got into the habit of getting up in the morning, I wasn't too good at that before. My body's got used to waking up. I'm going to continue on this path outside. Being in a halfway house will help." They must also state a sort of allegiance to the adjustment plan: "I know I'll need to be monitored. And my family will support me. But electronic monitoring will suit me well. I really want to be monitored." This is a performance that, between morality and psychology, combines rhetoric elements of guilt and redemption with taking responsibility for oneself and submission to the system. Inmates know that this is the price to pay for the possibility of release.

* * *

It is easier to enter prison than to leave. Or, to be more precise, it is easier for the state to take a person into prison than to prepare those it has locked up there for release.[13] While for more than a decade – but one might equally say, for more than a century – the leitmotif of penal policy has been prevention of recidivism, the combined practice of government, parliament, and the courts has consisted in doing the opposite of what scientific research has fairly unequivocally demonstrated and what a simple observation of life journeys renders almost self-evident: more people are being incarcerated for longer, at the risk of becoming detached from family, employment, and society; most of those imprisoned are released "cold," without having benefited from the conditions that would encourage resocialization. Just as the short-stay prison has been unable to provide most of them with the work, training, education, medical care and psychological support that could have both given some meaning to their time in prison and assisted their re-entry, so the correctional institution and the justice system are not in a position to implement a gradual transition from prison to society. But in pointing out this mismatch between declared intention (preventing recidivism) and actual realization (development of a policy that increases the risk of it), I do not mean to ascribe the main responsibility to agents, whether they be the probation and re-entry counselors or the directors and guards in the prison, or the sentencing judges and public prosecutor's representatives outside.

The problem is, in fact, essentially both a shortage of human resources, which forces the probation and re-entry services to limit the number of cases and restrict the category of inmates who can be presented for consideration, and a lack of availability that limits the time judges can dedicate to the sentence adjustment committees in which day release applications are discussed, and the parole hearings in which sentence adjustments are decided. But the lack of resources is not the whole story, and there is no certainty that, even if both these services were less constrained, the majority of releases would not continue to be unsupported. For there are two other factors that cannot be disregarded – one relating to the public officials, the other to inmates.

On the one hand, probation and re-entry counselors, and still more judges, are extremely cautious in their allocation of electronic monitoring, external work, and training placements, and particularly day releases, which take place under minimum surveillance. The rare incidents that receive widespread media attention and are used by politicians making an issue of the infractions committed by individuals on parole have destabilized the prison and court systems. "Everyone's a bit timid in their decisions these days," notes the director of the probation and re-entry service. "In my view, we shouldn't just think in the short term, you have to see the bigger picture. You have to dare to take the wager at the same time as minimizing the risk. We can't just have an obligation of means without a performance obligation." And she adds that, conversely, she does not see how prison can contribute to the prevention of recidivism: "Fights in the exercise yard, pressure and rackets among inmates, every day you're told what time to get up, to shower, to go out: that's not the way to support reintegration." But this view is not translated in the practices of agents, either those working within the prison or among the magistrates. One young sentencing judge explains her doubts: "To oversimplify, I'd say we often have the choice between being too lenient and being too harsh. In the first case, you're not protecting society well. In the second, you're not taking into account how the inmate has changed and the efforts he's made, and you risk discouraging him." Thus a two-stage selection takes place, first through the choice of cases made by the probation and re-entry service, and then in the sentencing judge's decision whether to agree the proposed adjustment. If only one request in five is rejected, this is because the plans are thoroughly prepared by the counselors, but also because they have made a prior selection, only taking on one-sixth of those incarcerated.

On the other hand, not all inmates are well suited to an adjustment plan. Probation and re-entry counselors and sentencing judges know from experience that with some kinds of inmates there is a high risk of the re-entry plan failing and a return to crime. A man in his 50s, his face bearing the marks of alcohol addiction, is brought to a parole hearing for revocation of his suspended sentence with probation. He is charged with two recent infractions, which he denies, but which are added to a criminal record numbering 43 offenses, the sentences for which have already led him to spend a total of 28 years in prison. The judge seems as resigned as the man himself. "Do you realize you're going to spend your life in prison? – I have already spent most of it there. – What work do you do? – I'm unemployed. – What do you live on? – Nothing, I'm just with my family. – And what do they think? – That it's a tragedy, they'd never have wanted their son to turn out like this." The man himself asks for his suspension to be revoked and to return to prison. Admittedly, this is an extreme situation, but it is indicative of the difficulties the probation and re-entry services and the sentencing judges may face when they have to propose or decide on an adjustment.

This is particularly the case with individuals suffering from psychiatric disorders, or with fragile personalities, the paradox being that these are the inmates for whom a release without preparation and without transition needs to be avoided at all costs, and for whom very few, either within the prison management or in the justice system, are ready to take the risk of electronic monitoring, external work, or training placement – or even a day release. It is these individuals who swell the ranks of the 87 percent of inmates who leave the prison "cold." Usually, they are told their release date a few weeks or days in advance. Sometimes, the prison registry calls them in the afternoon to tell them they will be released that evening, to everyone's surprise, first and foremost that of the prisoners themselves. Sometimes, too, the registry summons them to inform them that an old sentence has just been noticed, and that they will have to stay longer.

"What they call re-entry is just bullshit," comments a pre-trial prisoner who is young but already disabused by some experience of prison. "A guy who's served his sentence, where's he gonna go with his kitbag? Is he gonna stay in the bus shelter?" In reality, there is often someone waiting for an inmate on release – a partner, a mother, a brother, a friend. In some cases, however, for non-nationals without legal residence whose situation had not been resolved during their time in prison, it is a police wagon that stands at the door, waiting to take them from the correctional facility to the immigration detention center.

Conclusion

The Meaning of Prison

> But then it crossed his mind to ask: suppose it were all a deception?
> Dino Buzzati, *The Tartar Steppe*, 1945

I began this inquiry in 2009, when Rachida Dati was minister of justice and Nicolas Sarkozy president. When I completed writing it up in 2014, Christiane Taubira was in charge of the ministry and François Hollande head of state. Apart from indicating the long duration of the study, this points to the need to consider the temporality of research relative to its object, particularly when it is so closely bound with contemporary realities.

The law of August 10, 2007 instituted "minimum sentences," a provision that led to more frequent and longer imprisonment. The law of August 15, 2014 abolished these, introducing instead "penal constraint" as an alternative to incarceration for offenses punishable by less than five years' confinement, as well as the requirement for an evaluation two-thirds of the way through the sentence, with a possibility of "release under probation." Put simply, the first measure filled prisons up, and the second reduced numbers entering jails and brought releases forward. More broadly, one prioritized custodial sentences and inflexibility in repression, while the other favored alternatives to incarceration and placed the emphasis on the path to re-entry. In short, a policy of punishment versus a policy of prevention. In these circumstances, the question arises of whether both the changes in penal thinking and the situation of the correctional world, as presented in this study, correspond to a page in the history of penalties and prisons already belonging to the past.[1] Are the observations reported and analyses put forward destined to become obsolete very quickly? Will the anthropology of the carceral condition reconstructed here be subject to continual revision in the light of history?

These are legitimate questions, and the study of contemporary societies must of course take into account their changes. Those of the past inform a genealogy of the contemporary issues; for those to come, the only reasonable prediction is that some will occur. As to those currently under way, the history of the social sciences invites a degree of caution in what can be said about them. In this case, however, contemporary reality does not offer any fundamental challenge to the descriptions and interpretations presented here, for reasons that are both circumstantial and structural.

First, differences should not be exaggerated, nor changes overstated. The 2009 law on prisons, brought in by a right-wing government, reiterates the need to reconcile the functions of sanction, neutralization, and reparation with that of re-entry focused on preventing recidivism, on the one hand, and introduces or promotes a number of new formal rights for inmates, particularly with regard to the inmate's right to present his case at hearings, on the other (although it required a change of government and, more particularly, condemnations in the courts for some articles to be brought into effect, such as the abolition of systematic strip searches). Conversely, the penal law of 2014, adopted under a left-wing government, takes a marked step back from the proposals put forward by the consensus conference on prevention of recidivism that inspired those who drew it up (political negotiations within the majority in power led to multiple compromises, in retreat from expected measures including those aimed at ending the centrality of prison and abolishing indeterminate sentences, and to many concessions, for example on the role of the police and gendarmerie in monitoring offenders on probation). In sum, the changes are real, but the shifts less substantial than has been suggested, and certainly less radical than the two ministers themselves in opposite ways would have liked.

Second, the phenomena I have analyzed, such as the inequalities in the distribution of penalties and the emptiness of time in prison, the limitations on rights imposed by the need for order and the proliferation of sanctions within the carceral world, like the logics that underlie them, relate to structural facts and processes on which modifications to the regulations can have only a limited impact, and at best only after some time. It is worth remembering that, after the circular on penal policy was issued by the minister of justice on September 19, 2012, instructing public prosecutors and magistrates to use prison with moderation and eschew automatic sentencing, the number of people incarcerated rose again in the year that followed. A magical belief in the performativity of political discourse and legislative texts too often leads to governments and parliaments being given exaggerated credit for their capacity to change realities long embedded within institutions, professions, buildings, and moral economies. Institutions are made to protect and perpetuate themselves. Professions are defined and reproduced through schools, routines, professional interests, and union demands. Buildings themselves, and their constituent components, resist through the resilience of their history and the inertia of their materiality. Finally, moral economies of punishment allow the sanction to be justified on the grounds that it is both a deserved penalty for the individual who has committed an offense and a just reparation for the victim.[2] All these elements are combined in the case of prisons.

Without understating the effects of the ministry of justice reforms, I hazard the thought that the inmates and staff in the prison I studied will not see their carceral condition change as a result of the new penal law as much as its defenders hope and its detractors fear.[3] Not only does the relative timidity of the legislation as it was finally adopted testify to manifest resistance, among both the conservative opposition and the socialist majority, which does not augur well for future consolidation of these limited gains, but even if these are maintained in the long term, their consequences for the practices of the police and judges are likely to be as modest as those that ensued from the 2009 law on prisons, as analyzed in a parliamentary report three years after it came into force. In both cases, political calculations and structural forces combine to reduce the impact of the new measures.

For the place and form of prison, a little over two centuries since their inception, are so profoundly anchored in the imagination of contemporary societies as to be effectively naturalized. As incarceration has become central to the penal system, and its coercive rather than disciplinary form has been imposed throughout the correctional world, it has become increasingly difficult to think of punishment apart from prison, and of prison apart from its punitive significance. Of course, the fact that the carceral paradigm, in its contemporary form, seems the obvious solution to both police and judges – those in government and ordinary citizens – does not preclude seeking alternatives to imprisonment and adjustments to sentences; nor does it prevent some material and juridical improvements in incarceration. However, even if the courts issue many other sanctions, privation of freedom is both the reference and the ultimate penalty, and even if reasons of deterrence or prevention are advanced to justify it (in contradiction to research), its true raison d'être remains retribution.

In his short story "Quiz at the prison," Dino Buzzati tells of a curious imaginary procedure at "a large penitentiary at the city limits." Once during his sentence, each prisoner is taken from his cell and led to the balcony of the facility, from where he is allowed a few minutes to address the crowd gathered below. If they applaud him, he is released; if they boo him, he serves out the whole of his sentence. The narrator explains that he has never known anyone to be released. One day his turn comes: the crowd, mockingly, exhorts him to speak of the injustice of his conviction, the suffering of his elderly mother, the harsh privations of detention. At first remaining silent, in the end he replies: "I have no intention at all of moving you. I am not innocent. I have no desire at all to see my family again. I have no desire at all to leave the prison. My life here is happy." Taken aback, the crowd hesitates, and then, as the narrator calls on them to boo, protests burst forth: "No! It would be too convenient for you!" Then comes the applause. The man is therefore freed.[4] Indeed, for society, prison must remain a punishment.

*　*　*

During a public debate in the spring of 2014, the director of the National Prison Administration, commenting on a paper I had just presented, complained that, like so many others, my research focused on a minority within her institution, given that prisoners accounted for only a little over a quarter of the people under sentence for whom her services were responsible; the other three-quarters mainly consisted of convicted offenders subject to supervision in the outside world. She saw this focus on prison as an ambiguous "fascination." This interesting remark is a useful reminder that the prison sentence is knitted into a fabric of penal provisions that grows ever broader and more densely woven. Over 30 years, from 1982 to 2012, the number of people under sentence rose much more quickly than the number of prisoners, tripling at a time when the number of people incarcerated "only" doubled.[5] Within this population, there are four times as many individuals being supervised outside prison for suspended sentences with probation, or doing community service under judicial supervision, or on conditional release as there were 30 years earlier, while the numbers of those serving out adjusted sentences in the form of electronic monitoring, external work placement, or parole have increased from a few dozen to more than 10,000 since 2005.

Prison, then, is only one part of the correctional sphere – and is neither the most important nor the most extensive. But it is the heart of it: not only because it represents the hard kernel in terms of severity of penalty, but also because it is an ever-looming presence behind the many structures of surveillance and monitoring outside detention, where failure to respect their rules exposes the offender to the permanent threat of incarceration. In other words, far from countering the centrality of prison, the words of the director of the National Prison Administration confirm it, at the same time as situating the carceral world within a broader correctional network where incarceration always remains on the horizon. The punitive state must therefore be understood to extend within and around prison, through both the carceral and the correctional. The various modes of electronic monitoring, at the beginning or end of the sentence, as part of a negotiated adjustment or an automatically applied measure, are simply tentacles that prison extends into society. If a person under sentence contravenes the protocol by leaving his authorized area or breaching his prescribed timetable, actual imprisonment may be imposed. To paraphrase a famous aphorism, in its contemporary configuration, the correctional world is the continuation of the carceral world by other means.

The way the statistics are analyzed is of crucial significance here. An optimistic version of recent developments asserts that the number of people incarcerated as a proportion of the total of those under sentence fell from 40 to 30 percent in three decades, suggesting that less recourse is being made to prison and alternative punishments are increasingly employed. Conversely, a realistic reading, focused on absolute rather than relative values, reveals that the number of people under sentence increased from 75,000 to 250,000 in 30 years, while the number of prisoners rose from 31,000 to 65,000. Without doubt, France is locking people up more, and for longer, than ever in its history. But the threat of incarceration is also being held over an even larger number of people. The carceral condition therefore needs to be understood in the light of a punitive society for which incarceration has, for two centuries, seemed the most appropriate method of managing certain groups that represent a problem for it; it extends the field of application both directly, by locking more people up, and indirectly, by developing liminal forms of the prison.

This is not a new argument, and studies of prison have apprehended its multifaceted reality for 50 years. However different they are in approach, one being sociological and the other genealogical, the two central texts on prison, Erving Goffman's *Asylums* and Michel Foucault's *Discipline and Punish*, have in common that they consider it within a broader context. Confinement bears not only upon criminals, but also on other categories of the population, first and foremost the mentally ill, who for Goffman are the principal object of his research, and for Foucault, the subject of his preceding book on the history of madness.[6] In Goffman's analysis, the concept of the total institution, which groups prisons and asylums together with leper colonies, boarding schools, and monasteries, serves to define the modalities of communal life when individuals are locked up under the authority of other individuals in an enclosed, strictly regulated space. The fact that these individuals and places are respectively designated "inmates" and "asylums" says much about the at once singular and universal significance assigned to the correctional and mental health facilities in this model. In Foucault's work, the relationship between knowledge and power, whether of philosophers or revolutionaries, criminologists or psychiatrists, determines the modern rationales behind the techniques of incarceration particular to each type of problem. Instead of interning all categories together, including the poor and vagrants, as was the case under the ancien régime, the new theories form the basis for constructing prisons for criminals and asylums for the mentally ill.

In his classic study *The Discovery of Asylum*, which appeared in the interval between the publication of Goffman's and Foucault's books, David Rothman provides a key to a historical reading of them, by reconstituting the conditions under which, in the early nineteenth century, a cluster of institutions designed to separately confine those deemed a threat to the moral order and the social order – criminals, juvenile delinquents, the mentally ill, the poor, orphans – emerged almost simultaneously. Focusing on the penitentiary experiment in the United States, in Auburn and Philadelphia, which is known to have been an influential model for France,[7] Rothman shows how a generalized practice of incarceration develops, and he identifies a number of common characteristics: a similar organization regardless of whether the mission is punitive, caring, or charitable; a radical separation from the outside world; a valuing of isolation and work; a population recruited among the lower sectors of society; and a disparity between the stated aims and the actual reality.

How did the carceral paradigm, applied to a whole range of deviances, come to be so quickly imposed and so widely disseminated? Historians' answers to this question vary, depending on whether they accord greater importance to the moral crisis or to the social crisis of the world at the time, to the fear of weakening of values revealed by crime, madness, and indigence, or to the fear instilled by the rise of dangerous classes. It is, moreover, possible that there were differences from country to country, and that the moral dimension prevailed in the emerging United States, while the social dimension was more marked in Europe at a time of revolution.

But one feature went unnoticed in these historical, sociological, and philosophical studies of incarceration. While the prison, the asylum, and a number of other institutions of confinement emerged at the same time, there was a marked divergence in their subsequent development. To take only the prison and the asylum, for which we have a long series of statistics dating, in the French case, back to the 1850s, the following facts can be observed.[8] While the rate of incarceration fell progressively for almost a century, the proportion of the population hospitalized in psychiatric facilities saw a contrary development over the same period. In 1940, in France, the proportion of the population in prison was half what it was in 1850, but the proportion of the population in asylums was five times higher. After the long, tragic parenthesis of World War II, which transfigured the demographics of both prisons (through the mass imprisonment of former collaborators) and asylums (owing to the extremely high mortality of the mentally ill, who were virtually abandoned during the war), the graphs are inverted. From the mid-1950s, the rate of incarceration increased markedly, while the proportion of the population confined in psychiatric hospitals fell still more spectacularly from the early 1960s. Relative to the population as a whole, the proportion of prisoners doubled in 50 years, while the proportion of mentally ill patients confined in asylums fell by two-thirds. This observation holds in most Western countries.[9] Although no such continuous statistics are available for the internment of the poor and orphans, it is likely that the demography of the corresponding institutions followed a similar trend as that described for asylums.

So while incarceration has for two centuries been the generalized mode of governing groups that are deviant on the legal, medical, and social levels, statistics reveal two great historical periods. From the mid-nineteenth to the mid-twentieth centuries, prison saw a decline, while the asylum flourished. The first of these developments has multiple origins, notably the introduction of suspended sentences and conditional release, and, to a lesser extent, exile and deportation to penal colonies; the second derives from the increasing exclusion of the mentally ill, for whom psychiatric facilities are places of abuse rather than treatment. By contrast, in the period since then, for a little over half a century the prison population has grown while the asylum population has decreased, in both cases strikingly. The rise in the prison population is due to the increased severity of the law and the courts and, more broadly, the repressive attitude of society toward even minor infractions; the fall in the asylum population originates in advances in therapy following the discovery of psychotropic drugs and changes in the conception of care for the mentally ill, linked to the campaign for deinstitutionalization. In addition, an interflow between the two groups began to occur, with a proportion of those suffering from mental illness, particularly psychotic or antisocial personality disorders, finding themselves in prison following a misdemeanor or felony often related to their condition, for which judges became increasingly reluctant to accept the argument that they did not bear criminal responsibility.

In the long history of incarceration, the contemporary period thus marks a major shift, characterized by an unprecedented decline in the various institutions of confinement, with one exception – prison.[10] The carceral paradigm, which for a time penetrated into the worlds of mental health, social assistance, and abandoned children, has retreated to a single function: punishment. Virtually the only reason people are locked up now is for retributive purpose. Henceforth, privation of freedom is only deemed legitimate for criminals and, above all, petty offenders: it should be remembered that felonies represent only 2 percent of prison sentences. Almost all people incarcerated are imprisoned for a misdemeanor, many of which have only recently become subject to correctional treatment or repression, indicating that a few decades ago these people would not have been imprisoned for these offenses, which were punishable by simple fines, or were even not subject to any sanction.[11] In other words, while punishment is now the only legitimate use of confinement, its field of application has expanded considerably.

There is a certain irony in the fact that the two key texts on confinement were written at the historical tipping point of the two great institutions on which their authors focused. Goffman published his study of the social condition of the mentally ill, which would be read by many as a radical critique of psychiatric hospitals, at a time when the asylum as a form had already entered into a sort of twilight. Foucault published his study of the birth of the prison, which culminates in the advent of disciplinary techniques and surveillance systems beyond the carceral world, just as ideas on the reform of individuals were going into reverse, with a return to the centrality of incarceration and an unprecedented growth in the prison population. However, this is not to say that they would have conceived their accounts very differently if they had written them today. Even the criticisms that can be made of them, or the disagreements that may be expressed with their views, are fundamentally linked not to their temporal relevance but, rather, to their theoretical and methodological premises. Goffman's approach consists in abstracting the missions taken on by the various institutions he studies (punishment, care, education, discipline) to focus on the general form of relations that flows from their common features. Foucault's interpretation rests on an analysis of discourses (of philanthropists, politicians, legal theorists, ordinary citizens) rather than the realities of life in prison. In both cases, these decisions proved particularly heuristic.

However, in my consideration of the carceral condition, I have proposed an inflexion of their perspective in two ways, in order to take into account both the content of relations (not just their form), and the everyday matter of practices (not principally the discourses developed about them). The issue is both epistemological and political. On the one hand, my aim is to historicize and differentiate. Even if prison retains a certain form of organization, both spatial and functional, from one country to another or one era to another, and even if similar intentions and criticisms are repeated over time and in different contexts – in other words, even if the form and the discourses remain relatively consistent – facilities change and differ from one another, and with them the sense of the experience of the carceral condition. The extreme isolation of inmates does not mean the same thing, and is probably not lived in the same way, in the Colorado maximum security facility that opened two decades ago and the Philadelphia penitentiary two centuries earlier. On the other hand, my point is to recognize that not everything is equivalent, which would come down to saying that nothing makes any difference. Within the same formal structures, and with reference to the same sets of discourses, conceptions of punishment, practices of local justice, and the attitudes of staff toward inmates can substantively alter the realities of prison, demonstrating how important both national and local policies are. The apparently identical process of admission to prison as observed half a century ago in Britain and today in France reveals, behind the series of similar stages, a very different meaning and experience. Both the researcher and the layperson need to be attentive to these differences, for democracy consists precisely in this capacity for discernment.

But this is not as easy as might be imagined. As far as respect for the rights of inmates or treatment by prison staff are concerned, it is probably better to be confined in a French prison as it is today than in a French prison of the mid-twentieth century or a US prison of the early twenty-first century. And yet, in contemporary correctional facilities in France there are proportionally five times more suicides than there were 50 years ago, and 12 times more than in similar institutions in the United States.[12] This spatial and temporal contrast, which troublingly articulates a dissociation between the objective and subjective aspects of imprisonment, invites further exploration of the world of prison and its contradictions.

* * *

How, then, are we to think of the contemporary carceral condition? It is a condition at once moral and social; this is nothing new, but my point is precisely to grasp its specific configuration at the present time.

From a moral perspective, the carceral condition is characterized by the central importance accorded to punishment in the implicit or explicit justification of prison. The retributive aspect has of course always been an integral part of what is known, significantly, as the penalty of imprisonment, but at various points this has been relegated to the background when redemption (in religious terms) or rehabilitation (in secular parlance) became the foremost concerns, or when prevention of recidivism prevailed. In this respect, the public discourses of politicians, on both the right and the left, when they call for tougher sentencing and stricter execution of sentences, are much more instructive than the carefully worded formulas of the preambles to legislation, which talk of protecting society and prisoner re-entry. The reason that we imprison so many, for so long, is first and foremost because we think that prison is a proper and just punishment. "The criminal gets what he deserves," is how we might sum up the moral philosophy of the carceral condition. The same logic prevails in society and within prisons: everything that is done for these men judged or presumed guilty is always too good for them. Public protests against the introduction of television into cells 30 years ago are echoed today in the remarks of a guard who sees prison as a holiday camp or a director who believes that the cells are more comfortable than an average hotel room. Even if not shared by everyone, this thinking pervades the prison system and the judicial extensions of it in the form of parole. It is this that explains both why the privation of freedom is supplemented by a multitude of other privations, even when it would be relatively easy to eliminate them without risk to order or security, and also why offenses committed within the prison walls are now subject not to a single penalty, as would be the case outside, but by a series of sanctions affecting all aspects of the inmate's life. Furthermore, this punitive principle is so embedded in the prison world that even when a disciplinary board is convinced of the innocence of an inmate accused by a guard or of the existence of extenuating circumstances relating to the officer's known prior history, a sanction is still considered the appropriate response, at least in the form of a suspended penalty, in order not to alienate the staff.

From a social perspective, the carceral condition is characterized by the fact that inmates are recruited predominantly from the lower sectors of French society. There is nothing especially new in this either, if we reflect that, ever since prisons came into existence, it has been working-class groups who populated them. But the composition of this lower sector has changed. In the nineteenth century, it was made up of workers and foreigners, particularly Italians; in the twenty-first century, it consists principally of young men of working-class background but often unemployed, of African descent but generally French nationality, living in urban areas designated "sensitive." This points to the colonial inheritance and the racial dimension as new features of carceral demographics that imbricate with older ones, such as economic precarity and spatial segregation or male gender and youth. This social differentiation of prison reflects the thinking behind penal policies that focus repression on low-income neighborhoods. On the one hand, petty crime, such as theft and receiving stolen goods, has become the focus of much greater attention and severity on the part of lawmakers, the police, and the courts than offenses committed primarily in better-off circles, such as financial fraud and tax evasion; on the other, for the same offense – for example, possession of drugs or driving without a license – the police focus much more on minorities than on the majority and on the projects than on well-off neighborhoods of detached housing, while the court procedure for real-time processing penalizes disadvantaged groups compared to the middle and upper classes. But penal policy is not the only issue, since, prior to this, it is the ensemble of economic, residential, and ethnoracial disparities that explains the chaotic life journeys, curtailed education, chronic underemployment, and family instability known to increase the risk of a criminal career.

Analysis of the carceral condition thus makes it possible to answer a question that frequently recurs in the reflections of historians, sociologists, and philosophers engaged in the study of prison: how can an institution so often criticized for its dysfunctional nature, its high cost-benefit ratio, its ineffectiveness in combating crime, and its failure to live up to democratic values not only maintain itself and develop over more than two centuries, but also appear to the majority as the only possible solution? The answer to this question lies in the conjunction of the moral and social dimensions of the carceral condition. Prison offers a morally acceptable solution (because it deals with those who are guilty, or presumed to be so, who must therefore be punished) for the exclusion, during a shorter or longer period, of individuals who are socially undesirable (less because they are thought to have deviant habits, which are tolerated in other social categories, than because they are rejected for what they are and what they represent). My point is not to deny the reality of criminal practices and the legitimacy of sanctioning them, but the focus on minor offenses and marginalized population groups indicates clearly that repression is not aimed toward equitable punishment of the offenses most damaging to society.

Hence, the function of prison is not simply to sanction crimes, but to convey a repressive response to the social question, basing it on a moral line of argument. The recent rapid expansion of the prison population, at a time when not only are inequalities and precarity worsening, but discrimination against and stigmatization of people of immigrant origin have become an accepted part of public discourse, is no mere coincidence. The increase in the number of prisoners derives principally from the sectors most affected by inequalities and precarity, discrimination and stigmatization. In France, as in most other Western countries, the punitive state is a way of governing inequality. But the removal of those concerned from society is aimed less at neutralizing a dangerous class by physically excluding it for long periods, as in the United States (in France the average stay in prison, even if it has increased substantially over recent years, is a little under a year) than at inculcating in those who constitute it the idea of their place in society; it is a recall to the social order rather than to the moral order.

The deteriorating material condition of prisons forms part of this work on minds and bodies. The overcrowding of facilities with miserly budgets and insufficient staff; the inability of services to guarantee the minimum of well-being in terms of healthcare and privacy; the chronic shortage of work, training, and education that results in a sense of emptiness; the impossibility of making provision for adjustment and re-entry for three-quarters of inmates owing to a lack of human resources; the ever-present threat of sanctions for breaching the rules or protesting an injustice: all these elements contribute to inmates' apprenticeship in their place in society, including the pointlessness and demeaning nature of the daily tasks accomplished, which give them a sense of the low esteem in which they are held. The price of this learning process is marginalization for the inmate himself and, in terms of his family, owing to loss of income and the subsequent difficulty of finding a job, a weakening of conjugal relationships and deleterious effects on the development of children. The way in which society treats not only prisoners but also prisons has consequences for the facilities themselves and for those who work in them, who often suffer from an undeservedly poor reputation as a result of a moral contamination from both their institution and those it houses. Thus the carceral condition includes – to varying degrees and in different forms – all those who "are" in prison.

In proposing that we consider these prison worlds in terms of a carceral condition, my point is to understand the meaning and the experience of an institution that, above and beyond changes of ministers and shifts in policy, has for more than 200 years maintained its durability, its growth, and particularly its self-evident existence at the heart of the punishment system. It is not that we should not mark certain recent tendencies, in particular the substantial decrease in the prison population in Germany and the Netherlands since the early 2000s, compared to France which saw one of the highest increases in Europe.[13] And it is not that we should fail to take into account the substantial material improvements made in recently constructed facilities, which serve as store windows for a prison estate that is still largely dilapidated, and which make it possible to try out modes of accommodation that are less damaging to human dignity, as well as more efficient methods of surveillance.[14] But while it is important to analyze in detail the multiple and sometimes contradictory implications of these variations, they make little difference to the moral and social characterization of the contemporary carceral condition that I have presented here.

There is in prison something that resists transformations of form and developments of discourse, a sort of hard kernel that is barely touched by new legislation and new buildings, as the persistently high suicide rates indicate. This ineradicable component of prison is formed, despite the efforts of some of those who work there, from the vacuity of time in prison, a time that "serves no purpose," as inmates repeatedly say, and which instills in them, by throwing it into heightened relief, the feeling of their own worthlessness. The ultimate truth of the carceral condition, if there is one, thus resides in the fact that prison is a place empty of meaning, and that those who are locked up there gradually and indefinitely experience this void. The pain of the penalty is in this apprenticeship.

* * *

One final remark on the two founding texts of contemporary thinking about incarceration. There is a tension between the central theses of Erving Goffman and Michel Foucault. The former, in identifying and describing "total institutions," constructs prisons as places outside society, obeying rules that are specific to them.[15] The latter, by contrast, analyzing the "carceral archipelago," sees it as a device for surveillance and punishment that embraces the whole of society.[16] What I believe my study shows is that this tension can be resolved by taking the opposite position to each of these assertions. First, the correctional institution is less total than it appears.[17] One could almost say that everything gets in: the law, private enterprise, television programs, cellphones, but also lawyers, visitors, journalists, and even social scientists. Both advances in technology and a certain democratic culture make prison permeable to everything that goes on in the outside world. Second, the carceral world does not, for all that, dissolve into the social space.[18] Granted, the desire to discipline and punish takes many forms: camera systems in public and private places and data mining of telecommunication companies, electronic monitoring of prisoners and community service work. But the intellectual seductiveness of this panoptical, multicentric model comes up against the stubbornly inert, insurmountable singularity of cells and prisons, with their high walls and barbed wire, their isolation and overcrowding, their chains of privations and sanctions. Thus the carceral condition needs to be considered dialectically, both as it is traversed by the reality outside, and as it remains an irreducible fact.

To think about the carceral condition therefore also means thinking about society, which continually reinvents incarceration without altering its refractory core. The manner in which prison is designed and organized, filled and emptied, how those housed or employed there are considered and treated, the way extensions or alternatives to it are imagined – all these material and symbolic, legal and correctional elements represent so many pointers that can be used to read the contemporary world. The carceral condition is not this world's shadow[19] because of those who are locked up in prisons, as common sense and political discourse would have it, but because of the social inequalities it contributes to reproducing and the everyday injustices it helps to legitimize.

Epilogue

Ethnography Regained

> ... that way out of oneself, that connecting road which, though private,
> opens onto the highway along which passes what we learn to know
> only from the day when it has made us suffer: the life of other people.
>
> Marcel Proust, *The Captive*, 1923

"To understand something, you have to live it," an elderly inmate told me one day – guards had told me of his vast knowledge of the carceral environment, acquired over the course of two long sentences. Speaking with benevolent certainty, he sought to alert me to the pointlessness of my enterprise: "You can't do an objective study of prison. You're going to write on the basis of what we say. But to be able to analyze something, you have to experience it." A striking paradox, in which he seemed to be asserting that subjectivity was the necessary condition for objectivity.

Despite the apparent contradiction in terms, there is a profound truth in this observation, and the long hours spent, over four years, within the prison do not enable me either to completely grasp or to faithfully reproduce what is lived by inmates or, albeit in a different way, by staff. Moreover, despite their daily cohabitation, the officers are evidently no better placed to grasp the experience of prisoners, of whom they like to say, as if remaining blind to the carceral condition: "All they are missing is freedom."

But does the impossibility of "understanding" what one does not "live" and of "analyzing" what one does not "experience" mean that the effort to give an account of what plays out in the world of prison is doomed to fail (and beyond the singularity of this particular environment, would the question not evidently hold whatever the place, group, and subject studied)? Ethnography is an attempt to respond to this question.[1] It is an exploration of this "life of other people" that Proust refers to – a "way out of oneself," a displacement of one's own field of vision that enables one to embrace the perspective of people other than oneself.

However, unlike the novelist who puts himself inside the skin of his characters, thinks and decides for them, brings them into existence like a demiurge, the anthropologist maintains a careful distance from the protagonists of the world he studies.[2] He listens to them and watches them, strives to understand their actions and to contextualize them in a network of meanings, but without holding any illusion that he can ever enter into their thoughts or explain their decisions – at least, never entirely, never for certain.[3] To the omniscience and ubiquity of the writer, who knows everything about his subjects and moves with detachment from one to the other, the ethnographer counterposes the modest observation that human beings are not transparent to him.

This is not just the epistemological cautiousness of one who is well aware that his description could have been different and that his interpretation will always be subject to contestation. It is also the ethical conviction that individuals retain a portion of privacy, ambivalence, obscurity – in a word, of subjectivity – that remains inaccessible to analysis.[4] No ethnography can ever give a sufficiently accurate description of the anguish of incarceration and the torments of a first night in prison, the slow attrition of long sentences and the harrowing pain of solitary confinement. No ethnography will ever establish with definitive certainty the reasons for an inmate's act of violence, a guard's helpful gesture, or the judgment pronounced by a disciplinary board. The anthropologist must restrict himself to an account of the facts, what he has seen and heard, what he has understood, and what he can offer to render the meaning of that which he has witnessed.

But the observer is also a participant. He is so simply by virtue of being where he is, however discreet he tries to be: "We didn't even notice you were there; I don't know how you do it, but you really know how to make people forget you," I was told several times by directors or officers after a delicate situation had arisen, where outside scrutiny was not necessarily appropriate. The observer is also a participant through his interactions with the various actors in the carceral world, well beyond what he imagines: "I'll tell you honestly, I'm not sure if I should talk to you, I'm worried it might harm my case," said one inmate with whom I had had several conversations. Thus the anthropologist is at once an alien and a familiar presence, furtive and bothersome, reassuring or dangerous, a presence that intrigues (inmates asked if I was the new director) or arouses expectations (guards said they could not wait to read my book).

As a general rule, I tried to interfere as little as possible with the activities of the prison, while at the same time becoming assimilated into them. I kept in the background during arrival interviews and disciplinary board meetings, I stayed close to the monitoring post or near the entrance to the visiting rooms, I followed the morning rounds when cells were opened for showers and the journey of the meal trolley when lunch or dinner was served, I accompanied trips to the exercise yard during the day and cell inspection rounds at night, I sat with the inmates at cultural events and alongside the representatives of the prison management at parole hearings. My verbal exchanges with the guards consisted of brief conversations as they carried out their tasks, interspersed by requests from inmates. By contrast, interviews with directors, counselors, judges, ministers of religion, and members of support organizations almost always took place in the offices outside the prison proper, allowing for more substantial discussions, to which all lent themselves with great good will.

During the first two years of my research I principally developed relationships with the various categories of staff, but did not manage to engage in any real contact with inmates. The few interviews I had at the beginning, in the inmate interview rooms in each block, were too formal, and placed me too much on the side of authority, for me to be able to draw reliable conclusions – and this leads me to question the limits of validity of the many studies conducted, in Britain and the United States especially, on the basis of questionnaires distributed to hundreds of prisoners. Over the last two years of my study, I spent much more time with inmates, often at their invitation, sometimes at the suggestion of a guard. The conditions in which these conversations took place were very different, generally with a man alone in his cell, occasionally in a group in the larger and more welcoming cell of an auxiliary – and these situations became so routine that sometimes a guard would inadvertently lock me in with my interviewee.

I attribute this development of the research to a gradual reciprocal building of trust: on the one hand, the staff, accustomed to my presence as I had been there longer than quite a number of them, left me freer to move around, while the inmates began to see my work as a rare opportunity to be heard; on the other, I myself felt more at ease in the facility and with its various actors, giving me more scope to act on my own initiative. The length of the study, in terms not only of days spent in the field but still more of the stretch of time between its beginning and its end, is in fact an essential component of ethnographic work, distinguishing it from other forms of investigation such as journalism.

*   *   *

As a participant observer, should the anthropologist then take sides? The question may seem surprising. Yet it has lain at the heart of debates in the social sciences for at least 50 years. "Whose side are we on?" asked Howard Becker, in a text that is often taken up and discussed, in which he was responding to the reproach often addressed to social scientists that they take sides with the subordinate, the dominated, and the deviant.[5] According to Becker, in view of the hierarchy of credibility that, in the social world, always means that the version of authority, the dominant, and moral entrepreneurs prevails, proposing an alternative version, generally delegitimized, is effectively to re-establish a balance of truth. In relation to prison, the question would then be to decide whether one chooses to side with the staff or with the inmates.

But is this really the best way of posing the problem?[6] In reality, the question "Whose side are we on?" can be understood in two different ways. On the methodological level, it is a matter of knowing whether one is focusing research on staff or on inmates. On the political level, the issue is to decide whether one is championing the cause of the former or the latter. Most sociological studies, proceeding by interviews or questionnaires, focus on one group or another.[7] The choices their authors make are thus based on methodological rather than political grounds. But ethnography proceeds otherwise. It aims to grasp the facts observed in their entirety, to understand the rationales of all protagonists, to give an account of the diversity of their points of view. It is not that anthropologists can imagine they have a panoptical gift that allows them to comprehend the institution in its totality, but they do not decide before they start what should be watched and what should be listened to.[8] They deal in scenes and moments, conversations in the course of events rather than structured interviews, dialogues they hear instead of questionnaires they distribute, details and singularities to which they pay as much attention as to structures and regular patterns, actions and decisions in which they seek to reconstitute the processes, the determinants, the stakes, and the possible meanings.

Can we then say that the ethnographer is objective? Certainly not in the common understanding of the term, according to which the description of the facts should be independent of the describer – but he can in the sense in which Nietzsche understands the concept.[9] For Nietzsche, contrary to the Kantian idea of pure reason, all knowledge is the product of a perspective that is bound to both a historical context and a social position. The perspectives of the inmate and the guard, the judge and the director are historically and socially situated, and, depending on their biography and their environment, the perspectives of a middle-class white inmate and a working-class inmate of African descent, of a director who has climbed the career ladder from the post of correctional officer and one who came into the job direct from university can of course be very different. None can claim to hold the truth of prison.

But ethnographers treat all of them with equal importance. They gather them, compare them, note their similarities and their differences, but also identify the context and the position from which they are put forward. "The more eyes, different eyes, we can use to observe one thing, the more complete our 'concept' of this thing, our 'objectivity' will be." This Nietzschean understanding of objectivity, as being in some sense the conjunction of multiple subjectivities, offers a response to the observation of the older inmate who told me that one had to live something to understand it, and that without experiencing it, I could not give an objective account of it.[10] Hence objectivation – without ever being able to claim absolute objectivity – consists not only in gathering subjective perspectives, but also in situating them. For while it is important to take all of them into account, they do not all carry the same meaning.

Consequently, ethnography must be supplemented by a historical gaze and a sociological approach. This is what I have attempted to do in this book, setting the various visions of a given reality – concerning the production of violence, the recognition of rights, the logic of order, the conception of security, the use of sanction, the preparation for release – both in the contemporary context of the relationship to punishment and inequality, and in relation to the positions occupied by all those involved in the social space. In this way we can go beyond particularism, which would restrict reflection to the world of prison (we need to understand how decision-makers, lawmakers, the police, judges, journalists, and society as a whole make this world what it is at any given time) and relativism, according to which all points of view are equally valid (yet inmates, guards, counselors, directors, judges, and outside contractors speak for different interests and ethos). It is in this sense, I think, that we can speak of a critical ethnography.

*   *   *

But there is an aspect of ethnographic work that is rarely evoked, owing to the fear that mention of it would risk undermining its always threatened epistemology: this is the affective dimension. In fact, the Proust of *The Captive* and the Nietzsche of *The Genealogy of Morals* are unexpectedly at one on this point: we can only know "the life of other people" to the extent that "it has made us suffer," asserts Proust; there is no "pure, will-less, painless, timeless knowing subject," so seeking "to suspend each and every affect, supposing we were capable of this" would amount to "castrate the intellect," argues Nietzsche. What is true of literary and philosophical knowledge also holds for scientific knowledge.[11] But it is probably in scientific knowledge that the legitimacy of the affective dimension is most strongly challenged.

However, in the case of the social sciences in general and anthropology in particular, ethnography is not just a method; it is also an experience. A human experience of the encounter with others, of recognizing how they differ from one another and from oneself, and still more how they participate in a common world: "The work of anthropology is not to promote alterity but to reduce it," writes Jean Bazin.[12] But if this is an intellectual experience, it is also an affective one. There is no ethnography without a certain relation of sympathy with those among whom one is conducting it; this sympathy in itself is a way in which we know one another.[13] In this respect, much more than in many other fields of research, the anthropologist working in prisons is affected by what he sees and what he hears, by the suffering and the violence he witnesses, by the individuals who confide in him and the fragments of life they offer him. To take up the neologism proposed by Jacques Derrida, we could say that all ethnography of the carceral world is a hauntology.[14] At the end of their days and nights spent in the field, and long after the end of their study, researchers remain profoundly marked by the scenes they have witnessed in a walkway, during a visit, or at a parole hearing, and by the stories of these men who have shared moments of their lives, confidences about their condition, sometimes simply silences and smiles. This book would not be what it is without this experience.

When, during my investigation, a guard or an inmate asked me what the purpose of my research was – a question both challenging and legitimate, as every social scientist knows – I replied that I was striving to "humanize" prison (I can picture the incredulous raised eyebrows of those reading such an admission, and I am as aware as they are of how clichéd this formula sounds in the context of current public discourse about the "humanization of prisons"). But I explained to my informants (who seemed to understand) that I was using this term not in a moral sense (rendering the carceral world more humane) but more modestly, as an empirical proposition (showing that it is made up of human beings). This may seem a trivial idea, but it is perhaps less anodyne in light of the social science literature of recent decades and even more of the state of the public debate about punishment.

The "curious eclipse of ethnography of prisons at a time of mass incarceration" finds its echo in the observation that "criminologists tend to present their analysis of prison in the form of inhuman data."[15] The importance of rehabilitating the "human" reality of prison, which has been at the heart of a series of recent studies in France, is not just a scientific issue, it is also a political one. Showing a man standing in front of the only window in the prison that is not covered with a dense rubberized grid, dreaming of the day when he will be able to go and pick up his little girl from school, or a lieutenant taking time before she goes home to offer a few words of comfort to an old inmate when she hears he has just lost his niece; describing the suffering of a man banging his head against the wall of his solitary confinement cell, or the embarrassment of a director who feels obliged to sanction an inmate to avoid angering guards, is to reveal the contradictory realities of prison, and perhaps alter the representation society has both of those who are locked up there and those who work there.

* * *

Without doubt, what one is reading as one engages in a writing project offers a pointer to what one is attempting in one's own undertaking. When I began this book, I was reading neither Foucault nor Goffman – my book was Dostoevsky's *Memoirs from the House of the Dead*.[16] Not that a nineteenth-century Russian labor camp and a twenty-first-century French prison have much in common. The short-stay facility I studied was a place of the living. And it was precisely the *life* of the institution, with its order and rigor, its habits and eruptions, and the indissolubly linked *lives* of those who cohabit there, one group constantly busy while the other slowly languishes, that formed the matter of my investigation. This is also the case with Dostoevsky's memoir, and his detachment and reflexivity, descriptive power and analytical lucidity, withholding of judgment and concern for truth were, for me, a source of inspiration. But above all, in this unique and singular work by a novelist, there was a resolute determination to understand and to lead others to understand the nature of the carceral world. The point was not only to tell the prisoners' stories, even though some of them would return in the form of characters in subsequent novels, but to recreate a world so that his readers, discovering it, could decide whether it corresponded to the kind of punishment by which they wished to sanction those who transgressed the law. Contemplating the place where he had been imprisoned for four years, and which he was about to leave, for one last time, Dostoevsky, rarely so explicit, for once offered a hint of his response to this question: "How much youth had gone to waste within those walls, what great powers had perished uselessly there!"

Ethnography derives from a similar project, whereby the anthropologist strives to bring some intelligibility to the world. While to begin with, during the investigation, it is an encounter with those with whom he shares moments of life, it subsequently becomes, through writing, an encounter with publics, whose responsibility it to some degree engages. For, ultimately, it is only these publics that can decide how society should punish.

Notes

Introduction – The Expanding Prison

1 For a history of "prison before prison," see the article by Edward Peters (1998), as well as volumes by Cécile Bertrand-Dagenbach et al. (1999) for antiquity and by Isabelle Heullant-Donat, Julie Claustre and Elisabeth Lusset (2011) for the Middle Ages.

2 On the prehistory of prison as institution, see Spierenburg (1998), and for France, Castan and Zysberg (2002).

3 *The Oxford History of Prison*, edited by Norval Morris and David Rothman (1998), offers a historiographic perspective on prison in the Western world; for France, a remarkable chronology has been established by Christan Carlier and Marc Renneville (2007) on the Criminocorpus website.

4 Beccaria's treatise *On Crimes and Punishments* (1995/1764) proposed a radical revision of what the author defends as the "right to punish," seeking to make the punishment proportional to the crime, but also to render it more effective than the death penalty as a deterrent to criminals. Bentham's *Panopticon* (2002/1791) proposed a new architecture and organization for prisons, which allowed guards to view all prisoners without being seen by them, and could thus reduce the number of prison staff while strengthening security. Michael Ignatieff's classic study (1978) and Randall McGowen's synthesis (1998) offer an analysis of the prison in Britain.

5 The ideas put forward by Foucault (1977: 231, 82) have led to a radical revision in the ways of thinking about the genealogy of incarceration. They were nevertheless almost immediately subjected to critique by historians both in France, as attested by Michelle Perrot's edited volume (1980), which set up a debate around *Discipline and Punish* with the author, and in the English-speaking world, as evidenced by Michael Ignatieff's discussion, in which he re-examined his own work (1981). Foucault was criticized in particular for basing his work too much on the projects of reformers of the penal system and the conceptualists of prison design, and as a result drawing conclusions that remain uncorroborated by studies of what actually goes on in prisons. As is well known, he is an analyst of discourses, not a historian of practices.

6 See Jacques-Guy Petit et al.'s history of prisons over the last two centuries (2002), and particularly Michelle Perrot's preface.

7 In his study of the prison system in the Victorian era, Sean McConville (1998) analyzes the role of scientists and experts in legitimizing the harshness of the punishment system.

8 As David Rothman (1971) shows in his book on the parallel development of prison and asylum in the United States in the early nineteenth century.

9 According to Nietzsche (1989/1887: II 13–14), one of these reasons appears more profound than the others: "Punishment is supposed to possess the value of awakening the feeling of the guilt in the guilty person." However, he sees this view as an error that is belied by the facts: "It is precisely among criminals and convicts that the sting of conscience is extremely rare; prisons and penitentiaries are not the kind of hotbed in which species of gnawing worm is likely to flourish."

10 In Rawls's view (1955: 4), the problem of punishment is not whether it is justified, which most people agree that it is: "The difficulty is with the justification of punishment: various arguments for it have been given by moral philosophers, but so far none of them has won any sort of general acceptance."

11 According to the International Center for Prison Studies, the rate of imprisonment of 710 people per 100,000 of the population puts the United States at the top of the world rankings, far ahead of Russia and China, with a rate seven times higher than that of France (Walmsley 2013). Of course, mass incarceration does not eliminate the execution of some convicts, but the figures indicate the relative importance of these two systems of punishment: there were 46 executions in the US in 2010 (Snell 2013), compared to a prison population of 2.3 million in that same year (Glaze 2011); the number of executions has been falling since the late 1990s.

12 This classic triad takes up the categorization put forward by Philippe Combessie (2009: 19), who also refers to "expiation" in relation to the retributive element of imprisonment.

13 As Grégory Salle (2011: 20) notes, "the history of prison can only be partially captured by attempts at periodization." The author contrasts "definitive chronological divisions," which suggest straightforward evolution, with "the structural inertia inherent in institutions," which emphasizes the constant return of the same problems and the same debates. At the risk of oversimplification, it is useful to take the measure of imprisonment over a long period as it reveals the circumstantial nature of tendencies often seen as inevitable, or even necessary.

14 Marie-Danièle Barré's 1986 study of historical demographics begins in 1831, but she notes that the data for the years before 1852 are of doubtful reliability. Her count relates only to local and regional prisons, and thus excludes reformatories for minors, and the penal colonies overseas, where an estimated total of 97,000 convicts served sentences between 1850 and 1938.

15 In their chapter on the "Republican Prison," Petit et al. (2002: 147) note, not without irony, that this period is marked by a "crisis of repression."

16 Relating these figures to the population of metropolitan France, in 1955 there were 20,086 prisoners out of a total population of 43,227,872 inhabitants,

representing a rate of 46 per 100,000. In 2005 there were 58,344 prisoners out of a total population of 60,963,000, a rate of 96 per 100,000, thus more than double the earlier figure.

17 The statistics for the increase in the number of people in prison over this period are drawn from the data published by Marie-Danièle Barré (1986), supplemented by the *Key Figures in Prison Administration of 2013* (*Chiffres clés de l'Administration pénitentiaire 2013*). The figures for detention of undocumented immigrants are taken from the *Report of the Activities of the General Inspector of Places of Incarceration of 2012* (*Rapport d'activité du Contrôleur général des lieux de privation de liberté 2012*).

18 The change in the number of homicides has been analyzed by Laurent Mucchielli (2008). One might take the view that the number of homicides has fallen precisely because more and more potential murderers are in prison and thus rendered harmless. Studies in the United States, where "mass imprisonment" has been accompanied by a fall in crime, seem to counter this apparently common-sense hypothesis, mainly because there is neither a temporal nor a geographical correlation between the two: the decrease in the murder rate emerged before the explosion in the prison population, and it was no more marked in places where the rate of imprisonment is higher (King et al. 2005). Besides, it also occurred in neighboring Canada when the prison population was conversely decreasing. If there is a causal link between the two phenomena, due to the incapacitation of certain criminals, it is a minor one, probably reversed by other factors.

19 According to Salas (2005), this "penal populism" is characterized by a dual "pathology" of punishment and representation.

20 According to Garland (2001), the period of "penal welfarism" runs from the 1890s to the 1960s, and corresponds to a time of relative optimism about the possibility of reducing crime through social programs as much as through repressive policies.

21 In his nostalgia-tinted study of the "decline of the rehabilitative ideal," Francis Allen (1981) notes these two lines of criticism, but clear-sightedly adds two major elements that contribute to understanding this decline: the lack of theoretical and practical coherence in the model itself, which led to wide variations in the ways it was put into practice, and the reduction in public spending on this policy, which effectively doomed it to failure.

22 In a celebrated and influential article entitled "What works?" sociologist Robert Martinson (1974) offered such a scathing review of the policy of rehabilitation in prisons that his work is often referred to by the phrase "Nothing works!" which has become a sort of recurring motto for conservative commentators.

23 Amongst the abundant literature on US prison demographics, see in particular the report *Unlocking America* (Austin et al. 2007).

24 This reciprocal movement, whereby the pauperization of the social state parallels the extension of the penal state under the Clinton administration, has been analyzed by Loïc Wacquant (2009/2004).

25 The total prison population rose from 31,551 in 1982, the lowest level in recent history, to 64,782 in 2012. During the first decade of the twenty-first century, a period for which we have reliable and comparable statistics (Aebi and Delgrande

2011), France had the second highest increase in prison population in Western Europe, after Spain. During this period the prison population fell in several countries, notably Germany and the Netherlands.

26 As Pierre-Victor Tournier (2013: 87–91) emphasizes, these circumstantial factors have substantial impact. On the one hand, until 2007, each newly elected president has ritually pardoned criminals sentenced for minor offenses in a sort of sovereign gesture. On the other hand, the emotion provoked by the killings committed by Jean-Claude Bonnal in 2001, when socialist Lionel Jospin was prime minister, and Tony Meilhon in 2011, when conservative Nicolas Sarkozy was president, in both cases shortly after these murderers had been released, led to restrictions on parole and probation. The first phenomenon emptied the prisons, the second one filled them.

27 In an interview with me in March 2015, Robert Badinter took pride in having been the minister of justice who had emptied French prisons the most significantly in recent times.

28 Gaullist Jacques Chirac became prime minister in 1986, with Charles Pasqua as minister of the interior and Albin Chalandon as minister of justice; they were succeeded, in these respective positions, by socialists Michel Rocard, Pierre Joxe, and Pierre Arpaillange in 1988, then right-wing Édouard Balladur, Charles Pasqua, and Pierre Méhaignerie in 1993, then by left-wing Lionel Jospin, Jean-Pierre Chevènement, and Élisabeth Guigou in 1997, and finally by conservatives Jean-Pierre Raffarin, Nicolas Sarkozy, and Dominique Perben in 2002.

29 These figures, issued by the ministry of justice, are cited in a study by Annie Kensey (2010) and in the annual report of the Directorate of Prison Administration (2013). The figures for July 1, 2013 are retrieved from: www. justice.gouv.fr.

30 According to Kensey (2010), between 2001 and 2010 convictions for culpable homicide fell from 10.6 percent to 6.9 percent, and those for sexual assault from 25 percent to 15.6 percent, of the total prison population. However, between 1999 and 2009 the number of people imprisoned rose from 77,000 to 84,000, and the average length of sentence increased from 8.1 to 9.4 months. Moreover, the number of short sentences (less than six months) shot up over the same period: there were only 4,200 in 2002, compared to 8,900 in 2010.

31 In the study by Annie Kensey and Abdelmalik Benaouda (2011), the rate of imprisonment for repeat conviction within five years of release is 45 percent. It is only 32 percent for those who were initially given probation after being convicted, but, for those who were actually incarcerated, it rises to 47 percent when they were later released on parole and 56 percent when they served their full prison time. Furthermore, short sentences also result in a higher reoffending and reincarceration rate than average: 57 percent.

32 The lack of discussion by the authors of the way in which selection is operated through legislative, policing, and judicial processes could suggest that the composition of the prison population simply represents the reality of the criminal population (Cassan, Toulemon and Kensey 2000), which is clearly not the case, as will be discussed later.

33 In a polemical text, Faugeron and Houchon (1985: 115) write: "Traditional

penology has too often addressed prison 'in and of itself,' as if what happened behind the walls could form the object of independent study. This is to forget that prison is just one element in a vast play of morality that begins elsewhere."

34 The analyses and quotations that follow are taken from Book 1, "The Function of the Division of Labor" (Durkheim 1997/1893: 29–31, 33–40).

35 In the United States in 2013, 3,278 people were sentenced to life imprisonment without parole for nonviolent acts such as possession or sale of marijuana (*The Economist*, November 16, 2013); 3,125 people were sentenced to death in the 33 states and two federal districts that continue to impose this punishment (*Death Row USA Winter 2013*, www.deathpenaltyinfo.org/documents/ DRUSAWinter213.pdf). The 2008 financial crisis resulted in 5.5 million people losing their jobs, and 500,000 families being evicted from their home (*The Pew Charitable Trusts*, www.pewtrusts.org/our_work_report_detail.aspx?id=58695). Although it is difficult to determine precisely where the responsibilities for the advent of this crisis lay, the few sentences that were handed down consisted of fines that, despite being large sums, had little impact on the banks and bankers concerned: e.g., $4 billion for J. P. Morgan Chase, $1.2 billion for Deutsche Bank, $1.25 billion for Morgan Stanley (*New York Times*, February 4, 2014).

36 According to an epidemiological study conducted by a team of researchers from the University of Washington, between 2003 and 2011, the number of deaths directly or indirectly due to the war in Iraq, initiated on the pretext that the country held weapons of mass destruction, is estimated at 461,000, of which 60 percent were violent deaths, often of civilians (*PLOS Medicine*, www.plosmedi-cine.org/article/info%Adoi%2F10.1371%2Fjournal.pmed.1001533). In May 2012 a Malaysian court symbolically convicted George W. Bush, Dick Cheney, and Donald Rumsfeld of crimes against humanity, and passed the case file to the International Criminal Court (*Foreign Policy*, www.foreignpolicyjournal.com/ 2012/05/12/bush-convicted-of-war-crimes-in-absentia/). No court action has been initiated against the United States.

37 From the law of February 2, 1981, known as the "Security and Freedom" Act, which was drawn up by justice secretary Alain Peyrefitte and interior minister Christian Bonnet, to the law of March 14, 2011, promulgated by justice secretary Michel Mercier and interior minister Claude Guéant, the legislation of three decades has focused on petty crime. At the same time, the government has often accused the courts of being over-lenient, and a series of laws that are both more repressive of crime and more restrictive for judges has been submitted to Parliament and voted through (*Le Monde*, February 7, 2011). By contrast, the government's tolerant attitude toward financial crime and corruption has been the subject of severely critical reports, particularly from the Organization for Economic Co-operation and Development (OECD): the government examines an average of only three cases per year; in 12 years, only five companies have been convicted, moreover with little dissuasive penalty (*Transparency International*, www.transparency-france.org/e_upload/pdf/exporting_corrup tion_report_2013_final_for_web.pdf). The effects of corruption are generally assessed purely in financial terms (the additional cost), but its consequences can be wider and more tragic (Black 2007).

38 The study considered nearly 400,000 cases from the period 1952 to 1978 (Aubusson de Cavarlay 1985). Prior to this Nicolas Herpin (1977) conducted a survey of inequality in relation to the courts.

39 The analysis reveals an equally unfavorable ratio for "French nationals from the overseas territories" in relation to "metropolitan French nationals," thus reinforcing the racial interpretation (Lévy 1985).

40 *A National Disgrace* (*Une humiliation pour la république*) was the subtitle of Jean-Jacques Hyest and Guy-Pierre Cabanel's report (2000) to the Senate on "conditions of detention in prison establishments in France."

41 This two-way shift is considered in a collection of essays presenting an ethnography of the police, the courts, prison, the social services, and mental health services (Fassin et al. 2013).

42 The same holds true in the United States, with the distinction between local jails, which house all those held as a result of penal policy, and where the problems concerning overpopulation are more serious, and state prisons, which, together with federal prisons, generally hold those serving longer sentences. In a recent study, John Walsh (2013) points out that the former have been subject to much less analysis than the latter. The classic work on state prisons remains John Irwin's book (1985).

43 According to *Key Statistics of Prison Administration 2013* (*Les chiffres clés de l'administration pénitentiaire 2013*), of the 190 establishments in France, 98 are short-stay prisons, 85 are long-term prisons (including 43 penitentiary centers incorporating also short-term blocks), 6 are penitentiary establishments for minors, and 1 is a secure mental health facility at Fresnes.

44 As Faugeron and Le Boulaire (1992) put it: "The standard prison is the short-stay one: this is the most frequently used correctional facility. And it is where the most serious overpopulation occurs." Two decades on, their observation holds even more true.

45 I began my research in April 2009. Because I moved abroad, it continued over a series of short periods that totaled seven months: April to July 2009, June 2010, December 2012, January 2013, and finally June and July 2013. This extension over time, due largely to circumstances external to the research, allowed me on the one hand to observe developments linked both to modifications of penal and prison regulations and to changes in management and administrative personnel, and, on the other, to establish long-term relationships that fostered a sort of trust from individuals toward me as well as in myself with respect to a field that, probably more than others, needs time if it is to be mastered.

46 Zone Urbaine Sensible (ZUS) – zones designated as high priority for city intervention and development, on grounds of high levels of public housing and unemployment, and low educational achievement [translator's note].

Chapter 1   For Whom the Cell Fills

1 French prison staff are split into three levels. At the line level, trainee officers (*élèves* and *stagiaires*) and correctional officers (*surveillants*) correspond to junior

ranks, while chief officers and sergeants (respectively *premiers surveillants* and *majors*, also collectively called "*grades*," represent senior ones. The command staff comprises lieutenants, captains, and commandants. The management staff consists of wardens (directors and deputy directors) and interregional directors.

2 Various studies have assessed the effects of prison overcrowding on prisoner behavior, the incidence of violence, and the rate of reoffending following release. A classic study of British prisons established that, while prison size appears to have little effect on these variables, overcrowding increases both violence and recidivism (Farrington and Nuttall 1980). Subsequent studies have concluded that overcrowding is probably not directly a causal factor, but rather an aggravating one (Gaes 1994).

3 Figures from the *Journal officiel* of April 21, 2009, p. 3875, supplemented by *Key Statistics for Justice 2012* (*Les Chiffres clés de la Justice 2012*, www.justice. gouv.fr/art_pix/chiffres_cles_2012_20121108.pdf). For the period prior to 2004, there are no figures for the number of people under prison sentence, which was approximately the same as the number of people in prison. Since 2005, the two figures have been calculated separately, as the number of people receiving a prison sentence but not incarcerated is rising, from fewer than 1,000 in 2005 to more than 12,000 in 2014, most of them under electronic surveillance.

4 These data are taken from Kensey's (2010) note on the decade 2000–10, supplemented by *Key Statistics for Justice 2012*.

5 The first document cited is the *Information Report on Ways of Combating Prison Overcrowding* (*Rapport d'information sur les moyens de lutte contre la surpopulation carcérale*), presented by representatives Dominique Raimbourg and Sébastien Huyghe (2013). The second is the *Report on Conditions of Detention in Penitentiary Establishments in France* (*Rapport sur les conditions de détention dans les établissements pénitentiaires en France*), drawn up by senators Jean-Jacques Hyest and Guy-Pierre Cabanel (2000). The quotation is from Jean-Pierre Dintilhac, Public Prosecutor for the Paris District Court.

6 The program, characterized by the simultaneous introduction of the private sector into the prison system and of neoliberal concepts into thinking about prisoners, is analyzed by Madeleine Akrich and Michel Callon (2004).

7 The report appended as an annex to the law of March 27, 2012 states unequivocally: "The primary aim of the present law is quantitative adaptation of prison real estate to the needs foreseeable in the year 2017, by bringing it up to 80,000 places by that date. As of October 1, 2011, prison capacity was 57,540 places for 64,147 people incarcerated. The most likely scenario for the development of the prison population is a prediction of 96,000 people under prison sentence by 2017" (www. legifrance.gouv.fr/). In May 2011, Michel Mercier had spoken of 20,000 new places (*Le Figaro*, May 5, 2011). In September 2011, Nicolas Sarkozy went further, pushing the figure up to 30,000 (*Le Monde*, September 13, 2011).

8 The incoming minister of justice limited new construction to those projects that had already been started (*Le Monde*, September 28, 2011). The penal reform passed by the French parliament in 2014 proposes alternatives to prison, and a new mode of probation (*Le Nouvel Observateur*, June 10, 2014).

9 The Consensus Conference "For a New Public Policy on Prevention of

Reoffending," chaired by Françoise Tulkens, former vice-president of the European Court of Human Rights, submitted its report to the prime minister on February 20, 2013. The first recommendation was headed: "Prison, One Penalty Among Others" (http://conference-consensus.justice.gouv.fr/wp-content/uploads/2012/10/CCR_DOC-web-impression.pdf).

10 Published in the *Journal officiel* of October 18, 2012, this circular, which was much commented on, marked the official beginning of the change in policy. While careful of judges' sensitivities, and anxious to avoid the criticism of undue leniency, the minister of justice stated that "all decisions must be individualized, even in the case of contentious repeat offenders," and that "the custodial prison sentence should only be handed down as a last resort" (www.legifrance.gouv.fr/affichTexte.do?cidTexte=JORFTEXT000026503698).

11 It should, however, be noted that over the same period, the number of people sentenced to prison but not jailed increased by 1,142, a rise of more than 11 percent. In other words, the total number of sentences issued rose rapidly, with a slightly higher increase for electronic monitoring than for custodial sentences (www.justice.gouv.fr/art_pix/mensuelle_internet_juillet_2013.pdf).

12 To give just one example among many others, the journalist Brice Couturier, in a radio program on the 2014 prison reform, expressed surprise at the abolition of mandatory minimum sentences and the creation of conditional probation, a development which, he claimed, "demonstrated leniency toward criminals at a time when public opinion was calling, on the contrary, for the courts to be more strict" (*France Culture*, June 10, 2014). This "penal populism," as Denis Salas (2005) calls it, is doubly problematic: first, the assertion about polls reflects the journalist's opinion more than that of the public, and second, the reasoning implies that democracy should be guided by public opinion.

13 Under the heading *Growing Pressure from the Public and the Media*, the authors of the report offer a critical analysis of the "public opinion" argument used to justify penal policy (Raimbourg and Huyghe 2013).

14 Moreover, "the problematics offered by the polling agencies are subordinated to political interests, and this very strongly governs both the meaning of the answers and the meaning given to them on publication of the findings. The opinion poll is an instrument of political action" (Bourdieu 1998/1980: 150). The history of how this "public opinion" has been manipulated by those in power and instrumentalized in governing populations goes hand in hand with that of Western democracies (Blondiaux 1998).

15 In a speech a few days after the murder, Nicolas Sarkozy declared: "When an individual like the alleged perpetrator is released from prison without ensuring that he will be monitored by a probation and reentry counselor, it is a mistake. Those who covered up or allowed this mistake to happen will be sanctioned: that is the rule" (*Le Point*, February 3, 2011). Judges responded by announcing a strike.

16 The subheading of the article suggested a wide support of Nicolas Sarkozy's statement about magistrates: "In a survey conducted by IFOP for *Le Figaro*, the vast majority of respondents agree that judges who make mistakes should be sanctioned" (*Le Figaro*, February 13, 2011). "It seems that public opinion is calling for change," the article concluded in a populist tone.

17 As Pierre-Victor Tournier (2013: 93) shows, comparison of the first quarter of 2010 with the first quarter of 2011 reveals an increase of 9 percent in decisions for immediate incarceration, 11 percent for those awaiting trial, and 8 percent for those sentenced to one to three years' imprisonment.

18 The minister of justice stated that she was informed about this study in October 2011, shortly after she took up her post (*Le Monde*, October 6, 2011). A year and a half later, the 2009 study was finally published. The authors argued that prison "scares people," with more than 50 percent of them thinking that they "might one day be put in prison, because 'it can happen to anybody' or because of a 'driving offense'" (Belmokhtar and Benzakri 2013).

19 Driving offenses are one of the four categories that have seen a spectacular rise in convictions since the 1990s, the three others being drug offenses, assault, and insulting an officer and resisting arrest (Timbart 2011). The detailed figures for convictions in 2011, drawn from the National Criminal Records Statistics (Casier Judiciaire National), can be found in a 2013 official publication (www. justice.gouv.fr/art_pix/stat_conda2011.pdf).

20 Road deaths reached a peak of 16,545 in 1972. From this date on, there was a virtually regular decrease from year to year, falling to 3,250 in 2013. Expert and campaigner Claude Got devoted a book to "road violence" (2008).

21 Each year the ministry of the interior produces a report entitled *The Points-Based License* (*Le Permis à point*), summarizing its activity and results (www. interieur.gouv.fr/Publications/Statistiques/Securite-routiere/Bilan-du-permis-a-points/Bilan-2011).

22 In 2000 there were 4,500 convictions for driving with an invalid license. In 2011 the total was more than 22,100 (Timbart and Minne 2013).

23 It is difficult to determine the exact role played by tougher enforcement in the spectacular fall in road traffic mortality since the 1970s. First, there have been considerable improvements in vehicle safety and road design since the prevention policy was introduced in 1972, and this accounts for part of this positive change. Second, taking the year 2003, which marks the repressive turn in terms of the points-based license and blood alcohol limit, as a benchmark, it is noteworthy that mortality had already plummeted to one-third of its previous figure in the three preceding decades, that the decline was 43 percent over the following 10 years, and, more generally, that the rate of decrease was virtually unchanged over the entire period, and thus does not indicate a specific effect of imprisonment for driving offenses (see the *Road Safety Report 2013, Bilan 2013 de la Sécurité Routière*, www.securite-routiere.gouv.fr/).

24 Sentences of six months or less accounted for 21 percent of those entering prison in 2006, compared to 28 percent in 2008 (www.justice.gouv.fr/art_pix/1_1_rapport_evaluation_peines.pdf).

25 This detailed study (Leturcq 2012) is supplemented by more sporadic data gathered by two magistrates who drew up a copiously documented pseudonymous report (Forseti and Paul 2014).

26 The criteria for immediate appearance are detailed in Articles 393 and following of the Code of Penal Procedure.

27 In their study of "emergency justice" in nine district courts, Benoît Bastard and

Christian Mouhanna (2007) emphasize this reorientation of priorities, quoting a public prosecutor on real-time prosecution: "Real-time prosecution concentrates all the public prosecution energies on trivial misdemeanors, and deprives more complex areas, like economic and financial crime, environmental crime, and public health offenses, of resources. We lose sight of long-term cases."

28 The data on the increase in convictions and sentencing for drug offenses and driving without a license relate to the period between 2000 and 2009 (Timbart 2011; Timbart and Minne 2013). The data on corporate crime relate to the period 1999–2011 (Delabruyère et al. 2002 and the report *Convictions for the Year 2011* [*Condamnations Année 2011*]).

29 According to a study of more than 1,000 immediate appearance trials observed in 2007 and 2008 by the Lyon Council for the Respect of Rights (Conseil lyonnais pour le respect des droits) (Debard et al. 2009), 75 percent of defendants are brought in as prisoners in this way. The hearing lasts on average 31 minutes, six of which are devoted to the public prosecutor's case, eight to the case for the defense, and six to the lawyer for civil parties if there is one. This very precise description corresponds closely to my own observations.

30 In her study of immediate appearance trials in two courts in the Paris region, Angèle Christin (2008) emphasizes the time pressure due both to the overloading of this system, which leads to judges working late into the evening, and the method used to evaluate the work of courts, which is based primarily on the number of cases tried. This pressure is, moreover, so internalized that, in my experience, even when there are few cases to be tried, speed prevails.

31 In 2002 there were 38,300 immediate appearance trials, and 37,400 traditional procedures. In 2011, the respective figures were 43,000 and 17,000 (Raimbourg and Huyghe 2013).

32 The figures for immediate appearance trials are taken from the following studies and reports: Nantes and Nimes (Zocchetto 2005), Toulouse (Welzer-Lang and Castex 2012), Lyons (Debard et al. 2009). The figure for France as a whole is for 2009 (Timbart 2011).

33 The parliamentary report (Zocchetto 2005) cannot be accused of bias against immediate appearance trials, since the title of the section devoted to them is: "A disparaged but indispensable and relatively well-practiced procedure."

34 The authors of the report conclude: "People judged under this procedure are thus not only very frequently sentenced to custodial jail terms, but also imprisoned immediately, making it impossible to adjust the sentence prior to implementation" (Raimbourg and Huyghe 2013).

35 The journalist reporting on the issue wrote of "an apocalyptic picture of failures of communication between the various departments of the Ministry of Justice" (*Le Monde*, June 21, 2011).

36 There were substantial differences in execution rate in relation to the length of the sentence, with two out of five being executed when the penalty was less than three months, compared to three out of four when it was over six months. Close analysis of the phenomenon offered a much less dramatic view of it (Torterat and Timbart 2005).

37 The report by the General Inspectorate of Judicial Services was commissioned

by Justice Minister Rachida Dati in 2008 (www.justice.gouv.fr/art_pix/1_1_rapport_evaluation_peines.pdf).

38 The point at which Foucault was appointed to the Collège de France coincided with this shift from the archeological phase of his work to the genealogical phase – or in terms of the field of research, from psychiatry and medicine to the courts and prison (Foucault, *Résumé des cours 1970–1982*).

39 In his lectures, Michel Foucault describes how the privileged class fixed the rules of the game in order to control what would be punished and what would not (2015/2013).

40 On changes in wages, see: www.insee.fr/fr/themes/tableau.asp?ref_id= NATTEF04114; on social benefits, see: www.insee.fr/fr/ffc/tcf/tef2010/T10F054/T10F054.pdf; on unemployment rates see: www.insee.fr/fr/themes/series-longues.asp?indicateur=taux-chomage-sexe; on income inequality, see: www.inegalites.fr/spip.php?article632. Between 2001 and 2011, the average standard of living of the poorest decile rose by 70 euro, an increase of 0.9 percent, while that of the richest decile rose by 8,115 euro, an increase of 16.4 percent. Since 2008, as a result of the economic and financial crisis, the poorest have even seen a fall in their resources, while the richest have enjoyed an increase in theirs.

41 For a comparative approach to inequality, see: http://inequalitywatch.eu/spip. php?article58&lang=en. For international data on rates of imprisonment, see: http://dx.doi.org/10.1787/factbook-2010-95-fr. The United States has both the highest ratio between the income of the richest decile and the poorest decile (15.1 in 2008, before the crisis which is known to have increased disparities) and the highest rate of imprisonment (760 per 100,000 of the population).

42 Although I do not take up his theoretical distinctions, which offer a much more complex picture, David Garland (1990) puts forward an analysis of the various sociological theories of punishment.

43 The pioneering work in this neo-Marxist strand is *Punishment and Social Structure*, published in 1939 (Rusche and Kirchheimer 2009/1939). With regard to the contemporary period, the writings of Loïc Wacquant partially follow this line but complicate it; he writes: "America has clearly opted for criminalization of poverty, as an adjunct to the generalized spread of wage and social insecurity" (1999: 151).

44 This approach is in certain respects that of *The Division of Labor in Society* (Durkheim 1997/1893). David Garland's approach is in part derived from it.

45 For an account of the moral economy, seen from the point of view of a history of the concept, a reformulation of its definition and its relation to political economy, one can refer to my essay (Fassin 2009).

46 It is in this light that we can read Philippe Robert's synthesis (1985) of the debates around relations between insecurity, public opinion, and policy on crime.

47 In *The Illusion of Free Markets*, Harcourt (2011) critically questions the consensus according to which the economic domain should be regulated by the market, while crime repression should be exercised by the state – a paradox in the United States where the official discourse is that of neoliberalism.

Chapter 2   A Well-Kept Public Secret

1 The example provided concerns the Colombian police officers and soldiers who, at the height of the civil war, would force passengers to get off the bus in which they were traveling to be checked and searched, when everybody knew without ever saying it that they were themselves even more deeply involved in acts of terrorism and drug trafficking than the guerillas they were fighting (Taussig 1999: 5–6).

2 In the early years of the twenty-first century, the prospect of incorporating data on origin or skin color in surveys of discrimination generated heated debate in France (É. Fassin 2010).

3 The cautious analysis by Cheliotis and Liebling (2006) reveals both the existence and the complexity of these phenomena, the differences between groups in the ways they experience prison, relationships with prison staff and with other prisoners, respect and dignity, and the sense of security.

4 As shown by Western and Pettit (2010), these racial inequalities, which are also social inequalities, date back to the first half of the twentieth century, during the very period when the abolition of slavery and the erosion of the Jim Crow laws might have pointed toward a reduction in disparities, and have remained steady despite the gains made by the civil rights movement.

5 In this respect, it is worth noting the pertinence of the surveys conducted by the National Institute for Statistics and Economic Studies (Insee 2002), in collaboration with the Directorate of Prison Administration, and based on the 1999 census. These shed more light on the social background, family history, and marital relations of men in prison (Cassan et al. 2000; Kensey et al. 2000; Cassan and Mary-Portas 2002).

6 This, despite the fact that representatives of the state continue to use the expression "indigenous French people" in naturalization ceremonies, thus explicitly instituting, amid the ceremonial trappings of the Republic, a distinction among French people based on their origin (Fassin and Mazouz 2007).

7 It was only in the late 1990s that, under pressure from advocacy groups and in response to European requirements, the word "discrimination" entered the public arena and political debate in France. The adjectives "ethnic" and "racial" were rarely used to qualify discrimination in official documents, which preferred the circumlocution "by reason of real or supposed origin" (Fassin 2002).

8 For example, the very comprehensive *Report on Activity 2013* by the General Inspector of Prisons and Detention Centers (2014) refers only to inequality between facilities. The word "discrimination" appears only in relation to dietary regulations linked to religious practices, and to access to treatment for certain health conditions.

9 Statistics show that in English and Welsh prisons, black prisoners made up 13.2 percent of the 83,000 inmates, although they represent only 2.8 percent of the general population (Berman and Dar, 2013).

10 This leads Michael Tonry (1994) to suggest that, contrary to popular belief, the overrepresentation of black people in prison is slightly less marked in the United States (6.4) than in Britain (7.1), bearing in mind, nevertheless, that at the time

the rate of incarceration of black people was three times higher in the United States (1,860 per 100,000 of the population, compared to 547 per 100,000 in Britain).

11 The rate of incarceration of black people was 4,749 per 100,000 inhabitants, compared to 1,822 for Hispanics, and 708 for whites (West 2010). As a point of reference, it was 97 per 100,000 in France in the same year.

12 Bruce Western's 2006 book, from which these statistics are taken, represents the most systematic attempt to describe and analyze inequalities in "mass incarceration" in the United States.

13 According to Angélique Hazard (2008b), the number of foreigners in prison fell from 15,322 in 1993 to 11,140 in 2007 – a drop that is all the more remarkable given that the prison population grew from 33,880 to 46,742 over the same period.

14 According to Philippe Combessie (2009: 40), 51.2 percent of prisoners have a father born outside France, compared to 25.2 percent of the general population; for Africa specifically, the corresponding proportions are 30 and 7.6 percent.

15 The three factors offer different and complementary information. The family name is traditionally used in studies of discrimination, but it is inadequate in a number of ways: for example, a black person may have a European family name and a Christian forename, or Arab family name and forename. The photo largely helps to correct this problem, but does not identify some minorities, particularly Roma, who are not physically distinct from non-minority whites; however, they can sometimes be identified by their family name, or by notes occasionally appended to the file. Finally, nationality offers very different, juridico-administrative parameters: it makes it possible to distinguish between foreigners and French nationals within minority groups and, for example, between people from North Africa and French people of North African origin. It also makes it possible to pick out certain minorities identified on criteria of nationality alone, such as Romanians and Turks. Nevertheless, this trio of factors in no way implies an essentialization of the groups differentiated in the study: on the one hand, there is the possibility of errors in classification; on the other, and more importantly, the categories only indicate one of the possible identifications of individuals. Nevertheless, given the impossibility of conducting a study of the prisoners themselves, this is a reasonable approximation of the racial characteristics of the population of one prison.

16 The figures used relate to the year 2007 (Hazard 2008b). In terms of the composition by national origin, the main difference is in the higher proportion of sub-Saharan Africans (25 percent compared to 18 percent), and the lower proportion of North Africans (30 percent compared to 36 percent), in the population in my study.

17 The parallel obviously has limits. Not only is the rate of incarceration in the United States incommensurate with that in France and Britain, but the average length of sentence there is much higher than in the two latter countries.

18 The national study "Trajectories and origins" ["Trajectoires et origines"] (Beauchemin et al. 2010) offers some indirect information: the "majority population" represented 76 percent of all people aged between 18 and 50; we

can thus deduce that minorities, i.e. immigrants and children of immigrants as well as natives of the French overseas territories and their children, represent 24 percent, and compare this figure with that observed in prison. But this operation is doubly problematic: first, the minorities thus defined are as likely to include Portuguese individuals and their children as Malians and their children, which makes it difficult to evaluate the specifically ethnic and racial dimension; second, the reference population of this study is national, while the catchment area of the prison is essentially local.

19 The Leuven Lecture, addressed to jurists and criminologists, relates more specifically to avowal in a judicial context, but already offers an introduction to what was to be the subject of the last Lecture at the Collège de France: *parrhēsia*, that is, the courage of truth (Foucault 2014).

20 Tournier and Robert's study (1989) came at a time when the right had returned to power after five years of left-wing coalition government, and when the interior minister, Charles Pasqua, substantially increased the number of government initiatives on immigration and crime, bringing repressive legislation before parliament, particularly the laws of September 9, 1986, on conditions of entry and stay of foreigners, and December 31, 1987, on combating drug trafficking.

21 The pioneering work of Nicolas Herpin (1977), René Lévy (1985), and Bruno Aubusson de Cavarlay (1985), cited above, remains remarkably relevant in the contemporary situation. However, there has been virtually no further such work carried out, and contemporary research has rarely addressed the theme of inequality.

22 A juridical analysis of this law, and more generally of disparities in the fight against drugs, appears in Kara Gotsch's paper to the American Constitution Society for Law and Policy (https://www.acslaw.org/sites/default/files/Gotsch_-_After_the_War_on_Drugs_0.pdf).

23 The proportion of convictions for breach of the law on drugs is almost identical, at 13.9 percent. These statistics on offenders entering prison in 2008 were gathered by Philippe Combessie (2009).

24 These figures are taken from Ivana Obradovic's very comprehensive analysis (2012) of changes in the penalization of drug use since the 1980s.

25 The report, known as the Henrion Report, was submitted to Simone Veil, then minister of social affairs (Henrion, 1995). Figures from the French Office for Drugs and Drug Use support its analysis. In 1995, arrests for cocaine use were 56 times less frequent than those for marijuana use, and over the preceding decade the numbers had risen by 156 percent and 205 percent respectively. As for dealing, it was much less subject to repression than simple use: half as likely to be the subject of arrest and conviction in the case of cocaine, and one-twelfth as likely in the case of marijuana; the respective increases over 10 years were 64 percent and 138 percent. In other words, the police prioritized repression of marijuana over that of cocaine, and repression of use over that of dealing.

26 According to the study "Trajectories and origins," "immigrants and descendants of immigrants" make up over half (52.3 percent) of the population aged 18–50 in Sensitive Urban Zones (with people originating from the African continent accounting for one-third of the total), but only one-tenth of the population

living outside these zones (Observatoire national des zones urbaines sensibles 2012).

27 The only French study on racial discrimination in identity checks showed that, in Paris railroad stations, black and Arab people were checked respectively six and eight times more often than whites. It is significant that this unique study was commissioned by a foreign organization (Open Society Justice Initiative 2009). No such observational study has been carried out in the suburban neighborhoods of cities.

28 I have developed this point in *Enforcing Order* (Fassin 2013c), and more specifically in my article on police discretion (Fassin 2014a).

29 A study conducted in New York over more than 20 years (Golub et al. 2007) shows that African Americans, and to a lesser degree Hispanics, are more likely than whites to be arrested for simple use of marijuana, more often charged when they are arrested, and more harshly punished when they are charged, with this offense representing 15 percent of all crimes.

30 A national study (Beck et al. 2011) defines users as those who have consumed the drug at least once in the previous year, and regular users as people who have used it at least 10 times during the previous month. People who have tried marijuana at some point number 13.4 million, and daily users 550,000.

31 In the ESCAPAD study of 17-year-olds, categorized by the father's occupation, the odds ratios were 0.73 for staff members, 0.62 for blue-collar and 0.52 for the unemployed, compared to 1.0 for white-collar workers, and 0.9 for independent entrepreneurs (Legleye et al. 2009). In the study "Life events and health," among 18–34-year-olds, regular marijuana use was 7.3 percent for those who had not finished high school and 6.1 percent among those who had at least two years of higher education, while recent use was 15.7 percent and 1.5 percent respectively (Beck et al. 2010).

32 According to the national study "Living environment and security," 20 percent of people living in residential neighborhoods, 27 percent in housing projects, and 39 percent in Sensitive Urban Zones say they have observed drug use or dealing (Rizk 2010); 14 percent in the Paris suburbs, 19 percent in the capital, and 25 percent in Sensitive Urban Zones say they are troubled by drug-related issues – compared, for instance, to 61 percent of Parisians who say they are troubled by pollution (Le Jeannic 2007).

33 A detailed analysis of "the chain of decisions that lead to constructing a 'user of illicit substances' in the penal sense of the term" was conducted by Marie-Danièle Barré (1996), who notes that "between visible use in a public space ... and charges being brought through a police procedure, there is plenty of room for maneuver."

34 The expression "police property" was proposed by Canadian criminologist John Alan Lee (1981) to designate the "dangerous classes" that the police are delegated to repress.

35 In his study of the criminal investigation police, René Lévy (1987: 145) already noted this phenomenon.

36 This results-driven policy, and more broadly the problems posed by the

production of statistics on the police, have been analyzed by Jean-Hugues Matelly and Christian Mouhanna (2007).

37 Arrests for use of drugs rose fivefold, increasing twice as fast as arrests for dealing and resale. The latter have been falling since 2010, while the former continue to rise (Observatoire français des drogues et des toxicomanies 2013).

38 Thus, between 2002 and 2009, arrests and placements in police custody increased by 9 percent for dealers, 42 percent for resellers, and 91 percent for simple users (Cour des comptes 2011).

39 These figures are taken from Ivana Obradovic's book (2012), where she notes that, despite a reduction in the total number of sentences for simple use, the increase in the number of custodial sentences resulted in a virtual doubling of the total number of prison years handed down, which rose from 1,530 to 2,890.

40 While in the United States, where the fight against drugs has indeed been the main vector of mass incarceration, discrimination in this domain has been the subject of rigorous research, in France there have been no studies specifically documenting such discrimination. It is worth remembering that, according to a frequently cited study by the American Civil Liberties Union (2013) concerning repression of simple possession of marijuana in the United States, the proportion of arrests is 3.73 times higher among blacks than among whites, despite a similar rate of consumption in the two groups. A sociohistorical analysis explaining how legislation, the police, and the courts have contributed to the racialization of this war on drugs has been conducted by Doris Mary Provine (2011).

41 Of the 88,930 custodial sentences implemented in 2008, 14.36 percent related to traffic offenses, 14.19 percent to breaches of drug laws, and 1.36 percent to failure to respect public authority (Combessie 2009). Alongside these three types of crime, a fourth offense, assault, saw a rapid rise in convictions between 1990 and 2009 (Timbart 2011).

42 These data are drawn from city-wide and regional analyses carried out by Insee, and the statistics recorded for Sensitive Urban Zones (www.insee.fr/fr/).

43 Unemployment among those with a Certificate of Vocational Training or a Diploma of Vocational Skill ranges from 13 percent to 27 percent. It is 30 percent for those without qualification, and 8 percent for those with higher education (Martinelli and Prost 2010).

44 The data on young people are drawn from an Insee study (Jugnot 2012); the statistics for the adult male population appear in a Dares study (Minni and Okba 2014).

45 A number of studies in the United States have confirmed the existence of these practices that consist of stopping vehicles to check them depending on the skin color of their drivers (Warren et al. 2006). The distinction between categorical discrimination, based on prejudice, and statistical discrimination, based on probability, was put forward by Michael Banton (1983).

46 Under article 395 of the Code of Penal Procedure, "if the maximum prison sentence specified by the law is at least two years, the public prosecutor, when he considers that the combined charges are sufficient and that the case is ready to be tried, may, if he judges that the charges concerned justify immediate appear-

ance, bring the defendant immediately to court." In the case of flagrante delicto, a maximum sentence of six months is sufficient condition.

47 According to studies conducted in criminal courts in Lyons (Debard et al. 2009) and Toulouse (Welzer-Lang and Castex 2012), and by Chowra Makaremi in the Paris suburbs (Fassin et al., 2013), the individuals in immediate appearance trials can be characterized as follows. Socially, they are young men, generally isolated and in precarious circumstances: in the Lyons study, 97 percent were male, 53 percent were under 30, 63 percent were single, divorced, separated, or widowed, 69 percent had no stable income, and more than half of these were entirely without resources. In addition, while the vast majority were of French nationality, many of them belonged to minorities: 65 percent in the Toulouse study, where the authors based their classification on individuals' appearance, and 80 percent in the Paris region, based on their family name. In terms of penal circumstances, the defendants often had a criminal record, having already been convicted and even being recidivists, in terms of the legal definition, as they had repeated the same offense: of the defendants in Lyons, seven in ten had a criminal record, while three-quarters of defendants in the Paris region did. The offenses they were accused of were principally traffic offenses, use and possession of drugs, insulting behavior, and resisting arrest, but also domestic violence and aggravated robbery.

48 This was the first study to include data on the racial characteristics of defendants in court decisions in France (Jobard and Névanen 2007).

49 In her significantly titled book *Judging Mohammed*, Susan Terrio (2009) shows how some sociologists, notably Hugues Lagrange and Sebastian Roché, have, through their interpretations of juvenile crime in terms of cultural difference, played an important role in the production and legitimization of magistrates' and politicians' prejudices toward minorities.

50 The historian (Perrot 1975) bases her analysis on the *General Report of the Administration of Criminal Justice* [*Compte général de l'administration de la justice criminelle*].

51 At the end of his book focused mainly on the United States, Loïc Wacquant (2004: 295–9) strives to describe what he calls the "French style of prison aberration," describing prison as a "vacuum cleaner for social trash" who are constituted mainly by "young people from low-income backgrounds, of North African immigrant origin, parked in peripheral housing projects that have been eviscerated by three decades of economic deregulation and state retreat from urban planning."

Chapter 3   Ye Who Enter Here

1 In a questionnaire from the Parliamentary Committee on Ways of Combating Prison Overpopulation, the Magistrates' Union, the largest trade union for court session judges, responded thus to a question about magistrates' failure to visit short-stay prisons: "It has to be recognized that the main reason they do not fulfill this legal obligation is essentially lack of time. The question is therefore

not whether the number of visits prescribed by the law should be increased, but rather to ensure that these visits are effective and can take place without warning" (www.union-syndicale-magistrats.org/web/upload_fich/publication/rapports/2012/surpopulation_carcerale_oct2012.pdf).

2 The first version of these rules was adopted in 1973, and the most recent revision dates from 2006. Signed by the 48 member states of the Council of Europe, the 108 recommendations are being progressively implemented by each state, and within each, by the facilities concerned (https://wcd.coe.int/ViewDoc.jsp?id=955747). On January 30, 2012, the independent certification body Veritas awarded the "EPR" logo to 110 of the 167 correctional facilities in France.

3 The European Prison Rules provide a framework of standards, and their acceptance by the prison management, followed by certification by the official certification body, indicates that the facility conforms to these general principles. As noted by the International Prison Observatory (Observatoire international des prisons 2012: 48–50), there is considerable variation in the actual implementation of these rules from one facility to another, and hence also in the consequences for inmates, from the level of comfort in cells to the amount of telephone credit they receive.

4 Sometimes "admission procedures and obedience tests may be elaborated into a form of initiation that has been called the 'welcome,' where staff or inmates, or both, go out of their way to give the recruit a clear notion of his plight" (Goffman 1968/1961: 18). The episode concerning the Irish youth is taken from the autobiography of writer and campaigner Brendan Behan.

5 Applicable, in the widest sense, to barracks and monasteries equally, "the handling of many human needs by the bureaucratic organization of whole blocks of people . . . is the key fact of total institutions" (Goffman 1961: 6).

6 According to Douglas North, "Institutions are the rules of the game in a society, or more formally, are the humanly devised constraints that shape human interaction" (1990: 3).

7 The epigraph of this chapter comes from the inscription at the gates of hell that ends with the famous injunction: "Lasciate ogni speranza, voi, ch'entrate!" ("All hope abandon, ye who enter here!") (Dante 2012/1472, Canto III). The expression "descent into hell" is also used by Anne-Marie Marchetti (2001: 23) in relation to people who have committed crimes subject to very long or even life sentences. Gilles Chantraine (2004: 149) notes that ex-prisoners speak of "hell" in referring to their arrival in prison.

8 One account of entry into prison exposes the limits of the impact of human intervention: "The ritual of admission is necessarily degrading however it is carried out by the correctional officers, whether they attempt to reassure an individual in obvious distress, or treat a group of new arrivals as another batch to be dispatched to the cells" (Lhuillier and Lemiszewska 2001).

9 The recommendations in question are paragraphs 17.3, 18.6, 18.7, and 18.8 of the European Prison Rules issued by the Committee of Ministers of the Council of Europe (https://wcd.coe.int/ViewDoc.jsp?id=955747).

10 The law of March 4, 2002, relating to the rights of sick prisoners, known as the Kouchner Act, allows for a suspension of sentence on medical grounds in the

case of a life-threatening condition. Ten years after it was passed, 1,200 people had died in prison, while around 600 had benefited from this humanitarian measure (*Le Figaro*, March 5, 2012). Among the beneficiaries was Maurice Papon, who spent the last four years of his life at home, released amid a controversy that centered less on the gravity of the charges against him (complicity in crimes against humanity) than on the favorable treatment he received, while so many others imprisoned for minor offenses, like the Tunisian man mentioned by the guard, ended their days in prison (*Le Parisien*, September 19, 2002).

11 A DNA sample may be taken from a person who has committed or is suspected of committing an offense. Initially reserved for specific convictions for sexual offenses or child abuse, the practice has been generalized to all those receiving prison sentences, and all those charged with offenses that could result in such a sentence (www.senat.fr/lc/lc157/lc1570.html). On August 31, 2012, according to the National Committee on Electronic Data and Freedom (Commission nationale de l'informatique et des libertés, CNIL), the National DNA Database contained data for a little over two million individuals, one-fifth of whom had been convicted, while the other four-fifths had merely been charged.

12 The study of 306 prisoners conducted by the head of the Regional Medical-Psychological Service for the Lille-Loos-Sequedin region, using evaluation scales, offers a quantitative assessment of a "general psychic suffering," a "feeling of having failed in life," and "sleep disturbances" during the 48 hours following arrival in prison (Archer 2008).

13 The authors of the report also point out the ambivalence expressed by correctional officers toward these innovations, with some considering that what is good for inmates is good for guards, while others feel that everything is being done for inmates and nothing for them (Chauvenet and Rambourg 2010).

14 This is the dual perspective put forward by the International Prison Observatory (Observatoire international des prisons 2012: 45–50): recognizing the satisfaction of inmates, and emphasizing the administration's public relations strategy, the authors title one section of their report "The European Prison Rules as 'fig-leaf.'" For a short time there was a newsletter, *News on the European Prison Regulations* (*Actualité des règles pénitentiaires européennes*), which continued for five issues until January 2010 (www.justice.gouv.fr/art_pix/LettreRPE5.pdf).

15 For analysis of the tensions between the penal state, grounded in punishment, and the liberal state, grounded in law and rights, see the conclusion of *At the Heart of the State* (Fassin et al. 2015).

Chapter 4   Life in Prison: A User's Manual

1 According to the prison's statistics, of the nearly 300 pre-conviction prisoners in the facility, 70 percent had their cases under investigation, and the remainder were divided almost equally between those whose immediate appearance trial had been postponed, and those appealing the court's decision or applying to the Court of Cassation. Of course, in terms of flow rather than stock, nonconvicted prisoners in custody prior to their immediate appearance trial represented a

much larger proportion, because they stayed only a few weeks if their trial had been postponed, or even a few days if they had been committed during a weekend, for trial the following week.

2 The island of W is an imaginary place where "there are two worlds, the world of the Masters and the world of the slaves. The Masters are unreachable, and the slaves tear at each other," but the Athlete trains, devoting all his energy "to simply waiting for that alone, to that single hope of a paltry miracle which will get him out of beatings, whippings, humiliations, fear," of "this huge machine, each cog of which contributes with implacable efficiency to the systematic annihilation of men" (Perec 1988/1975: 160–1).

3 According to the precious *Prisoner's Guide* (*Guide du prisonnier*) published by the International Prison Observatory (Observatoire international des prisons 2012: 114), "typical departmental sanitary regulations specify that 'the toilet cubicle should not open directly onto the room where cooking is done'," while "the European Committee for Prevention of Torture believes that the absence of partitions in 'a cell occupied by more than one inmate' is 'unacceptable', and recommends that 'sanitary facilities should be fully partitioned'."

4 According to a published recommendation by the General Inspector of Prisons and Detention Centers following his visit to the Villefranche-sur-Saône short-stay prison in 2008: "The installation of grids plunges cells into quasi-darkness during the day, giving the inmates a powerful feeling of isolation and gloominess. These devices can even deprive them of any view of the sky. They make life in the cells, which is already difficult or very difficult, even harder, and foster feelings of depression or anger." While recognizing the efficacy of this measure in reducing disposal of trash and the exchange of objects, the authors recommend alternative solutions (*Journal Officiel*, January 6, 2009).

5 Overpopulation is translated here into doubling-up in cells. In some French facilities populations are substantially higher. For example, in 2012 the administrative court ordered the state to pay compensation, with interest, to seven former inmates of the Dunkerque short-stay prison who had complained about their conditions of incarceration in a 250-square-feet space with three sets of double bunks (*La Voix du Nord*, February 16, 2012). Even more striking, in the United States, jails often have dormitories with rows of dozens of structures comprising two or three narrow metal platforms one above the other, covered with a thin mattress, with tables between them for meals. One panel of federal judges in 2009 ordered the state of California to reduce the number of prisoners from 150,000 to 90,000 within a year, declaring that the overpopulation was unconstitutional (*New York Times*, August 5, 2009).

6 Launched in 1986 by then minister of justice, Albin Chalandon, this program envisaged the construction of 13,200 prison places. Its two principal features were an architectural and technological modernization that was supposed to enable better surveillance of inmates and thus reduce the risk of the kind of disorders that had broken out in prisons over the preceding decade, and the delegation of a substantial proportion of the operation of correctional facilities to private contractors, on the basis of tenders under which these contractors took on functions such as catering, prison work, and facilities for families, while the

surveillance functions remained in the public sector. The program was criticized for relegating the re-entry of prisoners to the background (Gallo 1995: 87–8).

7 This almost permanent enclosure, known as the "closed-door regime," is characteristic of short-stay prisons in France. On the one hand, long-term facilities, which are in principle reserved for convicted prisoners serving sentences longer than two years, have an "open-door regime" during the day, which normally allows prisoners to move around the prison and go about their occupations. However, this regime has become stricter over recent years, as central prisons have also gone over to permanently "closed doors," while the introduction of differential regimes of imprisonment has led to the same constraints being imposed on some inmates in other facilities. This increase in exceptions from the daytime "open-door regime" for prisoners serving long sentences has been criticized by the European Committee for the Prevention of Torture (Observatoire international des prisons 2012: 106). On the other hand, in some neighboring countries, in facilities with standard levels of security, prisoners move much more freely around fairly extensive areas of the prison, in line with the European Prison Rules, which state that "this regime shall allow all prisoners to spend as many hours a day outside their cells as are necessary for an adequate level of human and social interaction" (https://wcd.coe.int/ViewDoc.jsp?id=955747).

8 In his interviews with ex-prisoners, Gilles Chantraine (2004: 167–72) distinguishes two forms of this disuse of time: "hollowed-out time," which derives from a certain "conformism," consists of simply killing time; "anesthetized time," which reflects a total "apathy," represents a sort of obliteration of the self and evasion of time, mainly through drugs. What I propose here is somewhat different: linking the reality of the emptiness of prison time with the feeling of wasting the time of one's life and considering the objective and subjective dimensions of temporality together.

9 As Goody (2002: 17) remarks, while the physiological substrate of the senses seems common to all humans, sensorial experiences are culturally constructed, varying over time, and in different societies. What is perceived as normal or abnormal, pleasant or unpleasant, for example, in the contemporary West, differs from what is perceived in this way in other social environments. Sensitivity to light, the perception of noise, and the awareness of odors are not uniform in prison.

10 In an interview following the release of Jacques Audiard's film *A Prophet*, the director of the Nanterre short-stay prison, where some of the film's scenes were shot, stressed that it was "extraordinarily accurate," citing the sonic environment as an example: "It was shot in the studio, but the sound was recorded in prisons" (*Le Figaro*, August 26, 2009).

11 Light deprivation during the day has marked negative effects on the cerebral metabolism, with concomitant alterations of both physical activity and psychological state. Numerous animal experiments have demonstrated the existence of harmful effects on the brain, including the death of neurons producing the neurotransmitters involved in emotion and cognition, with long-term signs of psychomotor retardation; these symptoms can be reversed by treatment with anti-depressants (www.scientificamerican.com/article/down-in-the-dark/).

Observations in human subjects have identified a specific pathology linked to seasonal lack of natural light, with depressive symptoms that respond to light therapy (www.mayoclinic.org/diseases-conditions/seasonal-affective-disorder/basics/definition/con-20021047).

12 The famous poem, from Verlaine's collection *Wisdom* (*Sagesse*), was written in 1881 when Verlaine was imprisoned in Brussels. This line was taken as the title for the fine documentary *Si bleu, si calme* (*So Blue, So Calm*) that Éliane de Latour made with inmates of La Santé prison. It is through the window-grilles in the cells of these inmates that the Parisian sky is glimpsed in the film (www.film-documentaire.fr/Si_bleu_si_calme.html.film.1531).

13 Cells in maximum security prisons offer black and white TV with programs selected by the facility, both in order to control what prisoners watch and to add to the punishment of incarceration (http://solitarywatch.com/about/fortressesof-solitude-part-1/).

14 On his tour of French prisons in 2005, the European Commissioner for Human Rights made a similar observation when he visited Fleury-Mérogis, the largest short-stay prison in France: "We noticed a large building in the middle of one of the detention complexes. The prison director informed us that it was a gymnasium intended for the inmates. The gymnasium was built eight years ago with European funding. Apparently, however, the designers of this innovatory project unfortunately failed to include secure entrances in their plans for this building, which has prevented it from being put into service. This story is so grotesque that it might have been amusing if it had not been so sad" (Gil-Robles 2005).

15 The Conference of National Museums, as well as a number of other major museums, have launched "beyond the walls" initiatives, aiming to make art available to "excluded audiences," especially in hospitals and prisons (www.grandpalais.fr/fr/article/hors-les-murs-lexposition).

16 One famous precedent is Germaine Tillion's *Verfügbar aux Enfers* (*The Campworker Goes to Hell*), an operetta written and performed at Ravensbrück. In making reference to this work, my intention is not of course to compare either the conditions of incarceration in a German concentration camp with those in French prisons, or the creative work of Tillion and her collaborators with those of the prison inmates, but simply to suggest a convergence from the point of view of the meaning of the action, as the performance was both a form of release and an act of resistance, a gesture of humor and of mockery (*Le Monde*, May 29, 2007).

17 Management at the Luynes short-stay prison, near Aix-en-Provence, has been innovative in this respect, allowing a hip-hop show to be organized within the prison, which involved three young prisoners being selected from among 200 who put themselves forward, and then writing and recording a rap album (http://rue89.nouvelobs.com/rue89-culture/2013/12/08/star-ac-a-petite-frangine-rap-prison-shtar-academy-248195). Named the Shtar Academy ("shtar" being prison slang for "jail" and the name of the show being a parody of the well-known French television talent show *Star Academy*), the group has received the accolade of an entry in English-language Wikipedia (http://en.wikipedia.org/wiki/Shtar-Academy).

18 There is a remarkable documentary, *Visiting Hours*, by Didier Cros, who spent a year in the Châteaudun long-term prison, and filmed these meetings between prisoners serving long sentences and their visitors with great sensitivity (http:// cinemadocumentaire.wordpress.com/2013/01/21/parloirs-un-documemntaire- de-didier-cros/). "It is much easier for the spectator to identify with a visitor than with an inmate, whose words are never heard, because they are not deemed valid. Through the medium of families, the visiting room thus allows the viewer to project him- or herself into the problematic context of prison," says Cros.

19 The survey by the National Union of Regional Federations of Prisoner Family Support Centers (UFRAMA, *Union nationale des féderations régionales des maisons d'accueil de familles et proches de personnes incarcérées*) interviewed 2,100 individuals, 71 percent of whom were visiting inmates in short-stay prisons. Among them, 56 percent made the journey by car. A quarter of journeys to short-stay prisons were made by bus.

20 On June 14, 2014, a demonstration was held in the town of Bayonne, calling for better conditions of imprisonment for the 103 Basque prisoners. All political parties, most of the local politicians, mayors, and members of parliament, called on people to support the demonstration. The campaign's first demand was for prisoners to be placed closer to their families (*Le Monde*, June 14, 2014).

21 This is the case particularly for wives and partners, as shown by Megan Comfort (2008) in her book on San Quentin State Prison, where she analyzes the ordeal that imprisonment of their partner represents for these women.

22 Some sense of this can be gained from the fragments of text collected by Jean- Pierre Guéno (2000) under the title *Paroles de détenus* (*Prisoners' Words*). But the variety of these experiences, and the reflexivity of those who live them, are revealed much more extensively in the often remarkable blogs written by prisoners who keep a journal of their time in jail (especially: http://lavieenpris onraconteeparundetenu.blogs.nouvelobs.com/ and http://brunodesbaumettes. overblog.com/). The information website Rue 89 has also published pages from a blog by an "unknown convict" (www.rue89lyon.fr/2013/12/24/la-parole-est- la-prison/), while the *Nouvel Observateur* magazine website presents a former prisoner's blog under the title "View on prison" (http://laurent-jacqua.blogs. nouvelobs.com/).

Chapter 5   In the Nature of Things

1 Erving Goffman (1968/1961: 187) is rarely credited with having been perhaps the first to have accorded their due importance to materials and the "make-do's" they offer to those incarcerated, in the chapter of his book *Asylums* dedicated to "hospital underlife."

2 There is a long history of study of the "social life of things" in the social sciences, both in cultural anthropology (Appadurai 1986) and in the study of science and technology (Daston 2000). My aim here is to extend this approach, both by focusing on contemporary everyday objects, and by adding a political and moral reading to it.

3 As Foucault puts it: "It is not an ideology; it is not exactly, fundamentally, or primarily an ideology. First of all and above all it is a technology of power" (2007: 49).

4 This is the subject of Scott's book *Weapons of the Weak*, which focuses on the peasants of the developing world: "These Brechtian – or Schweykian – forms of struggle have certain features in common. They require little or no coordination or planning; they make use of implicit understandings and informal networks; they often represent a form of individual self-help; they typically avoid any direct, symbolic confrontation with authority" (1985: xvi).

5 In 24 facilities spread throughout France, 47 workshops contribute to the activity of this manufacturing authority, in the spheres of information technology, clothing manufacturing, printing, leatherwork, metalwork, agriculture, tailoring, and woodworking. They provide work for more than 1,000 prisoners, and have a turnover of 23 million euros. The objects produced include office furniture, but also "prison furniture," household linens, as well as "security equipment," described in the "products catalogue" (www.sep.justice.gouv.fr./art_pix/sepr_produits.pdf).

6 In his study of a medium-security prison in Britain, Ben Crewe (2009: 370–2) lists five ways that drugs enter the facility. The usual procedures are packages thrown in or brought in during visits. Temporary release offers another possibility. Corruption of staff is the most "fruitful," as it enables larger quantities to be smuggled. The most surprising, but most restricted technique is by mail, with drugs being fixed underneath the stamp or between a folded-over sheet of paper. Larger objects such as phones are difficult to bring in after temporary release, given the strip search on return, and obviously can never get in through the mail.

7 In her study of long sentences in France, Anne-Marie Marchetti (2001: 214) makes the same observations with regard to smuggling in general, and drugs in particular. Quoting a "lifer," she explains that "guards, who are not searched, are the best placed to bring in drugs (or other commodities!)." When she asks what happens if the inmate is caught, her interviewee replies: "We don't snitch on the screw. We don't snitch so he'll carry on doing the dirty work." In some cases, the facts came to light and correctional officers were arrested following an investigation. One lawyer who has defended several of them has described the substantial profits they made from this lucrative trade (*Le Monde*, September 7, 2012).

8 As an example of the first type, a version of "Harlem Shake," in which inmates of the Montmédy prison complex, their faces concealed in hoods or behind scarves, dance to a hip-hop track with the repeated lyric "*Con los terroristas*," appeared on the front page of a freesheet (*20 Minutes*, December 4, 2013). As an example of the second, a brutal intervention against inmates in the Roanne long-term prison who were refusing to leave the exercise yard in protest against their conditions of incarceration, filmed from the window of a cell, found its way onto the *Nouvel Observateur*'s "View on prison" site, with commentary from the blogger Laurent Jacqua: "Screws, we can screw you too: we reveal your brutality" (http://laurent-jacqua.blogs.nouvelobs.com/tag/eris).

9 Interviewed on July 17, 2014, shortly before she was appointed to the Council

of Ministers, Adeline Hazan, the General Inspector of Prisons and Detention Centers, stated that she was in favor of authorizing cellphones "provided that the number of contacts used is limited," and with the aim of "supporting the maintenance of family relations." In this she took up a proposal formulated by her predecessor in this post, Jean-Marie Delarue (www.rtl. fr/actu/societe-faits-divers/prison-le-controleur-favorable-a-l-autorisation-des-telephones-portables-7773268397).

10 The reference is to Sganarelle's eloquent speech at the opening of Molière's play: "Whatever Aristotle and the other old philosophers may say, there's nothing so fine as snuff. All the best people are devoted to it, and anyone who lives without snuff doesn't deserve to live. Not only does it purge and stimulate the brain, it also schools the soul in goodness, and one learns in using it how to be a true gentleman. You've noticed, I'm sure, how whenever a man takes a pinch of snuff, he becomes gracious and benevolent toward everybody, and delights in offering his snuff-box right and left, wherever he happens to be. He doesn't wait to be asked, but anticipates the unspoken desires of others – so great is the generosity which snuff inspires in all who take it."

11 The term "mouse," used for these small packages attached to a string which distantly resemble a rodent, led one journalist to state erroneously: "Reports suggest that some inmates have even trained rats to transport small packages" (http://tempsreel.nouvelobs.com/societe/20130715.OBS9546/sequedin-qui-a-aide-redoine-faid-a-s-evader.html).

12 A parallel could be traced with Maurice Godelier's analysis (1972/1969), in an entirely different context, of salt as currency among the Baruya of New Guinea: "Salt is a prized commodity, but is it a 'currency'?" he wonders. "For a commodity to function as a currency, it must be able to be exchanged for all other commodities; it must function as their general equivalent." He shows that this is indeed the case. With regard to tobacco in the prison I studied, a more systematic study would be required to formally determine its role as currency.

13 David Scheer (2014) offers a fine-grained analysis of prison architecture, in one of the studies that takes this material aspect of prison most seriously.

14 See, for example, Corinne Rostaing's richly detailed study of women's prisons in France, where she describes her theoretical approach thus: "In this study, prison will be defined as a structured complex of social relations between actors of varying status" (1997: 4). I would suggest adding "objects" to "actors."

15 One exception is Lorna Rhodes's pioneering study of high-security prisons in the United States, where she offers detailed descriptions and even photographic illustrations of the "technologies of control" used by prison officers, or more frequently, showcased in the advertising of specialist providers: the "violent prisoner chair" in which the inmate is strapped down after being "gassed," or the "stun belt," which delivers a powerful electric shock to the aggressive inmate, and is considered a "clean" form of coercion (2004: 51, 91).

16 The so-called "ontological turn" in anthropology, proposes a shift of perspective from the anthropocentric viewpoint of the social sciences. It ascribes particular importance to nature and objects, which are endowed with their own essence, assumed to be in some way external to the human world. A short

text by Eduardo Kohn introduces this approach: www.culanth.org/fieldsights/
463-what-an-ontological-anthropology-might-mean. My proposal is symmetrical: I start from objects in order to shed a new light on human actions.

17 A photograph of the permitted version and a description of the banned version
of the stinger, known in French under the diminutive "toto," can be found in
the excellent glossary of the organization Ban Public, which disseminates information on prisons in Europe (http://prison.eu.org/rubrique.php3?id_rubrique=
220). As one blogger who writes a fascinating diary from the Les Baumettes
prison puts it: "The stinger works fine for heating a cup of water and making
an instant coffee, but it's not great for real cooking" (http://brunodesbaumettes.
overblog.com/chapitre-premier-la-chute.html#11/09b).

18 The report from an expert medical assessment of the toxicity of the solid fuel
stove sold by the prison management can be accessed on the Ban Public site
(http://prison.eu.org/spip.php?article13335). A video detailing the method for
constructing a home-made heater, called "chauffe" in French, using a sardine
can as oil container, three soda cans as a support, and paper napkins inserted
into the end of an empty tube of mustard as a wick, recorded by a prisoner
named Roby, can be seen at Dailymotion (www.dailymotion.com/video/xa89ra_
fabrication-de-la-chauffe-en-prison_lifestyle).

19 The anthropological, and even historical, approach to objects could be broadened by extending the analysis beyond those embedded in the world of prison,
to focus on their presence throughout the system of punishment, as Philip Smith
(2008) does for the guillotine and the electric chair.

Chapter 6   A Profession in Search of Honor

1 A longitudinal study of the 130th class of correctional officers to gradu-
ate from the National School of Prison Administration (École nationale de
l'administration pénitentiaire, ENAP) shows that, when asked about their future
or present profession, at the time of graduation, only 52 percent answered that
they were going to become correctional officers, while a few years after having
started to work in the prison system, 64 percent of them said what their job was.
Thus, half of young graduates and one-third of experienced officers acknowledge that they do not "admit to" their profession (Benguigui et al. 2008).

2 The year 2002 saw a succession of damaging accounts: the scathing report
by Véronique Vasseur, chief medical officer at La Santé prison (2000), which
received wide media coverage; a report by the National Assembly entitled *La
France face à ses prisons* (*France Face-to-Face with Its Prisons*) (Mermaz and
Floch 2000); and a senate report under the heading *Prisons: Une humiliation
pour la République* (*Prisons: A National Disgrace*) (Hyest and Cabanel 2000).

3 The example that Hughes gives is Nazi Germany where, he writes, the majority
of the "good people" accepted, or even supported, Hitler's project but closed
their eyes to what those who executed the "dirty work" were doing (Hughes
1962). My intention is, of course, not to draw a parallel with the activity of
correctional officers. Even so, one day a director spontaneously offered the

disillusioned remark: "It's always the same: the way people talk, you'd think we were Nazi torturers!"

4 The authors ask "why the image of the correctional officer is so negative, when all he does is carry out the task society sets him, specified down to its smallest details"; they speak of a "process of displacement onto one professional category, correctional officer, of the bad conscience associated with the condemnation of others, the penalty inflicted in the name of the law and society, by judges and jurors" (Chauvenet et al. 1994: 50, 59).

5 This chronology is drawn from Carlier and Renneville's *Histoire des prisons en France* (*History of Prisons in France*) (2007), on the Criminocorpus website.

6 See the memorandum of September 2, 2011, published in the *BOMJL* (ministerial bulletin), No. 2011–09 (www.textes.justice.gouv.fr/art_pix/JUSK1140047C. pdf).

7 The SIG-Sauer Pro, carried by correctional officers tasked with prisoner transport, is a semi-automatic pistol. The SP2022 model they are issued is the same as that carried by the national police and the gendarmerie. But it is not altogether true that prison officers do not carry weapons. Guns are used in some intervention situations, or by some categories of officer (Razac 2008).

8 In what follows, I base my characterization of law enforcement officers and their work on this research, conducted from 2005 to 2007 (Fassin 2013c).

9 The available research at both facility and national level does not give details of place of birth, only (at best) place of residence, making it impossible to render a precise account of the frequent migrations from hometown to be nearer the workplace. In the prison I studied, one-quarter of the correctional officers lived in the Nord-Pas-de-Calais region, while individuals from the Caribbean made up one-fifth of the staff. At the national level, it has similarly been noted that residents of the Lille region account for the largest proportion in the classes graduating from ENAP, followed by those from the Overseas Territories. Within the groups from these two jurisdictions, children of blue-collar workers and clerks make up one-third of the total, those whose parents are unemployed 15 percent, while children of executives account for only 4 percent, confirming the predominantly working-class origins of correctional officers (see, for example, http://www.enap.justice.fr/pdf/156SVT.pdf).

10 Léonore Le Caisne (2000: 339) notes that candidates for these professions, "in the vast majority of cases, only enter prison after failing the examination or training for other sectors," with correctional officers "generally having taken the examinations for the police, the customs or the postal service." In fact there are significant variations from one year to another, with 64 percent having attempted entry to other professions in the 149th graduating class, compared to only 23 percent in the 158th. However, recent years have seen a relative stabilization, with roughly half of all candidates having sought entry to other professions. Thus among the 185th graduating class, 48 percent had taken another examination, of which 70 percent had applied to enter the police or the gendarmerie, the customs, or the army. "The large majority of these students thus wish to work in a public security service," the authors of the report conclude (www.enap.justice.fr/pdf/sociodemo_svt185.pdf).

11 To my knowledge, however, no other researcher has conducted successive studies in the two professional worlds. Laurence Proteau might have been an exception: after studying police detectives in a provincial precinct, she became interested in prison officers, but she was unable to go beyond the exploratory stage: "the reasons I gave up have largely to do with the structural differences between the two 'worlds.' Officers in the police detective branch prove to have some signs of social mobility, whereas officers in prison administration accumulate indicators of loss of social status. Their positions in their respective institutions, the characteristics of their work, and their image in society – police officers held in high esteem, prison officers undervalued – places them high or low on the scale of social values and recognition. This sociological configuration constructs the visions of the world that the two have, and makes it very difficult for a researcher to pass from one field to the other" (Le Caisne and Proteau 2008: 125). My experience was different, and the problematic valorization of one profession and unjust deprecation of the other are probably part of the reason for my interest in the two professions and the comparison between them.

12 If we consider the police in terms of *policing* – that is, in the broad sense of a practice that aims to manage social order – or of *the police* – that is, in the more restricted sense of an institution to which the state delegates part of its monopoly on the legitimate use of physical force – it is clear that there are substantial overlaps between police officers and prison guards (Liebling 2000).

13 For a detailed analysis of discourse and practices around the "Roma question" from 2010 onwards, first under a right-wing government and then under a left-wing president, see É. Fassin et al. 2014.

14 The mayor, who was also a representative for the Union of Democrats and Independents (UDI), was threatened with dismissal but chose to resign three days later (*Le Monde*, July 24, 2013). Six months later he was convicted of "glorifying crimes against humanity," and sentenced to . . . a suspended fine of 3,000 euro (*Libération*, January 25, 2014).

15 Conducting a study in two short-stay prisons in the Paris region under the aegis of the European research program I was then leading, Yasmine Bouagga (2015) also noted the absence of racialized discourse and racist remarks among prison staff. She explained this in terms of the presence of guards originating from the overseas territories, and the inculcation of the ideals of the French republic. There are many studies of racism and discrimination among the police, particularly in Britain and the United States, that concur in noting the universality of racism and the frequency of discrimination, although the former does not necessarily lead to the latter. There is no equivalent in the French sociological literature, but my ethnographic research offered local confirmation of these observations (Fassin 2013c).

16 As a development from the civil rights movement, and following riots in prisons, a policy of diversification of prison officers was undertaken in the United States, on the theory that staff who were from a social environment and minority background similar to those of the prisoners would treat them better. While the first research appeared not to support this hypothesis (Jacobs and Kraft 1978), subsequent studies reveal differences between groups, with black guards experi-

encing their work as more dangerous and unsatisfying, but showing themselves to be more sensitive to rehabilitation and collegiality than their white colleagues, though there was no difference between the groups in terms of their punitive conception of prison or their work-related stress (Van Voorhis et al. 1991).

17 In her study of the issue of racialization and racism in British prisons, Coretta Phillips (2012: 172) notes that they seem, if not entirely absent, at least very rare in the life of the two correctional facilities she studied.

18 Appropriating the Weberian concept of ethos, Pierre Bourdieu (1998/1980: 86) describes it as "an objectively systematic set of dispositions with an ethical dimension, a set of practical principles." It is precisely this that questionnaires are unable to grasp: "One forgets that people may prove incapable of responding to ethical problems being quite capable of responding *in practice* to situations raising the corresponding questions." Thus, asking prison officers in a survey what they think of someone "who does not wear a seat belt" or "does not buy a railroad ticket" in order to draw up a "legalism rating" (Benguigui et al. 2008: 49–51) may be interesting, but it does not tell us about the actual relationship to the law or regulation in question in specific cases: these have to be observed first hand.

19 Although the concept of institutional racism was first used in the United States, it gained popularity through the report by Sir William Macpherson in Britain, following the murder of black teen Stephen Lawrence by a racist gang. As the London police had done nothing to find the culprits, despite pressure from the Lawrence family and campaigning groups, a commission of inquiry was set up. It exposed operational failures that were due not only to the incompetence of police officers, but also to prejudices and discriminatory practices deeply rooted in the police as an institution. The concept of institutional racism, a powerful campaigning tool but a notion that is still underconceptualized, has become more established in the public arena than in the world of scientific research (Phillips 2011).

20 Under Article D.221 of the Code of Penal Procedure, members of prison staff "may not maintain relations that are not justified by the requirements of their work with persons placed or having been placed by the courts under the authority or control of the facility or service for which they work, or with their family or friends."

21 It was in *Protestant Ethics and the Spirit of Capitalism* that Weber (2001/1905: 39–50) analyzed the twin aspects of *Beruf*, drawing on the thinking of Martin Luther. But he returned to the term in the title of the two famous lectures he gave in 1917 and 1919, *Wissenschaft als Beruf* and *Politik als Beruf* (published in English as *The Vocation Lectures*, Weber 2004).

22 Analysis of the 186th graduating class, published in February 2014, shows that 14 percent of officers say they chose to become a correctional officer "out of interest in human relations professions," and 13 percent for "helping to maintain public order" (www.enap.justice.fr/pdf/socio-demo_svt185.pdf).

23 This research studied the 130th graduating class, whose members entered training in 1993 and were interviewed five times over the subsequent decade. Significantly, in the closed question about reasons for choosing the profession of

correctional officer, the authors of the study did not include a response relating to "human relations," as if it was impossible even to imagine. Yet in response to the question "What do you like about the job of correctional officer?" "human contact" is cited by 40 percent of students and 30 percent of those actively employed, for whom "working in a team" tops the list (Benguigui et al. 2008).

24 In his introduction to *The Use of Pleasure*, quoted at the opening of this chapter, Foucault (1985/1984: 25–6) distinguishes three levels of morality: the "moral code," which is a prescriptive ensemble transmitted in a diffuse manner by the institution; the "morality of behaviors," which designates the way the institution's rules and values are applied; and the "ethical subject," which constitutes the individual as such, in a relationship of self to self and self to others that goes beyond mere application of prescriptions. As the intermediate level is simply the translation of the first level, it is more interesting to reflect on moral code and ethical subjectivity as they allow for an analysis of the tension between institutional and individual thinking.

25 In his report on French prisons, the former European Commissioner for Human Rights also notes: "How many times have I heard stories about prisons where the conditions are alleged to be more comfortable than in the homes of people of modest means who have never broken the law? I have even heard that the conditions in prisons are now similar to those of a good hotel since it is possible for prisoners to have television in their cells" (Gil-Robles 2005).

Chapter 7   Violent, All Too Violent

1 In their book on prison violence, Chauvenet et al. (2008: 211–43) distinguish two types of violence between prisoners – acts that are "without immediate motive," prime among which are attacks on "diddlers"; and those "which have a motive," including attacks on "snitches." In the first group, "explosions," which have "interchangeable targets," are juxtaposed with "scapegoats," among whom "the most stigmatized are pedophiles." In the second, "drug-related violence" is grouped together with "lack of respect," which may be inferred from "nothing more than a look." These two heterogeneous groupings do not shed light, however, on the way in which, in the case of both "diddlers" and "snitches," a similar application of norms and values leads to negative moral categorizations that justify the violence (hence there are motives for the rough treatment of sex offenders just as much as for individuals suspected of informing).

2 In this case, the man himself recounts this episode to me, including the circumstances in which the violence arose, leaving me to suppose (even though he does not say so) that he is in prison for a sexual assault. However, in the world of prison, such assumptions are far from always based on information about the inmate's criminal record, and may be based on extrapolations from factors such as age (older), social background (middle class), skin color (white), and length of sentence (in the case of a convicted prisoner). Léonore Le Caisne gives an example of this in her study of the Poissy central prison (2000: 134).

3 Rape of rapists is a common punishment in prison. The influential report by Human Rights Watch on rape in US prisons, entitled *No Escape* (Mariner et al. 2001), analyzes how the aim of this practice is to emasculate the victim by humiliating him, both other prisoners and guards demonstrating their contempt toward him. The statistics cited in the report, drawn from two studies in penitentiaries, indicate that around 20 percent of prisoners have been subject to sexual violence from other prisoners; between one-third and one-half of these assaults take the form of nonconsensual anal penetration.

4 Challenging the stigmatizing categorization is the only way of avoiding violence. As Edgar et al. note (2012: 34), if the victim cannot prove he does not deserve the humiliating designation, he will be ostracized and may be assaulted. But informing on others is an accusation that is especially difficult to counter once the seed of doubt has been sown.

5 Obviously, not all prisoners adhere to this dominant model in the same way. In a study conducted in Great Britain, Evans and Wallace (2008) distinguish three groups: those who adopted it a long time ago, and hold onto it; those who, although socialized in this norm, have moved away from it to some extent; those who define themselves outside this code.

6 In their edited collection on prison masculinities, Sabo et al. (2001: 3) talk of "gender-blind criminology," taking up James Messerschmidt's formula.

7 The question is raised more readily in the United States, where, admittedly, violence is much more of a problem. Programs aimed at deconstructing hyper-masculinity have been developed in some prisons (Karp 2010).

8 In *Code of the Street*, Elijah Anderson analyzes the "moral life" of working-class black neighborhoods in Philadelphia: "Manhood on the streets means assuming the prerogatives of men with respect to strangers, other men, and women – being distinguished as a man . . . One's physical safety is more likely to be jeopardized in public *because* manhood is associated with respect. In other words, an existential link has been created between the idea of manhood and one's self-esteem, so that it has become hard to say which is primary" (2000: 91).

9 The law on prisons of November 29, 2009 states: "Persons incarcerated have the right to freedom of opinion, conscience, and religion. They may practice the religious office of their choice, under conditions appropriate to the organization of the facility, without limits other than those imposed for the sake of security and the good order of the facility" (http://legifrance.gouv.fr/affichTexte.do?cidTexte=JORFTEXT000021312171). The possession of religious books is specifically authorized. For the month of Ramadan, the short-stay prison I studied had permitted inmates to receive parcels from their family with food for the breaking of the fast, and had also organized the preparation and distribution of special meals that catered for Muslims' dietary practices during this period.

10 The same concern to rectify this common prejudice about prison inspires the British author of a "survival guide to prison" written by "a guy who was recently released." Under the heading "Violence," he notes: "Considering the media hype and most people's vicarious view of prison, violence is relatively rare" (http://ldmg.org.uk/survival_guide_to_prison.pdf).

11 In Jacques Audiard's 2009 film *A Prophet*, the hero, Malik El Djebena, is forced by a Corsican gang to execute another inmate; in Gary Gray's 2009 film *Law Abiding Citizen*, the main character, Clyde Shelton, savagely and gratuitously murders his cellmate. In both cases the scenes are spectacularly gory.

12 In 2012 there were 2 homicides and 111 attacks on staff resulting in temporary incapacity for work (www.justice.gouv.fr/art_pix/Chiffres_cles_2013_opt.pdf).

13 As early as his study of British prisons, conducted in the 1970s, psychologist William Davies (1982: 150) noted: "There are degrees of aggression and violence which lie on a continuum, for example: shouting, 'squaring up,' pushing or shoving, slapping, scratching, butting, punching, biting, elbowing, kneeing, kicking, knifing, shooting, exploding. In prison an inmate might find himself on a violence disciplinary report for virtually any of these activities." In France, official statistics have included a growing variety of incidents, with threats or spitting, or even a simple hostile remark, carrying the same statistical weight as slashing with a razor blade.

14 In 2007, only 367 incidents of violence between prisoners and 491 attacks on staff were recorded (www.anvp.org/offres/file_inline_src/58/58_P_4246_3.pdf).

15 The press regularly trots out this increase in the figures without examining what it signifies – a legitimate growing concern about violence, rather than an increase in violence itself (two examples: "La marmite carcérale et ses débordements" ("The prison pot boils over") (*Le Monde*, October 22, 2005), and "Les agressions contre les surveillants augmentent" ("Rise in attacks on prison officers") (*Le Parisien*, April 2, 2010).

16 According to the *Key Statistics in Prison Administration* (*Chiffres clés de l'administration pénitentiaire*) the number of homicides of prisoners in the years from 2007 onward was 1, 3, 2, 4, 3, and 2 respectively. The figures for attacks on staff leading to temporary incapacity for work, cited in the same source since 2009, are: 113, 109, 129, 111 (www.anvp.org/58_p_5791/statistiques-judiciaires-et-penitentiaires.html).

17 This is also the case in the United States, where rates of homicide in state prisons plummeted from 54 to 4 per 100,000 between 1980 and 2002, and fell less sharply, from 5 to 3 per 100,000, in county jails between 1983 and 2002. This represents a total decrease of 93 percent over the two decades marked by the largest increase in the prison population. However, it should be pointed out that homicides represent only 1.5 percent and 2.1 percent of prison mortality in state prisons and county jails respectively (Mumola 2005).

18 In his "Critique of violence," Walter Benjamin outlines his project: "The task of a critique of violence can be summarized as that of expounding its relation to law and justice" (1995/1921: 277, 287). This relation is based on the dual dimension of violence as lawmaking and law-preserving. Benjamin uses the death penalty as an extreme example of this dual violence, but any punishment, by its very nature, is a manifestation of it.

19 As noted in the Senate report on conditions in prison (Hyest and Cabanel 2000), it was the seriousness of the AIDS epidemic in prisons that triggered this important reform. The evaluation of the operation of the new healthcare system within prisons nevertheless draws ambivalent, if not contradictory conclusions. On the

one hand: "Aside from the specific issue of dental care, prisoners enjoy a quality of care almost equivalent to that experienced outside, and in any case massively superior to what they have been used to outside." On the other: "Nevertheless, the medicine practiced in prisons, where the rules of the Code of Penal Procedure sometimes sit uneasily alongside those of the Public Health Code, necessarily remains a 'medicine of extremity.'"

20 For a sociological analysis of the healthcare relationship in French prisons, particularly its gendered aspect, see Bessin and Lechien (2002), and for mental health more specifically, see Fernandez and Lézé (2011).

21 For example, on July 23, 2014, the administrative court in Lille ordered the French state to pay 34,000 euros to the family of a prisoner who died from repeated epileptic seizures, for which the night shift had failed to call the paramedics (www.oip.org/index.php/publications-et-ressources/actualites/1162-deces-d-un-detenu-suite-a-plusieurs-crises-d-epilepsie-l-etat-condamne-pour-n-avoir-pas-appele-les-secours).

22 The circular emphasizes that these units are based on experience in other countries, and conform to international recommendations (www.textes.justice.gouv.fr/art_pix/boj_20090002_0000_0018.pdf). As of June 1, 2013, there were 74 FLUs in 22 prison facilities. There were also 33 family visiting rooms in 9 facilities. This means that 153 other facilities had neither (www.justice.gouv.fr/prison-et-reinsertion-10036/la-vie-en-detention-10039/le-maintien-des-liens-familiaux-12006.html).

23 On sexuality in prison and its relationship to the violence of both the institution and inmates, see the pioneering study by Welzer-Lang et al. (1996).

24 Homel and Thompson's essay (2005) presents a succinct and clear review of the literature. The study by Chauvenet et al. (2008) combines empirical and theoretical approaches to violence in French prisons.

25 The authorship, or at least the first exposition, of this model is attributed to two classic texts: Donald Clemmer's study, first published in 1940, on the "prison community" was conducted in an unnamed facility that "possesses many features common to all American penitentiaries"; Gresham Sykes's 1958 study of "the society of captives" was conducted in the New Jersey State Maximum Security Prison in Trenton, "a social system in which an attempt is made to create and maintain total or almost total social control."

26 The critique of the culturalist model (the prison's system of values) and the functionalist interpretation (inmates' practices aim to adapt them to their environment) was advanced most prominently by John Irwin and Donald Cressey (1962: 145). Without denying the reality of the influence of the carceral world, they take the view that the "'indigenous origin' notion" of violence ignores the fact that, while there is indeed a "prison code," it is also "part of a *criminal* code, existing outside prisons." This is simply the manifestation of a more general sociological reality, that the members of a group borrow their understanding of the world from cultures that are not necessarily those of the group in which they find themselves at any given moment.

27 Since Charles Thomas's pioneering research into the phenomena of *prisonization* (1977), various studies, including some recent ones, have proposed an

articulation of the privation and importation theories (Blevins et al. 2010; Mears et al. 2013).

28 Although he analyzes the literature relating to the characteristics of violent prisoners, such as their age, gender, ethnic or racial origin, and criminal antecedents, Anthony Bottoms (1999: 212, 235) devotes most of his attention to "environmental factors" in the prison world, focusing particularly on experiments conducted in some facilities to understand or reduce violence.

29 A whole strand of criminology has recently developed around what are called "situational" theories and methods (Wortley 2002). This approach, often behaviorist and applied, tends to put forward scenarios, and sometimes suggests responses. I have attempted rather to develop a reading that accounts, as it were, more "thickly" for these situations that generate violence.

30 On the basis of research carried out in five British penal institutions, with the assistance of Helen Arnold, Alison Liebling (2004: xviii) uses the term "moral performance" to reflect on the fact that prisons are "moral places" in which the questions of justice, trust, respect, and well-being are crucial, and in which values and emotions are at work.

Chapter 8   Rights, Interrupted

1 The precise formulation used by Berlin (1969: 169) is a little more complex when he differentiates between the two senses of the word liberty: "The first of these political senses of freedom or liberty (I shall use both words to mean the same), which (following much precedent) I shall call the 'negative' sense, is involved in the answer to the question 'What is the area within which the subject – a person or group of persons – is or should be left to do or be what he is able to do or be, without interference by other persons?' The second, which I shall call the 'positive' sense, is involved in the answer to the question 'What, or who, is the source of control or interference that can determine someone to do, or be, this rather than that?'." The two questions are clearly different, even though the answers to them may overlap.

2 *Conditions of Incarceration in France* (*Les Conditions de détention en France*) is published by the International Prison Observatory (Observatoire international de prisons 2011), and offers a critical overview of life in prison; the *Prisoner's Guide* (*Guide du prisonnier*), issued by the same organization (2012), specifies, in more than 700 systematic and pedagogically informative pages, the rights of prisoners and their families in all areas, with precise references to the legislation concerned. This is a document that is accessible and valuable to anyone with an interest in the subject.

3 Taking into account the respective demographic weight of the states in question, and of course the duration of the suspension of voting rights following the end of the sentence in those that practice this extension, the disenfranchised population comprises approximately one quarter inmates, one quarter individuals on parole, and almost one half ex-felons. It has risen fivefold in 30 years. African Americans account for the highest proportion of those suffering this restriction,

and in some states more than 20 percent of them cannot vote (Uggen et al. 2012).

4 The General Inspector raises "the question of the compatibility of the organization of work in prison with the most basic social justice" (www.cglpl.fr/wp-content/uploads/2013/06/Com-de-press_CGLPL_QPC-travail.pdf).

5 This situation is sometimes challenged in the courts. For example, on February 8, 2013, a prisoner won a case at the industrial tribunal in Paris, in which she had argued that the ending of her work for a call center should be considered dismissal, thus giving her access to the relevant rights (www.huffingtonpost.fr/2013/02/08/detenue-prison-application-droit-du-travail_n_2645103.html).

6 In an analysis of the Constitutional Court's decision and of the response from the minister of justice, the International Prison Observatory noted that in 2009, during a parliamentary debate on the law on prisons, "the socialist group in the National Assembly, which included [current justice minister] Christiane Taubira, [current president] François Hollande and [former prime minister] Jean-Marc Ayrault," had filed an amendment stating that it was necessary that "the incarcerated individual has a contract of work specifying his duties and also giving him access to all social rights," and asserting that "none of the arguments invoked in rejecting the introduction of a contract seems justified" (www.oip.org/index.php/component/k2/item/1083-le-conseil-constitutionnel-consacre-le-non-droit-du-travail-en-prison-satisfaction-du-ministère-de-la-justice).

7 These data are drawn from *Key Statistics in Prison Administration: 2013* (www.justice.gouv.fr/art_pix/Chiffres_cles_2013_opt.pdf), and the audit report on the prison service drawn up by the National Court of Audit (Cour des Comptes) in 2010.

8 The importance of vocational training should not, however, be underestimated. Three courses were available: janitor, kitchen porter, and table service. Each of these comprised 350 hours of training, 24 hours per week. They included a substantial theoretical element – too much for many of the inmates who felt there was not enough practical activity – which enabled them to reach a certain standard, for example in math. Trainees also received remuneration and a certificate at the end of the course. Vocational training in prisons is tending to become decentralized, with regional bodies taking over (www.ladocumentation-francaise.fr/var/storage/rapports-publics/144000083/0000.pdf).

9 Delegated management is subject to the rules of open invitations to tender. The 20 or so prison facilities covered by the law of June 22, 1987 are distributed among a small number of companies, the main ones being Siges (a subsidiary of the Sodexo group), Gepsa (a subsidiary of the Suez group), and Idex (http://prison.eu.org/spip/php?article6069).

10 The National Court of Audit report (Cour des Comptes 2010) does not exclude the more global economic difficulties in its explanation of what, outside prison, would be considered an unemployment rate of 70–80 percent, but it notes that the variations in performance among the delegated contractors do not correlate with the situation in the local jobs market in the regions in which the corresponding prison facilities are located, strongly suggesting differences in the quality and intensity of activity engaged in finding contracts outside prison.

11 The businesses that do make use of labor concessions do not publicize the fact that they employ prisoners (www.jounaldunet.com/economie/enquete/travail-emploi-detenus-prisonniers/1-des-entreprises-tres-discretes.shtml). The scandal that hit Ikea after it was revealed that the Swedish company used East German workers during the 1980s centered on two elements: the fact the company used a captive workforce, and the fact that these were political prisoners (*Guardian*, November 16, 2012).

12 Some prison facilities, including short-stay prisons, also provide in-cell work. This has the triple advantage – for the employer and the management – of enabling much longer working hours, saving on workshop space, and eliminating the need for guards to be present. For prisoners, it often leads to harsher exploitation (Observatoire international de prisons 2012: 197).

13 In an article devoted to work in prisons, based on research conducted in five facilities, Fabrice Guilbaud (2008) offers an interesting comparison with work outside. He demonstrates the importance of remuneration, occupation of time, and psychological support, depending on the kind of work, particularly for prisoners serving long sentences, but also describes how inmates "slack off," partly as a way of increasing the rate paid per piecework. However, probably because he focuses his analysis on this parallel, Guilbaud misses one essential dimension that I here term tactical, and which is specific to the carceral world: the focus on obtaining secondary benefits.

14 For nineteenth-century British prisons, see William James Forsythe's book (1987). For penitentiaries in the southern United States, see Alex Lichtenstein's work (1996).

15 In O'Brien's words (1982: 11): "The prison *was* a workplace and prisoners *were* workers." The structure was modeled on a factory, establishing a link with the outside world.

16 The shift from the galleys to forced labor, and the move from the strictly punitive function to a focus on "discipline and production" during the 1820s are discussed in a chapter of André Zysberg's book (1980), while in her text on "revolution and prisons" Michelle Perrot (1980) analyzes the return of corporal punishment marked by the Montalivet circular of 1839, which reinstated the punitive function of the sanction, made prison conditions harsher, and stated that work should henceforth form part of the punishment and that the tasks should prioritize repetition in order to increase productivity.

17 By contrast, in the United States, this aspect is openly acknowledged. According to the *Left Business Observer*, the prison-industrial system in federal prisons supplies "100 percent of all military helmets, ammunition belts, bulletproof vests, ID tags, shirts, pants, tents, bags, and canteens." Added to these are a very high proportion of other items for the US military, including office equipment and airplane components. During the 1990s the number of prison industries grew by 500 percent and in 1998 there were more than 2,500 industries employing prisoners. To take just one example, the Correctional Corporation of America (CCA), one of the largest companies operating private prisons, with a turnover of $300 million, calculated that in 2005, at a daily wage of $28.89 for its inmate employees, it made a profit of $50.26 per inmate per day (Barak 2009: 145–8).

18 As is well known, Karl Marx (1933/1867: 698–703) uses the term "industrial reserve army" to describe a surplus population capable of "sudden expansion and contraction" that "creates an ever-ready supply of human material fit for exploitation" ready to respond to the needs of the economy. He sees this as a central element in the regulation of supply and demand, and hence in determining wage levels. The very minimal numbers of the prison population working under labor concessions in France render this effect insignificant. In the United States, by contrast, the prison workforce can be not only attractive, but competitive with the free market, and businesses sometimes choose to relocate their activity within prisons: such was the case of a factory in Texas manufacturing computer components for IBM and Compaq, which sacked its 500 employees and recruited inmates of the nearby Lockhart private prison. It even occurred with a *maquiladora* (factory operating in a tax-free zone) on the Mexican border, which closed and then reopened inside the giant San Quentin prison in California, on the basis that inmates were an even cheaper workforce than Mexicans (www.globalresaerch.ca/the-prison-industry-in-the-united-states-big-business-or-a-new-form-of-slavery/8289?print=1). Evidently, prison serves not only to exclude from the labor market a surplus poor population that is no longer of use, as Loïc Wacquant rightly notes (2000), but can also internalize part of this market by using inmates as a coerced, docile, and low-paid workforce.

19 As Philippe Combessie puts it (2000): "When you lock up poor people, you impoverish the incarcerated." A study of poverty in prison by Anne-Marie Marchetti (1997), based on research in seven prisons, shows that short-stay facilities are the worst affected by poverty, that poor people are, on average, more often incarcerated and for longer, and that their poverty results in harsher living conditions in prison.

20 The reference text was the circular of July 20, 2001 on combating destitution (www.justice.gouv.fr/bulletin-officiel/dap83d.htm).

21 As Bronislaw Geremek showed (1987), in his history of poverty beginning in the early Middle Ages, sometimes the poor inspire pity, and sometimes they end on the gallows – hence the title of his book.

22 For an in-depth discussion of these modes of allocation of assistance, relating specifically to the one billion francs in the French government's Urgent Social Fund in 1998, see my article on justice principles and judgment practices (Fassin 2003), in which I show that, in application letters, demonstration of merit is what brings the highest returns in terms of assistance received, while the description of needs, and appeals to compassion, are less effective.

23 The title of this circular itself suggests the shift, speaking of "combating poverty in prison." The memo states that "one-quarter of the penal population is thought to be in precarious circumstances," and that "prison administration should set targets to support the most impoverished individuals, including guaranteeing the dignity of those incarcerated" (http://circulaire.legifrance.gouv.fr/pdf/2013/05/cir_37054.pdf).

24 According to a survey conducted during the census (Insee 2002: 141), 70 percent of prisoners aged 18–24, 62 percent of those aged 25–29, 64 percent of those

aged 30–34, and 70 percent of those aged 35–39 had left school before the age of 18. Only 1 percent of those aged under 40 had continued their education beyond the age of 25.

25 According to data from the tracking that is now systematically conducted, "4.7 percent do not speak French, and 5.1 percent speak only rudimentary French" (*Key Statistics in Prison Administration: 2013*: http://www.justice.gouv.fr/art_pix/Chiffres_cles_2013_opt.pdf).

26 In his classic work on the reform of prisons, Charles Lucas, the theoretician of incarceration (1836: 130), exclaims: "What is the prison system but a system of education?" In an appendix, he quotes from Lord Russell's 1835 instruction to "the Sheriffs of England": "For each prison where the prisoners number more than 50, there shall be a schoolmaster." For historical overviews of prison education, see O'Brien (1982); for the nineteenth century, see Petit et al. (2002).

27 This is an approximate figure. As I have noted, until the year 2003 the prison population was calculated on the basis of the number of people under sentence, hence without differentiating between those housed in facilities and those on parole. From 2004 the two figures were distinguished. As far as education in prisons is concerned, what counts is of course those actually in prison. A comparison can reasonably be drawn between the number of inmates in 2013 and the number under sentence in 2003, given that in the early 2000s, very few sentenced individuals were granted parole. For example, in 2004 there were 59,246 individuals under sentence and 58,942 prison inmates, a difference of 0.5 percent. The data relating to teachers are drawn from Jean-Pierre Laurent and Jean-Luc Guyot's report on education in prisons (2010).

28 GENEPI (Groupement Étudiant National d'Enseignement aux Personnes Incarcérées) is an organization set up in 1976, as part of a movement of intellectuals and public figures following the suppression of prison riots in the early 1970s. It works both within prison facilities, organizing short courses, and in the public arena, mobilizing public opinion around the issue of prison (www.genepi.fr/).

29 The tensions and contradictions between education and security concerns are analyzed by Fanny Salane (2011), in a review of the trajectories of prisoners serving long sentences who pursue education beyond the high-school leaving certificate.

30 A sociological approach to law in prison can be found in Corinne Rostaing's article (2007) and Yasmine Bouagga's book (2015). Noteworthy works by jurists include those by Giudicelli and Morais (1998) on inmates' litigation within prisons, Poncela (2001) on the law as applied to sanctions, and Céré (2003) on disciplinary law in prison.

31 Two examples of approaches to inmates' rights are the *Prisoner's Guide* (Observatoire international de prisons 2012) and the annual reports of the General Inspector of Prisons and Detention Centers (www.cglpl.fr/).

32 In a published lecture, Dan Kaminski (2010) opposes the normalizing project of prison and the reduced voting rights of prisoners, as contravening inmates' rights.

33 On April 1, 2014, there were 15,310 foreigners among the 80,740 people under

prison sentence, amounting to 19 percent (www.justice.gouv.fr/art_pix/trimes-trielle_avril_MF2014.pdf). The 2011 census counted 64,933,400 people living in French territory, of whom 3,888,977, or 6 percent, were non-nationals (www.insee.fr/fr/ppp/bases-de-donnees/recensement/populations-legales/default.asp).

34 In 1993, the number of non-nationals under prison sentence was 15,322, compared to 33,8880 French nationals, or 31.1 percent of the total prison population (Hazard 2008b). In 1990, according to the census, there were 3,750,000 non-nationals out of the 58,111,000 people living in France, or 6.3 percent – a slightly higher proportion than today (www.insee.fr/fr/ffc/docs_ffc/ref/IMMFRA12_g_Flot1_pop.pdf).

35 The law of November 26, 2003, introduced by then minister of the interior Nicolas Sarkozy, made possible a degree of mitigation of this "double penalty," which had been a key campaigning issue for human rights organizations. However, bans on remaining in France, internment, and deportations continued, including for fathers of children born in France (www.gisti.org/IMG/pdf/200604_livre_noire_dble_p.pdf).

36 Cimade, the Ecumenical Mutual Support Service, was founded in 1939 under the name Comité inter-mouvements auprès des évacués (Interfaith Committee for Evacuee Support), with the aim of assisting the displaced populations of the French provinces of Alsace and Lorraine, and continues to be known under its original acronym despite the change of title. During World War II, the organization offered support to internees in the Vichy regime's camps, and direct assistance to people in danger from the Nazis. Today its two most important fields of practical activity are with undocumented migrants in immigration detention centers, where they have paid workers, and prisons, where they send volunteers. Cimade currently operates in 71 prisons (www.lacimade.org/poles/enfermement-eloignement/rubriques/39--trangers-en-prison).

Chapter 9   Land of Order and Security

1 See the statement by the Director of Prison Administration announcing the setting-up of ERIS on February 27, 2003 (http://prison.eu.org/spip.php?article3465). The scope of operation of these teams, which are sometimes compared to the gendarmerie's Special Intervention Group, was redefined and extended by the decree of April 24, 2012 (www.textes.justice.gouv.fr/art_pix/JUSK1240026A.pdf).

2 The ERIS uniform for each season is specified in the decree of April 14, 2004 (www.justice.gouv.fr/bulletin-officiel/dap94b-annexes.htm). The gear comprises, in addition to helmet and shield, a flash-ball – a weapon generally described as sublethal.

3 See the evidence from an inmate at Clairvaux, who was beaten up in his cell (http://laurent-jacqua.blogs.nouvelobs.com/archive/2012/04/27/e-r-i-s-ou-l-impunite-de-la-violence.html). ERIS have been condemned for violent or humiliating practices several times in the European Court of Human Rights (http://hudoc.echr.coe.int/sites/eng/pages/serach.aspx?i=001-107152).

4 For the case of France, see, in addition to parts of my own study (Fassin 2013c), the chapter by Christian Mouhanna (2009) on new forms of police intervention in the management of riots. In the United States, the police response to demonstrations following the death of a young black man killed by a police officer on August 9, 2014 in Ferguson, Missouri, is seen as a decisive contributory factor in the continuation of riots, and occasioned a national public debate on the militarization of the police: recourse to SWAT – Special Weapons Attack Team trained by the army and supplied with military equipment, including armored vehicles and heavy weapons – is now routine even for arrests made in suspects' homes (American Civil Liberties Union 2014).

5 Technical specifications sheet No. 2 of the circular of April 11, 2011, regarding the methods for control of incarcerated persons, describes the procedure thus: "The officer proceeds to full body search in the following order. He asks the inmate to pass his hand through his hair and to push his hair away from his ears, in order to verify that nothing is hidden there. If necessary, he asks the inmate to take out his earphones. Depending on the character of the inmate or the situation, he may ask him to open his mouth and lift his tongue in order to remove any dentures (for example, when the inmate is in the habit of hiding razor blades in his mouth, or has just put something in his mouth). He then checks the armpits by asking the inmate to raise and lower his arms, before inspecting his hands and asking him to spread his fingers. As various objects can be hidden between the legs, the officer must ask him to spread his legs in order to check for these. He then proceeds to examine the feet of the inmate, particularly the soles and toes" (www.textes.justice.gouv.fr/art_pix/JUSK1140022C.pdf).

6 In a case brought by the International Prison Observatory, the Council of State ordered the director of the facility to stop conducting systematic strip searches following visiting hours (www.conseil-etat.fr/fr/communiques-de-presse/regime-des-fouilles-integrales-systematiques.html).

7 The circular of October 15, 2012 specifies the conditions under which this nationwide list is held: it includes persons involved in organized crime or terrorist movements, those with a propensity to violent acts or public order disturbances, and those who have attempted or are suspected of having attempted to escape (www.textes.justice.gouv.fr/art_pix/JUSD1236970C.pdf).

8 A classic study of eight US prisons compared three models of management: control, involving the strict application of norms, for both inmates and guards; responsibility, which gave more autonomy to both; consensus, which was intermediate between the two. The first model correlated with a greater number of incidents, both minor and serious (Reisig 1998). A study of 371 prisons, also in the United States, concluded that violence among inmates and against staff is much less frequent when programs that enhance inmates' lives, particularly in terms of work or education, are provided (McCorkle et al.1995). Other research has produced similar results (Homel and Thompson 2005).

9 A number of rulings by the European Court of Human Rights refer to violation of Article 3 of the European Convention on Human Rights: "No one shall be subjected to torture or to inhuman or degrading treatment or punishment," for example, in the case of an inmate who had been subjected to several strip

searches, with video-recorded visual examination of the anus, each day (www. cncdh.fr/fr/publications/arret-el-shennawy-c-France).

10 The director of the Department of Corrections for the Île-de-France region, Jean-Marc Chauvet, was asked to draw up a report on prison security (2001). In a sign of the times and the place, a large proportion of this document is devoted to combating escapes by helicopter.

11 In his report on prison security, Chauvet (2001) was already arguing that it was impossible to stem the flow of cellphones, and suggested jamming communications.

12 In their analysis of this development, Duthé et al. (2011) note: "In the late 1940s, the suicide rate in prison was roughly equivalent to that observed among men aged 15–59 in the general population. Since then, the gap has widened." They also point out that during the 1990s, the reduction in prison overcrowding (but not in the overall prison population) was not followed by the fall in the suicide rate that might have been expected.

13 Comparisons between countries should of course be analyzed with caution, as Aubusson de Cavarlay (2009) points out in a critical note on the indicators used. However, it has to be noted that even if, as he proposes, we modify the reference population, for example by relating suicides to the population entering prison rather than the imprisoned population at any given moment, as is generally done – in other words, calculating on the basis of flow and not stocks – France remains top of the list (with the exception of Luxembourg, which is generally not included in comparisons because of the small numbers involved).

14 Aubusson de Cavarlay's analysis (2009) shows that some countries, such as the United Kingdom, where the prison suicide rate is half that in France, still have a comparable excess suicide rate in prison, indicating a similar specific effect of incarceration, while others, such as Germany, have both a general suicide rate and an excess prison suicide rate about half that in France.

15 From this point of view, rather than saying, as Duthé et al. (2009) maintain, that it is difficult to compare European prison suicide rates because penal policy differs in different countries (with some, like France, making extensive use of pre-trial detention, while others, such as Finland, hardly have recourse to it at all), one might venture that it is precisely these differences that need to be analyzed, because they make it possible to highlight the "suicidogenic" effects of these policies.

16 These figures are drawn from a study by Angélique Hazard (2008a). The most recent data in her survey are for the years just prior to the beginning of my research.

17 Jean-Louis Terra's report (2003) was highly regarded by the ministry, and correctional officers who expressed a desire to do so were invited to take "Terra training" (as 70 percent of guards nationally did, according to *Key Statistics in Prison Administration: 2013*).

18 Gaëtan Cliquennois (2010) undertook a sociohistorical analysis of suicide prevention in France. He places particular emphasis on the tensions between healthcare practitioners and guards.

19 In her study of these supermax facilities, Lorna Rhodes (2004) reveals the highly

pathogenic conditions imposed on inmates, many of whom have mental health issues, and the resulting contradictions between the logic of control and that of care.

20 A report by Paul-Roger Gontard (2010), commissioned by then secretary of state for justice, Jean-Marie Bockel, reviews the European experience in this domain. Denmark, Sweden, and Finland make extensive use of this model. Great Britain, Austria, and Belgium also have some open facilities. In France, only the Casabianda prison in Corsica operates on this principle: the majority of inmates there are convicted of sexual offenses.

Chapter 10   The Never-Ending Punishment

1 The decree of June 8, 1842 states that "the lash, the birch, and the cat-o'-nine-tails" are forbidden, as is shaving the head of women (https://criminocorpus.org/legislation/12851/).

2 Charles Perrier (1902: 53) wrote a remarkably detailed description of the functioning of prisons in his time, including a section devoted to "delation and punishment."

3 A regularly quoted parliamentary report (Hyest and Cabanel 2000) offers a similar analysis: "In reality, in some facilities, the disciplinary procedure appears to be an 'internal communications' operation, with the decision being made – in most cases – in the guards' favor. Management is careful not to discredit an officer in front of inmates, which does indeed have deleterious consequences. It is difficult for it to judge impartially."

4 Hence, explains Perrier (1902: 3), the only decision to be made is the harshness of the penalty, which depends on the "services" rendered to the facility and previous conduct.

5 There were in fact two rulings dated February 17, 1995, one relating to a sailor, called the "Hardouin" ruling, the other to a prisoner, known as the "Marie" ruling, that created new case law in deeming that disciplinary issues in the military and in prison were not a matter solely for internal order processes, but could be investigated by the administrative judge in case of an appeal. The prisoner in question had lodged an appeal against a decision by the director of the facility where he was incarcerated, punishing him with seven days in solitary confinement, suspended, because he had filed a complaint against a physician in the short-stay prison who was ignoring his requests for healthcare (www.conseil-eta.fr/fr/presentation-des-grands-arrets/17-fevrier-1995-hardouin-et-marie.html).

6 Guillaume Ferrus (1850: xii–xiv) put forward the following proposal: "We have noted that the disciplinary hearing is today the director's administrative tribunal … It would be better, assuming the adoption of measures that seem just to us without asserting that they are practicable, for a council, composed of the director and two persons from outside the internal administration, to sit permanently in the prison for this purpose."

7 In view of their level of funds, most inmates received statutory legal aid, and the

lawyers were thus paid by the state. The fee tariff was initially set at 88 euros per case, exclusive of all other remuneration (www.justice.gouv.fr/bulletin-officiel/ sadjpv86b.htm). In 2013, a government attempt to reform legal aid failed, following a campaign by lawyers (www.liberation.fr/societe/2013/09/17/les-avocats-inquiets-pour-l-aide-juridique-aux-plus-pauvres_932496).

8 The circular begins with this soothing sentiment: "The disciplinary activity incumbent upon prison management personnel, under the authority of heads of facility and the supervision of interregional directors, aims to facilitate the development of harmonious community life" (www.textes.justice.gouv.fr./art_pix/JUSK1140024C.pdf).

9 Figures provided by the International Prison Observatory (Observatoire international des prisons 2012) on the basis of data from the ministry. This increase represents a 13 percent rise in sanctions, over a period when the number of persons incarcerated fell by 0.2 percent (www.justice.gouv.fr/art_pix/Chiffresclesjanv2010_opt.pdf).

10 The report (Hyest and Cabanel 2000) came out prior to the recent major reforms of disciplinary law, which reduced penalties but did not alter the classification of misdeeds.

11 These variations in the way cases are assessed are also found in comparisons between facilities. In his 2012 report, the General Inspector of Prisons and Detention Centers compares 12 facilities: the frequency of sanctions by solitary confinement ranges from 34 to 75 percent of sanctions; the rate of suspension of sanctions is between 6 and 53 percent; isolation is ordered in between 0 and 30 percent of cases; mere warnings are given in 4–9 percent of cases; acquittals account for between 5 and 18 percent of decisions. On the basis of the available data, the prison I studied lies midway through the range: during the same period, in 2011, the breakdown of disciplinary sanctions was as follows: 60 percent sentenced to solitary confinement, 23 percent to isolation, 4.5 percent given warnings, and 4.1 percent acquitted (the slightly different data I give elsewhere in the text are calculated for a three-year period).

12 Confinement in an isolation cell can be implemented either within the main prison, or in the isolation block. It is accompanied by suspension of activities. Although in principle this is not a disciplinary sanction but a "precautionary measure," it sometimes tends to be substituted for solitary confinement (www.justice.gouv.fr/bulletin-officiel/dap73c.htm).

13 The case of Philippe El Shennawy offers an extreme example of these accumulated sanctions. Convicted in 1977 of armed robbery and false imprisonment, the 13 sentences added to his initial penalty resulted in a total of 56 years in prison. Following a campaign calling for the quashing of his mandatory sentence, his penalty was adjusted and he was released under electronic monitoring after 38 years in prison, 19 of which had been spent in isolation. France was condemned in the European Court of Human Rights for "inhuman and degrading treatment" of El Shennawy. His accomplice in the initial case had committed suicide three years after he was imprisoned, while in solitary confinement (*Le Monde*, January 22, 2014).

14 This triple ordeal is unique and cannot be experienced by someone who, as an

experiment, has himself locked up in these conditions. In a powerful symbolic gesture, the director of prisons for the state of Colorado spent 20 hours in solitary confinement, no doubt as a way of condemning the dangers of it, but certainly not of living the reality (*New York Times*, March 16, 2013).

15 The research, published in an international journal (Falissard et al. 2006), was based on an interview conducted by two psychiatrists, who then compared their diagnosis. Three figures were calculated for each pathology: a condition diagnosed by one of the two clinicians, a condition diagnosed by both, and a diagnosis revised by consensus. The first two statistics obviously represent the ends of the scale (the highest and lowest), while the third, where the two doctors ultimately agreed, is intermediate. It is this latter rate that I have used here, for the purposes of clarity.

16 The conditions of confinement are admittedly extreme in the United States, in terms of duration and material environment, but it has been demonstrated that punitive isolation gives rise to a specific psychiatric syndrome which resembles that observed in some acute brain disorders (Grassian 2006).

17 These figures relate to the years 2006–7 (Hazard 2008a), showing a rise in the rate from 11 to 16 percent over five years. In the United States, some see suicides in "disciplinary cells" as an unofficial "death row," which causes more fatalities than the "real" death row housing inmates sentenced to the death penalty (http://solitary-watch.com/2012/06/04/suicides-in-solitary-confinement-in-arizonas-prisons).

18 A study by James Marquart (1986), conducted in a Texas prison, shows how the ranking officers teach young guards to resolve order issues at the least with slaps and kicks, and at worst by torturing manacled and naked inmates. A number of recent scandals, for example in the Rikers Island juvenile facility in New York, have revealed that these practices not only persist, but are tolerated by the authorities: the magistrates who have tried to inquire into them have been removed under pressure from the guards' union (*New York Times*, March 16, 2013).

19 Pioneering studies include the research by Parton et al. (1987) on disciplinary boards, and the survey by the Harvard Center for Criminal Justice (1972) on judicial interventions into the prison world. In France, Fabrice Fernandez devoted a study to the work of a disciplinary board in the program that I coordinated (Fassin et al. 2015).

20 In fact, in its modern institutional form, the more accurate reference is not the dungeon, but the penitentiaries of Pittsburgh and Philadelphia, Pennsylvania, in the early nineteenth century. The total isolation of prisoners day and night, which was supposed to allow for their moral reform at the same time as their individual punishment, constituted a contrasting model to the Auburn prison in New York State, in which inmates were segregated at night and worked together during the day (Rothman 1971).

21 These figures are drawn from the Federal Bureau of Justice statistics, and aggregate statistics for administrative, disciplinary, and protective isolation. The first two of these account for 70,000 prisoners, and correspond to solitary confinement in France. In California alone, of the 1,111 individuals housed in 2011 in solitary confinement, 513 had been there for more than 10 years, and 78 for more than 20 years (http://solitarywatch.com/facts/faq/).

22 There are various organizations that campaign for the abolition of solitary confinement, including, in France, Ban Public, the "gateway to information on prisons" (http://prison.eu.org/spip.php?article14105).

Chapter 11   An Unfinished Business

1 The four studies cited are respectively those by Carrasco and Timbart (2010), Josnin (2014), Tournier (2005), and Kensey and Benaouda (2011). It should be borne in mind that Kensey and Benaouda, in their calculations, take into account the fact that a person sentenced to imprisonment often has a more substantial criminal record and has committed a more serious offense than a person who has not. The rates calculated by Tournier, and the odds ratios estimated by Kensey and Benaouda, are therefore in this sense valid for the case of "all other things being equal."

2 In particular, Lipsey and Cullen (2007) carried out a review of the literature and a meta-analysis of the available research.

3 This is the analysis put forward by Feeley and Simon (1992), in a classic text that offers a critical analysis of the founding principles of the new penology.

4 The law of May 27, 1885 lists, in exhaustive detail, the forms of repeat offending punishable by this extreme sentence: two convictions "to forced labor or isolation," or a single conviction relating to two offenses such as theft, vagrancy or begging, or seven convictions of which two were serious and the remainder for vagrancy etc. (https://criminocorpus.org/legislation/16687/). Almost simultaneously, as a counterpoint, the law of August 14, 1885 introduced the process of rehabilitation for those sentenced to an "afflicting or dishonoring penalty," the official definition of a sentence in the middle of the range of severity (https://criminocorpus.org/legislation/16688/). This period saw highly charged parliamentary debates (Petit et al. 2002: 144, 147).

5 This delicate balance is outlined, albeit somewhat rhetorically, in Article 1: "The regime of execution of the penalty of privation of freedom reconciles protection of society, punishment of the offender, and the interests of the victim with the need to prepare for the integration or reintegration of the incarcerated individual, so that he can lead a responsible life, and to prevent the perpetration of further offenses" (http://www.legifrance.gouv.fr/affichTexte.do?cidTexte=JORF TEXT000021312171&categorieLien=id).

6 According to the circular of March 19, 2009 relating to the responsibilities and working methods of probation and re-entry services, "the ultimate aim of the work of the probation and reentry service is prevention of recidivism" (www.textes.justice.gouv.fr/art_pix/boj_20080002_0000_0004.pdf).

7 Nationwide, 57 percent of those released in 2013 had spent at least six months in prison (www.justice.gouv.fr/art_pix/ppsmj_2014.pdf).

8 The affair in question is the "Laetitia case," already referred to: in January 2011, in the town of Pornic, a young woman was abducted and murdered by a prisoner on a suspended sentence with probation. The president pointed the finger at the judges and the police. A subsequent inquiry raised questions about the

monitoring by the probation and re-entry service, despite the fact that the future murderer had been released from prison at the end of his sentence, therefore not under the terms of an adjustment, and that the crime for which he had previously been incarcerated was not a sex offense but insulting a magistrate, which did not imply a special follow-up (*Libération*, February 18, 2011).

9 In their report, senators Jean-René Lecerf and Nicole Borvo Cohen-Seat (2012) write: "The results from PSAP and SEFIP appear limited and disappointing in light of the energy expended in implementing them" (www.senat.fr/rap/r11-629/r11-62912.html).

10 See, in particular, the report on prison management of the National Court of Audit (Cour des comptes 2006). A more recent report by the General Inspectorate of Judicial Services offers a more up-to-date assessment of probation and re-entry services (Lacoche et al. 2011).

11 This discussion of the sedimentation of roles is based on legislative texts published on the Criminocorpus site, which registers laws, decrees, orders, and circulars (https://criminocorpus.org/legislation/12877/). In her study of the profession of probation and re-entry counselor, Yasmine Bouagga (2012) rightly emphasizes the "judicialization" of the training for and practice of the profession, but concludes too quickly that there has been a "shift from an axis of 'compassion' to one of 'repression.'" Observation of practices suggests rather a shift from the "social" to the "preventative."

12 The circular of June 29, 1945 formalized the "establishment of a prison social service" with "a social support worker in every facility" (https://criminocorpus.org/legislation/12879/). The circular of February 1, 1946 gathered the associations for "sponsorship of released prisoners" into a federation, principally focused on "finding accommodation, where necessary, and a job" for these inmates (https://criminocorpus.org/legislation/12880/).

13 A field of research that was long neglected, the onward trajectory of former prisoners has, particularly in the United States, been the subject of studies that aim to understand the obstacles to reintegration and the incidence of recidivism, on multiple levels, from the individual level through that of family networks to that of government policy (Morenoff and Harding 2014).

Conclusion – The Meaning of Prison

1 The anthropologist of the contemporary world is often faced with such questions, especially when working on highly politically topical subjects, as I experienced when I was conducting research on undocumented migrants. I had just corrected the proofs of a collection of essays that I was coediting on this theme when the chief executive of the publishing house called me to express concern. It was June 1997, the left had just returned to power, and my interlocutor thought that it would not be long before the problem on which our book focused was resolved. He was wondering whether there was still any point in publishing it, and whether we should at least rewrite the introduction so as to point to the likelihood that the situation would soon be radically altered. I reassured him.

First, the analysis and observations on which our book was based dealt with structural phenomena linked to immigration policy, and would therefore remain valid above and beyond any reorientations introduced by different governments. Second, the socialists' accession to power had little chance of effecting a major shift in this area and resolving the issue of undocumented migrants once and for all. Despite the real improvements introduced by the circular of June 24, 1997 on legalization of migrants, and the law of May 11, 1998 on non-nationals' rights of entry and stay, subsequent events unfortunately confirmed that the book had lost none of its relevance.

2 Recent research in experimental psychology and brain imaging tend to indicate a deep root to the desire to punish, independent of any other consideration such as prevention, leading some to suggest that penal policies and practices should be agreed on the basis of "the moral intuitions of the governed community" (Darley 2009). This is a sophisticated form of what might be termed scientific populism.

3 Here "carceral condition" should be understood in the sense of what is inherent in the carceral world, in other words in the broad understanding of Hannah Arendt (1998/1958) when she talks of the "human condition" in relation to the three activities of labor, work, and action.

4 The crowd "were disoriented and disappointed. As if they were seeing their prey escape," writes Buzzati (1984: 81).

5 The year 1982 marks the low point in punitive policies in the recent period: 31,551 people with custodial sentences, 45,785 monitored outside prison, making a total of 77,336. In 2012 the respective figures were 73,780; 173,063; and 246,843 (www.justice.gouv.fr/art_pix/ppsmj_2014.pdf).

6 Significantly, Robert Castel's important book *L'Ordre psychiatrique* [*Psychiatric Order*] (1977) appeared in English in 1988 under the title *The Regulation of Madness: The Origins of Incarceration in France*. Although the translated title bears no relation to the original, it links the asylum and the prison, madness and incarceration, in line with the books that, at that time, were proliferating on these two themes in the United States.

7 In the two great studies and calls to action of Charles Lucas's *Du Système péni-tentiaire en Europe et aux États-Unis* [*On the Prison System in Europe and the United States*] (1828) and Gustave de Beaumont and Alexis de Tocqueville's *On the Penitentiary System in the United States and its Application in France* (1979/ 1833). Beaumont and Tocqueville proved more enthusiastic promoters of the US model than Lucas.

8 The figures for prison demographics are taken from Marie-Dominique Barré's study (1986), supplemented for the recent period by the *Statistics Series for Persons Subject to Justice* (www.justice.gouv.fr/art_pix/ppsmj_2014.pdf). The data on asylum demographics are drawn from the studies by France Meslé and Jacques Vallin (1981), supplemented for the recent period by the figures published by François Chapireau (2007).

9 The United States represents an extreme form of this dual tendency, with the number of people imprisoned increasing fivefold since the 1960s, and the number of psychiatric beds falling to a 20th of what it was, creating opposite problems of excess and shortfall, with equally damaging consequences. With

regard to prisoners, see the data in Sentencing Project (http://sentencinproject. org/doc/publications/inc_Trends_in_Corrections_Fact_sheet.pdf). For data on hospital beds for mentally ill patients, see the report by the Treatment Advocacy Center (www.treatmentadvocacycenter.org/storage/documents/the_shortage_ of_publichospital_beds.pdf).

10 To which we should also add immigration detention centers and other places specifically designed for non-nationals, which are effectively virtual ad hoc prisons that allow the individuals detained there to be channeled more quickly toward the place from which they will be deported, as documented in the 2014 report by the Open Access campaign, *La Face caché des camps d'étrangers en Europe* [*The Hidden Face of Camps for Non-Nationals in Europe*] (www. migreurop.org/IMG/pdf/facecachecampsetrangers-okweb.pdf).

11 One example of offenses that have recently become punishable by imprisonment is traffic offenses, particularly if one already has points on one's license. An example of an offense newly subject to repression is breach of the drug laws for simple possession of marijuana. The most recent figures available show that in 2011 a total of 603,000 offenses were the subject of a conviction: 1,896 felonies resulted in short- or long-term custodial prison sentences, while prison sentences were issued for 285,658 misdemeanors, of which 85,493 were custodial sentences (www.justice.gouv.fr/art_pix/stat_conda2011.pdf).

12 The suicide rate in French prisons rose from 4 to 19 per 10,000 inmates between 1960 and 2008 (Duthé et al. 2009). The suicide rate in US state prisons and local jails was respectively 1.4 and 4.7 per 10,000 inmates in 2002 (Mumola 2005). For reasons that are poorly understood, new prisons seem more conducive than older ones to suicide; there was a string of suicides in the facilities of Lyon-Corbas (with 8 suicides out of 900 inmates in two successive years following its opening), and Nantes (with 3 suicides out of 600 inmates within three weeks in early 2013) (www.politis.fr/Pourquoi-se-suicide-t-on-plus-dans.21759.html).

13 According to the Directorate of Prison Administration, between 2001 and 2012 the number of individuals sentenced to prison fell from 78,706 to 69,268 in Germany, and from 15,246 to 11,324 in the Netherlands, but rose from 47,005 to 76,407 in France. This represents falls of 12 percent and 26 percent respectively in the former two countries, and an increase of 62 percent in France (www.justice.gouv.fr/art_pix/ppsmj_2014.pdf). For a comparison of prison policies, and more generally of the issue of prison in France and Germany, see Salle (2009). It is interesting to note that, even in the United States, the number of individuals incarcerated has seen an admittedly modest fall in recent years.

14 Inaugurated in 2014 with a theoretical capacity of 768 places, the Orléans-Saran prison complex, which replaced the crumbling short-stay prisons of Orléans and Chartres, has, for example, five family life units (*La Nouvelle République*, July 26, 2014), while the Alençon-Condé-sur-Sarthe prison complex, opened in 2013 with a capacity of 204 places, is described as "the most secure prison in France" (*Le Monde*, February 17, 2014).

15 Toward the end of his analysis of total institutions, Goffman (1968/1961: 106, 111) does devote a few pages to "qualifications and conclusions," as a way of

softening his somewhat too systematic model, noting in particular the "permeability" of the "total institution."

16 In the final chapter of his book, Foucault (1977: 304) writes: "The carceral archipelago transported this technique from the penal institution to the entire social body."

17 Challenges to claims of the total nature of the prison institution are quite common. The critique has been particularly developed by Keith Farrington (1992).

18 Discussion of this carceral network, which binds society in a "continuum" that includes medicine and education, and heralds biopolitics, was opened up in a debate with Jacques Léonard (1980).

19 The original French title of this book is *L'Ombre du monde*, which means, literally, "The world's shadow."

Epilogue – Ethnography Regained

1 I am considering ethnography in both its genealogical and its etymological sense. On the one hand, it is a practice of inquiry (closely tied to the totemic figure of its inventor, Bronislaw Malinowski) that is based on long presence and participant observation; on the other, it is a practice of writing (as indicated by the Greek origin of the second part of the word, *graphein*), which implies a twofold exercise of translation of the material into text, and communication of this text to an audience (Fassin 2013a).

2 I use the word "anthropologist" here; I could equally well have written "sociologist." In the French tradition that can be traced back to Marcel Mauss, anthropology and sociology form part of a single science of the social, which also includes history. In the US tradition, originated by Franz Boas, what is known as cultural anthropology is associated with physical anthropology, linguistics, and archeology, with the result that the social becomes somewhat distanced. On the relationship between ethnography and fiction, see my discussion of the similarities and differences between their projects from the point of view of the real and the truthful (Fassin 2014b).

3 "But did he ever murder anyone, Dostoevsky?" asks Albertine, astonished by the way crime recurs in the Russian novelist's works. The narrator replies: "It's possible that creative writers are tempted by certain forms of life of which they have no personal experience" (Proust 1992/1923: 432–3).

4 As Rod Earle (2014) points out when, describing his dual experience as an ex-prisoner turned criminologist studying the carceral world, he distinguishes "serving time" (serving out the time of one's sentence) from "spending time" (spending time in prison, in his case for the purposes of research).

5 The text of the paper Becker presented as president of the Society for the Study of Social Problems was published the following year (1967).

6 For example, while acknowledging the impossibility of achieving neutrality, Alison Liebling (2001) pleads for an approach that recognizes the points of view of both the subordinate and the authorities.

7 To cite only the sociological literature in French, the work of Chauvenet et al. (1994), among others, is based on interviews with guards, while the studies by Marchetti (2001) on long sentences and Chantraine (2004) on a short-stay prison are drawn from interviews with inmates. Some studies, however, link the two groups, like those by Rostaing (1997) on the carceral relationship, and by Chauvenet et al. (2008) on prison violence. The collection edited by Benguigui et al. (2008) brings together studies conducted in parallel, using interviews and questionnaires with inmates and various categories of staff.

8 As an indication of the vitality of ethnographic research on prisons, the *Annual Review of Anthropology* devoted two reviews of the literature to the field in a little over 10 years (Rhodes 2001; Cunha 2014).

9 In section 12 of the third essay of *The Genealogy of Morals*, Nietzsche (1989/ 1887: III, 12) argues: "There is only a perspective seeing, only a perspective 'knowing'."

10 What I have proposed to call critical perspectivism consists precisely in recognizing the incommensurability of perspectives, but going beyond this potential impasse by resituating them in a historical and sociological context that renders them, if not compatible, at least co-intelligible (Fassin 2013b).

11 This is how we should understand the concept of the moral economy of science put forward by Lorraine Daston (1995), who speaks of "a web of affect-saturated values" that, more than rationality alone (in the idealist version) or calculation alone (in a strategic reading), underlie scientific work.

12 As Bazin (2008: 48–50) continues: "The anthropological experience consists in displacing oneself, not necessarily very far and sometimes only in thought or through a simple reorientation of the gaze, but enough to concretely experience and undergo apprenticeship in an unfamiliar world. It is in the extent to which what goes without saying for these people does not go without saying for me, observing them, that I am in a position to have to learn how they act."

13 A recent trend in social science research on prisons, significant though very much in the minority, emphasizes the importance of taking into consideration researchers' own involvement in their field and their position in relation to their informants (Sutton 2011); some even talk of autoethnography (Jewkes 2012).

14 Himself inspired by Marx's famous dictum "A specter is haunting Europe – the specter of communism," Derrida (1994: 10) uses the term hauntology to refer to this "logic of haunting" whereby the past resurfaces in the present. In their pioneering study of the world of correctional officers, Chauvenet et al. (1994: 16) say they were "consciously and unconsciously invaded by prison, often having dreams and nightmares about it." This physical and psychological experience – "sometimes we broke down" – derives from their dual understanding of the "weight of the unspoken in punishment" and the "shared lot of the work of correctional officers."

15 The first of these statements forms the title of an article by Loïc Wacquant (2002); the second is taken from an article coauthored by a researcher and four prisoners (Bosworth et al. 2005).

16 Begun two years after the end of his four-year spell in Siberia and completed six years later, this work represents the most remarkable ethnography of the

carceral world (Dostoevsky 2001/1862). By comparison, Marquet de Vasselot's *Ethnographie des Prisons* [*Ethnography of Prisons*] (1854/1841), published at almost the same time in France, appears a pompous pamphlet offering little empirical information.

References

Aebi, Marcelo, and Delgrande, Natalia (2011). *Space I: Annual Penal Statistics: Survey 2009*. Lausanne: Lausanne University and Council of Europe.

Akrich, Madeleine, and Callon, Michel (2004). "L'intrusion des entreprises privées dans le monde carcéral français: Le Programme 13 000," in *Gouverner, enfermer. La prison, un modèle indépassable?*, ed. Philippe Artières and Pierre Lascoumes, 295–317. Paris: Presses de Sciences Po.

Allen, Francis (1981). *The Decline of the Rehabilitative Ideal: Penal Policy and Social Purpose*. New Haven: Yale University Press.

American Civil Liberties Union (2013). *The War on Marijuana in Black and White*. New York: ACLU.

American Civil Liberties Union (2014). *The War Comes Home: Excessive Militarization of American Policing*. New York: ACLU.

Anderson, Elijah (2000). *Code of the Street: Decency, Violence, and the Moral Life of the Inner City*. New York: Norton.

Appadurai, Arjun, ed. (1986). *The Social Life of Things: Commodities in Cultural Perspective*. Cambridge: Cambridge University Press.

Archer, Evry (2008). *Recherche sur l'évaluation de la souffrance psychique liée à la détention*. Loos: ADNSMPL.

Arendt, Hannah (1998/1958). *The Human Condition*. Chicago: University of Chicago Press.

Aubusson de Cavarlay, Bruno (1985). "Hommes, peines et infractions: La légalité de l'inégalité," *L'Année Sociologique* 35: 275–309.

Aubusson de Cavarlay, Bruno (2009). "Note sur la sursuicidité carcérale en Europe: Du choix des indicateurs," *Champ Pénal/Penal Field* 10 (http://champpenal. revues.org/7558).

Austin, James, Clear, Todd, Duster, Troy, et al. (2007). *Unlocking America: Why and How to Reduce America's Prison Population*. Washington, DC: IFA Institute.

Banton, Michael (1983). "Categorical and statistical discrimination," *Ethnic and Racial Studies* 6(3): 269–283.

Barak, Gregg (2009). *Criminology: An Integrated Approach*. Lanham, MD: Rowman & Littlefield.

Barré, Marie-Danièle (1986). "130 années de statistique pénitentiaire en France," *Déviance et société* 10(2): 107–128.

Barré, Marie-Danièle (1996). "Toxicomanie et délinquance: Relations et artefacts," *Déviance et société* 20(4): 299–315.

Bastard, Benoit, and Mouhanna, Christian (2007). *Une Justice dans l'urgence. Le traitement en temps réel des affaires pénales.* Paris: Presses Universitaires de France.

Bazin, Jean (2008). *Des Clous dans la Joconde. L'anthropologie autrement.* Toulouse: Anacharsis.

Beauchemin, Cris, Hamel, Christelle, and Simon, Patrick (2010). *Trajectoires et origines: Enquête sur la diversité des populations en France.* Paris: Ined-Insee.

Beaumont, Gustave de, and Tocqueville, Alexis de (1979/1833). *On the Penitentiary System in the United States and its Application in France,* trans. Francis Lieber. Carbondale: Southern Illinois University Press.

Beccaria, Cesare (1995/1764). *On Crimes and Punishments,* in *On Crimes and Punishments and Other Writings,* trans. Richard Davies and Virginia Cox. Cambridge: Cambridge University Press.

Beck, François, Guignard, Romain, and March, Laura (2010). "Les pratiques addictives des jeunes adultes," in *Violences et santé en France: État des lieux,* ed. François Beck, Catherine Cavalin, and Florence Maillochon, 203–219. Paris: La documentation Française.

Beck, François, Guignard, Romain, Richard, Jean-Baptiste, Tovar, Marie-Line, and Spilka, Stanislas (2011). "Les niveaux d'usage des drogues en France en 2010," *Tendances* 76 (OFDT).

Becker, Howard (1967). "Whose side are we on?" *Social Problems,* 14(3): 239–248.

Belmokhtar, Zakia, and Benzakri, Abdellatif (2013). "Les français et la prison," *Infostat Justice* 122.

Benguigui, Georges, Guilbaud, Fabrice, and Malochet, Guillaume (2008). *La Socialisation professionnelle des surveillants de l'administration pénitentiaire.* Nanterre: Université Paris X–CNRS.

Benjamin, Walter (1995/1921). "Critique of violence," in *Reflections: Essays, Aphorisms, Autobiographical Writings,* trans. Edward Jephcott. New York: Schochen Books.

Bentham, Jeremy (2002/1791). *Panopticon; or, the Inspection-House: Containing the idea of a new principle of construction applicable to … penitentiary houses, prisons … and schools, with a plan of management, etc.* London: T. Payne.

Berlin, Isaiah (1969). "Two concepts of liberty," in *Liberty.* Oxford: Oxford University Press.

Berman, Gavin, and Dar, Aliyah (2013). *Prison Population Statistics.* London: Library of the House of Commons.

Bertrand-Dagenbach, Cécile, Chauvot, Alain, Matter, Michel, and Salamito, Jean-Marie (1999). *Carcer. Prison et privation de liberté dans l'Antiquité classique,* Paris: De Boccard.

Bessin, Marc, and Lechien, Marie-Hélène (2002). "Hommes détenus et femmes soignantes: L'intimité des soins en prison," *Ethnologie française* 32(1): 69–80.

Black, William (2007). "Corruption kills," in *International Handbook of White-Collar and Corporate Crime*, ed. Henry Pontell and Gilbert Geis, 439–455. New York: Springer.

Blevins, Kristie, Listwan, Shelley Johnson, Cullen, Francis, and Jonson, Cheryl Lero (2010). "A general strain theory of prison violence and misconduct: An integrated model of inmate behavior," *Journal of Contemporary Criminal Justice* 20(10): 1–19.

Blondiaux, Loïc (1998). *La Fabrique de l'opinion: Une histoire sociale des sondages*. Paris: Seuil.

Bosworth, Mary, Campbell, Debi, Demby, Bonita, Ferranti, Seth M., and Santos, Michael (2005). "Doing prison research: Views from inside," *Qualitative Inquiry* 11(2): 249–264.

Bottoms, Anthony (1999). "Interpersonal violence and social order in prisons," *Crime and Justice* 26: 205–281.

Bouagga, Yasmine (2012). "Le métier de conseiller d'insertion et de probation: Dans les coulisses de l'état pénal?," *Sociologie du travail* 54(3): 317–337.

Bouagga, Yasmine (2015). *Humaniser la peine? Enquête en maison d'arrêt*. Rennes: Presses Universitaires de Rennes.

Bourdieu, Pierre (1998/1980). *Sociology in Question*, trans. Richard Nice. London: Sage.

Buzzati, Dino (1984). "Quiz at the prison," in *Restless Nights: Selected Stories of Dino Buzzati*, trans. Lawrence Venuti, 78–82. Manchester: Carcanet.

Carlier, Christian, and Renneville, Marc (2007). "Histoire des prisons en France," Criminocorpus-Chronologie (https://criminocorpus.org/outils/15717/).

Carrasco, Valérie, and Timbart, Odile (2010). "Les condamnés de 2007 en état de récidive ou de reiteration," in *Cahiers d'études pénitentiaires et criminologiques* 108. Paris: Direction de l'administration pénitentiaire.

Cassan, Francine, and Mary-Portas, France-Line (2002). "Précocité et instabilité familiale des hommes détenus," INSEE *Première*, 828.

Cassan, Francine, Toulemon, Laurent, and Kensey, Annie (2000). "L'histoire familiale des hommes détenus," INSEE *Première*, 706.

Castan, Nicole, and Zysberg, André (2002). *Histoire des galères, bagnes et prisons en France de l'ancien régime*. Toulouse: Privat.

Castel, Robert (1977). *L'Ordre psychiatrique: L'âge d'or de l'aliénisme*. Paris: Minuit.

Céré, Jean-Paul (2003). *Droit disciplinaire pénitentiaire*. Paris: L'Harmattan.

Chantraine, Gilles (2004). *Par-delà les murs: Expériences et trajectoires en maison d'arrêt*. Paris: Presses Universitaires de France.

Chapireau, François (2007). "L'évolution du recours à l'hospitalisation psychiatrique au xxᵉ siècle," in *La Prise en charge en santé mentale*, ed. Magali Coldefy, 127–142. Paris: La documentation française.

Chauvenet, Antoinette, Orlic Françoise, and Benguigui, Georges (1994). *Le Monde des surveillants de prison*. Paris: Presses Universitaires de France.

Chauvenet, Antoinette, and Rambourg, Cécile (2010). *De quelques observations sur la mise en œuvre des règles pénitentiaires européennes*. Agen: École nationale de l'administration pénitentiaire.

Chauvenet, Antoinette, Rostaing, Corinne, and Orlic, Françoise (2008). *La Violence carcérale en question*. Paris: Presses Universitaires de France.

Chauvet, Jean-Marc (2001). *La Sécurité des établissements pénitentiaires et des personnels*. Paris: La documentation française.

Cheliotis, Leonidas, and Liebling, Alison (2006). "Race matters in British prisons: Towards a research agenda," *British Journal of Criminology* 46(3): 286–317.

Christin, Angèle (2008). *Comparutions immédiates: Enquête sur une pratique judiciaire*. Paris: La découverte.

Clemmer, Donald (1966/1940). *The Prison Community*. New York: Holt, Rinehart & Winston.

Cliquennois, Gaëtan (2010). "Preventing suicide in French prisons," *British Journal of Criminology* 50(4): 1023–1040.

Combessie, Philippe (2000). "Quand on enferme les pauvres, on appauvrit les enfermés ... ," *Panoramiques* 45: 30–35.

Combessie, Philippe (2009). *Sociologie de la prison*. Paris: La découverte.

Comfort, Megan (2008). *Doing Time Together. Love and Family in the Shadow of the Prison*. Chicago: University of Chicago Press.

Cour des comptes (2006). *Garde et reinsertion: La gestion des prisons*. Paris: La documentation française.

Cour des comptes (2010). *Le Service public pénitentiaire: Prévenir la récidive, gérer la vie carcérale*. Paris: La documentation française.

Cour des comptes (2011). *L'Organisation et la gestion des forces de sécurité publique*. Paris: La documentation française.

Crewe, Ben (2009). *The Prisoner Society: Power, Adaptation and Social Life in an English Prison*. Oxford: Oxford University Press.

Cunha, Manuela (2014). "The ethnography of prisons and penal confinement," *Annual Review of Anthropology* 43: 217–233.

Dante Alighieri (2012/1472). *The Divine Comedy*, trans. Robin Kirkpatrick. London: Penguin.

Darley, John (2009). "Morality in the law: The psychological foundations of citizens' desires to punish transgressions," *Annual Review of Law and Social Science* 5: 1–23.

Daston, Lorraine (1995). "The moral economy of science," *Osiris* 10: 2–24.

Daston, Lorraine, ed. (2000). *Biographies of Scientific Objects*. Chicago: University of Chicago Press.

Davies, William (1982). "Violence in prisons," in *Developments in the Study of Criminal Behaviour*, vol. 2, ed. Philip Feldman, 131–161. New York: John Wiley.

Debard, Mireille, Gachet, André, Bergnes, Karine, and Pidoux, Chantal (2009). *Comparutions immédiates*. Lyon: Conseil lyonnais pour le respect des droits.

Delabruyère, Dominique, Hermilly, Jocelyne, and Ruelland, Nadine (2002). "La délinquance économique et financière sanctionnée par la justice," *Infostat Justice* 62.

Derrida, Jacques (1994). *Specters of Marx: The State of the Debt, the Work of Mourning and the New International*, trans. Peggy Kamuf. New York and London: Routledge.

Dostoevsky, Fyodor (2001/1862). *Memoirs from the House of the Dead*, trans. Jessie Coulson. Oxford: Oxford University Press.

Durkheim, Emile (1997/1893). *The Division of Labor in Society*, trans. W. D. Halls. New York: Free Press.

Duthé, Géraldine, Hazard, Angélique, Kensey, Annie, and Pan Ké Shon, Jean-Louis (2009). "Suicide en prison: La France comparée à ses voisins européens," in *Population & Sociétés* 462. Paris: Institut national d'études démographiques.

Duthé, Géraldine, Hazard, Angélique, Kensey, Annie, and Pan Ké Shon, Jean-Louis (2011). "L'augmentation du suicide en prison en France depuis 1945," *Bulletin épidémiologique hebdomadaire* 47–48: 504–508.

Earle, Rod (2014). "Insider and out: Making sense of a prison experience and a research experience," *Qualitative Inquiry* 20(4): 429–438.

Edgar, Kimmett, O'Donnell, Ian, and Martin, Carol (2012). *Prison Violence: The Dynamics of Conflict, Fear and Power*. Abingdon: Routledge.

Evans, Tony, and Wallace, Patti (2008). "A prison within a prison? The masculinity narratives of male prisoners," *Men and Masculinites* 10(4): 484–507.

Falissard, Bruno, Loze, Jean-Yves, Gasquet, Isabelle, et al. (2006). "Prevalence of mental disorders in French prisons for men," *BMC Psychiatry* 6(33): 1–6.

Farrington, Keith (1992). "Modern prison as total institution? Public perception versus objective reality," *Crime & Delinquency* 38(1): 6–26.

Farrington, David, and Nuttall, Christopher (1980). "Prison size, overcrowding, prison violence, and recidivism," *Journal of Criminal Justice* 8(4): 221–231.

Fassin, Didier (2002). "L'invention française de la discrimination," *Revue française de science politique* 52(4): 403–423.

Fassin, Didier (2003). "Justice principles and judgment practices in allotting emergency state financial aid in France," *Revue française de sociologie*, Annual English Selection 44(S): 109–146.

Fassin, Didier (2009). "Les économies morales revisitées," *Annales: Histoire, sciences sociales* 64(6): 1237–1266.

Fassin, Didier (2013a). "Why ethnography matters. On anthropology and its publics," *Cultural Anthropology* 28(4): 621–646.

Fassin, Didier (2013b). "Scenes from urban life: A modest proposal for a critical perspectivist approach," *Social Anthropology* 21(3): 371–377.

Fassin, Didier (2013c). *Enforcing Order: An Ethnography of Urban Policing*. Cambridge: Polity.

Fassin, Didier (2014a). "Pouvoir discrétionnaire et politiques sécuritaires: Le chèque en gris de l'État à la police," *Actes de la recherche en sciences sociales* 201–202: 72–86.

Fassin, Didier (2014b). "True life, real lives: Revisiting the boundaries between ethnography and fiction," *American Ethnologist* 41(1): 40–55.

Fassin, Didier, et al. (2013). *Juger, réprimer, accompagner: Essai sur la morale de l'État*. Paris: Seuil.

Fassin, Didier, et al. (2015). *At the Heart of the State. The Moral World of Institutions*. London: Pluto Press.

Fassin, Didier, and Mazouz, Sarah (2007). "Qu'est-ce que devenir français? La naturalisation comme rite d'institution républicain," *Revue française de sociologie* 4(4): 723–750.

Fassin, Éric (2010). "Statistiques raciales ou racistes? Histoire et actualité d'une controverse française," in *Les nouvelles frontières de la société française*, ed. Didier Fassin, 427–451. Paris: La découverte.

Fassin, Éric, Fouteau Carine, Guichard, Serge, and Windels, Aurélie (2014). *Roms et riverains: Une politique municipale de la race*. Paris: La Fabrique.

Faugeron, Claude, et Houchon, Guy (1985). "Prison et pénalités: De la pénologie à une sociologie des politiques pénales," *L'année sociologique* 35: 115–151.

Faugeron, Claude, and Le Boulaire, Jean-Michel (1992). "Prisons, peines de prison et ordre public," *Revue française de sociologie* 33: 3–32.

Feeley, Malcolm, and Simon, Jonathan (1992). "The new penology: Notes on the emerging strategy of corrections and its implications," *Criminology* 30(4): 449–474.

Fernandez, Fabrice, and Lézé, Samuel (2011). "Finding the moral heart of carceral treatment: Mental health care in a French prison," *Social Science & Medicine* 72(9): 1563–1569.

Ferrus, Guillaume (1850). *Des prisonniers, de l'emprisonnement et des prisons*. Paris: Germer-Baillère.

Forseti, Andréa, and Paul, Anna (2014). *Pour en finir avec les peines plancher*. Paris: Terra nova.

Forsythe, William James (1987). *The Reform of Prisoners 1830–1900*. London: Croom Helm.

Foucault, Michel (1977). *Discipline and Punish: The Birth of the Prison*, trans. Alan Sheridan. London: Penguin.

Foucault, Michel (1985/1984). *The Use of Pleasure: The History of Sexuality, vol. 2*, trans. Robert Hurley. Harmondsworth: Penguin.

Foucault, Michel (2007). *Security, Territory, Population: Lectures at the Collège de France, 1977–78*, trans. Graham Burchell. Basingstoke: Macmillan.

Foucault, Michel (2014). *Wrong-doing, Truth-telling: The Function of Avowal in Justice*, trans. Stephen W. Sawyer. Chicago: University Press of Chicago.

Foucault, Michel (2015/2013). *The Punitive Society: Lectures at the Collège de France, 1972–1973*, trans. Graham Burchell. Basingstoke: Macmillan.

Gaes, Gerald (1994). "Prison crowding research reexamined," *Prison Journal* 74(3): 329–364.

Gallo, Ermanno (1995). "The penal system in France: From correctionalism to managerialism," in *Western European Penal Systems: A Critical Anatomy*, ed. Vincenzo Ruggiero, Mick Ryan, and Joe Sim, 71–92. London: Sage.

Garland, David (1990). *Punishment and Modern Society: A Study in Social Theory*. Chicago: University of Chicago Press.

Garland, David (2001). *The Culture of Control: Crime and Social Order in Contemporary Society*. Chicago: University of Chicago Press.

General Controller of Prisons and Detention Centers (2012). *Rapport d'activité 2011*. Paris: Dalloz.

General Controller of Prisons and Detention Centers (2014). *Rapport d'activité 2013*. Paris: Dalloz.

Geremek, Bronislaw (1987). *La Potence ou la pitié: L'Europe et les pauvres, du moyen âge à nos jours*. Paris: Gallimard.

Gil-Robles, Alvaro (2005). *Report by Mr. Alvaro Gil-Robles, Commissioner for Human Rights, on the Effective Respect for Human Rights in France*. Strasbourg: Council of Europe.

Giudicelli, Catherine, and Morais, Anne-Marie (1998). *Le Contentieux administratif des détenus: Éléments de jurisprudence*. Paris: Ministère de la Justice.

Glaze, Lauren (2011). *Correctional Population in the United States, 2010*. Washington, DC: Bureau of Justice Statistics.

Godelier, Maurice (1972/1969). "'Salt currency' and the circulation of commodities among the Baruya of New Guinea," in *Studies in Economic Anthropology*, ed. George Dalton, 52–71. Washington, DC: American Anthropological Association.

Goffman, Erving (1968/1961). *Asylums: Essays on the Social Situation of Mental Patients and Other Inmates*. Harmondsworth: Penguin.

Golub, Andrew, Johnson, Bruce, and Dunlap, Eloise (2007). "The race/ethnicity disparity in misdemeanor marijuana arrests in New York City," *Criminology and Public Policy* 6(1): 131–164.

Gontard, Paul-Roger (2010). *Le Régime ouvert de détention peut-il être étendu dans le champ pénitentiaire français? Mission d'étude de faisabilité*. Paris: Ministère de la Justice.

Goody, Jack (2002). "The anthropology of senses and sensations," *La Ricerca Folklorica* 45: 17–28.

Got, Claude (2008). *La Violence routière: Des mensonges qui tuent*. Paris: Lavoisier.

Grassian, Stuart (2006). "Psychiatric effect of solitary confinement," *Washington University Journal of Law & Policy* 22: 325–383.

Guéno, Jean-Pierre, ed. (2000). *Paroles de détenus*. Paris: Librio-Radio France.

Guilbaud, Fabrice (2008). "Le travail pénitentiaire: Sens et articulation des temps vécus des travailleurs incarcérés," *Revue française de sociologie* 49(4): 763–791.

Harcourt, Bernard (2011). *The Illusion of Free Markets: Punishment and the Myth of Natural Order*. Cambridge, MA: Harvard University Press.

Harvard Center for Criminal Justice (1972). "Judicial intervention in prison discipline," *Journal of Criminal Law, Criminology and Police Science* 63(2): 200–228.

Hazard, Angélique (2008a). "Baisse des suicides en prison depuis 2002," *Cahiers d'études pénitentiaires et criminologiques*, Direction de l'administration pénitentiaire 22.

Hazard, Angélique (2008b). "Étrangers incarcérés," *Cahiers d'études pénitentiaires et criminologiques*, Direction de l'administration pénitentiaire 25.

Henrion, Roger (1995). *Rapport de la Commission de réflexion sur la drogue et la toxicomanie*. Paris: La documentation française.

Herpin, Nicolas (1977). *L'application de la loi: Deux poids, deux mesures*. Paris: Seuil.

Heullant-Donat, Isabelle, Claustre, Julie, and Lusset, Elisabeth, eds. (2011). *Enfermements. Le cloître et la prison IVIe–XVIIIe siècle)*. Paris: Publications de la Sorbonne.

Homel, Ross, and Thompson, Carleen (2005). "Causes and prevention of violence in prisons," in *Corrections Criminology*, ed. Sean O'Toole and Simon Eyland, 101–108, Sydney: Hawkins Press.

Hughes, Everett (1962). "Good people and dirty work," *Social Problems* 10(1): 3–11.

Hyest, Jean-Jacques, and Cabanel, Guy-Pierre (2000). *Les Prisons: Une humiliation pour la république. Les conditions de détention dans les établissements pénitentiaires en France.* Paris: Sénat.

Ignatieff, Michael (1978). *A Just Measure of Pain: The Penitentiary in the Industrial Revolution, 1750–1850.* New York: Pantheon.

Ignatieff, Michael (1981). "State, civil society, and total institutions: A critique of recent social histories of punishment," *Crime and Justice* 3: 153–192.

Insee (Institut national de la statistique et des études économiques) (2002). *L'Histoire familiale des hommes détenus.* Paris: Insee, Synthèses 59.

Irwin, John (1985). *The Jail: Managing the Underclass in American Society.* Berkeley: University of California Press.

Irwin, John, and Cressey, Donald (1962). "Thieves, convicts, and inmate culture," *Social Problems* 10(2): 142–155.

Jacobs, James, and Kraft, Lawrence (1978). "Integrating the keepers: A comparison of black and white prison guards in Illinois," *Social Problems* 25(3): 304–318.

Jewkes, Yvonne (2012). "Autoethnography and emotion as intellectual resources: Doing prison research differently," *Qualitative Inquiry* 18(1): 63–75.

Jobard, Fabien, and Névanen, Sophie (2007). "La couleur du jugement: Discriminations dans les décisions judiciaires en matière d'infractions à agents de la force publique (1965–2005)." *Revue française de sociologie* 48(2): 243–272.

Josnin, Rémi (2014). "Une approche statistique de la récidive des personnes condamnées," *Infostat Justice* 127.

Jugnot, Stéphane (2012). "L'accès à l'emploi à la sortie du système éducatif des descendants d'immigrés," in *Immigrés et descendants d'immigrés en France,* 61–75. Paris: Insee.

Kaminski, Dan (2010). "Droits des détenus, normalisation et moindre éligibilité," *Criminologie* 43(1): 199–226.

Karp, David (2010). "Unlocking men, unmasking masculinities: Doing men's work in prison," *Journal of Men's Studies* 18(1): 63–83.

Kensey, Annie (2010). "Dix ans d'évolution du nombre de personnes écrouées de 2000 à 2010," *Cahiers d'études pénitentiaires et criminologiques,* Direction de l'administration pénitentiaire 35.

Kensey, Annie, and Benaouda, Abdelmalik (2011). "Les risques de récidive des sortants de prison: Une nouvelle evaluation," *Cahiers d'études pénitentiaires et criminologiques,* Direction de l'administration pénitentiaire 36.

Kensey, Annie, Cassan, Francine, and Toulemon, Laurent (2000). "La prison: Un risque plus fort pour les classes populaires," *Cahiers de démographie pénitentiaire* 9.

King, Ryan, Mauer, Marc, and Young, Malcolm (2005). *Incarceration and Crime: A Complex Relationship.* Washington, DC: The Sentencing Project.

Lacoche, Sarah, Berbain, Hugues, Monnet, Emmanuel, et al. (2011). *Les Services pénitentiaires d'insertion et de probation.* Paris: La documentation français.

Laurent, Jean-Pierre, and Guyot, Jean-Luc (2010). *L'Enseignement en milieu pénitentiaire: Rapport annuel 2010.* Paris: Direction de l'administration pénitentiaire.

Le Caisne, Léonore (2000). *Prison: Une ethnologue en central.* Paris: Odile Jacob.

Le Caisne, Léonore, and Proteau, Laurence (2008). "La volonté de savoir sociologique à l'épreuve du terrain: De l'enchantement du commissariat au désenchantement de la prison," *Sociétés contemporaines* 4(72): 125–149.

Lecerf, Jean-René, and Borvo Cohen-Séat, Nicole (2012). *Loi pénitentiaire: De la loi à la réalité de la vie carcérale.* Paris: Sénat français.

Lee, John Alan (1981). "Some structural aspects of police deviance in relations with minority groups," in *Organizational Police Deviance: Its Structure and Control,* ed. Clifford Schearing, 49–82. Scarborough: Butterworths.

Legleye, Stéphane, Spilka, Stanislas, Le Nézet, Olivier, and Lafiteau, Cécile (2009). "Les drogues à 17 ans: Résultats de l'enquête ESCAPAD 2008," *Tendances* 66 (OFDT).

Le Jeannic, Thomas (2007). "On pardonne tout à son quartier sauf ... l'insécurité, les dégradations, le bruit," *Insee Première* 1133.

Léonard, Jacques (1980). "L'historien et le philosophe," in *L'Impossible prison: Recherches sur le système pénitentiaire au xixᵉ siècle,* ed. Michelle Perrot, 9–28. Paris: Seuil.

Leturcq, Fabrice (2012). "Peines planchers: Application et impact de la loi du 10 août 2007," *Infostat Justice* 118.

Lévy, René (1985). "Police et sociologie pénale en France," *L'année sociologique* 35: 61–82.

Lévy, René (1987). *Du suspect au coupable: Le travail de la police judiciaire.* Paris: Méridiens-Klincksieck.

Lhuilier, Dominique, and Lemiszewska, Aldona (2001). *Le Choc carcéral: Survivre en prison.* Paris: Bayard.

Lichtenstein, Alex (1996). *Twice the Work of Free Labor: The Political Economy of Convict Labor in the New South.* London: Verso.

Liebling, Alison (2000). "Prison officers, policing and the use of discretion," *Theoretical Criminology* 4(3): 333–357.

Liebling, Alison (2001). "Whose side are we on? Theory, practices, and allegiances in prisons research," *British Journal of Criminology* 41(3): 472–484.

Liebling, Alison, with Arnold, Helen (2004). *Prisons and Their Moral Performance: A Study of Values, Quality, and Prison Life.* Oxford: Oxford University Press.

Lipsey, Mark, and Cullen, Francis (2007). "The effectiveness of correctional rehabilitation: A review of systematic reviews," *Annual Review of Law and Social Science* 3: 297–320.

Lucas, Charles (1828). *Du Système pénitentiaire en Europe et aux États–Unis.* Paris: Bossange et Béchet.

Lucas, Charles (1836). *De la réforme des prisons, ou De la théorie de l'emprisonnement, de ses principes, de ses moyens et de ses conditions pratiques.* Paris: Legrand et Bergounioux.

Marchetti, Anne-Marie (1997). *Pauvretés en prison.* Ramonville Saint-Agne: Erès.

Marchetti, Anne-Marie (2001). *Perpétuités: Le temps infini des longues peines.* Paris: Plon.

Mariner, Joanne, et al. (2001). *No Escape: Male Rape in US Prisons.* New York: Human Rights Watch.

Marquart, James (1986). "Prison guards and the use of physical coercion as a mechanism of prisoner control," *Criminology* 24(2): 347–366.

Marquet de Vasselot, Louis-Augustin-Aimé (1854/1841). *Ethnographie des prisons.* Paris: Boutarel et Garnot.

Martinelli, Daniel, and Prost, Corinne (2010). "Le domaine d'étude est déterminant pour les débuts de carrière," *Insee Première* 1313.

Martinson, Robert (1974). "What works? Questions and answers about prison reform," *Public Interest* 35: 22–54.

Marx, Karl (1933/1867). *Capital.* London: J. M. Dent & Sons.

Matelly, Jean-Hugues, and Mouhanna, Christian (2007). *Police: Des chiffres et des doutes.* Paris: Michalon.

McConville, Seán (1998). "The Victorian prison: England, 1865–1965," in *The Oxford History of the Prison: The Practice of Punishment in Western Society,* ed. Norval Morris and David Rothman, 117–150. Oxford: Oxford University Press.

McCorkle, Richard, Miethe, Terance, and Drass, Kriss (1995). "The roots of prison violence: A test of the deprivation, management, and 'not-so-total' institution models," *Crime & Delinquency* 41(3): 317–331.

McGowen, Randall (1998). "The well-ordered prison: England 1780–1865," in *The Oxford History of the Prison: The Practice of Punishment in Western Society,* ed. Norval Morris and David Rothman, 71–99. Oxford: Oxford University Press.

Mears, Daniel, Stewart, Eric, Siennick, Sonja, and Simons, Ronald (2013). "The code of the street and inmate violence: Investigating the salience of imported belief systems," *Criminology* 51(3): 695–728.

Mermaz, Louis, and Floch, Jacques (2000). *La France face à ses prisons: Rapport à l'assemblée nationale.* Paris: La documentation française.

Meslé, France, and Vallin, Jacques (1981). "La population des établissements psychiatriques: Évolution de la morbidité ou changement de stratégie médicale?" *Population* 36(6): 1035–1068.

Minni, Claude, and Mahrez, Okba (2014). "Emploi et chômage des descendants d'immigrés en 2012," *Dares analyses* 23.

Molière (2011). *Don Juan,* trans. Richard Wilbur. San Diego: Harvest.

Morenoff, Jeffrey, and Harding, David (2014). "Incarceration, prisoner reentry, and communities," *Annual Review of Sociology* 40: 411–429.

Morris, Norval, and Rothman, David, eds. (1998). *The Oxford History of the Prison: The Practice of Punishment in Western Society.* Oxford: Oxford University Press.

Mouhanna, Christian (2009). "The French police and urban riots: Is the national police force part of the solution or part of the problem?" in *Rioting in the UK and France: A Comparative Analysis,* ed. David Waddington, Fabien Jobard, and Mike King, 173–182. Cullompton: Willan Publishing.

Mucchielli, Laurent (2008). "Une société plus violente? Une analyse socio-historique des violences interpersonnelles en France de 1970 à nos jours," *Déviance et société,* 32(2): 115–147.

Mumola, Christopher (2005). *Suicide and Homicide in State Prisons and Local Jails.* Washington, DC: Bureau of Justice Statistics.

Nietzsche, Friedrich (1989/1887). *On the Genealogy of Morals,* trans. Walter Kaufman. New York: Vintage Books.

North, Douglass (1990). *Institutions, Institutional Change and Economic Performance*. Cambridge: Cambridge University Press.

Obradovic, Ivana (2012). "La pénalisation de l'usage de stupéfiants en France au miroir des statistiques administratives: Enjeux et controversies," *Déviance et société* 36(4): 441–469.

O'Brien, Patricia (1982). *The Promise of Punishment: Prisons in Nineteenth-Century France*. Princeton: Princeton University Press.

Observatoire français des drogues et des toxicomanies (2013). *Rapport national 2013 à l'OEDT*. Saint-Denis: OFDT.

Observatoire international des prisons (2011). *Les Conditions de détention en France*. Paris: La découverte.

Observatoire international des prisons (2012). *Le Guide du prisonnier*. Paris: La découverte.

Observatoire national des zones urbaines sensibles (2012). *Rapport 2012*. Saint-Denis: Éditions du Comité interministériel des villes.

Open Society Justice Initiative (2009). *Police et minorités visibles: Les contrôles d'identité à Paris*. New York: Open Society Institute.

Parton, David, Stratton, John, and Shanahan, Michael (1987). "The use of discretion in prison disciplinary boards," *American Journal of Criminal Justice* 9(1): 82–93.

Perec, Georges (1988/1975). *W, or the Memory of Childhood*, trans. David Bellos. London: Collins Harvill.

Perrier, Charles (1902). *La Vie en prison*. Lyon: A. Storck & Cie.

Perrot, Michelle (1975). "Délinquance et système pénitentiaire en France au xixe siècle," *Annales* 30(1): 67–91.

Perrot, Michelle, ed. (1980). *L'Impossible Prison: Recherches sur le système pénitentiaire au xixe siècle*. Paris: Seuil.

Peters, Edward (1998). "Prison before the prison: Ancient and medieval worlds," in *The Oxford History of the Prison: The Practice of Punishment in Western Society*, ed. Norval Morris and David Rothman, 3–43. Oxford: Oxford University Press.

Petit, Jacques-Guy, Faugeron, Claude, and Pierre, Michel (2002). *Histoire des prisons en France (1789–2000)*. Toulouse: Privat.

Phillips, Coretta (2011). "Institutional racism and ethnic inequalities: An expanded multilevel framework," *Journal of Social Policy* 40(1): 173–192.

Phillips, Coretta (2012). *The Multicultural Prison: Ethnicity, Masculinity, and Social Relations Among Prisoners*. Oxford: Oxford University Press.

Poncela, Pierrette (2001). *Droit de la peine*. Paris: Presses Universitaires de France.

Proust, Marcel (1992/1923). *The Captive*, trans. C. K. Scott Moncrieff and Terence Kilmartin, rev. D. J. Enright. London: Chatto & Windus.

Provine, Doris Marie (2011). "Race and inequality in the war on drugs," *Annual Review of Law and Social Science* 7: 41–60.

Raimbourg, Dominique, and Huyghe, Sébastien (2013). *Rapport d'information sur les moyens de lutte contre la surpopulation carcérale* 652. Paris: Assemblée nationale.

Rawls, John (1955). "Two concepts of rules," *The Philosophical Review* 64(1): 3–32.

Razac, Olivier (2008). *L'Utilisation des armes de neutralisation momentanée en prison*. Dossier thématique 5. Agen: CIRAP.

Reisig, Michael (1998). "Rates of disorder in higher-custody state prisons: A comparative analysis of managerial practices," *Crime and Delinquency* 44(2): 229–244.

Rhodes, Lorna (2001). "Toward an anthropology of prisons," *Annual Review of Anthropology* 30: 65–83.

Rhodes, Lorna (2004). *Total Confinement: Madness and Reason in the Maximum Security Prison*. Berkeley: University of California Press.

Rizk, Cyril (2010). "Les phénomènes de consommation et de trafic de drogue dans le cadre de vie des personnes de 14 ans et plus," *Angle* 23.

Robert, Philippe (1985). "Insécurité, opinion publique et politique criminelle," *L'année sociologique* 35: 199–231.

Rostaing, Corinne (1997). *La Relation carcérale: Identités et rapports sociaux dans les prisons de femmes*. Paris: Presses Universitaires de France.

Rostaing, Corinne (2007). "Processus de judiciarisation carcérale: Le droit en prison, une ressource pour les acteurs?" *Droit et Société* 67: 577–595.

Rothman, David (1971). *The Discovery of the Asylum: Social Order and Disorder in the New Republic*. Boston: Little, Brown & Co.

Rusche, Georg, and Kirchheimer, Otto (2009/1939). *Punishment and Social Structure*. New Brunswick: Transaction Publishers.

Sabo, Don, Kupers, Terry, and London, Willie (2001). "Gender and the politics of punishment," in *Prison Masculinities*, ed. Don Sabo, Terry Kupers, and Willie London, 3–17. Philadelphia: Temple University Press.

Salane, Fanny (2011). "Faire des études en prison: Logique sécuritaire contre logique scolaire," in *Prisons sous tensions*, ed. Georges Benguigui, Fabrice Guilbaud, and Guillaume Malochet, 250–275. Nimes: Champ social.

Salas, Denis (2005). *La Volonté de punir: Essai sur le populisme penal*. Paris: Hachette.

Salle, Grégory (2009). *La Part d'ombre de l'État de droit: La question carcérale en France et en République fédérale d'Allemagne depuis 1968*. Paris: Éditions de l'École des hautes études en sciences sociales.

Salle, Grégory (2011). "1975: Une date marquante dans l'histoire de la prison? Petit essai de mise en perspective," in *Prisons sous tensions*, ed. Georges Benguigui, Fabrice Guilbaud, and Guillaume Malochet, 20–56. Nimes: Champ social.

Scheer, David (2014). "La prison de murs troués … Essai d'analyse d'une micro-architecture carcérale de l'embrasure," *Champ pénal* 11 (http://champpenal.revues.org/8833).

Scott, James (1985). *Weapons of the Weak: Everyday Forms of Peasant Resistance*. New Haven: Yale University Press.

Smith, Philip (2008). *Punishment and Culture*. Chicago: University of Chicago Press.

Snell, Tracy (2013). *Capital Punishment, 2011: Statistical Tables*. Washington, DC: Bureau of Justice Statistics.

Spierenburg, Pieter (1998). "The body and the state: Early Modern Europe," in *The Oxford History of the Prison: The Practice of Punishment in Western Society*, ed. Norval Morris and David Rothman, 44–70. Oxford: Oxford University Press.

Sutton, James (2011). "An ethnographic account of doing survey research in prison: Descriptions, reflections, and suggestions from the field," *Qualitative Sociology Review* 7(2): 45–63.

Sykes, Gresham (2007/1958). *The Society of Captives: A Study of Maximum Security Prison*. Princeton: Princeton University Press.

Taussig, Michael (1999). *Defacement: Public Secrecy and the Labor of the Negative*. Stanford: Stanford University Press.

Terra, Jean-Louis (2003). *Prévention du suicide des personnes détenues: Évaluation des actions mises en place et propositions pour développer un programme complet de prévention*. Paris: Ministère de la Justice and Ministère de la Santé.

Terrio, Susan (2009). *Judging Mohammed: Juvenile Delinquency, Immigration, and Exclusion at the Paris Palace of Justice*. Stanford: Stanford University Press.

Thomas, Charles (1977). "Theoretical perspectives on prisonization: A comparison of the importation and deprivation models," *Journal of Criminal Law and Criminology* 68(1): 135–145.

Timbart, Odile (2011). "Vingt ans de condamnations pour crimes et délits. *Infostat Justice* 114.

Timbart, Odile and Minne, Marie-Dominique (2013). "Le traitement judiciaire de la délinquance routière," *Infostat Justice* 123.

Tonry, Michael (1994). "Racial disproportion in US prisons," *British Journal of Criminology* 34, Special Issue: 97–115.

Torterat, Jérémie, and Timbart, Odile (2005). "L'exécution des peines d'emprisonnement ferme," *Infostat Justice* 83.

Tournier, Pierre Victor (2005). "Peines d'emprisonnement ou peines alternatives: Quelle récidive?" *Actualité juridique: Pénal* 9: 315–317.

Tournier, Pierre Victor (2013). *La Prison: Une nécessité pour la république*. Paris: Buchet-Chastel.

Tournier, Pierre Victor, and Robert, Philippe (1989). "Migrations et délinquances: Les étrangers dans les statistiques pénales," *Revue européenne des migrations internationales* 5(3): 5–31.

Uggen, Christopher, Shannon, Sarah, and Manza, Jeff (2012). *State-Level Estimates of Felon Disenfranchisement in the United States*. Washington, DC: The Sentencing Project.

Union nationale des fédérations régionales des associations de maisons d'accueil de familles et proches de personnes incarcérées (2008). *À propos du vécu des familles et proches de personnes incarcérées*. Saintes: UFRAMA.

Van Voorhis, Patricia, Cullen, Francis, Link, Bruce, and Wolfe, Nancy Travis (1991). "The impact of race and gender on correctional officers' orientation to the integrated environment," *Journal of Research in Crime and Delinquency* 28(4): 472–500.

Vasseur, Véronique (2000). *Médecin-chef à la prison de la Santé*. Paris: Le Cherche-midi.

Wacquant, Loïc (1999). *Les Prisons de la misère*. Paris: Raisons d'agir.

Wacquant, Loïc (2000). "The new 'peculiar institution': On the prison as surrogate ghetto," *Theoretical Criminology* 4(3): 377–389.

Wacquant, Loïc (2002). "The curious eclipse of prison ethnography in the age of mass incarceration," *Ethnography* 3(4): 371–397.

Wacquant, Loïc (2009/2004). *Punishing the Poor. The Neoliberal Government of Social Insecurity*. Durham: Duke University Press.

Walmsley, Roy (2013). *World Prison Population List*. London: International Centre for Prison Studies.

Walsh, John (2013). *The Culture of Urban Control: Jail Overcrowding in the Crime Control Era*. Plymouth: Lexington Books.

Warren, Patricia, Tomaskovic-Devey, Donald, Smith, William, Zingraff, Matthew, and Mason, Marcinda (2006). "Driving while black: Bias processes and racial disparity in police stops," *Criminology* 44(3): 709–738.

Weber, Max (2001/1905). *The Protestant Work Ethic and the Spirit of Capitalism*, trans. Stephen Kalberg. Chicago: Fitzroy Dearborn.

Weber, Max (2004). *The Vocation Lectures: "Science as a Vocation"; "Politics as a Vocation,"* trans. Rodney Livingstone. Indianapolis: Hackett Publishing Company.

Welzer-Lang, Daniel, and Castex, Patrick, eds. (2012). *Comparutions immédiates: Quelle justice?* Toulouse: Erès.

Welzer-Lang, Daniel, Mathieu, Lilian, and Faure, Michaël (1996). *Sexualité et violence en prison: Ces abus qu'on dit sexuels*. Lyon: Aléas.

West, Heather (2010). *Prison Inmates at Midyear 2009: Statistical Tables*. Washington, DC: Bureau of Justice Statistics.

Western, Bruce (2006). *Punishment and Inequality in America*. New York: The Russell Sage Foundation.

Western, Bruce, and Pettit, Becky (2010). "Incarceration and social inequality," *Daedalus*, Summer: 8–19.

Wortley, Richard (2002). *Situational Prison Control: Crime Prevention in Correctional Institutions*. Cambridge: Cambridge University Press.

Zocchetto, François (2005). *Rapport d'information sur les procédures accélérées de jugement en matière pénale* 17. Paris: Sénat français.

Zysberg, André (1980). "Politiques du bagne (1820–1850)," in *L'Impossible Prison: Recherches sur le système pénitentiaire au xixe siècle*, ed. Michelle Perrot, 165–205. Paris: Seuil.

Index

Michael Taussig - a "public secret" cited 59)

"peo do know w/out having actual knowl. 57)
[voluntary ignorance,]

244 Disc hearing critique.

status a "modern inmate" 249

sys of punitive inflation 256

Solitary - the sanction that goes w/o
saying. 255

* Solitary: phys exp of the bareness of the
carceral cond. 259

* privation of freedom 26~
place of constraint / plac of rights 262

262 prison discipline - concern for internal
order in a place of constraint.

* a way of governing inequality? ↦
264 by prioritizing repression over prevention
"pro under sentence" not "prisoners" =
surveillance

287+ carceral/correctional. tentacles that
prison extends into society.

288 Criminal form of the prison
David Rothman, The Discovery of
Asylum.

290 Punishment. , func of incarcerat
retributive purpose. 290 of incarcerat
felonies 2% of prison sentences.

392 Colonial inheritence + racial dimension,

393 The ques [= abolition] was only solution.